D·I·R·E·C·T·I·N·G

FILM TECHNIQUES
AND
AESTHETICS

Second Edition

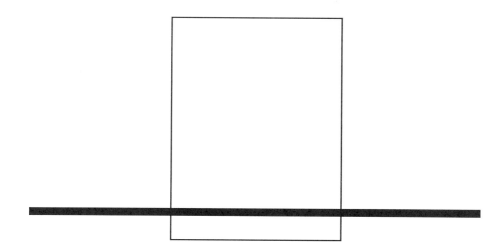

D·I·R·E·C·T·I·N·G
FILM TECHNIQUES AND AESTHETICS

Second Edition

Michael Rabiger

Focal Press

Boston   Oxford   Johannesburg   Melbourne   New Delhi   Singapore

Focal Press is an imprint of Butterworth–Heinemann

 A member of the Reed Elsevier group

 Recognizing the importance of preserving what has been
written, Butterworth–Heinemann prints its books on acid-free
paper whenever possible.

Library of Congress Cataloging-in-Publication Data
Rabiger, Michael.
    Directing : film techniques and aesthetics / Michael
Rabiger.—2nd ed.
       p. cm.
    Includes bibliographical references and index.
    ISBN 0-240-80223-3 (pbk. : alk. paper)
    1. Motion pictures—Production and direction. 2. Motion
pictures—Aesthetics. I. Title.
PN1995.9.P7R26 1996
791.43'0233—dc20   96-18886
                                                              CIP

British Library Cataloguing-in-Publication Data
A catalogue record for this book is available from the British
Library.

The publisher offers discounts on bulk orders of this book.
For information, please write:
Manager of Special Sales
Butterworth–Heinemann
313 Washington Street
Newton, MA 02158–1626
Tel: 617-928-2500
Fax: 617-928-2620

For information on all Focal Press publications available,
contact our World Wide Web home page at:
http://www.bh.com/fp

10 9 8 7 6 5 4 3 2

Printed in the United States of America

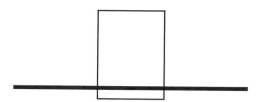

To my wife Nancy Mattei, the very best supporter and critic,
and to the memory of Gladys her mother.

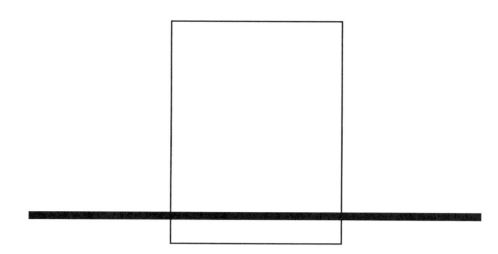

C·O·N·T·E·N·T·S

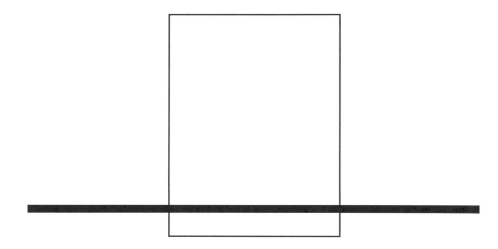

I·N·T·R·O·D·U·C·T·I·O·N

Here is a practical and comprehensive manual to help you become a director. No matter what genre you work in, no matter whether you work in film or video, this new edition will answer your needs. Whether you are a novice in film school, learning on your own, or making a career change as an industry professional, it will occupy your head, your heart, and your hands with meaningful work, for it is aimed at those who learn by doing.

Extensively revised in structure and expanded in content, this Second Edition contains much that is new. There are new sections on screen grammar and the basics of screen production. There is an extensive short form writer's workout devised as a game of chance; greater emphasis on the importance of dramaturgy and story editing tools; and more about form and structure. A new feature is the Form and Aesthetics Questionnaire (end of Part IV Checklist) which will yield a useful overview of any project, past, present or future. The themes and archetypal situations behind all drama are listed and discussed in the new section of story editing. Blocking and camera movement get more attention, there are more production projects, more about actors and controlling the inner lives of the characters, and more on how a director must think, feel, and act while creating a work for the screen having a unified "voice" and vision. Throughout there is a strong emphasis on tackling the supreme challenge in directing, to control point of view. To help in this, an important new section focuses on the director's quest for an artistic identity. For those wanting an education and eventual career, there is an expanded guide to international film schools and a career guide.

You may wonder why a production manual devotes twenty-five chapters to the thought and activities preceding production. The simple fact is that films (and videos, of course) succeed or fail largely because of two factors. One is how credible and compelling the human presence is on the screen—which means there is a huge amount to learn about drama, actors, and acting. The other factor is the originality in the writing, dramatic, and visual design stages. For these reasons the director's artistic identity, basic screencraft, writing, aesthetics and authorship, acting and actors, textual interpretation, and rehearsal all require far more explanation than shooting and editing, which one might liken to capture and presentation.

The book's organization suggests a rather idealized and linear process for film production, but this will help you find information in a hurry. Throughout I stress the circularity and organic nature of filmmaking art: how important it is to adapt to the individuality of actors, to be ready with improvisatory methods, to solve problems through creative dialogue, and to adapt flexibly to exigencies and opportunities rather than rigidly carry forward an assembly line process. In particular I caution against treating the script as finished and immutable when it too is an organic entity that must either grow or die. This outlook and its resulting practices make survival possible for the low-budget independent, but film industry users have also told me how important this affirmation has been as they swim upstream against some of the industry's more philistine beliefs.

Learning to make films is like learning to become a musician. You can't master the skills with your head alone. Mostly you'll need practice, practice, practice if you are to internalize your art. For this reason the book urges a vast amount of practical work, all of which has abbreviated conceptual instructions, technical and artistic goals, and judgment criteria to help you monitor where your strengths and weaknesses currently lie. When production reveals specific difficulties, you can turn to the other chapters or the index for help in solving your particular problem. Since the *why* is as important as the *how,* practices and self-development are all integrated by a commonsense theory of film derived from everyday perceptual experience.

Some of this edition's many changes have been stimulated by technological developments in filmmaking itself, such as nonlinear digital editing, and those in the arena of artistic form. Cutting-edge directors seem to be moving away from the long-dominant mode of objective realism. Today's films are more likely to thrust us into characters' subjective, inner lives by using more elliptical and impressionistic storytelling techniques. These may include a greater subjectivity in point of view, a less linear narrative development and one likely to be driven by a character's stream of consciousness. In addition, editing, music, and sound design are also more likely to draw the audience into the visceral life of the characters, as one sees in Jane Campion's *The Piano* (1993). But since realism still dominates public taste, and since it still presents a huge challenge to a new director, it remains central to the book's training purposes.

Throughout I aim to dissolve the artificial barriers between the aesthetic and the technical, a segregation as rampant in film schools as in the film and television industries themselves. This split—a symptom, I suppose, of the way our culture makes a class division between artists and artisans—is particularly unreal for filmmakers since nobody in film or video can long hide from the technology that makes screen utterance possible. It has been difficult to draw a line between what does or does not concern a director, so I have tried to cover the creative process in all of its many aspects, and to at least outline whatever else the director must understand or supervise. Budgeting, however, along with fundraising and legal matters, I have thankfully left aside. For this and other specialized information, consult the bibliography.

Nobody writes a book like this alone. Many ideas for this edition grew out of the innumerable relationships with past and present students whose names would halfway fill this book. I have benefited equally from interaction, advice, and criticism from colleagues at Columbia College Film/Video Department—in particular Doreen Bartoni, Robert Buchar, Dr. Judd Chesler, Gina Chorak, Dan Dinello, Chap Freeman, Paul Hettel, and Joe Steiff. I have also learned much from my overseas teaching spells in Norway, Iceland, Holland, Germany, New Zealand, and the Czech Republic, and from the many impassioned film educators I have been lucky enough to encounter along the way.

Special thanks to: Tod Lending for teaching me more about dramatic form; Ken Jacobson of Focal Press for advice on the book's original substance; Karen Speerstra of Focal for enduring support and encouragement; and to Milos Stehlik of Facets Multimedia in Chicago for pictorial assistance.

Michael Rabiger, Chicago, 1996.

P·A·R·T I

ARTISTIC IDENTITY

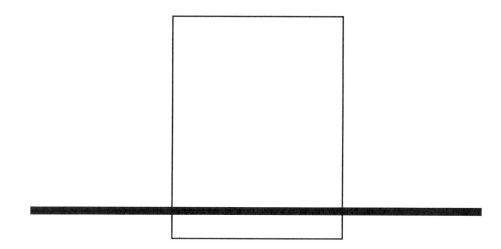

C·H·A·P·T·E·R 1

THE JOB OF THE DIRECTOR

To become an outstanding screen director demands that you either have, or develop, a strong artistic identity. There are also certain qualities and skills required for the job, but first we should look at the job itself, the need for new talent, and the present-day working environment for filmmakers. I should warn video purists that I use the word "filmmaking" to include both film and video production, for I believe they are not different media so much as different delivery methods. Why then is a "made for TV" film usually inferior? Only because it is made by a factory process and with a certain audience in mind, not because an electronic medium is used. The people who make material for television usually think of themselves as efficient processors of entertainment, not producers of anything with profound meaning.

ENVIRONMENT

Purists in both video and film camps must face the fact that digital nonlinear editing is rapidly replacing film editing altogether. Video origination is also making steady advances in quality so that in a festival which interchanges video and film projection, one can sometimes discover one has been watching a video production after assuming it was film. The celebrated documentary *Hoop Dreams* (1994) was shot on Betacam and transferred for general cinema viewing to 35mm film. Few patrons can have been any the wiser. Mobility between technologies is a fact of life and shows all the clearer that they take similar directorial skills.

Now is a good time to study filmmaking. Profound changes are happening in the cinema industry itself, once a closed and father-to-son business like some medieval craft guild. Today's filmmakers emerge from film schools and are more broadly experienced, more versatile, and better educated in the cinema than any preceding generation. Camcorders and tape editing have encouraged more hands-on experience and faster maturation of skills. Looking ahead, digital sound, camera, and nonlinear editing equipment promises the rapidity, access, and diversification that low-cost tape recording offered popular music in the 1960s, and from which came a revolution in forms. We should expect great diversity of cinematic form in the next decade, as more people are able to experiment, and more productions search for more narrowly focused audiences.

The means of production has moved out of studio control, and the equally vital areas of financing and distribution show strong signs of becoming decentralized and more like publishing. The evidence is in the bookstores which now sell audio and video cassettes, CD ROMs, and even computer software. And as cable television, phone companies, and home video/computer equipment move toward making the moving image available at home on individual demand, the market for diverse, original, and contemporary screen works must rise.

But this picture is offset by the fact that becoming a feature film director is a long, uphill process. For every *wunderkind* leaping fully armed from film school there are a handful of others who will take twenty years working their way up from editing, camera, or writing. There are a legion who don't make it at all. The insight and range of skills required for even minimally competent directing is staggering, and to reach a professional level requires the same guts and practice as you need to become a concert pianist. Then if you can't get into one of the better film schools, there's the problem of learning and getting information. Acting and writing are thoroughly documented while practical information on directing is almost nonexistent. What exists is either derived from the theater, or is the anecdotal material (less politely, war stories) published by or about working directors.

You should also know that your dream is rather widely shared. Every entering film student wants to direct, but most learn from their baptismal ordeals that they are better suited to specialize in one of the other crafts. This is wise since virtually nobody can raise money to direct without first proving themselves over the long haul in editing, camerawork, or screenwriting. On the other hand, I firmly believe that the best film crew members have the nascent skills to direct. Such people have a holistic rather than fragmented relationship to the project's soul. They truly know why collaboration, not competition, gets films made.

So before you commit time and funds to preparing yourself you should examine this book very carefully indeed, particularly Part VIII: Career Track.

WHO CAN DIRECT?

Directors come in all human types—tall, short, fair, dark, introvert, extrovert, loquacious, taciturn, male, female, gay, straight. The only common qualities seem to be tenacity, vision, inventiveness in the face of obstacles, and a love for the filmmaking process. More men than women think they have these qualities, but happily this is changing. With a multi-disciplinary craft requiring social skills as well as intellect and character, it is almost impossible to predict who will be truly capable. The best way to prove your capacity is to just do it.

While this book assumes you have no prior knowledge of film directing or of acting, you will need to acquire some screencraft basics. There are development projects but no equipment handling instructions, for which there are many good manuals (see Bibliography). Don't agonize over cinematic techniques; people who have something to say will soon figure out better ways to say it. Don't listen to those who say you must first learn the tools before you can have something to say. Tools, not authorship, is their purview.

You will need keenly realized, strongly visual stories. This material, which is usually but not always a screenplay, needs to be thoroughly felt, comprehended, and believed in. After that you will need a competent crew and a well-chosen cast, and the skills and strength of character to get the best out of everybody.

Directing means bringing together people of very different skills. It takes long and lonely struggle to keep them going and to hold onto your original vision. You will need to fully understand the actor's frame of reference and the various states of consciousness they pass through. You will have to understand how to use the screen dynamically, and how to fulfill the emotional, psychological, and intellectual needs of the common person—that is, your audience. Happily they are quite a lot like yourself. After shooting, you will then need further skills and persistence in the cutting room to work with an editor at uniting the fragments into an optimal version.

Good directing means demanding much from cast and crew while making each individual feel valuable to the whole. For all this you need the self knowledge, humility, and toughness to be a good leader. Above all you need to be a doer.

Asking for all these qualities in one human being is a tall order. For the beginner, trying to develop so many skills is like learning to juggle. Your first efforts (of which you are so proud) soon embarrass you with their inexpert writing, amateurish acting, and turgid dramatic construction. There has been no help in print, and without access to professional mentors, reliable guidance is hard or impossible to find. Well used, this book can be your best friend. It is an indexed, integrated, and comprehensive approach and has advice, examples, and explanations to cover most predicaments. It cannot, however, provide the perseverance and faith in oneself that characterizes those who survive in the arts and crafts. This you supply.

PARTICULARLY FOR THE EXCLUDED

Filmmaking has long been a white male preserve, but women and minorities are entering in increasing numbers, and bringing their individual talents and blessedly different ways of seeing. Is this you? My hope is that your experience and sensibilities will dislodge the sick preoccupation with power and violence presently dominating mass culture. Apologists claim that it reflects and does not lead our society. But if this were true there would be no such thing as an advertising industry. But just as pornography arrives and wanes in societies emerging from decades of sexual repression, so perhaps the present emphasis on violence is a passing reaction to widespread feelings of frustration and personal insignificance. Maybe new visions and new voices can show us who we really are.

WITH LOW BUDGETS IN MIND

Most users of this book will be working with modest equipment and slender budgets. One can make excellent films without elaborate settings, or expensive props, costumes, equipment, or special effects. Everyone respects the ability to make much out of little. Accordingly most of my film examples come from modern low-budget cinema. The search for useful examples leads inevitably to resourceful, original minds that are sometimes working far afield in other countries and other cultures—a link that can only be good.

SHORT FILMS OR LONGER?

Anyone serving on a festival jury soon discovers that films reveal their strengths and weaknesses within two or three minutes and often within two or three shots. The trapped juror wishes ardently that the filmmaker had sought feedback from an audience after five minutes of screen time instead of a mind-numbing forty-five. The implication is important: short films still require their makers to conquer the full range of production, authorship, and stylistic problems—but in a small compass and at small cost. The economy is in shooting costs and editing time, not in brainwork. For like poetry in relation to the novel, one must still establish characters, time, place, and situation, and set appropriate limits on the subject. These are tough skills to learn and take much practice. Getting seen is the precursor to getting noticed, and for actuarial reasons alone short films are always more likely to be shown in festivals than long ones. But most film schools use feature films as teaching examples since features drew both students and faculty to film in the first place. So students often receive inadequate guidance on framing short subjects. Films by neophytes are consequently often like zeppelins, all size and no substance or agility. There is a special section in Chapter 16 on short forms.

FILM OR VIDEO?

Directing methods for screen drama are the same for both film and video, though the scale of operations and the path to completion may be different. Passions run high as to what medium one "should" use, so it is worth running over some pros and cons—especially as they affect the acquisition of skills.

Costs in professional production may come out relatively equal for film and video, so film is often the preferred camera medium, even though postproduction is moving toward being wholly done in digital video. Currently the 35mm film process records a much more detailed image and permits a higher fidelity sound recording, but this superiority only shows up in a well-equipped, well-run film theater (most are neither). Since so much viewing is in the home and on video, the superiority of film is often a wasted virtue.

High definition television (HDTV) will prolong film's life by making location recording temporarily so expensive that Super 16mm film, with its wide screen format, will be the economic choice—for a while. It must also be said that anything on film is widely regarded as automatically of higher *class* than video, so film remains the medium of visual choice for festivals where most short films begin (and end) their careers.

Audience consumption patterns will inevitably shape future production methods; only cinemas need film and they are unlikely to show more films if cablecasting can offer instant and wide choice in the home. What they will show is likely to be high-budget spectacle.

For the filmmaker in training, video offers the massive advantage that one can shoot ample coverage without regard to expense. This alone is an educational revolution. Film is something special and wonderful to handle in editing but takes massive effort to splice, file, and retrieve. Sound tracks transferred to 16mm optical sound track (unavoidable for composite, that is, sound-on-picture prints), are truly atrocious. Sixteen millimeter film is emphatically *not* the medium of choice for anyone who cares about filmmaking in any holistic way.

High band 8mm video (Hi8) with its digital Pulse Code Modulation (PCM) tracks, is up to CD disk quality, and so is the computer audiovisual workstation. The latter functions like a word processor—able to cut, move, and copy both sound and picture materials. It is the basis for the nonlinear video editing setups like Adobe Premiere, Lightworks, D/Vision, Avid and a host of competitors. Once picture and sound materials have been digitized (that is, compressed into a digital signal and stored in a computer's hard disk) the editor has virtually instant access to any frame in the hours of material, and can assemble, change, and view either old or new assemblies at will. Further, one can make optical effects or titles with none of the delay and uncertainty occasioned by the need for laboratories. Time and energy saved is time and energy with which to create.

Linear videotape editing on the other hand uses an electronically controlled transcription process between videocassette player and recorder. Although for the beginner it is physically easier than film editing, it is more arduous in the long run because additions and deletions are not as easy as they are with a film workprint. Film editing is like making a chain; it can always be broken into, and links added or subtracted. The links are the separate pieces of sound and picture, and one can see and feel what one is doing. Linear videotape compilation on the other hand is like a spinning operation that produces a continuous filament whose middle cannot be retrospectively altered.

Presently most video editing is offline, that is, it uses low-level equipment to produce an artistically viable fine cut that is several generations away from the camera original and is of degraded technical quality. Once the fine cut has been achieved and an Edit Decision List (EDL) has been compiled, the project moves to the online editing stage. This uses the EDL and an array of expensive computerized video and sound equipment to produce a fine-quality release print from camera original tape.

Nonlinear editing design is moving inexorably toward the fusion of these stages; future equipment will be wholly digital and there will be no need for two processes because digital copying does not degrade through generations. A broadcast quality version in both sound and picture will result from every stage of editing.

With some experience and a lot of drive, you can use small-format tape like Super VHS, Hi8, or digital video to produce sophisticated work. This you can use to argue persuasively for support to use the more expensive formats like Betacam or film. Whether you use linear or nonlinear editing will be a matter of time and budget.

What matters most is to get experience with different kinds of filmmaking. People not machines make films.

WHY USING HOLLYWOOD AS A MODEL CAN'T WORK FOR BEGINNERS

To appreciate which educational approach functions best, one must first compare the professional feature team's process with that of the struggling independent group. Differences show up when one compares schedules and budgets of a 90-minute professional feature with a typical 30-minute student production.

Priorities in professional feature films are determined more by dollar economics than by artistic requirements: scriptwriting is relatively cheap, while tying up stars, equipment, or crew is very costly. Reliable performance is valued and risky experiment is to be feared. Actors are cast for their ability to produce something usable, immediate, and repeatable. The director is under economic pressure to shoot a safe, all-purpose camera coverage that can be "sorted out in the cutting room" afterward.

Locked into such a production system, the director has little option but to fight narrowly for what he (only rarely she) thinks achievable. Hollywood-style films, too profitable to change from within, are often as packaged and formulaic as supermarket novels, and look like it. A box office success can make back millions for its financiers in a few weeks, so backers always prefer the standard process to the new or the personal.

Now consider how professionals acquire and maintain craft skills. During a feature shoot, a hundred specialists may each carry forward their particular part of the communal task, each having begun as an apprentice in a lowly position and working half a lifetime to earn the senior levels of responsibility. Many, like my-

Production Aspect	90-minute low-budget professional feature	Typical 30-minute student film
Script development period	6 months to several years, innumerable drafts	2–6 months, probably 2 drafts only
Preproduction period	4–12 weeks	3–5 weeks
Rehearsal period	Little or none	0–7 days
Shooting period	6–12 weeks	7–15 days
Postproduction period	4–6 months	3–14 months
Format	35mm	16mm or Super 16mm
Budget in $$$	8 million dollars	35 thousand dollars

FIGURE 1-1

Typical professional and student productions compared.

self, come from film families and have had their youth in which to absorb the mind-set that goes with the job. The significance of this heritage cannot be overstated. But, though apprenticeship is a vital factor in the continuity of skills, it is also a conditioning force that deeply discourages self-evaluation and change.

Little of all this is evident to the newcomer, who naturally thinks one should emulate the professional system—often with the misplaced encouragement of professionals. Look again at the beginner's schedule in Figure 1-1. The big giveaway is the postproduction period. Enormous time and effort is spent in the cutting room afterward trying to recover from the problems embedded in the script (beyond the writer/director's experience), inadequate acting (poor casting, insufficient rehearsal), and shooting (hasty, too much early coverage, too little later). I mean only to warn, not to discourage or disparage. The number of variables to be brought under control by the director is literally enormous, and the newcomer cannot help but underestimate the process.

VITAL DIFFERENCES FOR THE LOW-BUDGET FILMMAKER

Because the low-budget (or no budget) director seldom has a wide choice of crew or actors, he or she needs different methods that will shape nonprofessionals into a well-knit, accomplished team. Nonprofessional actors need extended rehearsals in which to develop empathy with their characters and the confidence that alone gives their performances conviction and authority.

Under these circumstances the director cannot afford to be immovable about the script: cast limitations require that it be responsive to the actor rather than vice versa. In any case a script is always a literary blueprint and by its nature unfulfillable except through intelligent (which means flexible) translation. One can elude some of these shortcomings by choosing a subject and treatment requiring no elaborate events and environments. One can schedule more time for rehearsal (if one knows how to use it), and so on. But setting the whole low-budget situation alongside big-industry norms, it is overwhelmingly apparent that low-budget filmmakers must set different priorities and use special strategies.

ALTERNATIVE ROUTES

You can and must aim at professional-level results, but you must travel by a road that uses trial and error as a developmental process, and makes of it a strength. As we shall see, a convincing human presence on the screen is only achieved (by amateur and professional actor alike) *if the director can see the actors' problems and remove the blocks causing them.* Left undisturbed, these obstacles will sabotage the entire film, no matter how accomplished the rest of the production process. And without a top-notch, screen-trained cast, these problems are virtually guaranteed.

The development process outlined in this book creates and cements bonds between members of the ensemble, and gives the director and writer (if they are indeed two people rather than one) a positive exposure to the singularities of each cast member. The director must in turn be ready to adapt and transform the script in order to capitalize on cast members' individual potential.

In sum, what the Hollywood filmmaking army does with its marines and machines can be matched only if the low-budget filmmaker enters the fray as a guerrilla combatant using cautious, oblique, and experimental tactics. Once this principle of organic, mutual accommodation is accepted, the rest of the process follows logically and naturally.

Nothing about this is radical or untried. A little reading will show similar strategies to have been used by talents like Allen, Altman, Bergman, Bresson, Cassavetes, Fassbinder, Fellini, Herzog, Leigh, Resnais, Tanner, and many others who give primacy to the contribution by actors.

ABOUT DRAMATIC PRESENTATION

In relation to actors, the director's main task is often misunderstood. It is not to goad actors into doing something extraordinary, but instead to remove a myriad of psychological obstacles. These smother both the ordinary and the extraordinary from happening. For effective screen acting lies not in a range of arcane techniques but in the actor being relaxed, honest to his emotions, and free of misconceptions. A misguided self-image, for instance, puts the actor's attention in the wrong place and makes him behave unnaturally. The perfectly normal psychological defenses that everyone develops are therefore a major barrier to naturalness in acting, and even more so are popular ideas about acting itself. Novice actors in particular, and even trained actors who should know better, often feel they must produce something heightened to deserve attention and entertain the audience. Instead of *being,* the player discharges his responsibility onscreen by signifying, that is, by telegraphing thought and emotion. This is so thought-laden and artificial that it precludes any true experiencing. The actor becomes self-conscious and disunited; while he "acts," another part of him anxiously watches and plans the next phase of the performance. Pitilessly, the camera reveals this divided and unnatural state of affairs. Michael Caine has some compellingly illustrated arguments to make in *Acting in Film: an Actor's Take on Movie-Making* (BBC TV tape, NY: Applause Theatre Publishers, 1990).

However, when actors "signify" it is not solely inexperience or misguided effort. The impulse to stylize dramatic material has a long and respectable history in live theater. Until modern staging and lighting methods became possible in the nineteenth century, stage performance made little attempt to be naturalistic. Greek drama was played in masks that concealed the actors' psychological identity and projected archetypal human qualities like nobility, wisdom, or greed. Japanese Kabuki theater used elaborate, ritualized costumes and an operatic verbal delivery which, like western opera, invites the audience to attach itself to the groundswell of human passions beneath the surface. Likewise, medieval Christian mystery plays, mime, mummers, and the Italian *commedia del arte* all employed traditional characters, gestures, episodes, and situations. All of this was deliberately nonrealistic and nonindividualistic.

Why should the person of the actor be concealed, yet the interpretation of a stock character be so prized by audiences? Prior to the Renaissance the very idea of individual worth was a vanity amounting to blasphemy against God's purpose. The transience of life, and the religious explanations rationalizing this bleak state of affairs, made people see themselves as ephemera in a God-determined whole.

One's life was just a brief thread in God's great tapestry, with each individual destined to carry out a role allotted by accident of birth and patterned by such constants as ambition, compassion, love, and jealousy. Realistic presentation, at least to a small audience, was never impossible but one sees how verisimilitude and psychological accuracy were irrelevant to the predicament audiences knew as their own.

With the focus shifting to individual potential that began during the Renaissance, and particularly after the impact of Darwin in the nineteenth century, audiences were increasingly ready to accept the significance of the individual life and to see it as a struggle for survival, rather than as a temporary stay in which to earn merit for an afterlife. Writers increasingly reflected ideas about the individual's inner life and about his (rarely her) individually wrought destiny. Acting styles were slower to change, and remained declamatory and stylized as late as the early phase of the movies.

In Russia just after the revolution, at a time of bold rethinking in the arts and advances in psychology, Stanislavski developed the modern theory of the actor's consciousness that underlies any distinctive performance. The advent of sound cinema brought audiences eyeball to eyeball with the remains of feigned naturalism, and both actors and dramatists were forced to give new attention to what could pass for credible human interchange.

Modern audiences now expect screen characters to be no less believable than their realistically photographed settings. So unless a film strives for a subjectively perceived environment (as in German expressionist cinema of the 1920s and 1930s, or any of the nonrealist modern genres such as horror), audiences expect real people behaving realistically in real settings. This is easy to understand and hard to produce.

Rightly or wrongly the preponderance of cinema aims at the appearance of verisimilitude, so realistic acting should be the student director's first goal. Done well, it looks effortless, but the process of filmmaking compels a circuitous artifice to get there. With shooting fragmented by lighting changes, talent availability, and budget, it is not even a good training ground for actors. The best usually come from strong theater backgrounds, where the continuity of performance and the closed loop of communication with an audience have given the actor confidence in his instincts. The film actor on the other hand must perform in fits and starts; no feedback is possible since during filming the only audience is the director and crew, who must in any case be dismissed from consciousness while the camera is rolling. Acting for the camera should be like living unwatched. The camera sees everything, spying at close range upon characters in their most private and intense moments. Actors can afford no lapse in experiencing their characters' inmost thoughts and feelings. Such a lapse, called "losing focus," is immediately visible.

Good actors can shut out the technical process. During his apprentice days, Aidan Quinn did an improvised scene of considerable power with a woman actor in a directing class of mine. It was taped documentary style (more about this later). During the very intense scene, the camera snaked all around the actors and came within two or three feet of them. After the director called "cut," the actors turned to me and said, "We should have taped that one." They had been totally unaware of the camera's presence.

As in documentary, the camera-as-witness compels actors, when they are to be convincing, to undergo a series of actual emotions. They can seldom wear a mask, either actual or psychological and instead must go naked to merge with the part—whether that character is good or bad, attractive or ugly, intelligent or stupid.

There is a problem that is particularly acute in love scenes. How to behave with spontaneity before camera and crew in take after take. This throws formidable demands upon the actor's concentration, ego, and self-assurance, for it is unacceptable to merely signify villainy, impersonate weakness, or mime erotic attraction. The actor must dig deeply into his or her own emotional range in order to uncover whatever is demanded. Searching within himself for an "unpopular" or revealing emotion, the actor may have to confront embarrassing or even hateful aspects of himself. Ralph Fiennes, who so powerfully played the Nazi camp commander Amon Goeth in Steven Spielberg's *Schindler's List* (1993), found his part emotionally excruciating, so much did he despise his character. Some of the Polish extras hired to play anti-Semitic townspeople are said to have wept after being asked to yell anti-Semitic abuse at actors playing Jewish prisoners.

A further threat to the actor's ego may be that of accepting and building upon critical feedback from an undemocratic audience of one: the director. A far-ranging, seemingly effortless performance onscreen will thus be the result of an extraordinarily disciplined mind drawing widely upon its owner's emotional experience. For actor and director to achieve such a performance, they must navigate a minefield of problems together.

ON MASKS AND THE FUNCTION OF DRAMA

In various ways throughout this book I shall seek to demonstrate a curious and little appreciated fact: *A cinema audience does not really go to see the film, it goes to see into itself, to imagine, think, and feel as others do.* This is no different from the reader of a novel, who reads not to see language or print, but to participate in that structured, waking, and intensely personal dream that we call reading. For this reason, perhaps, film with its hypnotic appeal to the senses has often been likened to dreaming.

Now we discover another purpose behind the traditional actor's masks and stock characterizations. By denying us the literal identity of the actors, stylistic devices encourage us to fill in our own mental images, just as the literary phrase "her beauty was incomparable" does for a reader. Theatrical reality is representational, blurred, and held at a distance to allow us to experience not specific human attractiveness or malevolence, but the immeasurably richer beauty and terror of our own beholding mind. Ancient dramatists discovered something the infant cinema is having to learn—that if dramatic art is to fulfill its potential it cannot simulate reportage; it must evoke our co-creation.

Here we collide with the cinema's limitation—the prosaic realism of the camera, showing literally and to the last open pore whatever is placed before it. Used unintelligently the camera purveys a surfeit of the real but leaves nothing to the imagination. This is a severe handicap for an art medium. How can you possibly *show* "incomparable beauty?" Films that break out of this stockade always in some way connect us to myth and archetype, that stock of tragi-comic human equations constructed somewhere in the distant past which unfailingly trigger our deeper emotions. The character of Garance in Marcel Carné's *The Children of*

FIGURE 1-2

Carné's *Children of Paradise*, a story of unattainable love based on the Pierrot and Columbine archetypes (courtesy Museum of Modern Art/Film Stills Archive).

Paradise (1945) will be undyingly lovely while one print survives and one audience member lives to see it. She is so not just because the actress Arletty is beautiful, or because the black and white cinematography and the lighting are unearthly, but because her enigmatic character hides so much. She is the legendary character of Columbine reborn, the fickle, unattainable, free spirit whom poor Pierrot can never hold because he's too sincere and earthbound. In short, she evokes the poignancy of our own lost loves.

DEVELOPING CINEMA ART

A progressive cinema form must work to activate the audience's imagination, opening up interior spaces to be filled from the hearts and minds of the viewers. Here we are talking about richness and ambiguity of character and theme, and about a cinematic language that must further develop if it is to show less and imply more. Only thus can it direct the audience toward something of greater worth than the superficial and the sensational. We are talking about looks, glances, averted profiles, turned backs, enigmatic silences, the suggestive voices of nature, and of primeval landscapes inhabited or abandoned by humans. We are talking of a cinema able to alert us to what exists at the very edges of our perception, and beyond.

The more the cinema invites the audience to exercise its judgment and to draw on its own buried culture, the more it will approach the emotional release of music and match the intellectual power of literature. One day it may even be able to justify robbing literature of its fans.

The cinema is several arts rolled into one. But to develop your potential as an artist you will have to look for the component parts outside cinema. You will have to step outside the smug envelope of the present to learn how the other arts function and how they act upon us. And you will need strong, clear, and critical ideas about your contemporaries and their time. This is at the core of an individual artistic identity and the story material it chooses, which is the subject of the next two chapters.

THE ROAD TO AUTHORIAL CONTROL

This book is intended to take the beginner up to the most advanced levels of filmmaking. As such it sets forth many guidelines for the *auteur* filmmaker, that is, the writer/director wanting to exercise an integrated control across the spectrum of the writing and realization processes. Such control can only be exercised when one understands advanced concepts about how work of depth and resonance is created, how screen works achieve a strongly individual identity, and how the narrative form itself might be expanded and developed.

Curiously, the *auteur* exists both at the beginner level and at the pinnacles of the world film industry, but much less apparently in the middle ground. A typical evolution begins in film school where the filmmaker starts as a Renaissance figure doing anything and everything. Wanting to produce more sophisticated work, he or she soon specializes in one of the crafts. Competently handled, that craft becomes the bridge into the film industry where initially he or she makes a slender living as a free-lancer. Now a specialist technician, our filmmaker becomes known and established and living becomes less precarious. If during the following years the drive to direct results in an opportunity, early directing work is likely to be cautious and commercial, for death at the box office means dropping down the ladder again. With two or three modest successes a director can expand into more personally meaningful work. Even when limited by survival instincts and money interests to doing popular work, the astute director can flex artistic muscle and learn to control the medium. This is even true to a more limited degree in commercials.

When a director gains a mature control over the medium and over what he or she needs to say through it, audiences begin to detect and be excited by an authorial identity at work. The filmmaker who in youth at film school once had total control over a very small film now regains similar ubiquity over an immensely expensive and popularly significant medium. The *auteur* reemerges, now driving a better car. This same person, now humbled from some years of teamwork, would be embarrassed to proclaim himself an *auteur* even though the control is as much his as it will ever be. Those heartfelt thanks given to film crew members during Academy Awards night are no meaningless ritual. They acknowledge the true source of creativity in such a collaborative art form.

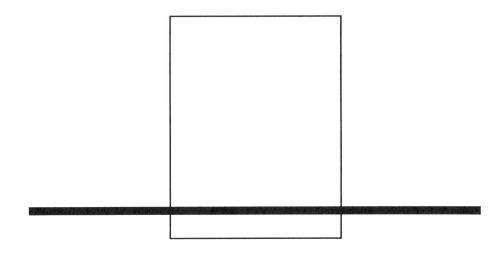

C·H·A·P·T·E·R 2

IDENTIFYING YOUR THEMES AS A DIRECTOR

When you have gained technical control over using the screen, if not long before then, you will want to shoot films that are meaningful to you. Filmmaking is too long and arduous to commit one's energies to doing just anything. In any case, people attracted to the arts are there for a purpose, whether they know it or not. By nature human beings are seekers and one's chosen art form becomes the vehicle for the quest. The nature and direction of each person's search varies but all of us seek meaning. When we do find an answer, it glitters—but only for a while. Soon we face a more profound question underlying it.

Perhaps the act of search is what lends us grace, rather than any of our occasional discoveries. At any rate, you will want your filmmaking to be *about* something. Whether you write your own stories, have someone else write a script, or choose something to adapt, you will still face a central question: How am I going to use my developing skills in the world? What kind of subject should I tackle? What can I be good at? What is my artistic identity?

Those with dramatic life experience (say, of warfare, survival in labor camps, or of being orphaned) seldom doubt which subjects to tackle. But for the rest of us who live more ordinary lives, placing an identity on one's undoubted sense of mission can be baffling. One faces a conundrum; you can't make art without a sense of identity, yet it is identity that you may be seeking through making art.

Many are attracted to the arts because they feel the need for self-expression, but this phrase has a variety of applications. The most prevalent is that of self-affirmation, but this suggests that art and therapy are synonymous. Art is about doing work in the world, while therapy is acquiring wellbeing. Nothing wrong with that. Everyone seeks recognition because everyone privately feels under-appreciated. Self-affirmation in the arts, however, can become the slippery slope to self-display, and any inventory of one's beliefs and achievements leads rather too easily to homily. Trying to prove one's individuality and worth is to be avoided at all costs if only because one's liberation almost certainly rests on ideals, role models, and ideologies that are already common property.

Another approach to self-expression rests with form. Some people think that by mastering particular styles and genres, one can carve out an identity different from everyone else's, but I think this too is another misguided quest for individuality in a society uncomfortably locked together by mass media. We live in an age that elevates the notion of individuality. It tells us that Self is that which is different from everyone else. But historically this is a recent western idea which gathered force when man began abandoning the notion of God and made himself the center of the universe. The Hindus have a very different belief. To them, Self is that which you *share* with all creation. Significantly, one ideology is inclusive, the other isolating. I find that most who are trying to create something actually subscribe to both ends of the spectrum. They want to be individual and recognized, but they also want to create something universal. Another conundrum.

You may be asking, does all this really matter so early in one's career? Maybe not, but most beginners are anxious to find what they are best equipped to handle. I think their instincts are right. Indeed, without some persuasions about cause and effect in life, without a perception of its order, one lacks the vision to create vision. How, then, to go about defining oneself in order to direct fictional films?

In reality, one's choices are mercifully few. Each person's life has marked him or her in unique ways, and these marks—whether one knows it or not—play a determining role in how one lives one's life and what one chooses to pursue. You can struggle against this, and deny the marks you carry, but this is merely evidence of their power over you. Looking back we can often see patterns to our lives; we suddenly see what has been driving us. Even more clearly can we see these patterns in those we know well. Each person's path is chosen in relation to these psychic marks, and thus we play a major part in making our own destiny.

Let me illustrate from personal experience. Some time back, as part of a study program, I was required to watch all my documentary films and to write a self-assessment. To my astonishment I discovered that though they were all about different topics, they did have a common theme. It was that "most people are imprisoned but the inventive are able to adapt, rebel, and escape." How could I have unknowingly made over twenty films with this one constancy?

I began searching for explanations. I grew up in a family relocated by the war into an English agricultural village. We were middle class and isolated among the rural poor. For the first several years my father, a foreigner in origin, was away serving on merchant ships and my mother found nothing in common with most of her neighbors. Going to a local school, I had to contend with the other kids who jeered at the way I spoke. I was derided, my possessions envied, and even ambushed. Though I thought we were "better" than the local people, I learned several things: that I was different and unacceptable to the majority; that fear was a constant; and that one had to handle it alone because adults were preoccupied. I discovered that one could get out of tight spots by making people laugh, and that outside home it was best to become a different person. One day my parents realized I had a different voice for outside home.

Eventually I saw that my torment was not my fault for being cowardly, nor was it even personally intended by my tormentors. I represented a class that was viscerally hated by their parents, so I became the scapegoat. Blindly we played out roles of which we were unaware. When I learned in later years how the rural poor had been suppressed and exploited in previous centuries, I understood the other kids' hostility to what I represented. Losing my fear, and with it an inculcated sense of class superiority, my relationship with fellow conscripts in the Royal Air Force—where the whole thing might easily have been repeated—was quite different and very gratifying.

To summarize: In earlier life I lived on both sides of an invisible barricade. Needing survival strategies, I became equipped to empathize with others in a like predicament: the black person in a white neighborhood, the Jew among Gentiles, the child among adults. Now if I am drawn to foreigners or the displaced, or to people with unorthodox vision, it is through no unaccountable quirk. Having once worn the scarlet letter myself, I now easily enter the reality of others similarly placed. I am intensely moved by the plight of the unaware individual caught in a web, blindly struggling to survive, to adapt and perhaps escape. Any story containing these trace elements quickens my interest. But for many years I was hardly aware of it, and even less was I aware that I had a vision of life as a variation of successive imprisonments from each of which, for the determined few, there is the possibility of escape.

Different personalities respond to different issues. Countless male directors, working in an industry that preeminently respects power, end up making autobiographical films about men achieving manhood and authority. A woman's path may be very different. Donna Deitch in *Desert Hearts* (1985) explores the different kinds of love that women can give. Alain Tanner has repeatedly made films about people trying to live out their impractically romantic ideals in a drearily unimaginative setting. Oliver Stone in *Platoon* (1987) focuses on a young Everyman patriot who is catapulted into a war so indecipherable that he must concentrate on physical and spiritual survival. A biography by Paul Michaud about the late François Truffaut links such films as *The 400 Blows* (1959), *Jules and Jim* (1961), *The Wild Child* (1969), and *The Story of Adèle H.* (1975) with trauma Truffaut suffered as a child on being estranged from his mother. His characters' rootless lives, their naïve impracticality, and even his study of Adèle Hugo's neurotic, self-destructive hunger for love all reflect aspects of the Truffaut his friends knew. This does not reduce or "explain" Truffaut so much as point to an energizing self-recognition as the source of his prolific output, and to suggest how diverse are the means by which self-recognition can be expressed and made universal.

You too carry the marks of a few central issues as your formative experience. Reminders of these unfailingly arouse you to strongly partisan feelings. Though the issues may be few and personal, they will deeply touch your audience and keep you busy for life if you explore them sincerely and intelligently. We are not talking about autobiography, but a core of experience as a theme to which there are endless variations.

FIND YOUR LIFE ISSUES

There are right and wrong ways to come into possession of your own particular life issues. A wrong way is to regard someone else's tastes and judgment about you as more authoritative than your own. Change authority and you change identity—but do you?

To find what your own life issues really are means confronting yourself honestly and paring away everything alien to your abiding concerns. This is not easy because of the shimmering, ambiguous nature of actuality itself. What is real? What is cause and what is effect? Perhaps because film appears to look into the world rather than into the person or people making the film, most filmmakers stop at an extremely superficial understanding of their own drives. Drama, if it is to have any spark of originality, is really about developing a dialogue—with oneself and with an audience.

PROJECTS

Here are a few exercises to begin that process that you may find helpful.

PROJECT 2-1: THE SELF-INVENTORY

To uncover your real issues and themes, and to therefore discover what you can give others, make a nonjudgmental inventory of your most moving experiences. This is not as difficult as it sounds, for the human memory jettisons the mundane and retains only what it finds significant.

1. Go somewhere private and write rapid, short notations of each major experience just as it comes to mind. Keep going until you have at least ten or a dozen experiences in which you were deeply moved (to joy, to rage, to panic, to fear, to disgust, to anguish, to love, etc).

2. Now stand back and organize them into groups. Give names to each grouping and to the relationships between them. Some moving experiences will be positive (with feelings of joy, relief, discovery, laughter) but most will be painful. Make no distinction, for there is no such thing as a negative or positive truth. To discriminate like this is to censor, which is just another way to prolong the endless and wasteful search for acceptability. Truth is *truth*—period!

3. Now examine what you've written as though looking objectively at someone else's record. What kind of expressive work should come from someone marked by such experiences? You should be able to place yourself in a different light and find trends, even a certain vision of the world, clustering around these experiences. Don't be afraid to be imaginative, as though developing a fictional character. Your object is not therapy, but to find a storytelling role that you can play with all your heart.

Even though you have a good handle on your underlying issues, try making the inventory anyway. You may get some surprises. Honestly undertaken, this examination will confirm which life-events formed you and this in turn will urge that your work explore the underlying issues they represent. You will probably see how you have resonated to these issues all along in your choice of music, literature, and films, not to mention in your friendships, love affairs, and family relationships.

PROJECT 2-2: ALTER EGOS

It is often useful to make an oblique approach to finding one's deeper aspirations and identifications. Particular characters or particular situations in films, plays or books often trigger a special response in us, and this in turn offers useful clues to one's own makeup, the larger part of which will always remain a mystery. The purpose of this project is to discover one's resonances.

1. List six or eight characters from literature or fiction with whom you have a special affinity. Arrange them by their importance to you. An affinity can be hero-worship, but it becomes more interesting when one is responding to darker or more complex qualities.
2. Do the same thing for public figures like actors, politicians, sports figures, etc.
3. Make a third list of people you know or have known, but leave out immediate family if they complicate the exercise.
4. Take the top two or three in each list and write a brief description of what, in human or even mythical qualities, each person represents, and what dilemma seems to typify them. If, for instance, O.J. Simpson were on your list, he might represent someone whose jealous passion destroyed what he most loves.
5. Now write a self-profile based on what the resonances suggest. Don't hesitate to imaginatively round out the portrait as though it were a fictional character. The aim is not to define who you are (you'll never succeed) but to build a provocative and active picture of *what you are looking for and how you see the world.*

PROJECT 2-3: USING DREAMS TO FIND ONE'S PREOCCUPATIONS

Keep a log of your dreams, for here the mind expresses itself unguardedly and in surreal and symbolic imagery. Unless you have a period of intense dream activity, you will have to keep a record over many months before common denominators and motifs begin showing up. Keep a notebook next to the bed, and awake gently so you hold onto the dream long enough to write it down. If you get really interested in this work, you can instruct yourself to wake in the night after a good dream, and write it down. Needless to say, this will not be popular with a bedroom partner.

Dreams frequently project with great force a series of tantalizing images that are often symbolically charged with meaning. The British novelist John Fowles started both *The French Lieutenant's Woman* and *A Maggot* from single images, one of a woman gazing out to sea toward France, the other of a mysterious group of horsemen crossing a hillside accompanying a lone woman. Whole complex novels came from investigating the characters "seen" in these alluring glimpses.

You have hidden patterns and propitious images waiting in the wings to be recognized and developed.

FINDING YOUR WORK'S PATH

This search for your own path, for the truths underlying your formation and patterns, starts feeding itself once you make a commitment to expressing something about it. This sustains the artistic process: at the beginning you get clues, clues lead to discoveries, discoveries lead to movement in one's work, and movement leads to new clues. A piece of work—whether a piece of writing, a painting, a short story, or a filmscript—is therefore both the evidence of movement and a prime mover in making further progress in the search for meaning. One's work becomes the trail of one's own evolution.

FOLLOW YOUR FASCINATIONS

In getting ready to produce, search for that special element that fascinates you. It might be expressed through mountaineering, the rescue of animals, something involving water and boats, or love between schoolfriends. You explore that fascination by producing something external to your own thoughts: the piece of work. What begins as a circumscribed personal quest soon leads outward. You might take two opposing parts of your own character during a trying period of your life and make them into two separate characters, perhaps making imaginative use of two well-known political or historical characters to do so. Profiling historical personalities, social assumptions, political events, or the temperaments of the people most influential in your life will all contribute to further shaping your consciousness. Doing such things well entertains and excites your audience, who are also—whether they know it or not—pursuing a private quest and starving for a sense of direction.

C·H·A·P·T·E·R 3

DEVELOPING YOUR STORY IDEAS

A writer changes hats as a matter of course and the two worn most often are "story development" and "story editing." These two modes of functioning use quite different operations: intuition, emotional memory, and following instincts on the one hand, and intellectual analysis and structuring on the other.

Screenwriting manuals and screenwriting teachers often suggest that one begins from an outline, but this is actually a later stage. One often begins from nothing more than a germ of an idea, or a persuasion. This, born hesitantly from personal feelings, is a fragile flame that is easily snuffed out. The best work comes from the artistic process being practiced in its purest form while hack work comes from industry formulae. There is something to be learned from them, but later. At an idea's inception one must move slowly, carefully, and without preconceptions.

If you sit down to write something "new" and purely from imagination you will soon discover you are paralyzed by all the other creative minds who have got there first. Truly, no story is original. So don't give a thought to being "good" or "original" or any of those other judgmental words. Work at it, and little by little something will emerge, for the truth is that you belong in a historical stream and it's impossible not to borrow from the human story—that is, from life and from other creators. In the writing chapters there is a list of themes, plots, and situations, because there are really not too many. But that doesn't limit you, for there are limitless interesting characters walking the face of the earth, and an unending number of variations and combinations to emerge from the basics. So have no compunction when you borrow from life or other art; in making a film you are going to put the starting materials through a long and complex transformation. If you start from a given story or myth that has special meaning, you can change one or two of the elements in this borrowed framework, develop your own characters, and the meaning and impact of the entire work will be affected, probably beyond recognition.

Like many writers you will probably want to start from something actual. At first, searching for stories, it may seem that nothing dramatic has ever happened in your life to draw upon. Perhaps the tensions you have witnessed or experienced never matured into any action. But the writer's gratification—and it may even be the chief reward of authorship—is to make happen what should have happened but didn't. Precisely because an event or situation has etched itself into your consciousness, it can almost certainly be shaped into something expressive of particular themes and a particular vision of life. This, depending on your tastes and temperament, may be tragic, comic, satiric, realistic, surreal, or melodramatic. By projecting the familiar into the confrontation and change you wish had happened, you can follow the road not taken. A real-life situation that contains characters, events, situations, and conflicts already has the elements of drama, and the potential to become a full-blown story.

Imagine, for example, that you want to make a film which projects the incompatible natures of your parents to some point of resolution. Since they have never expressed anything more than irritation with each other, you do not know how to do it. In the newspaper, however, you see a true story about a peaceable civil servant, married for thirty-eight years, who flipped and did the unthinkable. This catches your eye because you're interested in what makes people conform all their lives, do tedious or meaningless work, and then at one particular triggering moment shear off at a tangent into new territory. This man at Thanksgiving suddenly rose up from the dinner table because his wife put the salt shaker back in the wrong place on the table. Irrevocably crossing some inner threshold, he left home to look for a childhood sweetheart. And since the article doesn't tell you what happened, you decide to invent the consequences.

Now you face a dilemma. You can digress imaginatively from biographical fact or you can stick closely to it. Here are two examples of feature films that followed the biographical path. John Boorman's *Hope and Glory* (1987) is modeled on the lives and emotional evolution of his family during World War II when he was a boy, and explores with imagination and sympathy his mother's unfulfilled love for his father's best friend. Another British film, Terence Davies' *Distant Voices, Still Lives* (1989), uses an impressionistic and associative narrative style to explore his Liverpool family's life as he grew up. The whole family stands in the shadow of a harsh and sometimes brutal father. Out of this, Davies shows that it is never by intentional words that ordinary people reveal their inner lives but more often by gestures, tastes, and the sentimental songs of the period.

There is another path, sometimes followed by those who *have* had dramatic life experience, which is to embrace biography as though it were dramatic. But without vision of the underlying causes, without sensitivity to the nuance of the actual, and how unexpectedly people really behave under pressure, you will fall into stereotype. Nothing is more mysterious and full than the actual, and nothing is so untrue as stereotype.

COLLECTING RAW MATERIALS

The seeker is the person committed to a search for a larger picture among the many baffling clues, hints, and details that life provides. Some seek for personal respite and go to a therapist, others do it out of a need to entertain—that is, to share what it means to be alive with others. But assuredly the stories you need to tell probably won't be on hand when you want them. It will take a resolute search process. Then your materials will begin emerging in bits and pieces, and often unexpectedly.

Because of the singularity of your identity, you may find you have only one story in you. But—and this is an article of faith—telling it successfully will eventually open the way for the next one. Even prolific artists often mine a single, deep-seated theme—their work being the obsessive pursuit of ever deeper understandings.

If you are by nature a storyteller, you will already be doing some of what I am about to describe, which are ways to collect and sift material that can be made into a story, *the* story you need to tell. You will have to collect materials, and examine your collection diligently as it grows. You are actually searching for the outlines of the collector, the shadowy self that is implacably assembling what it needs to represent its own preoccupations.

JOURNAL

Keep a journal and note down anything that strikes you, no matter what its nature. This means carrying a notebook at all times and being willing to use it publicly and often. If you use a computer, you can file incidents in a database under a variety of tags, and call up material by particular priorities or in a particular order. One result of typing and storing material is that you explore it and remember it better. The alternative to recording is to notice much but remember little, and to find oneself empty-handed when you need story materials. There is no special virtue to a computer over, say, index cards except that it lets you juggle experimentally with your collection of materials by using the database sort function to experiment with different structures.

Rereading your journal becomes a journey through your most intense ideas and associations. This primes the creative pump and suggests alternatives when you run dry of inspiration. Inspiration is a most unreliable handmaiden, so most working artists develop routines to keep them active. The more you consciously note what catches your eye, the nearer you move to your underlying themes and interests. This is an example of changing hats—when you move from collecting to analyzing. Good analysis also helps you know what you need to collect!

NEWSPAPERS

There is nothing like real life for a profundity of outlandish and true tales. Keep clippings or transcribe anything that catches your interest and classify them in groups or families. Listing and classifying is vital because it's really about searching for underlying structures. Going back through the files of fifty-year-old newspapers will supply you with a profusion of rich sources. Maybe you find a story about two business partners, one of whom absconds with the company bank balance to blow it all in Las Vegas. It reminds you of your best friend's father, and the ruin a similar incident caused her family. That sets you thinking about your role in trying to help her through the period of disaster, and what you both learned. Here, you realize, are characters and a plot; all you need do is put it in the present, find a point of view, and start helping the story to develop itself.

The agony columns, or the personals, even the ads for lost animals can all suggest subjects and characters. Newspapers are a cornucopia of the human condition at every level, from the trivial to the global. Local newspapers are particularly fertile because the landscape and characters are accessible and reflect local economy, local conditions, and local idiosyncrasies.

With every source, you have the same fertile possibility: to cross-pollinate ideas by bringing together your overall interests with plots, characters, and situations available from elsewhere.

HISTORY

History doesn't happen, it gets written. Look at *why* history is written and you see not objective truth but someone's interpretation of what he or she thinks is significant. History is all about point of view.

The past is a rich repository of figures who have already participated in the dramas that interest you. The playwright John Osborne explored the predicament of the anti-establishment rebel through Martin Luther; Alan Bennett resurrected George III to investigate paternal authority as it veers over the brink of insanity; and Steven Spielberg brought alive Oskar Schindler so he could explore the awful predicament of being Jewish in Nazi-dominated Europe. Jane Campion recreated the dark and isolated beginnings of fellow New Zealander Janet Frame in *An Angel at My Table* (1991) and her next film *The Piano* (1993) uses a nineteenth-century setting to develop the themes of isolation and eroticism. In both films she explores a woman's point of view in breathtakingly imaginative ways.

No matter what happens to fascinate you—be it charismatic leaders who go wrong, practical jokers who get taken seriously, crooked doctors who find real cures, polygamous family groups who end up at war, neglected inventors, or old ladies who fill their houses with stray animals—there is a wealth of fully realized characters awaiting employment. A little diligent research and you can find just what you want in the great casting agency of the past.

MYTHS AND LEGENDS

Legend is inauthentic history; by taking a historical figure and developing your own version of his or her life and actions, you are making or furthering a legend. Every culture has its legendary icons (George Washington, Al Capone, Robin Hood, Queen Victoria, William Tell, Adolf Hitler) who reflect the national sense of demons and geniuses. You can choose or make your own.

Each culture also has its favorite myths, many translatable into a modern setting. Myths are useful because they enshrine conflicts that man has found enduringly insoluble, and therefore must be accommodated. The human truths in Greek mythology (for instance) do not lead to easy or happy resolution, but instead leave a bittersweet aftertaste that is perversely uplifting. Each generation regenerates myths for its own purposes, using them to frame contemporary characters and action that is usually unresolvable. This quality of paradox and the unanswerable is peculiarly modern. Happily we have left an age of anodyne resolutions and entered one which recognizes that we face many questions that have few answers.

FAMILY STORIES

All families have favorite stories defining influential members. My grandmother Lily May Russell was said to find things before people lost them. In all respects conventional, she had mild kleptomania where flowers and fruit were concerned. At an advanced age during breaks in long car journeys she would hop over garden walls to borrow a few strawberries or liberate a fistful of chrysanthemums. How a family explains and adjusts to these characteristics might be the subject of a short film. My other grandmother began life as a rebel in an English village, became an Edwardian hippy, married an alcoholic German printer called Rabiger who beat her and abandoned her in France where she stayed the rest of her life. She and her children lived lives too richly fantastic to be believable in fiction, but there are many single aspects I could borrow and develop.

Family tales can be heroic or they can be very dark, but being oral history they are always vivid. Sometimes one is told almost nothing, yet the surviving information is so trenchant that it demands that one develop the rest of the character. One of my great-grandfathers (Robert Russell, the father of Lily) was a Scottish milliner who began life selling ribbons and fabric from a pony and trap in southern England. My grandmother's family, instead of saying he liked drink, related how his horse would embarrass him by stopping automatically outside every pub when he took his family out for a Sunday drive. He had eight children, all did well and some of the boys ended up either collecting pubs or navigating southern England by car using a list of pub names. Yet none was an alcoholic. Who was this man Robert Russell?

CHILDHOOD STORIES

Everyone emerges from a childhood war zone. If you write down two or three of the most intense things that happened, you will have several ready-made short film subjects that are intensely meaningful, have a strong and inbuilt visualization, and contain great thematic significance for your subsequent life.

One that springs to mind is when, at the age of five or so, I found a pair of scissors and cut my own hair. My mother was so dismayed that I put on a hat and wore it steadfastly when my father came home. But thereafter when my hair was unruly my mother would say it was because I had cut it myself. This incident lay, emblematically, at the root of a discomfort with my body and my appearance for decades after. *I had cut my own hair and ruined it!* What a childish absurdity. But wait, let's look deeper. Behind it is the idea that one can make a fatal, self-mutilating mistake for which one suffers ever afterward. And it turns out that my mother—I am realizing this as I write it for you—had in fact made such a mistake. As an eleven-year-old she let her foot be run over by a streetcar, hoping that an accident would bring her feuding parents together. Repairing and setting the broken foot caused her agony, and it did bring her parents together. But only for a couple of years, and the streetcar driver who had been her friend was devastated.

So many invisible influences direct one's destiny. How far have you explored yours?

DREAMS

Your dreams are a sure indicator of your underlying concerns. Keep a notebook by your bed and write down each dream immediately while you still remember it. You can even train yourself to wake during the night after a good one. Don't edit or try to shape them, just scribble down the essentials.

Look back over an accumulation of entries and you will see a pattern of recurring motifs and archetypal characters. Here are your deepest concerns expressed in surreal action and imagery. What more could a filmmaker ask?

SOCIAL SCIENCE AND SOCIAL HISTORY

If for example you are interested in how factory workers have been exploited, you can find excellent books and case studies on the subject, many containing bibliographies. The list of works will tell you what other accounts exist, perhaps in both fiction and nonfiction. The more modern your source, the bigger the bibliography. Some books now contain filmographies too.

Case histories can be a good source of trenchant detail. If you are writing a part for a shoplifter, reading about actual shoplifters will supply you with what is typical (you need to know that) and also with detail that is quirky and interesting, so your shoplifter character doesn't remain a stereotype.

Case histories generally come with an interpretation, so the dramatist can find both good material and ideas about its possible significance. Social scientists are chroniclers and interpreters; their work can confirm your instincts and provide the kind of background information that allows you to root your fiction in what we know about the real world.

SUBJECTS TO AVOID

Many subjects come to mind easily because they are in one's immediate surroundings or are being pumped up by the media. Stay away from:

- worlds you haven't experienced and cannot closely observe,
- any ongoing, inhibiting problem in your own life (you won't find a new perspective on it while directing a film unit; see a good therapist),
- anything or anyone that is "typical" (nothing real is typical, so nothing typical will ever be interesting or credible),
- preaching or moral instruction of any kind, and
- films about problems to which you already have the answer (so does your audience).

Your films will be your portfolio, your precious reel that alone tells others who you are and what you can do. Try to make films for the outside world and not just for your film school peers. If you show short films that look into a larger world and that do not have a central character suspiciously like yourself, you will avoid the narcissistic tunnel vision afflicting many student films.

Try taking what you have learned the hard way in your own life and applying it to a character or characters unlike your own to say something about the human condition.

DISPLACE AND TRANSFORM

After a period of careful inquiry and reflection, take the best issues you discover and, even though they are temporary and subject to change, assume they are your own real ones. If you are working directly from events and personalities in your own life, *transform the screen version away from the originals.* This has numerous benefits. It frees you from self-consciousness and allows you to tell all the underlying truths instead of only those palatable to friends and family. Most importantly, it allows you to concentrate on dramatic and thematic truths instead of getting tangled up in biographical accuracy.

You can obscure your sources by giving characters alternative attributes and work, making them composites by amalgamating the attributes of two life models, placing the story in a different place or epoch, or even by switching the sex of the protagonists. One student director whose script told his own story—about the painful choice he had made to abandon a suburban marriage and a well-paying job to become a film student—inverted the sex of the main characters and made the rebel into a woman. In rethinking the situation to give her credible motivations, he made himself inhabit both the husband's and wife's positions and came to more deeply investigate what people trapped in such roles expect out of life. Displacement forced him into a more objective relationship with his characters and raised the level of his film's thematic discourse.

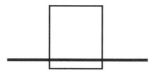

CHECKLIST, PART I
ARTISTIC IDENTITY

The recommendations and points summarized here are only those most salient or the most commonly overlooked. To find more about them or anything else, go to the Contents at the beginning of this part, or try the Index at the back of the book.

To Get on Target for Becoming a Director:

- get hands-on knowledge of all the production processes you are most likely to oversee
- accept that you'll need to know writing, acting, camerawork, sound, and editing
- confront your temperament and creative track record for clues about which specialty to take as your craft stepping-stone toward eventual directing
- resolve to make lots and lots of short films

As a Director You'll Need to:

- become a tough-minded leader
- be able to function even when feeling isolated
- be ready to make much out of little
- be interested and knowledgeable in other artforms
- have original and critical ideas about your times

To Make Educational Progress:

- don't listen to the film snobs; use film or video as resources allow since finishing lots of film projects is what matters, not the delivery medium
- use short works to argue for your competency at directing longer ones
- become computer literate fast if you aren't already doing so
- be ready to adapt and improvise when working low-budget (people and imagination make films rather than equipment)
- be ready to rewrite the script around the actors
- shoot rehearsals documentary-style and judge from the screen so you learn to make correct judgments in the moment
- use trial and error in a long developmental process prior to production to arrive at professional-level results

When You Deal with Actors:

- learn to see actors' obstacles and how to remove them
- use an intense developmental period prior to production to lower fears and create an ensemble
- remember that the camera sees and hears everything; actors must *be,* not perform
- egos are threatened when actors must play bad characters, or their character's bad parts

To Entertain Your Audience Means:

- giving mental, emotional, and imaginative work, not just life's externals
- making work that activates the mind and heart of the viewer
- using myth and archetype to underpin anything you want to be powerful
- using screen language that suggests, not merely shows, so your audience can imagine

Authorship Essentials Require:

- using your work to search for your identity, not illustrating what you know
- picking a form after you've found a story—remembering that form follows function

Questions to Help You Travel Inward and Develop Your Ideas:

- what marks has your life left on you?
- what ongoing dialogue are you privately having with yourself?
- what is the unfinished business in your life? (Your next story can use and further this quest but it's best to do it in a displaced rather than autobiographical form)
- after you make a self-inventory, what authorial role would you project for anyone else having that kind of major emotional experience?
- what are the major conflicts you face, or which seem to perennially interest you?
- what kind of heroes or heroines do you respond to, and what does this say about the issues and needs in your own life?
- what constants keep turning up in your dreams?
- what visual images remain with you, charged with force and mystery, waiting for you to investigate and develop?
- what areas of life do you find abidingly fascinating?

Resources to Probe:

- what genres fascinate you?
- what themes and preoccupations emerge from your journal?

- what kind of characters and themes turn up regularly in the clippings you make from newspapers?
- who do you identify with in history?
- what mythic or legendary figures are peculiarly your own, and which would you like to develop?
- what major characters or situations can you use from your family history?
- what are the childhood stories that seem to epitomize your growing up?
- what constant themes emerge?

Avoid:

- self-consciousness and libel by displacing the actual into the fictional, so you can be truthful
- worlds you don't know unless you're willing to do enormous research
- any personal topic for which you really need a therapist
- anything or anyone typical
- anything that is generalized
- preaching
- illustrating what you know
- any idea, situation or character already familiar or clichéd (rejection of cliché brings better and better substitutes when you persist).

P·A·R·T II

SCREENCRAFT

C•H•A•P•T•E•R 4

SCREEN GRAMMAR

This chapter is not a conventional screen grammar since plenty of good texts already exist. Instead I want to share an approach to film language that should keep you from losing your bearings once, as a director, you get caught up in the demands and delights of technique. In this state it is fatally easy to forget that making films is really about communicating with the audience. For film is consumed like music; not for a demonstration of theories or technical virtuosity, but in order to enter different realms of feeling and idea.

This chapter explains how much film language is really an analogue for human perception, action and reaction. If you never let go of this, your filmmaking will come not just from the head but from the heart.

All languages have their grammar and conventions, and that of the screen is no exception. It developed from the 1890s when the early cameramen and actors (and eventually directors) competed to put simple stories before audiences. At first their films were naïvely simple, but within a couple of decades and in spite of the absence of sound, they invented most of the screen language that we now take for granted. In the various filmmaking centers of the world, they found out what worked by trial and error, with the Russians alone making a concerted effort in the 1920s to formulate what the screen could do. In fact, theory among working filmmakers is still notable for its absence. We should not be surprised; spoken languages of great subtlety flowered long before anyone thought of philology.

Film language is a set of collectively generated conventions that enable us to tell stories to each other through the medium of images, actions, sounds, and words. It exists because human beings of every culture share complex processes of perception and logic. Those in the time arts who routinely make creative decisions—at no matter what level of sophistication—focus most of their discussion on how some aspect of drama "works." Over and over again the criterion applied to an action, a shot, a line, or a character's motivation is whether it "works." The implication is important; artistic decisions are made in the light of shared instincts of recognition. If it were otherwise, cinema and drama generally could not exist.

Most people learn film technique by copying other filmmakers. This is as natural and risky as actors studying other actors, so we too should heed Stanislavsky's warning—that actors should search for the roots of their craft in life itself, not among other actors. Put another way, a copy of a copy is always degraded. Your ideas and feelings about life should be preeminent, and you should use screen techniques as the vehicle for their realization. We certainly learn to speak that way, acquiring language because it gets us what we need. My elder daughter's first sentence was "Meat, I like it." Language is a tool to do or get something (more meat!).

From this rather fundamental perspective let's look at the different units of film language.

THE SHOT

A shot is a framed image placed on record by someone who thinks it holds meaning. If you view someone else's rushes or "dailies" (that is, footage straight out of the camera) you find yourself constantly trying to figure out what the makers (camera operator and director) were thinking, feeling, and seeking. You assess this not only from what is in the shot, but also *from what it excludes*. A shot of a man staring offscreen may exclude what he sees, and in the process, focuses us on how, rather than what, he is studying.

The more remote the material is in time and place, the easier it is to see the filmmaker searching for meanings, and to see how susceptible he or she was to the received truths of the day. The corollary is true: we are more likely to accept present-day footage of familiar scenes as "objective" and value free. But records, whether of actuality or of life enacted or reenacted, are always *constructs,* they are always subjective, and they always invoke a triangular relationship between content, storyteller, and viewer.

Let me elaborate. Imagine you are hunting through World War II archival shots in a film library, as I once did at the Imperial War Museum in London. After you recover from the atmosphere of a place so packed with sad ghosts, you notice from the library stockshots that by today's standards their cameras and film stock were less developed. Even so, each shot testifies, in addition to its subject, different kinds of involvement from its makers, that is, different emotion, emphases, and agendas.

Imagine you run a shot that some librarian has labeled "Russian soldiers, vicinity of Warsaw, running into sniper fire." From the first frame you notice how emotionally loaded everything seems: it's shot in high contrast black-and-white filmstock that accentuates the mood, and the air is smoky because lighting comes from behind the subjects. Though here as elsewhere, filming is undeniably a mechanical process of reproduction, everything is polarized by the interrelationship of human choice, technology, subject, and environment, and all of these things are contributing to what you feel. The camera enters the soldiers' world because it runs jerkily with them instead of shooting from a sheltered tripod. You catch your breath when a soldier falls because the cameraman almost trips over his fallen comrade. The camera recovers, continues onward leaving the wounded soldier to his fate. Then suddenly it plunges to the ground. The camera motor runs out framing some out-of-focus mud. With slow horror you realize you have just accompanied a cameraman in his last seconds of work. Feeling desolated, you replay his shot several times. You notice that when you hold on particular frames, it seems as though time and destiny can be replayed, reentered, and relived. Even when you replay something and "know" what's going to happen, *film is always in the present tense.*

Now someone brings you a photo of a dead cameraman lying face down on the battlefield, his camera fallen from his hands. It's him. Your poor cameraman. You recognize the knob of mud from his last seconds of film. Left alone with him, you ponder the combination of forces that made him willing to gamble his life to do this work. You wonder whom he left behind, and whether they learned how he died. You are his witness, but you have also *become* him, taken on his destiny. He will always be with you, somewhere. You have grown and will always *be* him, somewhere in the recesses of your own being.

Really, a shot's meaning can go very far beyond its subject.

SHOT DENOTATION AND CONNOTATION

If you can identify a shot's content you know what a shot denotes, but to grasp its connotations means looking beyond surfaces and interpreting how and why it might be used to imply more than it depicts. This speculation in turn prompts us to wonder about the heart and mind behind its making. This is very obvious when a shot communicates the death of its maker, but much less so when we see calm shots of a flower or a hand lighting a candle. The shots *denote* a flower and a candle being lit but—depending on context—might *connote* "natural beauty," "devotion," or a host of other ideas. Connotation is a cultural activity which depends on how far the filmmaker can draw the audience along a path of metaphysical association.

SHOTS IN JUXTAPOSITION

When two images are juxtaposed, or cut together, we infer a meaning from their relationship. Figure 4-1 shows some examples with explanations.

The examples in Figure 4-1 illustrate an engaging disagreement between two early Russian editing theorists. Examples 1–5 illustrate Pudovkin's categories of juxtaposition in which exposition and building a story line are paramount. Examples 6–12 show some of the preferred categorizations of Eisenstein, to whom the essence of narrative art lay in conflict and dialectics. His juxtapositions therefore highlight contrast and contradiction, and argue as much as they inform.

Meaning and signification, like all communication, are culturally based and are in slow but inexorable evolution. Signification depends on a collusion between

	Shot A	Shot B	Shot B in relation to A	Type of cut
1	Woman descends interior stairway	Same woman walking in street	Narrates her progress	Structural (builds scene)
2	Man runs across busy street	Close shot of his shoelace coming undone	Makes us anticipate his falling in front of a vehicle	Structural (directs our attention to significant detail)
3	Hungry street person begging from doorway	Wealthy man eating oysters in expensive restaurant	Places one person's fate next to another's	Relational (creates contrast)
4	Bath filling up	Teenager in bathrobe on phone in bedroom	Shows two events happening at the same time	Relational (parallelism)
5	Exhausted boxer takes knockout punch	Bullock killed with stun gun in an abattoir	Suggests boxer is a sacrificial victim	Relational (symbolism)
6	Police waiting at road block	Shabby van driving erratically at high speed	Driver doesn't know what he's going to soon meet	Conflictual (still vs. the dynamic)
7	Giant earthmoving machine at work	Ant moving between blades of grass	Microcosm and macrocosm coexist	Conflictual (conflict of scale)
8	Geese flying across frame	Water plummeting at Niagara Falls	Forces flowing in different directions	Conflictual (conflict of graphic direction)
9	Screen-filling closeup of face, teeth clenched	Huge Olympic stadium, line of runners poised for pistol start	The one among the many	Conflictual (conflict of scale)
10	Dark moth resting on white curtains	Flashlight emerging out of dark forest	Opposite elements	Conflictual (dark vs. light)
11	Girl walks into funfair	Distorted face appears in funfair mirror	The original and its reflection	Conflictual (original vs. distorted version)
12	Driver sees cyclist in his path	In slow motion driver screams and swings steering wheel	Event and its perception	Conflictual (real time vs. perceived time)
13	Driver gets out of disabled car	Same image, car in foreground, driver walking as a tiny figure in distance	Transition—some time has gone by	Jump cut

FIGURE 4-1

Examples of juxtaposed shots or cuts.

audience and communicator, a set of conventions that must be learned before their purpose becomes evident. For instance, ethnographers have remarked after projecting edited footage to isolated tribesmen that their subjects understood the "story" until the film cut to a closeup. The tribesmen lost concentration because they could not understand why the camera eye suddenly "jumped close." They were about to learn that a closeup does not a collapse space so much as temporarily diminish the field of attention and clear away what surrounds and obscures the center of interest.

But *whose* center of interest? The film technician along with the critic will answer, "the audience's." Our answer is more complex, and infinitely more useful to directing films because it places the persona of a storyteller ahead of the audience's reception of the story.

Perception by a camera is a mechanical process in which a focal plane is affected by incoming light. Perception by you and me is radically different because we evolve an intellectual and emotional framework within which to organize what our senses tell us. The convention of the internal monologue, or "voice over" illustrates this because it verbalizes this process. For our purpose let's say that *perception is our inner life of ideas and feelings proceeding in counterpoint with our environment of outer, visible and audible events.* I want to stress that this interior activity is not just passive reaction; it also directs our attention as we try to confirm impressions, hopes, fears, interests, and hypothetical explanations. The object of the oral or literary storyteller is to recapture, sustain, and modulate this vital activity. Because film is always in the present tense, the film storyteller is a presence guiding our attention rather than a reteller. You can't retell the present; but you can observe, navigate, and even narrate it, interpreting it as it unfolds.

We are going to examine the way this perceptual process works in a notional figure I'll call the Concerned Observer. This person is an involved onlooker who forms ideas and anticipations while seeing and hearing. At a later point we are going to make the Observer into the more active and participatory Storyteller, whose function is absolutely central to conscious, integrated film directing.

I am trying to make perception as personal and nonabstract as possible here because in everyday life perception is so routine that we seldom notice *how* or why we observe. Even the word "observe" has misleadingly passive, scientific association, when in reality it is a highly active process and freighted with an intricate interplay of feelings, associations, and ideas, all of which lead constantly to actions.

THE AXIS

The next time you are near two people having an animated discussion, notice how your attention shifts from one to the other. Figure 4-2 represents A and B being watched by the observer O. It's useful to think of O as a child, because children are highly observant, have strong emotions, and often invisible to their seniors. As the Observer, your eyeline moves back and forth, led from A to B and back again as they talk. Your eye follows the line of tension between them, the active pathway of words, looks, awareness, and volition. This is called the *scene axis* and is really the subject-to-subject axis.

Every scene has, in addition to the probable subject-to-subject axis, an observer-to-subject axis which in my example is at right angles to the scene axis between A and B. This is called the *camera axis* or camera-to-subject axis. But the term is misleading because it depersonalizes its function into something technical-sounding when really it is intensely human. The Observer (yourself watching the

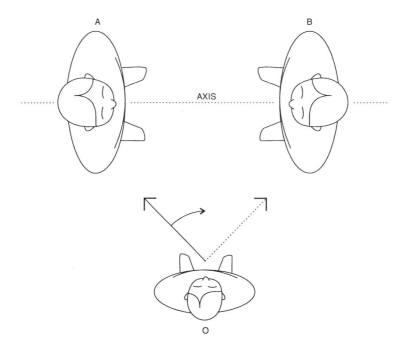

FIGURE 4-2 ──

The Observer watching a conversation.

two people in conversation, for instance) has a strong sense of his own relationship to each person (his axis), to the invisible connection between them (their axis), and to what passes between them.

In turning to look from person to person, the Observer can be replaced by a camera *panning* (that is, moving horizontally) between the two speakers. Now let's see in Figure 4-3 what happens when O moves closer to A and B's axis.

Not to miss any of the action, the Observer must switch fast between A and B. Under such circumstances human beings blink their eyes to avoid seeing the unpleasant blur between widely separated subjects. To the brain this produces two static images with virtually no period of black in between. Cutting between two camera angles taken from the same camera position reproduces this familiar experience. Historically this cinematic equivalent probably emerged when someone tried cutting out a nauseatingly fast pan between two characters. It "worked" because its counterpart was already part of human experience.

THE ACTOR AND THE ACTED UPON

During a conversation you sometimes merely look at whoever speaks next. Other times, when the talk becomes heated, you find yourself looking at the listener, not the speaker. What's going on here? Any human interaction is like a tennis game.

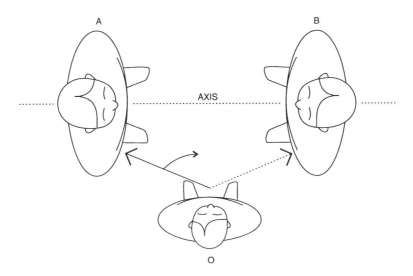

FIGURE 4-3

The Observer moves close to the characters' axis.

At any given moment, one player *acts* (serves the ball), the other is *acted upon* (receives the ball). When a player prepares to make an aggressive serve our eye runs ahead of the ball to see how the recipient will deal with the onslaught. We see her run, jump, swing her racquet, and intercept the ball. When it becomes certain she's going to succeed, our eye flicks back to see how the first player is placed, how she will handle the return. The whole cycle has been reversed because our eye jumps back to the original player before the ball returns.

We monitor every interaction this way because we know that consciously or otherwise everybody is *constantly trying to get or do something,* no matter where, what, or who the people are. A game ritualizes this interchange as a competition, but a conversation is likely to be just as complex and structured.

Of course, we nice middle-class people hate to think of ourselves making *demands.* We picture ourselves as patient, tolerant victims acted upon by a greedy and selfish world. Seldom do we see ourselves as acting upon others, except during our occasional triumphs. But the fact is—and you must take this to heart if you intend to work in drama—that *everyone acts upon those around him, even when he uses the strategy of passivity.*

To the Observer, at any given moment one person is the actor, and the other is the acted upon. Often the situation alternates rapidly. But it is through their action and reaction that we routinely assess a person's character, mood, and motives.

Now look at how you watch two people conversing. Your eyeline switches according to your notion of who is acting upon whom. As in watching tennis, you'll find that as soon as you've decided how A has begun acting on B, your eye switches in mid-sentence to see how B is taking it. Depending on how B adapts and acts back, you soon find yourself returning to A.

Once you know this principle, a lot of shooting and editing decisions become obvious.

SUBTEXT

While you watch a conversation you search for behavioral clues to unlock the hidden motives and inner lives of the characters. Beneath the visible and audible surface lies the situation's *subtext,* or hidden meaning—something we are always seeking. Most of the work a director does is not with the text but with the subtext. The text is what the characters do, or what action they take verbally. But why do they say what they say, and do what they do? This is the purview of subtext, something developed in drama by the director and the actors, and something continuously developing during rehearsal, shooting, and even in editing where it is the editor's job, in addition to putting the piece together, to liberate those subtextual possibilities that eluded everyone else.

DOLLYING, TRACKING, OR TRUCKING

Dollying, tracking, or trucking are names given to any movement where the camera itself moves horizontally through space. In life we are sometimes motivated by our thoughts and feelings to move closer or further away from what commands our attention. We move sideways to see better or to avoid an obstacle in our sightline. Sometimes in accompanying someone important, we look sideways at them. The point is that camera movements all need *motivation,* either in response to the action or, more interestingly, as part of the strategy of story revelation adopted by the Storyteller.

CRANING UP OR CRANING DOWN

Craning up or craning down is a movement vertically up or down, and is similarly motivated. The movement corresponds with the feeling of sitting down, or standing up—sometimes as an act of conclusion, sometimes to "rise above," sometimes to see better.

SCREEN DIRECTION

Screen direction is a term describing a subject's direction or movement, especially when a subject's movement links several shots, as in a chase. An important screen convention is that *characters and their movements are generally observed from only one side of the scene axis.* Let's imagine you ignored this and intercut one part of a parade moving screen L–R (left to right) with another going R–L. The audience would expect the two factions to collide, such as when police move up to a position where they can block a demonstration.

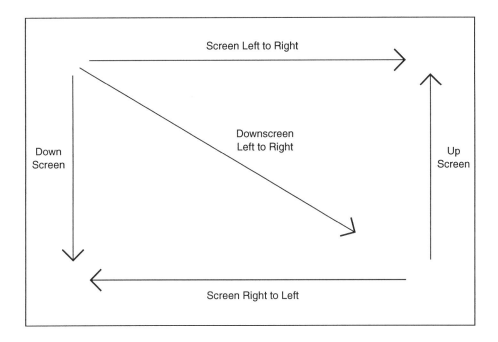

FIGURE 4-4 ───

A range of screen directions and their descriptions.

Now suppose you run ahead of the parade in order to watch it file past a landmark. In the new position you would see marchers entering an empty street from the same screen direction. But in life you might cross the parade's path to watch it from the other side. This would be unremarkable because you initiated the relocation. But in film to simply cut to a camera position across the axis must be specially set up on the screen or it causes confusion for the audience.

CHANGING SCREEN DIRECTION

Changing screen direction can be done if we see the change onscreen. You can make a parade change screen direction by filming at an angle to a corner (see Figure 4-5). The marchers enter in the background going R–L, turn the corner in foreground, and exit L–R. In essence they have changed screen direction. If subsequent shots are to match, their action will also have to be L–R. Another solution to changing screen direction is, during a gap in the parade for instance, to dolly so the camera *visibly* crosses the subject's axis of movement (see Figure 4-6). Remember that any change of observing camera orientation to the action must be shown onscreen.

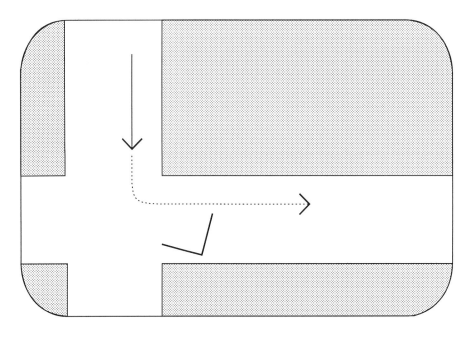

FIGURE 4-5 ——

By shooting at a corner, a parade or moving object can be made to change screen direction.

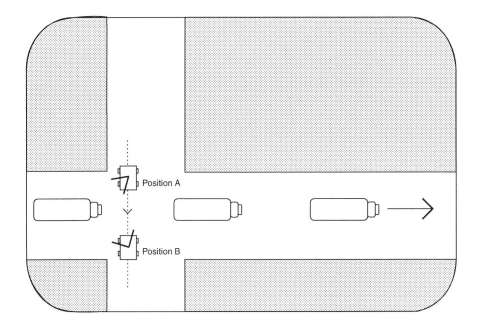

FIGURE 4-6 ——

Dollying sideways between floats in a parade changes the parade's effective screen direction, but the dollying movement must be shown.

DIFFERENT ANGLES ON THE SAME ACTION

So far we have found everyday human correlations for every aspect of film language. But can there be one to justify using very different angles to cover the same action? We said earlier that cutting together long and closer shots taken from a single axis or direction suggests, by excluding the irrelevant, an observer's changed degree of concentration. But now imagine a scene of a tense family meal that is covered from several very different angles. Though it's a familiar film convention, surely it has no corollary in life? Ah, but wait. This narrative device—switching viewpoints during a single scene—was a prose convention long before film was invented; so probably it has rather deep roots.

In literature it is clear that multiple points of view imply not physical changes of location but shifts in psychological and emotional points of view. The same is true when this strategy is used onscreen. But film is misleading because unlike literature it seems to give us "real" events. So we must constantly remind ourselves that film gives us a *perception* of events, a "seeming" that is not, despite appearances, the events themselves.

Here's an example from your own life. When you've been a bystander during a major disagreement between friends, you got so absorbed that you forgot all about yourself. Instead you went through a series of internal agreements and disagreements, seeing first one person's point, then another's. You got so involved that you virtually experienced each of the protagonists' realities.

Screen language evokes this heightened subjectivity by using a series of privileged views. These correspond, we have learned, with the way an observer may identify with different people as time unfolds. Under such close examination, our sympathy and fascination migrates from person to person as events unfold. What's important in screencraft is that the *empathic shifts must still be rooted in a single "storyteller's" sensibility* if they are to have a naturally integrated feel. The state of heightened and embracing concentration is not one we normally maintain for long.

ABSTRACTION

The alternative pole to this state of probing emotional inquiry is that of withdrawal into mental stocktaking, or abstraction. We alter our examination from the whole to a part, or a part to the whole—whatever suffices. Watch your own shifts of attention; you will find that you often do this to escape into a private realm where you can speculate, contemplate, remember, or imagine. Often detail that catches your eye turns out to have symbolic meaning, or is a part that stands for the whole. Thus a car doorhandle near a swirling water surface can stand for a whole flood. This much-used principle in film is called *synecdoche* (pronounced sin-eck-dockee). Often our eye alights on something symbolic, that is, something conventionally representative much as a scale represents justice, or a flower growing on an empty lot might represent renewal.

This act of abstraction can, of course, have different causes. It may not be withdrawal or refuge by the Observer, but rather looking inward in an intense search for the significance of a recent event. Selective focus is a device used to suggest this state. When an object is isolated on the screen, and its foreground and background are thrown out of focus, it strongly suggests abstracted vision, as does abnormal motion (either slow or fast). These are just a few of the ways to represent how we routinely dismantle reality, and objectively distance ourselves from the moment. We may be searching for meaning, or simply refreshing ourselves through imaginative play.

SUBJECTIVITY/OBJECTIVITY

We experience a world full of dualities, oppositions, and ironic contrasts. You drive your car very fast at night, and then, stopping to look at the stars you become aware of your own insignificance under their light which has taken millions of years to reach your eye. Human attention shifts from subjectivity to objectivity, from past to present and back again, from looking at a crowd as a phenomenon, to looking at the lovely profile of a woman as she turns away. There is screen language to replicate every phase of the Observer's attention. As a filmmaker if you make the shifts in the stream of images consistently human, you will create the sensation in your audience of an integrated being's presence—that of our invisible, thinking, feeling, all-seeing Observer.

DURATION, RHYTHM, AND CONCENTRATION

Human beings are directed by rhythms that begin in the brain and control heartbeat and breathing. We tap our feet to music, or jump up to dance when the music takes us. Everything we do is measured by the beat, duration, and capacity of our minds and bodies. The duration of the feature film is said to be governed by the capacity of the human bladder! Screen language is governed by other human capacities. The duration of a shot is determined by how much attention it demands, just as the decision when to cross the road is governed by how long we take to scope out the traffic. The speed of a movement on the screen is judged by its context, where it is going, and why.

Speech has inherently powerful rhythms. The Czech composer Leos Janacek was so fascinated by language rhythms that his late compositions draw on the pacing and tonal patterns of people talking. Films, particularly those with long dialogue scenes, are similarly composed around the speech and movement rhythms of the characters. Here screen language mimics the way an observer's senses shift direction and reproduces the way we maintain concentration by refreshing our minds through search. These are the most difficult scenes to get right in editing because subtextual consistency depends on delicate nuances.

Rhythm plays yet another important role in film viewing. Early and enduring stories like the Arthurian legends and the Norse sagas were composed in strict rhythmic patterns because it made memorization easy by the troubadours reciting them from court to court. The rhythms of poetry not only aid concentration but make extensive memorization possible. Equally significant is that when spoken language has strong rhythmic structure, audiences can concentrate for longer periods.

Film language makes use of every possible rhythm—those of speech and others. Many sounds from everyday life—bird song, traffic, the sounds from a building site, or the wheels of a train—contain strong rhythms to help in composing a sequence. Even static pictorial compositions contain visual rhythms such as symmetry, balance, repetition, opposition, and patterns to intrigue the eye.

SEQUENCE

In life there is a flow of events and only some of it is memorable. A story about a life takes only the significant parts of a life and jumps them together. The building blocks are segments of time (the hero's visit to the hospital emergency room after a road accident), the events at a location (the high points of his residency in Rome), or of a developing idea (as he builds his own home his wife loses patience with the slowness of the process). Because time and space are now being indicated, there are junctures between the narrative building blocks that must be either indicated or hidden, as the story demands.

TRANSITIONS AND TRANSITIONAL DEVICES

Most of the transitions we make in life—from place to place, or time to time, are slow or imperceptible because we have other preoccupations. Stories either replicate this by hiding the seams between sequences or by indicating or even emphasizing them. An action match between a woman drinking her morning fruit juice and a beer drinker raising his glass in a smoky dive minimizes the scene shift by drawing attention to the act of drinking. A dissolve from one scene to the other would indicate, in somewhat dated screen language, "and time passed." A simple cut from one place to the next leaves the audience to fill in the blank. However, in a scene of a teenager singing along to the car radio in a long, boring drive, followed by flash images of a truck, screeching tires, and the teenager yanking desperately at the steering wheel is intentionally a shock transition. It replicates the violent change we go through when taken nastily by surprise.

Sound can be a transitional device. Hearing a conversation over an empty landscape can draw us forward into the next scene (of two campers in their tent). Cutting to a shot of a cityscape while the bird song from the campsite is still fading out gives the feeling of being confronted with a change of location while the mind and heart lag behind in the woodland. Both these transitional devices imply an emotional point of view.

All transitions are in fact narrative devices, ways of handling the necessity of moving, montage fashion, between the discontinuous. Each implies an attitude or point of view either on the part of characters or the Storyteller.

SCREEN LANGUAGE IN SUMMARY

Screen language is routinely misunderstood as some kind of professional packaging. Used as technique for documenting events for an audience, it can easily lack soul. But whenever as viewers we sense the integrity of a questing human intelligence at work, life onscreen becomes human and potent instead of mechanical and banal.

Imagine that you go to your high school reunion and afterward see what another participant filmed with his little video camera. It is his eyes and ears, recording whatever he cared to notice. Afterward you find that his version of the events gives a strong idea of his personality. You see not only who he looked at and who he talked to, but from how he spent time with each person and event you see into his mind and heart at work, and even into the inner workings of his character.

Likewise, a good fiction film's handling of its events and personalities creates an overarching heart and mind doing the perceiving. Under the *auteur* theory of filmmaking, this is the director's vision. But controlling how a whole film crew and actors create the perceptual stream is simply beyond any one person's control, so I prefer to personify the intelligence behind the film's point of view as that of the Storyteller. This is not the simple "I" of the director, but a fictional entity as complex and dependent on artistic serendipity as any created by an actor or novelist.

Less obviously this is also true for documentary and other nonfiction forms. All are constructs, even when they take their materials directly from life. At its most compelling, *screen language implies the course of a particular intelligence at work as it grapples with the events in which it participates.* People who work successfully in the medium seem to understand this instinctively, but I have never heard or read what I have just written. If you happen to lack this instinct, simply pattern your work around the natural, observable processes of human perception, human action, and human reaction. You can't go far wrong if you are true to life. As you do this, your film will somehow take on a narrative persona all its own, and this you should encourage.

To prepare yourself for this responsibility, you can either read all of Proust and Henry James, or if you don't have the time, simply get into the habit of monitoring your own processes of physical and emotional observation, especially under duress. You'll constantly forget to do this homework because we are imprisoned to the point of forgetfulness within our own subjectivity. In ordinary living we see, think, and react automatically, and notice so very little. Now compare this with what you are used to seeing on the screen. The camera's verisimilitude makes events unfold with seeming objectivity. Well used, it gives events the force of *inevitability,* like music that is perfect. Students often assume that the cinema process itself is an alchemy that will aggrandize and ennoble whatever they put before the camera. But the cinema process is primarily a framer and magnifier; through it truth looks more true, and artifice more artificial. Small is big, and big is enormous. Every step by the makers of cinema relentlessly exposes their fallibilities along with their true insights.

The process, far from automatically delivering objective and inevitable cinema, delivers a metamorphosis of scale. Anyone present when something was filmed and who later saw the film version, has experienced how different it is from on-the-spot impressions. Not only has content been inescapably chosen and mediated by a string of human judgments, but it has also been transformed by the lenses, lighting, filmstock, or video medium used, and even the context in which one saw the movie (crowded cinema, motel TV, with your family, etc).

If you want to use the medium successfully you will need to understand a lot about the human psyche. You will need to feel what your audience will make of what you give it. This is rooted not in audience studies or theory, but in your instinct for human truth and human judgments.

Let's say it again: A film delivers not just a filtered version of events but also, by mimicking the flow of a human consciousness at work, implies a human heart and mind doing the observing. Screen some of the world's first filming and you'll comprehend this. The Lumieres brothers are palpably present behind their wooden box camera, winding away at the handle until their handmade filmstock runs out. It is through their minds as well as their cameras that we see workers leaving the Lumieres factory, or the train disgorging those passengers who are so unaware of the history they are making.

Film conventions are modeled on the dialectical flow of our consciousness whenever we are following something of importance to us. Our emotional responses play a huge part in this by literally directing our sight and hearing. You can test this out. Try noting down what you remember from a striking event you experienced. What most people recall of an accident, say, is highly visual, abbreviated, selective, and emotionally loaded. Just like a film!

C·H·A·P·T·E·R 5

SEEING WITH A MOVIEMAKER'S EYE

The four study projects in this chapter will make you familiar with some essentials of composition, editing, script analysis, and lighting. Collectively they yield the basics of seeing with a moviemaker's eye and will be immensely useful to your confidence when you begin directing.

PROJECT 5-1: PICTURE COMPOSITION ANALYSIS

A stimulating and highly productive way to investigate composition is to do so with several other people or as a class. Though what follows is written for a study group, you can do it solo if circumstances so dictate.

Equipment Required: For static composition, a slide projector and/or an overhead projector to enlarge graphics are best but not indispensable. For dynamic composition you will need a video player, preferably with freeze-frame and slow speed scan functions. Four-head VCRs have better scan and freeze frame capability than two-head, which usually break up a static picture unrecognizably. Your monitor set can be a domestic TV receiver, but it is best to connect VCR sound (usually labeled "line out") to the auxiliary input (or "line in") socket of a hi-fi. Reproduction is better, and you won't get that infuriating waterfall roar each time you stop the player.

Object: To learn the composition of visual elements by studying how the eye reacts to a static composition and then how it handles dynamic composition, or composition in movement.

Study Materials: For static composition, a book of figurative painting reproductions (best used under an overhead projector so you have a big image to scan), or better, a dozen or more 35mm art slides, also projected as large images. Slides of Impressionist paintings are good, but the more eclectic your collection the better. For dynamic composition use any visually interesting sequences from a favorite movie on videotape, though any Eisenstein movie will be ideal.

ANALYSIS FORMAT

In a class setting it's important to keep a discussion going, but if you are working alone, notes or sketches are a good way to log what you discover. Help from books on composition is not easily gained since many texts make composition seem intimidating or formulaic, and may be difficult to apply to the moving image. Sometimes rules prevent seeing rather than promoting it, so trust your eye to see what is really there and use your own nonspecialist vocabulary to describe it.

STRATEGY FOR STUDY

If you are leading a group, you will need to explain what is wanted something like this:

> We're doing this to discover how each person's visual perception actually works. I'll put a picture up on the screen. Notice where your eye goes in the composition first, and then what course it takes when you examine the rest of the picture. After about fifteen seconds I'll ask someone to describe what path his eye followed. You don't need any special jargon, just let your responses come from the specifics of each picture. Please avoid the temptation to look for a story in the picture, or to guess what the picture is "about," even when it suggests a story.

With each new image pick a new person to comment. Since not everyone's eye responds the same way, there will be interesting discussions about the variations. There will usually be a great deal of agreement, so everyone is led to formulate ideas about visual reflexes, and about what compositional components the eye finds attractive and engrossing. It is good to start simple and graduate to more abstract images, even to completely abstract ones. Many people, relieved of the burden of deciding a picture's "subject," can begin to enjoy a Kandinsky, a Mondrian, or a Pollock for itself, without fuming over whether or not it is really art. After about an hour of pictures and discussion, encourage your group to form some compositional guidelines.

After the group has formed some ideas and gained confidence from analyzing paintings, I usually show both good and bad photos. Photography, less obviously contrived than painting, tends to be accepted less critically. This is a good way to discover just how many classical elements can be found in what appears to be a straight record of life.

Here are questions to help you formulate ways of seeing more critically. They can be applied after seeing a number of paintings or photos, or you could direct the group's attention to each question's area as it becomes relevant.

STATIC COMPOSITION

1. After your eye has taken in the whole, review its starting point. Why did it go to that point in the picture? (Common reasons: brightest point in composition, darkest place in an otherwise light composition, single area of an arresting color, significant junction of lines creating a focal point.)

2. When your eye moved away from its point of first attraction, what did it follow? (Commonly: lines, perhaps actual ones like the line of a fence or an outstretched arm, or inferred lines such as the sightline from one character looking at another. Sometimes the eye simply moves to another significant area in the composition, going from one organized area to another and jumping skittishly across the intervening disorganization.)

3. How much movement did your eye make before returning to its starting point?

4. What specifically drew your eye to each new place?

5. If you trace an imaginary line over the painting to show the route your eye took, what shape do you have? (Sometimes a circular pattern, sometimes a triangle or ellipse, but can be many shapes. Any shape at all can reveal an alternative organization that helps one see beyond the wretched and dominating idea that every picture tells a story.)

6. Are there any places along your imaginary line that seem specially charged with energy? (Often sightlines: between a Virgin's eyes and the baby's, between a guitarist's and his hand on the strings, between two field workers, one of whom is facing away.)

7. How would you characterize the compositional movement? (For example, geometrical, repetitive textures, swirling, falling inward, symmetrically divided down the middle, flowing diagonally, etc. Making a translation from one medium to another—in this case from the visual to the verbal—always helps one discover what is truly there.)

8. What parts, if any, do the following play in a particular picture:
   a. repetition   f. straight lines   k. non-naturalistic coloring
   b. parallels   g. strong verticals   l. light and shade
   c. convergence   h. strong horizontals   m. human figures
   d. divergence   i. strong diagonals
   e. curves   j. textures

9. How is depth suggested? (This is an ever-present problem for the director of photography who, if inexperienced, is liable to take what I think of as the firing squad approach: that is, placing the human subjects against a flat background and shooting them. Unless there is something to create different planes, like a wall angling away from the foreground to suggest a receding space, the screen is like a painter's canvas and looks what it really is—two-dimensional.)

10. How is the individuality and mood of the human subjects expressed? (This is commonly through facial expression and body language, of course. But more interesting are the juxtapositions the painter makes of person to person, of person to surroundings, or of people inside a total design.)

11. How is space arranged on either side of a human subject, particularly in portraits? (Usually in profiles there is lead space, that is, more space in front of the person than behind them, as if in response to our need to see what the person sees.)

12. How much headroom is given above a person, particularly in a closeup? (Sometimes the edge of a frame cuts off the top of a head, or may not show one head at all in a group shot.)

13. How often and how deliberately are people and objects placed at the margins of the picture so you have to imagine what is cut off? (By demonstrating the frame's restriction one can make the viewer's imagination supply what is beyond the edges of the "window.")

VISUAL RHYTHM: HOW DURATION AFFECTS PERCEPTION

So far I have stressed the idea of an immediate, instinctual response to the organization of an image. When one shows a series of slides without comment, one moves to a new image after sufficient time for the eye to absorb each picture. Some pictures require longer than others. For a movie audience, unless shots are held to an unusual length as in Antonioni's *L'Avventura* (1960), this is how an audience must deal with each new shot in a film. Unlike responding to a photograph or painting, which can be studied thoughtfully and at leisure, the filmgoer must interpret within an unremitting and preordained forward movement in time. It is like reading a poster on the side of a moving bus: if the words and images cannot be assimilated in the given time, the inscription goes past without being understood. If, however, the bus is crawling in a traffic jam, you may have time to absorb and become critical or even rejecting of the poster.

There is an optimum duration for each shot to stay on the screen; this depends on the complexity of its content and form, and the accessibility of its significance, that is, how much work the viewer must do to extract the shot's authorial meaning. Shot duration is also affected by an invisible third factor, that of expectation. For the audience will either work fast at interpreting each new image, or slowly, depending on how much time the film allowed one to process the preceding shots.

This principle, in which a shot's duration is determined by content, form, significance and expectation, is called visual rhythm. As you would expect from such a musical term, a filmmaker, like a musician, can either relax or intensify a visual rhythm. There are consequences in this for both the rate of cutting, and for the tempo of camera movements.

Ideal films for the study of compositional relationships in film and visual rhythm are the classics by the Russian, Sergei Eisenstein, such as *The Battleship Potemkin* (1925), *Que Viva Mexico* (1931–32), *Alexander Nevsky* (1938), and *Ivan the Terrible* (1944–46). His origins as a theater designer made him very aware of the impact upon an audience of musical and visual design. His sketchbooks show how carefully he designed everything in each shot, down to the costumes. More recent films with a strong sense of design are Ingmar Bergman's *The Seventh Seal* (1956), Stanley Kubrick's *A Clockwork Orange* (1971), or David Lynch's *Blue Velvet* (1986).

Designer's sketches and the comic strip are perhaps the progenitors of the storyboard (see example in Figure 6-2 in the next chapter) which is much used by ad agencies and conservative elements in the film industry to lock down what each new frame will convey. Storyboarding is particularly helpful for the inexperienced, even when your artistry is as lousy as mine and doesn't run much beyond stick figures.

DYNAMIC COMPOSITION

When images move there are more compositional principles at work. With dynamic composition a new problem emerges, for a balanced composition can become disturbingly unbalanced should someone cross the frame, or leave it altogether. Even the turn of a figure's head in the foreground may posit a new eyeline (subject-to-subject axis), which in turn demands a compositional rebalancing. Then again, zooming in from a wide shot demands reframing since compositionally there is a drastic change, even though the subject is the same.

To study dynamic composition find a visually interesting sequence, such as the chase in John Ford's *Stagecoach* (1939), or that in William Friedkin's *The French Connection* (1971), or almost any part of Andrew Davis' *The Fugitive* (1993). Here your VCR's slow-scan facility will be very useful. See how many of these aspects you can find:

1. Reframing because the subject moved (look for a variety of camera adjustments)

2. Reframing as a consequence of something or someone entering the frame

3. Reframing in anticipation of something or someone entering the frame

4. A change in the point of focus to move attention from background to foreground, or vice versa. (This changes the texture of significant areas of the composition from hard focus to soft.)

5. Strong movement within an otherwise static composition. (How many can you find? Across frame, diagonally, from background to foreground, from foreground to background, up frame, down frame, etc. Eisenstein films are full of these compositions.)

6. How much does one feel identified with each kind of subject movement? (This is a tricky issue, but in general the nearer one is to the axis of a movement, the more subjective is one's sense of involvement.)

7. How quickly does the camera adjust to a figure who gets up and moves to another place in frame? (Usually subject movement and the camera's compositional change are synchronous. The camera move becomes clumsy should it either anticipate or lag behind the movement. Often camera movements are *motivated* by changes like this from within the composition.)

8. How often are the camera or the characters blocked (that is, choreographed) to isolate one character? What is the dramatic justification?

9. How often is the camera moved or the characters blocked so as to bring two characters back into frame? (Good camerawork, composition, and blocking is always trying to show *relatedness*. This helps to intensify meanings and ironies, and reduces obvious signification through cutting.)

10. How often is composition more or less angled down sightlines, and how often do sightlines cross the screen? (Here there is often a shifting of point of view from subjective to objective.)

11. What does the change of angle and change of composition make you feel about or toward the characters? (Probably more involved, than more objective.)

12. Find several compositions that successfully create depth and define what visual element is responsible. (An obvious one is where the camera is next to a railroad line as a train rushes up and past. Both the perspective revealed by the rails and the movement of the train create depth. In deep shots, different zones of lighting at varying distances from the camera, or zones of hard and soft focus, can also achieve this.)

13. How many shots can you find where camera position changes to include more or different background detail in order to comment upon foreground subject?

INTERNAL AND EXTERNAL COMPOSITION

So far we have been looking at composition that is internal to each shot. Another form of compositional relationship is the momentary relationship between an outgoing shot and the next or incoming shot. This, called external composition, is a hidden part of film language; hidden because we are unaware how much it influences our judgments and expectations.

A common usage is when a character leaving the frame in the outgoing shot leads the spectator's eye to the very place in shot B where an assassin will emerge in a large and restless crowd. The eye is conducted to the right place in a busy composition.

Another example might be the framing of two complementary close shots in which two characters have an intense conversation. The compositions are similar but symmetrically opposed. In Figure 5-1 the two-shot (a) gives a good overall feel of the scene, but man and child are too far away. The close shots, (b) and (c), retain the feel of the scene but effectively cut out the dead space between them. Note that the heads are not centered: each person has lead (rhyming with "feed") space in front of his face, and this reflects their positioning in the two-shot. The man is high in the frame and looking downward, and the child lower in the frame and looking up—just as in the matching two-shot.

Other aspects will emerge if you apply the questions below to your sequences under review. Use the slow-scan facility to examine compositional relationships at the cutting point. Go backward and forward several times over each cut to be sure you miss nothing. Try these for yourself:

1. Where was your point of concentration at the end of the shot? (You can trace where your eye goes by moving your finger around the face of the monitor. Your last point in the outgoing shot is where your eye enters the composition

FIGURE 5-1

Wide shot and two complementary closeups. Notice lead space in front of each CU character, and how the height and placing in the frame of each mirrors the composition of the master shot.

of the incoming shot. Notice how shot duration determines the distance the eye travels in exploring the shot. This means that on top of what we have already established about shot length it is also a factor in external composition.)

2. What kinds of symmetry are there between complementary shots (that is, between shots designed to be intercut)?

3. What is the relationship between two different-sized shots of the same subject that are designed to be cut together? (This is a revealing one; the inexperienced camera operator usually produces medium shots and close shots of the same scene that cut together poorly because proportions and compositional placing of the subject are incompatible.)

4. Examine a match cut very slowly and see if there is any overlap. (Especially where there is relatively fast action, a match cut, to look smooth, needs about four frames of the action repeated on the incoming shot. This is because the eye does not register the first three or four frames of any new image. This built-in perceptual lag means that when you cut to the beat of music, the only way to make the cuts look in sync with the beat is to cut three or four frames *before* the actual beat point.)

5. Find visual comparisons in external composition that make a storyteller's comment (for instance, cut from a pair of eyes to car headlights approaching at night, from a dockside crane to a man feeding birds with arm outstretched, etc.).

COMPOSITION, FORM, AND FUNCTION

If form is the manner in which content is presented, then visual composition is not just embellishment but a vital element in communication. While it interests and even delights the eye, good composition is an organizing force when used to dramatize relativity and relationship, and to project ideas. Superior composition not only makes the subject (content) accessible, it heightens the viewer's perceptions and stimulates his imaginative involvement, like language from the pen of a good poet.

I believe that form follows function, and that one should first involve oneself with content before looking for the appropriate form to best communicate it. Another way of working, which comes from being more interested in language than content, is to decide on a form and then look for an appropriate subject. The difference is one of purpose and temperament. Content, form, structure, and style are analyzed in greater detail in Chapters 12–16.

So far we have looked at pictorial composition, but a film's sound track is also a composition, and critically important to a film's overall impact. The study of sound is included next in the editing study project.

PROJECT 5-2: EDITING ANALYSIS

Equipment Required: VCR as in Project 1.

Object: To produce a detailed analysis of a portion of film using standard abbreviations and terminology; to analyze the way a film is constructed; to learn the conventions of film language so they can be used confidently.

Study Materials: Any well-made feature film will do, but I particularly recommend Nicholas Roeg's *Don't Look Now* (1973). Adapted from a Daphne du Maurier short story, the film is set in Venice and fully exploits its exotic location. The narrative style is admirably compact and allusive, relying heavily upon editing to telescope each event into a brief montage of essential moments. Roeg's background is in camerawork, so not only does he value the visual above the spoken, but his composition and camera use are masterly. The film also has a dense and highly evocative sound track. The narrative, which develops out of the trauma a couple suffer at the loss of their child, moves freely backward and forward in time, and this is particularly evident in the lovemaking scene.

Other feature films I would recommend for study are Terence Malick's *Days of Heaven* (1978) for its evocative cinematography and its unusual and effective pacing; Peter Weir's *Witness* (1985) for the superb Amish work sequences and for the ways it contrasts urban and Amish lifestyles; and Martin Scorsese's *King of Comedy* (1982) for the wide variety of material and moods it encompasses.

For an adaptation of a classic Ambrose Bierce short story there is Robert Enrico's *Occurrence at Owl Creek Bridge* (1962), which tells its complex story with virtually no dialogue and uses the camera with great subtlety. The film is especially impressive for the way it uses rhythms and sound effects, for its creative distortion of time, and for its agile camera with many matching angles, each contributing a piece of revelation to the whole.

FIRST VIEWING

Whatever work you choose, first see the whole film without stopping, and then see it a second time before you attempt any analysis. Write down all the strong feelings the film evoked, paying no attention to order. Note from memory which sequences sparked those feelings. You may have an additional sequence or two that intrigued you as a piece of virtuoso storytelling. Note these down too, but whatever you study should be something that hits you at an emotional rather than a merely intellectual level.

ANALYSIS FORMAT

What you write down is going to be displayed in split page format, where all visuals are placed in the left half of the page, and all sound occupies the right half as in Figure 5-2.

First transcribe the picture and dialogue, shot by shot and word by word, as they relate to each other. Your draft transcript should be written with wide line spacing on numerous sheets of paper so you can insert additional information on subsequent passes. Once this basic information is on paper, you can turn to such things as shot transitions, internal and external composition of shots, screen direction, camera movements, opticals (such as fades, dissolves, superimpositions), sound effects, and the use of music. You will need to make a number of shot-by-shot passes through your chosen sequence, dealing with one or two aspects of the content and form at a time.

It is better to do a short sequence (two to four minutes) very thoroughly than a long one more superficially, since your object is to extract the maximum information about an interesting passage of film language. Script formats, either split-page or screenplay, must only show what can be seen and heard. Some of your

```
                    T.B. Sanatorium Sequence

ACTION                              SOUND
F/I L.S. Ruins of sanitorium. Camera   Birdsong, distant jet, sounds of
pans left around buildings, stops with softball players more distant still
two small figures walking slowly

Cut to CS two pairs of feet walking    F/I sound of elderly man coughing, F/O
on brick path, weeds growing up

2S SILVIA and AARON in profile         YOUNG MAN's voice: "Dad?  Dad?"

POV shot of residential building, many AARON: "This was his last home.  Where
windows broken                                I saw him...

Telephoto shot of gutter with ferns           ...last.  You know what he
growing against skyline                       missed the most?"

                                       SILVIA: "Your mother?"

LS through ruined greenhouse, SILVIA   AARON:  "No.  His garden.  His damned
and AARON in B/G                              garden!"

POV shot sapling growing up through    AARON: "Why did they let this place go?
broken glass roof                             It used to be so beautiful"

CS AARON's hand opening creaky gate    SILVIA: "How long did you come here?"

                                       AARON:  "Just over a year.  He had a
WS enclosure with vegetable plots, one        vegetable plot here.  Towards
old man working in B/G.  SILVIA and           the end I had to do everything
AARON enter shot from camera right.           for him."

                                       SILVIA: "That's how you became such a
                                               gardener?

2S, AARON looks off camera left,       AARON:  "I used to see that thing all
SILVIA follows his gaze                        the time while I was
                                               digging...

POV shot, electricity generator                ... it seemed to be waiting
building with high chimney                     for him to die".

Neglected rock garden, pond dry with   AARON:  "When I was a kid and Dad had
weeds growing out of cracks                    left us, I used to try and
                                               hate him, but I never could.
                                               It was a mistake to come back
                                               here."

Frontal 2S.  SILVIA puts arm around
AARON who is disconsolate.
```

FIGURE 5-2

Split page format, also known as TV script format. Picture is always on the left, sound on the right.

notes (for example, on the mood a shot evokes) will clutter the functional simplicity of your transcript, so keep notes on what you felt separately.

MAKING AND USING A FLOOR PLAN

For a sequence containing a dialogue exchange, make a floor plan (also called a ground plan) sketch as in Figure 5-3. In the example, the character Eric enters,

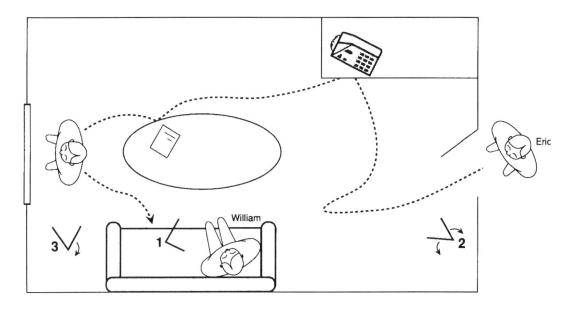

FIGURE 5-3

Floor or ground plan showing entry and movements of character Eric, and the camera positions to cover the action.

stands in front of William, goes to the phone, picks up a book from the table, looks out the window, and then sits down on the couch. The whole action has been covered by three camera positions.

When you analyze a sequence, make a floor plan. It allows you to recreate what the room or location looks like in its entirety, to record how the characters moved around, and to decide how the camera was placed. This will help you in future to decide where to place your own camera. It will also show how little of an environment need be shown for the audience to infer the whole, that is, create it in their imaginations.

STRATEGY FOR STUDY

Your split page log should contain action-side descriptions of each shot and its action as well as sound-side notes detailing the content and positioning of dialogue, music start/stopping points, and featured sound effects (that is, other than synchronous, or "sync" sound. Sound that logically arises from the location is called *diagetic sound*. Nondiagetic sound is that which has been applied as counterpoint, for example, the sound of a loud heartbeat placed over a man trapped in an elevator.

Scrutinize the sequence by categories. I have listed them in a logical order for inquiry, but do not hesitate to reorder my list if you prefer.

Very important: *read from film rather than read into it*. Film is a complex and deceptive medium; like a glib and clever acquaintance, it can make you uneasy about your perceptions and too ready to accept what should be seen or should be felt. Recognize what you felt and connect your impressions with what can actually be seen and heard in the film.

To avoid overload, concentrate on a few of the given aspects at a time and try to find at least one example of everything so you understand the concepts at work.

First Impressions   What was the progression of feeling you had watching the sequence?

Definition and Statistics

What determines the beginning and ending points of the sequence? Is its span determined by:

- being at one location?
- being a continuous segment of time?
- a particular mood?
- the stages of a process?
- something else?

How long is the sequence (minutes and seconds)?

How many picture cuts does it contain? The duration of each shot and how often the camera angle is changed are aspects of a director's style but they are just as likely to be derived from the sequence's content. Try to decide whether the content or its treatment are determining the number of cuts.

Use of Camera

How many different motivations can you find for the camera to make a movement?

- does the camera follow the movement of a character?
- does a car or other moving object permit the camera to pan the length of the street so that camera movement seems to arise from action in the frame?
- does it lay out a landscape or a scene geography for the audience?
- is the move one that gets closer, and intensifies our relationship with someone or something?
- does the camera move away from someone or something so we see more objectively?
- does the camera reveal significant information by moving?
- is the move really a reframing to accommodate a rearrangement of characters?
- is the move a reaction, panning to a new speaker, for instance?
- what else might be responsible for motivating this particular camera move?

When is the camera used subjectively?

- when do we directly experience a character's point of view?

- are there special signs that the camera is seeing subjectively? (For example, an unsteady handheld camera used in *Owl Creek* creates the running man's point of view.)
- what is the dramatic justification?

Are there changes of camera height?

- to accommodate subject matter?
- to make you see in a certain way?
- for other reasons?

Use of Sound
What are the sound perspectives used?

- complementing camera position (near mike for close shots, far from mike for longer shots and so replicating camera perspective)?
- counterpointing camera perspective? (Robert Altman's films are fond of giving us the intimate conversation of two characters distantly traversing a large landscape.)
- uniformly intimate (as with a narration, or with voice-over and "thoughts voices" that function as a character's interior monologue)?
- other situations?

How are particular sound effects used?

- to build atmosphere and mood?
- as punctuation?
- to motivate a cut? (next sequence's sound rises until we cut to it)
- as a narrative device? (horn honks so woman gets up and goes to window where she discovers her sister is making a surprise visit)
- to build, sustain, or defuse tension?
- to provide rhythm? (meal prepared in a montage of brief shots to the rhythmic sound of a man splitting logs; last shot, man and woman sit down to meal)
- to create uncertainty?
- other situations?

Editing
What motivates each cut?

- is there an action match to carry the cut?
- is there a compositional relationship between the two shots that makes the cut interesting and worthwhile? (*Don't Look Now* is obsessed with these.)

- is there a movement relationship that carries the cut (for example, cut from car moving left-to-right to boat moving left-to-right)?
- does someone or something leave the frame (making us expect a new frame)?
- does someone or something fill the frame, blanking it out and permitting a cut to another frame that starts blanked and then clears?
- does someone or something enter the frame and demand closer attention?
- are we cutting to follow someone's eyeline, to see what they see?
- is there a sound, or a line, that demands that we see the source?
- are we cutting to show the effect upon a listener and what defines the right moment to cut?
- are we cutting to a speaker at a particular moment that is visually revealing? What defines that moment?
- if the cut intensifies our attention, what justifies that?
- if the cut relaxes and objectifies our attention, what justifies that?
- is the cut to a parallel activity (that is, something going on simultaneously)?
- is there some sort of comparison or irony being set up through juxtaposition?
- are we cutting to a rhythm (perhaps of an effect, music, or the cadences of speech)?
- other reasons?

What is the relationship of words to images?

- does what is shown illustrate what is said?
- is there a difference and therefore a counterpoint between what is shown and what is heard?
- is there a meaningful contradiction between what is said and what is shown?
- does what is said come from another time frame (for example, a memory of one of the characters or a comment on something in the past)?
- is there a point at which words are used to move us forward or backward in time? (That is, can you pinpoint a change of tense in the film's grammar? This might be done visually, as in the old cliché of autumn leaves falling after we have seen summer scenes.)
- any others?

When a line overlaps a cut, what is the impact of the first strong word on the new image?

- does it help identify the new image?
- does it give it a particular emphasis or interpretation?
- is the effect expected (satisfying perhaps) or unexpected (maybe a shock)?
- is there a deliberate contradiction?
- other effects?

Where and how is music used?

- how is it initiated? (often when characters or story begin some kind of motion)
- what does the music suggest by its texture, instrumentation, etc.?
- how is it finished? (often when characters or story arrive at a new location)
- what comment is it making? (ironic? sympathetic? lyrical? revealing the inner state of a character or situation? other?)
- from what other sound (if any) does it emerge (segue)?
- what other sound does it merge (or segue) into at its close?

Point of View and Blocking

Blocking is a theatrical term meaning the way that actors and camera are moved in relation to the set. The term "point of view" goes beyond whose literal eyeline the audience shares and includes the notion of whose reality the viewer most identifies with at any given time. This turns out to be a much more complicated and interesting issue than it first seems, for a film like a novel can present a main point of view (probably through a point-of-view character) and also multiple, conflicting points of view that are associated with other characters. The author's statement is largely achieved through the handling of point of view, yet the work's appearances can be deceptive unless you look very carefully.

Sometimes there is one central character, and one point of view, like Travis Bickle's in Scorsese's *Taxi Driver* (1975). Or there may be a couple whose relationship is at issue, as in Woody Allen's *Annie Hall* (1977). Successive scenes may be devoted to establishing alternate characters' dilemmas and conflicts. Altman's *Nashville* (1975) has nearly two dozen central characters, and the film's focus is the idea of the music town of Nashville being their point of convergence and their confrontation with change. Here, evidently, we find the characters are part of a pattern, and the pattern itself is surely an authorial point of view that questions the way people subscribe to their own destiny. In Quentin Tarantino's *Pulp Fiction* (1994) and Robert Altman's *Short Cuts* (1993) both use serpentine storylines with characters who come and go and appear in different permutations. Each sequence is liable to have a different point-of-view character. Both films deal with the style and texture of groups, and their time and place.

Following are some ways of digging into a sequence to establish how it covertly structures the way we see and react to its characters. First a word of caution. Point of view is a complex notion that can only be specified confidently after considering the aims and tone of the whole work. Taking a magnifying glass to one sequence is therefore a way of verifying your overall hypothesis. The way the camera is used, the frequency with which one character's feelings are revealed, the amount of development he or she goes through, the vibrancy of the acting—all these factors play a part in enlisting our sympathy and interest.

In your sequence under study, to whom at different times is the dialogue or narration addressed?

- by one character to another?
- to himself (thinking aloud, reading diary or letter)?

- to the audience (narration, interview, prepared statement)?
- other situations?

How many camera positions were used? (Use your floor plan.)

- show basic camera positions and label them A, B, C, etc.
- show camera dollying movements with dotted line leading to new position.
- mark shots in your log with the appropriate A, B, C camera angles.
- notice how the camera stays to one side of subject-to-subject axis (an imaginary line that the camera avoids crossing) to keep characters facing in the same screen direction from shot to shot. When this principle is broken, it is variously called *crossing the line, crossing the axis,* or *breaking the 180-degree rule,* and has the effect of disrupting the audience's sense of spatial relationships.
- how often is the camera close to the crucial axis between characters?
- how often does the camera subjectively share a character's eyeline?
- when and why does it take an objective stance to the situation (that is, either a distanced viewpoint, or one independent of eyelines)?

Character Blocking: How did the characters and camera move in the scene? To the location and camera movement sketch you have made, add dotted lines to show the characters' movements (called blocking). You can use different colors for clarity.

What points of view did the author engage us in?

- whose story is this sequence if you go by gut reaction?
- taking into account the angles on each character, with whose point of view were you led to sympathize?
- how many psychological viewpoints did you share? (Some may have been momentary or fragmentary, and perhaps in contradiction to what you were seeing.)
- are the audience's sympathies structured by camera and editing? Or are they molded independently by perhaps acting or the situation itself?

FICTION AND THE DOCUMENTARY

Most of these analytical questions apply equally to the documentary film and one realizes that the two forms have much in common. This is more than a similarity in film language, for some of the important questions cannot be applied to most nature, travelogue, industrial, or educational films. These genres generally lack what distinguishes the fictional and documentary forms—authorial vision. That is, they often lack a point of view, a changing dramatic pressure, and a critical perspective upon what it means to be human. These elements are crucial in providing the feeling of an authorial voice, of a human sensibility unifying the events it shows, even though (and we must never forget this) the making of a film is collaborative. We sense the presence of a storyteller's sympathy and intelligence, and what in lesser hands might be technical or formulaic becomes vibrantly human.

This kind of vision is the best sort of leadership, for unegotistically and by example it invites us to see a familiar world with new eyes.

PROJECT 5-3: A SCRIPTED SCENE COMPARED WITH THE FILMED OUTCOME

Object: To study the relationship between the blueprint script and the filmed product.

Study Materials: A film script and the finished film made from it on videotape. Don't look at the film until you have planned your own version from the text. The script must be the original screenplay and not a release script (that is, not a transcript made from a finished film). A suitable script is to be found in Pauline Kael's *The Citizen Kane Book: Raising Kane* (New York: Limelight Editions, 1984). Another is Harold Pinter's *The French Lieutenant's Woman: A Screenplay* (Boston: Little, Brown, 1981). The latter has an absorbing foreword by the author of the original novel, John Fowles, which not only tells the story of the adaptation, but describes from a novelist's point of view what is involved when one's novel makes the transition to the screen.

If obtaining an original script is a problem, an interesting variation is to use a film adapted from a stageplay, and to study an obligatory scene, that is, one so dramatically necessary that it cannot be missing from the film version. Good titles are:

Arthur Miller's *Death of a Salesman*

Laslo Benedek's 1951 film version with Fredric March

Wim Wenders' 1987 TV version with Dustin Hoffman. Interesting for its expressionist sets and because a theatrical flavor is retained.

Edward Albee's *Who's Afraid of Virginia Woolf?*

Mike Nichols' 1966 film version

Peter Schaffer's *Equus*

Sidney Lumet's 1977 film version

Tennessee Williams' *A Streetcar Named Desire*

Elia Kazan's 1951 film version

STRATEGY FOR STUDY

Study the Original
Try to select an unfamiliar work and read the whole script (or stage play). Choose a scene of four or five pages.

14. Imagine the location and draw a floor plan. (See Figure 5-3 for an example.)

15. Make your own shooting script adaptation, substituting action for dialogue wherever feasible, and making use of your location environment. (See Figure 7-1 for standard screenplay layout.)

16. Mark in characters' movements on floor plan.
17. Mark in camera positions (A, B, C, etc., and indicate camera movements). Refer to these in your shooting script.
18. Write a brief statement about (a) what major themes you think the entire script/play is dealing with, and (b) how your chosen scene functions in the whole.

Study the Film Version
First see the entire film without stopping. Then run your chosen scene two or three times, stopping and rerunning sections as you wish. Carry out the following.

1. Make notes on film's choice of location (imaginative? metaphoric?).
2. Make a floor plan and mark in camera positions, movements of characters.
3. Using a photocopy of the scene, pencil in annotations to show what dialogue has been cut, added, or altered.
4. Note actions, both large and small, that add significantly to impact of the scene. Ignore those specified in the original, as the object is to find what the film version has added or substituted to the writer's version.
5. Note camera usage as follows:
   —any abnormal perspective (that is, nonstandard lens used. A standard lens is one that reproduces the perspective of the human eye. Telescopic and wide-angle lenses compress or magnify perspective respectively.)
   —any camera position above or below eye level
   —any camera movement (track, pan, tilt, zoom, crane). Note what you think motivated the camera movement (character's movement, eyeline, storyteller's revelation, etc.).
6. Note what the thematic focus of the film seems to be, and how your chosen scene functions in the film.

Comparison
Compare your scripting with the film's handling and describe the following:

1. How did the film establish time and place?
2. How effectively did the film compress the original and substitute behavior for dialogue?
3. How, using camerawork and editing, is the audience drawn into identifying with one or more characters?
4. Whose scene was it, and why?
5. How were any rhythms (speech, movements, sound effects, music, etc.) used to pace out the scene, particularly to speed it up or slow it down?
6. What were the major changes of interpretation in the film and in the chosen scene?
7. Provide any further valuations of the film you think worth making (acting, characterization, use of music or sound effects, etc.).

Assess Your Performance
How well did you do? What aspects of filmmaking are you least aware of, and need to develop? What did you accomplish?

PROJECT 5-4: LIGHTING ANALYSIS

Directors do not need to understand the technique of lighting; that is the DP's role. But they do need to know what effect each different lighting setup produces, and what terminology one uses to effectively describe it.

Equipment Required: VCR as in previous projects. It will be helpful to turn down the color control of your monitor so that initially you see a black-and-white picture. Adjust the monitor's brightness and contrast controls so the greatest range of gray tones are visible between video white and video black. Unless you do this you simply won't see all that is present.

Object: To analyze common lighting situations and understand what goes into creating a lighting mood.

Study Materials: Same as in previous project, only this time it will be an advantage to search out particular lighting situations rather than sequences of special dramatic appeal. The same sequences may fulfill both purposes.

LIGHTING TERMINOLOGY

Here the task is to recognize different types and combinations of lighting situations and to apply standard terminology. Every aspect of lighting carries strong emotional associations which can be put to work in drama to great effect. Technique and the terminology to describe it are therefore powerful tools in the right hands. Here are some basic terms:

Types of Lighting Style
High-key picture: The shot looks bright overall with small areas of shadow. In Figure 5-4 the shot is exterior day, and the shadow of the lamppost in the foreground shows that there is indeed deep shadow in the picture. Where shadow is sharp, as here, the light source is called *specular.* A high-key picture can be virtually shadowless so long as the frame is bright overall.

Low-key picture: The shot looks dark overall with few highlight areas. These are often interiors or night shots, but in Figure 5-5 we have a backlit day interior that ends up being low key, that is, having a large area of the frame in deep shadow.

Graduated tonality: The shot has neither bright highlights nor deep shadow but consists of an even, restricted range of midtones. This might be a flat lit interior, like a supermarket, or a misty morning landscape as in Figure 5-6. Here an overcast sky diffuses the lighting source, and the disorganized light rays scatter into every possible shadow area so there are neither highlights nor shadow.

FIGURE 5-4 ——

High-key scene, hard or specular lighting, high contrast. Notice compositional depth in this shot compared with the flatness of Figure 5-5.

FIGURE 5-5 ——

Backlit low-key scene, subject silhouetted against the flare of backlit smoke.

FIGURE 5-6 ——————————————————————————————————————

Graduated tonality scene, low contrast because key light is diffused through morning mist.

Contrast

High-contrast picture: The shot may be lit either high or low key, but there must be a big difference in illumination level between highlight and shadow area, as in Figure 5-7 which has a soot-and-whitewash starkness. Both Figures 5-4 and 5-5 are also high-contrast images although the area of shadow in each is drastically different.

Low-contrast picture: The shot can either be high or low key, but with shadow area illumination level near that of highlight levels. Figure 5-6 is high key, low contrast.

Light Quality

Hard lighting: This is any specular light source creating hard-edged shadows; for example, sun, studio spotlight, or candle flame. These are all called "effectively small" light sources because a small source gives hard-edged shadows. Figure 5-4 is lit by hard light (the sun), while the shadow under the chair in Figure 5-5 is so soft it is hardly discernible.

Soft lighting: Any light source is soft when it creates soft-edged shadows or a shadowless image as in Figure 5-6. Soft light sources are, for example, fluorescent tubes, sunlight reflecting off matte finish wall, light from overcast sky, or a studio soft light.

Names of Lighting Sources

Key light: This is not necessarily an artificial source, for it can be the sun. The key is the light that creates intended shadows in the shot, and these in turn reveal the angle and position of the supposed source light, often relatively hard or specular

FIGURE 5-7 ——————————————————————————————————————

High-contrast image with very few midtones owing to back lighting and no fill.

(shadow-producing) light. In Figure 5-4 the key light is sunlight coming from rear left and above the camera. In Figure 5-5 it is streaming in toward the camera.

Fill light: This is the light used to raise illumination in shadow area. For interiors it will probably be soft light thrown from the direction of the camera, which avoids creating additional visible shadows. There are shadows, of course, but they are hidden from the camera's view by the subject. Especially in interiors fill light is often provided from matte white reflectors, through diffusion material, or is derived from bounce light, that is, hard light bounced from walls or ceilings to soften it.

Back light: This is light thrown upon a subject from behind, and often from above as well as behind, as in Figure 5-5. A favorite technique in portraiture is to put a rim of light around a subject's head and shoulders to separate them from the background. Rain, fog, dust, or smoke (as in this case of garage barbecuing) all show up best when backlit.

Practical: This is any light appearing in frame as part of the scene; for example, table lamp, overhead fluorescent, or, as in Figure 5-8, the candles on a birthday cake. Usually practicals provide little or no real source of illumination. Here the candles light up the faces, but not the background.

Figure 5-8 illustrates several lighting points. The girl in the middle is lit from below, a style called "monster lighting" and rather eerie for a birthday shot. The girl on the left, having no backlight or background lighting, disappears into the shadows, while the subject on the right is outlined by set light, that is, light falling on the set. The same light source shines on her hair as a backlight source and gives it highlights and texture.

FIGURE 5-8 ——————————————————————————————————————

Practicals are any lights seen in frame, like these birthday candles. Strong set light prevents the background from going dark.

Types of Lighting Setup

Here the illustrations are of the same model lit in various ways. The effect and the mood in each portrait varies greatly as a result. The diagrams show the positioning of the key and fill lights. In a floor plan diagram such as these, one cannot show the height of the shadow-producing light sources, only the angle of throw relative to the camera-to-subject axis. Heights can be inferred from the areas of highlight and their converse, the shadow patterns.

Frontally lit: The key light in Figure 5-9 is so close to the camera-to-subject axis that shadows are thrown backward out of the camera's view. You can see very slight shadows in the folds of the subject's shirt, which show that the key was to the right of camera. Notice how flat and lacking in dimensionality or tension this shot is compared with Figures 5-10 and 5-11.

Broad lit: In Figure 5-10 the key light is some way to the side, so a broad area of the subject's face and body is highlighted. Key light skimming the subject lengthens his face, revealing angles and undulations. There are areas of deep shadow, especially in the eyesockets, but these could be reduced by increasing the amount of soft fill light.

Narrow lit: The key light in Figure 5-11 is to the side of the subject and beyond him, so that only a narrow portion of his face is receiving highlight. The majority of his face is in shadow. This portion of the face is lit by fill light, or we would see nothing. Measuring light reflected in the highlight area and comparing it with that reflected from the fill area gives the lighting ratio. Remember when taking measurements that fill light also reaches highlight areas but not vice versa, so you can only take accurate readings with all the lights on.

Silhouette: Here in Figure 5-12 the subject reflects no light at all, and shows up only as an outline against raw light. This lighting is sometimes used in docu-

FIGURE 5-9

Frontal lighting: flattens the subject and removes much of the face's interest. Most flash photography is frontal and correspondingly dull.

 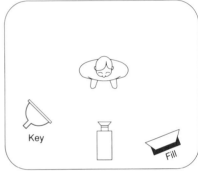

FIGURE 5-10

Broad lighting: illuminates a broad area of the face and shows the head as round and having angularities. Revelation becomes interesting because lighting is selective.

 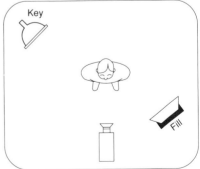

FIGURE 5-11

Narrow lighting: illuminates only a narrow area of the face. More fill used here than in Figure 5-10. The effect is decidedly dramatic.

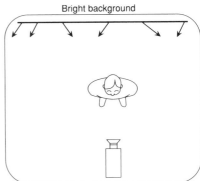

FIGURE 5-12 ———

Silhouette: all light is from the background and none reaches the subject's face.

mentaries when the subject's identity is being withheld. Here it produces the ominous effect of someone unknown confronting us through a bright doorway.

STRATEGY FOR STUDY

Locate two or three sequences with quite different lighting moods, and using the definitions above, classify them as follows:

1. Style: high-key/low-key/graduated tonality?
2. Contrast: high or low contrast?
3. Scene: intended to look like natural light or artificial lighting?
4. Setup: frontal/broad/narrow/back lighting setup?
5. Angles: high/low angle of key light?
6. Quality: hard/soft edges to shadows?
7. Source: source in scene is intended to be _____
8. Practicals: practicals in the scene are _____
9. Time: day for day/night for night/dusk for night/day for night? _____
10. Mood: mood conveyed by lighting is _____
11. Continuity: any differences of lighting to show that wide and close shots can, within limits, be handled differently?

After you have analyzed several different sequences, turn up the color to see if you can spot patterns in its use. These should suggest how the DP (director of photography) sets about interpreting the emotional associations of the location and requirements of the script. Predominant hues and color saturation level (meaning whether a color is pure, or "desaturated" with an admixture of white) have a great deal to do with a scene's effect on the viewer. For instance, Hitchcock's *The Trouble with Harry* (1955) places its unwanted, unburied corpse in the serene beauty of autumnal New England. In Louis Malle's *Pretty Baby* (1978) DP Sven Nykvist produces with great economy of means the ruby-shaded opulence of 1917 New Orleans bordellos. Scorsese's *After Hours* (1985) has many threatening night exteriors in New York City, and a lot of dark, "cold" colors.

Two classically lit black-and-white films are Orson Welles' *Citizen Kane* (1941) with cinematography by the revolutionary Gregg Toland, and Jean Cocteau's *Beauty and the Beast* (1946) whose lighting Henri Alekan modeled after Dutch painting, especially its interiors. A much more recent B&W film by Alekan is Wim Wenders' poetic *Wings of Desire* (1987).

C·H·A·P·T·E·R 6

SHOOTING FUNDAMENTALS

If you have dipped into this book and want to jump right into the "doing" part, its design is meant to encourage you. Although one kind of learner likes to read, understand, and be thoroughly prepared before entering practical work, there are others (myself included) who must try things by doing them. I find it hard to learn stage two of anything practical without first exploring stage one for myself. So start production if you wish, and use the rest of the book to solve the questions and problems you encounter. That, after all, is the history of the film industry. The projects in this book allow you to explore techniques of expression but you should make each a vehicle for your own ideas and tastes. After every one I have included questions to help you probe your work's aspects, strengths, and weaknesses. You can freely modify the projects in character, location, or action without loss if you hold onto the learning goals.

These two projects and their variations represent a fairly complete workout in basic filmmaking. If they appear purely technical, look closer, for they can be used to explore what it takes to build a character, a situation, and the audience's involvement through nonverbal, behavioral means. They also allow you to build an authorial point of view and the disparate perspectives of the characters themselves.

HOW BEST TO EXPLORE THE BASICS

You can shoot these exploration projects on film or videotape but tape has most of the advantages; it's cheap, can be watched in B&W or color, has sync sound, and needs no turn-around time for lab processing. Most importantly, its low cost permits you to shoot extensive coverage in search of a high level of actor performance and camera control. Film uses reliable, mechanical tools compared with video and it imposes some instructive limitations because of its high-image quality and high costs, but experimenting and developing the actors' performances may be very expensive. With few chances to get things right, you either lay careful and effective plans or fail ignominiously.

This is the school of hard knocks which teaches you a lot about teamwork and organization, but first screen lessons that stress planning and parsimony are likely to shortchange the human presence onscreen. By encountering cinema as equipment and logistics, student directors delay facing what is so hard in fiction: putting spontaneity and legitimate emotion on the screen. Unless one wants to work in genre films where character is unimportant, *a legitimate and gripping human presence on the screen is mandatory.* This requires a knowledge of actors and what it means to act for the camera, something utterly distinct from what you need to produce well-directed camerawork, and far more important to the audience (your camera crew is unlikely to agree).

I believe that good screen fiction requires multidimensional characters striving after their goals in truthful and interesting ways. How can something that looks so easy and natural in the cinema be so difficult to produce? And why are the directorial skills to accomplish this so misunderstood?

The answers lie somewhere in the evolutionary history of the film industry and in that of its very recent offspring, the film school. They are not really germane to this book. What does matter is that *any production with parts that are less than credible will fail to hold its audience,* no matter how inventive or exquisite all the other craft and camerawork happens to be. Students and even teachers often seem to avoid or deny this unpalatable truth. When a student director discovers this Achilles heel in himself it often happens when he or she is a senior and a return to basics seems no longer feasible. Hence the melancholy stereotype of student films as a genre of distended, poorly written and poorly acted films shot in stunningly lovely Eastmancolor.

Learn directing fundamentals using the fast and inexpensive medium of video. After a period consolidating your skills you can start directing on the more expensive medium. First let's look at what video offers.

Camcorders are reliable, reasonably controllable, and WYSIWYG (What You See Is What You Get). You can even watch each take on a monitor as you shoot and concentrate on directing rather than arguing the mysteries of film exposure, latitude, depth of focus, lighting, and so on. You'll be doing what many feature directors now do; use a video assist—that is, they view a video monitor hitched to the film camera rather than viewing the action itself. Shoot as many takes as you need to get the best out of your cast. Video will further allow several people to edit multiple and experimental versions—important in a class learning about narrative strategies, compression, and the individual voice each editor imposes on the material.

Most of the objections to video arise from the restrictions of linear (tape transfer-based) editing. Alter the length of one shot, and everything thereafter must be retransferred. Film, on the contrary, allows one to interpose or transpose at will, as if one were working on a chain made of replaceable links. However, reconstituting a film workprint is time consuming and a heavily spliced print can become virtually unprojectable. Now with the advent of Avid, Lightworks, and a host of other computer-based NLE (nonlinear editing) systems, the arguments for using video in film education increase dramatically, especially as the film industry itself has adopted digital NLE instead of film editing.

Diehards will continue to oppose the use of video under any circumstances. This may be clinging to the past, but it often signifies a deep appreciation for the matchless acuity (ability to render fine detail) of film and the narrative power of its beauty and particular transformation characteristics. Nobody can argue with this. However, that is the province of cinematography, not directing.

ON DEVELOPING YOUR TECHNIQUE

The projects that follow will help you develop a broad and representative range of directing and editing skills. Technique should not become an end in itself. "Art," said Thomas Hardy, "is the secret of how to produce by a false thing the effect of a true." This applies wonderfully to the artifice that goes into filmmaking. Good technique is transparent and goes unnoticed by the audience because the film grips the viewer's imagination. Poor technique or virtuosity misapplied is technique which draws attention to itself and fails to serve the film's purpose. I am not including here reflexive films which are about filmmaking and necessarily draw attention to their own means.

The first projects explore basic techniques and embody modest subject matter. Do not be deceived by their simplicity into thinking they are too easy. Where a project requires lighting, keep it basic and simple, so you avoid getting sidetracked by the joys of cinematography.

I have supplied requirements, procedures, and hints, leaving much of the problem solving, always the most rewarding area of learning, to your ingenuity and resourcefulness. For additional information, use the table of contents at the front of the appropriate production phase, or the Glossary and Index at the book's end.

Shooting assignments are best assessed in a group or class; here you get used to working with collaborators and listening to an audience's reaction. Some of the projects have a great number of critical assessments, too many to monitor while watching a cut. Each person in a group can watch out for a few particular facets. This ensures a discussion of depth from which everyone learns—particularly the maker, whose job it is to listen and take notes, not to explain anything.

ASSESSMENT METHOD

After each project is a list of desirably positive facets such as "Project imagery is well composed" for you or your class to score according to agreement. Numbers aren't in themselves useful, but having to make quality decisions is. I use the following five-point scale:

Not true or not applicable	0
Only minimally true	1

Somewhat so	2
Average and acceptably so	3
Considerably so	4
Unusually and strikingly so	5

PROJECT 6-1: BASIC TECHNIQUES: GOING AND RETURNING

This project is without dialogue and concerns building the character and situation of a character who looks forward to arriving at a building but discovers she has lost her keys. In the discovery and returning to her car to look for them she can go through a range of subtle emotions—irritation, anxiety, relief, perhaps even amusement. While creating this character you get a workout in film grammar basics such as screen direction and matching.

Skills:

- maintaining relevant screen direction
- panning and tilting to follow action
- picture framing and composition to suggest depth
- editing: action match cutting
- cutting together different sizes of similar image
- cutting together complementary angles on same action
- telling a story through action and behavior, and without words
- ellipsis (compressing real time into a more cinematic shorthand)
- editing to music
- making a long version (first assembly) and a short version (fine cut)

6-1A: PLAN, SHOOT, AND EDIT LONG VERSION

A car draws up. The car's occupant, Mary, approaches a house looking up at a window in pleased anticipation. She mounts a flight of steps to the front door. There she discovers she does not have her keys. Perplexed, she returns to her car, which she expects to be open. Finding the door locked, she curses, thinking her keys are locked in. Looking inside, she sees that the ignition lock is empty. Patting her pockets and looking around in consternation, she spots her keys lying in the gutter. She picks them up, relieved, and returns toward the house.

Figure 6-1 is a specimen floor or ground plan. Adapt yours to your location (mine is a one-way street to allow the driver to drop her keys in the nearside gutter). The floor plan shows Mary's walk and the basic camera positions to cover the various parts of the action. No sound is necessary.

Figure 6-2 is a storyboard of representative frames for each camera position. For your coverage make your own ground plan and show camera positions and storyboard key frames. Here is a sample shot list as it relates to the ground plan and key frames A through G.

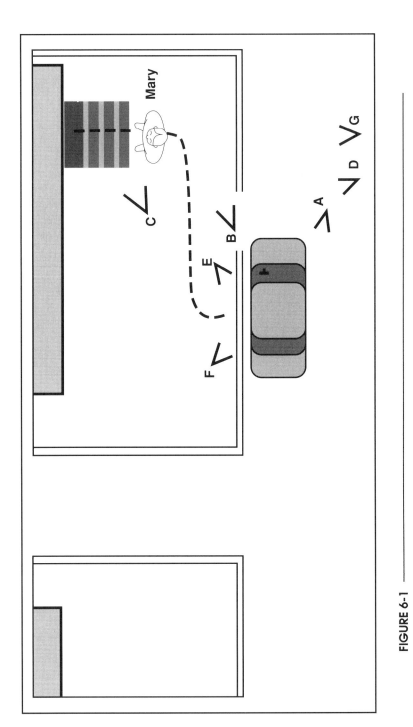

FIGURE 6-1

Specimen floor plan for the "Mary Sequence." Camera positions are marked as A through G.

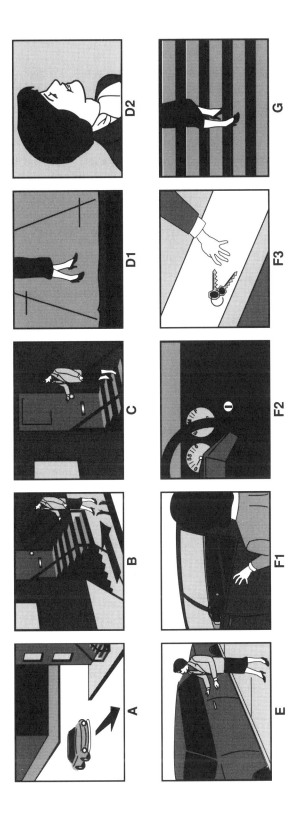

FIGURE 6-2

Storyboard frames showing setups for the various camera angles in Figure 6-1.

1. Establishing shot of locale from camera position A with car arriving as in Frame A.

2. Medium shot (MS) panning with Mary L–R (left to right). When she turns the corner in the path she changes her effective screen direction ending up as in Frame B.

3. Medium-close shots (MCS) Mary's feet walking R–L and L–R on sidewalk and up steps as an all-purpose cut-in (also called insert) shot, as in Frame D1.

4. Big closeup (BCU) panning telephoto shot of Mary's head as she walks, looking up at window as in D2.

5. Feet enter shot descending steps, camera tilts down to follow action, Frame G.

6. Over-shoulder (OS) shot of empty ignition lock, F1.

7. Point-of-view (POV) shot, F2.

8. BCU keys in gutter, hand reaches into frame and takes them, F3.

In its simplest edited form the abbreviated sequence might look something like this:

Camera Position	Shot Number	Action
A	1	Car arrives, Mary gets out, slams door, exits bottom right of frame.
B	2a	Mary enters L–R, begins crossing frame.
D2	3	CU Mary smiles up at window.
B	2b	This is the rest of shot 2a. Mary continues L–R, turns corner of path, walks R–L toward steps and up them.
C	3	Mary rises into frame from R–L, fumbles for keys, can't find them, looks back at car, turns back out of frame.
B	4	Mary descending steps, across frame L–R, turns corner, crosses frame R–L.
E	5a	Mary arrives from screen R, walking R–L toward car, fails to open door, curses.
F1	6	She crosses frame, repositions herself looking R–L to see if key is in ignition, peers inside.
F2	7	Her POV of empty ignition.
E	5b	Mary straightens up, pats pockets, sees something out of frame on the ground.
F3	8a	CU keys lying in gutter from Mary's POV.
E	5c	Mary reacts, stoops down.
F3	8b	CU of keys, hand enters frame, takes them back up.
E	5d	Mary straightens up looking relieved and exits into camera, making frame go black. End of sequence.

Notice that shot 2 is intercut with a CU, while the action in shot 5 has been intercut three times. When directing for intercutting like this, it is not advisable to shoot short individual pieces to exactly fit a slot in the script. More consistent, and easier on the actors, is to shoot a large section or even the whole action in the two different sizes of shot, afterward selecting the fragments you require from the continuous take during editing.

Also notice that at the end of shot 5, when Mary returns with the keys, her movement is used to black out the screen by walking right up to the camera lens. To make a transition to another shot, start with the actor's back against the lens and have the actor walk away from the lens. In the transition the screen goes from action to black then from black to a new scene. This is one of many transitional devices of which the simplest is the humble cut. Overuse the fancy ones, and you run the risk of being tricksy.

- cut this first, long version together, taking into account cutting from shot 2a to 3.
- make sure Mary's walking rhythm is maintained and that you do not inadvertently make her take two steps on the same foot. A rhythm match will be required for other walking shots, too.
- when cutting from 5a to 6 there will probably be an action match. Below are some of the few rules in filmmaking.

Cutting On Action: This is always strongest because the eye locks onto the action. When an attention-commanding action flows across a cut, the eye hardly notices the change of composition or subject. Action matches are best when the outgoing shot initiates the movement and the incoming shot takes over and completes most of the action.

Match Cut Rules: For the best action match,

Step 1: establish the start of an action in the outgoing shot using only as much as is necessary to recognize what the action is going to be.

Step 2: complete the majority of the action in the incoming shot, but be aware that if the action flowing across the cut is at all fast, you must *repeat three or four frames of the action at the head of the incoming shot.* This is because the eye does not register the first three or four frames of any new image. Though a frame-by-frame analysis shows a slight action repeat, shown at normal speed the action will appear smooth and continuous.

- cutting from 5c to 8b, same principle. Let Mary just begin to stoop and then cut to keys with hand entering at top of frame shortly afterward. If you leave too much footage before the incoming hand appears, you will imply that Mary is eight feet tall.

Criteria: Run your cut version. Make an exact minutes and seconds count of its length. Now try rating your agreement for each of these criteria on the 1–5 rating outlined above. Circling the scores will give you clues to which aspects of your work are strong and which need more work.

Editing	Action match cuts are smooth and natural-looking	0 1 2 3 4 5
	Uses match cuts on major moments of action to bridge shots wherever possible	0 1 2 3 4 5
	Match cuts between two sizes of same action use image size change large enough to make a natural-looking cut. (If change is too small it looks like a messy jump cut)	0 1 2 3 4 5
	Rhythm of footsteps is perfectly matched	0 1 2 3 4 5
	Cutting from angle to angle feels natural and motivated	0 1 2 3 4 5
	Overall editing rhythm feels natural	0 1 2 3 4 5
Camera operating	Camera movements are so smooth they seem motivated by subject's movements	0 1 2 3 4 5
	Pans and tilts sync with the motivating action, not ahead or behind	0 1 2 3 4 5
Composition	Camera height is varied to create interesting angles	0 1 2 3 4 5
	Framing and composition on static shots is excellent	0 1 2 3 4 5
	Compositions create perspective and depth	0 1 2 3 4 5
	Lead space ahead of subject well judged	0 1 2 3 4 5
	Compositional proportions around subject is maintained between images of different sizes	0 1 2 3 4 5
Blocking	Screen direction of subject remains logical	0 1 2 3 4 5
	Does not "cross the line" (If you did, try using safety coverage such as close shots of feet walking to space out and disguise the mismatched shots)	0 1 2 3 4 5
Human presence and continuity	Actor looks so unself-conscious that footage could pass for documentary	0 1 2 3 4 5
	Nature and speed of actions is consistent from angle to angle	0 1 2 3 4 5
	Mood changes and development make a character of compelling interest	0 1 2 3 4 5
	Where she's come from and where she is going is suggested interestingly by acting, props, costuming, etc.	0 1 2 3 4 5
Dramaturgy	Sequence has a natural and satisfying arc of development and conclusion	0 1 2 3 4 5

6-1B: EDITING A MORE COMPRESSED VERSION

Run your cut and consider which moments in the action are vital, and which are link material. Surely a lot of the walking is of secondary importance. If, for instance, Mary turns to look back in the direction of the car, we don't need to see her cover every inch of ground to arrive at it. Amend the first cut by making a compressed version. Here's where the unused bridging closeups come in, signified in the new abbreviated list with an asterisk:

Camera Position	Shot Number	Action
A	1	Car arrives but cut before it comes to a complete halt.
B	2a	Mary enters L–R, begins crossing frame.
D2	3	CU of Mary smiling up at window.
D1	*	Her feet L–R.
B	2b	Mary arrives at corner of path, turns R–L; cut immediately to . . .
C	3	Mary almost at door, fumbles for keys, can't find, looks back at car and turns.
G	*	Feet descending a couple of steps.
D1	*	CS feet walking on sidewalk R–L.
E	5a	Mary almost at car, fails to open door, curses.
F2	7	CU to her POV of empty ignition lock.
E	5b	Mary straightens up, pats pockets, sees something on ground.
F3	8a	CU keys lying in gutter, her hand enters frame to pick them up.
E	5d	Mary leaving car walks into camera, turning screen black.

Discussion: How long is the sequence this time? It should be thirty to fifty percent shorter, yet lose nothing of narrative importance. See if you can cut it down further, to perhaps as little as thirty to sixty seconds overall. Keep running it and you will find shots or parts of shots that can be eliminated. Set the audience up to infer what is not visible, and they will. This way, instead of passively witnessing something that requires no interpretation, the audience actively participates and uses its imagination. This is treating your audience as active and intelligent collaborators rather than passive vessels to be filled up with "information."

6-1C: SETTING IT TO MUSIC

Having discovered how much leeway there is to the length of many of the shots, you can now turn Mary into a musical star. Find a piece of music with a strong beat that enhances the mood of the sequence. Reedit the materials placing your cuts and major pieces of action on the beat or on the music's instrumental changes. Be aware that *for each cut to appear on the beat, they must occur three or four frames before the actual beat point* because of the perceptual lag when you cut to a new image. The only nonnegotiable aspects of your earlier cut are the action match cuts. There is only one way to make them look right.

Discussion:
- how tightly does the action fit the music?
- does cutting on the beat become predictable? If so, try cutting on a musical subdivision.

- how much compromise did you have to make with the tight version to adjust the action to fit the music?
- what does the music add to the earlier version's impact?

PROJECT 6-2: CHARACTER STUDY

Skills:

- revealing a character through action
- using mobile *cinéma vérité* handheld coverage
- blocking camera and actor for mutual accommodation
- developing counterpoint between words and action
- imposing a second point of view

6-2A: PLAN, REHEARSE, AND SHOOT LONG TAKE
CHARACTER-REVEALING ACTION

Alan, alone, makes breakfast in his own way. Depending on your actor, this is an opportunity to show someone smart, dreamy, ultra-methodical, or slobbish making his breakfast in a particular state of mind and emotions. Have fun with it, and in your coverage incorporate:

- action of about four minutes that is emotionally revealing of Alan's basic character, particular mood, and immediate past and future,
- idiosyncratic interaction with objects (no other people, no phone conversations),
- a single, nonstop handheld take using wide-angle lens only,
- camera movement (pan, tilt, handheld tracking shot, etc.) to follow or reveal as necessary,
- close and long shots produced by altering subject-to-camera distance as necessary. This may be done by moving the camera in and out, or by blocking Alan to move close or far from a static camera,
- thorough exploitation of the domestic setting,
- lots of rehearsal with camera to make all of the above look smooth and natural, and
- safety cutaways, point-of-view shots, inserts.

The difference between an insert and a cutaway is that an insert magnifies something already in frame while a cutaway shows something outside its complementary shot's framing. Cutaways need motivation or they look contrived. For instance, in wide shot, Alan glances across frame, so use this glance to motivate cutting to your cutaway shot of a clock.

Discussion: You have probably discovered that the rehearsal process needs to be organized in stages:

- first determine Alan's character
- then his situation
- then figure out how to externalize these as action for the audience

Camera coverage will develop:

- first out of what the actor improvises
- then blocking can evolve from mutual accommodation between camera and actor

Some actions will have to be slowed down to look normal on the screen. You may need to reblock the action, that is, have the actor turn some actions around or move to a marked point so the action is visible without the camera having to move. You will probably need lighting; for this semi-documentary approach try placing light stands in a tight group against the least interesting wall, so your camera has maximum freedom to move without picking up telltale stands and supply wires.

Looking at your results, apply these criteria:

Blocking and location use	The setting is used throughout to great advantage. (Sometimes settings get used only as a generalized "container" rather than active components in the story)	0 1 2 3 4 5
	The essential action is always visible	0 1 2 3 4 5
	The action is in wide shot whenever necessary	0 1 2 3 4 5
	The action is in close shot whenever necessary	0 1 2 3 4 5
	Alan's movements are predominantly contrived to happen down the depth of the frame and create depth	0 1 2 3 4 5
	One always sees a transitionary movement or action when one needs to see it	0 1 2 3 4 5
Acting	We learn something about Alan from everything he does	0 1 2 3 4 5
	He looks naturally occupied throughout	0 1 2 3 4 5
	One can guess something about the day he anticipates	0 1 2 3 4 5
	One gets a sense of how he spent significant time previous to this scene	0 1 2 3 4 5
	Is there variation of mood and rhythm in what he does?	0 1 2 3 4 5
	Is he natural or are there dips in credibility?	0 1 2 3 4 5
	One gets the sense of a whole character with some issues bearing upon him	0 1 2 3 4 5
Dramaturgy	The piece is consistently interesting to watch	0 1 2 3 4 5
	There is an overall sense of development in the piece	0 1 2 3 4 5

	We see a whole complex character emerge	0 1 2 3 4 5
	There is evidence of personality conflicts and unfinished business	0 1 2 3 4 5
	The pace of the development does not lag or get stuck	0 1 2 3 4 5
	The piece feels resolved and finishes satisfyingly	0 1 2 3 4 5
	The high spot in the piece occurs where it should, not late or early	0 1 2 3 4 5
	The piece accomplishes its mission within the four-minute time requirement	0 1 2 3 4 5
Camerawork	The camerawork feels natural and unobtrusive	0 1 2 3 4 5
	The variations in camera height are all motivated	0 1 2 3 4 5
	The camera seeks to relate Alan to everything he is doing. (For instance, shoot over the toaster at Alan's face waiting for toast to pop up, rather than show toaster, then pan to Alan waiting)	0 1 2 3 4 5
	Composition is always in control. (Action isn't held safely wide so one feels one is watching a stage performance)	0 1 2 3 4 5
	Alan's movements onscreen are always at the right distance, never so close that the audience feels seasick	0 1 2 3 4 5
	The camera was never taken by surprise	0 1 2 3 4 5
	The camera never illegitimately anticipated what will happen next	0 1 2 3 4 5

Discussion:

- what in general might make fluid camerawork seem intrusive or objectionable?
- what is the drawback of long take coverage?
- what are its advantages?
- what is the difference in feeling when the action takes place across the frame instead of down its depth?
- what are the consequences for framing and camera movement?
- when can the camera look away from Alan and take its own initiative, make its own revelations? (Showing, for instance, that while Alan is searching for eggs, the frying pan is smoking ominously.)
- when is it legitimate for the camera to be caught by surprise or to show it knows what is going to happen next?
- does the audience feel it is spying on Alan unawares, or is there guidance, a feeling that the camera has its own ideas about him and is deliberately showing particular aspects of him?
- what might determine which storytelling mode to use?
- how much of the take is dramatically interesting and where are the flat spots of dead or link material?

6-2B: ADDING AN INTERIOR MONOLOGUE

Add an interior monologue track as a voice-over (VO) in which we hear Alan's thought process. In planning this you will need to consider the following:

- which actions does a person do automatically from long habit?
- which of them require thought?
- on what grounds is each decision made?
- at what points are a character's thoughts in the present?
- at what points do they fly away elsewhere, and why?
- when do we mentally refer to what we are doing, and why?

Do not forget to shoot monologue "presence track" or atmosphere (also known as buzz track or room tone) to serve as necessary "sound spacer" should you want to extend pauses in the VO.

Assessment:
When you have completed the assignment, assess or discuss,

- where the interior monologue voice is overinforming the audience
- where it is underinforming
- where there is a loss of dramatic tension from hearing Alan's state of mind rather than inferring it from his actions
- where does it set one up to notice or interpret something that follows
- where does it comment on something that has just happened
- whether losses are offset by gains in information, humor, or other aspects
- whether you used overall too much or too little VO

6-2C: VOCAL COUNTERPOINT AND POINT OF VIEW

Working again with the original piece, now write and record an alternative VO track that, instead of complementing what one sees, as Alan's VO does, contrasts revealingly with it. Action should suggest one meaning, sound another, and the conjunction of the two should yield a more complex set of possibilities. The aim here is to develop tensions between picture and sound, a series of deliberate ambiguities or even contradictions that invite the audience into making its own decisions about the discrepancies. Here you are impelling the audience to actively develop ideas about Alan's character. Suggested voices are:

- Alan telling his psychiatrist how his compulsions are going away when clearly they aren't
- Alan rehearsing how to convey his efficiency and foresight in an upcoming and important job interview
- Alan's mother telling him how to eat well now that he is on his own
- Alan's wife loyally telling a friend how easy he is to live with
- a private eye interpreting Alan's villainy from his innocuous actions

Discussion: Of course there is ample scope for comedy here, but try creating sympathy for your central character rather than making him a buffoon. The VO will have to be carefully written, timed against picture, and rehearsed. Be aware that though the first two are both apparently Alan's view of himself, they should allow the audience to develop an independent sense of Alan that might confirm what a psychiatrist or job interviewer suspected. The remaining three suggestions are perspectives that might better serve to profile the speaker.

Do not forget to shoot room tone as necessary sound spacer should you want to extend pauses in the VO.

When you have completed your first version, apply the assessment and see how you did.

Acting	The VO sounds natural, not like somebody reading. (Avoid this by showing the actor the ideas, then have him/her improvise lines. Edit them to the action. This reliably produces spontaneity)	0 1 2 3 4 5
Editing rhythm	There are ample spaces in the VO during which we can look and interpret for ourselves. (Too much VO will suffocate the audience's own perceptual process)	0 1 2 3 4 5
	Sometimes there are some really ironic juxtapositions of words and actions	0 1 2 3 4 5
	The juxtapositions sometimes add information that we cannot otherwise get. ("It's my birthday tomorrow")	0 1 2 3 4 5
	The juxtapositions sometimes provocatively contradict what we see. (keeps the audience guessing and therefore actively involved in decision-making)	0 1 2 3 4 5

Discussion:

- were you able through using VO to lift the bridging actions to the interest level of the best action? (It's wise to use VO to raise the dull parts and let eloquent actions speak for themselves.)
- did you leave interesting sound effects in the clear? (To do this, lay VO as a second sound track, then mix the two, raising the level of sync original track in the spaces between VO blocks.)

PROJECT 6-3: EXPLOITING A LOCATION

Skills:

- developing a mood
- shifting the mood from objective to subjective
- making use of cause and effect
- capitalizing upon inherent rhythms
- implying both a point of view and a state of mind
- suggesting a development

- using sync sound as effects
- using music to heighten or interpret the environment

6-3A: MOOD SEQUENCE

Select an interesting location which can be any authentic interior or exterior setting. It might be a harbor, motorcyclists' cafe, farmyard, teenager's bedroom,
stock exchange, fairground, book shop, airport lounge, or anything else that is
mainly a physical entity rather than a human event. This assignment has considerable documentary aspects and you will need to spend some hours just observing
with a notebook in hand. Afterward work your observations into a script, using
everything you can that is reliably likely to happen. You can use a POV Observer
character of your own so long as he or she looks unquestionably credible. Without using any speaking characters develop a mood sequence of about two minutes
that changes and intensifies. In planning your sequence, consider:

- what is inherently present that might structure the sequence? (Passengers arriving in an airport and going off to the departure gate? Time progression? Increasing complexity in the action? Forward exploratory movement of
  camera?)
- what cause-and-effect shots you can group together into subsequences?
  (Within a winter forest scene, you may establish icicles melting, drops of
  water falling past a shack's window, drops falling in a pool, or a rivulet of
  water flowing through ice, etc.)
- if there are inherent rhythms to be exploited (water dripping, cars passing, a
  street vendor's repeated cry, dog barking, etc.)
- if the sequences move from micro to macro view, or the reverse. (Start with
  BCU water droplets and develop to view of an entire forest; or conversely,
  start with aerial view of the city and end on a single overfilled trash can.)
- if you can create a turning point that marks the onset of a heightened or altered sensibility. (For instance, in a deserted sandy cove the camera discovers
  a single smoking cigarette butt. Thereafter, coverage suggests the uneasiness
  of wondering if one is being watched by a lurking human presence.)

Here fiction filmmaking merges with the documentary; the environment has
become a character under study by the storyteller. We make the same dramatic demands, asking that the environment grow and change so it makes us react and become involved. As always, contrasts and contradictions are the richest stimulant
to awareness. In a seaside scene it is juxtaposing frenetic game players with corpu-
lent sun-worshipers that provides the astringent comparisons, or the waves compared with the stillness of the rocks. Every setting like every character contains
dialectical tensions, those unreconciled and coexisting opposites that define the
subject's scope and subjective meaning to the observer.

Depending on who the storytelling Observer is (a child, an old man, a foreigner, a thief, an explorer, someone revisiting his past, etc.), the environment can be
interpreted very differently and even suggest the observing consciousness of a particular person in a particular mood, even though that person is seldom seen and
never heard.

Assessment: When you have edited your sequence together, consider:

Structure	There are clear developmental phases in the sequence like acts in a play	0 1 2 3 4 5
	The sequence has an overall rhythmic development that is satisfying and "right"	0 1 2 3 4 5
	There is a clear peak and "turning point"	0 1 2 3 4 5
	The sequence is neither too short nor too long	0 1 2 3 4 5
Form	The sequence flows and does not seem fragmented (if it does, this will point to a lack of subsequences each with its own beginning, middle, and end)	0 1 2 3 4 5
Content	A strong mood is established	0 1 2 3 4 5
	The piece deals with what one expects of that setting	0 1 2 3 4 5
	The piece shows some of the unexpected	0 1 2 3 4 5
Point of view	There is a strongly defined observing consciousness at work here (anger, fear, lethargy, hedonism, etc.)	0 1 2 3 4 5
	The point of view develops	0 1 2 3 4 5
Use of sound	Natural sound plays a narrative part in the sequence	0 1 2 3 4 5
	Natural sound supplies an emotionally laden atmosphere	0 1 2 3 4 5
Impact	The sequence has a strongly sensual impact and mood	0 1 2 3 4 5

Discussion:

- was the sequence dependent on what impressions each image and activity suggested or upon the movements and words of a central human subject?
- did you find inherent rhythms in the material?
- did you let the shot duration be decided by its context?
- was there a beginning, a middle, and an end to the sequence? (just as if you were writing a dramatic scene, but the developments must come from the rhythms and activities of the setting itself)
- the sequence should come from a response to the location and not be an attempt to impose some spurious usefulness on it for the purposes of a story.

6-3B: ADDING MUSIC

Now add music to your sequence, choosing it carefully (no songs; the aim is to work with emotional associations and behavioral narration, not a verbal one). By taking a cassette of several possible pieces of music into the editing room you can try each against your scene before deciding which works best.

Music can augment what has been created pictorially, or, more interestingly, suggest something underlyingly different; for example, a peaceful harvest scene accompanied by an ominous marching tune, or abandoned houses in a blighted urban area seen against an impassioned Bach chorale. Antiphony leads the observer to hunt for hidden meanings to the scene, and suggests that it may either be subjective to a character in the film or to the storyteller—that young farmworkers go off to die on foreign battlefields, or that poverty and failure are somehow part of God's plan for mankind.

Assessment: Run your scene and ask:

Music use	The music made a valid, not facile contribution	0 1 2 3 4 5
	Places were left in sound mix for natural effects to "bleed through." (Music must be chosen that won't drown particular sound effects [SFX])	0 1 2 3 4 5
	Particular cuts or pieces of movement were effectively recut to fit the rhythmic dictates of the music	0 1 2 3 4 5
	Music started at a natural point in the sequence. (The start and stop of a camera or subject movement can motivate music in- and out-points, as can the ending or beginning of a strong diegetic sound effect. Study feature film practice for further guidance)	0 1 2 3 4 5
	Music ended naturally	0 1 2 3 4 5

Discussion:

- when do you feel it is legitimate to use music?
- when not?
- when is music being used creatively rather than programmatically (that is, as mere illustration)?
- what should music's relationship be to dialogue?
- what should it be to diegetic sound effects (that is, effects natural to the scene)?
- when should music belong to the world of the characters and when can it come from beyond their world?
- to what degree can music be motivated by the storytelling "voice" of the film?
- can you mix periods (use modern music on a historic subject, for instance)?
- what determines the texture and instrumentation of a music piece?

PROJECT 6-4: EDITED TWO-CHARACTER DIALOGUE SCENE

Skills:

- planning and shooting dialogue exchanges
- camera placement
- using verbal rhythms and operative words in editing
- controlling the scene's point of view

6-4A: MULTIPLE COVERAGE

Take a short scene (approximately three minutes) that includes some sort of game and prepare to shoot as follows:

1. Cast the actors.

2. Decide the location.

3. Make several copies of the script and mark up one with the "beats" (more about this later, but for now, treat beats as those points where one of the characters undergoes a major realization.

4. Rehearse the scene.

5. Develop the accompanying action, going beyond what the script calls for.

6. Make a floor plan of the location showing characters' moves and intended camera positions (see Figure 5-3 as an example).

7. Define what you want the scene to accomplish and whose point of view the audience is to (a) mainly and (b) partially share and understand.

8. Using another copy of the script and colored pens for each camera position, mark up the script with your intended editing plan. There is an example in Figure 6-3.

9. Plan to cut between angles at times of major subject movement so cuts will look motivated, and be sure to shoot generous overlap at intended cutting points or you will not have choices in places to cut—particularly troublesome if the cut is to be an action match.

10. Shoot, playing the whole scene through in each major angle, thus allowing yourself to experiment widely during the editing.

11. Edit strictly according to your plan.

12. Solicit audience critique.

13. Reedit according to what you now feel should be done.

14. Solicit new audience critique.

15. Now write directorial guidelines based on what you have learned.

Discussion: This project covers a huge amount of ground even though it is very short. It will take a fair amount of effort and organization. Do not shortchange yourself on the planning stage; much can be learned from first theorizing what you intend to do; doing it, and afterward assessing where your planning worked and where it went awry.

In a professional situation, shooting full-length multiple angles for long, intricate scenes would be viewed as a decisionless coverage wasting actors' energies, crew time, and filmstock. It indicates a lack of vision about the scene's final form, and an ominous willingness to delay decision-making until editing. I only recommend this type of coverage here because it allows you to both carry out what you intended, and to reedit in other ways. When you lack experience and confidence, and particularly if the scene is short, it may be counterproductive to shoot any other way. Limiting coverage to short customized segments would mean not only risking an inflexible coverage but puts the cast into a rapid stop-start mode that will probably prevent them ever hitting their stride.

Long takes make consistent success hard to achieve throughout, but you can allow imperfect sections when the shooting script, which you have marked up with your intended cut, shows that an inadequacy falls in the part of an angle you

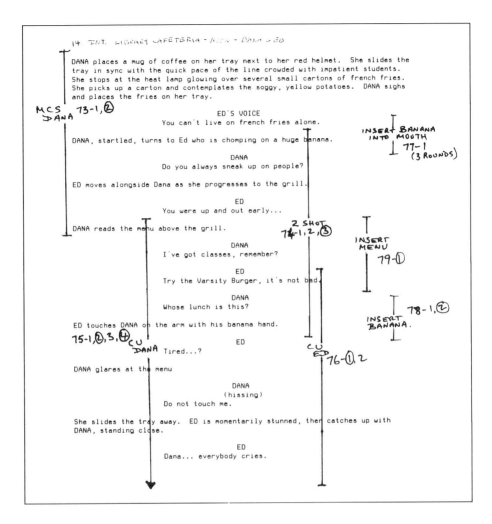

FIGURE 6-3

Marked-up script showing intended cut and generous overlaps to allow action matches and other kinds of alternatives in editing.

do not intend to use. Having this information at hand helps you decide immediately whether to call for another take.

A word on the pacing of a scene: comedy should be fast paced, about thirty percent faster than life if it is to look right on the screen. Serious scenes often need to be slowed, particularly at beat points so that pauses, silences, eyeline shifts, or an exchange of glances can be fully exploited. Experienced directors know that these are truly the high points of the scene. Dialogue leading to them is mere preparation. Beginners often reverse these priorities and strive to ensure that no silence, or silent action, ever threatens to "bore" the audience. Nothing could be further from the truth.

Once you are in the cutting room, it is heartening to see that wise coverage will let you double a pregnant pause; when you cut to a different angle you can add together the pauses from both. Conversely, if the moment was held overlong, you can abbreviate it through making the same cut between matching angles.

Although editors supplied with adequate coverage cannot speed up or slow down the way words emerge, they can control the rhythm and balance of action and reaction, which is a huge part of implying a subtext. Surefooted editing can make a vast difference to the degree of thought and feeling the audience attributes to each character. This in turn can greatly improve the sense of integration and consistency in the acting.

Assessment:

Editing	Action match cuts flow smoothly	0 1 2 3 4 5
	Screen directions are correctly maintained	0 1 2 3 4 5
	Room geography is revealed as necessary, and not confusing to a first-time viewer	0 1 2 3 4 5
	Convincing dialogue rhythms are maintained even when a picture cut happens in midsentence?	0 1 2 3 4 5
	Moments of significant action and charged silence have been fully exploited	0 1 2 3 4 5
	Changes of scene rhythm occur convincingly with changes in the characters' perceptions, thought patterns, and actions	0 1 2 3 4 5
	Eyeline shifts have been fully exploited. (The most natural of all cutting points occurs when a character shifts his eyeline; we expect to see what he now sees.)	0 1 2 3 4 5
	When a character moves or changes body position offscreen, he does not make his next appearance in a confusingly different position	0 1 2 3 4 5
	Editing shows actor or character acted-upon appropriately and consistently	0 1 2 3 4 5
Point of view	How the scene is shot and cut conveys a point of view (that is, effectively reveals the state of mind of the main character or of the storyteller)	0 1 2 3 4 5
	The scene breathes (moves us close or distances us where psychologically necessary)	0 1 2 3 4 5
	The game (or other shared activity) is used to effectively reveal psychological changes in the characters	0 1 2 3 4 5
Dramaturgy	The game develops convincingly	0 1 2 3 4 5
	The environment is utilized by the characters and made an active component in the drama	0 1 2 3 4 5
	There are no redundancies of dialogue, action, or angle, etc.	0 1 2 3 4 5

	The scene feels right in length (better to feel a little short than too long)	0 1 2 3 4 5
	The scene implies back-story and what might come after	0 1 2 3 4 5
Impact	The piece holds one's interest throughout	0 1 2 3 4 5
	The actors are engaging and natural throughout	0 1 2 3 4 5
	Significant subtexts are implied	0 1 2 3 4 5

Discussion:

- directing and editing a convincing dialogue scene is one of the more challenging tasks a director faces. How did you do?
- how was the writing once it became speech?
- would the acting in this scene pass as documentary shot with a hidden camera?
- what did you learn about directing actors from this experience?
- what did you learn about directing from a text?

6-4B: EDITING FOR AN ALTERNATIVE POINT OF VIEW

Reedit your scene to see if you can make the audience identify with a different point of view, such as the secondary character's point of view or an omniscient storyteller's point of view.

Discussion: Apply the same criteria as in Project 6-4A, but also ask what additional coverage you would need to make the audience more sympathetic with the new point of view.

PROJECT 6-5: AUTHORSHIP THROUGH IMPROVISATION

Skills:

- involving actors in script idea development
- spontaneous and creative interaction between actors and director
- directing an event for direct cinema coverage, useful where actors must merge, for example, with a large and uncontrollable public event
- editing documentary-style coverage
- script development from taped improvisations
- stylistic decision-making
- working intuitively and thinking on one's feet

6-5A: DEVELOPING A SHORT SCENE

Follow the instructions for *Exercise 15: Bridging Emotions* in Chapter 21 to develop a three- to four-minute scene between two characters. Then, once the scene is reasonably stable and secure, use a handheld camera to cover the complete scene favoring three different angles: character A, character B, and two-shot.

The goal is sufficient coverage to allow considerable freedom in cutting the scene together, and to be able to cope with the unavoidable variations inherent in multiple takes of an improvised piece. You will have to rely upon your camera operator for the quality of the coverage, so it is best to bring him or her in early to shoot rehearsals.

Cut together a complete version, and ask yourself the questions in Project 6-4A. In addition, consider:

- when was mobile, handheld footage stylistically appropriate and when not?
- what conclusions can you draw to help you make guidelines for the future?
- how acceptable is the dialogue track? (You will need to checkerboard your dialogue tracks in editing, and do a mix to get the best out of them.)
- was the coverage adequate or can one see that the operator was sometimes caught by surprise?
- what effect do these moments have upon the audience?
- how much does the unpredictability of the characters' movements prevent you from more deliberately showing their environment? (If, for instance, the philosophy of the piece is that "we are all figures in a landscape" yet the figures dominate to the exclusion of their surroundings, the improvisational form would be completely counterproductive.)
- how much does your coverage convey an integrated point of view?
- whose is it?
- does it arise more from the performance than from the camera treatment? (This is extremely hard to pinpoint, but nevertheless, too important to neglect.)
- did you have enough close detail (closeups, inserts, and eyeline cutaways that have to be grabbed by panning to the thing or person seen)?
- does the composition succeed in showing a revealing relationship between people (crestfallen son, for instance, in foreground, angry mother in background)?
- or between objects (miner grandfather's tombstone in foreground, the coal mine that killed him in background)?
- or between people and some aspect of their environment (forlorn, withdrawn child standing in a playground that looks like a concentration camp)?

Discussion: The mobility of handheld coverage generally projects the feeling of spontaneous human observation, as opposed to the godlike omniscience implied by perfect composition and rock steadiness. It injects an interesting sense of fallibility and subjectivity into the coverage. Sometimes, of course, this is intrusively wrong—for instance, during a sequence of misty mountain landscape shots at daybreak when nobody is supposed to be about. Here tripod shots are a must.

In "direct cinema," otherwise known as observational camera coverage, where the director cannot line up each shot, the creative initiative passes to the camera operator, who must have the mind of a dramatist, not just that of a technician or still photographer. You quickly find out whether your operator sees only composition through the viewfinder, or whether he or she is finding dramatic meaning and focus within a scene. Some do, some can learn, many will remain detached visual designers.

Sound coverage here is catch-as-catch-can (something your sound recordist may hate). While the camera must adapt to the action, the mike operator must try to pick up good sound in a swiftly changing, unpredictable situation and also stay out of frame. You will need to do a rough mix before you show your work to an audience, or the sound discrepancies will cause them to misread the piece's inherent qualities. One solution if you use a DAT multitrack recorder is to put a wireless mike on everyone who speaks, and record each on a separate channel.

Time your first cut for comparison with the next assignment.

6-5B: EDITING A SHORTER VERSION

Now edit your initial cut down, trying to make it tighter and more functional by eliminating verbal and behavioral padding. To do this you will have to debate with your editor the dramatic function of much that is said and done on the screen, and to devise methods of eliminating without trace whatever does not deserve to be there. Questions to answer are:

- what percentage of the original length did you eliminate?
- in what ways is the new cut more effective?
- how consistent is the pace of dramatic development?
- was all the expository detail necessary for the audience to understand the situation included by the actors? (It is fatally easy to overlook something vital.)
- was each new piece of expository information artfully enough concealed?
- did it come too early or too late?
- what did you feel about the acting?
- what would you do differently?

Discussion: The strength of improvisation is the spontaneity and realism of the acting and the conviction of the characters. Its weaknesses include:

- the difficulty of achieving a satisfying development. Improv often suffers from irregularly paced dramatic growth, with long plateaus during which both actors and audience feel the pressure for something to "happen."
- the temptation for actors when desperate to resort to manipulation so as to get the piece moving again.
- the difficulty of hiding exposition inside ongoing events. You do not want your audience to feel the presence of an editorializing hand during verbal exchanges, feeding such giveaway lines as, "Isn't it rough being out of work for three months, Ted?" and, "The last time we met—you remember, it was at the supermarket. You got mad because I couldn't give you back the money you lent me back in September."

Even if no clumsy authorial hand comes occasionally crashing through the backdrop in your piece, the probability is high that you will be dissatisfied with it. At times it is overcompressed, at times unavoidably flaccid. Editing removes a lot of padding, but it may also reveal inadequate joints and structural problems. However, if things go reasonably well, you end up with interestingly developed characters and a story line. Whatever you get can take you to the next stage.

6-5C: AN IMPROV SCENE MADE INTO A SCRIPT BEFORE SHOOTING

Transcribe the scene onto paper and rewrite it, aiming to keep the words the actors used, but compressing verbiage into pithy lines. Distribute and camouflage any expository information, and wherever possible transform dialogue into actions that do not require accompanying words. This way characters can show their feelings instead of telling them to each other. Now, using the same cast and location, rehearse and shoot the scene as in Project 6-4.

Discussion: Compare the two versions of the same scene.

- what was lost by turning an improvised performance, shot documentary style, into a scripted and more formally controlled scene?
- what was gained?
- what did you learn about authorship and directing through doing it?

PROJECT 6-6: PARALLEL STORYTELLING

Skills:
- intercutting two narrative lines
- counterpointing two moods or activities to imply a storytelling commentary
- advancing two story lines concurrently so each acts as a cutaway for the other, and both are kept to brief essentials
- showing separate, concurrent events developing toward a time of eventual convergency

6-6A: SEEING THE SCENES AS SEPARATE ENTITIES

Either write or improvise two whole scenes whose content will intercut meaningfully and provoke the audience to see a connection. Suggested subjects:

- man getting ready for a date
- woman in very different mood getting ready for the same date
- burglars getting ready to rob a house
- detectives making preparations to trap them
- man rehearsing how he will ask for a raise
- two managers discussing how they will fire him

Write each as a complete scene, then make photocopies and scissor them into sections that can be experimentally interleaved as a "paper cut" version of the eventual parallel storytelling. Before you intercut the scenes, first shoot and view each as a separate entity.

Now cast, shoot, and edit each scene separately and assemble them so that one whole scene follows the other.

Discussion: Do a reasonably tight edit on each sequence and then consider them as follows:

- what change in implications are there when you run them in reverse order? (The detectives, for example, may have arrived too late, and the firing may follow the request for a raise, instead of preceding it.)
- how long is each sequence?
- what do you gain in dramatic buildup by staying with each unbroken sequence?

6-6B: LONG INTERCUT VERSION

Now intercut the two sequences according to your paper cut, losing nothing of the original material.

Discussion: Consider the new version as follows:

- what ironies are you able to create? (Perhaps you counterpoint the fact that the woman preparing for the date has bought a new dress while the man forgets to clean his shoes.)
- what meaningful comparisons do you create? (Both the man asking for a raise and his managers think he is underpaid.)
- what causes and effects does the audience link together? (Both detectives and burglars have radios.)
- do both sequences appear to be happening at the same time, or is one retrospective in comparison with the other? (For instance, a son from abroad searching for his parents finds that his father is already dead. His father's death is intercut with his mother's account of it, which is softened to spare the son's feelings.)
- does one sequence foretell the outcome of the other? (In Roeg's *Don't Look Now* the famous lovemaking scene is intercut with the couple getting dressed.)

6-6C: SHORT VERSION

Now reassess the cut. Because it is no longer necessary to maintain the illusion of continuous time, you can pare away anything which the audience can infer and is thus nonessential. You will probably see new or different points at which to cut between the parallel stories.

Discussion: Now consider the new version asking:

- how much shorter is the new version compared with the two original sequences?
- how many of the ideas for your new cut arose out of the shooting, blocking, and playing of the scene?
- how much more information did you get from repeatedly watching the interplay of the two scenes?
- what kind of dramatic capital has been gained and what lost through intercutting?
- knowing what you know now, how should a writer plan the raw materials for such sequences?

6-6D: USING JUMP CUTS

Now experimentally reassemble each sequence in chronological order, retaining only the pieces you chose for the intercut version and using jump cuts. This is moving to coverage that uses discontinuous time.

Discussion: Eliminating the slack material between the high points does two things: it moves the story along faster, and it accentuates an authorial attitude or voice by discarding objective time and openly espousing just those pieces of time that matter. Flat-footed realism and its linear, continuous time has given way to something more challengingly subjective.

If you hate this version of your sequences, it is probably because the jump cuts themselves make ugly visual leaps. This would not be true had you been able to design them.

Similarity of Frame: For instance, you might cut from a bed with two people reading, to the same bed with them asleep, to a morning shot with one still there and the other dressing in the background. Older convention would dictate a long, slow dissolve between the three setups (which should be taken with the camera locked down in the exact same position so each composition is exactly the same), but the same narrative content can be done in a fraction of the time and at a fraction of the cost by jump cutting. Here the jump cut becomes not a mistake or contingency, but a formal storytelling device of great agility.

Difference of Frame: With a bold difference of composition you can simply jump cut forward in time. During a wide shot of people preparing to fire a piece of pottery you can cut to a close shot of the oven, somebody opens it, and the pot is already fired. We understand that a piece of insignificant time has been eliminated, even though dialogue continues with an unbroken sentence across the cut into the new time plane. The TV commercial has familiarized audiences with these cinematic shorthand devices.

Discontinuity allows a wealth of possibilities for a more authorial and staccato storytelling style, because it is freed from the literalness and "objectivity" of present-tense realism. Alain Resnais has pioneered the cinema's greater freedom in time and tense. His *Providence* (1977) sets up the fascinating labyrinth of a dying novelist's mind as he spends a night of pain anticipating a visit by his family the next day. As in his earlier *Last Year at Marienbad* (1961), Resnais departs from the present not only to plumb his point-of-view character's memory, but also to project us into the workings of his tortured imagination. This is like the conditional tense cinema of *Zero de Conduite* (1933) by the tragically short-lived Jean Vigo, which inspired Lindsay Anderson's disturbing but uneven *If . . .* (1968). Both films are ironic and satirical examinations of how power gets used (abused) in schools.

These developments are very significant if as a writer, director or editor you want to coopt the audience's imagination by using a cinematic language of greater flexibility.

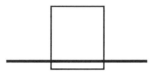

CHECKLIST, PART II
SCREENCRAFT

The recommendations and points summarized here are only those most salient or the most commonly overlooked. To find more about them or anything else, go to the Table of Contents at the beginning of this part, or try the Index at the back of the book.

Screen Grammar

- in everyday life pretend you are lining up shots. Determine their aspects and motivations according to the emotional context of an observer
- practice seeing each such shot for its connotations, not just denotation
- when you study a film, practice classifying shot juxtaposition by their type (illustrative, countpoint, contradiction, associative, tense-shifting, etc.)
- see how established directors handle the axis, particularly crossing the scene axis
- practice dividing up scenes in everyday life into their possible axes (subject-to-subject, and observer-to-subject axes; you may want to unobtrusively scan from different vantage points)
- make yourself aware of what makes a scene discrete (is it defined by time, location, mood, other?)
- screen language implies a particular intelligence grappling with events in which it also participates

Seeing with a Moviemaker's Eye

- notice when composition on the screen is being adjusted because of changing internal elements

- notice when visual rhythm is inherent to the subject matter or when it is being varied for authorial reasons
- notice external compositional relationships (the juxtapositional commentary created by two compositions cut, dissolved, or otherwise associated together)
- for practice make a floor plan of two rooms you live in, showing electrical outlets, windows and direction of ambient lighting, furniture placement, and door-swing directions
- practice being conscious of the layering in movies' sound tracks
- practice being aware of different kinds of light and lighting, in movies and in life, and make a mental note of the emotional associations
- notice in different situations how you experience time—what extends it and what truncates it

Shooting Fundamentals

- plan everything and make lists of everything you need to remember
- do floor plans showing camera placement for all your shooting
- mark intended camera positions on floor plan
- always check an exterior location for light direction at time of day when you plan to shoot
- check location for unwanted sound intrusions (like being in the flight path for an airport!)
- don't forget to get written permission for locations if you need them
- dialogue scenes are the hardest to shoot and cut well
- remember to inhabit your Storyteller's character while you direct. Shoot/see from his/her point of view. This won't be easy to remember
- always be aware of who is acting and who is being acted upon at any moment
- remember that characters are most alive when they are seeking to do or get
- direct to imply the subtext
- make storyboards if you are doubtful about how a sequence will cut together
- remember to shoot generous action overlaps between matching shots when you mean to cut them together
- decide when long comprehensive takes are called for, and when a more fragmented style suits the situation being filmed
- give your major attention to the actors and after initial consultation for each shot, leave directing the camera to the DP
- look carefully for what you may have forgotten before striking any camera position or set

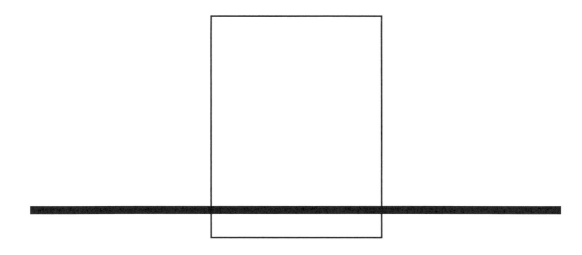

P·A·R·T III

WRITING AND STORY DEVELOPMENT

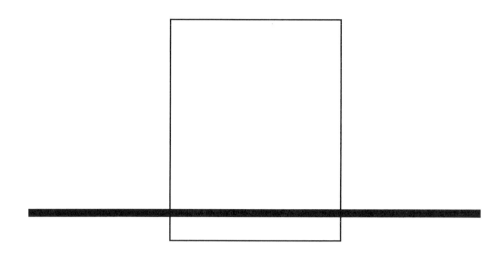

C·H·A·P·T·E·R 7

THE SCREENPLAY

If you are thinking of directing from someone else's screenplay this chapter will give you definite ways of assessing how practical and well-written it is. If you are about to produce your first screen work, this chapter will get you started with the writing. Even though your first films will probably be simple, read the chapters on writing, form, and structure. Even the maker of a short "exercise" piece faces options in point of view, genre, realism or stylization, as well as plot, and style. All of these are treated in further chapters.

WHEN YOU DIRECT FROM YOUR OWN WRITING

As a beginner, you will need to write and direct your own short films. In the early stages at film school, when everyone believes they are director material, it may even be expected of you. There is a huge amount to learn from writing and directing your own short work, but be prepared to learn as much from negative experiences as from positive ones. Also expect difficulty telling whether it is your directing or your screenwriting that was responsible for any failure. Later I will argue for collaboration with a screenwriter but for now, I will assume that you are a writer/director.

For any story in which you strongly believe, even for a 10-minute piece, allow much time and a number of drafts in which to complete the writing process, and *seek out honest criticism* at key stages. Doing so is like exposing your film to audience reactions in advance.

After a year or two of production, most film students realize that after school they will need to work professionally in one of the allied crafts before they feel mature enough to direct. They are helped in this by the virtual impossibility of finding directing work unless one emerges from one's training with a sensational piece of work, as Robert Rodriguez did at the Sundance Festival with *El Mariachi* (1993). If you are committed to directing professionally, start looking now for your natural collaborators. You can even form a creative collusion, writing for your best friend when she directs, and she writing for you when you do.

DECIDING ON SUBJECTS

Even when you make an exercise film to learn film grammar, take care to choose a subject you care about for a script. You will have to live with your choice and its ramifications for some time. Also involved will be other people's time and even funds. Once you shoot, you should be committed to completion, no matter what.

If this commitment sounds scary, it can at least be explored with the option of retreat all through the rewriting stages. Writing and rewriting, particularly when moving between the three different dimensions of screenplay, step outline, and concept (explained in detail later), all allow the director to *inhabit* a text, something virtually impossible from one or two detached readings. As always when you translate from one mode of presentation to another, you will discover aspects hidden from the more casual reader, no matter how expert. Whether your film is to be comedy, tragedy, horror, fantasy, or a piece for children, it must embody some issue with which you identify. Everyone bears scars from living, and everyone with any self-knowledge has issues within that await exploration. What you follow in your work will best sustain you when connected to something that moved you to strong emotions. This might be racial or class alienation; a childhood reputation for clumsiness; fear of the dark (horror films!), rejection by a family member, an obsession of any kind, a period of intense happiness, or a brief affair you had with someone very beautiful. It might be a stigma such as illegitimacy, or being foreign or unjustly favored—anything that has moved you to powerful feelings. Start a list. You will be surprised at how many subjects are already your own, and at the themes that emerge when you look for common denominators.

Filmmaking demands both creation and contemplation, an outward doing, and a parallel inner process of search and growth. This is the foundation of the artistic process. We have all passed through war zones. Your validity as a storyteller begins with the scars of experience rather than from ideas that lack the bedrock of experience. Work in any corner of existence about which you know something and want to learn more. Avoid debating problems or demonstrating solutions. The object is not to produce a film that preaches or confesses but one that deals, in some suitably displaced way, with something you really care about. Your story should show evidence of change, however minimal, in at least one of its characters. Find an area of life you know, one through which you can express your concern for others and one that reflects what it is like to be alive now. Those who pursue their art have simply made a job out of what most people can only do in their spare time—which is to attempt making sense out of things. The best filmmakers make films to better understand life's patterns and currents, and for the joy of practicing a craft well.

WHY READING A SCRIPT IS DIFFICULT

Whether you want to raise funds or just put your intentions before a crew and cast, communicating the nature of your film depends on the script. It seems simple—you just hand someone a script, don't you? But this may accomplish nothing useful; scripts are very demanding to read and a well-written one is purposely minimal. Because actors, director, camera crew, and even the weather all make unforeseeable contributions, the astute scriptwriter leaves a great deal unspecified. A good screenplay therefore consists of dialogue, sparse or nonexistent stage directions, and equally brief remarks on character, locations, and behavior. Until the shooting script stage there will be no directions for camerawork or editing. The reader must supply from imagination what is missing, something that everyone—director, technicians, actors—will do as part of their craft contributions.

A screenplay is a verbal blueprint designed to seed a nonliterary, organic, and experiential process. Rarely if ever does it give more than a sketchy impression of what the film will really be like. It gives little access to the thematic intentions behind the writing. These must be inferred by the reader, again at considerable effort. The lay reader, expecting the detailed evocations of a short story or novel, feels that inordinate mental effort and experience is required to decompress the writing. More arduous than reading poetry and much less rewarding, reading scripts is not pleasurable. Inside the film industry and out, most people resist reading any more scripts than necessary. Most production companies, receiving several hundred a week, throw the unsolicited ones away, or give them no more than a cursory glance, perhaps scanning every tenth page. Because the likelihood of finding anything usable is so small in the fifty thousand or so scripts copyrighted annually, professionals will usually only look at work forwarded by a reputable agent.

To earn money by screenwriting, first win the respect of a good agent. If you are a director looking for a script, expect a lot of hard and discouraging reading. First-rate scripts are extremely rare, and their qualities are immediately apparent. There is a terrible shortage of distinguished work. Looking for it will mean some bulk reading, but this negative learning will alert you to what clichéd thinking or hackneyed forms you need to avoid.

STANDARD SCRIPT FORMS

The industry standard for layouts is simple and effective and has evolved as the ultimate in convenience. Do not invent your own.

SCREENPLAY FORMAT

The specimen page in Figure 7-1 illustrates the rules for scriptwriting:

Scene Heading: each scene begins with a flush left capitalized scene heading that lists

- number of the scene (once all rewrites are complete),
- interior or exterior,
- location,
- main characters involved, and
- time of day or night.

Body copy: (action description, mood setting, stage directions) is double-spaced away from scene headings and dialogue, and runs the width of the page.
  Character names outside dialogue are capitalized.
  Dialogue sections are

- centered within extra margins,
- preceded and followed by a double space,
- headed by the speaker's name centered and in capitals,
- and accompanied when strictly necessary by stage direction inside brackets.
- Shot transitions like "Cut to," "Dissolve to," are placed either flush left or flush right and are only included when they are necessary to make sense.

Figure 7-1 is a page in pure screenplay form. There are no camera or editing directions. Industry practice varies; some commercial scripts are hybrid creatures trying to dramatize their contents by making it closer to a shooting script. This may help to sell the script in a particular quarter but has little practical value to the director. We shall do what is normal, and defer this degree of detail until the shooting script phase.

A TRAP FOR THE UNWARY

The screenwriter's most treacherous friend is the screenplay format itself, for its appearance and proportions suggest that films are built theatrically around dialogue. While this may be wretchedly true for soap opera, it is quite wrong for good screen drama, which is primarily behavioral. Actors and directors can also be lulled into assuming the primacy of the spoken over the behavioral. I do not mean to devalue the screenplay as the genesis of successful screen drama. Nobody has yet demonstrated that you can effectively coordinate actors and crew without a central structure, but that structure must be cinematic, not literary or theatrical. In fact there are ways to reach it apart from the traditional one of writing, but that we'll explore later.

SPLIT PAGE OR TV SCREENPLAY FORMAT

This format (Figure 5-2, page 57) is frequently used in multicamera television studio shooting when a complex drama must be enacted in real time. For this reason

14. INT. LIBRARY CAFETERIA — NOON — DANA & ED

DANA places a mug of coffee on her tray next to her red helmet. She slides the
tray in sync with the quick pace of the line crowded with impatient students.
She stops at the heat lamp glowing over several small cartons of french fries.
She picks up a carton and contemplates the soggy, yellow potatoes. DANA sighs
and places the fries on her tray.

                         ED'S VOICE
               You can't live on french fries alone.

DANA, startled, turns to Ed who is chomping on a huge banana.

                            DANA
               Do you always sneak up on people?

ED moves alongside Dana as she progresses to the grill.

                             ED
               You were up and out early...

DANA reads the menu above the grill.

                            DANA
               I've got classes, remember?

                             ED
               Try the Varsity Burger, it's not bad.

                            DANA
               Whose lunch is this?

ED touches DANA on the arm with his banana hand.

                             ED
               Tired...?

DANA glares at the menu

                            DANA
                          (hissing)
               Do not touch me.

She slides the tray away. ED is momentarily stunned, then catches up with
DANA, standing close.

                             ED
               Dana... everybody cries.

FIGURE 7-1 ──

Specimen page of screenplay format (from *A Night So Long* by Lynise Pion).

son the format is sometimes called a television script. In cinema-style shooting,
where each shot is created discretely and the sound "composed" afterward in the
cutting room, this density of detail may be irrelevant.

   Split page format is the best layout for logging and analyzing a finished
movie. Unlike the screenplay, it allows clear representation of the counterpoint between images, and between image and the various sound elements. Notice that the
left-hand picture column contains *only what you would see,* and the right-hand

sound column contains *only what you would hear.* Do not transpose them or the point of having a standard is lost.

Chapter 5: Seeing with a Moviemaker's Eye, strongly recommends that you make a split page transcript of a few sequences from your favorite contemporary movies. If you did it, you discovered how dense modern film language actually is. The exercise also demonstrates how effectively the split page format can toggle the reader's attention between dialogue and action. If you like what is called alternative cinema, which often uses dialogue, music, effects while intercutting different levels of footage (past, present, archive, graphics), you may find writing in screenplay format difficult or even paralyzing. Try using the split page format in the planning stage, and convert it to screenplay format later if you need to.

SPLITFORM CONFUSIONS

Publishers have caused confusion about the true nature of the screenplay by publishing a "continuity script" or "reader's script as the script of a popular film." Both are transcriptions of the finished product rather than the all-important blueprint that initiated it. The Glossary explains the differences. If you study scripts, be sure you know which you are reading.

PREPARING TO INTERPRET A TEXT

After first reading a screenplay, examine the imprint it left on you.

- what did it make you feel?
- who did you care about?
- who did you find interesting?
- what does the piece seem to be dealing with under the surface events?

Note down these impressions and read the screenplay once or twice again looking for hard evidence to go with your first impressions. Next ask what

- is the screenplay trying to accomplish?
- special means is it using to accomplish its intentions?

Again, note down your answers. Now leaf through the screenplay and make a flowchart of scenes, giving each a brief, functional description (example: "Scene 15: Ricky again sees Angelo's car: realizes he's being watched"). From this you will pinpoint the intended film's dramatic logic, something difficult to abstract any other way.

Having established some initial ideas about a screenplay's structure and development, we can now look at significant detail.

GOOD SCREENPLAYS ARE NOT OVERWRITTEN

Because a screenplay is a blueprint and not a literary narrative it is important to exclude embellishment. A good screenplay

- doesn't include any author's thoughts, instructions, or comments
- avoids using qualifying comments and adjectives because they will too precisely condition what the reader imagines
- leaves most behavior to the reader's imagination and instead describes its effect (for example, "he looks nervous" instead of "he nervously runs a forefinger round the inside of his collar and then flicks dust off his dark serge pants")
- underinstructs actors unless a line or an action would be unintelligible without guidance
- contains no camera or editing instructions.

The experienced screenwriter is an architect who designs the shell of a building knowing that the occupants will decide the walls, interiors, colors, and furnishings to their own tastes. Inexperienced screenwriters are often control freaks who, in architectural simile, design the doorknobs, lay carpet, and hang pictures and thus make the building uninhabitable to everyone but themselves.

The writer/director might seem to be a special case. Since he knows exactly what is to be shot, even where and how, why not write very specifically? One reason to avoid overinstructing your readers is that you prevent them from filling ambiguities with positive assumptions. Another is that it overlooks the reality of filming. Without unlimited time and money, nothing much works out as you envision, and it's unwise to specify anything that you can't in the end deliver.

OVERWRITING IS DANGEROUS

Overwriting is not just impractical, it is dangerous. Highly detailed description conditions your readers (money sources, actors, crew) to anticipate particular, hard-edged results. The director of such a script is locked into trying to fulfill a vision that disallows all variables, even the many that would contribute positively.

LEAVE THINGS OPEN

An open script invites cast members to create their own input while the overspecific, closed one signals that actors should conform to the actions and mannerisms minutely specified in the text, however alien. To challenge actors does not mean trying to minutely control them; on the contrary, it means getting from each his own different, and distinct personal identity. The good screenplay assists this by leaving the director and players to work out how things will be said and done. This depends on the personal qualities of the cast members and the chemistry between them and their director.

BEHAVIOR INSTEAD OF DIALOGUE

The first cowboy films made a strong impact because the American cinema recognized the power of behavioral melodrama. The good screenplay is still predominantly concerned with behavior, action, and reaction. It avoids static scenes where people verbalize what they think and feel.

PERSONAL EXPERIENCE NEEDS TO BE ENACTED NOT SPOKEN

Everyone is moved by their own life and everyone includes autobiography in their writing. But a writer needs to distinguish the intensity of life experienced from what is powerful or exciting seen by its externals in the cinema. In a moving personal experience, one is actively involved and acted upon, feeling the stresses subjectively and within. In screen drama, the characters' inner thoughts and emotions can only communicate to outsiders as they do in life itself, through outwardly visible behavior. Drama is doing. What matters on the screen is what people do. Every screen character who has any compelling quality is trying to do or get something all the time. Just as you are in your life, year to year, day to day, minute to minute. The trouble is, we are very aware of what we feel, and hardly at all aware of the infinitesimal things we do.

TESTING FOR CINEMATIC QUALITIES

A simple but deadly test of a script's screen potential is to examine how much the audience would understand and care if the sound were turned off. Examining each sequence this way will reveal how much is cinematic and how much is really radio with illustration. This is not to deny that we talk to each other or even that many transactions of lifelong importance take place through conversation. But life is inherently dramatic when you are one of the protagonists. Making drama means finding a way to make the inward struggles of other people visible through their actions. Dialogue should be used only when necessary, not as a substitute for action. *Dialogue should itself be action,* that is, people acting upon each other, not people telling things to each other (and the audience).

CHARACTERS TRYING TO DO OR GET

We judge an unknown person's character on the screen as we do in life, by looking first at all the visible clues—physical appearance, body language, choice of clothes as a key to the person's self-conception, and how the person wears them. We look at the person's belongings and surroundings, and over time watch how he or she handles their situations. We begin to see background, formative pressures, assumptions, and associates. We learn which among these the person chose and which he or she must unwillingly accept. How the person interacts—in particular with the unexpected or threatening—will tell us much, as do the reactions of friends and intimates. Such interaction also helps establish the relative temperaments and histories of the other characters.

Most of all we make character judgments from the moral quality of a person's deeds. Unexpected actions often modify or even subvert what has hitherto appeared to be true, perhaps giving the lie to what a character thinks he believes.

A character's path is not determined by personal history alone; there is also temperament, an active component in the person's makeup that exerts its own influences. "Character," said Novalis, "is fate." The astute dramatist knows this but also knows that in life many outcomes to a person's tastes and whims are inconclusive. It is important therefore to be selective without being too obviously programmatic. Without looking manipulative the dramatist shows only those acts, situations, and environments that show the protagonists' forward movement as each tries to do or get what lies in his or her agenda. It helps to build in contradictions so the audience can't quickly and easily key into a monolithic conception behind a character. Contradictions in a character's actions and beliefs are valuable and necessary if the person has any inner conflicts. Characters in realistic drama need to be complex if they are to have any magnitude and to seem whole and credible.

STATIC CHARACTER DEFINITION

When looking for a screenplay's potential, assess the characters by more than their "givens" such as age, sex, appearance, situation, and eccentricities. These supply a static summation, something like a photograph that typifies the character and makes development seem like something already accomplished. Watching this kind of character in a film is like seeing a photomontage in which each person is fixed in a typical role and attitude. This constriction is unavoidable in the TV commercial where, needing to be brief and propagandistic, character is set by one or two dominant characteristics. People in commercials are typical: a typical mother, a typical washing machine repairman, a typical holiday couple on a typical romantic beach. Homes, streets, meals, and happy families are all stereotyped. If a dramatic piece is conceived like this, players struggle vainly to breathe life into their static characters, but everything their characters do, everything that befalls them, falls back into that dominant and static conception. This prescriptive tendency denies and paralyzes the willpower, tensions, and adjustments present in even the most quiescent human being, and prohibits the very growth and changes that are the lifeblood of true drama.

DYNAMIC CHARACTER DEFINITION

What we need is a dynamic conception of character, one focusing on flux and that mobilizes the potential for development instead of paralyzing it. The secret, vital to writers and actors alike, is to put aside what a character "is"—which is inevitably static, complete, and isolating—and to concentrate on what a character is trying to do or get, which is dynamic and invariably interactive. To uncover this at any moment in a drama, ask:

- what is this character moving toward?
- what is this character moving away from?
- what does this character want to get or do?
- what specifically is stopping him/her?
- how does he/she adapt to this obstacle in order to try overcoming it?
- what new situation does this adaptation produce?

Trying to answer these questions will quickly reveal a script's handicaps and probably some of the solutions. These questions can be applied in a general way to the phases of a character's whole career, but their most practical function is in defining the development in a single scene, moment by moment.

In a good script you can see the development of each main character's inner will and say what he or she is trying to accomplish every step of the way. This will not be true of a poorly conceived story where the writer does not understand the importance of volition to characters.

CONFLICT, GROWTH, AND CHANGE

Though every prescription has its exceptions, dramatists agree that most stories need at least one character who shows some growth and change. This is generically called development, and can be true even for a minor character if he or she pursues an agenda; that is, struggles for something and faces inner conflict or outer opposition.

The six questions above seek evidence of conflict and movement. The screenwriter seldom supplies more than clues to the tensions in the characters. Making a character description alone does not solve the question of how to play that character because it is likely to be a static summary, what the character "is." But if there are consistent clues in what each character says and does, it is like completing a join-the-dots puzzle. When the clues add up, the character becomes someone who struggles for consistent ends and in so doing communicates the living quality of a real human being. To join the dots, the actors and their director must create the experiential basis for the character's actions. Most importantly, these are conceived in the actor's own coin, not centrally decided by writer or director.

Few stories that depend on a main or "point-of-view" character (or characters) will have energy or power unless at least one has to struggle, to change, and to grow somewhat in awareness. In a short film particularly, this may be minimalistic and symbolic, but its existence in a film that is either short or long is the cardinal sign of a strong story. That somebody grows in a story seems to answer our perennial craving for hope.

PLANNING ACTION

At its most eloquent the screen is a behavioral medium, one that shows rather than tells. Look at the list of sequences you made and rate each by how readily it could be understood without sound. In some sequences the film's narrative is evident through action. In others the issues are handled verbally, and could use translating into action. For example, in a breakfast scene while a father gives his young son a sermon about homework, you could work out "business" in which the boy tries to rearrange and balance the cutlery and cereal boxes, and the father, trying to get his full attention, tries to stop him. Though we do not see the precise subject in dispute, you have externalized the conflict between the two as action. Now whether this is best kept as work with the actors or whether it calls for script revision depends on your judgment. Will solving a particular problem encourage or inhibit your actors' creativity? Too little margin for imagination is stultifying; but too open, static, and empty a text may pose overwhelming problems.

Perhaps the scene can be rescripted as action. The boy comes home to find his father waiting with the schoolbooks set out. Reluctantly he sees what is at issue and silently takes the books into his room. Later his father looks in and finds his son sprawling in headphones listening to music. At breakfast the boy avoids his father's eye, but, unasked, goes to the doorstep to get his father the paper, guilt and remorse in his action. Now the need for confrontation and interaction has been turned entirely into a series of situations and actions, and avoids the theatrical set-piece conversation.

However you solve the problem, try to substitute every issue handled verbally by action of some kind. It may be minimal facial action, it may be movement and activities of a revealing metaphorical nature, or it may be movement that the character thinks will cover rather than reveal his true feelings. Action and conflict are inherently more interesting because action is the manifestation of will. Notice, however, that action becomes even more interesting when it conflicts with what a character says. Such contradiction reveals both his inner and outer dimensions, the conscious and the unconscious, the public and the private.

The antithesis of this principle is the script in which a tide of descriptive verbiage drowns whatever might be alive and at issue.

> ROSE
> Uncle, I thought I'd just look in and see how you are. It's
> so miserable to be bedridden. You're Dad's only brother and
> I want to look after you if only for his sake.

> UNCLE
> You're such a good girl, I always feel better when you look
> in. I thought I heard your footsteps, but I wasn't sure it
> was you. It must be cold outside—you're wearing your heavy
> coat.

> ROSE
> You are looking better, but I see you still aren't finish-
> ing your meals. It makes me sad to see you leave an apple
> as good as this when you normally like them so much.

> UNCLE
> I know dear, and it makes me feel almost guilty. But I'm
> just not myself.

I wrote this to show the worst abominations. Notice how the writing keeps the characters static, there is no behavior to signify feelings, and no private thought separate or different from the public utterances. Neither character signifies any of the feelings or hidden agenda that gives family interaction its undercurrents. Even between people who like each other there is always tension and conflict. But here the writing grips the audience in a vice of literalness, lacking even unspoken understandings for the observer to infer. Most damning, nothing would be missed by listening with eyes closed. It is the essence of soap opera.

By reconceiving this scene to include behavior, action, and interaction, one could prune the dialogue by 80 percent and end up with something animated by a lot more tensions. If, for instance, one of the scene's functions is to reveal that the old man is brother to Rose's father, there must be a more natural way for this to emerge. At the moment editorial information issues from her mouth like ticker-tape. Perhaps we could make her stop in her tracks to stare at him. When he looks questioningly back at her, she answers, "It must be the light. Sometimes you look so much like Dad." His reaction—whether of amusement, irritation, or nostalgia—gives clues about the relationship between the brothers.

DIALOGUE

In most movies people speak to each other a lot, and this raises the question of how to write good dialogue and how to write *different* characters since many writers create characters who all speak with the same voice.

Cinema dialogue sets out to be vernacular speech. Whether the character is a young hood, an immigrant waitress, or an academic philosopher, each may speak street slang, broken English, or in strings of qualified, jargon-laden abstractions. What type of thought, what type of speech, will each character use?

Dialogue in movies is different from dialogue in life. In the cinema it must sound true to life but cannot include life's prolixity and repetitiousness. It is far more succinct, though just as informal and authentically "incorrect." Dialogue must also steer clear of what the camera reveals, and avoid imposing redundant information ("You're wearing your heavy coat," as above).

Each character needs their own dialogue characteristics so writing good dialogue takes an extraordinary ear, or dedicated observation, and is an art in itself. Vocabulary, syntax, and verbal rhythms for each character have to be special and unlike another's. Eavesdropping with a cassette recorder will give you superb models, and if you transcribe everything, complete with "um's," "er's," laughs, grunts, and pauses, you will see that normal conversation is not normal at all. People converse elliptically, often at cross purposes, and not in the tidy ping-pong dialogue of the stereotypical drama. In real life little is denoted, much connoted. Silences are often the real "action" during which extraordinary currents are flowing between the speakers.

You will learn much by taking a piece of eavesdropped speech and editing it. You are doing on paper what an editor does when editing a radio documentary, that is, editing out most that is redundant yet retaining the individual's sense and idiosyncrasies. Any documentary editor will tell you how much stronger characters become when reduced in this way to their essence. This is the secret of a master of dialogue like Harold Pinter or any good mimic or comedian. They first learn to listen and in listening to search for the keys to behavior and thinking.

The best dialogue is really a form of action because in each line someone is aiming to do or get something. It is pressure applied even when it seeks to deflect pressure experienced. It is active and structurally indispensable to the scene, never a verbal arabesque or editorial explanation of what is visible. Least of all is it realistic padding. The best way to assess dialogue is to speak lines aloud and listen to their sound. If you write poetry all these questions will be familiar:

- is the line in character with the speaker?
- is there a better balance of words or sounds?
- can it be briefer by even a syllable?
- does it carry a compelling subtext (that is, a deeper underlying connotation)?
- is what it hides interesting?
- does it promote speculation and emotional response in the listener?

PLOT

The plot of a drama is the logic and energy that drives the story forward, taking the audience's interest with it. Because it is unavoidably complex and closely allied to a film's structure, I have dealt with it at greater length in Chapter 14: Structure, Plot, and Time. A story's plot is most visible in step outline form. It goes without saying that every step of the plot must seem logical and inevitable. What is unsupported, arbitrary, or coincidental will be the plot's weak points. In the plot-driven story, the movement of the story itself often compensates for characters of depth. In a character-driven movie, there may be inherent plot weaknesses that don't surface until several drafts later. Often by giving late attention to the plot you can appreciably strengthen a movie that depends on its characters. It is much more difficult to give depth at a late draft to characters in an action-dependent plot.

METAPHORS AND SYMBOLS

What makes the cinema so powerful is that settings, moods, objects, and actions often function as a revealing backdrop for a particular issue or as metaphors for the inner experiences of the main characters. This I suspect is the magic that draws people to cinematography and where it must serve more profound purposes than cinematography training usually embraces. The parched, bleached settings in *Paris, Texas* (1984) are emblematic of the emotional aridity of a man compulsively searching for his lost wife and child. In John Boorman's *Hope and Glory* (1987), the beleaguered suburb and the lush riverside haven dramatize the two inimical halves of the boy's wartime England. They also betoken his split loyalties to the different worlds and social classes of his parents. The film has many symbolic events and moments, one being as the boy disinters a toy box from the ruins of the family's bombed house. Inside are lead soldiers charred and melted in eerie mimicry of the Holocaust. Though the image is only on the screen a few seconds, everyone remembers it. It represents war and loss not only for the boy, who is the son of a soldier, but also for humanity immolated in warfare—particularly the victims of the Nazi Holocaust. It also suggests the poignant irreversibility of change itself, and the loss of childhood.

Symbols and symbolic action have to be artfully chosen because advertising has equipped audiences to decisively reject the manipulative symbol or overearnest metaphor before it has fully taken shape. Most importantly, *metaphoric settings, acts, and objects need to be organic,* that is, drawn from the world in which the characters live. They must not be imposed from outside or they easily become contrived and editorial.

One of the most breathtaking integrations of metaphor into screen drama is in Jane Campion's *The Piano* (1993), which sweeps the viewer up in its earliest scenes. That power is visible in the briefest summary: Ada, a young immigrant Scot who cannot (or won't) speak arrives with her illegitimate daughter and her piano on the wild New Zealand seashore of the nineteenth century. She is there to marry a man she neither knows nor loves, and who refuses to bring home her piano. Instead it goes to another man's home. Inevitably it is he and not her husband who listens to her music and it is to him that she gives her body and soul.

We are in a realm where nature is truly savage, love is denied by decorum, subtlety is beyond the reach of language, and where the soul reaches out by way of music and suppressed eroticism. Who could ask for a more potent canvas?

FOUNDATIONS: STEP OUTLINE, TREATMENT, AND CONCEPT

Though a screenplay shows situations and the quality of the dialogue writing, it offers little about point of view, that is, about the subjective attitudes that must be conveyed through acting, camerawork, and editing. It explains still less the subtexts, ideas, and authorial vantage point that we are supposed to infer and which supposedly motivate the writing in the first place.

If you are starting production work from a completed script, you will need to obtain from the writer, or better, make some short-form writing yourself to help you distill dramatic oversight from the piece in hand.

STEP OUTLINE

Writing methods vary considerably, but most writers produce a step outline first. Here the writer summarizes in short story, third-person, present tense form only what the audience will see and hear from the screen, allotting one numbered paragraph to each sequence. Making one during writing will invariably lead to departures and evolutionary changes of all kinds. Often the step outline has to be refashioned many times over to reflect each screenplay draft.

It should read as a stream-of-consciousness summation that never digresses into production details or into the author's philosophy. If you make the step outline, remember to set down *only what the audience will see and hear,* and stick to essentials. Write no dialogue, just *summarize in a few words each scene's setting, action, and any conversation's subject and development.*

Each numbered sequence is a step in the story's progression and the whole step outline is an extremely effective way of getting a bird's-eye view of the balance and progression of the material, whether the screenplay is a work in progress or is believed to be a final draft. In filmmaking the only final draft is the finished film. Everything else is experimental.

TREATMENT

A variation of the step outline is called a treatment. This is a narrative piece angled toward a smooth, present-tense short story form that nevertheless concentrates on what the audience will see and hear, and summarizes most dialogue exchanges. The term "treatment" is also used for the puff piece a writer must generate to get a script considered by a particular production company. Geared toward establishing the commercial potential of the film, treatments function like a trailer advertising a coming attraction, and often present the screenplay idiosyncratically for whoever is being targeted.

PREMISE OR CONCEPT

Neither the screenplay, treatment, or step outline articulates the ideas underpinning the film's dramatic structure and development. This, directly defined as the dramatic premise, is sometimes called the concept. It is a sentence or two expressing the dramatic idea behind the scene, or behind the whole movie. For *Don't Look Now* it might be, "A rational man who denies both the paranormal and his own repeated instances of clairvoyance must eventually be destroyed by the fate of which he is repeatedly warned."

If you and your writer are rewriting, you will find that examining and reexamining the concept will yield the paradigm to your latest labors and let you know if your work is still thematically focused. Like everything else in an organic process, the premise can metamorphose as writer and director journey deeper into the material. This is one of the most exciting aspects of making a film.

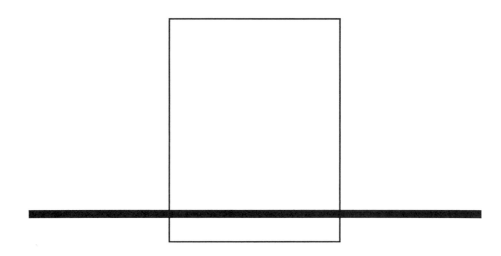

C·H·A·P·T·E·R 8

THE PROCESS OF WRITING

Screenwriting, once seen as a discrete craft and carried on quite separately from production, is now included in a larger authorial process which the director largely controls. Starting at the computer keyboard it develops through *mise-en-scène* and reaches its apotheosis in editing. That said, whether the script is generated by a writer alone or in a writer/director partnership, it largely determines the movie. At its best the script is the utopian vision which unites everyone involved in the film's realization.

When writing an initial script or screenplay, one tries to describe on paper the movie one runs in one's head. Naturally you can only set down what can be put in words, which can prescribe only a portion of cinema's gamut of effect. Then again, anything written does not necessarily translate into effective cinema. How, for instance, can you ever film "By the light of a melancholy sunset she broods upon the children she will never have?" A writer who doesn't understand the nature of film (and most don't) is working for the wrong medium, which must be why most screenwriting by the inexperienced is handled as a literary undertaking. Screenwriting needs to be visionary, yet guided by a knowledge of film both as medium and as production process. A *screenplay is a blueprint, not a complete form of expression,* and will be turned into a polished, professional movie by many other specialized and idiosyncratic minds—actors as well as camera, sound, art direction, props, and so on. Dialogue that a writer may imagine to have a set meaning can, in the mouth of an accomplished actor, acquire an unforeseen range of shading and subtlety. These nuances, even if you happen to think of them, are impossible to control in a script and the desire to do so produces unusable screenwriting.

Films are much less a transcription of language and ideas from paper than they are a self-referential stream—sights and sounds attuned like music to the outer edges of the Observer's and the audience's sensibilities. Making films goes far beyond what can be put on paper, but what the writer produces is crucial. The writer's working method and philosophy of film have very big consequences for a script's quality and originality.

WHY NOT YOUR OWN SCREENPLAY?

You may be thinking, "Can there really be any argument for using someone else's screenplay?" The *auteur* concept of filmmaking, emphasizing the integrity and control of one person's vision, influences many to believe that directing cannot be legitimate unless the writing is one's own. You should certainly do your first short work this way. Indeed becoming the total author should be a goal for your later career. But after mastering the basics most find it very wise indeed to work with a dedicated screenwriter. It allows you some distance on the work, and permits a highly specialized dialogue about essentials that is difficult or impossible to have with yourself. The screenwriter needs a director; the director needs a screenwriter. If you like writing, and you have a number of stories in you, why not function as a screenwriter to a trusted colleague who directs?

I am not saying don't write and direct, I am advising you not to do them for the same project. There is so much to control—even to produce competent but unremarkable cinema—that a director *must* rely on the creative collaboration of others, and most particularly in creating the blueprint. One example: most people's early writing naturally and properly uses autobiographical sources. If you then direct autobiographical material without a collaborator rigorously reading and critiquing it, you will find yourself trying to reanimate remembered situations and characters. You will encounter a troublesome disparity between the developing fictional world and the original purity and force of the experience. Actors sense the restrictiveness of this situation because fulfilling the director's expectations is impossible. A collaborator by their mere presence helps you displace the original into drama with its own internal dynamics. In film school or out of it, a director cannot do without a good team, part of whose function is to bring some objectivity.

Furthermore, there's the need to have confidence when you direct. If the script is a vital part of your life, anyone during production who queries its quality or credibility will in fact be questioning your self-knowledge and viability as a person. This can vaporize your whole self-esteem and directorial authority.

Directing, after you've served your apprenticeship learning film basics, means giving most of the control over the camera to someone specializing in cinematography and lighting, the sound recording to a recordist, the editing over to an editor, and writing to a writer. You work with each of these people, and you also work *to* them as though each were an audience member who needs convincing. This helps you attain some distance on the material so you can see it as an audience will see it.

WORK WITH A WRITER

I believe that the screen's strength, success, and relevance come from the process's division of labor; it enforces an additive process of creation with checks and balances. It is no secret that writing and directing a first large work is too much for one person to handle, but this is still what many do. They gamble everything, and when they don't win the jackpot, throw in the sponge. Nobody can say for sure whether a viable screenwriter, director, or editor might have developed, had the person not tried to be all three. It's like learning to juggle knives while learning to ride a bike across a high wire. Some skills are simply very demanding and need to be learned separately before combining them.

If I still haven't changed your mind, please consider bringing a co-writer on board to critique and story edit, and/or a more experienced producer to create a story editing partner. Most filmmakers of some confidence do instinctively seek out criticism at the scripting stage. It is the insecure who hide their work, and it is they who roll over dead after a screen failure.

Open your screenplay to criticism early and often. You cannot please everybody but you can make yourself listen, and you can recognize real problems early, particularly when several critics are saying the same thing. This is learning from an early audience much like a playwright who can evolve the play in light of audience reactions. But once a movie is completed, it becomes a fly set in amber. To survive and prosper, you must form the habit of submitting your work early to representational readers or audiences, seek out its weaknesses, and attend to them.

It is important, especially if you start directing really seriously, to find at least one good screenwriter with whom to collaborate—someone who really wants to write, not a director manqué. Even if you are an able writer yourself, film writing is often at its best as a shared process where ideas travel back and forth between equals. Working with a specialized mind that is focused on the priorities of the story will free you to concentrate on the separate problems of realization.

However, initial ideas or situations often originate from the director. The precursor to sharing your vision effectively with an audience is trying ideas on colleagues. Regrettably, this is the least practiced of necessary arts among film students, who walk in mortal terror of an idea being stolen. This is not completely unrealistic, but the dangers are very much exaggerated and should not inhibit you from profiting by intensive discussions. Reinvigorated cinema, like any art form, always seems to come from a group's profound exploration of fundamentals, a discourse that no individual would have the time, energy, or inventiveness to sustain alone.

WRITING YOUR OWN SCREENPLAY

Since most people reading this book want to be a writer/director, I'll proceed as though the director and writer were the same person. Even if you are working (as I hope) with a writer, the director needs to be deeply involved with what's written, and what is not. Writing is a big part of the creative process of fiction film, and results are deeply affected by how one sets about it. The act of writing is really the mind contemplating its own workings and thus being able to build upon its preliminary ideas and decisions. People who don't write are people who don't think in depth.

To write one should learn to type. Touch typing takes ten or fifteen hours of lessons. With computers making writing (and particularly rewriting) so much faster, touch typing is the most useful skill you will ever acquire. A word processor gives you easy changes, as well as a thesaurus, and spelling checks will catch typing errors.

WRITE NO MATTER WHAT

Set aside regular periods of time and make yourself write no matter whether the results are good or bad. The first draft is the hardest so do not wait to feel inspired, just keep hacking away. Write scenes that interest you, and write fast rather than writing well or in scene order. Get it all down any old how. Once a few things are down on paper, you can edit, develop, and connect what you have written.

Very important is to always *write as if for the silent screen.* Writing for the camera rather than thinking in speech exchange means dealing with human and other exteriors. To make your characters' inner lives accessible, keep in mind that *a person has no inner experience without outward signs in their behavior.*

If this or any other advice stops you writing, then write early drafts any way you can. Write any way, anywhere, anyhow—just write, rewrite and rewrite again.

IDEA CLUSTERING, NOT LINEAR DEVELOPMENT

Most who want to write but cannot are suffering the damage of doctrinaire teaching. The most common block results from trying to write from an outline in a linear fashion—beginning, middle, and end. At some point the writer ends up in a desert with nowhere to go. Perfectionism, which is fear of one's own judgment and that of others is another virulent paralyzer. I believe the saying that all unhappiness comes from comparison. Perfectionism is fine in its place—polishing one's crafted product to its ultimate form—but when applied to early work it's a killer. Most writing manuals are very prescriptive and will actually stop you writing.

At any stage when you hit the brick wall you can always resort to your associative ability. Where the pedestrian intellect fails, the exuberant subconscious will obligingly run rings around it. Here is one way to turn it loose.

Take a large sheet of paper and put down whatever central idea you are dealing with in the middle. It might be "happiness" or "rebuilding the relationship." Now, as fast as you can write, surround it with associated words, no matter how far removed or wacky. The circle of words should look like satellites around a planet. Around each individual idea put a further ring of words you associate with it. Soon your paper will be crammed with a little solar system.

Now examine what you have written and turn it into list form, classifying the ideas into families, groups, systems—anything that speaks of relationship. While engaged in this busy work all kinds of solutions to your original problem will take shape.

WRITING IS CIRCULAR, NOT LINEAR

Though finished writing is linear the process to get there is anything but. Scripts are not written in the order of concept, step outline, and screenplay, nor as beginning, middle, and end. Although the odd screenwriter may work this way, he or she is just as likely to write the most clearly visualized scenes first, making an outline to gain an overview, and later filling in the gaps and distilling the concept from the results.

Like any art process, scriptwriting—indeed filmmaking itself—looks untidy and wastefully circular to the uninitiated, and utterly alien to the tidy manufacturing processes dear to the commercial mind (your producer perhaps). This produces much friction and misery in the film industry, where artists handling people and concepts must work within financial structures imposed by managers, often from business backgrounds, who can only see inefficiency.

CREATE CHARACTERS

Fiction that is not entirely plot driven is driven by characters. Write down everything you can see happening to your characters as a way of getting to know them. Write what they look like, what they wear, what they like, how they live, where they come from, and what experiences have marked them. Most especially, write what they crave, what they are trying to get, and in what part of his spirit each one aches.

Strong characters will create their own plot, but a plot will not create characters, indeed it may cramp and desiccate them.

WORK TO CREATE A MOOD

Settings that are bland or unbelievable compel the audience to struggle with disbelief at every scene change, something unavoidable in the theater but eminently unnecessary when watching the screen. Using locations and sound composition intelligently can provide a powerfully emotional setting, and hurl the audience into the emotional heart of a situation.

Whenever you are out and about, make a point of noting major aspects of any place or situation that has a strong emotional effect. Later these can be incorporated in what you write. Like actors, good dramatists pay extremely close attention to what is around them and are constantly observing and researching in pursuit of their work. Making art is all about paying attention to life, something our escapist culture works to negate.

FILTER OUT RULING ESSENCES

After some initial writing, distill a dramatic premise. This is a sentence or two encapsulating the situation, characters, and main idea on which the whole movie is founded, such as, "An unfulfilled man adopted as a child is now having a troubled marriage. He sets out to find his biological mother. She is so different from what he has imagined that he returns to his wife with new appreciation."

Next make a step outline. As we have said, this is a third-person, present-tense description of each sequence's action with dialogue summarized, a new paragraph for each sequence. Reducing your work to essence allows you to gain control over what the script is truly about. It sounds paradoxical that as the writer one should need to discover one's own work's themes and meanings, but the creative imagination functions on different levels, and some of its most important activity takes place beyond the reach of the conscious mind. The summarizing, winnowing process of making outlines and concept statements is a discipline that will raise the submerged levels into view and make them more useful. The amended step outline and premise that you make after a new draft will energetically point the way to your next bout of revision and rewriting. Winnowing and summarizing makes analysis and development inevitable.

Only when the characters have been created, the action and plot have been worked out, is it wise to begin a screenplay.

WRITE FOR THE CINEMA'S STRENGTHS

To avoid filmed theater, try turning conversations into behavioral exchanges that a deaf person could follow. This means writing as though for a modern but silent cinema. Not only should dialogue be kept minimal, but the storytelling itself should try to use images to drive the story forward. David Mamet protests that "most Hollywood films are made . . . as a supposed record of what real people really did" (*On Directing Film*). Mainstream fiction tends to be expository realism, a stream of passively informational coverage that occupies the attention but does not challenge its judgments or imagination. Mamet advocates telling a story the way that "Eisenstein suggested a movie should be made. This method has nothing to do with following the protagonist around but rather is *a succession of images juxtaposed so that the contrast between these images moves the story forward in the mind of the audience*" (Mamet's emphasis). He goes on to say:

> You want to tell the story in cuts, which is to say, through a juxtaposition of images that are basically uninflected. Mr. Eisenstein tells us that the best image is an uninflected image. A shot of a teacup. A shot of a spoon. A shot of a fork. A shot of a door. Let the cut tell the story. Because otherwise you have not got dramatic action, you have narration. . . . Documentaries take basically unrelated footage and juxtapose it in order to give the viewer the idea the filmmaker wants to convey. They take footage of birds snapping a twig. They take footage of a fawn raising his head. The two shots have nothing to do with each other. They were shot days or years, and miles, apart. And the filmmaker juxtaposes the images to give the viewer the idea of *great alertness*. . . . They are not a record of how the deer

reacted to the bird. They're basically uninflected images. But they give the viewer the idea of alertness to danger when they are juxtaposed. That's good filmmaking. (*On Directing*)

This truly cinematic (as opposed to newsreel) method produces a dialectic of images and action that challenges the audience to follow the underlying authorial logic. It is also true to one's daily experience as a concerned Observer, our judgments causing our attention to jump from object to object to person to face to hand to doorway—and so on. In life we are forced to interpret people by their external appearances and deeds. Perhaps this is why Herzog did not telephone or write to his beloved mentor Lotte Eisner when she lay sick, but trudged all the way on foot from Munich to her bedside in Paris.

Characters in a movie should be seen in action; their actions should give clues to their inner tensions. They should speak not for realism or atmosphere or because their author needs to speak through them, but in order to act on each other. Dialogue is best when it is a form of action and sparse dialogue raises words to high significance.

These are all views for you to consider. I'm not asking you to agree or believe. Decide what qualities *you* really enjoy on the screen and compose your filmmaking to take advantage of them.

SCREENPLAY: FORM FOLLOWS FUNCTION?

Unfortunately because of the priorities and theatrical layout of the conventional screenplay, dialogue appears to be the major component. Here form doesn't follow function, form *swallows* function. Anyone trying to write the Eisensteinian screenplay is impeded, not helped. A better way to draft initial ideas is to use the split page form with an added third column where you draft the Observer's developing perceptions, as in Figure 8-1.

Using this layout you can draft what you want your audience to think, feel, question, decide (both rightly and wrongly), or to remember from earlier in the film. The word processor's drag-and-drop function is excellent for moving materials around experimentally but an agreeably low-tech alternative is to put your shots or sequences on index cards and move them around on a large table. Inventing your own way to experiment with ideas and intentions is important to developing your own creative process and style.

THE AUDIENCE IN MIND

If the drama you develop is to get beyond the egocentricity of therapy, you will have to think about your audience. This does not lead automatically to exploitation or fatal compromise. It means trying to conceive works that participate in modern thought and modern dilemmas, works that prompt questions and ideas which cut across conventional thinking and which will resonate in the lives of others. The only real way to picture this audience is to write for an audience of people very much like yourself in their values and intelligence, but lacking your experi-

Picture	Sound	Observer notices . . .
Wide shot car graveyard.		A mood of decayed hulks, family cars worn out and cast aside.
Shots of cars, their headlights making them look like faces.	Bird song, turns into the regular breathing of someone sleeping.	
Grass and ferns growing up through floors. Glass splintered in black sedan.	Mumbling, as of a dreamer.	Do cars have ghosts?
Executive at head of boardroom table waits for respectful silence.	Male group making businessman conversation. Sound diminishes to silence.	Important people once used this car. What does all this have to do with abandoned automobiles?
Bangs his hand down on table. Everyone jumps.	Child's voice begins nursery song, then . . .	Why's he angry?
Car graveyard again. A pair of gloves on a dusty seat. A plane passes through top of frame.	Bang!! Pigeon wings flapping, a voice in a large room says, "Are we all ready?"	Someone has left their gloves . . . another voice from another time . . . what's going to happen?
A muffled figure rises from back seat, stretches, yawns.	Sync sound.	Ah, someone lives here. A new character. Is this street person going to connect with those boardroom types?

FIGURE 8-1

Draft screenplay in split page form giving precedence to shots and their association to sound. In a third column the writer sketches the Observer's interior process while following the story.

ence and knowledge. Some people by nature share much with the greater world, some share little. There is nothing you can do about this except to change and grow as much as you can. Popularity in the cinema or out of it is not something anyone can plan. One can only use one's potential and be truly oneself. In this you have a lifetime's work.

STORY LOGIC AND TESTING YOUR ASSUMPTIONS

During the composition process one writes from experience, imagination, and intuition as well as from assumptions stored in the unconscious. What is least certain is not the original experience or what one wants to say about it, but whether one's intentions will get across to the audience. Most miscommunication arises from being unaware of assumptions the audience can't or won't share, and failing to provide timely expository framing. For instance, though a screenwriter knows that her character Harry would never perjure himself in court, her audience knows nothing of the sort. His honesty must first be established (the word "establish" appears a lot in screenwriting). To do this she might make Harry go back into a store after unthinkingly carrying a newspaper out with his groceries. Now his honesty is attested by his action of paying for it. She can even make him a white-collar criminal who has siphoned thousands from his corporation but who still goes out of his way to pay for his newspaper at the corner store. Complex moral codes are always interesting.

A story is a progression of logic that raises questions and offers clues (that are often delayed) to the answers. This you design and test through your planning process's third column. You will need to satisfy the audience's basic expectations for every human situation you set up. For instance, a film about a man adopted in childhood who searches for his biological mother would hardly remain credible if he failed to look for his birth certificate and never questioned his foster parents. These are basic steps that you must either show or establish as having been accomplished without satisfactory result.

Later when our adoptee finds his mother, it would be equally illogical for him to become happy and fulfilled. Everyone of any maturity knows that people finding their progenitors have very mixed emotions, not least pain and anger. Lasting euphoria would be untrue to human nature and make the character simpleminded. Either the character or the movie-makers are naïve. If it's the latter, the audience will quickly realize it is smarter than the movie—and move on.

CREATING SPACE FOR THE AUDIENCE

Whether a story is told through literature, song, stage or screen, the successful storyteller always creates significant spaces that the audience must fill from its own imagination, values, and life experience. Unlike the reader of a novel the film spectator does not have to visualize the physical world of the story, so all the more important is that he speculate about the characters' motives and morals. As a painting implies life beyond the edges of its frame, so dramatic characters and the ideas they engender should go beyond what we can see and hear.

CREDIBILITY, MINIMIZING, AND STORY TENSION

Fiction, though a self-contained world, still runs under rules drawn from life at large. The writer cannot capriciously violate the audience's knowledge of living. The story and its characters must be interesting, representative, and consistent if they are to remain credible. Other genres like documentary or folk tale are hardly less free; each is true in some important way to the spirit of reality, and all are governed by rules to which the audience must be willing to subscribe. This means that coincidences that happen in life are suspect once placed in a like fictional world.

While you write, anything you want to imply must first be named and fully explored before you move to minimize it. The creator always knows far more than gets shared with the audience but it is best to overspecify and then reduce.

Good storytellers withhold whatever they can and as long as possible because *successful storytelling absolutely depends on creating tension and anticipation.*

TEST EXHAUSTIVELY ON OTHERS

It is a good practice to explain one's ideas to anyone who will listen and be critical. If "the unexamined life is not worth living" the unexamined story idea is not worth filming. Hearing yourself is the very best way to see your ideas from another's point of view. Repeatedly exposing your ideas to skeptical listeners also flushes out the clichés in one's thinking (the power of positive embarrassment!). After all, one's first thoughts are the same junk as everyone else's. Original ideas come to those who work to reject the conventional.

As with initial ideas, so with the screenplay. In seeking responses:

- try to find mature readers whose values you share and respect
- keep your critics on track: you cannot be too interested in the film the respondent would have made
- ask what he or she understands from the script
- ask what the characters are like
- ask what seems to be driving them
- ask which scenes are effective
- ask which are not.

Shooting an imperfectly tested screenplay is opening a Pandora's box (I speak from experience). You should acquire a complete and accurate sense of what the audience knows and feels at each stage of the proposed film. Critical readers will have to be replaced over time as they become familiar with the material.

ACT ON CRITICISM ONLY AFTER REFLECTION

In an audience medium the director usually wants to be understood by a general audience whose experience does not debar them from entering the most arcane world if it is carefully presented. Seeking responses to a script can be very misleading and also be a test of self-knowledge. For if you resist all suggestions and argue the validity of the responses, you are probably insecure. If instead you agree with almost everything and in a mood of self-flagellation set about a complete rewrite, or worse, scrap the project, it means you are *very* insecure. If, however, you continue to believe in what you are doing but recognize some truth in what your critics say, you are progressing nicely. There will still be plenty of anguish and self-doubt. No gain without pain, they say.

Never make changes hastily or impulsively. Let the criticism lie for a few days then see what your mind filters out as valid. When in doubt, delay changes and don't abandon your intentions. Work on something else until your mind quietly insists on what must, or must not, be done.

Do not show unfinished work to family or intimates. Knowing you so well, they will want to save you by hiding your faults and naiveté from public view. Almost as damaging is total, loving, across-the-board praise. The best way to show them your work is with a general audience, whose responses will help shape your friends and family in theirs. How many artists have had nothing but resistance and dissuasion from their family only to see it all magically change once the world becomes accepting ("Well, now. I never thought you'd do anything with that damned guitar . . . ")

TEST ON A SCRATCH CAST

It is important when you cast and rehearse that you do not get taken by surprise. Before proceeding to production you should assemble a scratch cast to read the script through. Each actor, however inexperienced, will identify with one character and show you your script in an unfamiliar light. You should be able to wholeheartedly justify every word of dialogue and every stage direction in the script.

REWRITE, REWRITE, REWRITE

Be ready to keep changing the script all the way up to the day of shooting. A script is not an artwork with a final form; it is more like plans for an invasion that must be altered, if you are to survive, in the light of each hour's fresh intelligence. In filmmaking, finished versions cannot be tested on audiences the way they can be in the theater, so reshaping must be accomplished during the script development and cast rehearsal period. Editing, compressing, or expanding your material where needed, simplifying and even wholesale rewriting will shape the material to take advantage of the way players enact the piece. Feature films I worked on were regularly undergoing rewrites the day before shooting. Writers hate this compulsive rewriting, but their standards for completion arise from habits of solo creation, while filmmaking is an organic, physical process that must adapt to the unfolding reality of cast and shooting—both in negative and positive implication.

Rewriting is frequently omitted or resisted by student production groups out of inexperience or because it threatens the writer's ego. The director should take over the script if this happens and alter it as necessary. In the professional world, the writer *delivers* a script, and then loses control of it. There is a good reason for this.

ON DIRECTING FROM YOUR OWN SCREENPLAY

If you are preparing to direct from your own script, work hard to distance yourself by exposing it to tough criticism and making yourself behave as though it were someone else's work. Unless one has learned over a period of years to be professionally rigorous with one's own writing, there are many unexamined assumptions waiting to surface later as full-blown problems. They can easily sap the writer/director's confidence and authority. By carrying out all available analytical steps, you can with difficulty gain an objective understanding of your own work.

FIGHT THE CENSOR AND FINISH

It is very important to finish projects. Work left incomplete is a step taken sideways, not forward. It is tempting halfway through a project to say, "Well, I've learned all I can learn here so I think I'll start something new." This is the internal censor at work, your hidden enemy who whispers, "You can't show this to other people, it isn't good enough; the real you is better." One's work seldom feels good for long, but do not let that make you halt or change horses. Only intermittently will you feel elation, but finishing will always yield satisfaction and knowledge.

YOUR WORK IS NOT YOU

Your writing is not you, it is the work you did at a particular stage on your life's journey. Remember that your work is only an interim representation. The next piece of work will show changes, will strengthen you and sharpen your journey's purpose. Truffaut admitted late in life that it is just as difficult to make a bad film as a good one, and he became a kinder critic of other directors' work after he too had experienced the failures that prepare us to succeed. The integrity and perseverance of the explorer is what matters.

Keep going, no matter what. All writers say one thing, that one must write to a schedule. Some days it produces bad writing. Some days, trying to write produces little or none. Some days it produces more. But you must like the process and you must make yourself keep writing. Remember, better writing comes from rewriting bad writing.

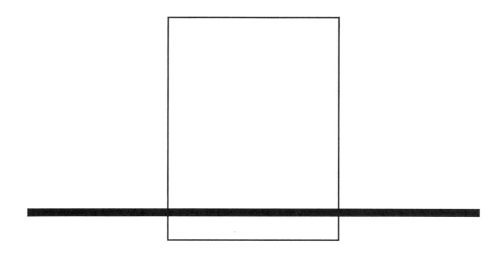

ADAPTATION FROM ART OR LIFE

There is a constantly growing supply of plays, novels, and short stories that might adapt well to the screen. Libraries keep copies of an amazing range of indexes and somewhere someone has already analyzed or indexed the very thing you are interested in by characters, subject, or theme. All you need do is to find the index. Short stories, for example, are indexed by theme.

The short story is a favorite source of material for both short and full-length films. Like all good literature it can be a quicksand to the unwary, for the magic of language can seduce the filmmaker into assuming it will make an equally fine film. Effective adaptation may actually be impossible if the author's writing style and literary form have no cinematic equivalency. A story relying upon a subtly ironic storytelling voice, for instance, might be a bad choice because there is no such thing as ironic photography or recording.

Effective literature never automatically contains the basis for a good film. Most of the criteria for judging material for an adaptation remain the same as those used to assess any script.

- does it tell its tale through externally visible, visual, behavioral means?
- does it have interesting, well-developed characters?
- is it contained and specific in settings?
- are the situations interesting and realizable?
- is there an interesting major conflict and is it dramatized rather than internal?

- does the conflict imply interesting metaphors?
- does the piece have a strong thematic purpose?
- is the thematic purpose one you can relate to strongly?
- do you find it inherently stimulating and in line with your own themes?
- can you invent a cinematic equivalency for the story's literary values?
- can you afford to do it?
- is the copyright available?

FAITHFUL ADAPTATION

Any well-known work comes with strings attached. Should J. D. Salinger person-ally hand you the rights to *The Catcher in the Rye,* you would not have a free hand at adaptation. Because the book has touched so many people, meeting their expectations would be well nigh impossible. For this reason alone, literature adapted to the screen almost always disappoints its fans. Other works, long or short, may pose narrative or stylistic problems that can only be solved through radically altering the form suggested by the original. For instance, John Korty's version of John Updike's five-and-a-half-page story "The Music School" (The American Short Story series) takes a story that happens contemplatively inside a man's mind, develops it into interwoven events, and propels them upon a musical theme of increasing texture and confidence. The result is a short film gem no less profound than Updike's overcompressed original, a good deal more accessible yet true to the original's spirit.

Karel Reisz's 1981 screen version of John Fowles' *The French Lieutenant's Woman,* however, suffers badly. Fowles' novels tend to overflow with ideas, and this one more than any. The movie version, although scripted by the supremely in-telligent Harold Pinter, is forced by time limitations to strip away most of the so-ciological exposition and philosophical speculation by which the novel assesses the nineteenth century against its twentieth-century offspring. Like most adapta-tions, the movie concentrates on the plot and action at the expense of discourse, and emerges with a bad case of malnutrition. This is a constant problem with BBC adaptations of literary masterworks. Over the years they have achieved the settled ways of an industry like furniture reproduction.

FREE ADAPTATION

A more fertile union of literature and screen can happen when, instead of process-ing literary or theatrical icons, the filmmaker takes aspects of a written work to seed a fully autonomous film. Inventive, original cinema takes what it needs from anything and everything, while "great" novels or plays processed for the screen are diminished, like paintings made into tapestry. Many of Godard's ground-breaking movies of the 1960s were free adaptations of theater or sociology, works by Alberto Moravia and Guy de Maupassant, and, most interestingly, transforma-tions of pulp fiction. The Quentin Tarantino movie *Pulp Fiction* (1995) however, adopts the style and values of pulp fiction without apparently having anything in its back pocket beyond style. Its undoubted professionalism and panache lead to an emptiness, a glorification of what it wants us to laugh at.

ADAPTING A SCREENPLAY FROM FICTION OR A REAL EVENT

By taking over a story framework (from a literary work or from a life situation) and substituting one's own choice of main elements, an entirely new work can emerge, since everything else, including the main issues, will be affected. In the search to integrate all the parts, the work will inevitably evolve and begin to impose its own demands that the writer must satisfy. Elements you might alter could be:

Characters: Placing a new character in any situation creates pressure for new outcomes (and therefore a changed destiny). Strong characters can steer a story to new conclusions that in turn express a different resolution and meaning.

Situations and conflicts: Changed characters almost certainly generate changes in the events, and changes in some or all of the main conflicts.

Period: One can tell an old story in a modern setting, as Leonard Bernstein did by adapting Shakespeare's *Romeo and Juliet* to New York City in the musical show *West Side Story.*

Settings: New characters demand their own settings to express what is particular to them. Changes of class, changes of region, or changes of occupation all have far-reaching consequences. A change of setting will produce changed pressures on the characters.

Point of view: In *The Wide Sargasso Sea,* novelist Jean Rhys reinterprets the situation in Charlotte Bronte's *Jane Eyre* by taking the viewpoint of the mad, imprisoned Mrs. Rochester. It is a radically different story that arises from Rhys' outrage at the injustices suffered by neglected wives, something she experienced during her early years in Paris. Any story that draws one emotionally into its web is capable of reinterpretation, especially if one violently disagrees with the conclusions reached by the original author.

Thematic purpose: You might keep similar characters but adjust the situations to produce a different thematic outcome. Here you may be attracted to interpreting the same events differently.

You are surrounded by rich resources for storytelling. You can legitimately borrow and adapt from any source, providing the new entity gains its own identity and purpose. Now your feeling should no longer be "Help, I don't have any stories to tell" but instead, "What is the basis for my choices and adaptations?" and "Why do I like this particular story so much?"

Whatever causes a deep response in you throws light on your underlying storyteller's identity. Growing self-knowledge will allow you to further build into your work whatever else fascinates you. The aim is to design a vehicle so freighted with personal significance that you become possessed by it, answering to characters, events, and situations that impel themselves forward to their own conclusion. Indeed, the sign of an effectively rigorous writing process is that your characters detach themselves from their originals and become autonomous within their own world. This independence comes from knowing that your story instills belief in its audience, that you can let go of any security blanket represented by remembered fact or respectable origins in established fiction.

COPYRIGHT CLEARANCE

If you make an adaptation bearing a likeness to its original you must make sure you have the legal right to use it. Copyright law is changed periodically. In the United States you can obtain current information from the Copyright Office, Library of Congress, Washington, DC 20559. Many works first published fifty-six years ago or more are old enough to be in the public domain, but do not assume this without careful inquiry, preferably through a copyright lawyer. The laws are extremely complicated, especially concerning a literary property's clearance in other countries.

ACTOR-CENTERED FILMS AND THEIR SCRIPTS

Another potential influence on the script is the cast. This will be more fully explored later, but this chapter would be incomplete without establishing the importance of actors' personalities and traits to an existing idea or script. Look at it this way: your vision reaches the audience through what you put on the screen and most of this will be the human presence. The credibility and quality of that human presence makes or breaks any film, yet seldom is the individuality of the very actors who bring it alive allowed to influence the text. Invariably, unless a powerful star is involved, the actors must adapt to the text. This is because most films are manufactured in a unidirectional process, and actors are fitted to a finished and funded script. This is neither desirable nor true for the low-budget filmmaker. Let's look at their situation.

Actors whose effortless-looking performances we take for granted arrive on the screen through a rigorous apprenticeship and selection process. But beginning or low-budget filmmakers must try to match this professionalism using actors with little or no experience. Most try doing this by following the industry's assembly line operation, when there's really something already wrong with professional norms. Jessica Lange, a film actress as professional as they come, has deplored the lack of rehearsal time in which to develop the emotional life of her characters (*American Film,* June 1987). So anyone using inexperienced actors, or nonactors, can hardly bring together people unknown to each other *and* unfamiliar with the process of filming yet expect them to be relaxed and focused in their roles. You need an induction process that will bring the anxiety levels down and build an ensemble able to be playful in its seriousness. For the inexperienced cast, there's an urgent need to explore and interact, so the prudent director plans time and activities in which cast and script can evolve. *Careful and lengthy rehearsal is a must,* using intelligent discussion and improv work to explore the ideas and emotional transitions in the script and to bring that magic quality of spontaneity to the screen.

Here is a scripting method that uses human beings as well as the typewriter. Though nontraditional it is in fact used increasingly and with significant results.

INTEGRATING THE CAST INTO THE SCRIPT

Some directors already write in an unconventional, actor-centered way, foremost among them Bergman, who does not favor the screenplay:

> If . . . I were to reproduce in words what happens in the film I have conceived, I would be forced to write a bulky book of little readable value and great nuisance. I have neither the talent nor the patience for heroic exercise of that kind. Besides, such a procedure would kill all creative joy for both me and the artists. (*Four Stories by Ingmar Bergman* [New York, Doubleday, 1977])

Bergman develops his films from an annotated short story. For *Cries and Whispers* (1972) he supplied notes about the artistic approach, intended characters and their situations, settings, and time period. There are also fragments from Agnes' diary, details of a dream, and the dialogue and narrative of the events. Materials like these Bergman hands to all participating, and the developmental work begins from a thorough discussion and assimilation of their possibilities. Much of the creation of characters and action then lies with actors whose careers and talents. Bergman has been instrumental in developing.

In the United States, actor/director John Cassavetes also gave primacy to his actors, either improvising completely as in *Shadows* (1959) or basing a written script on structured improvisations as he did in *A Woman Under the Influence* (1974). "The emotion was improvised," he said, "but the lines were written."

Alain Tanner, a Swiss director who came to feature films through television documentaries, has gradually evolved his fiction works toward the spontaneity of his documentary beginnings. For *Jonah Who Will Be 25 in the Year 2000* (1976) he showed photos of his chosen cast to writing collaborator, John Berger. The associations Berger made with each face became the basis for a script. In his more recent *In the White City* (1985) Tanner used no script at all, relying instead upon the ability of his fine actors to improvise upon a framework of specified ideas. This takes expertise all around.

In Britain Mike Leigh's films started out with bittersweet comedy but have developed into a darker criticism of English life. *High Hopes* (1988) and *Life Is Sweet* (1991) are comedies of character that make a poignant critique of English working-class powers of adaptation and survival when the mainstays of dignity—work and a place in the order of things—begin to disappear. *Naked* (1993) offers an apocalyptic vision of characters lost and in torment in a London where the have-nots roam the streets like hungry, wounded wolves. Leigh comes from the theater and bases his work on particular actors. His results show none of the hesitancy of pacing, bouts of self-consciously bravura acting, or uncertainty of structure visible in Cassavetes and other improv-based filmmakers.

FIGURE 9-1 ───

Tanner's *Jonah Who Will Be 25 in the Year 2000,* a film developed from its actors (courtesy New Yorker Films).

Before you line up behind any particular creed, it may be useful to glance at some fundamentals of modern realistic cinema. If the object is to create believable life on the screen and to expose credible contemporary issues, there must not only be viable ideas and situations, but above all, credible characters. Today's audience has spent upwards of eighteen thousand hours watching the screen and is an expert judge of acting. People are quite unmoved by the representational styles that audiences loved years back. So unless an actor finds an adequate emotional identification with his character, we will reject his performance and with it, much or all of the film.

Unsophisticated or untrained actors tend to model their performances not on life but upon ideas gleaned from other, admired actors. They will signify a character's feelings and "perform" to the mass audience they imagine existing just beyond the camera lens. The director must develop strategies for each actor to break through to something true. Their particular qualities and limitations should guide how you realize your authorial intentions. Even these may need rethinking if they are to align with the intrinsic and highly visible qualities of your cast.

As a developing director you must, as a matter of survival, give first priority to developing your actors' potentials. Good film acting looks like being, not acting at all. Your film can survive indifferent film technique, but nothing can rescue it from lousy acting; not good color, not good music, not good photography, not good editing. None of these—separately or combined—can change the true state of consciousness and the inherent human qualities that you cannot avoid capturing, documentary fashion, with your camera.

A SCRIPT DEVELOPED FROM ACTORS' IMPROVISING

Let us imagine you are going to make a film about the conflicts and paradoxes in a young man leaving home, and want to show it as an ordeal by fire. It is possible and even desirable to begin without a full-fledged script. The experience is so universal that most cast members will have strong feelings on the subject. You decide to find an interesting cast, knowing that each actor's ideas are going to be engaged in developing your thematic concerns. John Cassavetes' *A Woman Under the Influence* (1974) began this way. Cassavetes and his actress wife, Gena Rowlands, playing the wife in the film, were interested in what happens in an Italian-American blue-collar family when women's liberation ideas penetrate the home. The wife becomes aware that her role as wife and mother is preventing her from growing into an autonomous adult. The resulting script was founded on the experiences and personalities of the players. Uneven as the movie is, Gena Rowlands' performance is disturbingly memorable.

In Giles Walker's National Film Board of Canada comedy *90 Days* (1986) the subject grew out of a favorite actor's idea for making a film about an ordinary guy who orders an Oriental mail-order bride. After casting, the film was improvised in three stages, each section then scripted and shot as a prelude to conceiving the next. What makes this comedy so touching is that the main characters are all fully realized. Although the film is very funny, it also displays a wealth of sympathetic insight into everyday Canadian life, particularly the ordinary male's difficulties at articulating unfamiliar emotions.

By finding an interested cast and by posing the right questions, it is possible to draw out their interests and residual experience of life. When you turn up interesting and credible situations, you can have your cast experimentally play them out. As this happens, consistent characters begin to emerge from each player, and in emerging, demand greater clarity and background. You and your cast will find your attention turning from ideas to character development, and from character development inevitably to situations, and from situations and characters to the specific past events—personal, cultural, political—that seeded each character's present. Gradually you form a world out of the tensions and conflicts and it belongs to everyone taking part, because each has had a hand in the development.

A ship with several oarsmen needs a firm hand on the tiller. Directing a project of this nature takes subtlety, patience, and the authority to make binding decisions. Dramatically the results may be a mixed bag, but at the very least this process is a tremendous way of building rapport among cast and director. I find that the cast tends to retain what is successful by consensus, so that what began as improvisation gradually evolves as the ensemble increasingly deals with smaller details into a mutually agreed text. This is how folk drama was produced for hundreds of years.

Another more open-ended method is to start not from a social theme or idea, but from a mood or from the personality and potential of individual cast members. If "character is fate," let your characters develop their fates. By getting each to generate an absorbing character and by letting situations grow out of the clashes and alliances of these characters, themes and issues inevitably suggest themselves. A project like this is good for a theater company used to working together, or as a follow-up film project when the cast and director have come to trust each other and want to go on working together (not always the case!)

Though there are only 36 basic dramatic situations in the world, there is no limit to possible interactions between characters. Alternatively, both characters and issues might be developed from the nature and resonance of a particular location, say a deserted gravel pit, the waiting room in an underground car park, or a street market. Very potent is the site of a historical event, such as a field where strikers were gunned down, or the house where a woman who had apocalyptic visions grew up.

Experiments of this kind are excellent for building the cast's confidence to play scripted or unscripted parts with unself-conscious abandonment, and the daring to act upon intuition—all priceless commodities. Playful work of this nature generates energy and ideas, and when the dramatic output is rounded up and analyzed, a longer work can be structured. Firm guidance is imperative or the results will lack integration and fail to make any recognizable statement. This is true for all improv-generated ideas.

Techniques useful for this kind of work appear throughout Part V: Preproduction, and particularly in Chapter 21: Improvisation Work to Explore Acting.

THE VIDEO NOVEL: IMPROVISATORY APPROACH

Just as the theater in England was revitalized in the 1960s when local theater turned its back on cocktail plays in favor of more explosive local issues, it now seems possible, with increased local television programming and video equipment becoming widely available, that local fiction video groups will emerge to begin producing the modern equivalent of the regional novel. That nothing like it has yet happened is not because of the system, but because regional film production remains imitative and third rate. A few first-rate contemporary voices would send distributors rushing to invest in a new source of product.

The most likely point of origin is in city theaters producing works of contemporary social and political criticism, and having a fairly stable ensemble. It has been done before. Both the German director, Rainer Werner Fassbinder, and the fine actress, Hanna Schygulla, who played in his *Marriage of Maria Braun* (1978), emerged from such an institution, the Munich action-theater, which later became the *anti-teater*. The company made no less than six of Fassbinder's early films together, and his astonishingly prolific and creative film career was plainly rooted in the experience of creating instant theater from contemporary personal or political issues.

If it can be done in Munich, why not elsewhere? Of course, there are many arguments against a grass-roots screen drama movement. Funding, distribution, the continuity of the ensemble and the homogeneity of their vision are all difficult to sustain at the present time. Rather than debate these points I will just point out a possible niche for an enterprising group.

Let us take an example. During the last twenty years in Chicago the steel industry has gone silent and the hard-working ethnic communities that clustered around it have become unemployed. They have participated in the American Dream for two or three generations, and suddenly it has all died. What happens to such people? What happens to their sons and daughters? What happens when people whose sense of virtue was founded in hard, dirty labor now have no more "man's work" in the offing? How do they explain their losses? This story is being repeated all over the industrialized western world. Such people and their fate are of wide significance and of much interest. It is not hard to find out about them, for they have ample time for the researcher.

At first sight it seems more of a Barbara Kopple documentary subject, but when you begin to read articles and interviews, to visit with union leaders, local historians, doctors, and clergymen, as well as with the unemployed steelworkers and their families, you find that the story is diffuse and complicated. Some of the men live on false hope. Some drink too much. Some take meaningless jobs that pay only a fraction of what they earned before just to keep up their work ethic. The wives now begin to go out to work, and this changes the family dynamic. Their husbands feel a sense of failure. There is a dull anger, a depressed, moody resignation. There is also an ugly side to this resentment; the community becomes inturned and racist. There is a neo-Nazi group that meets in its own well-guarded headquarters. There are some demonstrations, some harassment of blacks in a neighboring district, a burning garage or two.

Then there are the young people. They either stay because for one reason or another they cannot leave, or they get out and go to college, leaving their parents' decaying neighborhood ever farther away, yet feeling guilty for betraying their embittered, once-proud parents by leaving.

What we have here is a situation with so many possibilities, so many things happening, that the only way to handle it is to decide which are specially interesting and make a dramatic construct out of those chosen. What we begin to see is perhaps a representative family whose members are composites inspired by people we met and who left an indelible impression. We make up a list of key events in the life of a composite fictional family:

- father loses job
- believes his skills will soon be needed elsewhere
- no job comes, no job can be found
- scenes of mounting economic and emotional pressure in the family
- the mother finds a job as a checkout clerk at a supermarket
- the daughter begins going to a college downtown
- daughter becomes increasingly critical of her family and its assumptions
- the son drops out of high school and hangs out on street corners, identifying more and more with the neo-fascist messages of revenge and hatred.

We have built up a series of pressures. Now we urgently need ideas about how these pressures will resolve, what kind of contortions this family and this bereaved community are going to suffer, and what "coming out the other side" may mean. A fictionalized treatment of these very real circumstances must, therefore, have an element of prediction to propose to its audience, a prediction about the way human beings handle this kind of slow-motion catastrophe.

To become a social analyst or prophet is an exciting job to give yourself. Do it well and you will arouse much interest, but you'll need the abilities of journalist, sociologist, documentarian, and novelist to make it work. But look what is already available: a host of characters to play minor roles; a landscape of windswept, rusting factories, and rows of peeling houses; a circuit of bars, dance halls, and ethnic churches with their weddings, christenings, and funerals. Sound too depressing? Then go to the amateur comedian contests and make Dad into an aspiring stand-up comic. The community where you are going to film has all sorts of regular activities to use as a backdrop, and within reason you can make the characters do and be anything you want.

What is happening in your area that needs to be understood? A rash of teenage suicides? A cult? A new and dangerous form of racing? A cosmetician who has found a way to get rich quick? A UFO society? An archaeological hoax by a hitherto reputable academic? A sexual purity movement among teenagers? Industrial espionage? An aging beauty queen who has run away with her priest? A computer nerd reorganizing the town's bank accounts for no personal profit?

Among novelists there have always been committed regionalists. You could become one. You could reach out to inhabit interesting, broadly significant local situations that can be filled out from imagination and experience. Newspapers, magazines, and bookshops are full of models, and you need only to choose well from the local storehouse.

Intelligently realized, the deeply local subject becomes the truly universal one.

STORY DEVELOPMENT STRATEGIES

While creating a story, the writer alternates between generating story materials and editing them in pursuit of development and unity. In the generating mode, give free rein to inspiration, writing organically and disconnectedly as ideas, scenes, characters, and situations appear in your imagination. This is letting the work help to create itself.

Then, once the blitz of a generating phase is over, you begin editing; that is, you review and analyze what you have produced in order to develop it. Like a manic potter who produces flawed and surplus goods among the useful, there comes a time when production must be halted to allow someone to organize, classify, tidy up and throw out the junk. Here you need methods by which to re-impose order. Whether one is a potter or a writer, nobody creates in a vacuum. Virtually all characters and situations, no matter how up to date, are variations of archetypal patterns. To deny this, or hide from it is not preserving one's originality so much as refusing the help of parentage that even great artists welcome.

Later in the chapter we will look at how to find and use archetypes. First, if you are assessing a completed script or especially if you are working on your own writing, you will need to get a dramatic oversight of the piece. This is true no matter whether it is five pages or a hundred and fifty. You will need to employ the analytic tools of the step outline, premise, concept, and treatment.

The step outline is like the framework of headings that I used to begin this book. Writing a book is a slow, circular activity like fumbling one's way through a dense forest. Even after starting from a clear plan I regularly lost an overview of what I was doing, and had to create content lists to see exactly where I had been and where I still needed to go. When you first picked this book up, you probably looked in the list of chapters, tables of contents, and index to see whether it contained what you wanted. These summations functioned for you and me both. Writing a story is a lot more complex than writing a manual, and more urgently needs periodic reorganizing and overview.

STEP OUTLINE

Writing methods vary considerably, but many screenwriters produce a step outline first. Here the writer summarizes in short story, third-person, present-tense form only what the audience will see and hear from the screen, allotting one numbered paragraph per sequence. It should read as a brief, stream-of-consciousness summation that never digresses into production details or the author's thoughts. It should include only the bare essentials, seldom dialogue, only summaries of each conversation's subject and development. Here is the beginning of something I have been working on:

> Step Outline for THE OARSMAN
> 1. At night between the high walls of an Amsterdam canal a murky figure in black tails and top hat rows an ornate coffin in a strange, high boat. In a shaft of light we see that MORRIE is a man in his late thirties whose expression is set, serene, distant.
> 2. Looking down on the city at night, we see a panoramic view over black canals glittering with lights and reflections, bridges busy with pedestrian and bike traffic, and streetcars snaking between crooked, leaning seventeenth-century buildings. As the view comes to rest on a street, we hear a noisy bar atmosphere where, in the foreground, a Canadian woman and a Dutch man are arguing fiercely.
> 3. Inside the fairly rough bar with its wooden tables, wooden floor strewn with peanut shells, wooden bar with a line of old china beer spouts, is JASMINE, a tough but attractive young Canadian in her late twenties. She is trying to leave the bar during a bitter argument with her tattooed and druggy-looking Dutch boyfriend MARCO. She says she's had enough.

Developing a step outline is an organic process, the premise can change as the co-creators journey deeply into the material's potential. When you come under the co-creative influences of your writer, crew, or actors, you should examine and re-examine the concept. You should be able to constantly find new aspects to your work and these can help it becoming progressively more focused. Like all periods of growth, it feels very good. Here is a potent source of energy and authority for a director.

EXPANDING AND COLLAPSING THE SCREENPLAY

The step outline is an excellent starting point for writing a screenplay but it is an equally useful tool for traveling in the opposite direction, that is, for simplifying the essentials of a completed screenplay draft. Working in screenplay format means that the basic structure often becomes obscured, even from its own progenitor. Particularly when a screenplay presents problems (and which doesn't?) it will help to make a step outline that reveals the plot and inherent structure.

Reducing the screenplay to step outline, then further reducing the step outline to a ruling premise are vital steps in testing a story's foundations.

STORY ARCHETYPES

During this century major work has been done surveying story archetypes. While archetypes are especially helpful to fiction writers in the editing and structuring phase of their work, you will almost certainly find them inhibiting as a starting point. Their completeness can be paralyzing. That's why I've held back this material to a section dealing with story editing tools. When you write initial drafts, put formulas out of mind and follow your inclinations. Create first, no matter how poorly; then shape and edit later when the world you have set in motion is firmly established. Myths and archetypes become most helpful for a story in difficulties or stuck.

In the Notes and Queries section of the *Guardian Weekly* a reader asked if it was true there are only seven basic stories in fiction. An obliging reader responded with eight:

1. Cinderella—virtue eventually recognized
2. Achilles—the fatal flaw
3. Faust—the debt that catches up with the debtor
4. Tristan—the sexual triangle
5. Circe—the spider and the fly
6. Romeo and Juliet—star-crossed lovers who either find or lose each other
7. Orpheus—the gift that is lost and searched for
8. The Hero that cannot be kept down

To these other readers added,

9. David and Goliath—the individual against the state/community/system, etc.
10. The Wandering Jew—the persecuted traveler who can never go home.

Another reader pointed out that it is fictional themes, not stories that are said to be limited to seven. They are:

1. Revenge
2. Survival
3. Money
4. Power
5. Glory
6. Self-Awareness
7. Love.

Yet another reader pointed to Georges Polti's *Thirty-Six Dramatic Situations* as the definitive listing of dramatic possibilities.

First written in French and copyrighted in English in 1921, this book is still in print (Boston, The Writer, Inc., 1977) and is a seminal work of dramaturgy. Polti lists each situation of human conflict with its elements and wonderfully categorized examples and variations. To whet your appetite Figure 10-1 shows the situations and elements.

	Situation	*Elements*
1	Supplication	A persecutor, a suppliant, a power in authority whose decision is doubtful
2	Deliverance	An unfortunate, a threatener, a rescuer
3	Crime pursued by vengeance	An avenger and a criminal
4	Vengeance taken for kindred	Avenging kinsman, guilty kinsman, remembrance of the victim, a relative of both
5	Pursuit	Punishment and fugitive
6	Disaster	A vanquished power, a victorious enemy or a messenger
7	Falling prey to cruelty or misfortune	An unfortunate, a master or a misfortune
8	Revolt	Tyrant and conspirator
9	Daring enterprise	A bold leader, an object, an adversary
10	Abduction	The abductor, the abducted, the guardian
11	The enigma	Interrogator, seeker, and problem
12	Obtaining	A solicitor and an adversary who is refusing, or an arbitrator and opposing parties
13	Enmity of kinsmen	A malevolent kinsman, a hated or reciprocally hating kinsman
14	Rivalry of kinsmen	The preferred kinsman, the rejected kinsman, the object
15	Murderous adultery	Two adulterers, a betrayed husband or wife
16	Madness	Madman and victim
17	Fatal imprudence	The imprudent, the victim or the object lost
18	Involuntary crimes of love	The lover, the beloved, the revealer
19	Slaying of a kinsman unrecognized	The slayer, the unrecognized victim
20	Self-sacrificing for an ideal	The hero, the ideal, the "creditor" or the person or thing sacrificed

FIGURE 10-1

Georges Polti's *Thirty-Six Dramatic Situations*. Reproduced by the kind permission of The Writer, Inc., Boston. Copyright 1977, 1993 by The Writer, Inc.

	Situation	Elements
21	Self sacrifice for kindred	The hero, the kinsman, the "creditor" or the person or thing sacrificed
22	All sacrificed for a passion	The lover, the object of the fatal passion, the person or thing sacrificed
23	Necessity of sacrificing loved ones	The hero, the beloved victim, the necessity for the sacrifice
24	Rivalry of superior and inferior	The superior rival, the inferior rival, the object
25	Adultery	A deceived husband or wife, two adulterers
26	Crimes of love	The lover, the beloved
27	Discovery of the dishonor of a loved one	The discoverer, the guilty one
28	Obstacles to love	Two lovers, an obstacle
29	An enemy loved	The beloved enemy, the lover, the hater
30	Ambition	An ambitious person, a thing coveted, an adversary
31	Conflict with a god	A mortal, an immortal
32	Mistaken jealousy	The jealous one, the object of whose possession he is jealous, the supposed accomplice, the cause or the author of the mistake
33	Erroneous judgment	The mistaken one, the victim of the mistake, the cause or author of the mistake, the guilty person
34	Remorse	The culprit, the victim or the sin, the interrogator
35	Recovery of a lost one	The seeker, the one found
36	Loss of loved ones	A kinsman slain, a kinsman spectator, an executioner

FIGURE 10-1 (Continued)

Lists like this may at first sight seem limiting. But myths, conflicts and themes are the DNA of human experience. Human beings will never stop enacting them, and so will never stop needing stories that explore their implications. You could make a long list of films for every one of the thirty-six situations above. Most films contain multiples of the basic situations.

Once you know which situations and theme (or themes) your script is handling, you can look up its collaterals. This will certainly give you ideas about modifications or additions. These are unlikely to change the nature or individuality of your piece; instead you are more likely to find and overcome your piece's weaknesses. Merely examining and testing the fabric of your story will toughen it and increase your authority as its director.

THE HERO'S JOURNEY

The lifetime work of Joseph Campbell, author of *The Mythic Image, The Masks of God,* and *The Hero with a Thousand Faces* was to collect myths and folk tales from every imaginable culture and to reveal their common symbolic denominators. "The hero," he says, "is the [person] of self-achieved submission." The terms of this submission may vary, but they reflect that "within the soul, within the body social, there must be—if we are to experience long survival—a continuous recurrence of birth (palingenesia) to nullify the unremitting recurrences of death" (*The Hero with a Thousand Faces,* Princeton University Press, 1972.)

Campbell recognizes that the hero's journey (he also means heroine's) always deals with a central character's struggle for regeneration against the forces of darkness. My purpose here is not to attempt to summarize his work, but to draw your attention to its profound implications for the maker of screen works. Just as Stanislavsky found the psychological and practical elements of acting from studying successful actors, Campbell discovered the recurring spiritual and narrative elements held in common by so many of the world's tales. If something you have created shares some of the archetype, you may find it useful to see what elements are missing, and whether their inclusion would strengthen your story. Campbell alleges that the hero generally makes a circular journey during his or her transformation. It includes departure, initiation, and return. You could apply this principle to a child going to her first day of school or to a cosmonaut making the first journey to a distant planet. Both go through severe trials and return changed. A few of Campbell's chapter headings in *The Hero with a Thousand Faces* show just how flexibly his analysis fits many film ideas:

Departure
    The Call to Adventure
    The Refusal of the Call
    Supernatural Aid
    The Crossing of the First Threshold
    The Belly of the Whale
Initiation
    The Road of Trials
    The Meeting with the Goddess
    Woman as the Temptress
    Atonement with the Father
    Apotheosis
    The Ultimate Boon
Return
    Refusal of the Return
    The Magic Flight
    Rescue from Without

The Crossing of the Return Threshold

Master of the Two Worlds

Freedom to Live

If this calls to you, read it for yourself. If you would like to apply the ideas directly to a screen work without getting lost in the fascinations of world literature, look into Christopher Vogler's *The Writer's Journey: Mythic Structure for Storytellers and Screenwriters* (1992, Michael Wiese Productions, CA). This is an intelligent and well-written book by a highly experienced story analyst who has worked for most of the major Hollywood production companies. Vogler's enthusiasm, his many examples from classic and contemporary films, his willingness to share everything he knows with the reader, and his ability to keep the reader focused on the larger picture of human endeavor, make this an unusually useful book. He concludes by saying, "The beauty of the Hero's Journey model is that it not only describes a pattern in myths and fairytales, but it's also an accurate map of the territory one must travel to become a writer or for that matter, a human being."

CHARACTER DEVELOPMENT PROBLEMS

A common problem is the character who refuses to develop and becomes a bore even to his creator. It usually happens because characters are being conceived to illustrate ideas rather than to dramatize situations, that is, to struggle with issues and conflicts. Contrast this with what Stuart Dybek says about his story "We Didn't" published in *Best American Short Stories 1994:* "As image begot anecdote, and as anecdote begot characters, I decided to let the characters take over and tell their story. They would have anyway, whether I'd let them or not." Authors commonly feel like servants to their characters but this can only happen when the characters are charged up with needs and desires that render them highly active. By the way, the annual *Best American Short Stories* series always contains superb and inspiring examples of short (and not so short) tales.

What to do when the characters are grounded? First find out what they want, what they are trying to get or do, and note down for each scene what they should be trying to get from each other or from their situation. Be aware that all interesting characters contain contradictory elements. Just think of who it is in your group that everyone always ends up talking about, and what it is that gets discussed. It's always what you can't reconcile, what doesn't make sense in the person's character.

Make sure that every major character has interesting character flaws and that these are manifest in interesting and hazardous ways. The definition of a tragic figure is, after all, a character of magnitude with a fatal flaw. Flaws don't have to be fatal and characters don't have to be tragic, but they should be fresh, interesting, and above all active.

One way to develop ideas about your characters is to try fitting them into different theories of personality and to consider what in the description you haven't used. Astrology offers a whole system of personality types and destinies which can jolt your thinking and help break out of monolithic characterization. Another system is that of the Enneagram, an ancient psychological system that goes back to the Sufis. Don Richard Riso's *Personality Types* (Houghton Mifflin: Boston, 1987) outlines the system and considers character under nine basic types; the reformer, the helper, the status seeker, the artist, the thinker, the loyalist, the generalist, the leader, and the peacemaker. Each type is broken down by a great range of healthy and unhealthy characteristics, all of which offer a wealth of insight and developmental possibility for the screenwriter.

THE MOST COMMON FLAW

The research I've cited above—focusing as it does on the paradigms of drama—further confirms what all the screenwriting manuals proclaim: that above everything the central characters must be active, doing, seeking, and therefore in conflict, rather than illustrative, passive or acted upon.

In my experience most screenplay failures lead back to many writers' limited concept of self. It is undoubtedly a widespread cultural flaw shared by writers who seem to see themselves (and often their point-of-view character) as someone acted upon, someone unable to significantly influence his or her destiny. If this is your sense of yourself, then you are going to create characters in that mold. In these scripts, if something good happens it is because of good luck rather than something earned by a character's action. If something bad happens, it is because bad things always happen to good people.

I have wondered why the culture of passivity is so pervasive. Maybe it's because the history of exploited and subject people renders down to a series of warnings about not antagonizing "them." Even the facial expressionlessness of some cultures, I suspect, can be traced back to forms of slavery where the expression of any emotion implied independence and led to immediate punishment. Coming myself from a nation that is still emotionally feudal, and knowing that a part of myself is conditioned to passive victimhood, I have pondered the question often, both personally and professionally. As a European I have been acculturated to a fatalism that is anathema to Americans. At a Munich film conference I heard a European filmmaker complain that the Americans had completely taken over the European film market because European films were too boring, and "because we don't know how to tell a story." I love too many European films to agree with the second statement, but the first—that American films dominate the cinema—is unassailable. It set me thinking about storytelling, and about the polarity between freewill and fatalism.

Why do world audiences prefer Hollywood fables? This can no longer be explained as it was in earlier decades as an international capitalist conspiracy. I believe the implications are more complex and interesting. Mankind has always had to fight against being overcome by fatalism, and as populations grow and the stress of competition increases, our personal significance diminishes. Each person must now resist the growing sense of being an anonymous supernumerary cog in a giant machine controlled by "them" somewhere else. Religion used to help us deal with this until Darwin convinced us we are just another species, red in tooth and claw from fighting to survive. Joseph Campbell's work seems to say that secular narrative is designed to help the individual deal with powerlessness. Folk tales about heroes remind both the teller and the listener that an individual has potential. But they also assert that the individual must acknowledge the moral laws of the universe if he or she is to merit regeneration.

An immigrant civilization like the United States, trying nobly to function under its extraordinarily visionary constitution, is by historic accident a laboratory of these values, and their antitheses. Freewill is an article of faith with Americans. An old-worlder like myself married to an American will frequently run up against reminders of a profound philosophical difference; under pressure I will hide behind irony and what I imagine is elegant fatalism; my American wife moves instead to combat and overcome the circumstances. An example: when I am ill I will generally accept what the hospital says it can do for me. But my wife goes into battle armed with pointed questions. Guess who uses more energy, and guess who gets better results from institutions.

The central question here, which matters enormously to writers, is whether to accept fate or whether to struggle against it. Neither course leads automatically toward better consequences. Revolution can be tragic and so can passive acceptance of circumstances. The only convincing explanation I've heard for the roots of the Holocaust points to passive acceptance of the authoritarian structure of the middle-European family at the time. Top-down authority in the home prepared people to unquestioningly carry out what their government told them to do, and to lack independent thinking or the moral authority to question their "duty."

Not surprisingly the energy of self-willed heroes comes as a refreshment to civilizations weary from bowing fatalistically to successive political and economic tyrannies. Somehow the better part of the American entertainment industry, so often led by immigrants with the energy and courage to reject the circumstances of their birth, has always offered visions—spurious or otherwise—of escape and moral triumph. This energy and optimism, widely equated with American immaturity, is in fact the very nutrient to be found in all of the world's folk drama.

Dramaturgy is really the art of orchestrating the contest of moral and emotional forces. For the competition to be serious, the contest needs to be balanced, as in Agnieszka Holland's *Europa, Europa* (1991) where the young Solomon Perel repeatedly escapes the dark force of his Nazi tormentors by a combination of luck and inspired ingenuity. Writers who on the contrary create from unexamined assumptions of passivity and victimhood deprive their audience of any true conflict. Since struggle is really the vehicle for moral and other debate, fatalism and victimhood tend to emasculate drama unless there are compensating elements, such as the elegaic beauty in Bo Widerberg's *Elvira Madigan* (1967) or Terence Malick's *Days of Heaven* (1978), or the humor in any of Woody Allen's "loser" films. This is partly the deficiency of film itself, which unlike literature cannot easily portray the inner reality of its characters.

So when you next look at a piece of writing for the screen, look critically at each scene and note down what the main characters are trying to do or get. Then survey the whole for the overall movement this creates. Use the tools describing paradigms to help you see deeper into the underlying dramatic structure, and to mend and reenergize what is deficient.

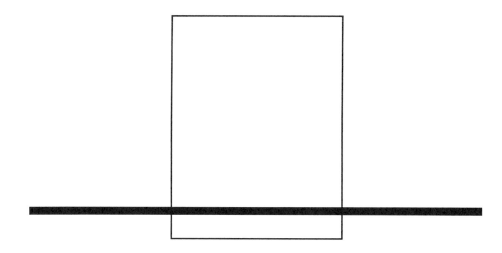

C·H·A·P·T·E·R 11

SCENE-WRITING EXERCISES

You can either use these short scene-writing exercises as you choose, or you can let chance give you the assignation. Then, facing unpredictable form and ingredients, you can test your flexibility and spontaneity. In a class or workshop the variety of interesting problems faced by the different writers will lead to interesting discussions about possibilities and difficulties that arise. Much useful learning can come out of these, as well as a greater sense of closeness and trust between writers.

TO PLAY

Work your way down the Lottery List gathering parameters for a piece of writing. H and T are heads and tails for that fairest of all taskmasters, the tossed coin. (Example: HHT = heads, heads, tails when you toss the coin three times). Whenever you throw a coin combination that is not listed, make a free choice for that section.

Before you begin, think of a number between 1 and 30 and remember it (you'll need it later).

SCENE-WRITING GAME

Words and/or Visual Language	H	Use dialogue sparingly
	T	Sound, music, effects but either no dialogue or not more than two lines
Gender of POV character	H	Same as yours
	T	Different from yours
Age of POV character	HHH	Same as yours
	HHT	2–9
	HTH	10–14
	HTT	15–20
	TTT	20–35
	TTH	35–50
	THT	50–65
	THH	Over 65
Genre	HHH	Comedy
	HHT	Tragedy
	HTH	Mystery
	HTT	Horror
	TTT	Western
	TTH	Sci-fi
	THT	Detective
	THH	Realism
Screen time	HH	One minute
	HT	Two minutes
	TT	Three minutes
	TH	Five to eight minutes
Scene crisis placement	HH	Near beginning
	HT	One third in
	TT	Two thirds in
	TH	At end
Number of beats	H	One per page
	T	Two or more
Number of characters	HH	One
	HT	Two
	TT	Three
	TH	You choose

Time	HHH	Morning
	HTH	Afternoon
	HHT	Late night
	HTT	Small hours
	TTT	Discontinuous (short overall time period)
	TTH	Discontinuous (long overall time period)
Main conflict	HH	Between characters
	HT	Between character & environment
	TT	Internal to POV character
	TH	Internal to other character

(Close your eyes, pick a number, 1 through 30, if you didn't do it when you began)

Title	1	First Time
	2	The Truth At Last
	3	Interlude with a Stranger
	4	Moment of Danger
	5	Last Bus
	6	No Turning Back
	7	Never forget
	8	Saved
	9	Finally
	10	Darkest Hour
	11	Embarrassing Moment
	12	Let It Be
	13	Paradise Lost
	14	Revisitation
	15	What Goes Around, Comes Around
	16	Live Now, Pay Later
	17	Bad Omens
	18	Go-Between
	19	Meant to Be
	20	Visitor
	21	Outsider
	22	Temptation
	23	First Love
	24	Persistence Pays
	25	Learning the Hard Way
	26	Jealousy

27	Memory
28	Bliss
29	Alienated
30	Speechless

When your first draft is finished

- put it away for a day or two
- reread it
- read it out loud, acting the movements and speaking the dialogue if there is any
- write more drafts
- economize on every word and every syllable
- shrink dialogue wherever possible
- replace dialogue with action wherever possible

Now rate your work, and have your class or any honest critics you can find rate it, according to these parameters (5 is highest in agreement, 1 or zero is lowest). Most of the criteria will clarify any scene in any screenplay.

SCENE ASSESSMENT CRITERIA

Characters	Gender identity of POV character is very convincing	0 1 2 3 4 5
	Each character pursues his/her own agenda through action	0 1 2 3 4 5
	The POV character's internal issues come across well	0 1 2 3 4 5
	What the POV character(s) tries to do or get really allows us to understand him/her/them	0 1 2 3 4 5
	The central characters are "round," that is, fully realized rather than "flat" support characters	0 1 2 3 4 5
	POV character's age is convincing in its concerns and characteristics	0 1 2 3 4 5
	All the characters have a dramatic function in the piece	0 1 2 3 4 5
	The characters each have different and characteristic actions	0 1 2 3 4 5
	There is really someone to like and care about here	0 1 2 3 4 5
Situation	The situation(s) developed from the scene title is original and compelling	0 1 2 3 4 5
Genre	The piece has a decided genre identity	0 1 2 3 4 5
	The character types really belong in this genre	0 1 2 3 4 5
	The story and the genre really complement each other	0 1 2 3 4 5

	The genre is fully utilized and explored	0 1 2 3 4 5
	The writer has imposed his/her own stamp on the norms	0 1 2 3 4 5
	The genre has been extended but not disabled by the writer's individual handling	0 1 2 3 4 5
Screen time	The piece feels neither too long nor too short	0 1 2 3 4 5
	The piece holds to its specified screen time	0 1 2 3 4 5
	It covers considerable ground for its screen time	0 1 2 3 4 5
Scene crisis placement	The high, or turning point of the scene came where it was supposed to come	0 1 2 3 4 5
	The lead up to it was wholly credible and well paced	0 1 2 3 4 5
	The lead up built tension	0 1 2 3 4 5
	The resolution after the scene crisis was convincing and well paced	0 1 2 3 4 5
Number of beats	The writer built in the required number	0 1 2 3 4 5
	Each beat was earned and effective	0 1 2 3 4 5
	There was a developing pressure leading up to the beat	0 1 2 3 4 5
	The beat caused changed consciousness (measurable in their behavior) by at least one character	0 1 2 3 4 5
Setting(s)	The settings are interesting and organic to the characters' situations	0 1 2 3 4 5
	Time and environment are evident and necessary	0 1 2 3 4 5
	The settings are used by the characters, not just included as backdrop	0 1 2 3 4 5
	The settings feel authentic	0 1 2 3 4 5
Conflict	Major issue or conflict is evident	0 1 2 3 4 5
	Conflict is organic to characters and their situation, not contrived	0 1 2 3 4 5
	Forces in opposition come to a point of confrontation	0 1 2 3 4 5
	Conflict results in material issues and changes	0 1 2 3 4 5
Plot	Necessary factual information is implied or evident	0 1 2 3 4 5
	Exposition is artfully disguised, not verbalized	0 1 2 3 4 5
	Events generate a forward movement	0 1 2 3 4 5
	Story logic and character motivation is impeccable	0 1 2 3 4 5
	Scene has energy and tension throughout	0 1 2 3 4 5
Structure	Time progression is well handled	0 1 2 3 4 5
	Events happen in their most effective order	0 1 2 3 4 5
	There is a clear sense of developmental phases through the scene	0 1 2 3 4 5

Theme	Thematic concerns develop naturally out of events we see	0 1 2 3 4 5
	The piece implies a substantial comment on the piece's thematic concerns	0 1 2 3 4 5
Dialogue	The dialogue rings true	0 1 2 3 4 5
	Each character speaks with his/her own voice and vocabulary	0 1 2 3 4 5
	There isn't a redundant word or syllable	0 1 2 3 4 5
Voice	The piece comes from the heart as well as the head	0 1 2 3 4 5
	The piece feels individual not derivative or imitative	0 1 2 3 4 5
	One can feel an individual human spirit behind the conception of this scene	0 1 2 3 4 5
Impact	Conflict is credible enough to have moral dimension	0 1 2 3 4 5
	Someone, however minimally, changes and grows here	0 1 2 3 4 5
	You really want to know what happens next	0 1 2 3 4 5

Discussion: Be a tough judge when you score. Nobody gains from feel-good criticism. If you don't know each other well enough to be candid, score the scene as a group and also talk to the writer as a group. No one person will feel responsible and the writer gets something like an audience reaction.

Numerical scores matter less than those aspects that were scored exceptionally high or low. Discuss the reasons you think are responsible. This feedback, and seeing how your readers' reactions match your intentions as the writer, are the real learning.

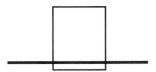

CHECKLIST, PART III
WRITING AND STORY DEVELOPMENT

The recommendations and points summarized here are only those most salient or the most commonly overlooked. To find more about them or anything else, go to the table of contents at the beginning of this part, or try the Index at the back of the book.

Writing as a Process
- investigate what differing techniques and permutations of characters can offer by doing the game of chance writing assignments in this chapter
- write sparingly and leave actions open for the actors to solve

- know what the characters are trying to do or get every step of the way
- what is each character's major conflict?
- use dialogue as the vehicle for action by one character on another
- write in step outline form first, NOT screenplay
- first drafts are dreadful
- write no matter what
- circle around between screenplay, step outline, premise and revise each as necessary
- don't be afraid to write by association, to let things happen and see where they lead
- really make us see the characters
- work to create a mood
- write visually and behaviorally, which is where the cinema excels
- write for the silent screen and let yourself resort to dialogue later
- distill a dramatic premise for the piece and one for each scene
- don't produce characters just as you need them; they have to be written in earlier
- pitch your idea to anyone who'll listen. You'll learn a lot from their reactions
- make your audience laugh, make them cry, but make them wait (for explanations)
- keep the audience in suspense and anticipation about as much as possible (but not past the point of patience)
- never use a line where an action could function as well
- don't cave in to critics. Wait to see what you feel is true.

The Screenplay

- to begin with, write and direct your own short works, three to ten minutes maximum
- choose subjects you really care about but avoid autobiography unless you have at least five years' distance on the events
- look for a reliable, compatible writing collaborator
- write about what calls to you, but write about that which you need to explore
- first work in step outline; do NOT write a script right away
- start developing the premise once you have the events mapped out
- use a computer and rewrite the piece as successive drafts
- just keep writing and rewriting regularly, don't wait for inspiration
- work on your characters first and foremost. Interesting characters are bound, sooner or later, to develop into a good story if you let them
- aim to tell a good story—don't set out to preach or advocate ideas
- practice pitching your idea (describing it briefly and well)

- use standard screenplay or split screen formats only
- write behaviorally as if for the silent screen and allow yourself dialogue later
- what do you want your audience to feel? And what do you want them to think?
- do a version of the script with a third column that details what the Observer (and therefore the audience) must notice
- write a premise
- write a treatment

Adapting a Book, Play, or Short Story

- adapting anything well-known presents many problems and you will probably have to stay faithful to the original
- cutting and compressing are always acceptable
- a free adaptation is more courageous, if the piece warrants it in translating to the screen
- short stories often make great adaptations, but get copyright clearance, and make sure you are choosing for cinematic, not literary, reasons
- you can base a film on adaptations or improvisations from your actors' lives
- a documentary approach involving research can be a potent way of laying the foundations for a good script

Story Development

- early versions of stories always need development
- make sure you begin each new round of work with an up-to-date step outline
- classify your tale according to the nearest basic dramatic theme and situation, any myths, legends, folk tales that parallel yours
- put the outline of your screenplay next to its archetypal collaterals and see what you can learn from an outline of the other work
- most stories are forms of a journey, so check your piece out against the archetypal Hero's Journey steps
- make sure major characters have interesting character flaws and contradictions
- apply the scene assessment criteria (end of Chapter 11)
- submit your work to as many objective readers as you can get, making sure that they don't lose their objectivity through reading more than one or two drafts.

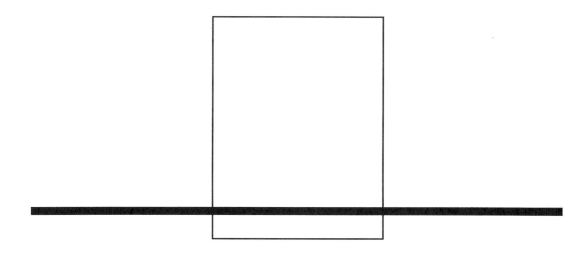

P·A·R·T IV

AESTHETICS AND AUTHORSHIP

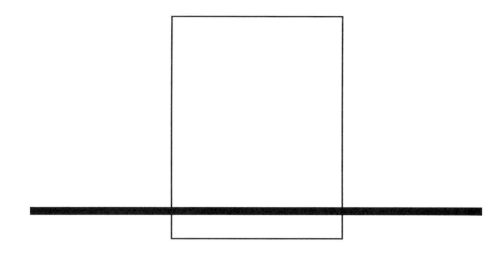

C·H·A·P·T·E·R 12

POINT OF VIEW

In film a point-of-view shot is a straightforward view from a character's physical location in the scene. But film also has its own version of literary point of view, a more diffuse impression in the audience of sharing a critical and psychological perspective on the events of the story. Though one can subjectively describe the point of view used in a scene, to say how it actually works is difficult, and how to control it harder still. This is because the screen does not affect us through a single channel like the language of literature. Language on the printed page is already complicated enough but at least it stands still while you analyze it. But film language is a complex interplay of moving images, each with an infinite content of words, symbols, sounds, color, movement, and music. How all interacts in our mind is simply beyond verbal analysis and formulation, but point of view is still within your influence and you should have ideas, intentions, and methods for controlling it.

Let's first look at how point of view works in the older and better studied medium of literature for some helpful parallels.

POINT OF VIEW IN LITERATURE

In literature there are two basic sources for a story's *narrating point of view*; one is *omniscient* and comes from outside the story, the other is by way of a *character within the story*.

OMNISCIENT POINT OF VIEW

The omniscient storyteller is outside the story and like God has unrestricted movement in time and place. An omniscient author can look into every aspect of the characters' past, present, and future and can even speak directly to the reader. A variation is the *self-effacing storyteller* who shows the tale without comment, remains essentially characterless, and expects us to make our own interpretation. Another variation allows a character within the story to have omniscient powers. This is easier to accept when the tale is in the past tense since the "tall tale" convention permits the narrator to affect greater knowledge and ability than would be credible in the events' present.

CHARACTER WITHIN THE STORY POINT OF VIEW

This is a more partisan and limited perspective routed through what characters in the tale experience, see, hear, and understand. The *naïve narrator* is one who either doesn't understand the implications of his situation or pretends not to. There is also, as we have said above, a tradition of omniscience for a participating character, who is usually heroic or outsize in some other way.

TYPES OF NARRATIVE AND NARRATIVE TENSION

There are two types or classes of narrative in literature. One is *simple narrative* which is primarily functional and supplies an exposition of events, usually in chronological order. The other is *plot-driven narrative* which may depart from chronology in order to reveal the events according to the story's type and plot strategy. Crudely speaking, simple narrative exists to inform while plot-driven narrative sets out to entertain by generating tension. In literature, a rich source of tension lies between the story's elements and the attitudes that the storyteller implies or manifests toward them. Withholding information is therefore an important way of generating tension.

POINT OF VIEW IN FILM

Screen language has some advantages over literature but also some major handicaps. Like any other art medium it must elevate some aspects and suppress others, and although the screen image's comprehensiveness allows it to dispense with literature's lengthy tracts of exposition and set up a situation and a mood in seconds, photography's undiscriminating inclusiveness presents the eye with an endless catalogue of detail. Part of the function of framing, camera movement, and editing is to keep the eye where it should be, and discourage wandering. When wandering is encouraged, as in Antonioni's *L'Avventura* (1959), the environment begins to overwhelm the characters.

The filmmaker must therefore direct the audience's attention if it is to successfully disentangle the intended subject from a surfeit of the authentic. A caricaturist would face the same problem if requested to work through life photography instead of line drawing. The "insistently descriptive nature of the film image," as James Monaco calls it, inundates both subject and subtext with irrelevant detail. Ideas and authorial clarity are therefore much harder to achieve than in literature.

Maybe for this reason when I first saw Terence Malick's *Days of Heaven* (1978) in the cinema I saw a beautiful and moving film, but only from a later television viewing did I fully grasp its underlying themes and allusions. The reduced image and enhanced importance of sound allowed me to look *into* it rather than *at* it.

Cinema relying on montage to channel our attention, the natural strategy for its narrative style is an omniscient POV with allusions to the individual character's viewpoints. Indeed there is said to be only one pure character-within-the-film POV movie, the actor/director Robert Montgomery's 1947 mystery *The Lady in the Lake,* in which the camera is the detective Philip Marlowe and characters address the camera when talking to him. We see him only when he looks at himself in the mirror. I saw a 1950s TV play in England using the same device. Why the characters treat the main character (the camera, that is) strangely and patronizingly is only revealed at the end when the main character goes to shake hands and we see that his hand is black. Simultaneously one discovered what it must feel like to experience systematic discrimination.

However, documentary author/camera operators like Robb Moss or Ross McElwee do become characters in their own films, just as the camera tends to become an observing character in any *cinéma vérité* document.

Fiction films need the advantages of omniscience, but since German expressionist times have understood the power of a psychologically subjective vantage point. It remains easier to imply what a character notices and feels than it is for the audience to explore what this really means to him. Let's look at the variations in POV available to the filmmaker and examine their authorial implication.

THE CONTROLLING POINT OF VIEW

The controlling point of view of a film is usually that of a central character. In *Anna Karenina* it would probably be Anna's but it could be Karenin's or anyone else's. In the novel *Wuthering Heights* the story is ostensibly told by a sympathetic servant who acts as a surrogate mother in a motherless household.

Film like literature often temporarily switches POV whenever it usefully augments the viewer's perceptions. This can be achieved through parallel action, through a choice of angle, or by subjective coverage that places us with the alternate character. Still more subtly, the switch can be made by an interaction that invokes our sympathy and needs no attention-guiding technique such as a special angle or shot. POV is after all intended to create an empathic insight into a character's feelings and thoughts—it isn't only what he or she sees.

Some films, like Truffaut's *Jules and Jim* (1962) or Alan Pakula's *Sophie's Choice* (1982) use a character's first-person voice-over narration to drive the film and locate its focus. Where there is no verbal narration, the controlling point of view is seldom made obvious. More often it is rooted in the consciousness of the person or persons at the center of the work. This follows the lead of omniscient literature. After Lewis Carroll's heroine passes through the looking glass, she enters a world of inverted logic that we experience from Alice's perspective. To the child in us, *Alice in Wonderland's* looming, swollen personages are alarming magnifications of those encountered in our own youth. Alice's bizarre world takes most of our attention, but through the way she copes with it we begin to empathically see into her psyche. What she confronts, and how she deals with it are the two sides of a single coin. This is more easily seen in Victor Fleming's *The Wizard of Oz* (1939). Dorothy makes a journey similar to Alice's through a bewitched landscape. She is joined by the Lion, the Tin Man, and the Scarecrow—alter egos whom she inspires to continue but which represent the threatened aspects of Self. When Dorothy awakes at the end of the movie we understand that her dream has been the means of reordering aspects of herself. Oz is therefore the setting for an allegorical quest for selfhood in which she seeks answers she needs in her "real" life on the farm.

Alice and Dorothy, the locus of attention in their particular worlds, are also surrogates for ourselves, and each heroine acts as a lens of temperament. As so often in stories, each character's journey begins by irreversibly crossing a threshold (as in Joseph Campbell's analysis of folk stories). Each character is the lens through which we see their world, and each creates and passes trials that justify their changed world and make it essential to their growth.

In *Kasper Hauser: Every Man for Himself and God Against All* (1974) Werner Herzog does something similar. In a setting of early nineteenth-century Germany, the viewer accompanies a young man into daylight for the first time. Like the feral boy in Truffaut's *Wild Child* (1969), Kasper has practically never seen, spoken to, eaten with, or walked among other human beings. Modeled on an actual wild child of the period, Kasper is truly innocent. He confronts all the beauty, complexity, and hypocrisy of civilization. In accelerated succession he suffers the amazements of childhood and the child's sense of bereavement at discovering the world's moral bankruptcy. It is an astonishing, sustained parable that makes one reexperience the familiar through Kasper's naiveté of spirit. But one also gets perspectives on Kasper through the professor of logic, the pastor, the traveling showman, the dandy, and the kindly family who teach him basic table manners—all those who try to help, classify, civilize or exploit the strange young man. By juxtaposition their views heighten our sense of Kasper, and his innocence is ultimately defined by the puzzled, derisive, or antithetical reactions of those who want to change him.

Many films establish powerful worlds through the eyes of young people, notably de Sica's *Bicycle Thief* (1949), Ray's *Pather Panchali* (1954), Truffaut's *400 Blows* (1959), Saura's *Cria* (1977), Schlöndorff's *The Tin Drum* (1979), Babenco's *Pixote* (1981), Bergman's *Fanny and Alexander* (1983), John Boorman's *Hope and Glory* (1987), and John Sayles' *The Secret of Roan Inish* (1995).

Notable films that create equally powerful worlds through an adult's point of view are Truffaut's *The Story of Adèle H.* (1975), Resnais' *Providence* (1977), Scorsese's *King of Comedy* (1982), Wenders' *Paris, Texas* (1984), Forman's *Amadeus* (1984), Luis Puenzo's *The Official Story* (1985), Paul Leduc's *Frida* (1987), Terence Davies' *Distant Voices, Still Lives* (1989), and Jane Campion's unnervingly visceral *The Piano* (1993).

VARIATIONS IN POINT OF VIEW

Variations in point of view not only show the physical viewpoint of a secondary character, but also elicit an emotional understanding, that is, they make us feel what that character may be feeling at a particular moment. Any good piece of fiction brings the minor characters alive, makes us feel that they too have lives, feelings, and agendas to fulfill.

FIGURE 12-1 —————————————————————————————————

Survival through the eyes of a street urchin in Babenco's *Pixote* (courtesy New Yorker Films).

BIOGRAPHICAL POINT OF VIEW

Biographical point of view implies the critical study of a central character who stands for larger qualities and ideas. *Kasper Hauser* focuses on the progress of a central character and keeps him center stage most of the time. The film's philosophical argument emerges from Kasper's collisions with different small-town factions, and by amassing a catalogue of their reactions. Boldly and poetically, the film imparts the violence of Kasper's sensations and of his chaotic inner life, beginning with a lyrical shot of a field of blowing corn. Over pastoral music a quotation is superimposed: "But can you not hear the dreadful screaming all around that people usually call silence?" At a stroke, Herzog establishes the juxtaposition of summer beauty and inner despair that will tear Kasper apart.

In the simple narrative sections we see Kasper objectively in his interactions with others, but Herzog's issue-driven plot and his use of music imply what Kasper feels, and cause us to infer Kasper's subjective experience. Herzog the storyteller frames and juxtaposes these viewpoints and intersperses sections of textual quotation to imply that Kasper is a tragically undefended and innocently good Everyman. This makes an impassioned and poetical comparison between the nobility of a human's potential, and the muddle and corruption we call civilization.

FIGURE 12-2

A novelist transforms his family into the characters of dark fiction in Resnais' *Providence* (courtesy Almi Distributors).

What could be more movingly appropriate from a child of World War II Germany?

CHARACTER WITHIN THE FILM

A film's apparent vantage point may come from a character within the film who directs us through the events, maybe by narrating them. Some of the most moving guides are children. In Malick's *Days of Heaven* (1978) there is a voice-over narration by the fugitive's young sister. The country lawyer's daughter is the narrator of Mulligan's *To Kill a Mockingbird* (1963), and the boy houseguest writing in his diary narrates Losey's *The Go-Between* (1971). In Truffaut's *Jules and Jim* (1961) the narrator is a novelist and participant in the love triangle. His limitations and distorted perceptions make us aware of his subjectivity and vulnerability, and this creates a rising sense of dramatic pressure. A character in extremity may perceive magic and monsters, and to portray these is really to dramatize that character's state of mind.

MAIN CHARACTER'S IMPLIED POINT OF VIEW

In mainstream omniscient cinema characters and their issues are often established through a meaningful juxtaposition of realistic events. Their world is "normal" and undistorted by how they perceive it. Lacking verbal narration, each charac-

FIGURE 12-3 ⎯⎯⎯⎯⎯⎯⎯⎯⎯⎯⎯⎯⎯⎯⎯⎯⎯⎯⎯⎯⎯⎯⎯⎯⎯⎯⎯⎯

Leduc's highly visual *Frida:* love and art through the transcendent vision of the Mexican painter Frida Kahlo (courtesy New Yorker Films).

ter's point of view must be implied rather than verbalized. The coolness and distance of this mode allow the audience to think as much as feel. Audience members long remain nonidentifying observers but eventually merge with the main characters through empathy. Jiri Menzel's *Closely Watched Trains* (1966) is about a youth adapting to his first job in a railroad station. Obsessed by the shameful fact of his virginity, he finds himself surrounded by the sex lives of others. This seems more the humor of the gods than a situation he has influenced. Tony Richardson's *A Taste of Honey* (1961), on the other hand, focuses on a provincial teenager who at a time of great loneliness gets pregnant, is abandoned by the father, and then befriended for a while by a homosexual boy. Showing how she is led by raw emotion from one situation to another, the film credits her destiny to the random interaction of environment, chance, and character. Her world, like that of the young Czech railwayman, is still an alien environment with which she must struggle, but she bears more responsibility for her destiny. This film (on which I worked as cutting room assistant) lost some of its documentary power in the transition from rushes to edited final version. Editing increases what we are able to see, but can also fragment the inherent power of a moment.

Each of Hitchcock's two most famous films hinges on the fallibility of a POV character's judgment. In *Rear Window* (1954) an injured photographer confined to his room is compelled to look at the building opposite and becomes so convinced that a murder has taken place that he takes on some of the guilt of the murderer. In *Psycho* (1960) Marion Crane battles to deny her instincts that something malign is afoot in the Bates Motel. In each case, the audience must constantly decide the nature of reality in relation to appearances, until at the end Hitchcock provides the famous keys that unlock the suspense.

Very different in intention is Fassbinder's *The Marriage of Maria Braun* (1978), which shows a German war bride working her way from rags to riches while always awaiting the return of her husband to begin the marriage proper. Maria seems to personify Germany's return from destruction and to imply that its passage to wealth is really a lengthening deferral of moral reckoning in connection with the Hitler years.

Two films about women center upon very different concerns. Teshigahara's *Woman of the Dunes* (1964) tells of a woman trapped in her house in a sand dune, who must dig constantly to prevent her home from being obliterated by the drifting sand. Villagers lure a male tourist into sharing her life and her fate. The film is notable for its abstract and erotically charged photography, so the viewer is constantly striving to relate the close-up shapes he sees to their parent whole— arm, knee, breast, sand dune, eddy, kitchen vessel—each shape threatening to engulf the viewer just as the woman's sandy environment threatens to engulf her. The film leaves a palpable feeling that sexuality and survival are symbiotic, as of course they are in Nature.

In another world altogether is the heroine of Polanski's *Tess* (1980), the film of Thomas Hardy's ballad-like novel. Tess, a country girl, is seduced by one man and later abandoned when her new husband learns about it. While the novel constantly but subtly thrusts the reader into understanding Tess's particular awareness, Polanski's version fails to find a cinematic equivalent to Hardy's poetic language so the viewer remains distanced. Further sabotaging the adaptation is the uncomfortable fact that the seducer is the only complex and interesting character.

DUAL POINTS OF VIEW

In Malick's *Badlands* (1974), Penn's *Bonnie and Clyde* (1967), and Godard's *Pierrot le Fou* (1965), the subjects are partnerships and so there are two point-of-view characters. All three films involve road journeys that end in self-destruction. In the two American films, the partnerships seem to exist so as to define male and female roles within a dissident or criminal subculture, while Godard's work uses the same self-immolating subculture as a vehicle to explore the incompatibilities between the male and female psyches. Each film studies the tensions generated between their characters, and uses the way each step is (or is not) resolved to energize the next move. *Pierrot le Fou* in particular makes a rewarding study of dramatic form, because character and dramatic tension are developed from action between the characters rather than from pressures applied externally by the chase.

Wim Wenders' *Alice in the Cities* (1974) is another journey but the dialogue is between characters initially quite unequal: a nine-year-old girl and the reluctant journalist who helps her search for her grandmother. Managing to avoid the pitfalls of kitsch sentiment the film explores the initial gulf between adults and children. By creating two lost and uncertain characters of wonderful dignity it shows how adults and children can achieve trust and emotional parity.

Gregory Nava's *El Norte* (1983) alternates between the vantage points of sibling accomplices as brother and sister escape Guatemala for the promised land of

FIGURE 12-4

A child's and an adult's world compared in Wenders' *Alice in the Cities* (courtesy Museum of Modern Art/Film Stills Archive).

El Norte (North America). As one episode of exploitation and disillusion follows another, one begins to realize that the siblings are also archetypal figures representing a whole class of vulnerable immigrants.

    Other films alternate points of view in order to mobilize a struggle between dialectical opposites. In Woody Allen's comedy of manners *Annie Hall* (1977) the duel is between Allen and Diane Keaton who are each neurotically self-protective New Yorkers; in Bergman's *Scenes from a Marriage* (1974) the tension is between the sundered halves of a marriage gone bad. Bergman's *Autumn Sonata* (1978) instead explores what is "mysterious, complicated and charged with emotion" in a mother/daughter relationship. A most imaginative and heightened duel comes in Babenco's *Kiss of the Spider Woman* (1985) in which a heterosexual political prisoner and his despised transvestite cellmate spar their way toward understanding and trust.

MULTIPLE POINTS OF VIEW

In Altman's two films *M*A*S*H* (1970) and *Nashville* (1975), as well as in Tanner's *Jonah Who Will Be 25 in the Year 2000* (1976), individual point of view is deliberately excluded because each character is meant to be a fragment within a mosaic. All three films have a cast of characters reaching into double figures, and all focus on the patterns that emerge during a collective endeavor rather than on the consciousness and destiny of any individual. This concern with the flow and texture of collective destiny reaches back to Lewis Milestone's *All Quiet on the Western Front* (1930), which follows a group of young German recruits during World War I from their schoolroom to their ignoble and futile deaths on the battlefield. Like Oliver Stone's *Platoon* (1987), it shows the disintegration of self-worth that comes with disillusion. But while Chris Taylor in Stone's movie remains an individual with individual choices, Milestone's boy soldiers are one by one stripped of life like cogs in a self-destroying machine.

One of Bergman's most remarkable films, *Cries and Whispers* (1972), sets in motion a dark web of guilt, blame, fear, and remorse spun by a family of women who attempt to close around one of their members dying of cancer. Within the lavish display of emotions expressed by the three sisters there glides the silent, caring servant Anna. Late in the film she cradles her dying mistress, regressed to childlike terror, against her bare bosom in a gesture that is stunning in its elemental tenderness. It stands in shocking contrast to the narcissistic emotion issuing from the sisters destined to survive.

AUTHORIAL POINT OF VIEW

Authorial point of view is difficult to separate from films containing individual points of view, but here for the sake of argument are three very different films, each dealing with ideas about humanity rather than the individuality of any protagonist.

Michael Cacoyannis' version of Euripides' *Iphigenia* (1978) is the least stagey of his trilogy that also includes *Elektra* (1961) and *The Trojan Women* (1971). By exposing a family to pitiless pressures, the film shows how Agamemnon rationalizes sacrificing his beloved daughter Iphigenia in return for favorable conditions in his war against the Trojans. Grievously betrayed by her father, Iphigenia must accept that the choice he has made was agonizing and for the larger good of their people. With a switch in time and place, you have the dissolution of a Tennessee Williams family. In both, the characters are more archetypal than individual. A similar thread runs through the genre of the western, which produced many archetypes and many stars but few deeply realized screen characters.

Volker Schlöndorff's adaptation of Heinrich Böll's novel *The Lost Honor of Katharina Blum* (1975) centers on a blameless young woman who harbored a fugitive radical. She is so hounded by a yellow press reporter that she finally acts contrary to her gentle, conforming nature and shoots him. So concerned is the film with the policeman's and journalist's distorting perspectives on Katharina's character that she remains strangely unindividualized even though she's onscreen for most of the film's 102 minutes. By the very fact that it fails to arouse identification with its central character the film is polemically successful and raises disturbing issues about rights—those of the state, of the public to news at any cost, and of the individual to privacy.

Orson Welles' *Citizen Kane* (1941) is also about perceptions and distortions in a person's character, but achieves its portrait by focusing on the late Charles Foster Kane as an enigma to be unraveled. While Katharina was a small person caught in the momentary spotlight of state security phobia, Kane is the great man whose driving motives remain tantalizingly obscure to the little people in his shadow. The key to Kane's underlying mood of unassuagable deprivation is revealed, and only to the audience, through the symbol of a sled that epitomized the loss of his home to Kane as a boy. It also lets Welles clinch his argument that pain fuels human creativity.

These storyteller point-of-view films, concerned with the mapping of cause and effect, employ characters to exemplify patterns of behavior rather than as objects of sympathy, although of course we must sympathize with the characters to care about the ideas they exemplify. The same might be said of Hitchcock's films, which dwell on the subtle, misleading interplay of human constants rather than seeking to confer recognition on human individuality. These dramatists are polemicists whose passions are of the head more than the heart.

Where a director's intelligence and character are repeatedly stamped in a body of work, one can trace the recurring signs of vision and philosophy. This we think of as the directorial point of view. Like that of a character, it may be interestingly polarized and in conflict. A storyteller like the novelist F. Scott Fitzgerald, who also wrote for Hollywood, may create a world of which he disapproves. Though Fitzgerald participated enthusiastically in the hedonism of the 1920s flapper generation, part of him loathed its privileges and egocentricity, and this ambivalence fueled his writing. Such fifth column critique is not unusual.

AUDIENCE POINT OF VIEW

There is still another point of view to be considered: that of the audience which measures the storyteller, his or her film, and the assumptions the film expresses. For us to look at a patriotic World War II film is to experience an eerie gap between our own values and those guiding the film's values. Individually, and collectively as an audience, we have our own perspective into which we fit the entirety of an artwork, including the authorial frame of reference within which it was originally fashioned.

SUMMING UP

The concept of point of view can be likened to a set of Russian dolls: the audience's point of view encloses the storyteller's (that is, the film's) point of view; the storyteller's encloses the point-of-view character's; and this in turn embraces that of the subsidiary characters, each of whom holds up a mirror to the others. It is the most difficult aspect of narrative art to conceive and control, and in many workaday films it often emerges by default, resulting from the subject in hand and the idiosyncrasies of the actors and team that made the film.

Point of view is difficult but important to bring under control. Perhaps the most practical approach is to think in terms of applied subjectivity. To expose this we might ask the following questions at any point while planning how to tell the tale:

- Whose mind is doing the seeing?
- What are the idiosyncrasies in the way they see?
- What disparity is revealed between their world and that of others?
- What is the function of a particular moment of subjective revelation?

We amassed four different point-of-view dimensions. Starting this time within the film frame, and backing away from the screen toward the audience, we find:

MAIN CHARACTER(S) OR CONTROLLING POINT OF VIEW

1. Main character(s) or controlling point of view, whose subjectivity affects the mood of both what is shown and how it is shown. This controlling point of view influences both content and form of the film and shows up in a number of ways:
    a. It may be explicit in the form of a character who speaks as a narrator to the audience, but more often it is
    b. implicit as we empathize with a particular character or characters. Usually artful *mise-en-scène* contributes heavily (see Chapter 27: Mise-en-Scène Basics).
    c. The characters' attention is usually directed within the action toward each other, perhaps in a dialogue, but may be
    d. a retrospective point of view (the body of the film is perhaps a diary or memoir) or
    e. a character may directly address the audience, as Woody Allen does.

SUBSIDIARY CHARACTERS' POINTS OF VIEW

2. Subsidiary characters' points of view, whose subjectivity is called upon where useful to heighten or counterpoint that of the controlling character. Sometimes a movie lacks a central character or characters, and concentrates on a texture of equal points of view.

AUTHORIAL OR STORYTELLER'S POINT OF VIEW

3. Authorial or storyteller's point of view. Authorship of a film is a collective effort, like that of an orchestra under a conductor, so the origin of authorial viewpoints remains uncertain; one cannot know that an actor rather than the director thought of a particular and effective feature. Authorial point of view has two main polarities which often overlap:
    a. A personal or *auteur* point of view in which the film expresses a central personality and attitude toward the characters and their story.
    b. In genre, authorial point of view is vested more diffusely in the handling of archetypes and archetypal forms, such as the film noir or the western.

AUDIENCE POINT OF VIEW

4. Audience point of view is the critical distance the audience senses between itself and the film. Escapist films, which seek to engulf the audience in sensation, lead the viewer to identify with a heroic figure and annihilate the audience's critical identity. Other directors, following the lead of Brecht in the theater, have stressed the cinema as an arbitrary show, not an escapist's substitute for reality. They intend the audience *not* to identify but to attain a heightened and critical perspective.

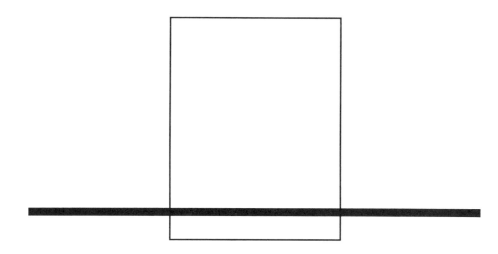

GENRE, CONFLICT, AND DIALECTICS

MAKING THE VISIBLE SIGNIFICANT

Throughout this book I have suggested that memorable cinema communicates an integrated point of view, not just as the occasional garnish by subjective camera angle or interior monologue, but as a feeling of access to a fellow spirit's inward and outward vision. We're talking not about the heroic and idealized characters enshrined by the star system, but rather the cinema through which one recognizes unfinished business in one's own life or in one's culture. Charles Foster Kane, for example, is a man blinded by his own rhetoric and corrupted by the power he has gathered, but *Citizen Kane* (1941) shows how much his actions are directed by the hurt child within. The lovers in David Lean's *Brief Encounter* (1945), at first stuffy and ludicrous, gain stature and poignancy as we comprehend the degree to which each belongs within a code of honor that places loyalty to commitments above passion and experiment. Somewhere in our lives, each of us has done the same, and suffered as much as these.

How should one go about reflecting such things on the screen? Robert Richardson goes to the heart of the problem filmmakers face in comparison with writers: "Literature often has the problem of making the significant somehow visible, while film often finds itself trying to make the visible significant" (*Literature and Film* [Bloomington, IN: Indiana University Press, 1969]). Unfortunately, film's surfeit of realistic detail invites the audience to look no deeper than the surfaces rendered so minutely and attractively by the camera. And this can lead us to make simplistic valuations. In Claude Jutra's *Dreamspeaker* (1978) the delinquent boy running away from the fire he has set in a remedial institution seems to be doing the inevitable, and the fact that he is sheltered by two Native Americans is a simple act of human goodness. By looking deeper, however, one sees that the story is really a parable comparing modern, clinical concepts of human care with ancient, animistic ones.

Film has the uniquely modern mission of finding and validating the spiritual underlying the material world. But Jutra had to solve the problem of making what is visible—the film's actions and its events—also function as the vehicle for a more probing, metaphysical inquiry. There are many subtle ways, of course, that film authorship can draw our attention to a film's subtext, but without an astute use of film language an underlying discourse can go completely unnoticed. Conversely if it is delivered in the wrong way, it may seem too literary or intellectually rarefied to raise its head amid the exuberant physicality of the material world.

Literature, portable as it is and consumed contemplatively at one's own pace, is still a superior forum for intellectual discourse. Here we must admit that screen drama, moving at a predetermined pace and compelled to approach the spirit by way of the physical, is handicapped. Though the VCR allows people to interrupt the movie and reexamine a passage, there's no evidence that anyone except the film buff does this. By its nature, film is sensory impressions that take root in the memory and imagination, inhabiting and haunting us for days or even years. Some screen works beckon one to return for the rest of one's life, like profound and uncompleted relationships.

The fiction film, the documentary, and the short story all have something in common. All are consumed at a sitting and so perhaps carry on the oral tradition which at one time carried (with religion) the entire burden of the ordinary person's education. Like the oral tale, these forms seem better suited to representing history that is personally felt and experienced rather than issues and ideas in abstraction. Surely any short, immediate form must entertain if it is to connect with the emotional and imaginative life of a mass audience. Like all entertainers, the filmmaker has a precarious economic existence, and either understands his audience or goes hungry. Richardson argues convincingly that the vitality and optimism of the cinema in contrast to other twentieth-century artforms is a result of its collaborative authorship and dependency upon public response. It would be foolish to claim that the appreciation of the common people is paramount, but surely the strength and endurance of ancient structures in modern cinema should remind us how much we share with the unacademic and intuitive tastes of our forebears.

Actually, the ordinary person's tastes and instincts—yours and mine—are not simple at all, but highly cultivated and accultured. But because we seldom discuss them or use them to make statements through art, we lack confidence when it is time to consciously live by them. Making a film is exciting precisely because it forces one to expose perceptions and judgments—for an audience and for oneself. The cinema's strength and popularity lies with its power to make an audience see and feel from someone else's point of view. In the cinema we see through different eyes and experience visions other than our own. For significant sections of the world, recently divested of thousands of years of spiritual beliefs, this is a reminder of community and something beyond self, whose value cannot be underestimated. Just as importantly, the best cinema is relativistic, that is, it allows us to experience other, related but opposing points of view. Used responsibly this is an immensely civilizing force to offset the conformity imposed by merchandisers striving to normalize us in every imaginable sphere.

OPTIONS

Anyone planning even the shortest film is forced to make some fundamental aesthetic choices at the outset. These are by no means free since all films depend on screen conventions. There are choices in screen language but other choices are driven by the type of story. Storytelling has deep roots that precede film, printing, and even written history. Undoubtedly literary convention owes most of its forms to those developed in the oral tale, which I contend is nearer to theater and cinema than is literature. Let's examine the idea of story as we experience it on the screen.

At its best the screen exercises our consciousness so successfully that a recently seen movie can afterward feel more like personal experience. Through the screen we enter an unfamiliar world or see the familiar in a new way. We share the intimate being of people who are braver, funnier, stronger, angrier, more beautiful, more vulnerable, or more beset with danger and tragedy than we are. Two hours of concentrating upon a good movie is two hours during which we set aside the apparent unchangeability of our own lives, assume other identities and live through a different reality. This world can be wonderfully dark and depressing, light or idealizing, or one that plumbs the unanswered questions of the present with wit and intelligence. We emerge from a "good" movie energized and refreshed in spirit.

This cathartic contact with the trials of the human spirit is a human need no less fundamental than eating, breathing, or making love. It is the essence of living fully. In our daily lives an excess of emotional movement or a lack of it will send us to the arts looking for reflected light. Quite simply, art, of which the cinema is the newest form, nourishes us in spirit by engaging us in surrogate emotional experience and implying what patterns lie behind it. It helps us make sense out of our past, helps us deal with our present, and prepares us for what might be coming. It shows us that what seemed isolatingly personal is really inside the mainstream of human experience. Art allows us to pass into new realities, become "other," and yet know we belong to the human family.

All art grows out of what went before it, even when the artist is deemed highly original. This means that you must choose an area in which to work, a language through which to speak to an audience, and perhaps some changes or variations that you want to make to the genre. Pushing the envelope of form cannot be done unless you are intimate with the conventions and the reasons they exist.

POINT OF VIEW AND GENRE

While realism presents a story in documentary fashion as interesting events in a world the audience accepts as real or typical, a genre projects us into a special world running under particular conditions. A slapstick or screwball comedy, a gothic romance, or a *film noir* each have emphases and limitations that are well understood by the audience. These arise from the area of life the genre deals with, but also from the heightened and selective perceptions of its protagonists. There is nothing inherently unreal, untruthful, or "distorted" about a genre once you accept that in life people not only contend with reality but also help to create it through selectivity and projecting their own perceptions. If "character is fate," then a collection of characters can collusively create their own reality. History and the newspapers are full of examples.

We enjoy genres like historical romance, sci-fi, or buddy movies because we need to experience worlds beyond the suffocatingly rational one of our normality. It's important to enter a "what if" world running under selectively altered circumstances. We buy into it by emotional choice, just as we learn the most vivid lessons from emotional immersion rather than from intellectual instruction. From watching Tolstoy's *Anna Karenina* we expect to enter the adulterous heroine's sufferings, not simply be told she is immoral. We want to know how it feels to be a young woman married to a stuffy older man, to feel isolated and loveless, and then to be approached by a romantic admirer. What can it be like to be tempted— and then viewed by society as the temptress?

When a movie is good, we imaginatively experience these conditions and come away expanded in mind and heart. To make this happen, the cinema must project us into a main character's *emotional* predicament, for our main and perhaps only desire is to inhabit the worlds of others. In a love triangle like *Anna Karenina* there is more than one emotional situation because separate and different perceptions are possible by each character—that is, Anna's, her husband's, and her lover Vronsky's. With the husband Karenin we might view Anna's liaison as a betrayal; with Vronsky, see it as a romantic adventure that turns sour; with Anna, feel night turn into brightest day, and then change into a long, bloody sunset.

Tolstoy's novel can be seen as the tragedy of the double standard that makes women into property and then denies them the same freedoms as men. But under a different shaping hand the story could emerge in the theater or cinema as a parable about the unfulfillability of romantic love. By favoring Karenin's point of view over that of his wife's in some scenes, the storyteller could imply without changing the events that Karenin is also a misunderstood and even pitiable figure. Another director might conceivably make the whole story into a metaphor for Mother Russia caught between servitude to the Czars and manipulation by the revolutionaries—thus making Tolstoy into a prophet of the Russian Revolution (something he would have hated!)

A story has dimensions beyond those understood by its inhabitants. In *Anna Karenina* there is also that of the storyteller Tolstoy, and still others superimposed by anyone reinterpreting the novel. Altered perspectives often require no change in the interactions specified by the original novel. They simply take the slant or filter of an adaptation, one that may draw on a contemporary mood or anxiety, or a personal perspective of the screenwriter.

Finally as we have said there is the point of view that the audience itself brings to the piece. This is affected by national culture as well as social, economic, or other contexts. A Chinese village audience does not interpret the film the same way as a San Francisco or Turin audience. Stories, domestic or foreign, are consumed by a culture in order to find reflected aspects and meanings for itself, which is why a Shakespeare play can be set in recent times and still resonate loudly in modern India.

To control a genre, a director needs of course to know what the special conditions of that genre are, and how to create and handle points of view within the film in order to build the subjectivity of a special world. The director must be able to analyze a story or screenplay and know whose subjectivity is important at any given point.

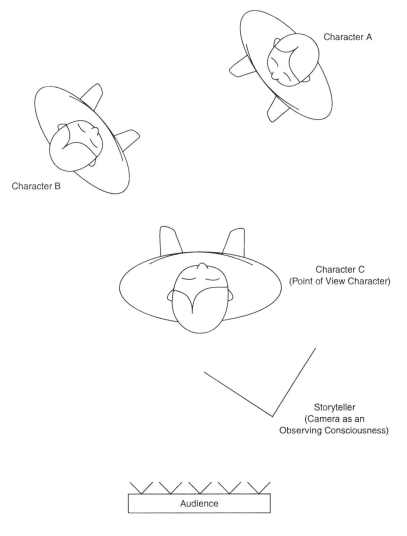

FIGURE 13-1

Diagram of characters, POV character and storyteller.

ON GENRE AND DRAMATIC ARCHETYPES

In French, *genre* simply means kind, type, or sort, and in English the word is used of films that can be grouped together. James Monaco's *How to Read a Film* lists under *genre:*

black film	gangster film	thriller
buddy film	horror film	war film
chase	melodrama	westerns
comedy (screwball)	musicals	youth
detective story	samurai	
film noir	science fiction	

For television it lists:

action shows	docudrama	soap opera
cop shows	families	
comedy (sitcom)	professions shows	

These classifications are evidently archetypal since each category contains characters, roles, or situations somewhat familiar to the audience. Each therefore promises to explore *a known world running under familiar rules and limitations.* The buddy film will always be about same-sex friendships, though it may contain works as diverse as Kramer's *The Defiant Ones* (1958), Hill's *Butch Cassidy and the Sundance Kid* (1969), and Hughes' *Planes, Trains and Automobiles* (1988). Ridley Scott's *Thelma and Louise* (1991) is a female version. You might think that Bergman's *Fanny and Alexander* (1982) makes a male/female buddy partnership, but most of the time Fanny is present only as a silent witness.

The gangster film, the sci-fi film, and the screwball comedy all embody subjects and approaches that function dependably within preordained limits. Understandably when so much is traditional, these genres do not normally strive for individual vision. This would require a recognizably personal signature in its style and content, more the province of the *auteur* film. In reality no film belongs entirely at either extreme and no film is authored by one person.

Screen archetypes, as we have said, have their roots in a cultural history infinitely longer than that of the cinema. Audiences have always craved alternatives to realism, so it is hardly surprising that horror and fantasy have been staples throughout cinema's short history. They are cinema's variation on folk tale and folk drama, forms through which humankind still indulges its appetite for demons, ogres, wizards, and phantom carriages. Under the guise of futurism, Schaffner's *Planet of the Apes* (1968) and Lucas' *Star Wars* (1977) are really old-fashioned morality plays whose settings obscure but do not efface their ancient origins.

Like any other drama, the morality play profits from a metaphorically charged setting, and twentieth-century space travel has refreshed the genre by providing a boundless new world for imaginative storytelling. By a nice paradox, sci-

FIGURE 13-2 ——

The human condition according to Jean-Luc Godard in *A Woman Is a Woman* (courtesy Museum of Modern Art/Film Stills Archive).

entific and industrial progress provides an excuse for Odysseus, Penelope, Hercules, Bluebeard, and Merlin to return in new outfits.

The profitability of the horror film makes one wonder why people will pay money to be frightened. Presumably the horror tale dates from times when our cave-dweller ancestors, bored during the long hours of winter darkness, told scary stories and dared one another to leave the campfire to tempt the wild beasts and evil spirits lurking in the shadows. Today in our hyper rational world we seek out Clouzot's *Les Diaboliques* (1954) or Carpenter's *Hallowe'en* (1978) to explore the same exquisite flirtation with dread. Inviting us to test our emotional reserves and belief systems, horror films are also rooted in the morality play and differ only in that disproportionate power is assigned to evil.

Though fiction cinema allows one to vicariously experience most imaginable fates, there has been a conspicuous silence on nuclear attack and the Holocaust, until Spielberg's *Schindler's List* (1994). Even here the film focuses on one of the few uplifting stories to emerge from that period of shame. True horror, it would seem, is nothing we really care to contemplate. Even those living through it have often chosen lifelong silence. With the possible exception of Resnais' *Hiroshima Mon Amour* (1959), Kramer's *On the Beach* (1959), and Kubrick's *Dr. Strangelove* (1963), global disaster is mainly displaced into the safer realm of high fantasy. Surely it is no coincidence that Japan, the only nation to yet experience nuclear attack, specializes in films and comic books featuring world-destroying monsters. It is fascinating to realize that in wartime when tensions and personal drama run at their highest, nations are most likely to produce realistic cinema about the trials of ordinary people. Then we become our own heroes, and the monsters and ghouls of folklore turn into the relatively human form of the prevailing enemy. Warfare may indeed persist because of our need to enact and not merely witness drama.

Comedy in its different forms offers worlds with constants to which we can turn with anticipation. Chaplin, Keaton, Mae West, W. C. Fields, Red Skelton, Laurel and Hardy, as well as Tati, Lucille Ball, Woody Allen, John Cleese, and Steve Martin all play types of character that are recognizable from film to film. Each new situation and dilemma pressures a familiar and unchanging personality with a new set of comic stresses.

Comedy's underlying purpose is surely to make audiences laugh at their own deepest anxieties and trauma. Harold Lloyd hanging from Manhattan skyscrapers and Chaplin working frantically to keep up with a production line or playing the dictator are obvious examples. But recent sex comedies in which women take over male preserves, homosexual couples take on motherhood, or sitcoms involving men taking over women's roles and identity all confirm how comedy functions as a safety valve to social change.

That audiences should want to vicariously investigate anxiety, fear, or deprivation is a good deal easier to understand than other kinds of experiment. The sexploitation film with its portrayal of women as willing objects of mysogenistic violence and the "slasher" film portraying sadistic brutality each prompt disturbing questions about manipulation and responsibility for the darker side of the (mostly male) human imagination. Perhaps secular middle-class living has so effectively banished fear and uncertainty that we recreate the primitive and supernatural to allay that worst of all bourgeois ills: terminal boredom.

Brecht's question remains. Is art a mirror to society or a hammer working on it? Does art reflect what is, or does it create it? The answers are likely to vary with the makers of the artwork, and to vary with history and even the age of those involved. What we can say with confidence is that in every period and in every part of the world, art has supplied a surrogate experience to exercise hearts and minds. Sometimes actuality is dramatic and mysterious enough on its own (as during war); at other times we gravitate toward works presenting elaborate metaphors for our condition, particularly as we approach taboos.

But how does the poor filmmaker, surrounded by the paraphernalia of scripts, budgets, and technical support, know when to abandon the kitchen sink realism so generic to photography? What we need here are guidelines to put individual perception into a manageable frame. I wish there were a magic formula, but instead we must talk about dialectical worlds that are animated by the creative tensions of opposition.

DUALITY AND CONFLICT

Have you ever received one of those photocopied family newsletters around Christmas time?

```
              The Russell News for the Year
David received his promotion to area manager but now has a
longer drive to work. Betty has completely redecorated the
dining room (with an avocado theme!) after successfully
completing her interior decorator course at Mallory School
of the Arts. Terry spent the summer camping and canoeing
and thoroughly enjoyed being a camp counselor. In the fall
he learned that he had a place at Hillshire University to
study molecular biology. In spite of what the doctor said,
Joanne has successfully adapted to contact lenses . . .
```

What makes this so insufferable is that the writer insists on presenting life as a series of happy, logical steps. In the Russell photo album everyone faces the camera wearing a smile. There will be nothing candid, spontaneous, or disturbing. The newsletter events are not untrue, but the selection method renders them lifeless, all the more so when you happen to know that David's drinking problem is getting worse.

By avoiding all hint of conflict, the account is rendered insipid. It totally suppresses the dissent, doubt, and eccentricity that makes every family turbulent. Family life is like a pond; calm on the surface but containing all the forces of warring nature below the surface.

So, too, is an individual. A person's life does not move forward in linear steps like an adding machine. Instead it moves like a flying insect in a zigzag pattern formed by conflicting needs and random conditions. Joanne Russell needs her mother's emotional support, but cannot bear the way she criticizes her. Terry Russell wants to go to college, but dreads leaving friends and home behind him. Each has conflicting feelings over these issues, and each feels contradictory impulses in dealing with them.

The individual psyche is like a raft on the ocean moving irregularly under the conflicting wills of oarsmen (the passions) rowing on all four sides. Most row peaceably together in one direction, but a few dissidents struggle to send the raft in their own direction. Imagine now several such rafts in conflict with each other, and we have a family.

Enlarge the analogy and make it an Elizabethan sea battle between two warring nations. With our all-seeing eye, we make out battle strategies, signaling, misunderstandings, failures, heroism, strokes of luck, changes of wind and direction, the onset of fog and storm. Then allies arrive and there are boardings, sinkings, the death of an admiral, and a rebellion by the men who toil below decks. By dawn the triumphant victors and their wounded go limping onward. This is an analogy for large-scale drama.

MICROCOSM AND MACROCOSM

Because drama reproduces on a large scale the warring elements found in an individual, the screenwriter can make drama from something like an exploded diagram of a single human being. By making each aspect of the subject's personality (usually his own) into a separate character, he can set it in conflict with all the others. This takes what would normally be an internal and mental struggle and transforms it into outwardly visible action—so necessary for the screen. In Wajda's *Ashes and Diamonds* (1958) the drama is an externalization of what is really Maciek's inner struggle on the eve of peace, what Wajda calls "the soldier's eternal dilemma, to obey orders or to think for himself." For the sake of dramatic legibility an individual's psychological interior has been turned inside out to make it large scale and visible, a microcosm turned into a macrocosm.

Conversely, when a diffuse, complex situation needs to be presented coherently, it can be miniaturized by reversing the process to make the macrocosm into a microcosm. Oliver Stone's *Wall Street* (1988) concentrates and simplifies trends in the stockbroking industry into a parable. A young stockbroker is seduced into illegal practices by the charisma of a powerful and amoral mentor. His counterbalancing influence is his pragmatic, working-class father. Interestingly a similar configuration of influences vie for the soul of the hero in Stone's *Platoon* (1987). In each case, a complex and otherwise confusing situation is simplified and made accessible because characters are created as representatives of moral archetypes. Then as the Everyman character makes choices, we see him tempered in the flame of experience.

Take care if you make a character into a torch-bearer for a human quality that he or she doesn't become monolithic and flat. It is enough for one quality to predominate; otherwise each character must be complex and facing some vital conflicts of his or her own.

HOW OUTLOOK AFFECTS VISION

When a piece is character-driven the storyteller's vision of the particular world will depend on the point-of-view character. When the piece is plot-driven, the storyteller's vision will hinge more on the settings, situations, and the idiosyncrasies of the plot. There are also temperamental and cultural factors shaping the filmmaker's choices. The political historian or social scientist, for instance, may see a naval battle as the interplay of inevitable forces, with victory or defeat being the result of the technology used and the different leaders' strengths and weaknesses. This is a deterministic view of human behavior that might produce a genre film. It is a relatively detached and objective kind of vision that will express itself similarly whether it works through the medium of comedy, mystery, or psychological thriller.

An *auteur* dramatist like John Boorman, probably more concerned with the individuality of human experience, would treat a battle differently—going below decks, looking into faces and hearts, and seeking out the conflicts within each ship and within each sailor, the great and the humble. Such a film might place us in the heat of battle to show not the constants in human history or the eternal repetition of human error, but the human potential inherent in moral choice. This kind of film is likely to show a more individual vision and a less predictable world, since it wants to raise questions about character and potential rather than to demonstrate the repetition of historical patterns.

Whether you show a deterministic world or one where individuals influence their destinies will be a matter of your temperament and what story you want to tell. It is also, as I say often, a matter of what *marks* life has made on you, and therefore what stories you need to tell. Luckily there are many limitations on choice.

DRAMA, PROPAGANDA, AND DIALECTICS

Drama and propaganda handle duality differently: drama sees the live organism of the sea battle while the propagandist, knowing before he starts where the truth lies, drives his audience single-mindedly through a token opposition to arrive at a prescribed truth. His drama is not a process of exploration but of jostling the spectator into accepting a predetermined outcome, much as salesmen's stories are directed at selling their merchandise. Television or cinema with a message arouses our defenses because we are being sold cheap goods under the guise of entertainment, and instinctively we resent it.

The dramatist, valuing the complexity, integrity, and organic quality of struggle and decision, treats audiences more respectfully. Truly dramatic writing evolves from exploring the author's fascination with particular ambiguities. To some degree it always represents a journey by its authors toward an unknown destination. The absence of this quality makes most well-intentioned educational and corporate product stultifyingly boring. The makers have either forgotten or are incapable of recreating the sense of discovery. The viewer is treated like a jug, a passive receptacle to be filled with information rather than an active partner in discovery. The educator with a closed mind wants to condition us, not to invoke free-ranging intelligence. This is why art under totalitarianism comes from the dissidents, never the establishment.

What we face is a range of dialectical oppositions between which any film will be suspended. Here are those mentioned so far as well as a few extra.

Either	*Or*
Auteur (personal, authorial stamp)	Genre (film archetype)
Subjective (character's) point of view	Objective (storyteller's) point of view
Nonrealistic	Realistic
Duality requires audience judgment	Conflicts are generic and not analyzed
Conflicts are interpersonal	Conflicts are large scale
Divergent and unresolved	Convergent and resolved
Outcome uncertain	Outcome satisfyingly predictable but not reached without struggle

Notice that these columns are neither prescriptions for good and bad films, nor do many films fall into predominantly one column or the other. They are simply alternates. How do you decide which oppositions to invoke in your particular piece of storytelling?

At the point of deciding what story and what kind of world the protagonists of the story inhabit, it may not be important. This will emerge later. It is important to recognize that anything or anybody interesting always has contradictions at the center, and that every story must be routed through the intelligence experiencing the story as it unfolds. For the sake of clarity we have personified this intelligence as the Concerned Observer.

BUILDING A WORLD
AROUND THE CONCERNED OBSERVER

You will recall that, relieved of corporeal substance the Observer is invisible and weightless like a spirit and sees all the significant aspects of the characters. Feeling for them, the Observer sometimes leaves the periphery to fly into the center of things, but remains mobile and involved, and always in search of greater significance and larger patterns of meaning.

The Observer develops empathy with, and knowledge of, the characters, and in so doing passes through a series of experiences that invoke his identification with the characters, strain his powers of understanding, and stress his emotions. Following are some invented examples for discussion.

SURVIVAL FILM

You have set your film in the rubble after World War Three. Your choice is to use realism to allow the audience no escape, and to make the audience identify with a family that has survived by a freak. There are some interpersonal conflicts (over what is the best direction to follow in search of water), but most of the struggle is between the family and the hostile environment. The trials faced are of survivorship that involve bravery and ingenuity rather than self-knowledge and human judgment. You want your audience to be affected by the bleakness of the environment, the tragedy of humankind wiping itself out, and the futility of your lone family's efforts. Their hope is to meet others. Their fear is of never finding enough food or shelter to survive an endless winter. You want to show the resourcefulness and compassion of a family unit under extreme duress.

LOTTERY WINNER FILM

An elderly widower goes from genteel poverty to stupendous wealth by winning the lottery. He decides to indulge his two best friends with everything they have ever wanted. Each according to his minor flaws becomes distorted by the bounty in a major way, and each finds that getting what you want brings more trouble than it is worth. In the end the three are forced to separate and begin new lives apart. Here you can show three different characters in three different phases of reality, all very subjective, and you can occasionally drop back to a more objective storyteller's mode. The conflicts each character suffers are mostly an internal conflict over suddenly having to opt for what makes one happy. There is much doubt and self-examination here, and perhaps conflict between the three friends as they find themselves in deep waters. The lottery winner feels responsible, and often we will see things through his eyes. The world which is first a desert becomes a cornucopia of delights; then it becomes complicated and troublesome. The lottery winner finds he likes his friends less and less until they all agree to give up the life they have taken on. The price of affluence is isolation.

Your intention is to show how security and a sense of self-worth comes from facing problems, and that people get into deep trouble when they suddenly have nothing left to push against. This is a subtle subject, for it shows how fragile people are when accommodating good fortune.

Neither of the above are unusual subjects, yet the world you show and the roles in which you successfully place the audience enable you to create a sequence of experiences that allows a great deal to emerge about the human condition. The same would be true for any form of film you choose, provided you decide not only upon the characters' careers, but also the role of the subjective, watching audience, a role that normally emerges by default rather than by conscious design.

OBSERVER INTO STORYTELLER

While the literary storyteller always tells a story that has already happened, the film storyteller summons us into a story that is happening here and now. In this respect, screen language is alien to human experience. We can't experience events through someone else's persona except in retrospect. Yet in our example earlier of seeing someone's documentary coverage of his class reunion party, we somehow do both; we experience the party happening not "then" but here and now and we know it is being filtered through a temperament, a process in life that normally takes place in the recounting afterward.

Both audience and filmmakers tend to resolve this psychic non sequitur by disregarding the storyteller, the subjective filter by which the world is seen in a certain way and with certain emphases as a result of individual persuasion and character. With distinguished (and distinguishable) cinematic authors such as Hitchcock, Godard, Resnais, Bergman, Fellini, Antonioni, Altman, and Peckinpah, you may not like their work, but there is no doubt about the individuality of the hands one is in. But much work for the cinema, and virtually *all* fiction made for television, lacks any individuality of vision whatsoever. As Mamet says, these movies are made "as a supposed record of what real people really did." In a faceless and servile manner the work becomes a newsreel taking its nature from the story and characters. Mamet's knowledge does not save him from falling into the same trap when he directs, so obviously it is not enough to understand the problem. I think the answer lies in three areas:

1. A director must make the film's storyteller have the subjectivity of a strong and interestingly biased personality. This is common to all effective storytelling voices. To obtain it for the film, the director must "play" this part while planning the film and while directing it. If this subjective vision is there, a good editor will recognize it with delight and work to enhance it. Editors are usually trying to *create* the storytelling voice which all too often is absent.

2. The director must control the process, not be controlled by it. This is a matter of having a strongly realized vision and of having the personal qualities of confidence, clarity, and obstinacy to get this vision out of the filmmaking process. The more "professional" the crew and actors think they are, the more the tail is likely to wag the dog.

3. You'll go where you aim. If it's to look professional, you will eventually do so—but facelessly. If you get a chance to direct a feature film, there are a hundred others equally qualified, equally professional. Nobody gives a damn about professionalism if that's all there is. The professionalism of one's beer is irrelevant if it has no character. And most beers are like most movies, characterless clones of the average.

Make your priority a good story seen in a specially appropriate way, and you will be readily forgiven any lack of professionalism. If you doubt this, take a look at Werner Herzog's earliest efforts at filmmaking. Technically rough they are already fascinating because the man has an abundant and poetic vision of humankind.

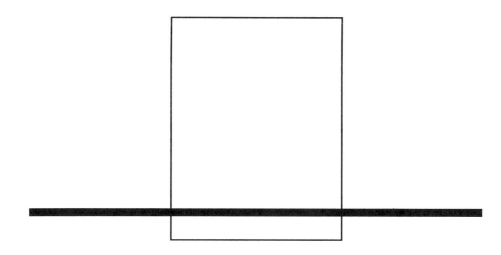

C·H·A·P·T·E·R 14

STRUCTURE, PLOT, AND TIME

The final structure of a film is a design that may have been influenced by any number of considerations. Composition, visual and aural rhythms, amount and complexity of movement within the frame, and length and placement of shots all help determine a film's final shape. Many of these elements are not, and cannot be, more than generally present in the filmmaker's mind at the outset. My intention here is to deal only with the largest dimensions to a movie's structure—the handling of plot, time, and thematic purpose.

There is a considerable and well-deserved backlash (among filmmakers if not general audiences) against the tightly plotted narrative film. It can often feel manipulative and contrived, and when one finds screenwriting manuals that not only prescribe three acts each having a certain length, but also the page number for the plot points, many would-be screenwriters head for the hills. This obsession with control of form would seem reductive and formulaic. But there is a considerable context missing from the picture. First, nobody in their right mind starts with the three-act form and all the page numbers. Writers begin with ideas, images, feelings, perhaps some incidents in their own or a friend's life. The first draft may be in shortstory form, in outline, or whole scenes in screenplay. That is how one generates material. At some point the writer starts to story edit, which means using a writer's toolbox to spot the narrative elements and archetypes, and to assess their effectiveness for a first-time viewer.

These archetypes are embedded in the oldest stories and the newest. Freud and Jung were highly conscious of them in their ground-breaking work on human psychology, and more recently Joseph Campbell made it his life's work to trace them in world mythology and folk tales. Independently, Hollywood's pragmatism led its screenwriters, as they studied what audiences liked, to arrive at similar conclusions though by a different route. While much about film form is hotly debated, some aspects are deeply established. "If anything is natural," says Dudley Andrew in *Concepts in Film Theory,* "it is the psychic lure of narrative, the drive to hold events in sequence, to traverse them, to come to an end."

My purpose here is not to argue the virtues of narrative or so-called nonnarrative approaches but to help you begin practical work. Suffice it to say that nonnarrative cinema is not lacking in structure. Consider this from a review of Richard Linklater's *Slacker* (1991): "An original, narratively innovative, low budget movie from the fringe, *Slacker* is a perfectly plotless work that tracks incidental moments in the lives of some one hundred characters who have made the bohemian side of Austin, Texas, their hangout of choice. . . . The two forces that hold the film together are its clear sense of place (specifically Austin, more generally college towns) and its intimate knowledge of a certain character type; the 'slacker.' . . . But the film's improvisatory, meandering style is actually carefully constructed" (James Pallot and the editors of Cinebooks, *The Movie Guide,* 1995).

If this movie is structured to show Linklater's ideas about a range of characters in a certain time and place, there are other patternings for drama. Traditional Indian drama is structured by a pattern of moods while Peter Greenaway's *A Zed and two Noughts* (1985) is structured around an operatic concatenation of events taking place between characters who work in a zoo. Interwoven are Greenaway's favorite fascinations; numbers, coincidence, philology, painting, wild life, decay, and taxonomies—just to mention a few topics that are explored and developed in this extraordinary film.

Organizing structure and a premise are inescapable while films are consumed in a linear fashion. The overformal structure common in Hollywood is really a paradigm abstracted from experience in cinemas and that happens—not surprisingly perhaps—to reflect developments in the consumption of literature and drama. There are other and innumerable variations and alternatives, but central organization of some sort, even for a short film, is inescapable.

PLOT

The plot of a drama is the design that arranges or patterns the incidents befalling the characters. Since we do not and cannot show everything that might happen to them, a film shows only certain incidents and actions while implying a whole world before or beyond what the film shows. By concentrating our attention, a film's plot therefore acts as a frame within which to focus authorial intentions.

The emphasis on plot may be light or heavy. Heavy plotting tends to place a stress upon the logical and deterministic side of life. In drama proceeding from a more existential philosophy, plot may be deemphasized in favor of a looser and more episodic structure where chance, randomness, and the imperatives of character legitimately play a large part. Your philosophy of life is bound to be reflected in the type and degree of plotting you use.

Though a film may ardently promote a theory of randomness in life, cause and effect is more fixed in the language it must use. The relationship between shots, angles, characters, and environments in film language is fashioned according to film language precedents. And though you have some latitude to modify the language, there's no more randomness in the basics than with any other language. You have to use the rules of English if you are to be understood by English speakers. Film language results from a historically developed collusion between filmmakers and audiences, but like all live languages it is in evolution. Plot plays its part in the pact not just by reconciling the characters' motivations—why character A manipulates a confrontation with character B, for example—but by steering our attention to the issues at hand. It should also maintain the tension that keeps the movie moving forward by making us want to see more.

Since a character's temperament largely determines his actions, plot must be consonant with character. Conversely, characters cannot be arbitrarily plugged into a plot, since plot and character must work hand in hand so that, as the story advances, each episode stands in logical and meaningful relationship to what went before. Plot failures will be those weaknesses or breaks in the chain of logic that cause a break in credibility. The audience will then feel confused or even cheated.

There is a distinction between how things happen in reality and what is permissible in drama. If in real life an oppressed, docile factory worker suddenly leaps to the center of a dangerous strike situation and averts a tragedy by inspired oratory, one will ponder what signs of latent genius were overlooked by his coworkers, but one cannot doubt it could happen. If, however, we model a fiction film upon such material, our audience will probably dismiss the events as untrue to life. Because the film is now fiction, we shall have to carefully rearrange or even add selected incidents to show that our hero's potential was visible (although nobody noticed it) and that it took the pressure of particular events to free him up to realize it.

Common weaknesses found in plotting are an excessive reliance on coincidence, or on the *deus ex machina,* the improbable action or incident inserted to make things turn out right. Audiences know when a dramatist is forcing a development in this way, so you must ask a great many searching questions of your screenplay to ensure that its plot is as tight and functional as good cabinetry. The well-crafted plot has a sense of inevitable flow, because it includes nothing gratuitous or facile. It generates a sense of energizing excitement, and each step—by obeying the logic of the characters and their situation—stimulates the spectator to actively speculate what will happen next. In dramaturgy, as we have said, this is a desirable commodity called "forward momentum."

THEMATIC PURPOSE

When directing a play or a film, one needs to be well aware of its intended final meaning or thematic purpose. Because most feature films are meant for a materialist and secular audience, they employ a realism that leaves little room for metaphoric or poetic expression. Yet I believe that audiences long for the resonance of deeper meanings, and crave drama that contains the seeds of hope.

Former generations, reared on the allusions and poetry of religious texts, were more attuned to thinking on multiple levels. So were citizens of the Eastern Bloc countries, who became accustomed to looking for hidden allusions smuggled past the nose of authority. The artist of today who wants to be noticed must recapture this skill, which is really that of using poetry to relay visions of what is, or what can be. Allegory and parable (from *parabola,* meaning curved plane or comparison) can hit a nerve in audiences very powerfully, as shown by Robert Zemeckis' otherwise predictable *Forrest Gump* (1994).

A helpful tactic for the filmmaker is to invent a graphic image or diagram to represent the movement of elements and characters in the story. This makes visible the film's underlying statements by posing a problem of translation (language to a graphic) that can only be solved by deep and sustaining thinking.

In *The Wizard of Oz* (1939) each of the characters exerts—for good or ill—different pressures upon Dorothy, who is like a hub at the center of a wheel having many spokes. Movement in the film is like a journey in which the wheel revolves a number of times, each spoke bearing upon her more than once. The image usefully organizes one's ideas about how *The Wizard of Oz*'s thematic design applies a rotation of pressured experiences, each testing Dorothy's stamina and resourcefulness.

Robert Altman's *Nashville* (1975) is very different. We have the trajectories of many characters converging at a single concert where there will be a gunshot. This one sound—to which everyone reacts—is the point of ultimate convergence, the one shared moment in all of their lives and the target (no pun intended) for all the film's lines of development. Because *Nashville*'s country music scene and its gunshot focal point are so quintessentially American, and because the film points to all those moments of terrible unity in American consciousness when leaders fell to an assassin's bullet, one can see how the film's design and metaphors are anything but arbitrary.

In identifying a thematic design, one may be trying to describe a journey that is emotional and metaphysical rather than physical and actual. Bo Widerberg's *Elvira Madigan* (1967) tells the true story of a nineteenth-century Swedish count who deserted both the army and his family to run away with a beautiful circus acrobat. The two, unequipped for practical life and perfectly in love, fail to take the material steps necessary to survival. Thematically their romantic flight is like the inverted elliptical flight of a doomed airplane, beginning as an ascent but flattening out before turning downward with increasing inevitability. This, or the pyramid shape, is actually the classical developmental shape (Figure 14-1) for tragedy.

This shape might be applied to a whole film or to a single episode among many. Another shape could be called the crossover, in which, for example, the strong is revealed as vulnerable, and the weak turns out to be strong. This happens in Chris Bernard's *Letter to Brezhnev* (1985) that was made on a low budget for Channel 4 TV in England. In this tale of two impoverished but feisty Liverpool friends it is the more conforming girl who eventually turns away from her home city to follow her Russian lover, not the more aggressive and demonstrative one. One might represent the stages of this movement as in Figure 14-2.

One might assign to Louis Malle's *My Dinner with André* (1982) the pattern of waves washing ashore as the tide goes out—a constant rhythm and repetition with a slow descent. Here we have two interlocking cycles; the undulation of the

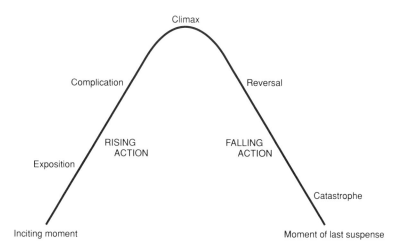

FIGURE 14-1

Development curve for the traditional tragedy.

waves in ceaseless motion, and the enclosing cycle of the tides. The tides represent the cyclical repetition of conversations through a person's life, and the waves represent the texture of the individual exchange. Implicit is the idea, too, of different seasons (the different ages and growth stages of a protagonist) and different weathers (moods) as well as the changelessness of the sea itself (human nature).

For Milos Forman's *Amadeus* (1984) one might graph Mozart's rise and fall in a repeating sawtooth fashion, as each of Mozart's successes are followed either by sabotage or self-inflicted setback.

The hero of Scorsese's dark comedy *After Hours* (1986) is like a rat trying to escape from a labyrinth. Indeed there is a caged rat in one scene where Paul finds himself trapped in a talkative woman's apartment. The film could be plotted out as a labyrinthine journey, each compartment holding out the promise of a particular experience but virtually all emerging as illusory and misleading.

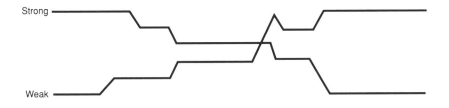

FIGURE 14-2

Graph representing the development of a character initially weak in relation to one stronger.

Sometimes the image for a film's thematic development is completely encapsulated in the film itself, as in Gregory Nava's *El Norte* (1983). The illegal Guatemalan immigrants cross the American border through a rat-infested land drain, which aptly miniaturizes their long, perilous journey fraught with dangerous, individual obstacles.

Each of my examples is no more than a rough beginning. Films under the microscope yield many additional thematic elements that cross-modulate within the larger pattern, as in the *My Dinner* example above. Each work's full design will only emerge at the end of postproduction. A problem in editing turns out to be a misjudged scene that subtly disrupts and negates the overall pattern, and must either be changed, moved, or eliminated. Often it is the discovery of a disruptor that establishes the harmony elsewhere, like one false note in an experimental chord progression that confirms by its wrongness the rightness of everything else.

Before you direct, make a close, written analysis of more than one film that moves you. This is true critical interaction and will help enormously when you come to abstract the thematic development from a script you intend to film. In developmental work following the initial script, produce a graphic representation of the whole film along the lines above, and then write about it. As always, the act of writing will further develop what had initially seemed complete and devoid of further development potential. Finding and illustrating the thematic progression in a script is of course a large step toward identifying the right structure for your film. The two are symbiotic.

HANDLING TIME

For every potential film there is an optimal structure, one that best presents the content and best delivers the film's underlying purpose. Arriving at it will always involve deciding how to handle time. As with all designing, the simplest solution is often the strongest. Less is more.

TIME PRESENTED CHRONOLOGICALLY

The most straightforward time structure is when a film's sequences proceed through time in a linear or chronological fashion. Chronological sequencing is likely to produce a relatively cool, objective film because the narrative flow is least interrupted or redirected by plot intentions. Effect follows cause in predictable but potentially unchallenging rhythm.

To depart from chronological time is always to court confusion in your audience, but something can also be lost when the conservative, linear approach is used. In Volker Schlöndorff's film version of Heinrich Boll's novel *The Lost Honor of Katharina Blum* (1975) the adaptors abandoned the flash-forward technique as too complex, substituting instead a conventionally linear structure that muted the novel's contemplative, inquiring voice. What emerged is a polemical film in the Costa-Gavras tradition.

NONLINEAR TIME AND SCENES FROM THE PAST

Chronology may be broken up and its blocks of time rearranged in response to the subjective priorities of a character's attention or recall, or because the storyteller has a narrative purpose for reordering time.

Resnais, perennially fascinated by the way the human memory edits and distorts time, intercut *Muriel* (1963) with 8mm movie material from the Algerian war to create a series of flashback memory evocations. In his earlier *Hiroshima Mon Amour* (1959), the French woman and her Japanese lover increasingly recall (or are invaded by) memories of their respective traumas—his, the dropping of the bomb on Hiroshima; hers, a love affair with a German soldier in occupied France. These are past events central to the present-day anguish suffered by each, and Resnais' thesis implies that lives are impelled by trauma. The placing and frequency of these recollections indicate the movement of their inner lives, and provoke us into searching for what in their developing love affair it is that brings these withheld memories to the surface. Both films pose questions about the effect of repressed personal history on present behavior.

NONLINEAR TIME AND SCENES OF THE FUTURE

A scene from the future can be a useful foreshadowing device. A familiar comedy routine illustrates this. After we see a man start walking, the film cuts ahead to a banana skin lying on the sidewalk. Cutting back and forth between the man and the banana skin creates expectation so that when he falls on it, we are in a state of receptive tension and laugh when chance takes its toll. To subvert this expectation would be to make him step unaware over the banana skin at the point where the pratfall should occur.

Since the victim is unaware of the banana skin, any revelation of what is to come necessarily arises from a storyteller's point of view, not that of the character. If instead the banana skin has been laid as a trap by a hidden boy, then flashing back and forth between victim and banana skin can only be the waiting boy's point of view, and has become a piece of continuous present. Point of view here determines the *tense* of the footage.

In an example of dramatic foreshadowing, Jan Troell's *Journey of the Eagle* (1985) starts with unexplained shots of human bones in a deserted arctic encampment. The film is about an actual balloon voyage to the arctic at the turn of the century, a hastily prepared expedition that concluded with the death of the aviators. We see the actual aviators' fate first, and then the fictional film reconstructing their tragic destiny.

Alain Tanner uses different foreshadowing in *The Middle of the World* (1974). The authorial narration at different stages counts down how many days remain in the affair we witness between the engineer and the waitress. Because the ending in both films is foreknown our attention focuses on human aspiration and fallibility rather than, as it normally would, on whether the couple will stay together.

An interesting flash-forward technique is used in Nicholas Roeg's *Don't Look Now* (1974). The lovemaking scene is repeatedly intercut with shots of the couple getting dressed later in a state of abstraction. The effect is complex and poignant, and suggests not only the idea of comfortable routine but also that each is preoccupied with what must be done after they have made love. The sequence implies that each act of love has not only its beginning, middle, and end, but a banal aftermath waiting to engulf it.

NONLINEAR TIME AND THE CONDITIONAL TENSE

A favorite device in comedy is to cut to an imagined or projected outcome, as in John Schlesinger's *Billy Liar* (1963), whose hero takes refuge in fantasy from his dreary undertaker's job. It is used altogether more somberly in Resnais' *Last Year in Marienbad* (1961), in which a man staying in a vast hotel tries to renew an affair with a woman who does not know him. Sometimes maddeningly experimental as it moves between past, present, and future, the film extends multiple versions of scenes to suggest repeated attempts by the central character to remember or imagine. Here Resnais is using film as a research medium and providing us with an expanded, slowed-down model of human consciousness at work on a problem.

TIME COMPRESSED

All time arts must select and compress in pursuit of intensification of meaning, juxtapositional irony, and brevity. Film does this supremely well. Presumably this came about because newsreels at the beginning of film history showed that audiences would infer something larger and more complete from adequate fragments of a recognizable scene. The audience imagined not only what was beyond the edges of the frame, but inferred ideas from the dialectical tension between images, compositions, and subjects. Over the decades this film shorthand has become more concise as audiences and filmmakers have evolved an ever more succinct understanding. Ironically, this process has been helped and accelerated by that thorn in our flesh, the TV commercial. In the cinema, Jean-Luc Godard probably did more than anyone to demonstrate that cumbersome transitional devices were superfluous. Since the jump cut (already familiar from home movies) showed a time leap for a single cut or for a transition from one scene to the next, a more compressed overall editing style became inevitable. But narrative agility is useless if a film is still based on a ponderous scripting style that overexplains and relies on hefty dialogue exchanges.

For a sustained narrative style that is elegant, compressed, and highly allusive, one can do no better than study Nicholas Roeg's *Don't Look Now* (1973). If the movie does not transcend the superficially explored goals in Daphne du Maurier's short story original, it is fully accessible and richly rewards analysis.

American experimental cinema of the 1960s and 1970s rebelled against the conservatism of Hollywood and tried drastically altering assumptions about audience attention and the length of films and their parts. Eight hours of the Empire State Building made a statement at the long end of the spectrum, while Stan Van-DerBeek's two-frame cuts and manic compression of scenes stand (or should I say streak) at the other. As the cinema has disentangled itself from television, the most conservative dramatic techniques have been left behind for the little screen and its older audience, even though MTV and the advertising used to attract the consumer's attention has become demented. Cinema films have matured into being longer, more reliant on mood and emotional nuance, and less tied to the laborious plotting associated with screen narrative formulas.

The danger with too much narrative compression is the risk of distancing the audience from a developing involvement with personalities, situations, and ideas, and of generating a general, even ritualized drama, like the western serials that at one time dominated television. Compressing or even eliminating prosaic details should not simply allow the makers to shoehorn ever more plot into a given time slot; it should make way for the expansion of what is significant. Here the Godard films of the early 1960s reign supreme.

TIME EXPANDED

The expansion of time onscreen allows a precious commodity often missing in real life—the opportunity to reflect in depth while something of significance is happening. Slow-motion cinematography is an easy way to do this, but we are a little tired of lovers endlessly floating toward each other's arms. The same hackneyed device bloated the race sequences of Hugh Hudson's *Chariots of Fire* (1981).

Two films that expand time successfully are Robert Enrico's masterly short, *Occurrence at Owl Creek Bridge* (1962) and Paul Leduc's *Frida* (1987). The first, though it contains the seminal slow-motion lovers, is a brilliant expansion of a Civil War victim's momentary fantasy of escape while he is about to be hanged. The second is a retrospect of her key memories by the Mexican painter and political activist Frida Kahlo during the night in which she dies. Both films dwell successfully and without regard for objective time upon the act of introspection.

Yasujiro Ozu's *Tokyo Story* (1953) and Michelangelo Antonioni's *L'Avventura* (1959) subverted the popular action form by slowing both the story and its presentation to expose the more subtle action within the characters. *Tokyo Story* is about an elderly couple journeying to the capital only to find that neither of their children has time for them. The two hours and fifteen minutes of film is engrossing, yet the film is almost entirely in medium shot, and has *one* camera movement, a gentle pan.

Both films center on the tenuousness of human relationships, something impossible to achieve with a torrent of action. Needless to say, an unattuned audience will find such films boring. *L'Avventura* was ridiculed at the Cannes Film Festival, but later found success in Paris and became a cornerstone in Antonioni's career.

OTHER WAYS TO HANDLE TIME

There is literal time, something almost never acknowledged in film form. Agnes Varda's *Cleo from 5 to 7* (1961) lasts two hours and shows exactly two hours in the life of a woman who has just learned she may be dying. Conceivably there could be retrograde time, or time played backward to a source point, which might be a format for handling a story about regression in psychiatry to a buried moment of truth.

There is continuous time or rather, the illusion of it in transparent cinema. This is cinema that aims to rid its techniques of all cinematic contrivance. The appearance of real time is a technique that masks the expansion and contraction of

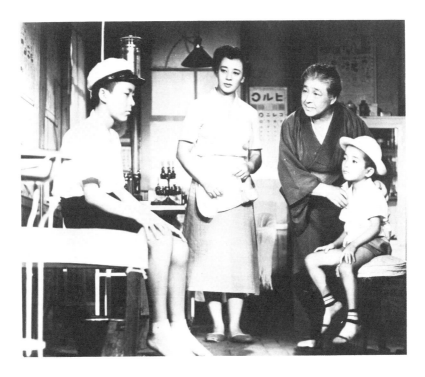

FIGURE 14-3

Technical minimalism and a slow pace concentrate attention on the tragedy of two old people in Ozu's *Tokyo Story* (courtesy New Yorker Films).

time behind the look of continuity. There is also discontinuous time, made possible by the jump cut, which dices time according to authorial purpose. And there is parallel time, or parallel storytelling, as pioneered by D. W. Griffith, who acknowledged a debt to Dickens.

Since the screen treatment of subjective experience is inseparable from perceived time and memory, there must be other designs for screen time yet to be explored.

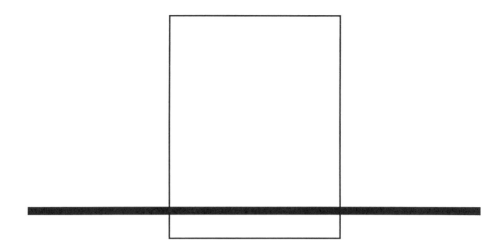

C·H·A·P·T·E·R 15

SPACE, STYLIZED ENVIRONMENTS, AND PERFORMANCES

Film abridges time in the interests of narrative compression, and can be equally selective with space. A protagonist eating dinner who suddenly remembers he hasn't put a coin in his parking meter will not be shown covering every step on his way to rectify the situation. Instead we will see him leap to his feet splashing soup, cut to him running toward the meter, then cut to the middle of an argument with the meter maid. Even where locations are used to set our expectations about characters, the movie may only show us key aspects. Three scenes in a baronial hall will be set against the fireplace, the great stairway, and a doorway flanked with suits of armor; our imagination will create the rest of the space. We may afterward "remember" seeing a wide shot of the whole hall.

In Scorsese's black comedy *After Hours* (1985), where the hapless office worker Paul escapes from one dark, tangled New York situation only to fall into a worse one, each location is shown only minimally. Though it feels as if one has seen every inch of Kiki's studio, Scorsese actually gives us very little. The spectator is always completing what has been suggested, and with only a few well-chosen clues our minds will construct a whole town, as in David Lynch's *Blue Velvet* (1986). Every setup in his small town America is obviously and garishly contrived to be surreal, and speaks of his origins as a painter. The film's early and brilliant predecessor is Lang's *Metropolis* (1926) where the stylized environment is so pervasively visionary that it becomes a leading component in the film's formal argument.

Such expressionism in any film, especially one set in the present, creates a *reality refracted through an extreme subjectivity*. Lynch's first film *Eraserhead* (1978), about an alienated man reacting to the news that his girlfriend is going to have a baby, is the ultimate example where subjectivity is taken to the limits of imaginable psychosis.

Stylization is often present in the sound treatment, as, for example, in Frank Tashlin's *The Girl Can't Help It* (1956) when a sequence about a man waking up with a hangover makes the smallest sound into an abrasive uproar. *Eraserhead* also makes full and frightening use of the potential of sound. As Bresson said, "the eye sees but the ear imagines." Our imagination is the ultimate dramatist; it is not what we see but what we imagine that is memorable and moving.

Film is such a relativistic medium that specific aural or visual devices can only be judged in their context, something beyond the scope of this book. This chapter will touch some issues that arise constantly for the film author and suggest some guidelines which show, I think, that point of view and environment are extricably intertwined. Making rules and drawing demarcation lines between realistic and the stylized, subjectively observed environment is too ambiguous unless tied to a specific example. Even then, a detectable stylization may be traced to nothing more remarkable than a choice of lens, a mildly unrealistic lighting setup, or an interestingly unbalanced composition.

A genre is a specialized world, and stylization serves to create that world by reflecting the special way in which characters perceive and interact with their environment. This illuminates their temperaments and moods, and makes their world a projection of their collective reality. In Polanski's *Repulsion* (1965) the apartment occupied by its paranoid heroine becomes the embodiment of threatening evil. Logically one sees how events are being created by her deluded mind, but one is nonetheless engulfed by what she perceives. The outcome is a sickeningly unpleasant sense of the psychotic's vulnerability. All this is being *demonstrated* by its storyteller—presumably for a larger purpose than to merely prove his power over our emotions. That Polanski's wife was later murdered by such people raises unanswerable speculation about the roots of art in its maker's subconscious.

The screen does not and cannot render anything objectively since time, space, and the objective world are all refracted through particularities that may be human, technical, or just plain random. The outcome is a partly deliberate, partly arbitrary construct. Every aspect of a complex film construct is likely to resonate with every other, like the stresses in a tent when one guy rope is tightened. For this reason alone, film has eluded attempts at objective analysis.

These chicken-or-egg questions are irrelevant to an audience, but bothersome to anyone trying to gain an overview of authorial method. The best advice is to accept that, no matter what film histories and books of criticism say, your only *control* over a live action film is to abort it. To control a film is like trying to control your life. You can't control either, but you can guide them. Your films will be a true record of how successfully you envision something and then capitalize on chance, which is why this book stresses planning a vision, advancing your self-knowledge, collaborating with others, and a willingness to improvise.

The ordinary viewer, however, sees a clear spectrum of possibility, with films of objective effect at one end, and films of invasively subjective impact at the other. As if sampling Mexican food, let's start with mild and move toward hot.

OCCASIONALLY STYLIZED

In mainstream omniscient cinema the stylized environment usually makes only a passing appearance—perhaps to reflect a character's temporary unbalance (euphoria, fear, insecurity, etc.), as a storytelling inflection, or to share confidential information with the audience much as a novelist might do in a literary aside. Withheld from characters, this privileged information (symbolic objects, foreshadowing devices, special in-frame juxtapositions) heightens tension by making us anticipate what the characters do not yet know is in store. By using a character's subjective vision minimally, realism lets us enter the main character's reality without having to give up our observer's superior sense of distance and well-founded judgment. In the famous shower scene in *Psycho* (1960) we temporarily merge with the killer's eyeline after he begins stabbing. The point of view switches to show the last agonized images seen by Janet Leigh's character. Finally the killer runs out, and as Janet Leigh's character is now dead, we are left with the Storyteller's point of view, that is, alone with the body in the motel room.

This brief foray into immediate, limited perceptions—first of the killer, then of his victim—is reserved for the starkest moment in the film, when Hitchcock boldly disposes of its heroine. Elsewhere we are allowed more distance from the characters. Were we to remain confined to the characters' point of view throughout we should often be denied exposure to Hitchcock's signs and portents of the terror to come. Often a storyteller raises the audience's awareness above that of the characters themselves and makes of the audience a privileged witness.

The deranged or psychotic subjectivity of *Psycho* and *Repulsion* is of course a favorite model for suspense movies. Many of the films listed earlier under single-character point of view expose us only sparingly to the point-of-view character's circumscribed vision, leaving most of the drama to be shown from a more detached standpoint. In Carpenter's *Hallowe'en* (1978) we mostly identify with the babysitter, but occasionally circle and stalk her with the vengeful but unseen murderer, occupying his reality even to the point of sharing the sensation of his breathing. While the switch to a subjective point of view catapults us into vulnerable perspectives at times of peak emotion, an audience's overall empathy builds because of the character's whole situation, not just at peaks or during closeups. The island scene in Carroll Ballard's *The Black Stallion* (1979) creates the boy's love for the stallion through a lyrically edited vision of the horse galloping free in the waves of the island foreshore, yet the camera is usually distant from both boy and horse.

So far we have dealt with movement from a safe base of normality into a character's subjectivity and back again, just as the closeup takes us temporarily closer than would be permitted in life in order to explore some development of high significance in a character, or as in the case of an object like a clock or a time bomb, some high significance to the mood or advancement of the story.

One must rely on the full range of storytelling to do this, not just editing. Indeed, to avoid stereotyped thinking about camera coverage and editing, it's important that you closely research what lies behind an audience's identification with a particular character. While getting an audience to identify with a main character is usually desirable, it is emphatically *not* the only purpose of drama. Brecht has said very cogently that drama also exists to spur thought, memory, and judgment, and these he contended were in abeyance whenever an audience member ceded his identity to that of a hero. But Mother Courage, for all her universality, is still a woman in a series of predicaments, and we must still empathize with her if we are to relate to the very human decisions she makes, and to make political judgments about emotion and expediency. I want to stress that sympathy and involvement in a film character's situation do not automatically arise because one happens to see from a character's location in space; it comes about because we have learned from her actions what she is made of, and from her situation what she must still face. Stylized camera coverage and editing do not alone create this, but they do serve it.

FULLY STYLIZED

Some films—to the purist, maybe all—set aside realism for a stylized environment throughout. Usually the film is deliberately distanced in time or place. Period films fall readily into this category, from Griffith's *Birth of a Nation* (1915) and Victor Fleming's *Gone with the Wind* (1939), to more recent nostalgia items as Barry Levinson's *Diner* (1982) and Coppola's *Peggy Sue Got Married* (1986), or Sayles' folk tale *The Secret of Roan Inish* (1995).

Since we more readily grant artistic license to what is filtered through imagination or memory, any story profits from being distanced in time and place from what is familiar. Indeed, the definition of "legend" is that which is unauthentic history. The cinema is thus furthering the notion of oral tradition where events are shaped and embellished to serve the narrator's artistic, social, or political purpose.

From a practical standpoint, it is straightforward (if expensive) to commission an art director to create a heightened or even caricatured past environment. In Lawrence Olivier's *Henry V* (1944) art director Carmen Dillon wonderfully evoked the atmosphere of medieval illustration. Alain Cavalier's *Therese* (1986) sets its story of a young girl in 1890s Lisieux, but uses strikingly minimalistic sets, even plain backdrops or pieces of furniture against a limbo background to evoke rather than show the Carmelite monastery. Wim Wender's television version of Arthur Miller's *Death of a Salesman* even capitalized on the play's origins by setting the piece in see-through sets that elicit both 1940s American suburbia and theater itself.

Nicholas Hytner's *The Madness of King George* (1994) uses the fact of the British king's mental unbalance to explore what happens when, as with eighteenth-century monarchy, personal power inhibits the right of subjects to question what might be normal behavior. The prerogative of royalty is a cover for writer Alan Bennet's continued fascination with the power in family dynamics. Remarkably, this "historical" film easily convinces us that we are privileged spectators of actual personalities in eighteenth-century England who are dealing with an actual political crisis. The king is a real, tragic yet funny person, not the posturing actor of so many treatments of history. This film is a must-see for American directors interested in history; the American screen seems unable to handle history without self-consciousness or posturing.

EXOTIC ENVIRONMENT

Instead of transporting the story in time, another way to achieve a tension between figures and their environment is to place them in a specialized or alien setting, such as the nuclear plant in Nichols' *Silkwood* (1983), or in Africa with Bogart and Hepburn in Huston's *African Queen* (1951). Herzog transplants his naïve Berliners to heartland America in *Stroszek* (1977), and Antonioni in *L'Avventura* (1960) imprisons his urbanites on an uninhabited island. Wherever the topic is a confrontation between antagonistic values, an alien setting allows the film to be impressionistic and create powerfully subjective moods. Vincente Minelli's *An American in Paris* (1951) allowed Gene Kelly to make Paris into a dream city of romance, while John Boorman's *Deliverance* (1972) thrust his four Atlanta businessmen into Appalachia's wilderness to put their "civilized" values to the test of survival.

FUTURISTIC ENVIRONMENT

The flight from the here and now includes not only myth but the future. Fritz Lang's *Metropolis* (1926) is the classic, but there is no shortage of other good examples. Chaplin's *Modern Times* (1936), Godard's *Alphaville* (1965), Truffaut's *Fahrenheit 451* (1966), and Gilliam's *Brazil* (1986) all hypothesize worlds of the future. Each shows Kafkaesque distortions in the social, sexual, or political realms that put characters under duress. Plucked from the familiar and invited to respond as immigrants to a world operating under different assumptions, we are often shown the totalitarianism of dehumanized governments made powerful through technology. However, in the drive to illustrate a thesis, secondary characters often emerge as unindividualized, flat archetypes as they do in *Fahrenheit 451* and *Brazil,* both of which owe a heavy debt to George Orwell's novel *1984*. If tales are traditionally vehicles for exploring our deepest collective anxieties, the realm of the future seems reserved for nightmares about the individual alone during a breakdown in collective control.

EXPRESSIONISTIC ENVIRONMENT

Some films construct a completely stylized world. Kubrick's strange and violent *A Clockwork Orange* (1971) is a picaresque tale played out by painted grotesques in a series of surreal settings. Even if one quickly forgets what the film is about, the visualization is unforgettable, and owes its origins to the expressionism of the German cinema earlier in the century. Robert Wiene's *The Cabinet of Dr. Caligari* (1919) borrowed its style from contemporary developments in the graphic arts which were seeking to advance a wholly altered reality—an endeavor utterly justified by subsequent history. Here characters may have unnatural skin texture, move without shadows in a world of oversized, distorted architecture and machinery. Fritz Lang's *Dr. Mabuse* (1922) and Murnau's *Nosferatu* (1921) sought to create the same unhinged psychology by a more subtle use of the camera. The proportions of the familiar have utterly changed and we find ourselves enclosed in a fully integrated, nightmarish world expressing an alien state of mind. It made its political and satirical comment much as Kokoschka, Grosz, and Munch were doing in the graphic arts of the 1920s and 1930s.

The modern equivalent to this world is the cinema of David Lynch. Whereas in *Taxi Driver* Travis Bickle insanely misreads a familiar world, the hero in an expressionistic film like *Blue Velvet* is thrust into an arbitrary and distorted cosmos. The audience must set aside normality for a heightened and subjective world vibrant with ominous metaphor. Central characters are often normal people under attack by a world running under inverted or alien rules. We are invited to identify with them and to survive and escape a system peopled by characters who neither reflect nor doubt. Expressionism is clearly the province of fairy tales like those by Hans Christian Andersen or the brothers Grimm. In the cinema Victor Fleming's *The Wizard of Oz* (1939) stands out as the classic of the genre, and more recently Steven Spielberg has made a whole industry out of providing modern fairy tales, most notably *E.T.* (1982).

ENVIRONMENTS AND MUSIC

Past, future, or distant settings can be selectively distorted to make a selectively biased caricature. But there are ways to remain in the present and yet display everyday transactions as heightened and nonrealistic. Musicals are one way. Jacques Demy's *The Umbrellas of Cherbourg* (1964), though visually formal and lyrical in composition and camera movement, tells a conventional small-town love story using natural dialogue. The difference is that it is sung, giving the effect of a realistic operetta (if that is not a contradiction in terms). The Gene Kelly films do much the same thing with dance, but use unashamedly abstract, theatrical sets. Busby Berkeley's dance films on the other hand veer toward fantasy by merging human beings into kaleidoscope kinetics.

Music itself, when its use surpasses conventional mood intensification, can impose a formal patterning of emotion upon the life onscreen. In Losey's *The Go-Between* (1971), Michel Legrand's exceptionally fine score starts with a simple theme from Mozart and develops and modulates it hauntingly, carrying us deep through a boyhood trauma and onward to the ultimate tragedy—the emotionally withered, unused life of the old man who survives. Peter Greenaway's use of Michael Nyman's minimalist scores in *The Draughtsman's Contract* (1983), *A Zed and Two Noughts* (1985), and *Drowning by Numbers* (1991) powerfully unites the mood of characters moving like sleepwalkers through worlds dominated by mathematical symmetry and organic decay.

THE STYLIZED PERFORMANCE

Perhaps the least stylized performance is that caught, documentary fashion by a hidden camera, as Joseph Strick often did in *The Savage Eye* (1959). Here we face a paradox: if the subject is unaware he is acting, he is not acting but simply being. Performers know they are performing, and make choices over what they present, consciously and unconsciously adapting to the situation. All performance is therefore stylized to a greater or lesser extent.

Here I'll draw a working distinction between the performance that strives for realism—the art that hides art—and that which is deliberately heightened for dramatic effect. The adaptations of Dickens' novels, such as George Cukor's *David Copperfield* (1934) or David Lean's *Oliver Twist* (1948), have a young person as their point-of-view character and use him to present a subjective view of the adult world. Fagan, Bill Sykes, and the other thieves verge on the grotesque, while Oliver remains a touchingly vulnerable innocent caught in their web. These are good examples of what E. M. Forster called flat and round characters, the round character being psychologically complete and the flat characters being filtered through Oliver's partial and vulnerable perception.

How much a secondary character should be played as subjective and distorted can be decided fairly easily by examining the controlling point of view. In Welles' version of Kafka's *Trial* (1962), it is the character of Joseph K. with whom we identify and through whose psyche all the characters are seen. Likewise, in *The Wizard of Oz,* Glenda and the Wicked Witch of the West are designed to act in oppositional ways upon Dorothy and dramatize her conception of benevolence and evil.

In films where a polarization is implied between the point-of-view character and those in the surrounding world, the oppositional characters are often analogues for the warring parts of a divided self. Often they are in dialectical opposition to each other and bear upon the (usually vulnerable) main character like the spokes of a wheel in relation to its hub. The morality play form, with its melodramatic emphasis on setting the innocent adrift among hostile or confusing forces, is a particularly useful way to externalize the flux within an evolving personality because the cinema, with its emphasis on externals, does not otherwise handle interior reality particularly well.

It is the writer's and director's task to set the levels of heightened characterization and to determine the nature and pressure of what each spoke must transmit to the hub, or point-of-view character. It will be crucial, too, that the level of writing and playing be consistent, and that there be change and development as the film is played out so that no part, whether spokes or hub, becomes static and therefore predictable.

The personification of human qualities implied by deliberately flat characters (as opposed to those who are dramatically undernourished) and by the stylized performance points back to the early theater's masks and stock characters mentioned in the subsection of Chapter 1 entitled "On Masks and the Function of Drama." Nonrealistic or flat characters are especially likely to function as metaphors for the conflicting aspects in the round character's predicament, and thus to forewarn us of a metaphysical subtext that we might otherwise miss.

NAMING THE METAPHORICAL

If characters play metaphorical roles in an allegory (and it is invariably revealing to analyze *every* script as if this were true), then it is important for the director to make up metaphors that describe each character, and to assign each an archetypal identity. These are potent tools for clarification and action, and the process is

FIGURE 15-1 ——————

Lovers amid encroaching darkness in Cox's *Cactus* (courtesy Spectrafilm).

equally useful for the worlds they inhabit. Paul Cox's *Cactus* (1985) portrays the developing relationship between an angry and desperate woman losing her sight and a withdrawn young man already blind (Figure 15-1). The man makes his refuge a cactus house where she visits him to explore her fate. The cacti are dry, hostile and spiky, but also phallic. So the setting becomes emblematic of his predicament as a man who has turned his back self-protectingly on intimacy of all kinds and who expects to survive without nourishment.

Having settings and predicaments dramatized and metaphors in hand as an explanation will greatly help you explain to actors how you want each to play his role, and why. We shall explore this principle much more fully when we come to analyzing the script and working with actors.

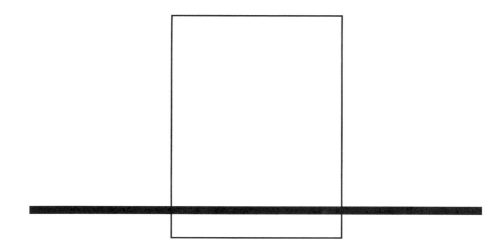

C·H·A·P·T·E·R 16

FORM AND STYLE

FORM

Form is the manner in which content is presented. For a film to have a coherent and provocative outlook on the human life that it shows, the story must be revealed in a particular and purposeful way; that is, the makers must find a form unique to the story's purpose and nature. If the possible variations seem unlimited they are in fact usefully confined by allied concerns, some of which we have already considered. Designing a film's form involves more than figuring out where to put the camera and what lens to use before shooting. It means articulating a clear and provocative purpose for telling the tale.

If, for instance, we want to show a holdup in a grocery store, we would need to first decide whose was the controlling point of view. It could variously be that of the store owner, the frightened clerk, a short-sighted old man, the off-duty policeman buying a loaf of bread, or the robber himself. Because each would see the events with a different significance, each would tend to notice different things, and this way of noticing lets the audience infer the nature and dilemma of that character.

So, in considering form, the chosen point of view can usefully limit and shape your decisions. Subsequent choice of lenses, camera positions and angles, and lighting all contribute to the cumulative impression you are building for the audience. This adds up to a progression of distinct moods and to a particular way of seeing.

We must also consider the structuring of time. The crime need not necessarily be shown in chronological order—one might also show it in portions, as remembered by a survivor, perhaps, or from the stage-by-stage retrospect of the court case following the arrest of the robber. Different witnesses might have conflicting memories of the different actions, and so on. Chronology, as these examples show, is really another facet of point of view.

Of overarching concern is the storyteller's nature and point of view, for it has an agenda and purpose distinct from that of the characters or even the director. This, for instance, might shift narrative focus between three of the characters, treating the point of view of each as equally important. The controlling point of view and the limitations inherent in the story's structure largely determine the form of any film, but good formal choices are seldom obvious nor can they be made without analysis and insight.

FORM, CONFLICT, AND VISION

Events do not achieve significance just because someone frames them. A quite average audience is already subconsciously aware that *good fiction is not a reproduction of life but an enactment of ideas about it.* If your topic is robbery, your audience expects you to reveal something fresh about what robbery means—socially, culturally, or emotionally. Who carries it out, where, in what way, and why—these are questions of basic story philosophy, all of which run back dependently to the film's vision of life. To answer such questions one should first put each major character under duress so his or her basic makeup is revealed. For every human being has a character that is a mix of innate temperament, environmental influence, and what his or her peculiar history has instilled. Almost all of what is visible about people's characters—what moves them to act the way they do and what causes them to forge their own destinies—arises from their personal baggage of unresolved conflicts, both the internal ones they carry everywhere and the external ones they confront, or cause.

Such conflicts already exist in you, the reader reading these words. They are your unfinished business in life. However old or young you may be, however much you feel yourself to be lacking in "interesting" experience, you are stigmatized in certain ways, and carry within you buried memories of events that still smolder. Their cause and effect you still feel deeply, and you will best find their significance by telling analogous tales. By this token, *the storyteller tells a tale not just to entertain, but to grow in spirit.*

Form, therefore, derives first from knowing what tale you want to tell, what you want to show through it, and then from finding the best framework and visual/aural language to impart it. The examples below are to highlight the elements of form you should take into consideration.

VISUAL DESIGN

This is the aspect of a film that people most readily notice, and it can be affected by lighting, choice of lenses, camera height and movements, costuming, set dressing, and by the locations and terrain themselves. A film gains power when it finds visual equivalencies to its thematic concerns. Wim Wender's *Paris, Texas* (1984) finds in the flat, depopulated, and arid terrain of Texas the perfect counterpart to the dehydrated emotions of the numbed, inarticulate man stumbling in search of his lost wife and child. *Elvira Madigan* (1967) used long takes and telephoto shots to merge the runaway count and his mistress into a lyrical, floating oneness with the Swedish landscape during its brief period of summer. Bergman's *The Seventh Seal* (1956) goes to the opposite extreme; set in the Middle Ages, when superstition and fear of the plague ruled men's hearts, the story takes place amid heavy forests. The dark figures, and low-key black-and-white photography make us experience the mixture of magic and superstitious terror at a time when life was "nasty, brutish, and short."

Jacques Rivette's *Celine and Julie Go Boating* (1974) has an ingenious and effective development in its visual style. Two young women break into a shuttered house where a stagey domestic drama is slowly unfolding. Obsessed with the characters and the play's outcome, they are compelled to keep returning, eventually discovering that they can enter the play's action—quite unnoticed by the other characters. As the piece develops, and as missing links drop into place, the characters and their setting gradually become more and more unnatural in color. What

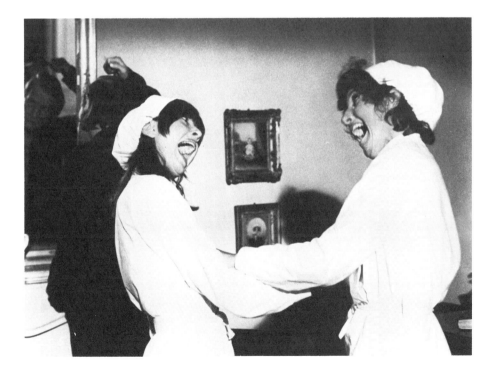

FIGURE 16-1

Two friends discover each is playing the same part in the drama they have infiltrated. Rivette's *Celine and Julie Go Boating* (courtesy New Yorker Films).

starts as realism gradually becomes more surreal, distanced, and artificial until it has become a dynamic genre painting.

SOUNDTRACK DESIGN

Too often film sound is merely diagetic, that is, it does no more than provide the logical and realistic accompaniment to what we see on the screen. Remember what Bresson said, "the eye sees, but the ear imagines." The cooing of doves floating in through a sunny bedroom window, the echo of footfalls in a church, the calling of children distantly playing hide-and-seek, or muffled weeping in a darkened room can work miracles upon our imagination and receptivity. Dialogue can be used in poetic counterpoint, as in Chris Marker's extraordinary short film made of still photos, *La Jetée* (1963). Songs and sayings, snatches of story, old recordings, street sounds, the sounds of the natural and the manmade world, as well as the shock and tension of silence can all be composed into a *musique concrète* that is poles away from the literal world of what-you-see-is-what-you-hear.

RHYTHMIC DESIGN

Rhythmic design probably suggests music or sound (such as footsteps and clocks ticking) to supply a rhythmic identity to a scene, but there are many elements in a film that can supply rhythms:

- sound effects
- speech patterns (and breathing)
- frequency of sound changes
- frequency of picture cuts
- inherent rhythm of shot (affected by content and its movement, movement of camera, and less definably by composition)
- inherent rhythm of action itself
- inherent rhythms of particular characters (this also varies according to their mood, time of day, predicament, and so on).

Cinematic rhythms emanate from several sources at any given time. A good editor and an experienced director are acutely sensitive to their combined effect, and know as instinctively as any musician when the combined effect is, or is not, working.

An audience's involvement, as any showman will tell you, is best sustained by variety. Shakespeare—who supported a large company of actors by satisfying the tastes of the common people—switches scenes from action to monologue to comedy, interspersing long scenes and short scenes, group scenes and duologues, duologues and soliloquys. Even while making a continuous thematic development through these varying orchestrations, he juxtaposes very different textures and rhythms. Without the sustaining music of consummate form and poetically dense language, Shakespeare could never have delivered such profound themes to unlettered audiences.

Good film technique likewise aims to refresh ear and eye with variations and comparisons that cause us to keep experiencing differently, to pass through a succession of perspectives and moods. Similar to variations in rhythm is the idea of changes in dramatic pressure. One can increase or relax the audience's sense of pressure by ringing the appropriate rhythmic changes. Surely this is the reason Bergman insists that film is a musical rather than a literary medium: "Film is mainly rhythm; it is inhalation and exhalation in continuous sequence" (Introduction, *Four Screenplays of Ingmar Bergman* [New York: Simon & Schuster, 1960]).

MOTIFS

These devices placed by the storyteller signify thematic aspects, as shots of flowing water might signify the theme of "life goes on no matter what." Any formal element, aural or visual, can signify a motif, and one that recurs is called a leitmotiv.

AURAL MOTIFS

In Carpenter's *Hallowe'en* (1978) there is a strange synthesizer sound accompanying the presence of the vengeful escapee. It is a nondiagetic sound (that is, heard by the audience and not by the characters) and serves to heighten our sense of their danger. Most films using specially composed music also use the leitmotiv principle, that is, a special instrumentation and/or special musical theme running through the film assigned to a character, situation, or sentiment. You surely know this from Prokofiev's delightful *Peter and the Wolf,* composed to introduce the different instruments of the orchestra and their tonal range to children through the medium of a fable.

VISUAL MOTIFS

Certain camera movements can be a motif, like the crabbing shots through the trees in Enrico's *Occurrence at Owl Creek Bridge* (1962) which signify a guilty, uneasy voyeurism. In Abraham Polonsky's *Tell Them Willy Boy Is Here* (1969) it is the action of running. The fugitive Indian is on the run throughout the film so that running itself becomes emblematic of his existence (as it once was for Polonsky, badly victimized during the McCarthy witch-hunt years). Shots of trickling sand in Teshigahara's *Woman in the Dunes* (1964) repeatedly characterize the woman's threatened situation. In Roman Polanski's *Tess* the use of color becomes a motif, as Thomas Hardy in fact specifies in the original novel. The young peasant heroine, moving unconsciously between what society sees as innocence and sin, is repeatedly associated with either white or red (the white dresses in the opening May walk, the red of the strawberry Alec puts between her unwilling lips, for example). The color red is also a motif connoting danger throughout Roeg's *Don't Look Now* (1973). Compositional balance or vantage (looking through foreground objects, for instance) or the use of sound and silence might all be pressed into service as motifs.

BRECHTIAN DEVICES COUNTERING AUDIENCE IDENTIFICATION

Cinema unlike literature is forced to view characters from the outside, and has subsequently favored action over contemplation. The suspense film and the action thriller go further, for they aim to make one *identify* with a particular character, and to "lose oneself," as the alarming success of the James Bond films testifies. It would be forgivable to assume that all films promote audience identification, certainly an assumption that was applied to the theater until Berthold Brecht's pioneering work when Germany began embracing the Nazis. Realizing how incompatible contemporary audience habits were with his purpose, Brecht redefined how theater might work. Wanting to stimulate his audience into thinking about the dialectics of political and social life, rather than letting them dream their way through the fate and fortunes of a unique individual, Brecht devised a theater of mixed and constantly changing forms. This he speculated would keep the audience aware it was watching a show with a dialectical purpose, and not an imitation of life.

The same constantly changing mode of address can be found in the work of Kluge, Godard, Tanner, and Greenaway, to name just a few. This style of discourse may employ an authorial narration, titles, songs, musical interludes, or surreal events peopled with bizarre, allegorical, or historical characters. Often using elliptical forms, these films deliberately disrupt the audience's ever present desire to lapse into that waking dream of identification which Brecht, surrounded as he was by incipient fascism, saw as suicidal escapism. Mass audiences are not yet drawn to Brecht's demanding alternative to traditional narrative form, but his work and that of those under his influence can be immensely moving and intellectually invigorating.

Keeping an audience thinking and not just feeling is a rare skill that awaits development on a wider scale in the cinema. Wim Wenders' two films about the angels over Berlin, *Wings of Desire* (1988) and *Faraway, So Close* (1993), point most excitingly in the right direction.

LONG TAKES VERSUS SHORT TAKES

Without abandoning his wish to keep the audience at a distance, Alain Tanner in *Jonah Who Will be 25 in the Year 2000* (1976) adopted a quiet and nonconfrontational technique by playing whole scenes as single takes. Using only the simplest of camera movements he lets us stand back and consider the meaning of the characters' lives rather than urging us to participate in their emotions. The result is a cool and welcome distancing that invites one to ponder with the characters how they should live out their ideals when their 1968 social revolution has failed.

To eliminate the need for editing, the long take needs astute blocking and rehearsal. In conventional technique, editing and mobile camerawork inject nervous excitement and enable the point of view to constantly migrate around a central character—both classic ways of seducing the spectators into identifying. Tanner uses some minimal camera movement to avoid making locations appear flat like a backcloth. Otherwise he uses one take per scene; yet one feels no loss of the conventional apparatus of cinema. In shooting, the level of playing and its consistency are of prime importance, so this apparently simple approach may save nothing in time or filmstock, since actors or technicians at any time may abort not just a take, but a whole scene. Hitchcock back in 1948 made his thriller *Rope* in the same way, but more as a technical challenge than because the story, based on the Leopold and Loeb murder case, called for it.

In the long take, the audience sees the whole picture, everything in its context, so far as practicable. Closeups are produced by blocking characters so they move close to the camera. In the conventionally shot and edited scene, the audience will more often be shown only enough important fragments (of a room, or of an action, for instance) to infer the whole. The act of completing their context in one's mind causes us to enter the reality of the person whose experience the scene represents. In so doing, says Brecht's notion, we yield intellect to sensation.

Somewhere between the extremes of Eisensteinian fragmentation—with its extreme control and manipulation of the spectator—at one end of the spectrum, and unbroken, uninflected presentation at the other lie the choices that reflect not just convenience, but, as always, your storyteller's special stance toward both story and audience. Surely there is a place for the emotions and the intellect in any intelligent film, though maybe not in every single scene it contains.

SHORT FORMS

Regrettably the short film subject is often considered beneath the director with serious intentions. This is like would-be novelists rejecting poetry and the short story as unworthy mediums. The short film is actually closest to the poetic form, for it requires deft characterization, a compressed narrative style, and something to say that is focused and fresh in voice. A good five- to ten-minute film is actually more demanding to make than a passable thirty-minute one.

For beginners it is essential to work in short form because it is inexpensive and places high demand on the control of craft and storytelling essentials. On grounds of brevity alone, good short films are more readily shown in film festivals than equally good longer films. To earn recognition, you need to win prizes; please be kind to yourself by saving time and money, getting invaluable experience, and by competing in the less restricted arena.

Think of it this way: you can make five eight-minute films for the price of one sixty-minute film. After this you will handle a long film five times as well because you have tackled five sets of demanding conceptual problems such as characterization, blocking, dramatic shape and flow, and editing. You will also have directed a host of actors and given life to a gallery of characters.

What makes a good short subject? Much like a good short story, a short film needs a limited but evocative setting, characters engaged in a significant form of

struggle, someone who develops however minimally to be significant, and a resolution that leaves one thinking about some aspect of the human condition. Such a
film can be a farce, a dark comedy, a lyrical piece, a Chaplinesque allegory (like
Polanski's early shorts), a sitcom—anything. However, it must declare its issues
and its personalities as quickly and deftly as animators do in their work. It should
be as well acted, as interestingly shot, and as tautly edited as the best five minutes
in a first-rate feature film. A superb short film is the ultimate advertisement for
what you could do with a bigger canvas.

The key to defining your best short film subjects lies in defining what situations you know that most test and reveal a given character. This will almost certainly include some turning point, where pressures have built up and the main
character is forced to take action. When he or she acts, there follow the inevitable
consequences to which he or she must adapt. Since the turning point marks the
onset of change, it may be the true starting point of the story for which the
buildup is only a prelude. In Polanski's nondialogue *The Fat and the Lean* (1961)
the thin man serves the fat man in all manner of humiliating ways, all the while
visibly yearning to escape toward the Paris skyline. Eventually, to our joy, he runs
away—only to be recaptured by the fat man, roused to action by the loss of his
slave. On one level a vaudeville comedy, on another a grisly political allegory, the
film shows how neither slave nor master are free. Who can wonder that Polanski
was soon entrusted with bigger things?

STYLE

The word "style" is often and confusingly interchanged with "form." Godard
when apparently speaking of form said, "To me, style is just the outside of content, and content the inside of style, like the outside and inside of the human
body—both go together, they can't be separated" (Richard Roud, *Jean-Luc Godard* [London: Secker & Warburg, 1967]).

The style of a film is really the visible influence of its maker's identity. This is
made messy by the fact that film authorship is usually collective. But a Godard or
a Lynch film, even if you hate it, is immediately recognizable. Partly this is content, partly the kind of tale and the characteristic forms each chooses, and partly
it is because they have the mark of individual personalities and tastes all over
them. It is this last, virtually uncontrollable, element that is properly style.

Just as you can't choose your identity at any meaningful level, so you should
let your film style take care of itself. You can and should locate your film within a
genre, and design its content and form to be an organic whole. If over the period
of its creation you serve each controllable aspect of your film well, people will
come to recognize in a succession of your films a continuity that is hard to pin
down, but that will be called your style. From your audience and your critics you
may even learn what it is—rather as (at considerable risk to one's equilibrium) one
extracts a sense of one's character from the reactions of friends, enemies, family,
flatterers, and detractors.

Setting out to develop a style or an artistic identity, as students often feel they
must do in fine art schools, leads to superficialities and attention-demanding gim-
mickry. Far more important is to develop your deepest interests and to make the

best cinema you can out of the imprint left by your formative experience. Working sincerely and intelligently is what can truly connect your work to an audience. Even with these qualities you must expect a long evolution while you internalize all the technical and conceptual skills.

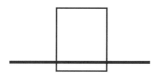

CHECKLIST, PART IV
AESTHETICS AND AUTHORSHIP

Note: There is an important Form and Aesthetics Questionnaire at the end of this section that will greatly help you during the development and preproduction stages of your film.

The recommendations and points summarized here are only those most salient or the most commonly overlooked. To find more about them or anything else, go to the table of contents at the beginning of this part, or try the Index at the back of the book.

Point of View

- making the audience experience a character's POV means making them experience a character's emotional situation as if it were their own
- complex drama often shows multiple POVs, which become poignant when the drama also shows their limitations, misperceptions, and miscommunications
- the eyes and mind through which we view the events (which we have personified as the Storyteller) also adds up to a very important POV, which may be philosophical, critical, amused, ironic, detached, excited, terrified, etc.
- everyone's POV, including that of the Storyteller, is stimulated and qualified by their own particular context (which is why juries are so carefully chosen)
- in everyday life make a point of backtracking whenever you have a sharp sense of someone else's reality to find out what opened the door for you
- make yourself aware of how POV is implied in literature, painting, photography, and theater as well as film. There are common denominators arising out of audience response that will strengthen your command in film
- it's important that we come to care deeply about at least one person in a story
- often films center on a main character's predicament and this person becomes the film's controlling POV. This does not exclude contrasting POVs, which can easily sharpen that of the main character or characters

- that we care about your characters and care whether they overcome their difficulties is a major component in the all-important area of suspense and dramatic tension
- to control POV requires a God-like ability by the story's creator(s) to see both from the characters' viewpoints and also from the audience's
- an omniscient POV gives the Storyteller the ability to be anywhere, see all, and know all (like God)
- a subjective POV means that the character through whom we are seeing is subject to special and very human limitations and passions
- an audience has its own subjectivity which the filmmaker may or may not be able to anticipate, depending on how distant the audience is from the filmmaker's own culture

Subtext and Making the Significant Visible

- the audience must know what it is looking for in a story so a story must declare its intentions
- merely *showing* events will probably leave the events' meaning buried under an avalanche of banal reality (a great hazard in filmmaking)
- much of what is meaningful in human life goes on below the surface and requires interpretation and judgment, skills that an audience loves to exercise
- what is cause and what is effect are plot considerations, but above these are the moral implications, which interest us above everything
- the events chosen, their artful juxtaposition, irony, and humor are all ways to signify an underlying meaning or set of values
- allegory, analogy, metaphor, symbol are more ways for the Storyteller to signify meanings
- the struggle between right and wrong is not morally testing like that between right and right

Genre

- a genre is a type of film that the audience recognizes as a world running under particular rules or norms
- film genres are often extensions of traditions begun in other media like painting, literature, music, or theater
- genre permits framing an area of life and seeing it through a particular prism of concerns or values
- subjectivity is inherently interesting and fertile in determining genre. "The public" as seen by an overworked postal clerk is a vastly different species from that seen by a newly ordained priest.

Duality and Conflict

- the clash of temperaments or values is the stuff of drama

- if drama is to be about people trying to get or do things, there must always be obstacles, difficulties, and unforeseen consequences, just as in life. This is conflict.
- conflict does not have to be something negative; we learn through solving problems and every problem involves solving conflicts ("gold is not tested save by flame")
- the core of every interesting personality lies in the person's conflicts or "unfinished business"
- every person and every situation contains opposites; actors are told when playing the bad character to find the good in him, and vice versa

Microcosm and Macrocosm

- the same truths are reproduced in large and small scales. An individual might represent a whole people, and dancers might be used to represent atoms. This can be useful
- nations behave with the passions of a myopic individual
- an individual's complex psyche can be split up and represented as a group of characters each representing different dominant traits

Drama, Propaganda, and Dialectics

- representation and typifying lead rather easily to flat characters and stereotyping. Work at defining the conflicts in every character you create, so he/she is interesting and realistically ambiguous
- like yourself, cinema audiences are drawn to the ambiguities in their own lives and not to other people's certainties (for which one joins a church)
- if you must promote ideologies, make their opposition strong and intelligent
- your audience is as intelligent as yourself. Safer to reflect human predicaments than be caught trying to tell people how to live
- duality and ambiguity in a movie invite the audience to make judgments. Using one's judgment is an important part of being gainfully entertained

The Difference Between Observer Filmmaking and Storytelling

- there is no right or wrong way to make any film, only effective and ineffective stories, and effective and ineffective forms for those stories
- some events are so powerful that they need only be relayed. They need little or no framing or implied commentary
- most fiction, however, needs a moral purpose in the telling, and a moral attitude on the part of the teller. This should never be simplistic—even for young audiences
- a story gains immensely from the added dimension brought by the critical intelligence of its Storyteller (good social criticism is less concerned with right and wrong than with enabling us to see more clearly and deeply)
- to the degree that the Storyteller can draw us emotionally into the film's world, we experience what it is like being other than we are. The audience longs to experience being *other*

- the story, the characters, the human predicaments in your movie are always going to be more important to get right than technique, which is at best a transparent vehicle for these

Structure, Plot, and the Handling of Time

- plot is the arrangement of incidents and the logic of causality, which needs to seem credible and inevitable at every step
- you can't be sure you have control of your movie's plot unless you maintain an up-to-date outline. This allows you to see it unobstructed
- a film's structure should create forward momentum by creating questions and appropriately delaying their resolution
- plot structure should never needlessly complicate unless the film's form is deliberately a maze. Clarity of Who/What/When/Where helps the audience concentrate on thematic issues and the Why, which usually centers on the characters and their situations
- a major organizing principle for any story involves how time is handled
- departing from chronological time usually signals that the film is routed through someone's subjectivity, either that of a character or of the Storyteller
- flashbacks generally slow and weaken the ongoing movement of a story
- heavy use of flashbacks (past tense) usually goes with a heavily determinist or even Freudian outlook (she does this *now* because of what happened to her *then*)
- have you graphed the intended rise and fall of pressures in your film?
- have you faced the faults this reveals?

Thematic Purpose

- the thematic purpose is your Storyteller's purpose for telling the tale
- the Storyteller is not necessarily you; more likely he/she is a dramatized intelligence who has particular needs to fulfill through telling the tale. Make sure you elucidate what they are for yourself, since this is the persona you are going to serve (play) when you direct, and it is the aura of this intelligence that gives the film a "voice" all its own
- you won't be in control of your movie's thematic purpose unless you maintain an up-to-date premise or concept
- examine your outline and screenplay for how well the movie serves the thematic purpose
- thematic purpose is often best discovered by searching for appropriate metaphors
- these metaphors will almost certainly suggest sound and visual motifs and even leitmotifs
- a well-developed theme unifies and justifies your movie
- it's important for your energy and focus that your movie serve a thematic purpose in which you deeply believe

- strong things are usually simple; don't feel your theme must be complex and all-embracing

Space, Stylized Environments, and Performances
- decide what kind of spaces your characters inhabit and what impression these should give
- depending on the film's system of POV's, you may want to show most, or very little, of the detail in each location
- a character can notice very little of their surroundings through familiarity, confusion, or because they are carrying out an urgent and narrowly defined purpose
- a character can notice very much about their surroundings because they have time on their hands, are in new surroundings, or have special reasons to take stock
- space may go noticed or unnoticed simply because that's the habit or temperament of the POV character
- stylization generally means a departure from the unremarkable
- in a movie a whole world may be stylized or only aspects of it
- stylization signals subjectivity on the part of characters, the genre, or their Storyteller

Music
- music can be misused as a dramatic crutch
- it can legitimately suggest the interior state of a POV character
- it can also signal the Storyteller's feelings about the story, which is useful because it makes you investigate what you're watching in particular ways
- for the audience music is like a drug habit; easy to start, difficult to end
- music can illustrate or it can counterpoint
- music can accompany and enhance whatever is inherently strong in emotion
- avoid music that duplicates what we can see or hear (for instance, lush pastoral music over shots of cows in a wide meadow)
- music can provide historical, social, or emotional context
- most music sold in libraries isn't worthy of the name
- better have no music than bad music
- too often bad music survives because it came free from a friend

Form and Style
- form follows function
- less is more
- simple is strong
- kill your darlings
- listen to your characters for what they need

- know where the movie belongs and where it departs from its genre
- don't neglect visual style; your cinematographer should be your ally here
- don't confuse visual style with directing; it's only part of the job and can lead you to neglect content and character
- design the sound track like a soundplay, don't just leave it to trail after picture
- remember that rhythms underlie everything in screen language, *everything*
- decide who or what you want your audience to identify with
- if you want to counter identification you will have to create it and subvert it
- only use long takes if your movie needs them; there are many other rewarding ways to challenge yourself
- short films are harder to make than long films; poetry is more demanding than prose
- short films get shown much more easily than longer ones
- let your film decide its style, not vice versa
- as far as your own style is concerned, you can only strive to become authentic to yourself. Personal style will take care of itself. In filmmaking you dress to impress at your peril

FORM AND AESTHETICS QUESTIONNAIRE

NAME _____

PHONE _____

FILM WORKING TITLE _____

Fill out this form to see how much you know about your film. Take time and refine your answers to fit into the deliberately small spaces. Notice that the questionnaire encapsulates the artistic process by starting with you, moving through information about your film and its characters, and ending with how you want to act on your audience.

1. **Statistics.**
My film will be _____ minutes long, will be shot on (format) _____ , is expected to take _____ shooting days, and to cost $ _____ . So far I have (check what applies):

__ rough idea, incomplete	__ thematic purpose	__ principal cast
__ rough idea, reasonably complete	__ premise	__ producer
__ beginning	__ treatment	__ production manager
__ middle	__ screenplay	__ director of photography
__ end	__ shooting script	__ all funds
__ step outline	__ all cast	__ %_____ raised,
		$ _____ to raise

2. Personal philosophy behind the making of this film.

"In life I believe that _____

_____

_____ "

3. Premise.

"The film explores my conviction by showing (here briefly write your film's premise):

_____

_____

_____

_____ "

4. Genre.

"The genre (type or family) of this film is

_____

and my film only departs from this genre in that it _____

_____

_____ "

5. Main characters, their dominant traits, and the major conflict for each (most important first).

(a) _____

_____

_____

(b) _____

_____

_____

(c) _____

_____

_____

(d) _____

_____

_____

More characters? Add on a separate sheet.

6. **Main situation affecting the main characters.**

"The major situation in which the characters find themselves is _____

_____

_____

_____ "

7. **Point of view.**

(a) "The point-of-view character is _____ and his/her biased way of

seeing is mainly _____

_____ "

(b) "Subsidiary characters are

_____

and their way of seeing, by contrast is _____

_____

_____

_____

_____ "

(c) "The Storyteller's characteristics are _____

_____

_____

and this makes him/her see in a particular way that is _____

_____

_____

_____ "

8. **Film's main conflict.**

"The major forces in conflict in this film are between

_____

_____

_____

and

_____

_____

_____ "

9. **Story resolution.**

"The resolution to the characters' unfulfilled desires is _____

_____

_____

_____ "

10. **Intended impact.**

"After they have seen my film I want my audience to:

(a) Feel _____

_____

(b) Think _____

_____

(c) Tell all their friends to go and see the film because _____

_____

_____

_____ "

11. **Other.**

Anything important not included above:

_____

_____

_____

_____

_____

_____

_____

_____

_____

_____

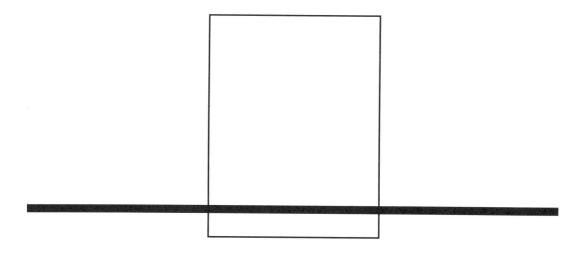

P·A·R·T V

PREPRODUCTION

CHAPTER 24
Director and Actor Prepare
a Scene

CHAPTER 25
Final Rehearsals and Planning
Coverage

CHECKLIST, PART V
PREPRODUCTION

C·H·A·P·T·E·R 17

INTERPRETING THE SCRIPT

THE SCRIPT

If you have already made the step outline and concept as previously described, you are coming to grips with the script's inner workings and practical implications. If not, do so. Since the screenplay is skeletal and open to a wide spectrum of interpretation, you will need all the help you can get to assess its potential and to build upon it methodically and thoroughly.

FIRST IMPRESSIONS

If the screenplay is new to you, read it quickly and without interruption, noting your random first impressions. First impressions are intuitive and, like those about a new acquaintance, become significant as familiarity blunts your clarity. Define the film's premise and make sure you have an up-to-date step outline showing each sequence's function.

DETERMINE THE GIVENS

Reread the script and carefully determine exactly what are the givens. This is your hard information directly specified in the screenplay. It includes locations, time of day, character details, clues to back story (events prior to the period covered by the film), and words used by characters. To each actor, for instance, the script provides everything known about his character's past and future. A character, after all, is like the proverbial iceberg—four-fifths out of sight. What is visible (that is, in the script) allows the actor to infer and develop what is below the "water line" (the character's biography, motives, volition, fears, ambitions, vulnerabilities, and so on). The givens serve as the foundations determining everything else. Much is deliberately and wisely left unspecified, such as the movements and physical nature of the characters and the treatment to be given the story in camerawork, sound, and editing. The givens must be interpreted by director, cast, and crew, and the inferences each draws must eventually harmonize to be consistent.

BREAK INTO MANAGEABLE UNITS

Next, divide the script or treatment into workable units by location and scene. This helps you plan how each unit of the story must function and this initiates the process of assembling a shooting script. If, for example, you have three scenes in the same day-care center, you will shoot them consecutively to conserve time and energy, even though they are widely spaced in the film. This will be laid out in the breakdown or crossplot (see Figure 17-4) described later in this chapter. When production begins, everyone must be well aware of the discontinuity between the three scenes or actors may inadvertently adopt the same tone, and camera crew shoot and light in the same way. In storytelling, one is always looking for ways to create a sense of contrast, change, and development.

PLAN TO TELL THE STORY THROUGH ACTION

Cinematic films remain largely comprehensible and dynamic even when the sound is turned off, so you should *devise your screen presentation as if for a silent film.* This will force you into telling your story cinematically rather than theatrically— that is, through action, setting, and behavior rather than through dialogue exchanges. This may require rewriting, which is a director's prerogative but some writers' idea of hell. Be sure to warn your writer of this likelihood well in advance. You don't want to find yourself battling your writer before you've even begun shooting.

DEFINING SUBTEXTS

The notion that every good text is a lifelike surface hiding deeper layers of meaning or "subtext" is invaluable. It reminds us that as dramatists we must always make evident the submerged stream of heightened significances flowing beneath life's surface. Much of the subtext arises out of what each character is really trying to do or get.

THE DISPLACEMENT PRINCIPLE

In life, people very rarely deal directly with the true source of their tensions. Characters often don't know themselves, or keep what they do know hidden from other characters (remember life with your family?). Instead, what takes place is a displacement. Two elderly men may be talking gloomily about the weather, but from what has gone before, or from telltale hints, we realize that one is adjusting to the death of a family member and the other is trying to bring up the subject of some money owed to him. Although what they say is that the heat and humidity might lead to a storm, what we infer is that Ted is enclosed by feelings of guilt and loss, while Harry is realizing that once again he cannot ask for the money he badly needs. This is the scene's subtext which we can define as "Harry realizes he cannot bring himself to intrude his needs upon Ted at this moment, and that his situation is now desperate." We cannot interpret the subtext here without knowledge gained from earlier scenes, and this emphasizes how much well-conceived drama builds and interconnects.

An important aspect of reading a script is to trace each event and character backward to see that the requisite groundwork has been laid. If a cousin arrives to show off a new car, and in so doing, reveals his uncle's plan to sell out the family business, that cousin needs to be established earlier, and so does the family's dependency on the business.

AMBIVALENCE, OR BEHAVIORAL CONTRADICTIONS

Intelligent drama exploits the way each character consciously or otherwise tries to control the situation, either to hide his underlying intentions and concerns or, should the occasion demand it, draw attention to them. Once as director and actors we know the subtext, we can contrive behaviors for each character that manifest the tensions between his inner and outer worlds.

Ambivalency like this is the audience's clues to a character's hidden life and underlying conflicts. When actors begin to act upon (not merely think about) their characters' conflicts and locked energies, scenes move beyond an illustrative notion of human interaction and we begin to truly feel the characters' emotions. The work now begins to imply the pressurized water table of human emotion below the aridly logical top surface. This surface tension means preserving a logical exterior in which he is rational, mannerly, and inscrutable and is all part of how a character keeps his agenda hidden. We all unconsciously do it, and most of the time.

DEFINING A PREMISE OR THEMATIC PURPOSE

Another concept vitally important to the director is that of the thematic purpose, or "superobjective," to use Stanislavski's concept. This is the authorial objective powering the work as a whole. One might say that the superobjective of Orson Welles' *Citizen Kane* (1941) is "to show that the child is father to the man, that the power-obsessed man's course through life is the consequence of childhood deprivation that no one around him ever understands."

It is vital for you to define a thematic purpose for a work in script form if you are to truly capitalize on the script's potential. Usually one has a strong intuition about what it is, but you should have it stated and to hand when you survey all the scene subtexts together.

To some degree a script's thematic purpose is a subjective entity derived from the author's outlook and vision. In a work of some depth, neither the subtexts nor the thematic purpose are so fixed and limited that interpretive choices for the director and cast are fixed and limited. Indeed, these choices are built into the way the reader reads and the audience reacts to a finished film, because everyone interprets selectively what they see from a background of particular experiences. These are individual but also cultural and specific to the mood of the times.

Kafka's disturbing story "Metamorphosis"—about a sick man who discovers he is turning into a cockroach—might be read as a parable about the changes people go through when dealing with the incurably sick, or it might be read more from a science fiction perspective as a grisly "what if" experiment that imprisons a human sensibility in the body of an insect. In the first example, the thematic purpose might be to show how utter dependency robs the subject of love and respect, while the second shows how compassion goes out to a suffering heart only when it beats inside a palatable body.

Whatever you choose as your thematic purpose, you must be able to articulate it with utter conviction, it must be consistent with the text, and you must be able to make it acceptable to your creative collaborators. Superficial readings of the screenplay will produce divergent, contradictory interpretations, so you must arrive at a shared understanding of the story's purpose or you won't have an integrated story. No matter how much work you put in, probing and intelligent actors will still take you into unexamined areas. That's part of the excitement of discovery.

GRAPHICS TO HELP REVEAL DRAMATIC DYNAMICS

Below are a couple of ways to expose the heart and soul of each scene. These methods for exposing what would otherwise remain undisturbed and unexamined are consciousness-raising techniques that allow the director to confront the implications of the material. They take time and energy to implement, but will richly repay your effort.

BLOCK DIAGRAM

Make a flowchart of the movie's content, with each sequence as a block. To do this conveniently, photocopy the Story Line/Editing Analysis Form (Figure 17-1). In the box name the scene, and under "Contributes" write two or three lines to describe what the audience will perceive as its dramatic contribution to the story line, as in Figure 17-2. This goes further than the step outline because it is pre-

```
 ┌─────────────────────────────────────────────────────────────────┐
 │   STORY LINE OR EDITING ANALYSIS FORM                 Page _____  │
 │   Production title _____ Length ____ mins │
 │                                                                   │
 │   Writer/Editor_____  Date ___/___/_____  │
 │  ──────────────────────────────────────────────────────────────  │
 │       Sequence Defined by       │    Sequence's Contribution to   │
 │        Brief Line Title         │    Film's Developing "Argument"  │
 │  ───────────────────────────────│──────────────────────────────  │
 │   ┌──────────────────────────┐  │     Contributes:               │
 │   │ Seq #____                │  │                                │
 │   │                          │  │   ............................ │
 │   │                          │  │   ............................ │
 │   │                          │  │   ............................ │
 │   └──────────────────────────┘  │                                │
 │  Ends:___'___"                  │              Length:___'___"   │
 │   ┌──────────────────────────┐  │     Contributes:               │
 │   │ Seq #____                │  │                                │
 │   │                          │  │   ............................ │
 │   │                          │  │   ............................ │
 │   │                          │  │   ............................ │
 │   └──────────────────────────┘  │                                │
 │  Ends:___'___"                  │              Length:___'___"   │
 │   ┌──────────────────────────┐  │     Contributes:               │
 │   │ Seq #____                │  │                                │
 │   │                          │  │   ............................ │
 │   │                          │  │   ............................ │
 │   │                          │  │   ............................ │
 │   └──────────────────────────┘  │                                │
 │  Ends: ___'___"                 │              Length:___'___"   │
 │   ┌──────────────────────────┐  │     Contributes:               │
 │   │ Seq #____                │  │                                │
 │   │                          │  │   ............................ │
 │   │                          │  │   ............................ │
 │   │                          │  │   ............................ │
 │   └──────────────────────────┘  │                                │
 └─────────────────────────────────────────────────────────────────┘
```

FIGURE 17-1 ──

Form for script or editing analysis.

dominantly concerned with dramatic effect rather than content. Expect to write descriptive tags concerning:

- plot points (unpredictable storyline shifts)
- exposition (factual and setup information)

```
┌─────────────────────────────────────────────────────────────────┐
│  STORY LINE OR EDITING ANALYSIS FORM                      Page 1  │
│                                                                   │
│  Production title ____A Night So Long_____ Length ____ mins │
│                                                                   │
│  Writer/Editor_____ Date ___/___/____ │
│  ─────────────────────────────────────────────────────────────── │
│          Sequence Defined by        ¦      Sequence's Contribution to │
│            Brief Line Title         ¦       Film's Developing "Argument" │
│  ─────────────────────────────────  ¦ ────────────────────────────── │
│   ┌──────────────────────────────┐  ¦                             │
│   ¦ Seq #_1__                     ¦  ¦       Contributes:          │
│   ¦ Bar Seq: Ed presses his com-  ¦  ¦  Establishes Ed's & Dana's charact- │
│   ¦ pany upon Dana and promises   ¦  ¦  .................................. │
│   ¦ to maintain a platonic rel-   ¦  ¦  ers and the sparring to come. │
│   ¦ ationship if that's what      ¦  ¦  .................................. │
│   ¦ Dana wants.                   ¦  ¦                             │
│   ¦                               ¦  ¦  .................................. │
│   └───────────────────────────────  ¦                             │
│  Ends:___'___"        ¦             ¦            Length:_3_'___"    │
│                       ψ             ¦                             │
│   ┌──────────────────────────────┐  ¦                             │
│   ¦ Seq #_2__                     ¦  ¦       Contributes:          │
│   ¦Garage Seq: Dana shows Ed her  ¦  ¦  More character details, that they │
│   ¦ motorcycle; each probes the   ¦  ¦  .................................. │
│   ¦ other's background            ¦  ¦  have country music in common, that │
│   ¦                               ¦  ¦  .................................. │
│   ¦                               ¦  ¦  each can be sentimental    │
│   ¦                               ¦  ¦  .................................. │
│   └───────────────────────────────  ¦                             │
│  Ends:___'___"        ¦             ¦            Length:_5_'___"    │
│                       ψ             ¦                             │
│   ┌──────────────────────────────┐  ¦                             │
│   ¦ Seq #_3__                     ¦  ¦       Contributes:          │
│   ¦ Len's Apt. Seq: Dana visits   ¦  ¦  Dana tries to have disconnected sex │
│   ¦ old boyfriend, makes love     ¦  ¦  .................................. │
│   ¦ with him, realizes it's a     ¦  ¦  and by failing, realizes that Ed │
│   ¦ mistake                       ¦  ¦  .................................. │
│   ¦                               ¦  ¦  is an unexpected force in her life │
│   ¦                               ¦  ¦  .................................. │
│   └───────────────────────────────  ¦                             │
│  Ends: ___'___"       ¦             ¦            Length:_4_'___"    │
│                       ψ             ¦                             │
│   ┌──────────────────────────────┐  ¦                             │
│   ¦ Seq #_4__                     ¦  ¦       Contributes:          │
│   ¦ Dana in Garage, Night Seq:    ¦  ¦  Dana has buried fears, but wants to │
│   ¦  Dana returns to face the     ¦  ¦  .................................. │
│   ¦  dark shadows                 ¦  ¦  confront them, no matter what. │
│   ¦                               ¦  ¦  .................................. │
│   ¦                               ¦  ¦                             │
│   ¦                               ¦  ¦  .................................. │
│   └───────────────────────────────  ¦                             │
└─────────────────────────────────────────────────────────────────┘
```

FIGURE 17-2 ───

Specimen of block diagram analysis of a script.

- character definition
- building mood or atmosphere
- parallel storytelling
- ironical juxtapositioning
- foreshadowing

Having to write so briefly makes one find the paradigm for each—a brain-strain exercise of the utmost value.

Soon you will have the whole screenplay diagrammed as a flowchart. You will be surprised at how much you learn about its structure and its strengths. Among weaknesses look for:

- expository scenes that release information statically and without tension
- unnecessary repetition of information
- information released early or unnecessarily ("Make them laugh, make them cry, but make them wait" said Wilkie Collins about writing mysteries. This is axiomatic for all drama.)
- factual information that comes too late
- confusions in time progression
- bunching of similar events or actions
- disappearances of lesser or even major characters for long periods
- characters suddenly appearing to serve a limited dramatic purpose
- use of coincidence to solve a dramatic problem ("Guess what, I've won the lottery!")
- a lack of alternation in mood or environment
- excitement too early leading to anticlimax
- similarity (and therefore redundancy) in what some scenes contribute
- multiple endings because of indecision over what (and therefore how) the story must resolve

GRAPH

Another way to dig below a script's surface is to graph out the changing emotional pressures or temperatures of each scene. It should be done after several readings of the script and before you start work with the actors. With a problematical scene it's good to do it collaboratively with the actors after some initial rehearsal. Time is the graph's baseline and tension is the vertical axis. You can do it for a scene and for each main character. If, for instance, you have a comedy scene between a dentist and a frightened patient, you could graph out the rise and fall of the patient's anxiety, and then rehearse the action to progressively escalate the patient's fear and link to it the rising irritation of the dentist. Each dramatic unit within the scene culminates in a moment of decisive realization for one or other of the characters, called a "beat." One such beat might take place in the reception area when the already nervous patient hears a yell from the surgery and decides to make a run for freedom once the receptionist's back is turned. Another might come when, finding she has already locked the door of retreat, he must face her contempt. (See "Finding the Beats" in Chapter 21 for more explanation.)

Before you begin shooting, make a "barometric" chart for your whole film's emotional dynamics. It won't be easy because you will have to invent graphing coordinates that reflect the issues in your particular film. You will be surprised at how much your homework reveals. I discovered the need for this exercise the hard way; in the cutting room I found I had directed a film in which many scenes had surreptitiously adopted a uniform shape and were restating the same emotional information.

To put the graphing method into action, here is a scene based on an experience of my father's in wartime London. Food was scarce and often acquired on the black market. Note that for a film treatment we put it into the present tense.

> Paul is a sailor from the docks setting out for home across London. On board ship he has acquired a sack of brown sugar and is taking it home to his family. Food of all kinds is rationed, and what he is doing is very risky. He has the sugar inside a battered old suitcase. The sugar is as heavy as a corpse, but he contrives to walk lightly as though carrying only his service clothing. In a busy street one lock of the suitcase bursts, and the green canvas sack comes sagging into view. Dropping the suitcase hastily on the sidewalk he grips it between his knees in a panic while thinking what to do. To his horror, a grim-faced policeman approaches. Paul realizes that the policeman will check what's inside the suitcase, and Paul will go to prison. He's all ready to run away, but the policeman pulls some string out of his pocket and gets down on his knees, his nose within inches of the contraband, to help Paul tie it together. Paul keeps talking until the job's done, then thanking him profusely, picks up the suitcase as if it contained feathers, and hurries away feeling the cop is going to sadistically call him back. Two streets later he realizes he is free.

The graph in Figure 17-3 plots the intensity of each character's dominant emotion against the advance of time. Paul's emotions change, while the unaware policeman's are simple and placid by contrast. Paul's stages of development roughly are:

• trying to walk normally to conceal weighty contraband,
• sense of catastrophe as suitcase bursts,

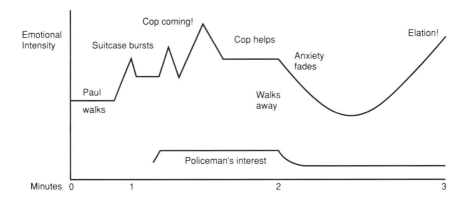

FIGURE 17-3

Graph expressing changes of emotional intensity in two characters.

- assuming policeman is coming to arrest him,
- realizing his guilt is not yet apparent—all is not yet lost,
- tension while trying to keep policeman's attention off contents,
- making escape under policeman's ambiguous gaze, and
- sense of joyous release as he realizes he's got away with it.

A visual of this kind brings clarity to where and how changes in the dominant emotions must happen. It shows the need to create distinct rising and falling emotional pressures within the characters, pinpoints where characters undergo major transitions, and focuses director and actor on the need to externalize these through action. A major problem with untrained actors is that they try to play all their character's characteristics along with whatever is happening in the moment. This muddies and confuses the playing, and drives the actor into an intellectual approach. *Good playing deals with one situation and its attendant emotions at a time, and finds credible ways to transition from one to the next.*

In the scene above, the policeman feels only a mild, benign interest, which falls away as the sailor with the successfully mended suitcase goes on his way. It is a very different situation for Paul. He must pretend he's an innocent man with a luggage problem. Knowing something the policeman does not know, the audience empathizes with the sailor's anxiety and appreciates his efforts to project petty concerns. What is missing from the scene is the knowledge of (1) the nature of the contraband, (2) where he is going with it, and (3) what he risks if he is caught. For the scene to yield its full potential, all these plotting points would need to be established earlier.

POINT OF VIEW

We could add a dimension to our scene by underscoring Paul's subjectivity. By having the policeman appear threatening as he approaches, we could make him seem to be testing Paul's guilt by offering to help. Only late in the scene would we reveal his benign motives. Camerawork, juxtaposing the bulging, insecure suitcase against the approaching policeman, would suggest visually the thoughts uppermost in Paul's mind.

Here we are trying to reveal Paul's point of view, which means *relaying evidence that makes us identify with him.* By switching to the policeman's point of view, we can also investigate his reality and show the POV of an apparently unsympathetic character as well as that of our hero. This is an important departure from the good/evil dichotomy of the simple morality play where only a main character is a rounded portrait and all the subsidiary characters remain flat.

The concept of subjective and objective points of view is enormously important to sophisticated storytelling. Unlike literature, which can easily move the reader from one person's consciousness to another, or pull away to an authorial bird's-eye view of human life, point of view is harder to shift in film because the camera tends to make such an impersonal inventory of its surroundings and thus to seem objective. However, in my example the audience has been led to participate in Paul's inner experience while seeing all the time how he conceals what he is feeling. Actors and directors of long experience carry out this duality intuitively and it is the clarity and force of subjectivity revealed in this way that contributes so much to a satisfying performance. For the beginner lacking unfailing instincts in this direction, nothing less than a detailed, moment-to-moment analysis will yield the insight to mold the scene effectively.

GENERALIZED INTERPRETATION
IS THE MOST COMMON FAILURE

Inexperienced players will, as I have said, approach a scene with a correct but generalized attitude gained from a reading or discussion. Applied like a color wash and without regard to localized detail, the unspecific, monolithic interpretation produces a scene that is fuzzy and muted where it should be sharp and forceful. When you direct, demand that each actor has clear specific goals within a scene.

CROSSPLOT OR SCRIPT BREAKDOWN
IN PREPARATION FOR REHEARSAL

Take the script and make a breakdown of characters appearing in each scene, like the one in Figure 17-4 made for a treatment of *Northanger Abbey*. A scene breakdown like this, allowing one to see at a glance which scenes require which location and what combination of actors, will be essential for planning the rehearsal schedule and the eventual shoot. It also indicates the film's inherent pattern of interactions and is yet another aid to discovering the work's underlying structures.

FIRST TIMING

A film's length absolutely determines the markets it can enter. Television has strict length requirements, so keeping control over length can be vital. Already you need to know how long the script will run. You can get a ballpark figure by allowing a minute of screen time per screenplay page. This should average out across many pages but will not necessarily work for specific passages such as a rapid dialogue exchange, or a succession of highly detailed images with long, slow camera movements. You can get a more reliable figure by reading over each scene aloud, acting all the lines, and going through the actions in imagination, or better, for real. Using a stopwatch, make a notation for each sequence, then add up the total.

Be aware that *rehearsal and development invariably slows material* by adding business not specified in the script. This kind of action must be present if the characters are to be credible and the film cinematic rather than theatrical.

If rewriting makes a scene too long, reexamine every line of dialogue to see if newly developed action makes any of it redundant. Likewise in rehearsal, never hesitate to cut a line if its content can be carried instead by an action.

```
                          NORTHANGER ABBEY
-----------------------------------------------------------------------
                  Script Cath- Isa-  John  Henry  James  Elean- Mrs.   General Mrs
Sc  Location      pages  erin  bella Thorpe Tilney Morland or    Allen  Tilney Thorpe
-----------------------------------------------------------------------
```

Sc	Location	Script pages	Catherin	Isabella	John Thorpe	Henry Tilney	James Morland	Eleanor	Mrs. Allen	General Tilney	Mrs Thorpe
1	The Dance	1-2	*						*		
2	Lower Rooms	2-6	*			*					
3	Pump Room	6-7		*							*
4	Mrs. Allen's	7-13	*	*	*		*				
5	Pump Room	13-20	*	*		*	*	*			
6	Mrs. Allen's	20-24	*	*	*		*		*		
7	On the Journey	24-25	*		*		*				
8	At the Theatre	25-27	*			*			*		
9	Mrs. Allen's	27-30	*	*	*		*	*		*	
10	Out Walking	30-35	*			*		*			
11	Mrs. Allen's	35-37	*	*							
12	In the Street	37-40	*		*						
13	At the Tilneys'	40-41	*						*	*	
14	Mrs. Allen's	41-43	*	*							

FIGURE 17-4

Typical scene and character breakdown table shows which characters, locations, and script pages are necessary for each scene.

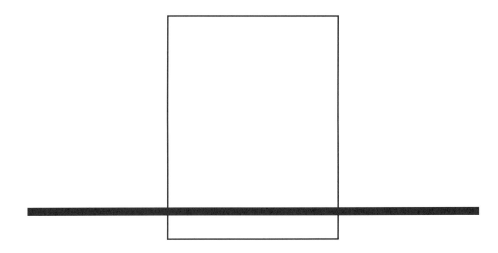

C·H·A·P·T·E·R 18

CASTING

CASTING

Good casting contributes massively to the success of any film. Beginning directors often do it poorly by settling for the first person who seems right, or who has already proved reliable.

The object of auditioning is to find out as much as you can about the physical, psychological, and emotional makeup of each potential cast member so you can commit yourself confidently to the best choice. Doing this means initially putting many actors through a brief procedure to reveal their character and to indicate how he or she handles representative situations. Later there will be semifinal and final rounds of auditioning. While procedures can be adjusted for actors with little or no training, the first aim is to identify the individual behind the façade. The director is therefore concerned with a potential actor's:

- physical self (features, body language, movements, voice)
- innate character (confidence, outlook, reflexes, rhythm, energy, sociability, imprint made by life)
- type of intelligence (sensitivity to others, perceptiveness of environment, degree of self-exploration, and cultivation of tastes)
- grasp of acting (experience, concepts of the actor's role in drama, craft knowledge)
- directability (interaction with others, flexibility, defenses, self-image)
- commitment (work habits, motivation to act, reliability)

THE DANGERS IN IDEALS

There are two ways to approach casting.

1. *Can this actor play the father in my script?*
Naturally you wonder whether this particular man is right for the character of the father in the script. There is, however, a hidden bias in this attitude. The actor is being held up to an ideal of the character, as though the character were already formed, and the actor either right or wrong. This puts emphasis upon a premeditated image of the character and makes you view the actor through a cookie cutter. By this measurement the actor must always fail. Casting a film from a mental masterplan is like marriage for the man who knows what Miss Right must be before he has met her.

2. *What kind of father would this actor give my film?*
By this approach you acknowledge that the role is capable of many possible character shadings. Casting becomes developmental rather than fulfillment. Very importantly, you are already treating the actor's physical and mental being as an active collaborator in the process of making drama.

ATTRACTING APPLICANTS

An essential principle running throughout every aspect of filmmaking is that of supplying yourself with an overabundance of choice. More than anywhere, apply this principle to casting, because the human presence on the screen is how you most directly and continuously command your audience's attention. Though this audience is not expert in any of the film techniques you might use, it is an absolute *authority* on the human presence. Here you can easily be more naive than your audience, especially if you cast a friend or loved one in a main part. I once edited a film where the director simply couldn't see how inadequate his wife was for the main part.

Despite these obvious dangers, casting among beginners is usually the least rigorous part of the whole process. Feeling uncomfortable with the power to choose among fellow aspirants, the embarrassed newcomer settles too early and too easily for actors who look right. Age and appearance matter, but this is only the beginning. All forty-year-old men are not alike, and to uncritically presume that one can take the right face and make its owner into the script's sentimental, spendthrift father is asking for trouble.

Inadequate casting usually arises from lack of:

- confidence in one's right to search far and wide
- knowledge about how to discover actors' underlying potential
- self-knowledge about who you can work with, and who you cannot

Learning how to audition helps to remove the crippling sense of inadequacy and embarrassment about making human choices. Knowledge and confidence are thus closely linked.

DEVELOPING CHARACTER DESCRIPTIONS

Before you can search for possible actors, make basic character descriptions to post in appropriate places (newspapers, theater or acting school billboards) or to give over the phone. A typical list might look like this:

<u>Ken</u>, 15, tall and thin, nervous, curious, intelligent, overcritical, obsessed with science fiction.

<u>George</u>, late 20s, medium height, medical equipment salesman, lives carefully and calls his parents each Friday. Husband of Kathy.

<u>Kathy</u>, early 30s, but has successfully lied about her age. Small-town beauty queen gone to seed after a steamy divorce. Met George through a dating service.

<u>Ted</u>, 60s, bus inspector, patriot, grower of prize chrysanthemums, disapproving father of George.

<u>Eddie</u>, 40s, washing machine repairman, part-time conjuror and clown at children's parties. Too boring to be married. Likes to philosophize.

<u>Angela</u>, 70s, cheerful, resourceful, a veneer of respectability that breaks down raucously after a couple of drinks. In early life made a fortune in something illicit. Determined to live forever.

Thumbnail sketches like these compress a lot into a few words and allow the reader to infer possible physical appearances. Finding people to fill these roles now becomes an attractive challenge.

ACTIVE SEARCH FOR ACTORS

With the exception of the oldest and youngest in the sample cast above, the rest are drawn from an age bracket normally immersed in daily responsibilities. Three of the adults are blue-collar parts, a social class least likely to have done any acting, and liable to feel inadequate and self-conscious. These are generalizations whose only function is to help focus the search and indicate what kind of inventiveness is needed to locate the exceptions with the necessary qualities and spare time.

Lacking a liberal budget, you must be resourceful in finding likely people to try out. Wherever possible, save time and frustration by actively seeking out likely participants. First contact key people in theater groups. Locate the casting director and ask if you can pay a brief visit. Whoever handles casting will be a mine of information about local talent. The next most knowledgeable people are the producers (who direct in the theater) and committed theater workers. Knowledgeable members will often respond enthusiastically with names you can invite to try out. When a theater group is successful enough to use only professional (union) actors, the response is likely to be cautious or even downright unfriendly. Theaters don't like their best cast members seduced away by screen parts, and may want to avoid prejudicing their relationship with the actors' union. You will probably get a tight-lipped referral to the actors' union.

If your budget is rock bottom, you will have to work hard. Actors well suited to specific parts can always be found, but it takes ingenuity and diligence. Never forget that if you have a good script *your film's credibility comes not from your film technique, but from how believable you can make the human presence on the screen.* Good film technique simply provides a seamless storytelling medium. The better it is, the more the audience dwells on that all-important human presence.

For the character of the fifteen-year-old Ken I would track down teachers producing drama in local schools and ask them to suggest boys able to play that character well. The teacher can ask the kid, or the kid's parents, to get in touch. This allays the nightmare that their child is being hunted down by a coven of hollow-eyed pornographers.

Elderly people are more of a problem. Since most cultures sideline the old, many become physically and mentally inactive. Your first task in casting Ted and Angela will be to locate older people who keep mentally and physically active. You may be lucky and find there is a senior citizens' theater group to draw upon, or you may have to track down individuals.

For Ted I would look among older blue-collar men who have taken an active and extroverted role in life, perhaps in local politics, union organizing, entertainment, or salesmanship. All these occupations require some flair for interaction with other people, and a relish for the fray.

Angela is a hard person to cast, but try looking among retired actresses or vocal women's group members such as citizens' and neighborhood pressure groups—anywhere you could expect to find an elderly woman secure in her life's accomplishments and adventurous enough to play a boozy, earthy woman with a past.

While you cast, remind yourself periodically that hidden among the gray armies of the conforming there are always a few individuals in any age group whose lives have been lived with wit, intelligence, and individuality. Such people rise to prominence in the often unlikely worlds to which exigency or eccentricity has taken them. Angela, for instance, might be the president of the Standard Poodle Fanciers Club, and Ted might be discovered in an amateur comedian contest.

Werner Herzog's actors, for instance, include nonprofessionals drawn from around him. The central figure in *The Mystery of Kasper Hauser* (1974) and *Stroszek* (1977) is played by the endearing Bruno S—, a street singer and Berlin transport manager whose surname has remained undisclosed to protect his job. Robert Bresson, who refuses to cast anyone trained to act, used lawyers in *The Trial of Joan of Arc* (1962) to play Joan's inquisitors. A lifetime spent defining details gave them just the right punctiliousness in their cross-examining. In his *Notes on the Cinematographer* (London: Quartet, 1986) Bresson gives a compelling rationale, akin to a documentary-making attitude, for using "models" (his word for players) who have never performed before.

PASSIVE SEARCH FOR ACTORS

If you live in a city, you can spread a large net simply by putting an advertisement in the appropriate papers. Be warned that large nets bring in some very odd fish and they may inordinately waste your time. If there is a fair amount of theater in your area, you may be lucky enough to find there is a monthly auditions broadsheet, or other professional periodical. In it, describe the project and give the number, sex, and age of the characters in a few words, and a phone number to contact.

SETTING UP THE FIRST AUDITION

FIELDING PHONE APPLICANTS

As each person calls up, you will need to amplify upon the role he or she fits, specify what the audition will demand, and, if the person sounds appropriate, give an audition slot on one of your audition days. Schedule people into slots so that they arrive at, say, ten-minute intervals and can be individually received by someone who can answer questions.

Be direct and realistic about the project and about the unit's level of expertise. If you are a student group, say so, and above all be truthful about the time commitment you will need for rehearsal and shooting. A cool response to the time commitment is a danger bell indicating the applicant's low level of interest or high ego. Many calling themselves actors are minimally experienced, or not experienced at all. The world is full of dreamers looking for a quick path to stardom; these should be avoided except for very brief, undemanding parts. A rigorous audition helps to weed out the half-hearted. You may want to add the obviously unskilled to a waiting list so that you can audition those claiming experience first.

A first call might ask actors to

- perform two contrasting three-minute monologues of their own choosing
- take part in a cold reading

THE AUDITION CALL

This session aims to net as many people as possible so later you can make callbacks for those deemed suitable. Many respondents in spite of what they said on the phone will be devoid of everything you require, or quite unrealistic about their abilities and commitment. In this winnowing operation, expect a lot of chaff for very little wheat.

GATHERING INFORMATION

Have actors wait in a separate area from the audition space, and give each a form to complete, so later you have on file:

1. name and address
2. home and work phone numbers
3. acting experience
4. role for which actor is trying out
5. special interests and skills

The last is purely to get a sense of what attributes the actor may have that indicate special energy and initiative. You might also have a further section asking actors to write a few lines on what attracts them to acting. This can reveal values and how serious and realistic the person is.

A good plan is to have assistants in the holding area who chat informally with incoming actors about what they have written on their forms. This helps calm actors' fears, but also affords impressions for your assistants, particularly about how punctual and organized the actor seems. These can be most valuable later.

INITIAL AUDITION

The actor can now be shown into the audition space where he or she will perform. Videotape the performances so you can review your choices later and make comparisons, especially if you see a lot of actors for one part.

Most people are extremely nervous and apprehensive at auditions, but this is not necessarily negative since it shows they attach importance to being accepted. The presence of a camera increases the pressure.

MONOLOGUE

It is good to require two brief monologues of the actor's choice that are very different in character. These can tell you:

- whether an actor habitually acts with the face alone or with the whole body
- what kind of physical presence, rhythm, and energy level he/she has
- what his/her voice is like (a good voice is a tremendous asset)
- what kind of emotional range he/she can produce
- what the actor thinks is appropriate for himself and for your piece

Whether they are well or badly performed and whether you can "see" the character the actor is playing is very important. The actor's choice and handling of material also indicate what he thinks he does best. The choice may reflect intelligent research based on what the actor has found out about your production, or it may indicate an enduring self-image. A man trying out for a brash salesman who chooses the monologue of an endearing wimp has probably already cast himself in life as a loser whose best hope is to be funny. This will hardly do for, say, the part of someone vengeful. Here you may sense a quality of acquiescence that makes the actor psychologically and emotionally unsuitable for this part, though perhaps interesting for another.

COLD READING

For this you will need several copies of several different scenes. Depending upon who is in your waiting room, you might want to try combining two men, two women, a man and a woman, or an old person with someone young, and so on. It is a good idea *not* to use scenes from your film, but instead to find something from theatrical repertory that is analogous in mood and characters. You don't want whoever you choose to become fixed by early impressions of your script.

Your assistant can decide from those waiting which piece to read next, and give each actor a copy of the scene in advance.

In the cold reading you will:

- see actors thinking on their feet
- see actors trying to give life to a character just encountered
- see the same scene with more than one set of actors
- have the opportunity to compare what quickness, intelligence, and creativity are evoked by the bare words on the page
- hear how each actor uses his voice
- see how some will inject movement
- find out who asks questions about their character or about the piece from which the scene is drawn

Performances and behavior will affect you differently and often in ways that pose interesting questions. In a reading with two characters of the same sex, you can switch the actors and ask them to read again, to see if the actors can produce appropriate and different qualities at short notice.

After actors have auditioned, always:

- thank them
- give a date by which to expect news of the outcome
- note down something positive about their performance to help you be supportive of those you have to reject

DECISIONS AFTER FIRST AUDITIONS

If you have promising applicants, run the tapes of their contributions and brain storm with your project coworkers. Discussing each actor's strengths and weaknesses usually reveals further dimensions in the candidates, not to mention insights into your crew members and their values.

Now comes the agonizing part. Call everyone who auditioned and tell them whether they were selected for callback auditions. Telling the bad news to those not selected is hard on both parties; mitigate the disappointment by saying something appreciative and positive about the person's performance. With the people you want to see again, set a callback date for further auditioning.

DANGERS OF TYPECASTING

Be careful about casting characters with prominently negative traits. It can, for instance, be disastrous during shooting to have an actor slowly become aware that he has been cast for his own negative qualities. If a very boring person were cast to play Eddie, the director would have difficulty calling out his boringness because it is patently reprehensible to exploit someone's weaknesses for an audience's amusement.

In varying degrees, all actors go through difficulties playing negative characteristics because of the lurking fear that these characteristics are really within their own makeup and will become visible. The less secure the individual is, the more likely such self-doubts will become acute. A sure sign of this insecurity is when an actor makes a personal issue of his or her character's qualities and argues to up-grade them.

To protect yourself, ask the actors you are considering to discuss their ideas about their characters' negative traits. Their underlying attitudes may influence your choice. Villains are easy to play, but playing a stupid or nasty character may either be viewed as an interesting challenge or as a personal sacrifice by the actor. There are no small parts, said Stanislavski, only small actors.

LONG- OR SHORT-TERM CHOICES

A great temptation is to cast the person ahead of the pack because he or she gave something quick and attractive during auditions. This actor may be brilliant or may later emerge as glib and inflexible, developing less than a partner whose audi-tion was less accomplished. Caution dictates that you investigate not only what an actor wants to do, but also how able that actor is to perform the unfamiliar, and how willing and interested to push beyond present boundaries. All actors of any experience are fervently committed in principle, but practice can reveal something utterly different. It involves the whole person, not just his ideas, and one may find that a genially accomplished personality coming under the threat of the unex-pected suddenly manifests bizarre forms of self-defense and resistance (See Chap-ter 20: "Actors, Problems").

THE DEMANDING PART OF THE CHARACTER WHO DEVELOPS

Not all parts require a high degree of adaptability to direction. To cast a surly gas station attendant for one short scene requires little in growth potential, whereas the part of a young wife who discovers that her husband is dominated by his mother will call for extended and subtle powers of development. The character must go through a spectrum of emotions during which she changes and develops, so the director must find an actor with the openness and emotional reach to un-dertake a grueling rehearsal and performance process.

FIRST CALLBACK

When you are ready to call back the most promising actors who auditioned, you will need to prepare some additional testing procedures.

A READING FROM YOUR SCRIPT

Give some background to the scene, which should be demanding but only a few minutes in duration.

1. Ask each actor to play his/her character in a specified way. After the readings, give the actors critical feedback and directions to further develop the scene.

2. Have them play the scene again and look for how the actors build on their in-itial performances, holding on to what you praised but altering the specified areas.

3. For a further run-through, give each actor a different mood or characteristic to see what he or she produces when given a radically different premise.

IMPROVISATION

Give two actors brief outlines of characters in the script, and outline one of the script's situations that involves them.

4. Ask your players to improvise their own scene upon the situation in the (unseen) script. The goal is not to see how close they get to the scripted original, but how they handle themselves when much of the creation is spontaneous.

5. After they have done a version, give them feedback about aspects you see developing in their version, and ask for a further version, specifying some change in behavior and mood. Now you will be able to see not only what they can produce from themselves, but how well they respond to direction.

SECOND CALLBACK

INTERVIEW

Give your best candidates the script to read, and tell them *not* to learn any lines. After they have read it, spend time informally with each, encouraging him or her to ask questions and to talk about both the script and themselves. By now you have formed ideas about the individual, which you try to confirm. Look for:

*   realism
*   sincerity
*   honesty
*   a genuine interest in drama itself

    Be wary of those who:

*   flatter
*   name-drop
*   give superficially good readings
*   are opinionated
*   leave you feeling they are stooping to do you a good turn
*   your instincts tell you are looking over your shoulder for something better

These are danger signs that foreshadow ego and commitment problems. On the positive side, it is a good sign if an actor is sincerely excited by a part because the script explores some issue that is genuinely central to his or her own life.

MIX AND MATCH ACTORS

When you have multiple contenders for a lead part, try them out in different permutations so you can assess the personal chemistry each has with the others. In part, this is to see how they will strike an audience. I once had to cast a short film about a man in his thirties who becomes involved with a rebellious teenage girl. We rejected a more accomplished actor because there was something indefinable

FIGURE 18-1

Actors have different development rates. Philippe Leotard in Tanner's *The Middle of the World* (courtesy New Yorker Films).

in his manner that made the relationship seem sinister. Another actor paired with the same actress changed the balance to give the girl the upper hand, as the story demanded.

It is extremely important that actors cast to play lovers be tried out extensively with each other because antipathy could spell disaster.

You also mix and match to look for the most dynamic chemistry between the actors themselves. Sometimes one can see early that two actors simply do not communicate well. This may be due to temperamental or philosophical differences, but whatever the cause, the result will be a wariness and stiffness in their playing that disables your film. Try to cast players who are responsive and interested in each other. Even when this is accomplished, you may encounter some common problem, such as Alain Tanner did in *The Middle of the World* (1974). The male lead usually produced his best work in an early take while the woman playing opposite him worked up to her peak over a number of takes.

FINAL CHOICES

In addition to the obvious question of body type and physical appearance, the director must, before making a final choice, review the overall advantages each actor offers, taking into account the actor's

- impact
- imprint on the part
- rhythms of speech and movement
- quickness of mind
- ability at mimicry, especially if he is to maintain a regional or foreign accent
- voice quality (extremely important!)
- capacity to hold onto both new and old instructions
- pattern of development, whether intuitive and immediate or slower and reflective
- commitment to the project
- commitment to acting as a discipline
- patience with filming's slow and disjunctive progress
- ability to enter and reenter an emotional condition for several takes and camera angles
- compatibility with the other actors
- compatibility with you, the director

CAMERA TEST

To confirm that you are making the right choices, shoot a short scene on videotape with the principal actors. Even then, you will probably remain somewhat uncertain and feel you have to make difficult decisions.

If you have an overwhelming urge to cast someone that your intuition says is risky, you should tactfully but directly communicate your reservations. You might, for instance, feel uncertain of the actor's commitment, or that the actor has a resistance to authority figures and will have problems being directed. Confrontation at this early point shows you how the actor handles uncomfortable criticism, and paves the way should that perception later become an issue or, God forbid, should replacement become a necessity. An actor who seems arrogant and egocentric will sometimes gratefully admit, when faced with a frank reaction to his characteristics, that he has an unfortunate way of masking uncertainty.

More than anything, people in all walks of life crave recognition. If the director is able to comment on the potential and the deficiencies masking it, the serious actor will respond with warmth and loyalty. Sharing and honesty is a goal in all director/actor and actor/actor relationships. It is the basis for trust and a truly creative working relationship. Every committed actor is looking for a director who can lead the way across new developmental thresholds. This is development not just at acting but in living. If you perform this function, that actor will place great loyalty with you and be your best advocate to other actors, who can sometimes hold back with a new director to find out if he or she is worth trusting.

When you make your final decisions, notify and thank all who have taken part. This signals your professionalism and maintains your good standing in the community. Needless to say, rejection is painful, and more so for those who made it all the way to the final round.

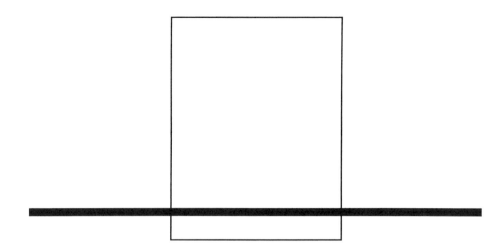

DIRECTING ACTORS

The most useful knowledge any director can acquire apart from basic filmmaking is of acting. You can and should read about it, but more important is to take classes and actually do it. Acting is a well-documented craft, so what follows is a brief digest of ideas and practices that I find particularly useful.

IN SEARCH OF NATURALNESS

While an animator creates a complete world according to a mental vision, live action cinema must fashion its tales using real objects and real people. The theater utilizes the same means but boldly forces the spectator to accept something patently untrue. Go to *Hamlet* and you must pretend that you are at a medieval Danish court with a missing wall. However, a cinema Shakespeare such as Kenneth Branagh's *Henry V* (1989) has little choice but to use authentic locations and costumes or to modernize the production. It is film's intimacy and minute realism that forces the need for realism in settings and psychological realism in the acting. In real settings audiences expect to meet people no less real than one encounters in documentaries.

This faces film directors with serious problems, especially those unable to afford experienced screen talent. You are going to need the combined skills of actor and drama coach if you are to meet your audience's expectations.

DIRECTING IS REMOVING OBSTACLES

In general, actors don't need special techniques or arcane information from their director. What they require is authoritative help in casting off layers of human insecurity so they can *be* rather than perform. Quite simply, freedom from tension is what permits this. The film actor should have no sense of there being an audience and no sense of even being seen except by the director. The biggest surprise to anyone watching a scene being filmed is the smallness and apparent inconsequentiality of the action. You think, "Nothing really happened—they can't have been filming!" Yet when you see the scene on the screen *everything* happens. The fiction camera captures life just as intimately and completely as you are used to seeing in a documentary.

The difference between theater acting and film acting is thus enormous, because *theater actors consciously draw on the audience's attention to help sustain belief in their roles.* When first transferred to the film situation, the theater actor feels robbed of this support and suffers a crisis concerning his or her ability and worth. The director is now the only audience and must wean the actor to a new, more internalized way of sustaining focus and belief. A nonactor will feel the same strangeness, because we all use other people's reactions to know what we are really doing. We shall need some methods to support nonactors as well as trained actors.

MAINTAINING FOCUS BY DOING

The film actor cannot lose focus even for a moment because the camera registers everything. An underoccupied actor being stared at by a camera becomes fatally aware of how he may look. This is a vicious circle, for soon the actor also becomes self-consciously aware of how unnatural it is to be thinking such things. Now fatally divided, one half of the actor is trying to act while the other half is trying *not* to be a judging audience. The battle against self-consciousness is lost until the actor can escape back into a state of natural preoccupation. The character's inner and outer actions offer this escape because they tend to engage the actor in the character's consciousness, deflecting the mind from consciousness of self. Doing is therefore the path to being. The actor will need a continuous flow of internal or external actions, of things to do.

FOCUS AND RELAXATION

The paradox here is that mental focus leads to overall relaxation of mind and body, which in turn further assists the actor to find and maintain the character's mental focus.

Always watch your actors' body language for signs of tension—particularly in their shoulders, face muscles, hands, and walk. It is usually within your power to undo this tension by using indirect ways to reassure actors that their work is effective or by redirecting their attention. When they care too much, they get tense. Have some improv games ready as a refresher to solve extreme cases.

EMOTIONAL MEMORY

The actor avoids paralyzing self-judgment by maintaining a flow of physical tasks. The experienced actor works hard to invent just the right action or task that resonates the character's present state of mind. Not only is the actor freed from self-contemplation but the truest actions also release powerful, authentic emotion during performance. Stanislavski called this curious psychic reflex emotional memory. Of his many discoveries about acting psychology, this is the most frequently misunderstood. To do it justice we must look at how the human mind works when an actor is *being* rather than *signifying*.

THE MIND-BODY CONNECTION

A person's body invariably expresses his or her state of mind. A brother knows what kind of day his sister has had from the way she gets off her bicycle. A class knows what kind of mood their teacher is in when she puts down her books. This intuitive knowledge of body language is present from our earliest years. Young children react intuitively to what adults express nonverbally and only become confused if the adult uses contradictory words. As people reach their teens they learn to value cerebral control over the intuitive and emotional. Even while being led by their emotions, teenagers come to regard all evidence of vulnerability as childish and lacking the control of adulthood. This is especially true for boys.

But remember our article of faith, that *no inner state exists without outward evidence*. We show what we feel. In the realm of acting this means that when an actor's mind is correctly occupied, when his actions are appropriate, his body will unconsciously express all that his character feels. Directing should therefore be concerned with arriving at a character's true state of mind, and helping the actor develop the actions that truly accompany it.

Conversely when an action feels false, the actor has either chosen poorly or has lost focus. Losing focus (that is, when he ceases to experience his character's thoughts and emotions), shows in his whole physical being, in everything he says and does.

Being focused is not peculiar to acting since it underpins everyone's sense of normality. In everyday life we maintain actions and pursue relationships from assumptions about who we are and how we appear to others. These are only challenged under exceptional circumstances. When someone we respect watches us, or when we must speak to a group, we become suddenly so self-aware that we stop functioning automatically and harmoniously. We cease, in fact, to behave normally. The implications are major for the film director, whose work so often centers on getting actors to reproduce the processes and feel of real life under conditions of intense scrutiny.

BUSINESS

Actor and director must generate plenty of "business" (appropriate action) while preparing each role. Instead of moving on because an actor correctly describes what the character feels, explore what the character might *do* in the circumstance. Doing might mean giving a scream, but it is more likely to be a small but significant action, like dropping the eyes, turning to glance out of a window, feeling for change in one's pocket, or recalling the image of an indulgent aunt. Many actions will be interior as well as exterior.

STAY BUSY IN CHARACTER

As an actor, the key to maintaining your character's flow of consciousness is not just to keep busy, but to *keep busy in character*. To exist realistically as a new character, you must have your attention fully occupied by your character's thoughts, memories, inner visions, and outward actions. Given any opportunity, your ever-anxious mind will begin to imagine how you must appear to those watching (foolish, undignified, heroic, handsome, deeply moving, etc.). This is disabling and leads immediately to the black hole called loss of focus.

LOSING AND REGAINING FOCUS

Insecurity of all kinds, even the fear of losing focus, leads to loss of focus ("We have nothing to fear but fear itself . . . "). In a moment, the audience sees a believable character crumble into a beleaguered actor. Unless the actor has learned how to recover, she can feel completely exposed.

An effective way to regain focus is to look narrowly at something nearby, such as a prop or the texture of one's sleeve. Because it is real, something in her character's here and now, her attention is stabilized. Now she can broaden her attention to include the character's whole sphere of awareness.

USING THE ACTOR'S EMOTIONS AS THE CHARACTER'S

What should the actor do when an irrelevant emotion intrudes itself, such as pain from a headache, or surprise over an unexpected move by a partner, or confusion from a misplaced prop? Part of any good actor's training is learning to employ every genuine emotion as part of the character's present. This means, in effect, embracing and coopting the invader instead of struggling to screen it out. Since every real emotion is visible, struggling to put a lid on the inappropriate will also be visible. The tactic of incorporating external emotion is thus inevitable.

By using every facet of an actor's self to maintain the character's physical and mental action, and by reacting to every nuance of any other character's behavior, the actor stays so busy every time the scene is played, and aware on so many levels, that he or she no longer worries about remembering lines or whether anyone is watching. Everything in the intense, subjective sphere of the character's reality recedes from consciousness. This intense state of focus is readily available for beginners to experience in improvisation work (which is what makes improv so valuable), but it is more difficult to maintain within the discipline of a text.

NEVER DEMONSTRATE

The director should always encourage the actor to find his own solution to a problem. Unless desperate, the director should never step forward and demonstrate what she wants. This implies you are an actor and want a mimicry of yourself, when actually you need something unique to the actor.

NEVER SAY, "BE YOURSELF"

This innocent request can set actors worrying: What did he really mean? How does he see me? Which me does he really want? Always focus your actor on aspects of the character's experience.

SET SPECIFIC, POSITIVE GOALS

Avoid negative instruction of all kinds ("Could you not be so noisy opening the closet?") You can get what you want by saying, "See if you can open the door softly this time."

Convey your wishes through redirecting attention to a particular kind of action ("I'd like to see you more irresolute as you turn away"). Less effective would be to say, "Be irresolute" without locating the character's doubt in particular moments of the scene. The actor may not agree but can negotiate another, specific place. Another way of effecting a change is through suggesting a different subtext to a particular action or line ("Try making your refusal more ironic" or "Try closing the door on him with finality instead of regret").

ACT AS IF NOBODY'S PRESENT

Instruct actors never to look at the camera, to ignore the crew's presence, and to act as if they were alone in real life. This prevents them from falling into the trap of playing to an audience.

OBSTACLES: HABITS OF BEING

MANNERISMS

Certain kinds of people do particular kinds of jobs, and some jobs generate mannerisms that are a liability in filmmaking. Lecturers and politicians tend to address invisible multitudes, instead of talking one-to-one as they did in rehearsal. Firemen talk in clipped official voices, salespeople may be ingratiating and so on. Unfamiliar circumstances like filming cause people to fall back on their conditioning, and many ingrained behaviors are hard or even impossible to change. The positive aspect is that many of the qualities for which you cast a particular person will survive the unnatural procedure of filming, to appear just as you wanted them on the screen.

Actors also have particular mannerisms that you will have to live with. To eliminate them would mean trying to change something so basic that you would disable their talents. Here the director must exert careful judgment before speaking up. As always, try to relocate actors' attention in the positive, rather than asking them to suppress the negative.

LIMITING AN ACTOR'S SPHERE OF ATTENTION

When an actor's misconception of his relationship to the camera must be altered, try to guess what is ingrained habit and what is only a misperception about filming. The latter you can probably correct. For instance, the theater-trained actor who addresses an audience can usually be redirected by saying, "Imagine there is a small bubble of space only big enough to enclose you and your partner. There is only one person, him, listening to you. Talk only to him, there is no one else, no camera present, just you two." Usually this reminder does the trick and keeps theatrically trained actors using authentic, unmagnified voices and actions. Interestingly, the scene intensity rises noticeably, which shows that theatrical technique can also function as a retreat from the danger of real feelings.

TACKLING SERIOUS PROBLEMS OF UNNATURAL ACTING

With an incurable voice projector or anyone who is habitually artificial, the best solution is to recast. If that is impossible, some selected video playback to the actor may forcibly communicate that he has a problem. Be aware, however, that most people are so shocked and depressed when they first see themselves on the screen that showing an unsatisfactory performance should be a last resort to be done privately and supportively.

Sometimes you will cast someone to play a small part and this person's concept of acting comes from TV commercials. Valiantly your housewife in the short scene projects a wacky personality. If she is playing a stage mom this could be just what you wanted, but in most other circumstances it would be a disaster. Take her aside and get her to talk through the character, perhaps getting the actor to recall someone similar whom she knows and upon whose image she can model herself. Trying to become an idea of the part is what is phony. Get your actor to develop her character's interior process through improvising an interior monologue or "thoughts voice" (see Chapter 22, Exercise 3: "Improvising an Interior Monologue"). Once she is busy maintaining her character's interior processes, the actor can no longer stand outside herself and make a presentation, which is the root of the problem. Fully inhabiting her character, she begins to speak and act out of a genuine consciousness. This at the very least takes care of realism.

C·H·A·P·T·E·R 20

ACTORS' PROBLEMS

The public, seeing accomplished performances as a matter of course, assumes that acting must be easy and pleasant. But the nature of their work places actors under a physical and psychic scrutiny that is very rare in ordinary life. This attention is the profession's allure but it also leaves the actor vulnerable and with nowhere to hide. Faced with a demanding part and a demanding director, even the experienced actor will doubt his or her worth, or, confronting an unfamiliar and unwelcome self-image, feel that it threatens his or her very ability to function. Under such conditions it is regrettably human to deny, to evade, and to blame others.

The accomplished actor is ready for these trials and does not need to be constantly on the defense. This is someone who maintains emotional and intellectual flexibility during criticism, and does not try to hide the nature or degree of problems. Such individuals are as rare in acting as they are everywhere else, and there is no one walking the face of the earth who does not have lapses. A thorough acting training seeks with painful and religious fervor to instill self-knowledge and self-discipline. This compels an actor to stand still and confront the worst rather than find ways to resist the director's demands. Few actors, especially those available to the low-budget filmmaker, have this degree of training.

Resistance to the work at hand is in any case remarkably constant and takes many forms. However frustrating you find it, you will need to treat it with understanding and respect, since it generally arises from insecurity, not ill will. Make no mistake, acting is a difficult and self-exposing craft. It aims to expose human nature, and the vulnerability of the person is never far away from the character being played. Nevertheless, you cannot afford to let any one person's needs and insecurities dominate those of the group or threaten the viability of the project.

LINES AND INSECURITY

Sometimes actors claim to need the book long after they should have learned the lines. This is a common insecurity symptom and it completely blocks a scene's development. If at a subsequent rehearsal and after due warning, the same individual still claims to need the book, simply take it and have a prompter supply whatever is missing. The difficulty and embarrassment of floundering through a scene in this way normally motivates the actor to come thoroughly prepared the next time. Insecure actors usually find it liberating to deal with the substance of the scene in this way instead of its letter.

When an actor again claims to need the book I say, "Well, you know what the scene's about so just make something up." The actor first looks appalled, but the results are usually good. The actor either knows the scene better than he or she thought, or, compelled to improvise from a general idea, takes a heightened interest in what is written. This exercise should not be undertaken punitively, but as a necessary way of getting on with business.

CLINGING TO THE LETTER OF THE SCRIPT

Clinging to the letter of the text or to "what we already decided" is also a form of resistance. The actor who is afraid to think, feel, and explore in character will often take refuge behind a structure of perceived "rules." These are what the actor learned from mentors elsewhere and the implication is that they are greater than you. You will rightly feel this as a threat to your authority and will have to deal with it as such. Be clear and definite about what you want and let the actor get there in his or her own way.

FEAR OF CHANGES

Sometimes your request to alter the performance in some way, or to change something set previously triggers an irrational unwillingness to adapt. Some people have a pattern of discomfort with authority figures (of which you are now one) and always have to rebel. Bear with this person, he is scared and probably doing the best he can. One way to disarm people with patterns of rebellion (or patterns of any kind) is to name the pattern, as affectionately as you can, when it next appears. "Uh oh—Anne's having another attack of existential doubt!" The company will laugh delightedly, and Anne will admit her problem instead of blaming the screenwriter. To carry this off you need to be sure the actor is insecure rather than angry.

ACTING IN ISOLATION

An actor who doggedly carries out what he or she has prepared regardless of the nuances of other performances is too unrelaxed to listen, watch, and work from life going on around. This actor will not feel the cup in his or her hand, smell the morning air, or feel the touch of his or her lover's lips. This type of actor is holed up inside a set of mental constructs, so it will be through physical detail that he or she best finds his way back to the here and now. It is particularly dangerous to let this person learn their lines, since internalizing the text is part of the armor. This person will be afraid of improvisation, and badly needs the relaxed security that having "played around" can bring.

OVERINTELLECTUALIZING

The tendency to intellectualize is another way an actor puts off the fearsome task of experiencing the character's (and his or her own) emotions. The actor who wants to debate every point feels safer discussing than doing, and may try to involve the whole cast in arguments about niceties of interpretation. These are delaying tactics, a bid to wrest control from the director, or both.

THE ANTI-INTELLECT ACTOR

This actor scorns discussion and the search for underlying structures, and may be someone intellectually insecure (lacking formal education, for instance) or someone unusually intuitive. Results will soon reveal which. It will be important to prevent this person, whose aura of conviction can be very influential, from derailing other cast members who work differently. As the director, avoid debates on method and stress the individual's freedom to use whatever method delivers the results you seek. This way you avoid the authority struggle that some actors seek, and remain flexibly accepting of each actor's needs.

CONTROL BATTLES

The actor who tries to control scenes, manipulate other actors, or resist directorial criticism is probably afraid to place trust in working partnerships of any kind. If you do not set limits this person may absorb a disproportionate share of everyone's energies. This actor often tries to direct other actors or to challenge the director's authority in public. Such a challenge can make a truly creative contribution, but it depends on the underlying spirit. Genuinely creative personalities sometimes overflow their territory and may need and want a firm hand to contain them. Combative energy of all kinds can get the company's collective adrenaline flowing.

PLAYWRITING

This actor plays against the flow of either a scripted or improvised scene, manipulates other actors, introduces inappropriate material, or in other ways undermines the validity of what others are doing. How you assert your authority will be important. Again, there may be a responsible spirit here who is working in inappropriate ways. Be careful not to be crushing.

INAPPROPRIATE HUMOR

Humor as everyone knows is often the precious elixir that gets people through difficult circumstances (hang out long enough with nurses and you'll see what I mean). But jokes or other diversions that disrupt the working atmosphere are often a means of delaying and diffusing a situation the actor finds threatening (like working without the book). When you are sure that sabotage is happening, cut into the saboteur's rigamarole and sharply rally the cast to work.

WITHDRAWAL

The actor who repeatedly deals with problems by withdrawing may be asking for special consideration, or may habitually evade the responsibility for solving problems. Try meeting one-on-one and naming the pattern.

UNPUNCTUALITY AND COMMITMENT PROBLEMS

This is very, very serious. Name the conditions for retaining the actor early and without compromise. An unreliable person who remains in the company gains increasing leverage daily as he or she gets more difficult to replace.

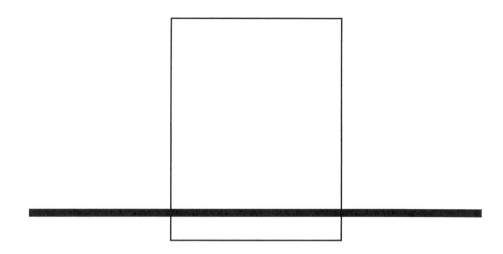

C·H·A·P·T·E·R 21

IMPROVISATION WORK TO EXPLORE ACTING

As the director you are really the coordinator between the text, the cast, and crew, and you set the parameters for everyone. You need to know what it feels like as an actor to expose one's body and emotions to a nonreacting camera and crew, and you need to thoroughly understand the mental and emotional process the player goes through. The best way to understand is to experience.

So here are some exercises for directing students. A class working together and rotating through the roles of director and actor will discover one must relinquish the social training we've all had at hiding and self-preservation. This conditioning prevents people from exploring their emotions in public, which is what acting is all about. Anyone can act, anyone at all, once the fears subside and the armor is laid down. Once people can do this, directing them becomes a matter of using the right keys to unlock each individual's potential.

Since discovering and using spontaneity is so important, the first twenty exercises are improvisational. Many will be familiar to anyone with an actor's training. It is important for each person in the ensemble to support and appreciate the others, particularly when they involve pushing limits. Acting together and making films together are not about competition, they are about collaboration. The whole can always be greater than its parts, but only when there's trust and courage, which go together.

FINDING THE BEATS AND DEFINING UNITS

Throughout improvs and scripted scenes alike the director searches for what are called beats. A beat is a moment of fulcrum in a scene when pressures culminate in a changed balance of forces. It's like felling a tree; you saw and saw, you push and pull, and then the tree begins to fall, and once it hits the ground you have a new set of problems to tackle. In drama, the moment of the beat is usually visible in an important change of consciousness in one or more of the characters, but a beat in a movie can be a revelation that the audience alone comprehends.

The change at the beat point may be subtle or it may be blatant; either way it represents a distinct step up the developmental stairway that drama always aims to be. An example might be the moment in Mike Newell's *Four Weddings and a Funeral* (1994) when Charles realizes that Carrie is going to marry her wealthy fiancé after all. The buildup of forces—of establishing the situation, building pressure, then of irrevocably changed circumstances that produce new pressures—can only be accomplished if the characters have mismatched volitions, and therefore harbor the potential for conflict. Conflict may be between characters, internal to a single character, between characters and a system, or between characters and their environment.

The first step in breaking down any text is to decide what the conflicts in the scene actually are, and to mark the beat points. Remember, *beats are moments of changed consciousness for one or more characters that produce a changed situation.* What leads up to the beat is unfulfilled needs in the characters and the consequent buildup of pressures. The timid Charles, in love with Carrie, is wondering how to tell her. Instead he discovers she is going to marry someone else, and the result is despair. The beat point is the moment of realization when his hopes and intentions must change. After that beat come new conditions (hopelessness) and a new set of volitions (escape, forgetfulness) that lead eventually to the buildup of another situation and the move toward a new minicrisis or beat. The material from one beat to the next is called a unit.

WHY IMPROV HELPS DRAMATISTS

Improv is a series of skill-building games that depend on spontaneously finding solutions as problem situations arise. It should be lighthearted enough to be fun, but serious-minded enough to have risks that pump the collective adrenaline. The object is for you to develop the confidence to act on impulse and intuition, something valuable to directors as well as actors. Improv is scary to do for the first time, and something of a Pandora's Box for an instructor who hasn't used it before. But you should try improv because:

- it is an unparalleled teacher of dramatic principle
- there are only a few principles, but they take courage and clear-sightedness to apply
- actors, writers, and directors can learn through doing
- a group can spontaneously explore their own abilities and temperaments

- having the courage to be silly is the threshold to more important things
- playing together helps dissipate the competitiveness that comes from insecurity
- improv lowers the stress of self-consciousness
- participants soon see when and why drama isn't working
- the dramatic situation is either black or white in improv, with few grays
- everything imaginable goes wonderfully wrong, but because it is a game there isn't too much at stake
- people learn important lessons *and* have fun
- directors have to act a part, too, in order to get lots of things done

In two-person improvs, for instance, you are likely to discover that:

- if each is to work off the other, each must watch and listen to the other
- the players must be completely in the present and cannot think ahead
- if a player uses preconceptions he will manipulate the other by "play-writing"
- each player must act on the other or one will fall into passivity and invite the other to take control
- taking control is as much the product of insecurity as is being passive
- anybody can be equal to the unexpected if they are relaxed enough to tap into their imagination
- improvs often get stuck on the same crucial elements
- solving problems takes failures
- courageous failures are successes
- safe successes are not successes at all
- actors can learn what's needed to unstick the piece and make it develop
- directors can learn to spot the class of problem in any piece of drama from experience gained in improv
- like jazz, everyone knows when a piece is "cooking"
- successful improvs have a natural ending
- improv covers much of the territory of dramatic art

Participants soon recognize from their experiments that drama only works when actors know what's needed to keep the dramatic cycle going. Ultimately drama is the actor's responsibility. Great actors are those who can take a poorly written part in a poorly directed movie, and still produce a character of life and depth. Good directors learn a lot about acting and about each actor, and learn to sense when an individual isn't living up to their potential.

THE JOURNAL

If you are part of a directing class, keep a journal. In it describe honestly your thoughts, observations, and feelings about assignments and peers. Periodically the instructor can collect them and report any trends or significant observations back to the class. No confidences or names are disclosed without the writer's prior permission.

The journal functions as a safety valve, a channel for feedback allowing the instructor to be fully aware of common insecurities and personal triumphs. Through it the instructor gets to know everyone on his or her own terms and can write confidential replies.

NOT ALL ACTING IS A DUET

The acting exercises below sometimes read as if acting always takes place between two people. Many times an actor will either be alone or in a large group and sustaining many interactions, but to allow for all this would produce unreadable English, so I have treated the duet as if it were the standard.

IMPROVISATION EXERCISES

WHAT THEY ARE

I use these exercises extensively with anyone, actors and nonactors, wanting to become directors. The exercises get people interested in the craft of acting and leave a residue of deep respect for the actor. They also create a vocabulary of experience that serves directors well. Sometimes the exercises incorporate a degree of premeditated structure, sometimes the actor has virtually no guidelines beforehand. Some of the exercises will be referred to later in the book because they are especially useful when actors get hung up during rehearsal or shooting.

ACTORS, MAKE YOUR AUDIENCE SEE

Using no props, see your surroundings and the things you handle with such conviction that the audience is able to see them too. When the actor sees, the audience sees, believes, and is captivated.

MIX IT UP

Be sure to change partners from exercise to exercise so that you work with people you do not know. Wear loose, comfortable clothing that you don't mind getting dirty. Try to play people whose characters, ages, and circumstances are removed from your own.

STAYING FOCUSED

The biggest challenge is to achieve and maintain focus; to think one's character's thoughts, to see one's character's mental images, and as a result, experience one's character's feelings. Because improvisation constantly springs surprises, the actor is repeatedly flushed out of hiding places. Through improv he can learn to trust his instincts, discover the supportiveness of other cast members, and gain confidence that dealing with the unexpected will not cause him to fall out of character.

THE DIRECTOR'S ROLE

To direct an improv seems like a contradiction in terms. Most of these exercises need nothing beyond the actors understanding the ground rules for the particular exercise. The more advanced exercises, however, will benefit from having a director select and coordinate cast ideas and make spot decisions so the piece can start without delay. Remember that the director is really the surrogate for an audience. All exercises will benefit from directorial feedback so the cast can tackle specific problems in subsequent versions.

DURATION OF SKETCHES

Either the instructor can call, "Cut!" or, as confidence develops, audience members give a show of hands when a piece runs out of steam. This way actors get used to satisfying audience demands and student directors learn to make independent judgments rather than relying on their instructor.

ASSESSMENT AND DISCUSSION

During an exercise look out for the combination of spontaneity and intensity that comes when actors fully accept the demands of a role. Reward courage with a round of applause at the end of the piece. After each exercise, brief and concentrated discussion is valuable, but the audience should speak mainly about what was communicated and *avoid discriminating between good and bad*. Avoid all theorizing; concentrate on what you felt and what specifically you saw happening at each stage. If discussion becomes academic it drains away the momentum. The director should not hesitate to suspend it. Actors and director should not justify what they did but instead listen to the comments attentively. In all your work, your audience is the most important arbiter.

EXERCISE 21-1: SEE OR BE SEEN

Purpose: Exploring the idea of focus.

Activity: Half the class is in the audience and remains seated. The other half, the performers, stand in a row facing the audience looking above them into space. Audience members should carefully study the faces and body language of the performers. The instructor:

- tells the performers to empty their minds and to concentrate on simply being themselves;
- after a minute or two, tells the performers to mentally visualize a room they know well and everything in it; and
- after another minute or two, tells audience and performers to switch roles and repeats steps 1 and 2 with the other half of the class.

Discussion: Address these questions to:

Performers: How did it feel to focus on being oneself?

Audience: How did the performers' feelings show in their behavior and appearance?

Both: What did you see when the performers switched to visualizing?

Performers: What kinds of work can an actor legitimately undertake to avoid feeling self-consciousness?

EXERCISE 21-2: DOMESTIC APPLIANCE

Purpose: To become in spirit something you are not.

Activity: First study a domestic appliance or activity in action. Announce in class what you are, then do a full impersonation using only your body and vocalized sound effects and trying to convey its spirit as well as its shape, actions, and sounds. The class should choose one for the instructor, who breaks the ice by going first (more than once I have been asked to be a flushing toilet). It is quite normal to feel foolish and painfully self-conscious. Use what you learned from Exercise 21-1 to maintain focus.

Examples:

Coffee percolator	Overfilled garbage bag removed
Toilet flushing	Cold car engine that will not start
Electric can opener	Tomato sauce pouring
Rubber plunger opening drain	Dripping faucet
Washing machine changing cycles	Upright vacuum cleaner
Autochange phonograph	Toothbrush at work
Blender with lumps	Electric toaster
Nutcracker	Rusty door lock
Honey pouring	Steam iron
Coffee grinder	Photocopier
Corkscrew	Ice cream cone melting
Garbage disposal unit	Clock radio coming on

Discussion:

1. When were you self-conscious?
2. Where in your body could you feel tension from self-consciousness?
3. Did you get into focus, and if so, how?
4. As an audience member, which impersonations made you see the real thing?

EXERCISE 21-3: FLYING BLIND

Purpose: Exploring trust and dependency.

Activity: The rehearsal space is made into a disordered jumble of obstacles. Divide into pairs. One person is blindfolded and turned several times to disorient him. He now walks as fast as he dares with his partner whispering instructions on which way to move. A variation is for the seeing partner to guide through touch. After a few minutes switch roles on the instructor's command.

Discussion: What were your feelings and sensations, being so utterly dependent on another person? (Instructor: what did the body language differences tell you about the different reactions to dependency?

EXERCISE 21-4: "TIMBER!"

Purpose: Exploring trust, equal partnership, and tactile defensiveness.

Activity: Using pairs (same sex or different), one person is a piece of timber, and the other must try to balance the timber upright. You can use any part of your body to catch and steady the timber except your hands. After a few minutes, swap roles on command.

Discussion:
- What are one's thoughts and feelings, being in bodily contact with someone you do not know well?
- How free and true to gravity was the timber? (Did he or she protect the two of you by making it easier?)
- How willing was the timber to trust you to catch him or her? To fall backward and stay rigid?
- Was one partner tending to control the situation?

Actors must be able to make physical contact and even play love scenes with people they may neither know nor find attractive. In any acting situation, each must share control equally, being ready to "catch" a partner, or be caught, yet neither taking more than momentary initiative. Neither should fall into a habitually dominant or a submissive acting relationship. When things are working right both actors are sensitive to each other, actively creating, conscious of the unique nuance of the moment, and able to work from it. This confidence comes from the relaxation that goes with having trust in one's partner and in the audience's approving reaction.

EXERCISE 21-5: MIRROR IMAGES

Purpose: Close observation and moment-to-moment adaptation without anticipating.

Activity: You arrive in front of the bathroom mirror, coming close to its surface, and go through your morning routine. Your partner is your image in the mirror, doing everything you do as you do it, inverted as a mirror image actually is. Swap roles after a few minutes.

Discussion:
- How successful was the "mirror" at replicating the actions?
- How difficult did the mirror find it to neither anticipate nor lag?
- Did the person stay in character?
- How frank and complete was the "person's" routine? Who took risks and was therefore self-revealing?
- What analogous situations is an actor likely to face?

EXERCISE 21-6: WHO, WHERE, WHEN, WHAT

Purpose: Immediate character and situation development without props.

Activity: Instructor designates an actor, then asks successive people for one each of who/where/when/what. The actor then carries out some appropriate action, in character, for a minute or two. The instructor calls "Cut!" when the action is long enough or if development levels off. The class reports what it saw happening and what was communicated. The actor then says briefly what he or she intended.

Example:

Who [is present]?	"Mary Jo Sorensen, thirty-five"
Where [is she]?	"In an airport lounge"
When [is this]?	"Christmas Eve, late at night"
What [is happening]?	"Waiting for her parents. She must tell them she has lost her job."

Our designated actress thinks a moment, then slips into character. She sits moodily tearing up a styrofoam coffee cup, looking sidelong with fatigue and distaste at some people nearby. From another direction she notices evidence of some change, and stands apprehensively, straightening her skirt.

Discussion: The class should say what it felt was going on inside the character. This may divide up into what was convincing, and what were false notes, intentions that did not come across as natural. In our example the actress focused on looking for her parents while feeling anxious, tired, and depressed, but did not forget to interact with her environment. Built into the action was a significant change, a heightening of awareness as her long wait suddenly promises to end. On balance the class believed that Mary Jo had not told her parents about the change in her employment, and liked the action with the styrofoam cup, which most "saw" in her hands. They also liked the irritability, but were unclear what was its source. One person thinks it was because of cigar smoke, another thought it was carousers the worse for drink. However, most felt that the change of awareness was imposed and that the actor lost focus at that moment.

The actress said she had believed in her character while she had the cup in her hands, but then had imagined a man with a loud voice but had been unable to see his image. In confusion she had decided to make her parents appear at the arrival gate, but this image too refused to materialize because she had forced it.

EXERCISE 21-7: SOLO, NO WORDS

(From this exercise onward, a piece can be ended when the majority of the audience, through raising hands, signifies to the director/instructor that dramatic development is past its peak.)

Purpose: Use unremarkable, everyday action to communicate something of the inner thoughts and feelings of a character whose life is quite unlike that of the actor.

Activity: From an action (the what) and using no props, invent a who, where and when to sustain your character sketch. Avoid storytelling or high drama of any kind. Try out any or all of these:

- alone in someone's house (whose?) where you explore: (a) the refrigerator, (b) the bathroom, (c) someone else's bedroom that you have been given
- finding a box of your childhood toys you haven't seen for many years
- unwrapping a long-awaited parcel
- waiting in the dentist's office
- making a grocery list
- trying on a new coat
- taking medicine
- caring for a pet
- taking a bike out after the winter
- cleaning out the attic
- wrapping a gift
- cleaning shoes
- looking out of the window
- waiting for a phone call
- dividing up the laundry
- watching a sport
- overhearing an interesting conversation in a store

Discussion: Audience: In a particular performance, what was interesting and what did it make you see? When did the player break focus? Why?

EXERCISE 21-8: DUO, NO WORDS

Purpose: Through interaction, communicate something of the inner thoughts and feelings of two characters using an everyday action that involves some element of conflict.

Activity: From an action (the what) and using no props, invent a who, where, and when to sustain your character sketch. Avoid storytelling or high drama of any kind. Try these:

- mending a car
- making a double bed
- buying a magazine
- pulling a sliver out of a finger
- carrying a heavy garbage can
- washing dishes after a special meal
- washing a child's hair
- photographing a model
- putting up a tent
- playing pinball
- maneuvering heavy furniture through doorway
- waiting in a doorway for a heavy rainstorm to ease
- writing out a speeding ticket after the talking is done
- watching a TV program; one likes it, the other does not
- a stranger in a plane who is falling asleep against you

Discussion: Did the actors create:

- two distinct character identities (who)?
- a believable and recognizable environment—country, area, city, place, or room—and use it (where)?
- a distinctive period and time of day (when)?
- a believable tension?
- a situation in which speech was not called for?
- an interaction in which neither was controlling the movement of the sketch? Was there communion and adaptation?

EXERCISE 21-9: GIBBERISH

Purpose: To use the voice as an expressive instrument and to compel the actors to use their bodies and voice quality as tools of communication. Too often actors cease to act with the whole body once they have lines to speak. This exercise stimulates speech but deemphasizes verbal meaning in favor of underlying intention.

Activity: Using the examples in Exercise 21-8 carry out an activity, with a conflict, using gibberish as the characters' language.

Discussion: As in Exercise 21-8. How did the actors handle the gibberish conversations? Did they become natural?

EXERCISE 21-10: SOLO, WITH WORDS

Purpose: To create a character, employing the usual who/where/when/what, and using both actions and speech.

Activity: In creating your character, remember to develop him or her through actions. Do not sit still and rely on a monologue. Here are some suggestions:

- a difficult phone conversation (phone has a long cord)
- reconstructing a painful conversation
- writing the opening remarks of an important speech
- rehearsing in front of the bathroom mirror for a traffic court appearance
- planning a dinner party
- getting ready to tell someone about a betrayal or infidelity
- working up to approaching your boss for a raise
- rehearsing the way you will evict a rich, peppery relative who came to visit and has long overstayed
- explaining to your new employer why you must start a new job in a gorilla costume
- imagining different approaches to someone who attracts you deeply but whom you hold in awe
- your head is stuck between the railings enclosing a war memorial. Someone has gone to call the fire department and you are trying to figure out an explanation.
- it is Judgment Day and you are rehearsing an explanation of your sins to a recording angel
- you are preparing to audition for the role of "Talk Show Host with a Difference"
- a practical joke has gone wrong and you must explain to the victim

Discussion: Did the actor:

- create a believable character?
- keep up a developing action?
- make the situation develop?
- make you see all the physical objects and surroundings?

EXERCISE 21-11: DUO, WITH WORDS

Purpose: To maintain conversation and developing action at the same time.

Activity: Each of these sketches requires both a conversation and accompanying physical action, which should be purposeful. Do not take it too fast, and do not feel you have to be talking all the time. Examples to try:

- eating a meal and discussing a prearranged topic
- demonstrating a kitchen appliance to a family member
- cleaning the car, discussing something
- getting a large piece of furniture through an awkward doorway
- discussing your son's or daughter's rotten grades
- asking for some money that you are owed
- buying something embarrassing from a pharmacist
- rearranging a room
- showing someone they have not done a good job of work
- teaching a friend to drive
- discussing a change in hairdo
- teaching someone a dance step
- meeting someone you had hoped to avoid
- a confession you would rather not hear

Discussion: Did they:

- keep both the topic and the actions going?
- keep the physical world they created consistent?
- work off each other?
- share the initiative equally?
- allow the piece to develop spontaneously?
- develop interesting characters?

EXERCISE 21-12: MAKE YOUR OWN CHARACTER

Purpose: To place the actor, as a character, in the hands of the audience.

Activity: Go before the class, in costume, as a character based on someone you know or have met who made a powerful impression on you. The class asks you probing questions about yourself. You answer in character.

Each character should be onstage for about ten minutes, and two or three performances per session is the maximum, as the interaction can be very intense.

Discussion: This, honestly undertaken, can be magical, a powerful exercise in portrayal that tells much about the actor's values and influences. There may be little need for discussion if the exercise goes well. Play it by ear.

EXERCISE 21-13: ENSEMBLE SITUATIONS

Purpose: To engage the whole group in a collective creation.

Activity: These are situations in which individual characters contribute to a whole. The where and when will need to be agreed beforehand. The aim is to keep up your character while contributing to the development of the piece. You might want to reuse a character developed earlier, perhaps the one from Exercise 21-12. Specimen situations:

- a tug of war
- dealing with an obstreperous drunk
- someone is hurt in the street
- surprise party
- a person faints in a crowded train
- bus driver stops bus because a passenger will not pay
- unpopular coach berates a team
- party interrupted by protesting neighbor
- busy hotel kitchen with waiters and waitresses coming and going
- airline with badly delayed flight dealing with irate passengers
- exercise class in an institution for severely disturbed people
- policeman tries to arrest person at demonstration; crowd argues
- subway train stops in tunnel due to power cut
- someone arrives with news that may have serious consequences

Discussion:
- how many subordinate actions were there going on during the main action?
- did everyone stay in character? (The temptation is to lose focus unless you are important.)

- how did the piece develop?
- what compromises did people make to sustain the whole?

EXERCISE 21-14: DEVELOPING AN EMOTION

Purpose: Here the actors are supplied with an emotion to reach for.

Activity: This exercise should not be attempted until the class has developed considerable rapport and experience. The players must invent characters and a situation, then develop it to the point where the specified emotion is reached. The class can stop the sketch when the emotion is reached, or if the piece is not going anywhere. Emotions one character might feel include:

anger	suspicion	sympathy
relief	jealousy	condescension
rejection	love	stupidity
disbelief	friendliness	release
superiority	empathy	suspicion

Discussion: This is a tricky demand because it asks that actors build to a known conclusion, and this tempts them to manipulate the situation. All the prior criteria apply, but important considerations here are:

- was the interaction credible?
- did it arrive at the specified emotion?
- if not, why not?
- was the development even or uneven?
- was the initiative shared equally?

This exercise can highlight the cardinal weakness of improvisation: unevenness of inspiration producing an inconsistent pace of development. The symptoms are lengthy periods when the actors are circling a problem, unable to break through or, alternatively, breaking through by decision instead of by the characters' process. This happens from frustration or panic at making the audience wait. A sign of confidence in both players and company (audience) is that the players do not short-circuit the process in pursuing the goal, and the audience remains supportive.

EXERCISE 21-15: BRIDGING EMOTIONS

Purpose: To make a credible change from one emotion to another.

Activity: Same as Exercise 21-14 except the players start in the middle of one emotion and find their way to the next. Start with two emotions, and then, if you want to make it truly challenging, specify three.

Discussion: Same as Exercise 21-14.

EXERCISE 21-16: GENERIC SITUATIONS ON TV

Purpose: To involve a group in immediate and unpremeditated invention.

Activity: Divide the class into players and audience. The audience is watching a TV program that leads up to one of the generic situations below. The players are TV actors who must instantly become a program showing the chosen situation. When the situation is running out of steam, an audience member may come up to the TV and change the channel and announce what the new program is. The players must now develop the same situation in the new program format, until someone changes the channel again. After a while, students swap roles. Here the accent is upon experiencing the same situation and probably the same emotions through very different characters, and feeding into different but set expectations in the audience. Suggested situations:

Persuasion	Being authoritative
Trapped	Avoiding something
Returning	Complaining
Interview	Disaster
Making a difficult request	Surprise
Successfully stopping an argument	Laughing out of relief
Jeering	Cheating

Discussion:
- how inventive were the players?
- how authentic were the situations to actual TV programs?
- how quickly were they able to make the change?
- how equally were roles distributed?
- did some actors fall into active/passive roles?

EXERCISE 21-17: VIDEO CONVENTION

Purpose: Same as Exercise 21-16.

Activity: Same ideas as Exercise 21-16 except the situation is a huge video dealer's convention offering unsold video programs at big discounts. The audience is comprised of potential buyers at a stand where everything imaginable is on sale:

do-it-yourself tapes on kitchen rehab or carburetor tuning, nature films, social documentaries, comedies, tragedies, slasher films, soft porn films, biology lessons, music videos, teen romances, farces, beauty procedures for the over-forties, etc. When the audience decides to see a new sample, an audience member calls out the title of the new video.

Discussion: Similar to Exercise 21-16. Accent is on spontaneity and speed of adaptation. Since these are videos that have not sold, they probably are obscure or third rate, and full of genre clichés. Did all the cast contribute equally?

EXERCISE 21-18: BLIND DATE

Purpose: To work with interior monologue.

Activity: A man and a woman have been set up by friends with a blind date. They meet in a bar and discuss how to spend the evening together. Character A has several conflicting personality traits, each represented by a class member. As the conversation between the two slowly proceeds, each of the voices chimes in, speaking its biased reaction or tendentious thought. Character A must listen to his or her interior voices, react realistically to his or her own "thoughts," and act upon the most appropriate in his or her next words or action. Character B must disregard everything except what Character A says or does. If you are playing Character A, you may get a chorus of inner voices, there may initially be none, the voices may overlap and argue with each other. Take all the time you need to react to them, remaining in character. Your personality traits (a voice for each) could include:

the need to be liked	fear of being manipulated
fear of rejection	worry about expense
the need to be different	guilt (feeling bad about something you've done)
the need to be normal	shame (feeling bad about who you are)
the need to make a conquest	pride

Discussion: This exercise is a lot of fun, and demands tremendous concentration from all concerned. It is a key to understanding that the actor who keeps his character's interior voices going will never lose focus, and will consistently bring a richness of ambiguity to each moment of the part. Remember, *the real action of any part is interior action which goes on behind the character's outward words and physical actions.*

- how did Character A handle all the input?
- what were his/her most noticeable influences?
- where did Character A break character?
- when did character B provide a good foil?
- what were the most interesting and convincing interior actions?

Once More: Now Characters A and B go through their scene again, but this time Character A internalizes the interior voices by imagining them. Often the scene will be strikingly rich in implications, and shows what real inner conflict brings to an actor's work.

EXERCISE 21-19: INNER CONFLICT

Purpose: To portray a character's contradictory tensions but never directly reveal them.

Activity: An actor is designated to play an intelligent person who wishes to be correctly understood. The character can be modeled upon someone prominent in the news. In this exercise, inspired by Richard Nixon and his "I am not a crook" speech, the character has gone through life denying certain aspects of his or her character, so sometimes "puts a good face on things" and rationalizes what he or she cannot change. The character begins with the sentence, "Because I think you may have the wrong idea about me, I'm going to tell you what most people don't know." After he or she has spoken for a while, the audience can help by asking questions. The actor must portray his or her character's conflicts by denial, which must flow from the character's rationale about what can or cannot be admitted in public.

Discussion:
- when was the character sincere?
- when suppressing the truth?
- how did you know?
- when was the actor's performance believable?
- when did it look contrived?
- what was interesting, what was less so?

EXERCISE 21-20: THROWN TOGETHER

Purpose: To bring together two characters in a common activity that each is using to gain emotional satisfaction from the other. The exercise seeks to explore the idea that in real life we almost never express what weighs on our minds; instead we recreate our own unsolved issues through the situation at hand and use them to seek satisfaction, occasionally with success.

Activity: Take two of the least compatible characters developed in Exercise 21-12 or 21-19 and put them together in a credible work situation. Within the bounds of ordinary, decent, civilized behavior, each follows his or her usual agenda in relating to other people. The actors should take the time to keep up an interior (and silent) monologue. No issues are ever named; their needs and reactions must be expressed through the work they are doing together. Whether they get along or whether they find mutual accommodation should not be predetermined.

Discussion:
- did each character develop?
- did each find a way to play out his/her issues through their work?
- did each choose a credible path?
- did they stay in focus and in character?
- did they find a believable way of cooperating?
- did you believe the outcome?
- did one "win?"
- did either or both find satisfaction? Neither?
- what was the obligatory moment in the scene?
- what made it the obligatory moment?

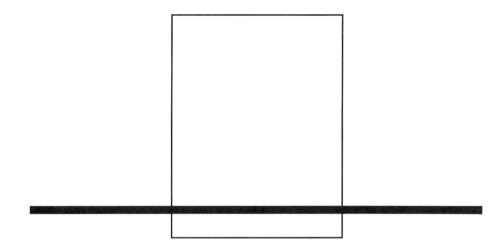

C·H·A·P·T·E·R 22

EXERCISES WITH A TEXT

These exercises, intended to develop particular skills, will be useful later in dealing with common problems that emerge in rehearsals or even shooting.

TEXTS

Because you should learn the rehearsal process without ever having to doubt the quality of the writing, it's smart at this stage to use a good one-act theater piece rather than your own writing. It won't be cinematic, but this part of your work concentrates on discovering the potential of text and cast, so this doesn't matter. Use something short so discussion can be narrowly (and therefore deeply) focused. Avoid comedy because it begs for a live audience, and you don't want your actors playing to the gallery. I have found several of Harold Pinter's short works to be ideal, in particular *The Dumb-Waiter*. In Pinter there is always a fascinating disparity between what characters say and what seems to be going on in their minds.

READ-THROUGH

The cast should carefully read the whole play, make brief definitions of the characters, and do an ensemble read-through of the whole piece. Actors must *not* learn lines until instructed, or they will internalize an unexamined understanding of the piece. Give time for discussions since you will learn a lot about both the play and your actors from listening and guiding these.

DEVELOPMENTAL PROCESS

Do not anticipate problems. Particularly when you direct actors of some experience, it is unwise to impose any developmental technique arbitrarily, as they may feel it is unnecessary or beneath them. Watch and listen very carefully, letting your actors get as far as they can with minimal directing. When problems arise, choose an appropriate technique to break the logjam. After one or two successes, your credibility will rise.

"USEFUL WHEN"

Each exercise is also a resource to help solve common problems during rehearsal or production of any work in progress. Its medicine-chest utility is given under "Useful When."

EXERCISE 22-1: WHAT THE ACTORS BRING

Useful When: You (as the director) want to adjust your thematic intentions for the piece around the cast and to make use of what each individual brings.

Purpose: To make decisions about the special qualities and characteristics of the actors for use in your thematic interpretation.

Activity: After the read-through:

1. Make notes for yourself that capture the intrinsic quality of each actor. This, for example, concerns an actor called Dale:

    Dale has a slow, quiet, repressed quality that masks a certain pain and bitterness. He is watchful, highly intelligent, intense, and his first reaction is often a protective cynicism, but really it matters very much to him that he be liked. He reminds one of a stray cat, cornered and defiant, but hungry and cold, too.

2. Make a projection of how the actors' qualities can legitimately be used to polarize the performances, and how this will affect your thematic interpretation of the piece. For example:

    Dale has the quality of honorable victimhood and this stacks the cards interestingly against the father, whom we assume has practiced subtle violence against his son in the distant past, without the mother being aware of it.

EXERCISE 22-2: MARKING BEATS IN A TEXT

Useful When: Actors cannot be relied upon to make an instinctive and complete dramatic analysis of a text.

Purpose: To find the beats, that is, the fulcrum points of emotional change. These will be extremely important to the actors and will need special consideration in the *mise en scène* (the combination of acting, blocking, camera placement and editing that produces the dramatic image on film).

Activity: Director and actors should separately study the scene looking for the beats. These moments of irrevocable change may be triggered by dialogue, by an action, or by outside information coming in, such as a phone call. Emotional change does not happen continuously and smoothly like the hands of a clock. It is more like the movement of a heavy object being pushed across a rough surface. Pressure against its immovability mounts and mounts until suddenly it slides a few feet. Those pushing regroup themselves and start exerting pressure again, until—boom!—again it moves.

In dramatic terms, the beat is the moment of yielding when emotional pressures overcome emotional resistance and compel a moment of changed awareness. From this definition it is apparent that each character must have a conception of what the conflict is, like two wrestlers who must make contact in order to compete. Finding beats, therefore, means finding the important moves in the match, and defining the strategy, from each protagonist's point of view, leading to each meaningful strike and counterstrike.

There may be one beat or there may be several in a scene. All the beats may belong to one character, or there may be beats for both, some even simultaneous and mutual. Either may remain unconscious of the other's change of consciousness, though the audience should be able to read the changes in both.

Discussion: In rehearsal agree where the beats are, and what causes them.

EXERCISE 22-3: IMPROVISING AN INTERIOR MONOLOGUE

Useful When: A text refuses to come alive, and you need a powerful method of getting actors to externalize their understanding. Also useful when you are far along in rehearsals and still have intransigent trouble spots. Asking a cast member for his inner monologue at such a trouble spot usually reveals a crucial lack of understanding at that point in the text, and also helps one know how to help. Sometimes the fault lies with the actor, sometimes with the writing.

Purpose: What an actor says and does is only the surface of his character's existence. In real life, we have a rich inner life going on all the time, and no fictional character can be interesting or complete without also having one. This exercise compels actors to fill the space between their lines and actions with the character's inner thoughts and feelings. Having an inner monologue can make what an actor has to do arise from a genuine inner life, and make everything that other characters do help *cause* that inner life.

Activity: For a troubling part of the text, ask your actor or actors to improvise their characters' interior monologue and then perform each line or action. A good solution is to use a loud voice for the line and a soft voice for the "thoughts voice" or interior monologue. If the cast is not used to doing this, they will find it hard or baffling, and the scene will go at a snail's pace. But having to create publicly and on the spot always yields deeper understandings because a high degree of commitment is unavoidable. When an actor has done this work and the results are still not making sense, asking for the inner monologue will reveal what part of her understanding needs changing. Generally this actor has failed to make sense of what her partner means, or to build upon her character's history. Here the director can be of great help. Demanding that an inner monologue be kept up is a sure way to immediately upgrade a so-so performance. It also helps stabilize players of unreliable timing because it supplies a repeatable interior process that will pace each forward step of a character's external behavior. This is work that actors habitually evade or forget, so the mere possibility that you will again ask them to do it aloud and in front of other actors usually keeps them working at it.

Discussion:

- do the inner monologues show that your actors are on the same wavelength?
- are you sharing the same interpretations?
- what did you (the director) learn from the actors?
- what did you learn about your actors?
- what did your actors seem to learn about you?

EXERCISE 22-4: CHARACTERIZING THE BEATS

Useful When: You need to clarify and energize a scene or a passage that is muddy and lifeless.

Purpose: To give each phase of buildup to the beat its own clear intention and identity, which in turn sharpens the beat or turning point itself. To focus attention on subtext, and on the actor's body language, movement, and voice range.

Activity:

1. Ask the actors to devise a brief tag line for each phase of the pressure that builds toward each perceived beat. So far as possible, phrase these tags in a way that always expresses volition (examples: "Leave me alone!"; "I need you to notice me"; "You're not going to hoodwink me again.") Be sure each tag is in the active, not passive voice ("Let me go to sleep" not "I am being kept awake") so that each tag line expresses active will even when the character is being victimized. Each tag line should contain an element of "I want . . . "

2. Now get the actors to approximate the actions and movements of the scene from memory, but speaking to each other using only the tags in place of dialogue. Where the text used verbal logic, now pressure can only be applied or parried by action that is highly defined by the tag, and using the voice and body as instruments. This necessity causes interesting developments in the actors' range of expression, shifting it from verbal/logical to physical/emotional, with a corresponding increase in power.

3. Now have the actors play the scene as scripted, and marvel at the difference.

Discussion:

- what did you learn about the actors from the movements they used this time?
- about their emotional range?
- about their communion when the exercise forced it into continuous existence?

EXERCISE 22-5: ACTIONS AT BEAT POINTS

Useful When: A scene seems monotonous, wordy, and cerebral. This technique can return the spotlight to the turning points.

Purpose: To focus and physicalize the beats and demarcate the phases of the scene behaviorally. This is the very opposite of playing a scene "in general" where the actors approach it with correct but generally applied ideas. A scene must be built of behaviorally authentic blocks, each containing a clear set of human strivings, however subtle. A scene containing several emotions in one character will be most effective when it builds each separately.

Activity: When the beat points are located and tagged, ask the actors to devise several of their character's actions during such a change of awareness. These can start out multiple and exaggerated in order for the director to choose which feels best. The chosen action can then be brought down to an appropriate level of subtlety. Of course, the actor should invent from his or her own emotional range, and the action should then be authentic to both actor and character.

Discussion:

- what is really at stake for each character at each beat?
- is there interpretational leeway?
- what is the range of options in terms of behavior that could be appropriate?
- which is the freshest?

EXERCISE 22-6: GIVE ME TOO MUCH

Useful When: One or more of your actors is under an emotional constraint, and the scene is stuck in low gear.

Purpose: To release actors temporarily from restrictive judgments they are imposing, and give them permission to overact.

Activity: Tell actors you feel that the scene is bottled up and that you want them to reach for the same emotions but exaggerate them. Exaggeration brings clarity, and it also licenses actors to go to emotional limits that they fear would look absurd if produced under normal conditions.

Discussion: You can now tell your cast what to change and at what new levels to pitch their energy and emotions. Often exaggeration alone clears a blockade. Ask actors how it felt to go so far beyond their previous levels. When actors switch from dabbling fearfully in the shallows to leaping with abandon off the top diving board, they often find they can now do the elegant dive. Frequently they will report letting go of a specific fear.

EXERCISE 22-7: LET'S BE BRITISH

Useful When: A scene has become overprojected, artificial, and out of hand. Actors may have begun to feel it will never work, that it is jinxed.

Purpose: To return the actors to playing from character instead of striving for an elusive effect.

Activity: Ask your actors to play the scene in a monotone, with emotion barely evident, but fully experiencing their character's emotion underneath the reticence.

Discussion: It is generally true that repressing emotion heightens it; for a scene that has turned into sound and fury, this may lead back to basics. Did it? What did the actors feel?

EXERCISE 22-8: SPOT CHECK

Useful When: A line or an action repeatedly does not ring true.

Purpose: To put a probe into an actor's process at a particular moment.

Activity: Simply stop a reading or an off-book rehearsal at the problem point and ask the actors what their characters' thoughts, fears, mental images, etc. were at that moment.

Discussion: Often you will find that someone has a misconception or is forcing an emotional connection and falsifying it. At worst, doing this acts as a sort of breathalyzer test, jolting the actors into keeping up the inner lives of their characters for fear you will pull them over. Use sparingly.

EXERCISE 22-9: SWITCHING CHARACTERS

Useful When: Two actors seem stalemated and not properly aware of the character each other is playing. This can arise when a defensive actor's overpreparation precludes him from adapting to nuances in a partner's playing. It may also be because your actors distrust each other or feel incompatible.

Purpose: To place each actor temporarily in the opposite role so later he or she empathizes with another character's predicament and achieves an interesting duality.

Activity: Simply ask actors to exchange parts, without regard for sex, age, or anything else.

Discussion: Ask each to say in a few words what he or she discovered about the scene when he or she carried the other role, and if they had any revelations about their original parts.

EXERCISE 22-10: TRANSLATING A SCENE INTO AN IMPROVISATION

Useful When: The cast seems unable to generate the emotion the scene calls for.

Purpose: To free the actors from the letter of the scene in order to create its spirit. It can also refresh a rehearsal session when energies are flagging. The less experienced your cast, the less are they able to concentrate and develop during long rehearsal sessions.

Activity: Take the main issue in the scene, or the one that is causing a problem, and translate it into two or three analogous scene subjects for improvisation. For example, if you have a scene about a conflict between a daughter and her suspicious and restrictive father, you might assign improvs on:

- a scene between an officious nurse and a patient who wants to leave the hospital
- a bus driver and a rider who wants to get off the bus before the next stop
- two customers in a supermarket checkout line, the younger of whom wants to jump the line because she only has three items

Each of these situations has a built-in conflict over rights and authority, and tackling them rapidly one after another will generate a wider emotional vocabulary that can be reimported into the original scene. At the very least, this exercise can ground the static electricity that builds up over repeated failures with the formal text. You can get even more mileage out of your improvs if you do a second round with the roles reversed.

Discussion: This either works or it does not, and there is not much to argue about. Try to keep improv equivalencies up your sleeve for any scene that may give trouble. Actors may initially resist your request, but usually come to enjoy the refreshment that improv brings when a scene has become oppressive and immobile. Few will be unimpressed that you can whisk out an alternative approach like this.

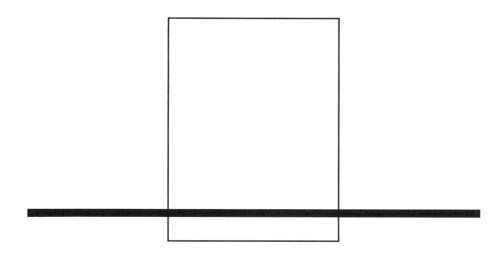

REHEARSAL AND DEVELOPMENT

Rehearsal is a much misunderstood activity. The misconceptions begin with the word itself, which suggests repetition and drilling. A much better word is *development*. To forgo development prior to filming is to forgo depth. Because movies are shot piecemeal it is often assumed that film performances, unlike theater, need little or no rehearsal and even that rehearsal damages spontaneity. This belief may be a rationalization for minimizing costs (rehearsal greatly increases them) or perhaps people think that only theater has to rehearse because of the problems of a continuous performance. It's true that good theater grows out of a radical and organic rehearsal process, even improvisatory theater. So why not film? The argument goes that film actors can learn the next day's lines the night before shooting, and since final movements depend on the logistics of the set and even of lighting, lengthy rehearsal is a waste of time and money.

Actors who create original characters do in fact study and rehearse as intensely as concert pianists practice. This preparation—both private and collaborative—seldom makes it into the movie gossip columns. But anyone who inquires how much Dustin Hoffman and Meryl Streep—to mention only two exceptionally versatile talents—prepare themselves cannot doubt that acting is an exceptionally demanding craft and that talent is the outcome of dedicated work.

If top professional actors must prepare, novices should work even harder. Few beginning filmmakers seem aware of this and the acting in student films is usually appalling. Too often student directors believe filming and editing is an alchemy that will turn lead into gold.

Before something good can emerge from the rehearsal process, the director must understand the importance of tapping into the actors' creativity, and not to think of them, however privately, as puppets. They must have the opportunity to become comfortable and interested in each other. To see the implications of this, we must examine an analogous life situation. Imagine an office birthday party where a group of people naturally integrate with each other and their environment. The outsider sees their familiarity and interdependence in everything they say and do. One could not bring in an impostor, however well briefed, without everyone knowing he was spurious.

Now think of a scene with a new cast developed from a text. Initially, at least, it is a convocation of such impostors whose pretensions to familiarity and interdependence show up painfully to every observer. Every piece of drama starts out cold in this way, but there's no need to *film* it, for heaven's sake. Yet that is what happens.

If instead you make the actors into an ensemble having its own dynamic of relationships and its own history together, you will make up in intensity what it might lack in longevity, and the company can begin to absorb dramatic situations into its own authentic reality. Fictional and actors' relationships become indistinguishably real.

That is our aim. The following stages produce a disciplined, creative quest, the expressive results of which are channeled through the sensibility of the director, the piece's first audience.

PLANNING

As soon as parts are cast, your assistant director (AD) should make a log of everyone's availability and work out possible rehearsal times. Warn actors new to the process that filming is very slow, and also warn them again of the temptations to deny the negative aspects of their characters. All human beings are made up of emotions that actors should see as neither positive nor negative but as simply true. Truth has a value that transcends popularity.

Most people find it easier to work to a predetermined schedule, and this also signals your professionalism. Allot more than enough time for the film's performances to evolve. A good rule of thumb is to invest at least one hour of developmental rehearsal for every minute of screen time. An easy three-minute scene thus needs a minimum of three one-hour rehearsals. Make rehearsals brief and frequent rather than long and comprehensive, since people doing unfamiliar work tire rapidly and lose the ability to concentrate.

FIRST READ-THROUGH

After everyone has studied the script, a first read-through will show how each actor interprets the piece and how well the nascent characters fit together. Expect to get first glimpses of where your biggest problems lie, in particular scenes, particular actors, or both.

Encourage actors to use as much natural movement as they can both during the read-through and subsequently, even though the primary focus is upon the meaning of words. Holding a script will inhibit movement, but the emphasis on doing reminds the cast to act with the whole body, not just the voice or the face.

Depending on the length and complexity of the screenplay, read it through in sections, or all at one go if possible. Have a list of fundamental questions ready for the actors. Give little or no direction; you want to see what ideas and individuality each spontaneously brings to his role and to the piece. Show that you expect actors to be partners in seeking answers to problems, for problem solving is at the heart of creativity. This also discourages actors from passively depending upon minute instructions, not usually a problem if your casting is good.

Although you may have strong ideas of your own, be receptive to your actors' input and individuality. It shows you expect them to dig into the piece and thoroughly explore what kind of people the characters are. They will have to judge what motivates each to do what he or she does, and to define what purposes lie behind the script as a whole. Any serious actor will find this approach attractive and challenging because it acknowledges his intelligence.

KEEP NOTES

A tough part of directing is holding onto important impressions during a rehearsal. Because you must monitor so many things simultaneously, early impressions get erased by later ones, and you can easily turn to the actors with a mind embarrassingly void of everything except the last impression, especially when you are fatigued. Avoid this by carrying a large scratch pad and without taking your eyes off the performance, scribble a key word or two. Glance down momentarily and place your pen at a starting point ready for the next note. Afterward you will have several pages of large wobbly prompts. These should trigger the necessary recall.

DIRECT BY ASKING QUESTIONS

Through probing questions you can guide the cast to discover what you may already know (this method also gives you time to think ahead!). Because of the energy and diversity a group brings to any enterprise, this process flushes out aspects that may never have occurred to you. Learning becomes a two-way street. Throughout production, even when everyone feels there can be nothing left to discover, the piece will continue to deepen, growing stronger as you and your cast stumble upon even more meanings and interconnections. Here lies much of the exhilarating sense of shared discovery and closeness that can develop between cast and crew, something everyone may recall nostalgically for years afterward.

Asking challenging questions is always a more effective way of briefing and coordinating a group than simply reeling off instructions. Orders, not least because of their authoritarian nature, are easily resisted or misunderstood, especially when they prove inadequate and must be modified or superseded. But people seldom forget what they discover for themselves. That is the philosophy underlying all the exercises and projects in this book.

NO LEARNING OF LINES YET!

At this stage, be absolutely clear that you want nobody to learn lines yet. Committing lines to memory also means transfixing whatever action and level of interpretation has been reached. Making changes becomes harder after the initial memorization. At this early stage there is insufficient knowledge of the piece to risk this.

SCHEDULING

Remind the actors before they leave of the next rehearsal and make sure each has a printed schedule. For the next meeting, ask the actors to set down notes on their character and develop a detailed biography to substantiate their conceptions. It may be safer to review these with each cast member separately than to review them in a group, where redirection at this early stage might damage someone's confidence.

FIRST DISCUSSIONS: FOCUSING THE THEMATIC PURPOSE

A theme represents an authorial system of values or beliefs that lies within the director's interpretation of the screenplay. To communicate yours on the screen, you will have to effectively argue it. Stating the thematic purpose of one's piece really means defining the steps and focus of this argument.

A story represents a limited but intense vision. Such a vision is made coherent and integrated, however subtly, by an underlying philosophy of cause and effect. Telling a story is really a way of constructing a working model of one's beliefs. If others are moved to conviction, the principles behind the model have been shared, acclaimed, and may be accepted as having merit. That is the best anyone can do.

A thematic purpose for your work need not try to encompass universal truth ("in our Western way of life the rich get richer while the poor get poorer") or be morally uplifting ("if people would just vent their real feelings, everyone could be free"). Audiences will feel they are being preached at especially when the scope of the film falls short of the global nature of its message.

Modest, solid, specific, and deeply felt aims are likely to have the most impact. Your thematic statement may focus the motivation for telling the tale onto a simple principle with profound consequences ("sometimes marriage between two good people is not practical and everyone suffers," or "though this idealogue is honest and sincere, he is dangerous to those that love him"). By taking a small truth and deeply investigating it, you can invest it with life and indicate larger truths of wider resonance. Put another way, *a thoroughly absorbing and convincing microcosm will effectively create the macrocosm.*

Your notion of the piece's thematic purpose will come from your study of the text but that does not guarantee that it will be shared by those who matter most: your cast. Regrettably, with small parts it may be expedient to simply tell players what the piece is about. But giving such instructions to anyone with a major role will be counterproductive since it suggests that the actor must discard any original or contrary impressions. In any case, limiting creative participation creates trouble down the road with all but the most passive actor.

A wiser approach is to form your own ideas and then either parlay your cast into accepting them, or into forming alternatives that are just as acceptable or (do not tell anyone!) superior. Again, make it very plain that actors must learn no lines until interpretations, meanings, and characters have been explored and agreed.

Now that the cast has had time to study the script:

1. Ask your players to discuss the purpose of the whole story. This reveals what spectrum of opinion exists. Encourage all points of view and impose none of your own at this time. Get the cast involved by expecting them to reason things out for themselves. Not only will this bring them closer, but you will acquire additional insights, since each is an advocate for a single character.

2. Ask the cast to formulate the "back-story" (what seems to have happened before the film begins).

3. Ask each actor to describe his character and to prepare a brief character biography for another meeting.

4. Turn the cast's attention to successive key scenes and ask the players to develop the subtext for each.

5. Ask the cast to review the main themes of the piece; say what you think is their hierarchy. During this process you should try to unify the body of opinion into a coherent thematic purpose for the piece.

If you cannot achieve agreement at this stage, at least agree to differ and let it go. Such disagreements often provide a creative tension that spurs closer examination during the next phases of work. Actors will probably be too busy with more immediate concerns to turn it into a running fight, and everyone will eventually arrive at a tacit agreement through shared problem solving or, failing all else, battle-fatigue.

You are now ready to begin developing the piece and to test your ideas through rehearsals. You have designed your plane and now you want to see if it flies.

ENCOURAGE ACTORS TO DEVELOP THEIR CHARACTERS' BACKGROUNDS

An essential resource for any conscientious actor is his character's biography, which he prepares himself. Without an explicit request some may not make the effort, especially if they have yet to understand its benefit. Others do the job inadequately or go off at a tangent through misreading the piece. This is a good time to meet alone with each actor to go over his or her ideas and to encourage, develop, or redirect. It is also a good time to discuss how the actor's character sees the other characters.

VALUES AND HAZARDS OF WORKING ONE-ON-ONE WITH ACTORS

Much of a part's future direction will develop from one-on-one exploratory sessions. Inevitably, the larger the cast, the less the director's undivided attention can be available to individual cast members. Since feedback is so vital to actors, most feel inadequately recognized most of the time. If the actor sees another actor alone with the director, he tends to resent the special attention unless the session is evidently remedial. Because of these pressures, try to work with a small cast, and to capitalize on relationships with good actors by using them again in subsequent productions.

A good solution to the demand for individual attention is to see everyone alone, even minor parts, at the outset. You will want to check the actor's ideas and approach, and establish a personal and supportive relationship. From then on try to rehearse collectively, reserving private discussion for special support, and the exchange of ideas or suggestions about problem areas. Develop something personal and supportive to tell each actor just before shooting begins.

REHEARSING ONE SCENE AT A TIME

Initially, try to rehearse scenes in script order. Later, as the piece becomes thoroughly familiar, adopt a plan of convenience and work around people's schedules or give priority to key scenes and those still presenting special problems.

At this stage the cast is still working with "the book." Actors are searching for their characters' full range of motivations, and developing a knowledge of how each scene functions in the piece as a whole.

DEAL ONLY WITH TOP-LEVEL PROBLEMS

At each of the initial run-throughs, deal only with a scene's most major problems or you risk burdening actors with too much information and blurring priorities. A rehearsal spirals backward and forward, oscillating between particular details and the more abstract areas of meaning and philosophy. As major problems get solved, others of secondary significance, such as single lines that lack conviction, will move to the top of the heap and claim everyone's attention. The rehearsal process is thus one of continuous discovery and refinement.

FROM BEAT TO BEAT, THE DRAMATIC UNIT

Once a scene's major difficulties are brought under control, you should go over everything within each beat, one unit at a time. This may be the only practicable approach if you have to rehearse and shoot all in the same day. Much of the value of working on each separate unit lies in preventing the actors' growing and embracing knowledge from pervading everything they do. The sign that this is happening is when the scene becomes muddy and lacking in dynamics. Characters should live keenly and restrictedly within their immediate present, experiencing one discovery after another, and reacting to what they discover.

THE ADVANTAGES OF VIDEOTAPING REHEARSALS

Once your cast is off the book and beginning to be reasonably confident, cover the rehearsals with a video camera. The most useful coverage is the documentary style called direct cinema. This is a continuous take by a handheld camera, moving close for closeups, and backing away and panning or tracking as the action requires. This treats the rehearsal as a happening to be recorded without any intervention on behalf of the camera. Because it tries to be in the right place at the right time, this coverage needs no editing. Taping rehearsals in this way produces a fascinating range of advantages:

- you can see a dramatically complete version within minutes of calling "Cut!"
- the mobile camera gives priority to the actors' freedom of movement
- the camera is choreographed into the process, rather than appearing later as a dominant and inhibiting newcomer
- the cast gets over its camera neuroses early
- the cast soon ignores the camera, and you can expect natural and unstrained performances
- the director judges what works on the screen from *seeing* what works on the screen
- the director, able to privately run and rerun rehearsals, gets an early sight of mannerisms, clichés, trends, and subtleties that would otherwise only make themselves known in rushes or postproduction
- the crew is integrated early, and can seek each scene's appropriate form in terms of camera angles, movement, lenses, lighting, and sound coverage
- the crew learns the imperceptible indications each actor gives when he or she is going to move, and what sightlines and movements can be expected
- during rehearsals director and crew evolve ways to cover stretches of action using fewer angles and longer takes
- compromises an actor must make in speed or destination to overcome a camera or microphone problem are solved before the shoot

  By the time formal shooting arrives:

- everyone is an old hand and there is little of the regression that normally accompanies the first shooting
- camera placements and movements most likely to show the scene to advantage are known, not theoretical
- first shooting is from a living reality, instead of something based on the static, heroic concepts of the storyboard approach

• improvisation and dealing with the unexpected is easier when everybody thoroughly knows the foundations

Especially when a group intends to function as a repertory company (like Fassbinder's early group) the cycle of performance and critical viewing is a superb way of helping people to get beyond shock and fascination at seeing their own image and to begin working on the places where their resistances lie.

A PLEA NOT TO COPY THE FILM INDUSTRY

The professional film industry often does without rehearsals for reasons of cost and spontaneity. You should not copy this practice. And if you do rehearse your cast, you absolutely must videotape what you do, or risk developing a theatrical performance that will look terrible onscreen.

Here are the reasons. If you are a location worker like a cameraperson or assistant director, and have watched a thousand setups and seen their effect onscreen, your experience will help you make good performance judgments if you direct. But for the inexperienced director who hasn't first apprenticed in the industry, *not rehearsing, or rehearsing without seeing the results on tape, leads inevitably to performances developed in a live-performance mode.* The resulting theatricality is impossible to change in the cutting room.

Another pitfall: newcomers to directing tend to delay evolving a *mise-en-scène* (camera treatment) until the last moment. This makes for a late and highly theoretical fragmentation of the material and coverage that errs on the side of caution to ensure against all possible editing problems. A production filmed this way has a processed look and lacks an integrated point of view. It is also expensive, takes longer to film, uses more filmstock, and exhausts the cast.

Taping rehearsals on the other hand gives constant and reliable feedback on both performances and coverage, and shows an acting company their work—if you choose to do so (see below). It is a wonderfully simple way for a director to develop an ensemble. It takes a little extra work, may slow the process of arriving at results, but guarantees a cinematic result. Can you afford *not* to tape rehearsals?

If you are still questioning whether this is "professional," remember that many directors use a video assist at film shoots. This is a video feed from the camera's viewfinder that lets the director see the action on a video monitor and hear sound through headphones instead of watching the take live from alongside the camera. If they need to see what is actually going on film, can you afford *not* to?

WHEN TO SHOW ACTORS THEIR PERFORMANCES

Taping rehearsals is not without risks. Cast members clamor for a showing, but are usually appalled on first seeing themselves onscreen. Thereafter individuals may depend more on your judgment, or they may go the other way and attempt to apply their own corrective action, giving you a new problem. If you show rehearsal footage regularly, inexperienced or untrusting actors can begin to direct themselves (or worse, other actors) instead of remaining inside their own characters' thoughts and experience.

If you show rehearsal tapes, you must persuade everybody well before the shoot to relinquish monitoring and judging his own performance and pass that responsibility over to you. You are the director and you represent the first audience. The actor who fails to do this, locked in defensiveness and mistrust, is a liability. Usually this person is of star status and terrified of losing his reputation—so you won't face this for a while!

Taping, showing rehearsals to actors, and debating the outcome is an evolutionary process that works well with a dedicated ensemble, but it takes time. If you are taping rehearsals but your schedule won't allow this degree of development, use the following procedure:

- warn that it is normal to hate the way one looks on the screen
- make a little footage available early in rehearsals for the curious
- be clear that you will show no tape footage later and no rushes during the shoot
- if there is protest, explain that actors in feature films are normally barred from seeing rushes because it is too unsettling and can ruin confidence

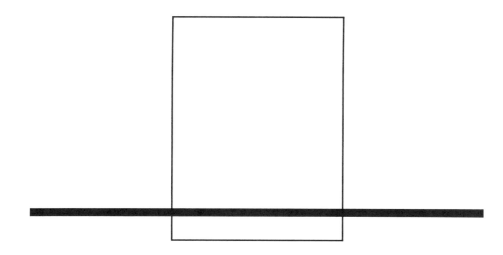

DIRECTOR AND ACTOR
PREPARE A SCENE

If collaborative work is to be truly effective, actors and their director should each work alone on the text before trying out a scene together. Their preparatory work will overlap, creating checks and balances in which action, motivations and meanings are examined from multiple perspectives. This helps avoid omissions, but it also draws valuable individual perceptions from the actors. These viewpoints will not necessarily be compatible, for each tends to see his or her character, other characters, and the piece itself from the partisan perspective of the character being played. In early group discussions the director leads the process of coordinating and reconciling them, making it a creative dialogue rather than a battle of wills. The director's vision should be nonpartisan, embracing, and holistic, a surrogate for the future audience.

Following are the responsibilities that director and actor bear at the outset of rehearsal. Description may make them seem like an intellectual exercise, but after you have gained some initial experience much becomes instinctive.

DIRECTOR

GIVEN CIRCUMSTANCES

Know the script so you're quite certain what locations, time frame, character details, acts, etc., are exactly specified, and what other detail is only implied or must be supplied by director and cast.

BACK-STORY

Using your intimate knowledge of the script, infer what took place prior to the script's action. This is the back-story. The remaining biographical details that substantiate back-story fall into the domain of the individual character's biography. This is best created by the actor playing the part. The director, however, needs to be ahead of the game to be considered authoritative by the cast.

NATURE OF CHARACTERS: WHAT EACH WANTS

It is vital to go beyond what a character "is" and to know what that character *wants,* and is *trying to get* or *do.* This conception gives the character not just a fixed, static identity worn like a monogrammed T-shirt, but an active, evolving quest that mobilizes willpower to gain each new end, moment to moment. For instance, there is a great difference between saying that "Paul is afraid" and saying "here Paul wants to deflect the policeman's attention away from his suitcase." In the static example the actor playing Paul is expected to play generalized fear, while in the active example his character has a series of definite ends to gain, each one specific to the moment. A succession of such small, precise goals utterly transforms a person's acting by showing his character in action, thus making the character's inner life visible.

NATURE OF ACTS

Finding authentic behavior is immensely important to storytelling in the cinema, for each genuine act, even the tiny ones, helps create a strong and unique identity for its doer. In the search for the authentic, labels or similes become a potent directive when communicating with actors. To say that a man leaves the table during a family feud is not enough, for it provides an instruction lacking any special identity. But naming his action "the tactical retreat" or "the first step in leaving home" gives it a quality and meaning immediately assimilated by the players, something memorable, specific, and valuable. A possessive mother's behavior when receiving her son's fiancée for the first time might be called "the snake dance" and a boy entering the funeral parlor where his father lies dead might be named "crossing the threshold of the underworld." *An evocative simile or analogy gives the nature of the act or action a precise and imaginative coloration.*

NATURE OF EACH CONFLICT

Because drama is powered by conflict, the director must know where and how each situation of conflict develops. It can appear as:

- tension within a character between the opposing parts of him- or herself
- conflict between characters, and
- conflict between characters and their situations

For any conflict to exist, a pattern of oppositions must emerge, tension build in stages (rising action), climax, and then resolve (falling action). When a scene's resolution leads to harmony, this is usually a temporary lull before fresh tensions develop, starting a new cycle. This cyclical movement, taking place within the scene as beats, has been likened to the cycles of an internal combustion engine (John Howard Lawson, *Theory and Technique of Playwriting* [New York: Hill & Wang, 1960]). The piston's compression stage is the gradual building of pressure inside the dramatic combustion chamber. At the moment of maximum pressure comes ignition and explosion, and this forces the motor forward into a new cycle of intake, compression, and explosion.

FINDING THE BEATS

A scene of tension between individuals is like a fencing match—much strategic footwork and mutual adaptation punctuated by strikes. Each strike threatens to alter the balance of power and puts the match's possible outcome in a new light. In drama, likewise, a scene's nature and apparent premise change at each impact moment, or *beat*. These beats are not rhythmical, and do not come regularly. They are moments of changed consciousness and high significance for at least one character, and they should be noticed by the audience. Each such moment is one where change is irrevocable. This is the beat, the heightened moment or "crisis adaptation" for which the scene has been working. There may be several such cycles or beats in a scene.

FINDING THE DRAMATIC UNITS

Between one beat and the next is the winding down from the old beat and the winding up, or rising action, leading to the crisis of the next. It can be minutes or seconds long. Mark the beat points in your script, and see how the scene's forward movement becomes a waveform charting a series of dramatic thrusts at the audience's emotions. This can be predictable and manipulative, or done in good taste it can be movingly true to human life. The difference is a matter of honesty, purpose, and taste in the writing.

Keep in mind all communication has two modes of operation: intellectual and emotional. As a screen audience *our ideas change only if we are also emotionally engaged*. Beginning filmmakers are often prepared by academia to seek control of an audience through the intellect. Unless taught by exceptional people, this closes rather than opens the student to the emotional implications in the material. To direct, you *have* to be able to enter the emotional realities of each character, see through their eyes, feel their feelings and changes.

BREAKING THE DRAMATIC UNIT INTO STEPS

Figure 24-1 is the first page in a scene where two characters, Tod and Angela, get lost while driving in a city outskirts, and have a fight because Tod won't stop and look at the map. The beat on this page is where Tod realizes that Angela is seriously upset and that he must do something different. There are several steps on the part of each character toward this moment, and they are decided by making an analysis of subtexts (that is, determining the paradigm underlying what the characters actually say or do). See if you agree that Angela's first three lines are all fueled by the same underlying idea, "I'm afraid we're really lost." When she realizes that their directions include a supermarket, and this as well as the gas

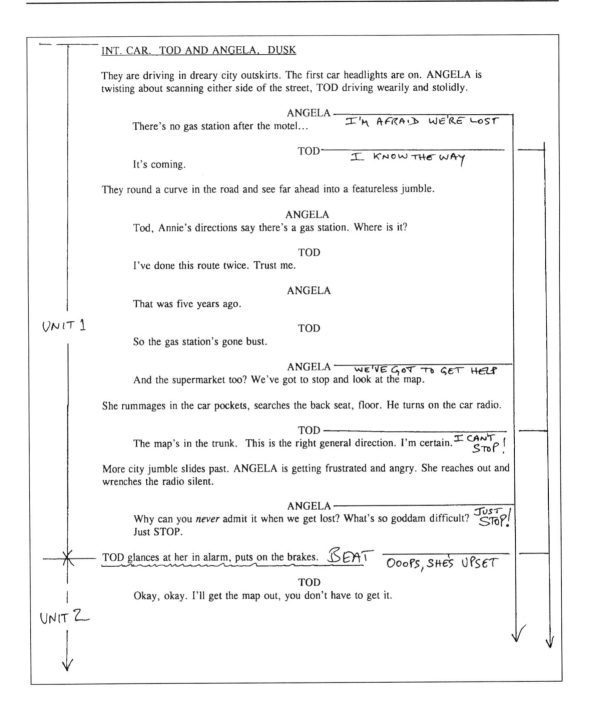

FIGURE 24-1

Script page with marked beat, dramatic units, and steps within the first unit delineated as tag lines.

station are nowhere to be seen, her subtext changes to "We've got to get help." Tod's lines are adaptations to Angela's expression of will, and pitted against hers. At the beat point, he realizes things have gone too far, stops the car, and a new unit begins.

This is analytic work that trained actors do, either consciously and with a pencil, or less consciously out of long training. Untrained actors won't have the first idea, and you will have to work with them until they understand the method. What it produces is a clear set of steps, each one fueled by a new emotion and volition. It is important to realize that a character's complex of emotions cannot all be played at once. They have to be built in steps, one clear emotion after another, with clear and appropriate action at each point. This is how it happens in life, but unfortunately we *remember* a situation in abstract, summary form in which all the fine and distinct experiences are mulched together and typified. This is where a good part of the confusion and misunderstanding arises about acting. Make a point of observing, in yourself and in others, how emotions really work. After you get into the habit of observing actuality, you won't fall for the stereotype renderings any more.

As a director, you must be ahead of your cast, breaking each scene down into units, and deciding precisely what you think drives each step for each character within each unit. You may learn something when you review the work the actors have done on their own, but they will be deeply impressed that you understand their parts so well. From preparation like this you derive your authority to direct, and your conviction about what you want. Actors seek clarity, decisiveness, and communication from a director—and seldom get more than a part of it. But the director who comprehends during a rehearsal or a take what each actor is giving, who describes it accurately back to the cast, is the conductor who can hear every instrument when the whole orchestra is playing. This is not a skill you are born with, it's something you work to acquire. Doing your homework on the script is the absolute foundation. Putting a screenplay under rigorous scrutiny also reveals definitively how functional the screenplay actually is, and what you need to do to improve it.

CHANGES IN A CHARACTER'S RHYTHM

Every character has his own rhythms for speech and action. These vary according to his mood (for instance, whether he is excited or tired). It is an actor's responsibility to keep the character's rhythms distinctive and varying according to the character's inner state, which is likely to change at a beat point. Monotony is an invariable indicator of performing by rote, so know where to expect rhythmic changes.

OBLIGATORY MOMENT

One of the intake, compression, explosion cycles described above will be the scene's "obligatory moment," the main moment for which the scene as a dramatic unit exists. This is the fulcrum point of the scene, the moment of change for which the whole scene exists. Subtract it and the scene is disabled or redundant. Make sure you define each scene's obligatory moment or your directing will have no focus.

FUNCTION OF EACH SCENE

Like a single cog in the gear train of a clock, each scene in a well-constructed drama has its correct place and function. Defining this early enables one to interpret the scene confidently and cause it to feed impetus into the larger pattern. Giving a name to the scene helps define it to yourself, and just as importantly, transfer this information rapidly and forcefully to someone else. It is definitely helpful to *mise-en-scène* decisions. Some of Dickens' chapter titles from *Bleak House* make good examples: "Covering a Multitude of Sins," "Signs and Tokens," "A Turn of the Screw," "Closing In," "Dutiful Friendship," and "Beginning the World."

THEMATIC PURPOSE OF THE WHOLE WORK

It is the director's prerogative to decide and to shape the authorial thrust of the whole work. This interpretation must remain consonant with the screenplay's content and be accepted by the cast. Unlike a published play, a screenplay is not a hallowed document and directors will take considerable liberties after it has been acquired—a cause of much bitterness among screenwriters. Whatever changes you make, you alter the thematic purpose at your peril, unless you define one that is more embracing.

ACTORS

Following are concepts important to an actor's preparation. Some, being identical to the director's, appear only in an abbreviated form. Though I have written in the third person as if addressing an actor, this is seldom advisable and you should use my direct address only to help you ask the right questions. The actor's job leaves him extremely vulnerable to criticism, so avoid the appearance of top-down instruction at all costs. If it must be done, couch it as respectful suggestions for experiment. This is all the more important when you are handling any technique or emotion you haven't directly experienced yourself. Your power as a director lies in recognizing the authenticity of the result, however the actor gets there.

BACK-STORY

Know the events that brought your character and the others to the script's present.

YOUR CHARACTER'S GIVEN CIRCUMSTANCES

Know at every point what circumstances, time, place, pressures, and other people are contributing to your character's physical and mental state.

BIOGRAPHY

Make up a full life story for your character, one that supports the back-story details implied by the script. This ensures that you know a great deal about the character you are creating and that everything your character says or does is rooted in the patterns created by his or her past. Without this integrity of experience and motivation, your character will lack depth and credibility. Your director will often question you during rehearsal about your character's background, usually centering on what is not yet coming across well.

BE ABLE TO JUSTIFY EVERYTHING YOUR CHARACTER SAYS AND DOES

You must know the pressures motivating your character's every action and every line. This process of justification has already been used to build your character's biography, and the biography in turn governs your character's choices and decisions. The script usually contains the relevant clues, but occasionally your character's action must be completely defined by you and your director.

DEFINE EACH ACTION WITH AN ACTIVE VERB

Onscreen actions are the most eloquent expression your character ever makes, so the linguistic tags by which you plan them matter a great deal. Take this example: "A woman is seen stepping away from her tipsy husband in embarrassment at a party when an indiscretion passes his lips." This description is in the commonly used passive voice, flat and only minimally informative. An actress might describe the action for herself as, "sidestepping the landmine," "she absorbs a punch in the gut," "she springs toward the bar," or "she reels aside after stepping in filth." All these descriptions use active verbs and illuminate the behavior and its motivation.

What about common actions, like opening a closet door? To perform the action in general, that is, without a specific motivation, is false to life. Giving each one a tag is a way to invest each action with a specific identity and therefore meaning. For instance, "he eases the door open" shows caution and perhaps apprehension. Substitute *jerks, rips, shoves, barges, slides, elbows, flings, dashes, heaves,* or *hurls* and you have a veritable catalogue of relationships between man and door, each coloring and particularizing the action to great effect.

Film expects actors to remain consistent over many takes and many angles, and a single scene may take a whole day. Consistency becomes a major problem, especially for the untrained actor, or the actor lacking screen experience. Verbal tags help stabilize this situation. Make them part of your preparation and each action can then have a clear quality and motivation that helps you remain emotionally consistent. Knowing the tag also makes communication with your director quick and clear, should it become necessary.

WHAT IS MY CHARACTER TRYING TO GET OR DO?

Answering this commonplace little question is a key to real acting. In everyday life most of us are unaware of how unceasingly inventive we are in pursuing what we want. Instead, we see ourselves as civilized, long-suffering victims sacrificing happiness and fulfillment to the voracious demands of others. But the word *actor* tells the whole tale: for your character to get what he or she wants (a smile, a cup of coffee, a sympathetic reaction, a rejection, a sign of guilt, a glimpse of doubt) he or she must actively adopt a strategy that is characteristic for your character alone, as he or she tries to realize the desire of the moment. As circumstances alter, the character's needs change and adapt. Incidentally, for an actor to be active like this is the only viable method to portray a passive person, who differs only in strategy.

WHAT ARE OTHER CHARACTERS TRYING TO DO TO ME OR GET FROM ME?

If your character constantly searches the other actors' characters for signs of will and intention, it means that your character is constantly and spontaneously moving between the defensive and offensive roles demanded by your character's ever-changing situation. In real life this happens within us automatically and unconsciously, but to master a role these reflexes must be deliberately patterned until you have fully internalized your character's spontaneous actions and reactions. Very importantly, this means that your character is alive to the real and unpredictable chemistry of the acted moment. A scene that has been done in untold takes and angles can still be alive at the end of a long working day because you and your partners are still working from the actual moment.

KNOW WHERE THE BEATS ARE

See "Finding the Beats" under "Director" above but be aware that an actor, sustaining a single consciousness, sometimes sees peaks of consciousness in his or her character that have been overlooked by the director. Don't be afraid to play these or be an advocate for your character.

HOW AND WHERE DOES MY CHARACTER ADAPT?

Your character has goals to pursue or defend and will perceive changes that signal either victory or defeat. To these you must, within the frame of the writing, make strategic adaptation. Spotting where and how these adaptations can be made helps build a dense texture for your character's consciousness. Maintaining this can become so much real work that you can stay effortlessly in focus throughout many takes.

KEEP YOUR CHARACTER'S INTERIOR VOICE AND MIND'S EYE GOING

In real life, people are enclosed in their own ongoing thoughts, hopes, fears, memories, and visions, some of which are indeed verbalized as an interior monologue. The good actor builds and maintains his or her character's stream of consciousness or "interior action." In your mind, hear or even speak your character's conflicting thoughts, summon up mental images from your character's past, remember and imagine in character, and you will be continuously convincing and interesting to an audience. When there is a consistent inner life, your actions and reactions will automatically be consistently paced and true. The actor's art is really that of developing a disciplined consciousness. A properly structured consciousness in turn liberates genuine feeling. This is why acting is so difficult and psychically demanding.

KNOW THE FUNCTION OF EACH SCENE

Not only must you know your character's objectives but you must know on a larger scale what the scene is supposed to accomplish and what your character contributes to the piece as a whole.

KNOW THE THEMATIC PURPOSE OF THE WHOLE WORK

The intelligent actor wants to grasp not just the character and the character's purview, for that leads surely to an adversarial relationship with other actors, but also to understand the meaning of the whole, so that his or her characterization can merge effectively with the thrust of the whole work.

REHEARSING WITH THE BOOK

EARLY WORK WITH THE BOOK

By now your actors should have done their homework. They have still not been given the go-ahead to learn their lines because, as we have said, this leads to actors internalizing an undeveloped interpretation. There is another hazard: learning lines fixes an actor's attention prematurely on words when, for screen acting, behavior (of which language is only a part) should receive the most attention.

Your cast will probably be bursting with questions and ideas. Running through each scene from the book (that is, actors reading from the script), you should concentrate on each actor's conception—of the character and of the scene itself. *Learning the scene is much more important than learning lines.* Early rehearsal work should be geared toward finding the focus and interpretation you want. Character consistency is slow to evolve, because it requires reconciling a character's actions in one scene with actions in other scenes. Expect discussion and disagreement over nuances of motivation behind the action and dialogue. This is not subverting your authority, but the heady and untidy excitements of discovery.

WHICH SCENES FIRST?

At the first rehearsal you will probably cover one or two scenes chosen for their centrality to the piece as a whole. These should have emerged while you made your dramatic breakdown and definition of thematic purpose. Work on these and the turning points in them will provide a sure framework for other linked scenes. Rehearsal should always deal with the most important issues first, like laying foundations to support a house.

REHEARSAL SPACE

It is a great advantage to rehearse in the actual locations to be used, but this is often impractical. Make still photos to show actors what the space for each scene is like. This helps them imagine the proportions in which the scene is to take place and feeds the overall image of their characters' lives. Rehearsal itself often takes place in a borrowed or rented space that is large and bare. Indicate placement of walls, key pieces of furniture, doors, and windows with tape on the rehearsal room floor.

The advantage of this sort of minimalist rehearsal is that there is nothing to distract from attention to the text and its characters; the disadvantage is that its abstract quality can lead to performing and theatrical projection toward an imagined audience.

MOVEMENT AND ACTION

Though reading from a text prevents actors from moving with any consistency or freedom, it is important to get each cast member to develop special actions to reflect his or her character's internal, psychological movement. This is particularly important at the beats. For example, a man being questioned one evening in the kitchen by his possessive mother decides he must soon confess he is engaged to marry. The text reveals what he eventually does, but we should see from what he does how he feels during these stressful minutes. The screenplay does not specify. Perhaps he starts drying the dishes, and repeatedly hands items to his mother to put away so her hands are never empty. When she becomes especially probing, he goes silent, and lets the water out of the sink, watching it drain away. As the last of it gurgles down the drain he turns and blurts out his secret. The domestic scene, the way he purges himself of the family china, the water running away like sand in an hourglass, all combine both as credible action and as metaphors for the pressure he feels to act on a "now or never" decision.

Spontaneous invention usually first produces a dramatic cliché, so the director will need to be demanding in order to get fresher and more unexpected action from the cast than the example I have invented here.

Without the ability to move and to truly interact with each other, actors' readings will remain inadequate, so content yourself with rough sketchwork at this stage. As soon as you are satisfied that character, motivation, and the right kind of ideas for action are agreed on in outline, instruct the actors to learn their lines for a scene.

REHEARSING WITHOUT THE BOOK

When work begins without the book, watch out that the increased meaningfulness of the lines doesn't usurp the development of physical action. Encourage the actors to approach the scene from a behavioral rather than textual standpoint. This confirms the importance of having a clear idea of the setting—what it is, what it contains, and what it represents to the characters themselves. Insist on exploring the meaning and spirit of lines, not on their strict accuracy. You can always tighten the readings later. You'll find Chapter 21, Exercise 9: "Gibberish" a useful resource here.

TURNING THOUGHT AND WILL INTO ACTION

Only a few significant actions are specified in the average script, and unless the director and actors approach the script as an extremely spare blueprint requiring extensive development, characters will move into position, deliver their speeches in an overwrought manner, and be done. This reliably produces a hollow, unconvincing movie.

The true power behind both speech and action is will. Imagine that you have a domestic scene between a mother and son under development. It might well develop as follows:

When Lyn tells her son Jon that the car bumper is twisted, she is willing her son to feel shocked and guilty. You and your cast know this from the rest of the script, but you want to translate this into action. At the beginning of the scene, Jon hears his mother walk to the garage, but instead of hearing her drive away, he hears her footsteps return. Now she must force her angry state of mind upon her son. You get your actress to slow her entry and make it wordless, accusatory. She stands in the door looking at him.

Now he must repel or subvert the pressure she is applying. The actor tells you he feels that his character wants to be busy. You decide he is building a model car and painting the kit parts, keeping this up so he can avoid his mother's accusing gaze.

How does she command his attention? From intuition you suggest to her, "Try throwing the car keys next to the box of parts." This interrupts the evasive activity to which he resorted and creates a charged moment culminating in a beat as their eyes meet.

You and your actors are elated because you feel instinctively that you have created a strong moment. Now when the mother says, "The front bumper's all twisted," she is no longer supplying information but pushing home an accusation that began with her silent reentry. We no longer have words as neutral information, or words initiating action. We now have action culminating in words that themselves seek an effect. Driven by conscious needs, words are themselves a kind of action seeking the gratification of a reaction. This is why a line loaded in this way is called a *verbal action*. In good writing, all dialogue is specific and has this potential for acting upon the person addressed. Good actors, good directors try to develop pressures in the characters, pressures that produce dialogue. Then the dialogue itself becomes action. It supplies momentum by energizing further action in the person addressed.

Developing a scene is therefore more than knowing the dialogue and where to move on such and such a line; it is working out a detailed flow of action to evidence the internal ebb and flow of each character's being. Primarily this is each actor's responsibility, but final choice and coordination is the director's job. Proof of success is when an audience senses what is going on without hearing a word. I do a lot of international travel and I seldom listen to the sound tracks of in-flight movies. I usually watch them silent to learn as much as possible from their nonverbal side.

SIGNIFICANCE OF SPACE

How characters use space in this flow of action becomes highly significant. Continuing our scene above, the mother and son are half the room apart when she enters but she walks up to him in silence. The pressure from her proximity causes him to make a painting error, and he lays down the work, looking up at her blamingly. "It's not my fault; you parked it too close to the wall," he says, continuing to look up. She turns away in frustration and turns on the TV. Both stare at the silent picture for a moment or two, hypnotized and taking refuge in habit before they return to the divisive issue of how the car got damaged.

It is now the action rather than the dialogue that is eloquent of their distress, yet in the script only a few bald lines of dialogue appear on the page. Action has been created to turn implication into behavior—*behavior being the ebb and flow of will*. If some dialogue is now redundant you can cut it. So much the better.

CHARACTER'S INNER MOVEMENT

A single moment of inner movement in a character can be broken down into four definite steps.

1. **Feels Impact:** Someone's expectation (via words or an action) enters character's consciousness.
2. **Sees Demand:** This, filtered through his temperament, mood, and current assumptions, is translated (correctly or otherwise) into a demand ("She wants . . . ")
3. **Feels New Need:** Forms a new need ("Now I must get . . . ")
4. **Makes Counter-Demand:** The new need is expressed through an action (physical or verbal) that he expects will get fulfilling results.

In the following example we have a discussion going on between a woman and a man about an outing they have planned.

It is early Friday evening. There is disagreement between Brian and Ann about which movie they should go to see. She wants them to drive out to the farther cinema and see a new comedy. Not really wanting to go out, he says the comedy was not well reviewed, so they might as well go to one of the nearer films. She produces a newspaper and says that on the contrary the movie got three stars in both papers. Looking at him, seeing he is not changing his mind, she turns abruptly and moodily kicks her shoes into the closet, saying that he never wants to go out with her any more. He looks concerned and protests that it is not true. They end up going to the movie she wanted to see and he enjoys it more than she.

Let's analyze a single moment of change. When Ann suggests the film at the faraway cinema, Brian, whose job we know requires him to drive daily far from home and who now wants to watch TV and relax, goes through interior changes as follows:

Feels Impact: "Drive ten miles to see a movie when I could settle down and watch the news! Oh boy, this is really something to come home to."

Sees Demand: "It's her day off and she wants us to do something together. The old complaint that I never consider her situation, but that's not true. . . . "

Feels New Need: "I really can't get back into that traffic again for forty minutes, I've really got to put this off somehow. . . . It's not even a decent movie."

Makes Counter-Demand: (Speaking to Ann while looking ineffectually through the accumulation of newspapers) "You know, I seem to remember that David What's-his-name in the *Times* only gave it one star."

Brian does not signal his feelings, but instead makes a direct, action-oriented leap between what he perceives to be happening and what he must do to cope with it.

In general our feelings are followed by action and only require conscious examination when we are in internal conflict. Brian is not divided in himself until he realizes that Ann is nearly crying with disappointment and frustration. To make him realize this, and to move him to action will require that we see Ann's changes and his adaptations to what she feels and does.

Of course, not all human interaction centers on disagreement, but it often happens in drama because drama centers on conflict, no matter whether it is comedy, tragedy, horror, or any other genre. Even when characters appear to be in harmony, one may be buying time, that is, going along verbally while turning the whole matter over in his or her mind. Since inner states always find outward expression, it is important to find a fresh, subtle action to evidence (not telegraph or illustrate!) what the character is experiencing inside.

ADAPTATION

Here we have something like two characters trying to stand up in a small boat. There are constant changes for which they must both compensate, each according to what one discovers is happening or judges to be the other's strategy. In this movement there are many feints, experiments, surprises, and mistakes.

KEEPING UP AN INTERIOR MONOLOGUE

So that actors maintain their characters' inner lives, you may need to demand inner monologues; that is, the conscious internal enunciation of the characters' thoughts and perceptions. A well-trained actor will have internalized this habit but you won't be in any doubt when it is absent. The character seems to lack a thought process, comes to life abruptly when he or she has something to say, then promptly goes dead while waiting for the next cue. Sometimes actors are actually visualizing the script page. This is certain death for a movie.

A good way to shift an actor out of this mode is to ask him or her to improvise a thoughts voice between lines, as in Chapter 22, Exercise 3: "Improvising an Interior Monologue." Improvising a monologue is also a superb way to examine a point where an actor repeatedly loses focus or when you suspect that the actor has a skewed understanding of a certain passage. The only way that an actor's character remains alive during times of reacting is also to make sure they remain internally active. Another benefit is that by having a reliable interior action to carry out, the actor is more likely to stay in focus and carry out actions at a consistent rate from take to take.

USING MISPERCEPTIONS

For characters in comedy or tragedy, subjective errors of perception arise out of a wide range of causes. There are emotional obstacles—such as fear, misplaced confidence, wrong expectation—to cause a character to read a protagonist wrongly. Other highly productive misapprehensions come from a character's unfamiliarity with the culture or with the personality of the antagonist, inattention, preoccupation, partial or distorted information, or habit, to name just a few. Misperception is a fertile source for comedy (think of John Cleese's Basil Fawlty in the *Fawlty Towers* series) and it just as easily produces tension in drama by provoking actions that, far from neutralizing a situation, drive matters forward to new heights of revelation about the characters' differences and inner lives.

The work of Harold Pinter, like that of many modern dramatists, exploits the tensions between the characters' surface conformity and the dark, groping, private worlds existing beneath. In *The Dumbwaiter,* for instance, two hired assassins are left waiting interminably in a disused kitchen for further instructions. The lengthening wait, punctuated with bizarre, unfulfillable requests sent down in the dumbwaiter, acts upon the two men's private fears and distrust. While trying to maintain the faltering normality of their working partnership, an increasing fear gnaws at each, and we see them regress out of sheer insecurity.

The subtext of the piece deals with masters and servants, order and chaos, security and insecurity. It presents the characters as an analogy for man waiting nervously to learn God's will. But without a response from director and actors to the possibilities of this grandiose subtext, the piece can come off as a light comedy of manners.

EXPRESSING THE SUBTEXT

An actor must develop not just an idea of subtext, but the physical expression of it, entering an intensive, created world where he or she lives out the thoughts and feelings of the character. The actor creates the character, yet also *is* that character and so can speak for him and be guided by a growing intuition about what works. This means feeling what action (given and received) truly sustains the flux of the character's emotions or it can mean, conversely, sensing what is going against the character's grain and which he needs to examine and change. Like ambitious parents to their child, each actor is shepherd and champion for his own character. The director encourages this, but also deals even-handedly with a cast so that a spirit of destructive competition doesn't set in.

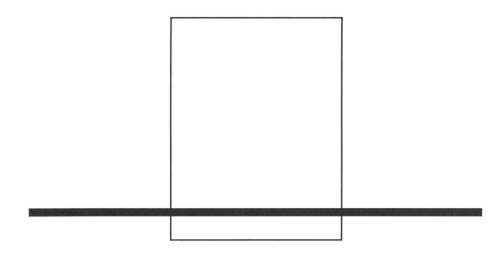

C·H·A·P·T·E·R 25

FINAL REHEARSALS AND PLANNING COVERAGE

THE DIRECTOR AS ACTIVE OBSERVER

So far, our rehearsal priorities have given primacy to the actors' sense of what their characters must do, moment to moment, with the director observing and steering the results by giving critical feedback. Soon the director must turn from interpreting the characters and text to planning their presentation on the screen.

Though it might be habit for the director to sit while observing and taking notes, this is dangerous because it leads to experiencing the action like a theater-goer, and to choreographing the action for a static camera placement. Clearly this is uncinematic and arises largely out of the director's immobility.

So, as the action unfolds, move around and adjust your position so you get the most involved and privileged view, either of the whole or of the significant parts. This leads naturally to your finding a point of view for the scene itself and the camera angles to reveal it. Your mobility also prevents actors from relating to one flat plane, that of you as the audience. Because they no longer know where you are, their action becomes inturned and enclosed as they play to and for each other—just as in real life.

When you need to fine-tune the blocking of actors and camera in relation to each other, and to break the action down into separate shots, it should now proceed with few conceptual problems.

FORM: SEEING IN AN UNFAMILIAR WAY

What makes films fresh and memorable is often not what is told, but how it is told. This is form as opposed to content and should be a concern all through the writing of the movie. Innovative storytellers are always searching for language that uniquely serves the tale in hand. Cinema form is influenced by many determinants such as photography, lighting, set and costume design, choice of location, story construction, and editing style.

Originality in form can be visual, such as the look of eighteenth-century English painting in Kubrick's *Barry Lyndon* (1976), the innovative deep-focus photography in Welles' *Citizen Kane* (1941), or the long lens compression and muted colors in Visconti's *Death in Venice* (1971). Originality of form can also lie in narrative style, such as the single take per scene of Tanner's *The Middle of the World* (1974), the edgy, compressed, and rapid movement of Roeg's *Don't Look Now* (1973), the predominance of stills in Marker's *La Jetée* (1963), or the surreal formalism of Greenaway's *Draughtsman's Contract* (1983). Formal freshness can reside in charismatic acting, as in Bertolucci's *Last Tango in Paris* (1972) or in Rafelson's *Five Easy Pieces* (1970). It can lie in a musical sensibility, as in Losey's *The Go-Between* (1971) or Godard's *Pierrot le Fou* (1965). More intangibly it can be located in a nontraditional approach to narrative itself, as in Tanner's *In the White City* (1985), Yvonne Rainer's *Kristina Talking Pictures* (1977), or Terence Davies' *Distant Voices, Still Lives* (1989) which is described as autobiography that is "part nostalgia, part nightmare." By an impressionistic and plotless sequence of scenes this film reveals a working-class postwar Liverpool family terrorized by its unpredictable and violent father.

The question of form—what options exist for best presenting a story's particular world—is at the very heart of original cinema, indeed of art itself. Form, seldom uppermost in the beginner's mind, is a difficult and elusive subject upon which to make generalizations. Even professionals tend to choose unconsciously and from what is normal. But the best and most enduring work evolves from a deeper awareness of how the arts, of which cinema is the most advanced synthesis, really function.

If you haven't already read it, Chapter 16, Form and Style contains a detailed account for you to consider. Here I want to draw your attention again to form's importance because your dialogue scenes should have a method of revelation that is special, not just get the all-purpose treatment. Remember that you occupy the position of the Observer; your Observer should have a special character and purpose so that we watch not mere observing but a Storyteller's tale.

BLOCKING

This ugly word, suggestive of building Stonehenge, refers to positioning actors and camera in relationship to each other. In my outline of a scene's development the director encourages the actors to freely develop movement and action without initial regard to filming restrictions. Where each character moves and why comes from what is in the script, what each actor feels the character needs, and what the director sees as necessary. With repeated rehearsal and especially if the rehearsal is going to be taped, this organic and experimental development will eventually settle into a tacitly agreed pattern of actions that express the flow of the characters' internal movements (perceptions, thoughts, feelings, will).

However, what emerges is by no means the only pattern possible. The exigencies of filming impose changes, and there are advantages that you simply discover. By altering a walk from one side of a table to the other, for instance, an additional camera angle and a lighting change can be saved. Such changes at the point of shooting seem like nothing but confusion to the cast, so avoid this disruption by trying to rehearse in the actual location and by involving the camera crew early. But blocking remains from first to last a process of mutual accommodation, and any part of which may change at a moment's notice. Actors, geared up for a big moment and then put on hold for a lighting change, are apt to become frustrated unless thoroughly forewarned of the changeable and sporadic nature of filmmaking itself.

For this and other reasons it is best to maintain an open attitude about how the scene may eventually be presented. This way you will not forfeit time and morale when shooting begins.

BENEFITS OF REHEARSING AT ACTUAL LOCATION

The script will often specify locations such as a convenience store or a drugstore that can easily be visualized. Everyone knows what a laundromat is like, or what it is like to wait in a typical train station, eat at a typical hot dog stand, or cook in a typical suburban kitchen. But wait, all kitchens are not equal! Each location in some way portrays its owners or its patrons, and a messy, greasy, dark kitchen imposes different physical and emotional conditions on the user than a light, airy, modern one.

A scene rehearsed to a hazy, generalized idea of the location and then transplanted into an actual kitchen at the moment of shooting will contain characters who barely connect with their surroundings, a serious deficiency. If rehearsals take place in the chosen location from the beginning, then actors can interact with their surroundings in a highly specific way.

When multiple on-site rehearsals are not practicable, take the actors for a research exploration, or at least show them photographs, so they have a distinct mental image. Director and actor alike can benefit from research. Michael Apted regularly sends his cast out ahead of shooting to research their characters. In the case of Aidan Quinn in *Blink* (1995), he spent time with Chicago detectives in order to play one himself.

Research for the director might include taping the actor at work in his or her own kitchen to note how the character and mood are subtly reflected in the actor's actions. Notice how often action is focused and purposeful, compared with the vagueness and gesturing of someone who only signifies living in a kitchen. Watch Peter Falk's performance as an old Polish baker in *Roommates* (1995).

Your aim in filming should be to make each location expressive and integral to the characters, and not a mere container for words and action. Try to see each setting as a character, worthy in itself of loving portrayal. This way you will set up an environment that makes the spectator imaginatively inhabit the movie, and maybe leaves him haunted by it long after. Any Wim Wenders movie is a lesson in making full use of settings.

HOW MUCH REHEARSAL IS ENOUGH?

Actors often express the fear that a scene will be overrehearsed. If rehearsal is drilling to a master plan, this is a real enough threat. But if it means digging into ever-deeper layers of meaning within the scene, of developing perceptions and restrictions that flow back and forth between the characters, of creating links and resonances with other parts of the script, then it can be unendingly productive.

Not all scenes merit such intensive work. Some exist merely to supply an uncomplicated story point—that a letter is delivered to the wrong address, for instance. Such a scene may require little or no rehearsal. Others are a gold mine of possibilities that richly repay persistent exploration. Decide which scenes need special work during your preparation but also be influenced by the ensemble's growing ability to focus upon problem areas and to discover their own solutions. This aspect, really a consequence of good leadership and good casting, can be the most rewarding aspect of collaborative work.

When an actor is convinced that developmental work cannot improve an impromptu performance, you as director may have to prove otherwise. Do not, however, extend rehearsing beyond where you can see a way ahead. When you reach your threshold switch to another scene. Seldom can one fully develop a scene on its own because of its dramatic interdependency on others. Spend time on related scenes in rotation rather than concentrating exhaustively upon one. This keeps actors' energies high and moves attention around the piece as a whole.

ONSCREEN LENGTH, REHEARSALS, AND
MAINTAINING A TIMING

Films intended for commercial showing have an optimum length related to their content. For television, length is also determined by the size of the "slot" and it will be precise to the second. A thirty-minute noncommercial TV slot usually requires a film of 28 minutes 30 seconds. Anything intended for commercial TV will have to be written with cliffhangers to accommodate commercials. Anyone who doubts the problems this brings should see Jack Gold's production for Hallmark of *The Return of the Native* (1995).

Most student films are limited more by budget than overall timing or commercial considerations, but the tendency is to shoot overlong scenes with too little coverage and far too much dialogue. Afterward it becomes apparent how much compression must somehow be accomplished in the cutting room. Invariably these problems are worse when rehearsals haven't been taped or timed.

Unsuccessful films often seem to be milking the longest possible film from available resources and story content. How long, though, should a film be? A good way to arrive at screen length in advance is to decide, on the basis of a bare story outline, what the shortest screen time you can imagine the story to be, and to budget time for each sequence accordingly. This calls for a professional economy in the writing. It also means that if you add anything to one sequence you must be ready to make savings in another. Lengthening your film beyond the original plan has consequences anyway on stock requirements and scheduling, so keeping an account of final screen time is vital.

At rehearsals someone—the assistant director if you have one—should time each scene with a stopwatch. If you are taping rehearsals, simply time the recording and mark the script accordingly. By adding scene timings together you get an up-to-date timing for the whole at any part of the process. This keeps you alert to consequences as scenes inevitably get longer. As each scene gathers "business," and as the characters increasingly adopt realistic thinking and authentic behavioral rhythms, individual scenes become shorter to watch but longer in real time. Be careful, for collectively they may not hold up. Your piece, a Prince Charming at the scripted thirty minutes, can easily turn out to be a forty-seven-minute toad.

As work proceeds, check new timings against earlier ones so you can *make necessary decisions affecting length prior to shooting*. While axing material is difficult or even traumatic with a tightly written piece, few scripts are really at their working minimum. So during rehearsal, be ready to review, edit, or tighten pacing as you go.

Can't it all be sorted out in the cutting room? Yes, they sometimes do miracles in the cutting room, but don't rely on them for more than minor savings, and certainly not unless you have provided sufficient coverage and cutaways. In fact, carry this written on the back of your hand as you shoot: "I will never end a scene without shooting full coverage, so help me God."

MAKING A TRIAL MOVIE

The best way to know whether a film holds up prior to the shoot is to assemble the best taped rehearsal versions and to watch the whole piece through. Seeing it in its entirety, especially if you bring in a small audience of filmmakers unconnected with the project, will give you an invaluable new perspective. True, the film will look awful, but even in this trial form it will alert you to redundancies, slownesses, expositional failures, restrictions or mannerisms in the performances, and afford definite guidance in pacing, coverage, and point of view. If the assembly is overlong (and it will be) you should run it several times until the textual cuts begin to call out to you. Since you are working on tape, they can even be tried.

All this is happening before you have begun shooting, and need not extend your schedule by more than a week. By this method you can painlessly make your film twice; the second version will profit immeasurably from the first.

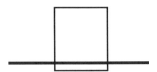

CHECKLIST, PART V
PREPRODUCTION

The points summarized here are only the most salient or those that are commonly overlooked. To find them or anything else, go to the table of contents at the beginning of this part, or try the Index at the back of the book.

Deciding On Subjects:
- choose your subject carefully; you are going to live with it for a long time
- through your film, be concerned for others
- choose a subject and issues you would love to learn more about

Questions When Assessing a Script:
- how behavioral and visually cinematic is it?
- how well would it play with the sound turned off?
- who did you care about and find interesting?
- is the plot credible, or can it be made so?
- what is the screenplay trying to do, and how is it going about it?
- in each scene decide what each character wants, moment to moment. What do they do to get it?
- what stops the character and how does he/she adapt to each obstacle?
- are the obstacles intelligently conceived to put the characters under test?
- are all characters integrated and multifunctional or are there convenience characters invented to solve particular situations?
- who grows and develops in the script and who remains only "typical?"
- from making a step outline, what do you learn?
- what is the screenplay's premise?
- what are the screenplay's thematic concerns and how effectively does it deal with the main one?
- what does making a flowchart for the film reveal, after you've named the function of each scene?
- what does a scene/character/location breakdown reveal?
- make a timing; does the film's story merit the time it takes onscreen?
- what problems emerge when you make an oral summary (a "pitch") to a listener?

SCRIPT EDITING

Plot and Character:
- relate storyline to basic dramatic situations and the "hero's journey" archetypes
- decide from parallel stories whether characters can be made more effective

Exposition:
- see if vital information comes early enough and whether any reinforcement is needed
- if it's spoken and too noticeable, hide it within action

Action:
- see how well the film would play if it were silent
- try reconfiguring dialogue scenes to play out as behavior instead of dialogue
- see what actions might better reveal each character's inner life and qualities

Dialogue:
- drop lines wherever possible
- convert discussion into behavior if possible
- tighten, compress, simplify remaining lines
- make sure it's in character's own vernacular

Scenes:
- mark beats and critically examine the working of each dramatic unit
- see if scene can create more interesting questions in audience's mind
- see if delay before these concerns are answered is too short or too long (often it's counterproductively short)
- eliminate scenes that repeat information or that fail to advance the story (get this information from your flowchart)

Dramaturgy and Visualization:
- decide whether convenience characters should be eliminated, amalgamated, or made properly functional
- from your flowchart assess how well the screenplay "breathes" between different kinds of scene, and consider transposing to improve variety
- from parallel works and archetypes, consider radical adjustments if these promise a better thematic impact
- check settings and events to see if these could be used more emblematically
- check for special imagery that is, or could, play a special part (visual leitmotifs, foreshadowing, symbolism, visual analogies, etc.)
- check that the screenplay's world is:
  - authentic
  - adequately introduced if it's unfamiliar
  - making full use of its connotations

CASTING

Organizing the Audition:
- write brief character descriptions; advertise appropriately
- actively search out likely participants for audition
- preinterview on phone before giving an audition slot
- thoroughly explain time and energy commitment
- ask actor to come with two contrasting monologues learned by heart

First Audition:
- receptionist chats with actors, has them fill out information form
- see actor's monologues and classify his or her self-image
- look for acting with whole body
- listen for power and associations of actor's voice
- ask "what kind of character would I get from this actor?"
- thank actors and give date by which decision will be communicated

Decisions Before Callback:
- call each actor and inform whether he or she is wanted for callback
- when rejecting, tell each actor something positive about his or her performance
- avoid casting people for their real-life negative traits
- carefully examine videotapes now and later for actor's characteristics relayed from the screen. Your impressions and intuitions here are everything

Callback:
- combine promising actors in different permutations
- have actors play parts in different ways to assess capacity for change
- test spontaneous creativity with improvisations based on the piece's issues
- redirect second version of improv to see how actors handle changes
- consider each actor's:
  - impact
  - rhythm and movements
  - patterns of development
  - imprint on part
  - quickness of mind
  - compatibility with other actors
  - ability for mimicry (accents, character specialties, etc.)
  - capacity for holding onto both new and old instructions
  - intelligence
  - temperament
  - type of mind
  - commitment to acting and to this particular project
  - concentration and attention span

- shoot camera test on principals
- consider confronting actors with your reservations before casting
- thank all for taking part and arrange date for notification

Developing the Crew:
- cast crew carefully, since they create the work environment
- shoot tests even with experienced members
- inquire into crew members' interests and values
- check reputation in previous collaborations
- assess flexibility, dependability, realism, commitment to project
- clearly delineate chain of responsibility
- begin with formal crew relationships

SCRIPT INTERPRETATION

- read all the points under "Script Editing" above
- determine the givens
- convert conversation into action that would relay the story without sound
- make sure screenplay establishes facts and necessary values for audience
- define point of view, subtexts, and characters' hidden pressures for each scene
- graph dramatic pressure changes for each scene, then string them together to graph out dramatic development for the film as a whole

REHEARSAL

- actors study the piece, make character biography, but do not yet learn lines
- director and actors break scene into dramatic units, with steps within each unit
- director encourages the search for action and movement at every stage
- meet principal actors singly to discuss his or her character
- expect actors to problem-solve
- keep notes during each run-through
- actors must play the scene not the lines

Focusing Thematic Purpose with the Players:
- discuss back-story and purpose of the piece with cast
- discuss subtext for key scenes and what it reveals about the characters
- develop a hierarchy of themes so you know what is most important

Rehearsal with the Book:

- tackle key scenes first
- thereafter point out what links these scenes
- deal only with top level of a scene's problems at each pass
- work on motivations
- develop possible actions
- find and characterize the beats
- develop special actions for the beat points
- within each dramatic unit, figure out the stages of escalation that lead to the beat
- rehearse in location or thoroughly brief actors on particularity of location
- now actors can learn their lines!

Rehearsal without the Book:

- dialogue should be a verbal action that seeks an effect
- film actors have no audience; they should be indistinguishable from real people coping with a real situation
- where an actor keeps losing focus, figure out the obstacle
- staying in character comes from staying appropriately busy in mind and body
- focus leads to relaxation
- watch your actors' bodies for signs of tension
- authentic physical action during performance liberates authentic emotion
- use improv to set level of focus to be matched in work from text
- give specific, positive goals for actors to reach toward
- characters' actions should generally seek an effect in other characters
- review the taped scene:
  - does it communicate effectively when viewed without sound?
  - is the cast using space effectively?
  - are characters fully using their physical surroundings?
  - can you see the characters' visions, memories, and imaginations at work?
  - does each character constantly pursue his or her own agenda?

Thinking Ahead About Coverage:

- set a timing limit for the scene and keep tabs on rehearsal timings
- prepare cast for blocking changes should exigency so require (it often does)
- cut dialogue or action to stay within timing goals
- note intentions for each scene while your memory is fresh

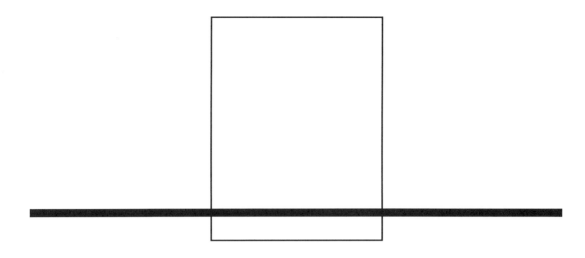

P·A·R·T VI

PRODUCTION

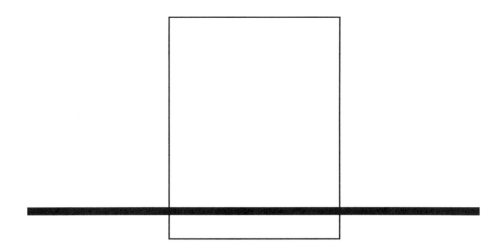

C·H·A·P·T·E·R 26

DEVELOPING A CREW

ON CREW AND ACTORS

Your crew will affect your actors so they should be "cast" for personal as well as technical capabilities.

USING PEOPLE WITH EXPERIENCE

I have titled this chapter "developing" rather than "choosing" a crew because even when experienced crew members are available you will still need to do some experimental shooting with them before the main shoot. Expect to continue developing standards and communication all through the production.

I have strongly advocated videotaping rehearsals using a documentary style of spontaneous coverage. There's another benefit apart from those already mentioned: it's an ideal way to find out ahead of time what developments or changes are required in key crew members. It may also tell you how equipment is functioning and how well you understand each other. A brief and unambiguous language of communication is always useful, but becomes mandatory if you are shooting material that takes advantage of transient location conditions, such as a brief crowd condition in a city or a sunset behind a flock of birds. At these times camera-position changes must be rapid and accurate. There is often little margin for misunderstanding between director and crew.

Even in highly controllable shooting circumstances, you will often discover that one operator's close-up is another's medium shot, depending on the work he or she has done before. Filmmaking is relativistic; framing, composition, speed of camera movements, and microphone positioning all come about through mutual values and adjustment, something that can only happen if crew members grasp each other's reflexes, terminology, and assumptions. From shooting rehearsals as well as test or exercise footage, you must expect to unearth wide variance of skill levels, differing interpretations of standard jargon, and incompatible assumptions about solving technical problems.

Such impediments confirm how important are formal, clearly understood lines of responsibility as well as a common language. These must be worked out ahead of the shooting, which brings enough problems of its own.

DEVELOPING YOUR OWN CREW

Let us take the most daunting situation—that you live in a place remote from centers of filmmaking, that you must start from scratch, work up your own standards, and find and train your own crew. We will assume you have access to a videotape rig comprising a camera, recorder, microphone, and monitor. How many and what kind of people will you need? What are their responsibilities?

First and foremost, everyone you recruit must appreciate your values and commitment to the importance of drama and to the project. Ideally they should share them. Naturally this is more important in a director of photography than it is in a grip or a cutting room assistant, but the small, low-budget enterprise needs to avoid all schisms of temperament and purpose, since so much of the groundbreaking work is sustained on belief and morale.

Before taking on crew members, examine not only their technical expertise and experience, but try also to assess their ideas and values. You might ask about favorite films, books, plays, hobbies, and interests. Technical acumen is important, but under stress a person's maturity and values become more so. Technical deficiencies can be remedied, but someone lacking positive responses to your choices of subject and treatment can quickly become a dead weight.

CREW MEMBERS' TEMPERAMENTS

A low-budget film crew is small, perhaps six to ten persons. A good crew is immensely supportive not only of the project, but also of the individuals in front of the camera, who may be acting for the first time. The crew's aura of commitment and optimism can easily be undermined by a single misfit with a bad attitude. Such people in important positions are like black holes, swallowing up energy, enthusiasm, and morale.

Crew problems vary; maybe a member needs some pressure to maintain focus on the job in hand. More seriously, at a location far from home or under pressure others may become unbalanced and regress into displaying bizarre hostilities. You may even find yourself dealing with someone actively subversive or emotionally out of control, as I have. This is not easy to foresee, but such people are an appalling liability in an activity so dependent on good relationships. Truffaut's *Day for Night* (1973) shows these all too human tendencies at work in the cast, but the problem can just as easily hit the crew. The crew united under benign but watchful leadership makes a huge contribution to morale, for their interest and implied approval is a vital supplement to that of the director. Conversely, any crew member's detachment or disapproval may be taken to heart by actors, whose work naturally makes them hypersensitive to reactions of any kind.

When recruiting, therefore, find out if a potential crew member has done film or other teamwork, and speak with people who worked with him or her. Filming is very intense, so former colleagues will know a person's strengths and weaknesses. If you are unable to verify a potential crew member's teamwork record, you may just have to rely on your intuition about how he or she bears up under stress.

In all crew positions, beware of people who:

- have only one working speed (it can be frenetic but it is usually medium slow). Faced with a need to accelerate, these insecure people usually either slow up in confusion or, go to pieces in a crisis
- forget or modify verbal commitments
- repeatedly fail to deliver what they promise on time
- habitually overestimate their own abilities
- show signs of a short attention span or who are easily distracted from their own field of responsibility
- act as though their work for you is a favor—they may also see you as a stepping stone to something better and step off in mid-production

I look for:

- a good sense of humor
- a nurturing temperament
- low-key realism
- reliability
- the ability to sustain effort and concentration for long periods
- people who will love the work we will do together
- people who know and like the kind of process that filmmaking is

ORGANIZE AREAS OF RESPONSIBILITY CLEARLY

No crew functions well unless roles and responsibilities are clearly defined and a chain of command is established, especially when it comes to dealing with contingencies. When the director is occupied with the cast, the director of photography leads the crew and makes necessary decisions. In most cases, crew members should take queries first to the director of photography and not to the director. The production manager, assistant director, and director of photography are there to take all possible burdens from the director, whose entire energies should go into the craft of directing, which includes a heavy responsibility to the cast. The director should not have to decide whether someone should put another coin in a parking meter.

When first working together, and for a long time after, *stick to a formal working structure* (see Figure 26-1). Everyone should take care of his or her own responsibilities, and refrain from action or comment in all other areas. As people come to know and trust each other, the formality can be relaxed by cautious and mutual consent.

In time, the members of a small film crew fall into roles. These may include such archetypes as prophet, diplomat, visionary, navigator, earth-mother, scribe, nurse, strong man, and fixer. Someone will always assume the role of jester or clown, for each crew develops its own special humor and in-jokes.

The feeling that comes from working effectively as a group is important: it can be the most exhilarating and energizing experience imaginable, and seems to be especially strong during times of crisis. Careful selection of the right partners makes anything in the world possible. A team of determined friends is unstoppable.

CREW ROLES AND RESPONSIBILITIES

Judging from a feature film's end credits, a unit has a bewildering number of roles and an army of people. Paradoxically the low-budget film may have more not less personnel in the titles. The answer is that many individuals have given only a day

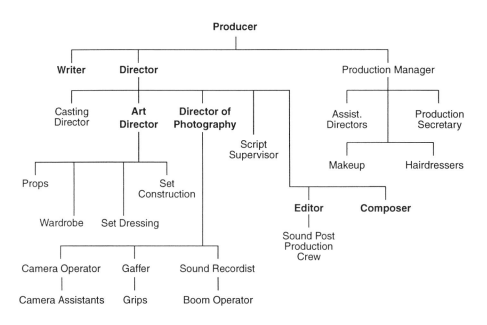

FIGURE 26-1

Lines of responsibility in a small-feature crew. Relationships may vary according to actual unit. Main creative positions are in bold.

or two of service. A "genealogical chart" of a small film unit, showing customary lines of responsibility, is included in Figure 26-1.

The role descriptions that follow are confined to the modest core likely to carry out the low-budget film or video shoot. I have assigned desirable personality types and backgrounds to the different crew positions, but, of course, in real life some of the best practitioners will be the exceptions. This list outlines each crew member's responsibilities and the strengths and weaknesses you can expect to find. To make it complete, I have included a summary of the director's role.

PRODUCER

Answerable to: Investors or studio heads.

Responsibilities: The producer assembles and administers the necessary funds, and oversees the project as a whole. Traditionally, the producer also has ultimate say in an artistic dispute between, say, a principal actor and the director. Since status is defined by a number of factors, relative influence may be unconventional and the producer must arbitrate such problems. Since the producer's role is primarily fiscal and logistical, the producer also heads the production department consisting of assistant producer, production manager, production secretary, and assistant directors.

Producers sometimes have assistants called *Associate Producers* or *Assistant Producers.*

Personality Traits: The ideal producer concentrates on being an enabler, supplier, and rationer of vital resources. To this end, planning, scheduling and accounting should be a producer's strengths, but if the producer is a person of taste he or she can also be a useful arbiter of the film's artistic progress. The ideal producer is a cultivated, intelligent, and sensitive business person whose goal in life is to nourish good work by unobtrusively supporting the artists and craftspeople hired to produce it.

And here is where it can all go wrong. Because they control money, producers have a great deal of power, and some, especially the inexperienced, assume that because artists and technicians are subordinates, their work and values are subordinate, too. Experienced filmmakers are wearily familiar with the crass philistine who has made money in insurance and now wants to express what he imagines to be his artistic side by producing a film. In the end, much energy is wasted in diplomatically trying to educate such a person into trusting the hired experts, but usually the film suffers as well as its makers.

Probably all producers want to control the artistic identity of the work, but the wise ones sublimate this impulse and retain respect for those whose artistry has taken many years to mature. Too many assume that the creative and organic process of filmmaking can be organized like a construction project.

Producers of some experience have a track record like anyone else, and you can find out from the grapevine what his or her reputation is. Never *ever* believe from the overtures that you will be treated better than your predecessors.

With producers of all different degrees of experience, look out for these danger signs:

- automatic distrust of everyone's motives
- a drive to personally control everything (micromanagement)
- inability to listen and learn from experts' explanations
- more interest in money and status and impatience with the film process

Filmmakers usually lack all flair for capitalism, and are only too aware of their dependency upon financial operators. It is in their interest to educate a producer, but this is sometimes frustrated by the unscrupulous financial operator's common compulsions:

- trying to play people off against each other
- the need to look aggressive and competent when he or she is not
- a willingness to trash anybody or anything that looks as if it can be bettered
- the desire to replace anyone who has seen the producer's ignorance show
- a willingness to take personal credit for other people's work whenever possible

These may all be part of the dirty tricks that won the producer ascendancy in the financial arena.

Anyone with access to money can call himself or herself a movie producer, for access to money is the prime qualification. In the last three decades I recall working for producers who were, variously, an insurance man, a real-estate developer, a gentlemanly hood, and a playboy draft-dodger. For one or two of them, hell already has room reservations. While the funds assembled by these people made production possible, their congenital distrust, crassness, and megalomania made the crews' lives into a tragi-comic rollercoaster ride. Using threats, sudden dismissal, and humiliation, such people survive only because filmmakers depend on financing to survive.

I also worked under producers who were principled, educated, restrained, and a source of support and discriminating encouragement to everyone. These men and women were the professionals—true leaders with a long history of deserving survivorship.

DIRECTOR

Answerable to: The producer.

Responsibilities: The director is responsible for nothing less than the quality and meaning of the final film. This means:

- writing or working with writers
- envisioning the film's scope, purpose, identity, and meaning
- researching locations

- auditioning actors
- assembling a cast and crew (though this may be done by the producer)
- developing both cast and script through rehearsals
- supervising makeup of the shooting schedule
- directing actors and crew during shooting
- supervising editing and finalization of the project

If there are no profits in view, the film may have no separate producer, so the director must additionally assemble funding before the making of the film and hustle distribution afterwards.

Personality Traits: A good director is:

- a person broadly educated in the arts
- possessed of a lively, inquiring mind
- someone who likes delving into people's lives looking for hypothetical links and explanations
- highly methodical and organized even when outwardly informal and easygoing
- able to throw away prior work if assumptions have become obsolete
- possessed of endless patience when searching out good ideas and good performances
- articulate and succinct
- able to make instinctive judgments and decisions
- able to get the best out of people without being dictatorial
- knowledgeable enough about each person's craft
- able to speak on terms of respectful equality with any practitioner
- able to understand technicians' problems and co-opt their efforts

If this sounds too idealistic, here are some of the negative traits that make even good directors decidedly human. Many

- are obstinate, private, even awkward beings who work in idiosyncratic ways
- find difficulty in giving appropriate time and attention to both crew and actors
- tend to desert actors for crew, and vice versa
- sink into a condition of acute doubt and anxiety during shooting
- suffer from sensory overload and find choice a painful effort

During production most show signs of acute insecurity (depression, manic energy, low flashpoint, panic, irresolution). If that is not enough to puzzle crew members, the director's mental state often generates superhuman energy and endurance that test crew members' patience to the limit.

The truth is that directing a reflection of life is a heady business. The person responsible for making this happen is living existentially; that is, fully and completely in the moment as if it were the last. The pressures of directing a movie usually make all this happen whether you like it or not. Especially is this true after an initial success: thereafter you face failure and artistic/professional death every step of the way. Like stage fright, the dread and exhilaration of the chase may never go away. But surely the portent of any worthwhile experience is that it makes you more than a little afraid.

CAMERA CREW GENERALITIES

Personality Traits: The camera crew members should:

- be image-conscious
- preferably have a background in photography and fine art
- have a sense of composition and design
- an eye for the telling details found in people's surroundings
- be decisive
- practical
- methodical
- dexterous

Depending on the weight of the equipment, they may also need to be robust. Handholding a twenty-pound camera for most of an eight-hour day is not for the delicate, nor is loading equipment boxes in and out of transportation. The job is dirty, grueling, and at times intoxicatingly wonderful. The best camera people seem to be calm individuals who do not ruffle easily in crises. They are knowledgeable and resourceful and take pride in improvising solutions to intransigent technical and logistical problems. What you hope to find is the perfectionist who still aims for the best and simplest solution when time is short.

Rather alarmingly, quite a number of experienced camera personnel isolate themselves in the mechanics of their craft at the expense of the director's deeper quest for themes and meanings. While it can be disastrous to have a crew of would-be directors, it can be nearly as frustrating to find you have a crew of isolated operatives. The best crew members comprehend both the details and the totality of a project and can see how to make the best contribution to it. This is why a narrow technical education is not good enough for anyone in a film crew.

DIRECTOR OF PHOTOGRAPHY

Answerable to: The director.

Responsibilities: Also known as lighting cameraperson, the director of photography (DP) is responsible for the look of the film and is the most important crew member after the director. That is, he or she collaborates closely with the director and takes all decisions about camera, lighting, and equipment that contribute to the camerawork. The DP is also

- the leader of the whole crew's work while the director concentrates on the actors
- responsible for specifying the lighting and camera equipment, lenses, film-stock, or their video equivalents
- responsible for testing and adjusting that equipment and for being thoroughly conversant with its working principles
- the person who reconnoiters each location in advance with the gaffer to assess electrical supplies and lighting design when the crew is small
- the person who decides and supervises the placement of lighting instruments
- the supervisor of the camera operator, and may indeed be the operator

No important work should ever be done without running tests as early as possible in order to forestall Murphy's Law, which is inexorable in filmmaking.

CAMERA OPERATOR

Answerable to: The director of photography.

Responsibilities: The operator is responsible for the handling of the camera, which means he or she takes an active role in deciding camera positioning (in collaboration with the director), and physically controls the camera movements such as panning, tilting, zooming in and out, and dollying.

It is also an advantage if your operator is alert to the many behavioral nuances that reveal character. In improvisation work as in documentary, the camera work is often "grab-shooting" so the operator must decide moment to moment what to shoot in a busy scene.

While the director sees content happening three-dimensionally in front of (or sometimes behind) the camera, the operator sees the action in its framed, cinematic form. The director may redirect the camera to a different area, but unless there is a video assist only the operator knows exactly what the action will look like on the screen. The director must be able to rely on the operator's discrimination, and this is also true for very controlled framing and composition, since movement within the frame often requires immediate and spontaneous reframing.

CAMERA ASSISTANTS

Answerable to: The camera operator.

Responsibilities: On a feature film there may be more than one assistant cinematographer (AC). Division of labor makes one a clapper operator and magazine loader, and another whose job it is to manually follow focus when the distance changes between subject and camera.

ACs keep the camera optics and film gate clean and manhandle the camera equipment from place to place. Their main requirements are to be highly organized, reliable, and zealous at maintaining the camera in prime condition, whether it is film or videotape. Because their responsibilities are almost wholly technical, it is more important they be good and diligent technicians. On a small unit, one camera assistant often does all the ancillary work, though this can lead to costly holdups.

GAFFER AND GRIPS

Answerable to: The director of photography.

Responsibilities: The job of the gaffer is to rig lighting and to know how to go about doing anything that needs to be fixed, mounted, moved, pushed, lifted, or lowered. The gaffer must have a good grasp of mechanical and electrical principles in order to improvise solutions for which there is no available piece of equipment. A good gaffer also understands not only the lighting instruments but the principles and practice of lighting itself, because he or she must be able to quickly grasp the intentions behind the DP's lighting instructions.

The job of the grip is to fetch and carry, and to rig lighting according to the gaffer's instructions. He or she also has the highly skilled and coordinated job of moving the camera support (dolly, crane, truck, etc.) from mark to mark as the camera takes mobile shots. Grips should be strong, practical, organized, and willing. On the minimal crew they may double up to help with sound equipment, camera assisting, turning on and off the videotape deck, and may leave the crew to fetch or deliver while shooting is in progress. A skilled grip knows something about everyone's job and is capable of standing in for some technicians in an emergency.

Personality Traits: Gaffers and grips need patience, since their work involves moving and maintaining large varieties of equipment, of which there never seems enough for the job at hand. While they work, production waits; while production is in progress, it is they who wait. When everyone else is finished, they go to work tearing down their masses of equipment and stow it, haul it away, then set it up again for the next day's shoot. All this must be good for the soul, for they are often highly resourceful and very funny. *Gaffer* is old English for grandfather, singularly appropriate for one who must know every imaginable way to skin the proverbial cat.

SOUND RECORDIST AND BOOM OPERATOR

Answerable to: The director of photography.

Responsibilities: In the inexperienced crew the unfailing casualty is sound quality. Capturing clear, clean, and consistent sound is either deceptively skilled, or sound recording does not have the glamour to induce people to try. Another obstacle is that even quite expensive videorecorders have a propensity for picking up every known electrical interference, allied to a sound quality that would embarrass the humblest sound cassette recorders. Hi8 and digital video with their pulse code modulation track of CD quality is a great improvement, but many older machines will survive to bring tears of rage to the low-budget filmmaker. DAT recorders make double system, multitrack sound shooting for video a highly practical alternative.

It is the sound recordist's responsibility to check sound and videotape equipment in advance, and to solve malfunction problems as they arise. The boom operator's job is to place the mike as close to sound sources as possible, without getting the mike in shot or creating shadows. In a complicated dialogue scene this means moving the mike around to catch each new speaker.

Personality Traits: The sound crew person needs to have patience, a good ear, and the maturity to be low man on the totem pole. In an interior setup, lighting and camera position are determined first, and the sound recordist is expected to somehow position the mikes without them being seen or causing shadows, and without losing sound quality. A shoot therefore turns into a series of aggravating compromises that the recordist is all too inclined to take personally. An alarming number of professionals turn into frustrated mutterers who feel that standards are routinely trampled. But it is the disconnected craftsman more than the whole filmmaker who fails to see the necessity and priority of compromise. Sound can be reconstituted in the sound studio later, but camerawork and actors' performances once shot are immutable.

The recordist is often kept inactive for long periods and then suddenly expected to "fix up the mike" in short order, so it helps to have someone who habitually thinks ahead. The unsatisfactory recordist is the one whose mind only begins to work when his setup time comes, and who then asks for a lighting change.

The sound recordist listens not to words but to sound quality, so it is essential to have someone who listens analytically, and actually hears the buzz, rumble, or edginess that the novice will unconsciously screen out. The art of recording has very little to do with recorders, and everything to do with the selection and placement of mikes, and being able to hear the difference. There is no independent assessment possible apart from the discerning ear. Only musical interests and, better still, a musical training seem to instill this critical discipline.

Sound recording is often brushed aside as easy and unglamorous among the uninitiated, and left uncritically to anyone who says he or she can do it. But poor sound disconnects the audience even more fatally than a poor story. Too many student films sound like studies of characters talking through blankets in a bathroom.

Handheld shooting is done with a Steadicam and a mobile sound unit. Without benefit of a conclusive rehearsal, the sound crew must keep the mike on the edge of the camera's field of view and close to the sound source without casting shadows or letting the mike creep into frame. With a camera on the move, this takes both skill and agile, quiet footwork. Nobody can wear construction boots or creaky leather jackets when shooting sound.

There are usually several solutions to any one sound problem, so a knowledge of available equipment and an interest in up-to-date techniques is a great advantage.

PRODUCTION MANAGER

Answerable to: The producer.

Responsibilities: The production manager (PM) might be considered a hard-to-find luxury on a minimal crew, but there are many people whose business background equips them to do this vital job surpassingly well.

    The PM is the producer's delegate and closely concerned with preproduction and production. He or she is a business manager based in an office who takes care of all the arrangements for the shoot. These might include being the contact person for the outside world, finding overnight accommodations, booking rented equipment to the specifications of camera and sound people, making up (with the director) a shooting schedule, negotiating travel arrangements, and locating restaurants near the shoot. The PM will watch cash flow and incubate contingency plans in case bad weather stymies exterior shooting. He or she will hustle to prepare the way ahead. All this lightens the load on the director for whom such things are a distraction from controlling the performances and visualizing the film as it evolves.

Personality Traits: The good PM is:

- organized
- trained in good business practices
- a compulsive list-keeper
- socially adept and diplomatic
- able to scan and correlate a number of activities
- able to juggle priorities
- makes decisions involving time, effort, and money
- the kind of person who is not intimidated by officialdom

    Good PM's make good producers.

ASSISTANT DIRECTOR

Answerable to: The production manager.

Responsibilities: On a feature shoot there may be a first, second, and third AD. ADs seldom become directors since their skills are not artistic but organizational and lean toward production management. Their job is to do all the leg work and take care of all the logistical needs of the production. ADs do

- scheduling
- arranging
- contacting

- reminding
- acquiring information
- calling artists
- herding crowds
- the director's barking

Sometimes in a director's absence an AD will rehearse actors, but only if he or she has a strong grasp of the director's intentions. The experienced AD may direct the second unit, but this more often falls to the editor.

Personality Traits: The main requirements for an assistant director are to be organized, have a good business mind, a voice that can wake the dead, and a nature that is both firm and diplomatic.

SCRIPT SUPERVISOR

Answerable to: The director.

Responsibilities: The script supervisor (also called *continuity supervisor*) must understand how the film will be edited together, and during shooting must continuously monitor what words, actions, props, and costumes are in use from shot to shot. Shooting on videotape makes checking a relatively simple (though time-consuming) matter, but with film no such record is visible until the rushes have been processed. An eagle-eyed observer who keeps a record of every significant variable is therefore the only safeguard that one shot will match another. If a video assist is used with a film camera, it is a simple matter to back up the script supervisor's notes by rolling a consumer VCR to keep a running record.

The script supervisor also assists the director by ensuring there is adequate coverage of each scene, and when time or resources must be saved, is able to define what can be omitted or shortened.

Personality Traits: The script supervisor

- needs to understand editing
- must know the script inside out
- must have fierce powers of concentration
- produces continuity reports that are extensively used on a feature film by the cutting rooms
- must be a fast and accurate typist

On films unable to afford a script supervisor, I have seen the editor do the job. The motivation is certainly there.

ART DIRECTOR

Answerable to: The director.

Responsibilities: To design everything in the film's environment so that it effectively interprets the script. This means overseeing props and costumes, as well as managing the interior design of sets and locations. If the film is a period production, the art director will research the epoch and its social customs to ensure that costumes and decor are accurate and make an impact. On a low-budget movie the art director will do his or her own set dressing, while on a larger production there is a special person, the set dresser, to take care of this responsibility.

Personality Traits: A good art director should

- have a fine arts background
- be able to sketch or paint fluently
- have a lively eye for fashion and social distinctions
- have a strong interest in the historical background of these phenomena
- have a strong grasp of the emotional potential of different color and color combinations
- be able to translate the script into a series of settings with costumes, all of which heighten and intensify the underlying intentions of the script

WARDROBE AND PROPS

Answerable to: The art director.

Responsibilities: Wardrobe and props' jobs are to locate, store, and maintain costumes and properties (objects such as ashtrays, baby toys, or grand pianos that dress the set), keep master lists, and produce the right thing in good order at the right time. When no wardrobe person is available, each actor becomes responsible for his own costumes. The AD should doublecheck beforehand what clothes each actor must bring for the next scene, so today's costume is not still sitting in the actor's laundry basket.

Personality Traits: Wardrobe and props people are highly resourceful and develop large numbers of contacts among antique, resale, theatrical, and junk shop owners. They must be practical, since things borrowed or rented must often be carefully operated and maintained. Costumes, especially ones that are elaborate or antique, take great expertise to keep clean and functional and may need temporary alterations to fit a particular actor. Props and wardrobe departments must be completely organized: each scene has its special requirements and the right props and costumes must appear on time and in the right place or shooting turns into a nightmare.

MAKEUP AND HAIRDRESSING

Answerable to: The production manager.

Responsibilities: The people in makeup and hairdressing produce the appropriate physical appearance in face and hair, often with careful attention to period details. A hidden part of the job is catering to actors' insecurities by helping them believe in the way they look. Where the character demands negative traits, the makeup artist may have to work against an actor's resistance. Makeup is particularly tricky; directors should shoot tests to make sure the makeup looks credible and is compatible with color stock and any special lighting.

Personality Traits: Diplomacy and endurance. My father was a makeup man and got to work before anyone else, preparing artists hours ahead of shooting when elaborate beards and whiskers were required. Apart from the usual kind of character or glamour preparation, his work included the bizarre, such as putting a black patch over the eye of Fagin's dog in David Lean's *Oliver Twist* (1948), applying the gold paint on the naked girl in *Goldfinger* (1964), and inventing ghoulish effects for Hammer horror films like flesh melting from a face to leave eyeballs staring out of bony eye sockets. Needless to say, it helps to be inventive and have a relish for the unusual, but he also spoke of the miseries of trying to make up foul-tempered alcoholics in the early morning. After the dawn rush, makeup and hairdressing must often sit idle, keeping a weather eye for when their handiwork needs repair.

EDITOR

A complete description of the editor's role and responsibilities is to be found in Chapter 32, Preparing to Edit.

C·H·A·P·T·E·R 27

MISE-EN-SCÈNE BASICS

The French expression *mise-en-scène* (literally, putting in the scene) is a usefully holistic term for those aspects of directing that take place during shooting. It includes blocking (movements of the actors, camera placement and movement) lens choice, and composition. Planning *mise-en-scène* for a scene means conceiving the scene's dramatic functions, relaying whose consciousness the audience should identify with, and doing all this in practical not simply intellectual terms. While the DP takes responsibility for everything concerning camera and lighting, the director must know what options exist and how to discuss them with the DP, undoubtedly the most important collaborator during the shoot. This is also a time when you can fall completely under the spell of your DP if he or she is strong-minded. And that would be another invitation to abdicate the director's role.

THE STORYTELLER'S POINT OF VIEW

Here David Mamet's protest should be remembered, that too much fiction film-making consists of *following* the action. Are you documenting happenings, or are you a Storyteller? The first is like passive surveillance, the second has an active identity that raises questions and implies a human heart and mind at work. What identity have you given your Storyteller, and what have you discovered as you watched the singularity of these unique characters and their situation grow?

These are not easy questions to answer, but *they will not answer themselves, and they will not be answered in the cutting room.* We can find help by using the connotations of the word "attitude." If the mind and intelligence and heart through which your audience sees your story has "attitude," how would you describe it? What will it be like? How will it show? Because that quest and that slant—which may be made up of any kind of relationship toward the story and its characters—must color the way the movie gets across. Somehow you have to signify your Storyteller's puzzlement, doubts, enjoyment, censure, opprobrium, delight, distrust, regret, fascination—whatever changing thoughts go into the Storyteller's "attitude."

By now you will have picked up ideas and perspectives towards the events in your script because the cast has made them "real." This is what you build on. Through moving around while the characters live out the pieces of their lives, you have begun to watch and identify according to a pattern. The pattern of watching is partly based on the intentions behind the writing, but much more importantly, it arises from the chemistry of personalities and situation. You must remain sensitive to this. Is how you notice, what you notice, and what you feel being reflected in the tape coverage? If not, why not?

By stopping to examine your impressions you can go further toward understanding their sources and their impact. *We can use our mind to examine our heart, and come away more strongly convinced of who we are and what we have seen.* A friend used to say, "Nothing is real until I have written about it." Make a point of writing the Storyteller's part as the invisible Observer, and develop further the symbiotic nature of the tale and the teller. They go together; one depends on the other. To create the Storyteller you have to bring the telling alive as well as the tale, that is, you must give it the integrity of a quirky human mind that sees, weighs, wonders, feels, and supposes as the story unfolds. Do that successfully and your work will acquire the magical quality of humor and intelligence that characterizes work having a soul. Not too many films have soul. But it is a quality that people seek and respond to universally. The process of filmmaking tends to overlook soul in the struggle for narrative efficiency and clarity, and to end up with a heartless, faceless record. The humanity, where there is humanity, is in the cast, and less in the way the film reaches us.

There is no formula for making a film with a soul. There is only the integrity of a way of seeing. Like everything else in fiction, this can be distilled, heightened, played with to the greater good. But it takes a director with a clear, strong identity—one that isn't overwhelmed by the people or the technology. You have your work cut out, don't you!

SCREENPLAY TO SHOOTING SCRIPT

Planning how to shoot each scene means first of all amplifying upon the screenplay, which thus far contains no camera directions. You can specify nothing that would be impractical for financial or logistical reasons, so the shooting script will be a plan to make the most of known resources, both human and material. If you have been taping rehearsals, these will be familiar and the question is not what to film, but how to film it. This stage comes after considerable rehearsal, location reconnaissance, conferring with the director of photography, checking whether financial resources allow special lighting or camera equipment, and so on.

The screenplay must now be turned into a shooting script. Scenes previously headed by titles alone (to avoid confusion from draft to draft) must now receive scene numbers. Necessary camera directions and transitions need planning. From rehearsals you should have a firm sense of the camera coverage required, but final codification with your DP will be dealt with later in this chapter. While simple poverty may make it difficult to impose an elaborately professional look upon a scene (dollying or craning shots, freeze frames, special titling, and optical work), this is slick packaging and its absence should never debilitate a worthwhile film. The responsibility for the graphic aspects of filmmaking lies variously with the director, cinematographer, and art director. Steven Katz's *Film Directing Shot by Shot* (Michael Wiese Productions in association with Focal Press, 1991) does the best imaginable job for a book at explaining the options for staging different kinds of scene. In its 366 pages of useful storyboards and diagrams it demonstrates how much graphic skill it takes to plan on paper two-dimensional coverage of a three-dimensional world. Many of the book's techniques depend on dollies, cranes, and take-apart sets common in Hollywood but beyond most low budget filmmakers' experience.

Be warned that even if you can afford this equipment, operating it adequately and making the lighting changes its use may demand will massively slow a production's progress, especially if its operators are learning on the job. This is very wearing on the cast. So keep in mind that decades of classic cinema were shot with limited equipment. You can function well by keeping to the simplest techniques that serve the film's artistic intentions. Resist your crew's desire to experiment with "better" equipment. The over-elaborate staging that you accede to (only because you don't want to disappoint your DP) may fail, and may sink a scene that would have worked perfectly well had it been kept simple. Always err on the side of simplicity.

With your DP decide what coverage is desirable for a scene, and then in consultation with your script supervisor, make pencil lines in a script copy to bracket portions of the scene. Each represents a camera angle and each has a brief identifying description, as in Figure 27-1. Now you can see at a glance what editing alternatives exist. To make editing possible, remember there must be a generous overlap of action from shot to shot. For editing to look smooth and seamless, *the best place to cut is always on a strong physical movement.* You will understand this best from analyzing well-made feature film scenes like the one you are planning, from the practical experiment of earlier work, and from what shows up in your direct cinema coverage of the rehearsals.

SCRIPT, CONCEPT, AND SCENE DESIGN

The design for a scene, while it must compromise with the limitations of cinematography, really proceeds from your gut impression of the scene as it exists, and also, of course, from its underlying function in the script. How, for instance, would you show a man who is being watched by the police get into his car and try to start it?

You might ask yourself these basic questions about the scene:

- what is the scene's function in the script?
- how much does the audience need to know about the scene's geographical layout at the outset of the scene? Later?

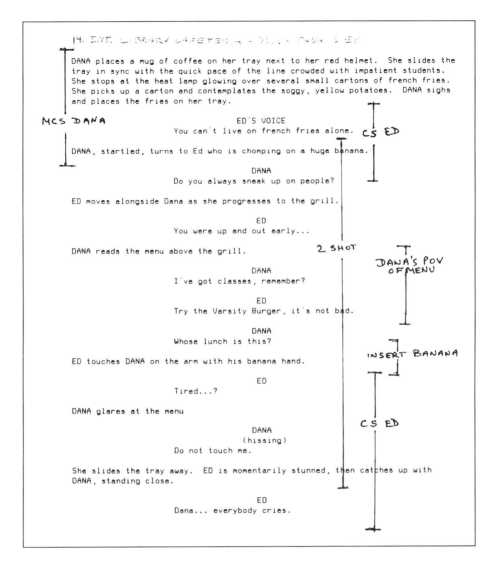

FIGURE 27-1

Script page marked up for shooting.

- what relationships need to be shown in terms of physical space?
- what elements can be compositionally juxtaposed to advantage?
- what are each character's expectations in the scene?
- how much does each character know about his predicament?
- what is the relationship between the watchers and the watched?
- is there anything the audience, but not the characters, should learn?

- what is special about the character that the actor has created and which you should try to reflect?
- what is the Storyteller's attitude to this scene compared with others?

Salient questions will vary with the scene depending on its contents, complexity, and what it contributes to the film as a whole. Defining what the Storyteller notices and feels helps you decide the means by which you reveal, and will help make everything much less arbitrary. Here you've got to develop instincts, and listen to them.

WHOSE POINT OF VIEW

Point of view is for many people a baffling notion. It is not literally "what so-and-so sees," though this may comprise one or two shots. Rather it attempts to relay to the audience how a character or characters in the film is experiencing particular events. We might, for instance, experience the trial of Joan of Arc from Joan's angle, or see the story from the perspective of a compassionate judge who wants her to admit she has invented her visions so he can let her go. For a heightened effect we might participate in a number of perspectives; then we'd feel with Joan how the inquisitors, the faithful, the crowd, and God, must be judging her.

Top priority will always be to ask, whose point of view is this scene to favor? A great many of your decisions about composition, camera placement, and editing flow from this. Returning to our man being watched by police, are we to see him getting into his car from the attitude of the policeman, or from a more omniscient (that is, Storyteller's) point of view in which we (but not the man) notice the cop? This will probably be decided on plot grounds but the characters themselves should influence your coverage, just as characters in real life influence who you choose to watch in any given situation.

Now imagine a more complex scene in which a child witnesses a sustained argument between his divorced parents. How should point of view be handled? We must first determine what the argument represents. Is it "child realizing he is a pawn," or is it "parents make bitter accusations, not caring that their child can hear?" Are we mainly interested in what the child sees or how the dispute acts upon him? Does new information come from the parents or are we focusing on the child's presence and reactions?

Questions like these determine whose scene it really is; the boy's, the father's, or the mother's. The scene can be shot and edited to polarize our sympathetic interest in any of these directions at any given moment in the scene. Remember that making no choice, no decision, leads to faceless, expressionless filmmaking, technical filmmaking with no heart or identity. There always remains the more detached way of observing the events, that of the omniscient storyteller. This point of view is useful to relieve pressure on the audience before renewing it again. Sustained and unvarying pressure would be self-defeating because the audience either adapts or tunes out. Notice how Shakespeare, in his tragedies, uses scenes of comic relief.

POINT OF VIEW CAN CHANGE

Imagine now, a scene in a clinic starting on a young and unhappy-looking doctor telling a patient that he has incurable cancer. As the patient begins to understand his predicament, we abandon the patient's point of view of the doctor and begin to watch the patient, keeping the doctor only as a voice, while we dwell on the sick man hearing his death sentence. The expression "point of view" really means the way our sympathy and curiosity migrates between patient and doctor, even though the film may finally be about the patient. Paradoxically, to understand and feel for the doctor, we need to share those moments when he empathizes with our central character, vacating his own protected reality to enter that of the man facing death. A character who never temporarily relinquishes his identity in this way would be someone alienated or inhuman. Even were that true (let us say we are making a biographical film about a Nazi despot), we might still move the point of view to the Nazi's victim, simply to allow the audience a vehicle for its pent-up feelings, and to force a comparison between the feeling and the unfeeling persons.

Guidance to deciding point of view comes from asking what makes dramatic sense to our friend, the Concerned Observer. Answers come from your instincts and from within the logic of the entire script. There may be no overriding determinant, in which case it is the editor who decides later, based on the nuances of the acting, *and if you've shot enough alternative coverage.* The corollary is, when in doubt, shoot enough to give the editor pov alternatives.

Sometimes a film will make us experience a situation from an intentionally detached (though no less interesting) perspective, such as in Tanner's *Jonah Who Will Be Twenty-Five in the Year 2000* (1976). This is the story of twelve individuals (six couples, actually) who are survivors from the turbulent 1960s. Each is trying to live out earlier ideals even though the social revolution for which he or she fought has failed. Tanner quite deliberately avoids aligning us with any couple or any individual, so we shall see them not as rebel individualists but rather as a tapestry of intentions.

A subjective point of view tends to use closeups and tends to be shot with the camera close to the axis or "line of psychic tension" between characters. An objective point of view tends to be a wider shot and further from that line (Figure 27-2). These generalizations are no more than a rule of thumb; point of view is something subtle that impinges on the audience through a unique combination of action, characters, lighting, mood, events, and context.

COMPOSITIONAL OPTIONS

SHOW RELATEDNESS

Returning to the boy and divorced parents scene: how are the protagonists to be spatially related? Showing the couple arguing in the same frame but the boy separated in a closeup reinforces his separation from both of them. Relating boy and mother in one frame to father alone in another suggests a different configuration of alliances or antipathies. There could be other factors—using foreground and background, the sides of the frame, different camera heights and different levels of

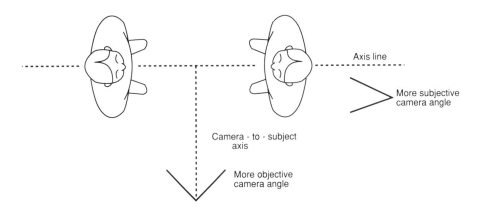

FIGURE 27-2

Camera-to-subject axis can be close or at right angles to the scene axis; this controls how subjective or objective the angle feels to the audience.

lighting—any combination of which might predispose the audience toward interpreting the scene in a particular way or from a particular point of view. It would be misleading and simplistic to suggest there are any rules here, since human judgment is made upon a multiplicity of nuances. What matters is the sensibility and rationale by which each shot is composed, lit, and blocked.

THERE ARE NO RULES, ONLY SENSITIVITY

Because in film everything on the screen is interactive and relativistic to the viewer, there can be few formulae: compositionally you are always showing the specifics of relationship between one object and another, one person and another, and implying the relationship of one idea, principle, or judgment to another. To do this you may also use editing or story construction (parallel storytelling, for instance, where you intercut a boxing match with a lover's feud). Whatever works, works through suggestion and implied comparison. It is more important to do, to try, to judge from what you see and feel, than rely overmuch on theory.

CAMERA PLACEMENT

USING LINES OF TENSION

Here are some reminders concerning the camera's relationship to what I call a scene's lines of tension. These invisible connections are the lines you would draw between the most important people and objects in a scene. Often they are also sightlines. They have great dramatic potential (changes of eyeline, for instance) and they often dominate the composition. Lines of tension and sightlines legitimize particular camera angles but also imply the emotional connections (and therefore points of view) associated with particular characters. This is not an easy concept to describe, and you will understand better if you have done the close editing analysis suggested earlier in the book.

SUBJECTIVE AND OBJECTIVE

No matter whose point of view your film favors, point of view itself will move. Changes in lines of tension or changes in their intensity are your prime clues. Let's look at the way the consciousness of an onlooker moves around, when observing the archetypal scene of two people in conversation.

The concept of there being a Concerned Observer is important. The observation itself is the normal, relatively objective movement of human perception, and we use it as a model for how the camera and editing moves our attention around within a scene. Quite simply, *camera work and editing together mimic the way any observer's ears, eyes, and psychological focus migrate within an environment* whether quiet or busy.

The changes of angle and shot are motivated by stimuli and also by pursuing lines of logical inquiry about the events. These come from the ideas and emotions released by the unfolding events. When perception is noticeably marked by the predispositions of the observer, the observer becomes the fully fledged Storyteller. Either way, whether the observation is that of a character within the film or of a biased, interestingly quirky Storyteller directing our attention, it tends to vary in intensity. The observation may start relatively detached, but in getting engaged with the predicaments and personal qualities of the characters, begins to manifest a more involved, identifying intensity that leads the Observer to become subjective. A film, like you or I in any commanding life-situation, will "breathe" between these two extremes. The difference can be dramatized by returning to the analogy of the tennis game.

You are watching two tennis players. The ball flies along the line of tension or axis between them. You can observe from the umpire's position near the net and see the game from a detached, objective position at ninety degrees to the axis, or one can walk in an arc around one corner of the court until you are looking over one player's shoulder. Here you become subjectively involved with the game, since you are now aligned with the predicament of one of the players by virtually standing in his or her shoes. This is also an angle where you make no choice; you are always seeing both players, though one from behind.

This principle, where the observer moves from being at right angles to the scene's axis to being almost on the axis itself, looking down the "firing line," applies to all situations of verbal, physical, or psychological interaction. It may be complicated by there being more than two protagonists, but coverage is always predicated upon the lines of tension that can be drawn. These lines are usually between major characters, but someone waiting anxiously might be connected by an invisible line of tension to an object like a clock, a phone, or a finger on the trigger of a gun.

The closer the camera is to a line of tension, the more subjectively involved the audience will feel. When complementary angles are used, the audience is switched rapidly between each protagonist's subjective experience, so the aggregate effect may be to enter the fray without necessarily identifying with one contestant over the other. This depends on the balance of editing as well as, less measurably, the power in each actor's characterization.

Not only do we have the Observer's relationship to the axes, but we also have differing degrees of closeness to the subject. Another way to see this is to consider close shots not as magnification alone, but as deliberate *exclusion* of other information. Juxtaposing subjects in antithetical relationship can be accomplished either by somewhat noticeable editing together multiple shots or, less obviously, by juxtapositional composition in a single shot.

SIGHTLINES AND LINES OF TENSION

Look at the floor plan for the argument between the mother and father who are being observed by the child (Figure 27-3A). The various psychic connections or possible lines of tension are in fact duplicated by the dotted-in sightlines. The major axis is between the parents, but others exist between each parent and the silent child. Each sightline suggests a camera position. What each camera angle covers is shown in the storyboard sequence (Figure 27-3B). Some angles are close (as in 4,

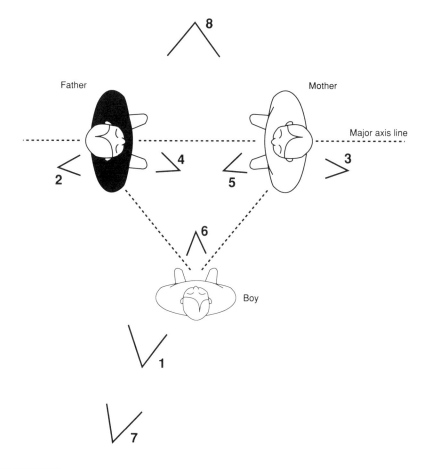

FIGURE 27-3A ————————————————————————————

Camera positions to cover a child's view of an argument between his parents. Lines of tension are indicated between characters.

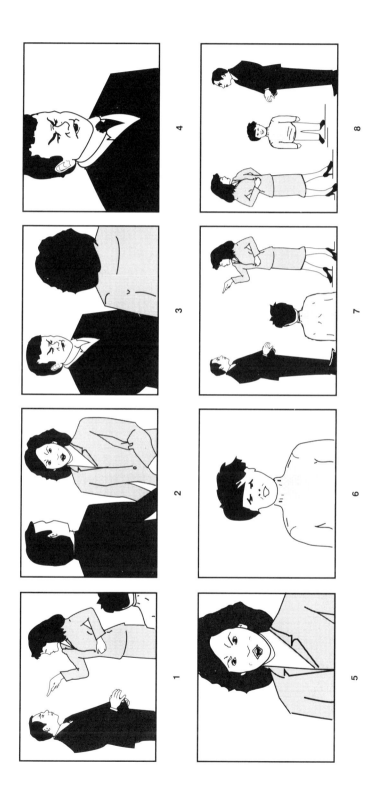

FIGURE 27-3B

Storyboard frames for camera positions 1 through 8. Note that in position 8 the two figures have reversed screen direction because the camera has crossed the major axis line.

5, and 6), some in medium two-shot (1, 2, and 3), and there are two master shots, further angles that take in everything (7 and 8). Positions 1, 2, and 3 are all to some degree omniscient because they are an outsider's view of the characters; that is, in pairs and related to each other. Position 7 is even more comprehensive, taking in all three. Positions 4, 5, and 6 are, however, close and subjectively involved, as if viewed by one of the other characters. Position 6 would be useful to show the child's eyeline shifts.

DO NOT CROSS THE AXIS!

Because the child remains in a fixed position, camera coverage that replicates his vision of his parents must stay on one side of the A to B axis line. The camera must not cross the axis if screen direction is to be maintained. If you cross this axis with your camera, as in position 8, your characters begin to look in the wrong screen direction, as you see in the storyboard sequence. In positions 1 through 7, the father always looks screen left to screen right, and the mother right to left. Even in the big closeups (4 and 5) the eyelines still show the characters maintaining the same screen direction. However, in camera position 8 that consistency disappears because the camera has strayed across the major axis line.

MOVEMENTS THAT LEAD TO REGROUPING MUST BE SHOWN

In a scene where characters sometimes move around, they regroup to face in new screen directions during the scene. This probably means that early and late reaction shots cannot be interchanged, and the scene cannot easily be restructured in the cutting room if so desired. *Movements that lead to regrouping must be shown onscreen.* They are the "reset" transitions that precede new compositional phases of the scene. Movements should also have dramatic significance, so you will want to show them anyway. Plan carefully so the scene will cut together effortlessly on the screen.

MOVEMENT IS THE BEST EDITING POINT

Plan to *use any pronounced movement in the scene as the cutting point between angles.* This is called an action match cut. The best guide is that you *initiate a little of the movement in the outgoing scene, and complete the bulk of it in the incoming shot.* Remember when editing that faster movements need three or four frames of repeated action on the incoming shot since the eye does not register the first three or four frames of any new image.

LONG TAKE VERSUS SHORT TAKE COVERAGE

To "cover" a scene means shooting enough variation of angle and subject so you can show it to advantage on the screen. Depending on the nature of the film this can mean long, intricately choreographed takes lasting for an entire scene as used by Hitchcock in *Rope* (1948) or it might call for a flow of rapidly-edited images as favored by such disparate filmmakers as Eisenstein in *The Battleship Potemkin* (1925) and Nicholas Roeg in *Don't Look Now* (1973).

The Long Take Method

The long take method generally requires a mobile camera and intricate blocking of both camera and actors to avoid a flat, stagey appearance. It requires virtuoso control by actors and technicians since even minor errors may consign an entire scene to take after take. There is also a risk which shows up later in the cutting room; because no control of individual scene elements is possible, the editor cannot rebalance the rhythm of the performances if they need it.

The Short Take Method

The short take method is inherently more likely to make the material look manipulated because it requires frequent cuts. At the kind of extreme favored by MTV the viewer is barraged with fragments from which to infer the whole. The filmmaker edits shots together because they create juxtaposition and tension, but for the audience, any cut always takes energy to interpret. Because a lot of cutting takes a lot of spectator energy, many directors try to reduce unnecessary calls on the audience's attention by choreographing their *mise-en-scène* as complex individual shots rather than rely on blowhard editing. Following the example of the wise virgins and the foolish virgins, they also shoot safety coverage in case longish takes turn out to be flawed. Be advised.

EDITING AS REFRESHMENT

Cutting between different angles is also a way to renew and refresh the spectator's perspective, showing different points of view, and invoking different kinds of experiencing. If the angles stayed close to the axis we should remain subjectively involved and eventually become desensitized. So for variation we cut to a more objective angle, causing the Storyteller to take us out of the firing line and to see more from a detached perspective. In a political meeting scene this might suggest a stepping away from the intensely personal to take a historical or sociological perspective. This, too, is a refreshment, a juxtaposition of impressions that interrupts what has become standard in order to push us into interpreting from another intellectual or emotional angle.

QUESTIONS TO ASK YOURSELF

Whichever combination of aspects you choose to show, in the scene, try to consider these factors:

GEOGRAPHY:

- What must the scene show to establish the environment satisfactorily?
- Does this orientation come early, or is it delayed for dramatic reasons?
- What combination of distance and lens will you need for the widest angle?
- Will you have enough lighting to shoot the most comprehensive shot?

MOVEMENTS BY CHARACTERS:

• At which points and why do characters move from one point to another?

• How will you show it? (Drop back to a wide angle? Move the camera with a character? Show another character's eyeline changing and hearing the moving character's footsteps?)

• What axis does the character move along at each stage of his movements?

POINT OF VIEW:

• At each significant moment, whose point of view are we sharing locally?

• Whose global point of view predominates in the overall story?

• When and why does point of view change?

• Is a particular change subjective or objective in direction?

• What emotion, thought, or preoccupation might the point of view convey?

EYELINES:

• What are the significant eyelines in the scene? (These motivate what the audience wants to see, and therefore motivate camera placement from shot to shot.)

• Where do eyelines change?

• Where should the camera look along an eyeline?

CAMERA MOVEMENT:

• When and why should the camera move?

• What feeling does its movement create? (In Robert Enrico's *Occurrence at Owl Creek Bridge* [1962] the tendency of the camera to slide sideways creates a sense of stalking, peering unease. A camera movement can suggest a retreat, a glance, a searching gaze, a running forward—a myriad of subjective sensations.)

• At what speed should the movement be? (Movements must be paced appropriately if they are to integrate with other aural or visual rhythms in a scene. Be careful of strobing when panning over repetitive patterns such as railings. See camerawork manual for further information.)

COMPOSITIONAL RELATIONSHIP:

• At what significant moments will it be necessary to show relationship? (One might frame a sleeping character supposed to be catching a plane with a clock in the background—more effective than laboriously intercutting the clock. Or one might play a whole mother-daughter argument in tight single shots to emphasize the adversarial, disconnected feel of their relationship.)

ISOLATION:

- What or who might legitimately be isolated from surroundings? (A misfit boy might frequently be shown alone, while the gang who try to recruit him always appear as a pack. A phone silently refusing to ring for someone waiting on tenterhooks for a call might also be shown as a single shot. In each case this isolation complements a dominant perception, either of someone within the film, or that of the Storyteller.)

SPACE:

- What is the significance of space between characters? (The changing distance between two characters having a conversation is highly indicative of who is gaining control, who is retreating or hiding. Camera position and the choice of lens can alter the audience's perception of space. For instance, a crowded street is often shot with a telescopic lens in order to compress cars and people into a bobbing sea, while someone reaching imploringly through prison bars might be shot with a wide-angle lens so his hand comes across a void and becomes enormous in the foreground.)

CRIB SHEETS

When directing your first films, work hard to brief yourself and make copious, organized reminder lists so you forget nothing in the hurly-burly of the set. As fatigue, the director's nemesis, sets in, your memory and imagination will shut down, and those notes (see Figure 27-4) will be a lifesaver.

When you define the story points you want to make, and have nailed down what you need from each sequence, you are directing from a plan of campaign instead of waiting to recognize success when it appears.

COVER IMPORTANT ASPECTS MORE THAN ONE WAY

Vital story points or important emotional transitions should be covered in more than one way, if you are later to have a choice and exercise maximum control over the telling moment. For instance, in a scene about a family reunion where the last of a set of wedding glasses gets broken by the mother, your major point may be to show her moment of realization and grief. The incident can, however, be given additional piquancy by shooting reactions on the part of others present. Her son may show anger at her clumsiness, her daughter may be surprised, her husband may be amused because he thinks it is just a minor accident, and her daughter-in-law may be concerned that she may have cut herself.

Covering these reactions allows for a variable richness in defining the moment. It also follows our often-mentioned principle of abundance, in which *one habitually generates more than strictly necessary to allow options and therefore control later.*

```
              Scene 15: TONY RETURNS HOME AFTER 5 YEARS' SILENCE.

Metaphor: Return of the prodigal son

Timing:   2 mins 25 secs

     Tony wants to:  avoid showing the love he feels for his father
                     evade specifics of the past
                     signify apology but evade admissions
                     make his father think he's returned out of duty
                     make contact with his childhood again
                     move his father to affection and thus forgiveness
                     retrieve mother's photo
                     convince Dad he's not a failure
                     ask for forgiveness

     Dad wants to:   keep Tony at an emotional distance
                     deny to himself that he's very moved by the boy's return
                     get him to think he's washed his hands of him
                     let him know the whole family disapproves of him
                     not act in the authoritarian way that alienated the boy
                     not let him know his bedroom has been kept unchanged
                     deny that he used the boy to get at his mother
                     signify that he loves him
                     ask for forgiveness

   Scene must convey that:  Tony has grown in confidence through travel
                            Dad has been ill and sees his own mortality
                            House is still as Mother left it
```

FIGURE 27-4 ————————————————————————————————

Example of director's crib notes.

CONTINGENCY PLANNING

Plan your coverage but ensure against surprises. Foresee weather changes, scheduling difficulties, and though you intend to show only one character onscreen during an intense exchange, shoot both. This allows you abundance—a fallback alternative if your plans are not fulfilled. This caution is not artistic compromise; only a fool takes a two-day water supply to cross a two-day desert.

THE FLOOR PLAN AND THE STORYBOARD

Draw a floor plan. It will help you consolidate your intentions for blocking and indicate how to use the fewest and most effective camera angles. On it show the characters' movements and the camera angles necessary for the edited version you want. Figure 27-5 is a floor plan for the scene you saw marked up in Figure 27-1. This diagram, growing out of the blocking developed during rehearsals and modified by location realities, helps further work out the editing in advance, and enables the director of photography to plan lighting and camera movements.

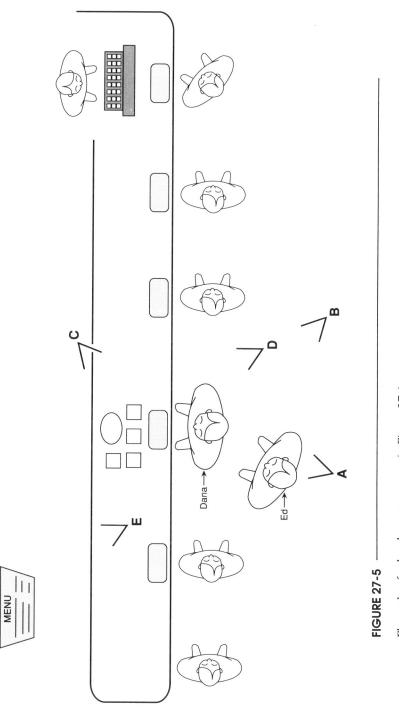

FIGURE 27-5

Floor plan for lunch counter scene in Figure 27-1.

On a tightly planned production the art director may make storyboard sketches for each angle as in Figure 27-3B. These help ensure that the contents of each composition are as interesting and relevant as possible. The suggestions each expert contributes may be so good that the director revises the original conception. As always in a true collaboration, the whole can always be greater than the sum of its parts.

Whatever the original intentions, the storyboard plan often goes out the window when you shoot. The particularities of a lens' field of view, problems with lighting, the needs of a character's movements, and even the size of the framing can all lead you to compose picture and block actors quite differently from the storyboard.

When storyboards are a fetish, it often foretells an overemphasis on physical design and an inability to deal with human and logistical variables during shooting. This bodes ill for the spontaneity necessary to naturalistic drama, and some of the history behind rigorous formal control is far from reassuring. The director most famous for compositional brilliance is Eisenstein, whose films were highly formalized and not at all concerned with spontaneity or even realism. As a Marxist visionary, he conveys powerfully the feel of inevitable historical process in a class-divided society, and the equally inevitable action and counteraction among its players. His films propose that individuals are part of a larger design, and elevate this into a historical analysis by using the rhetoric of a striking but highly theatrical visual design. Ironically, such techniques are equally serviceable in the service of the opposite camp. Leni Riefenstahl's *Triumph of the Will* (1936) seductively promotes Adolf Hitler as the benevolent god of the German people. Seductive form can be a kind of sophistry that substitutes for humanistic or truthfully intellectual content, as ten thousand TV commercials attest.

SPACE, PERCEPTION, AND BLOCKING

CAMERA EYE AND HUMAN EYE ARE DIFFERENT

The eye of the beholder during rehearsals is grossly misleading, for the human eye takes in a field of almost 180 degrees (see Figure 27-6). Although a 16mm camera lens of 10mm focal length is called a wide angle, it still only takes in fifty-four degrees horizontally and forty degrees vertically. This means that a reasonably comprehensive wide angle lens (before gross fairground distortion sets in) only has one quarter of the eye's angle of acceptance. This translates to a very restricted field of view indeed and one with resounding consequences for dramatic composition.

We compensate for such limitation by rearranging compositions so they trick the spectator into the sensation of normal distances and spatial relationships. Characters holding a conversation may have to stand unnaturally close before the camera, but look normal onscreen; furniture and distances between objects are often "cheated," either apart or together, to produce the desired appearance onscreen; and ordinary physical movements like walking past camera or picking up a glass of milk in closeup may require slowing by a third or more. Note however that comedy dialogue (though not necessarily movement) often needs faster than

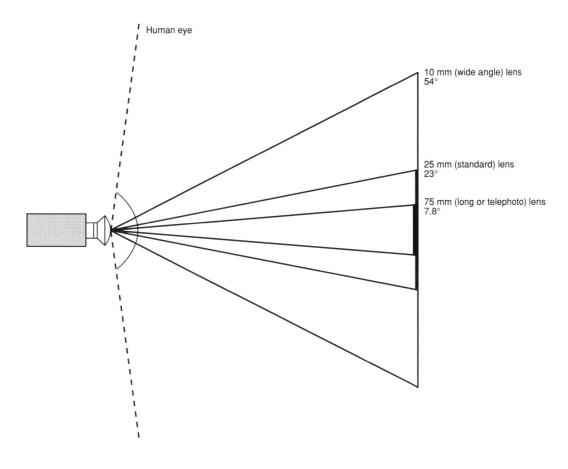

Human eye

10 mm (wide angle) lens
54°

25 mm (standard) lens
23°

75 mm (long or telephoto) lens
7.8°

FIGURE 27-6 ——

Human eye's field of vision compared with much more limited angle of acceptance for 16mm camera lenses. Note that vertical angles of acceptance (not shown) are twenty-five percent smaller still.

normal playing if it is to avoid looking slow onscreen. As always, screen testing helps you make all such decisions.

Packing the frame, achieving the illusion of depth, and arranging for balance and thematic significance in each setup's composition can all compensate for the screen's limited size and its tendency to flatten everything.

CHOOSING LENS SIZE

This is an area people sometimes find forbidding, but one doesn't need a physics degree to use lenses intelligently. Analogies from everyday life help one understand and memorize the principles involved. First, there is the normal sense of perspective as perceived by the human eye, and then there are departures on either side of normality. One such departure is represented by the telescope, which gives an almost miraculous sense of closeness but is hard to keep focused and steady. The

FIGURE 27-7 ————————————————————————————————————

Space and distance must be deliberately created on the screen. Still from Zsolt Kezdi Kovacs' *Forbidden Relations* (courtesy Spectrafilm).

telescope's image is somehow luminous and isolated in space compared with that of the eye. One sees the other extreme in the door security spyglass, which allows the cautious householder to see whether a visitor on the other side is friend or foe. The spyglass "sees" a lot of the hallway outside, but produces a reduced and distorted image. If your visitor is leaning with one hand on the door, you are likely to see a huge arm diminishing to a tiny, distorted figure in the distance. These familiar optical devices allow us to pursue the range of dramatic possibilities in the camera lens.

PERSPECTIVE

NORMAL LENSES

Depending on the camera format in use, the lens that gives a normal sense of perspective will vary as follows:

Format	*Focal length for normal lens*
8 mm	12.5 mm
16 mm	25 mm
35 mm	50 mm

You can see there is a constant ratio between the format (width of film in use) and the lens' focal length. The examples following discuss only 16mm format lenses, which are common to 16mm and most video cameras.

NORMAL PERSPECTIVE

Normal perspective (Figure 27-8) means the viewer sees an "as is" size relationship between foreground and background trucks and can accurately judge the distance between them. The same shot taken with a wide-angle lens (Figure 27-9) changes the apparent distance between foreground and background, stretching it out. A telephoto lens (Figure 27-10) does just the opposite, squeezing foreground and background close together. If someone were to walk from the background truck up to the foreground, the dramatic implications of their walk would be very different in the three shots; all have the same subject but a different formal treatment through the choice of lens.

FIGURE 27-8 ───────

Normal lens.

FIGURE 27-9 ───────

Wide-angle lens.

FIGURE 27-10 ──────────

Telephoto lens. Foreground
and background distances
appear quite different in
Figures 27-8 and 27-9.

PERSPECTIVE CHANGES ONLY WHEN CAMERA-TO-SUBJECT DISTANCE CHANGES

By repositioning the camera and using different lenses for Figures 27-8, 27-9, and 27-10, we are able to produce the same size foreground truck, as shown diagrammically in Figure 27-11. What all this means is that *changes of perspective result not from the lenses themselves, but from changes in the camera's physical distance from the subject* and its background. Now, examine Figures 27-12, 27-13, and 27-14. Each is taken with a different lens but from the same camera position. The size relationship of the stop sign to the portico background is the same in all three. Here, perspective has not changed, although we apparently have three different angles. Perspective is the product of camera-to-subject distance, for when this remains constant, so do the proportions between foreground and background—the means by which our eye assesses perspective.

MANIPULATING PERSPECTIVE

Using the magnifying or diminishing capacity of different lenses simply allows us to place the camera differently, so we can produce three similar shots (Figures 27-8, 27-9, and 27-10); and because camera-to-subject distance changes, perspective is different. Wide-angle lenses appear to magnify distance, while telephoto lenses appear to squash different distances into the same plane.

ZOOMING VERSUS DOLLYING IN FOR CLOSEUP

A zoom is a lens capable of infinite variation between its extremes (say 10 to 100mm, which is a zoom with a ratio of 10:1). If you keep the camera static and zoom in on a subject, the image is magnified but perspective does not alter. With a prime (fixed) lens and dollying in close, the image is magnified *and* you see a perspective change during the move, just as in life. One is movement, the other magnification.

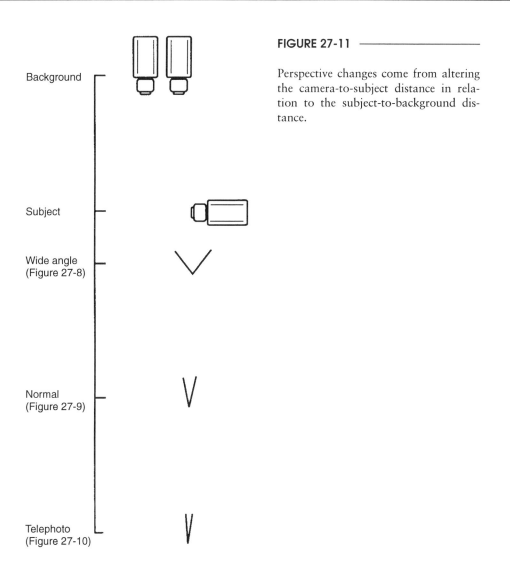

Background

Subject

Wide angle
(Figure 27-8)

Normal
(Figure 27-9)

Telephoto
(Figure 27-10)

FIGURE 27-11

Perspective changes come from altering the camera-to-subject distance in relation to the subject-to-background distance.

LENS CHOICE AFFECTS IMAGE TEXTURE

Examine Figures 27-12 and 27-14. The backgrounds are very different in texture. Although the subject is in focus in both, the telephoto version puts the rest of the image in soft focus, isolating and separating the subject from its foreground and background. This is because the telephoto lens has a very narrow depth of field and only the point of focus is sharp. Conversely, a wide-angle lens (Figures 27-9 and 27-12) allows a very deep focus. This can be useful, or it can produce a picture that drowns its subject in a plethora of irrelevantly sharp background and foreground detail. The telephoto has a "soft" textured background, the wide angle is "hard." Lens characteristics can be limiting or have great dramatic utility, depending on what you know and how you use it.

FIGURE 27-12 ————

Wide-angle lens.

FIGURE 27-13 ————

Normal lens.

FIGURE 27-14 ————

Telephoto lens. Figures 27-12, 27-13, and 27-14 are taken from a single camera position. Notice that the stop sign remains in the same proportion to its background throughout.

LENS CHOICE AFFECTS LENS SPEED

Lens speed is a deceptive term that describes nothing to do with movement, but instead how much light a lens needs for minimal operation. A "fast" lens is one in which the iris opens up wide so the lens is good for low-light photography. A "slow" lens is simply one that fails to admit as much light. By their inherent design, wide-angles tend to be fast (say, f1.4) while telephotos tend to be slow (perhaps f2.8). A two-stop difference like this means that the wide-angle is operative at one quarter of the light it takes to use the telephoto. This might end up making the difference between night shooting being practical or out of the question. Prime (that is, fixed) lenses have few elements so they tend to be faster than zooms, which are multielement. They also tend to have better acuity, or sharpness, because the image passes through less optics. Note that zooms have one lens speed over the whole range.

CAMERA HEIGHT

The old film manual adage says that a high camera position suggests domination and a low angle, subjugation. There are a host of other reasons to vary camera height—as many as there are relationships between compositional elements. The relationship may accommodate objects or persons in either the background or foreground, or accommodate a camera movement. This is covered below in the subsection "Relatedness: Separating or Integrating by Shot." If you carried out Chapter 5, Project 1: "Picture Composition Analysis" and took as your subject a film as cinematically inventive as Orson Welles' classic *Citizen Kane* (1941), you will have seen many occasions when the departure from an eye level camera position simply feels right. Often there is a dramatic rationale behind the choice, but don't turn them into a filmmaking ten commandments.

The veteran Hollywood director, Edward Dmytryk, in his book *On Screen Directing,* makes a persuasive case for avoiding shots at characters' eye level simply because they are dull. There may be another reason to avoid them. At eye level the audience probably feels itself intruding upon the action, just as we should feel both threatened and intrusive by standing in the path of a duel. Being above or below eye level positions us safely out of the firing line. This is something to remember whenever your camera approaches the axis.

LIMIT CAMERA MOVEMENTS

Apart from zooming, panning, and tilting, most camera movements spell trouble unless you have an expensive dolly and tracks, and a highly experienced team to operate them. Understandably, student camera crews like to hire advanced camera support systems because it gives them practice and makes them feel professional. The price of this education may be a production repeatedly paralyzed, while someone attempts to perfect a complex move that has little beyond egocentric virtuosity to offer the story.

HAVE THE COURAGE TO BE SIMPLE

The best justification for camera movement is often to limit the inherent fragmentation of cutting. Other camera movements are necessary to preserve composition and framing when characters are on the move, or to reveal something or someone formerly out of frame. The very best lessons in camera positioning and movement lie waiting in the best films in your chosen genre. Study them. You'll be surprised how good simple films look when they rely on a good story and good acting, rather than swishy camerawork.

MOTIVATION FOR CAMERA POSITIONING AND CAMERA MOVEMENT

ADAPTING TO LOCATION EXIGENCIES

It's hard to recommend rules for camera positioning and movement, since every situation has its own nature to be revealed and its own unique limitations. The latter are usually physical; windows or pillars in an interior that restrict shooting in one direction, or an incongruity to be avoided in an exterior. A wonderful Victorian house turns out to have a background of power lines strung across the sky, and has to be framed low when you wanted to frame high. Even when meticulously planned, filmmaking is always a serendipitous activity and often one's vision must be jettisoned and energy redirected to deal with the unforeseen.

For the rigid, linear personality, this constant adaptation may be unacceptably frustrating, but for others it represents a challenge to their inventiveness and insight. Nonetheless, you must plan, and sometimes things go according to intention.

WORK WITHIN YOUR MEANS

Any departure from the simple in cuts and camera movements should be motivated by the needs of the story if the audience is to feel it is sharing someone's consciousness. Good examples of subjectively motivated technique are Oliver's shock-cut view of the convict in the graveyard scene in *Oliver Twist* (1948) and dollying through the noise and confusion of a newsroom in *All the President's Men* (1976).

Such visual devices are dramatically justified, but for the low-budget filmmaker dollying, craning, and other big-budget visual treatments are not strictly necessary since few impressions cannot be achieved some other way. Whole films have been successfully made with a static camera always at eye level, or without cuts within a scene. Look at the opposite extreme: heavily scored music, rapid editing, and frenetic camera movement. These are mostly used as nervous stimulation to cover for a lack of content. Just roll around the channels on your TV, especially if you can get MTV.

Complex camera movement is sometimes absolutely justified. In a film about dance, like Emil Ardolino's *Dirty Dancing* (1987), Jeff Jur's camera cannot remain static on the sidelines. There are times when it must enter the lovers' dance and accompany them. Can this ever be done inexpensively? Using a wide-angle lens, an experienced camera operator, and a moving subject in the foreground to hold the eye, handheld camera work can often dispense with truckloads of shiny hardware and save mountains of cash. The Steadicam, a counterweighted body brace, can also in experienced hands produce wonderfully fluid camerawork at modest expense. See Wenders' *Faraway, So Close* (1993) for superb examples.

THE CAMERA AS OBSERVING CONSCIOUSNESS

Treat the camera as a questing observer and imagine how you want the audience to experience the scene. If you had a scene in a turbulent flea market, it would not make sense to limit the camera to carefully placed tripod shots. Make the camera adopt the point of view of a wandering buyer by going handheld and peering into circles of chattering people, looking closely at the merchandise, and then swinging around when someone calls out.

If, instead, you are to shoot a scene during a church service, with its elaborate ritualized stages, the placing and amount of coverage by the camera will be important, and it should be rock steady. Ask yourself whose point of view the audience is mostly sharing. Where does the majority of the telling action lie? With the newcomer? The priest? The choir or the congregation?

FIXED VERSUS MOBILE CAMERA

A camera on a tripod is able to zoom in and hold a steady close shot without physically crowding the actor. On the other hand, it cannot physically move to a new or better vantage point. The handheld camera gives this mobility, but at the price of a certain unsteadiness. A Steadicam in the right hands can solve this. But in the hands of someone inexperienced, you can lose half a day. Intelligent handholding may be the only solution if you are shooting a semi-improvised performance. The camera on a dolly or a crane can move through a predetermined cycle of movements, but these require great precision from both crew and cast, all of whom must hit predetermined chalk marks on the floor. Here the casualty may be spontaneity in the cast. A dolly and its crew are also apt to make some noise, so you may pay with more sound postproduction work and extra takes where floor creaks obscure dialogue.

SUBJECTIVE OR OBJECTIVE CAMERA PRESENCE

The two kinds of camera presence, the one studied, composed, and controlled, and the other mobile, spontaneous, reactive, and adaptive to change, will each give a different sense of observing presence. Each implies a relatively subjective or objective observation of the action. Camera-handling alone may thus alter the "voice" of the film, making it either more or less personal and vulnerable. Maintaining either mode becomes unremarkable, while shifting justifiably between them can be very potent.

RELATEDNESS: SEPARATING OR INTEGRATING BY SHOT

Composition and framing alters a scene's implications drastically. Isolating two people in close shots and intercutting them has a very different feel than intercutting two over-shoulder shots where the two are always spatially related. Their relationship in space and time looks much less manipulated by the filming process in the over-shoulder shots. In the single shots, the observer is always alone with one of the contenders and inferring the unseen participant. In cinema this isolation is the exception, for normally the limitations of the frame size make us use it to the utmost to show the relationship between everything and everybody.

BACKGROUNDS

Another camera positioning issue is deciding what part background must play in relation to foreground. If a character is depressed and hungry, there is a nice irony in showing that her bus stop is outside a McDonald's and that she is being watched by a huge Ronald McDonald. The composition will unobtrusively highlight her dilemma and suggest the temptation to blow her bus money on a large french fries. Sometimes the subject is in the middleground (a prisoner, bars in foreground, cell-mate in background at back of cell, for instance). Foreground compositional elements are an important part of creating depth.

CAMERA AS INSTRUMENT OF REVELATION

Looking down upon the subject, looking up at the subject, or looking at it between the trunks of trees in a wood can all suggest different contexts and different ways of seeing—and therefore of experiencing—the action that is the subject of the scene. The camera should seldom be a passive recorder, but should be used as an active instrument of revelation. While one can manufacture this sense of revelation through Eisensteinian dialectics and juxtaposition, this may be an intrusive way to get your point across. More subtle and convincing is to build this multileveled consciousness into the shooting itself. Exploiting the location as a meaningful environment and being responsive to the actions and sightlines of participants in a scene can create a vivid and spontaneous sense of the scene's dynamics unfolding. This is sharing the consciousness of someone intelligent and intuitive who picks up all the underlying tensions rather than sharing that of someone who merely swivels after whatever moves or makes a noise, as dogs do.

STUDY THE MASTERS

To know how best to shoot any particular scene, study the way good directors have shot analogous situations. In Chapter 5, Project 2: Editing Analysis, there is a film study project to help you define a director's specific choices and intentions.

COMPROMISES FOR THE CAMERA

When shooting action sequences, you may need to ask people to slow their movements down, since movement within a frame can look twenty percent to thirty percent faster than it does in life. Even the best camera operator cannot keep a profile in tight framing if the actor moves too fast or in focus if the actor strays from the chalk line on the floor. Such compromises on behalf of technology raise interesting questions about how much one should forgo in the way of performance spontaneity to achieve a visually and choreographically polished result. It will all depend on the expertise of your actors and your crew, but even the time of day you shoot may affect where you compromise, since tired actors are more likely to feel they are being treated like glovepuppets than fresh ones. Politics and expediency do not end here, for the crew can be disappointed or even resentful if you always forgo interesting technical challenges on behalf of the cast.

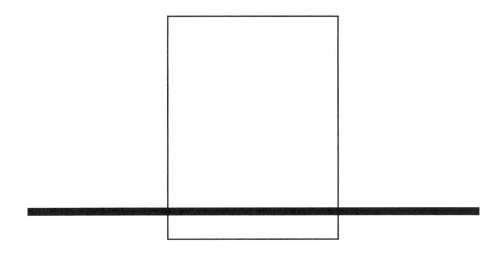

C·H·A·P·T·E·R 28

GETTING READY
TO SHOOT

EQUIPMENT SELECTION: DRAWING UP A WANT LIST

In a book like this it is impractical to be very specific over what equipment is desirable. To prepare for shooting, sit down as a group and brainstorm over what you really need. Make lists and do not forget to include basic repair and maintenance tools. Some piece of equipment is bound to need corrective surgery on location.

How the film looks, how it is shot, and how it conveys its content to the audience are decisions that affect your equipment needs, but these decisions are about the form of the film and need to be made organically from the nature of the film's subject. Plan to shoot as simply as possible, choosing straightforward means over elaborate ones. The best solutions to most problems are elegantly simple.

Overordering and overelaboration are always a temptation, especially for the insecure technician trying to forestall problems by insisting on the "proper" equipment, which is usually the most complicated and expensive. Since initially you will be trying to conquer basic conceptual and control difficulties, you may have little use for the sophistication of advanced equipment, and cannot afford the time it takes to work out how to best use it.

Learn as much as possible about the special technical requirements of the shoot so you, your DP, and your PM can decide what outlay is truly justified. Some extra items turn out to be lifesavers; others just cost money and never get used. Keep in mind it's human ingenuity and not just equipment that makes good films.

If your crew is at all inexperienced, make sure they study all equipment manuals beforehand; these contain vital and often overlooked information. Make sure you have equipment manuals with you on location. At the end of this book there is a bibliography to find more detailed information on techniques and equipment.

Do not be discouraged if your equipment is not the best. After all, the first chapters of film history which were so rich in creative advances were shot using hand cranked cameras made of wood and brass.

SCHEDULING THE SHOOT

A director needs to be familiar with details of the organization and scheduling that makes filming possible. Scheduling is normally decided by the director and the PM, and double-checked by principal crew members, in particular the DP. Much of the time you will have to make educated guesses since no film is ever quite like any other and there are few constants. Since time inevitably means money, your schedule must reflect your resources as well as your needs. Take into account any or all of the following:

- costs involved at each stage if hiring talent, equipment, crew, or facilities (see budget form in Figure 28-1)
- scenes involving key dramatic elements which may be affected or delayed by weather or other cyclical conditions
- availability of actors and crew
- availability of locations
- relationship of locations and travel exigencies
- availability of special or rented equipment, including props
- complexity of each lighting setup, and power requirements
- time of day to get available light coming from right direction

LOCATION ORDER

Normal practice is to shoot in order of convenience for locations and to take into account cast and crew availability. During a shoot, lighting setup or changes take the most time, so a compact schedule conserves on lighting changes and avoids re-lighting the same set. For all these reasons and more, it is unusual to shoot in script order. Lighting usually requires that one shoot wide shots, which may take all the lighting you've got, and close shots later, since close shots must match their wide-shot counterparts.

The character and location breakdown (Figure 17-4) described in Chapter 17 shows which scenes must be shot at each location. It is usual that scenes from the beginning, middle, and end of the film may all be shot in the same location. This makes rehearsal all the more important if actors are to move authoritatively be-

```
                    S H O R T   B U D G E T   F O R M
_____

                         Production Details

Working Title:............................................. Length: .....mins

Personnel:
       Director: ..............................Tel:..........(h)...........(w)
          Address ..............................
                  ..............................
       Dir. of Photog. ........................       ...........   ...........
       Sound:.................................       ...........   ...........
       Prod. Mgr:..............................       ...........   ...........

Format (circle all that apply):
       Video: Beta/VHS/³/₄"/1"
       Film:  b&w/color  negative/reversal  8mm/16mm/35mm

Project is at stage of (circle one):  Pre-Production/Production/Post-Production

Schedule at present is:
       Pre-Production from................to....................
       Production        ...............  ....................
       Post-Production   ...............  ....................

Brief Description of subject:




Thematic focus of film is:




_____
_____
```

FIGURE 28-1

Short budget estimate form. Note high and low estimate figures. A contingency percentage is always added to the budget total to cover the unforeseeable.

```
                        Pre-Production Costs


                                                              Low     High
Travel                                                        $...    $...
Phone                                                         ...     ...
Rehearsal                                                     ...     ...
Hospitality                                                   ...     ...
Other (_____ )           ...     ...


                                              Total           ...     ...
_____
                         Production Costs
Crew

Director     for .../....days at $...... per day              ...     ...
Camera        "   .../...  "   "   ......  "   "              ...     ...
Sound         "   .../...  "   "   ......  "   "              ...     ...
Gaffer        "   .../...  "   "   ......  "   "              ...     ...
Grip          "   .../...  "   "   ......  "   "              ...     ...
Prod. Mgr     "   .../...  "   "   ......  "   "              ...     ...


Equipment

Camera (film/Video)..... for   .../... days at $...... per day  ...   ...
Magazines (film).........   "   .../...  "   "   ......  "   "   ...   ...
Changing bag (film)......   "   .../...  "   "   ......  "   "   ...   ...
Clapper board (film).....   "   .../...  "   "   ......  "   "   ...   ...
Nagra recorder (film)....   "   .../...  "   "   ......  "   "   ...   ...
Video recorder..........   "   .../...  "   "   ......  "   "   ...   ...
Lenses..................   "   .../...  "   "   ......  "   "   ...   ...
Filter kit..............   "   .../...  "   "   ......  "   "   ...   ...
Exposure meter..........   "   .../...  "   "   ......  "   "   ...   ...
Color temperature meter..   "   .../...  "   "   ......  "   "   ...   ...
Camera supports: tripod..   "   .../...  "   "   ......  "   "   ...   ...
                baby legs   "   .../...  "   "   ......  "   "   ...   ...
                hi-hat..   "   .../...  "   "   ......  "   "   ...   ...
Tilt head...............   "   .../...  "   "   ......  "   "   ...   ...
Spreader................   "   .../...  "   "   ......  "   "   ...   ...
Dolly & Tracks..........   "   .../...  "   "   ......  "   "   ...   ...
Video monitor...........   "   .../...  "   "   ......  "   "   ...   ...
Headphones..............   "   .../...  "   "   ......  "   "   ...   ...
Mike boom...............   "   .../...  "   "   ......  "   "   ...   ...
Mikes:  gun.............   "   .../...  "   "   ......  "   "   ...   ...
        omni............   "   .../...  "   "   ......  "   "   ...   ...
        cardioid........   "   .../...  "   "   ......  "   "   ...   ...
        lavalier........   "   .../...  "   "   ......  "   "   ...   ...
        extension cords..   "   .../...  "   "   ......  "   "   ...   ...
        mixer...........   "   .../...  "   "   ......  "   "   ...   ...
Batteries...............   "   .../...  "   "   ......  "   "   ...   ...
Sun gun.................   "   .../...  "   "   ......  "   "   ...   ...
Open face quartz kit(s)..   "   .../...  "   "   ......  "   "   ...   ...
Softlight(s)............   "   .../...  "   "   ......  "   "   ...   ...
Spotlight kit(s)........   "   .../...  "   "   ......  "   "   ...   ...
Extension cords.........   "   .../...  "   "   ......  "   "   ...   ...
Tie-in cables...........   "   .../...  "   "   ......  "   "   ...   ...
```

FIGURE 28-1 (Continued) ───

```
  Materials

  Camera raw stock .../... rolls of type.... @ $....per roll (film)   ...    ...
  Nagra tape         .../...   "    "    " .... @ $.... "    "      "   ...    ...
  Develop          ...../.....ft of cam. orig @ $......per ft.    "   ...    ...
  Print            ...../..... " of workprint @ $...... per ft    "   ...    ...
  Sound transfer              ....hrs @ $..... per hr     "           ...    ...
  Sound stock (8mm/16mm/35mm)        ......ft @ $..... per ft     "   ...    ...
  Videocassettes .../...required of type........ @ $...... each       ...    ...


  Total......................................................$_____  $_____
  Talent
  _____ X _____days @ $......per day              ...    ...
  _____ X _____days @ $......per day              ...    ...
  _____ X _____days @ $......per day              ...    ...
  _____ X _____days @ $......per day              ...    ...
  _____ X _____days @ $......per day              ...    ...
  _____ X _____days @ $......per day              ...    ...
  _____ X _____days @ $......per day              ...    ...
  _____ X _____days @ $......per day              ...    ...
  Other_____      ...    ...


  Total.................................................. $_____  $_____


  Other

  Transport    ..../.... days        @ $...... per day.              ...    ...
  Subsistence ..../.... person days @ $..... per person per day      ...    ...
  Accomodation ..../....  "     "    " $.....   "    "      "    "    ...    ...
  Location or other fees                                             ...    ...

                                                Total                ...    ...
  _____

                          Post-Production

  Editor          ..../.... days @ $...... per day                  ...    ...
  Editing equipment ..../....  "    " $...... "    "                 ...    ...
  Time coding     ..../.... hrs  " $......  at $....... per hour     ...    ...
  Window dub      ..../....  "    " $......  " $.......  "    "       ...    ...
  Narrator        ..../....  "    " $......  per hr                  ...    ...
  Music                                                              ...    ...
  Titles                                                             ...    ...
  Sound mix       ..../.... hrs  @ $..... per hour                   ...    ...
  Transfer mag master to optical .../....ft @ $.......per ft  (film) ...    ...
  Conform cam original to workprint  ..../..... hrs @ $... per hr  " ...    ...
  Make first answer print...../.....ft @ $....... per ft          " ...    ...
  Make first release  "  ...../.....ft @ $....... per ft          " ...    ...
  On-line edit, timebase correction, etc  ..../....hr @ $.... per hr ...    ...
```

```
  Legal                                                              ...    ...
  Production Office                                                  ...    ...
  Miscellaneous:
        ...............................                              ...    ...
        ...............................                              ...    ...
        ...............................                              ...    ...
                                                Total                ...    ...
  _____

  Summary:

  Pre-Production  total.......................................... $  ...    ...
  Production      total..........................................    ...    ...
  Post-Production total..........................................    ...    ...

  Subtotal........................................................ $  ...    ...

  Contingency addition (12% of total)............................ $  ...    ...

  GRAND TOTAL..................................................... $.....  $....
```

FIGURE 28-1 (Continued) —————————————————————————

tween the different emotional levels required. The scene breakdown also displays which characters are needed, and this, too, in association with the cost and availability of actors may influence scheduling.

SCRIPT ORDER

Few films actually need to be shot in script order, however desirable this is for performance continuity. A film depending on a long, slow development—like the main character's decline into insanity in Nicholas Hytner's *The Madness of King George* (1995)—often calls for a long progressive change by actors in the main parts. Another type of film, depending upon a high degree of improvisation, might need to be shot in script order to maintain control over the evolving story line. Yet another still might take place entirely in interiors and have a small, constant cast so that shooting out of scene order is no advantage. But normally shooting in script order is not practical, so director, cast, and crew must be thoroughly prepared so that patchwork filming will assemble correctly.

SCHEDULE KEY SCENES EARLY

Some scenes are so dramatically important that there will literally be no film should they fail. Imagine that your whole film hinges upon the inevitableness of your heroine falling in love with an emotionally unstable man. It would be folly to shoot everything else trusting that your actors can make a difficult and pivotal scene work.

Such key scenes must neither be filmed too early when the cast has not yet reached its peak, nor too late, when failure or change might render weeks of work useless. If the scene is successful, it will give a lift to everything else you shoot; if the scene is not really working, you will want to reshoot in a day or two, and certainly before you commit yourself to shooting the bulk of the film. Problems should show up in rehearsals, but filming is only occasionally better than the best rehearsal, and often below it. While it is usual for the cast to feel more deeply during the first takes of a new scene, strong feeling is no substitute for depth of character development. When cast members realize they must sustain a performance over several angles and several takes per angle, they also begin to instinctively throttle back their energy level. Knowing this should make you try to mentally preedit your scene so you don't make undue and wasteful demands upon cast and crew. Drawing the line between adequacy and wastefulness is particularly hard for the new director, so it is best to err on the side of safety.

EMOTIONAL DEMAND ORDER

Scheduling should take account of the demands some scenes make upon the actors. A nude love scene, for instance, or a scene in which two characters get violently angry with each other should be delayed until the actors are comfortable with each other and the crew. Such scenes should also be the last of the day because they are so emotionally draining.

CONTINGENCY COVERAGE

Schedule exteriors early in case your intentions are defeated by unsuitable weather. By planning interiors as standby alternatives, you need lose no time. Make contingency shooting plans whenever you face major uncertainties.

BUDGETING SHOOTING TIME PER SCENE

Depending on the amount of coverage, the intensity of the scene in question, and the reliability of actors and crew, you might expect to shoot anywhere between two and four minutes of screen time per eight-hour day. Remember that traveling between locations, setup, or relighting in the same location all massively slow the pace of shooting. Some directors budget setup time for mornings and rehearse the actors while the crew is busy, but this cannot work as well outside a studio setting.

It is best to err on the side of underscheduling, since a tired crew and cast work progressively slower, and morale (not to mention tempers) becomes frayed. You can always shorten a long schedule, but it is unpopular or even impossible to lengthen one originally too short. Most nonprofessional shoots (and some professional) are seriously underscheduled. When crew and cast end up working twelve- or fourteen-hour days, artistic intentions go out the window and everyone ends up merely aiming to survive the ordeal. The sad part is that a promising film may be sabotaged by misplaced optimism rather than any inherent need to save money.

Be prepared for the first few days of shooting to be alarmingly slow because a crew is often still developing an efficient working relationship with each other. The first half of the shoot may fall seriously behind if the AD and PM do not apply the screws and keep the unit up to schedule. Not only does the inexperienced crew start slowly and over days get quicker, it also tends to reproduce this pattern during each day unless there is some determined progress-chasing by the DP and AD.

GOLDEN RULE NUMBER ONE: FORESEE THE WORST

Imagination expended in foreseeing the worst will forestall many potentially crippling problems before they take shape. That way you will equip yourself with particular spares, special tools, and emergency information, for example. Optimism and filmmaking do not go together. One blithe optimist left the master tapes of a feature film in his car overnight. The car happened to be stolen, and because there were no copies, the result of a vast amount of work was transformed instantly into so much silent footage.

The pessimist, constantly foreseeing the worst and never tempting fate, is tranquilly productive compared with your average optimist.

GOLDEN RULE NUMBER TWO: TEST IT FIRST

Arrive early and test every piece of equipment at its place of origin. Never assume because you are hiring from a reputable company that everything should be all right. If you do, Murphy's Law will get you. (Murphy's Law: "Everything that can go wrong will go wrong.") Be ready for Murphy lurking inside everything that should fit together, slide, turn, lock, roll, light up, make a noise, or work silently. His relatives hide out in every wire, plug, box, lens, battery, and alarm clock. Make no mistake; the whole clan means to ruin you. Make "test and test again" your true religion and leave nothing to chance.

SHOT AND SCENE IDENTIFICATION

Your crew must keep logs of important information when you shoot. These serve the same end for both videotape and film, but record-keeping and continuity observation is more stringent for film because it allows no instant replay.

CLAPPER BOARD

There are many fancy automatic film marking systems, but the exquisitely low tech clapper board, with only a piece of chalk and a hinge to go wrong, is my favorite. The clapper board ritual has three main functions. Visually it identifies the shot number and the production for the film laboratory; aurally the operator's announcement identifies the track for the sound transfer personnel; and in the cutting room the closing bar provides an exact picture frame against which to sync the bang on the recorded track.

Because video recording normally has sound and picture on the one piece of tape, sync is not an issue. No clapper board is needed unless you are shooting high-quality double-system sound (video picture with sound recorded separately on a high-quality sync recorder like a Nagra or DAT machine). For either film or video double system productions the clapper board allows sound to be synced to the picture.

You will still need a video shot numbering system to identify setup and take numbers even on a modest production. Using high-speed scan, one can run down to a chosen take without the need to search at sound speed for the camera stop and voice announcement. This is valuable on location when time spent reviewing tape is often stolen from much needed rest.

Film scene numbering boards carry a quantity of information used by processing labs, such as a gray scale, which includes white and black as a contrast reference, and a standard color chart for color reference. In video the color chart is electronically generated by the camera and is called the color bars.

To summarize, for film use a clapper board with announcement and for a video production use a number board with announcement only. For double system videotape use a clapper board and treat the operation like film, since sound will likewise have to be synced up to video action.

SETUP AND TAKE NUMBERS

The setup is the apparent position of the camera, which can be altered by a simple lens change as well as by physically moving the camera to a new position. There are two philosophies of numbering.

Method 1:   The *Scene/Setup/Take* system is favored in the Hollywood studio system. Numbering is based on the script scene number. For example: "Scene 104A, shot 16, take 3." Translated this means script scene 104A, setup 16, attempt number 3." Hollywood, making big highly supervised productions, needs lengthy factory part numbers. For the small, flexible production, this is unnecessary. The more elaborate a system is, the more susceptible it is to error and to breakdown if you depart from the script. Also, by taking longer to announce, it wastes precious film stock.

Method 2:   The *Cumulative Setup/Take* system is used in both documentaries and features in Europe. Shooting simply begins at slate 1 and each setup gets the next number. For example: "142 take 2." Shot numbers are often called slate numbers. This system is preferred for the overstretched small crew because it requires no liaison to coordinate numbers with the script, and needs no adaptation when the inevitable script departures come up.

SHOOTING LOGS

On a film shoot the camera assistant keeps a camera log (Figure 28-2) for each film magazine's contents by slate, take, and footages. Each magazine has a new camera roll number. This information comes into play during processing and later in editing. A day-for-night scene, for example, would be shot using a blue filter to give it a moonlit look, but if the lab lacked the relevant documentation it might easily treat the filtering as an error needing color-correction in the work print. The film sound recordist keeps a sound log (Figure 28-3) which records slate and take numbers, and whether each track is sync or "wild" (non sync voice or effects recording). The latter information is important to whoever does the transfer from 1/4″ master tape to 16mm, since there may be no pilot tone (electronic sync reference signal).

DOUBLE-SYSTEM RECORDING

Where sound is recorded by a mechanically and electrically independent recorder, film camera magazines or video cassettes do not stay in numerical step with their sound master roll numbers because their durations may be different, or because of wild tracks and atmospheres taken as the production progresses. Separate sound and camera logs are a necessity and film rushes actually travel to their destination in the cutting room by different routes (see production flow chart, Figure 28-4). The laboratory processes the negative and strikes a workprint for the editor, while the 1/4 inch magnetic master tape or DAT cassette goes to the sound transfer suite where a copy is made onto 16mm or 35mm sprocketed magnetic stock for use by the editor. Video master cassettes will be window dubbed for the editor and sound synced up in the cutting room. Thus, in double-system filmmaking, sound and picture are likely to come together for the first time under the editor's hand.

SINGLE SYSTEM

When shooting single system on video, records are simpler because both sound and picture are recorded side by side and on the same cassette (see flow chart, Figure 28-6). The deck operator keeps a master log by digital number and also makes a record of slate, take, and a brief description of the scene.

```
FILM CAMERA LOG     Production Title_____ Page_____

Operator_____ Camera #_____ Magazine #_____ Cam. Roll #____
Location_____ Film Type _____ Date ___/___/_____
------------------------------------------------------------------------------
Setup Take Comments                                                    Footage
_____|_____|_____|_____
_____|_____|_____|_____
_____|_____|_____|_____
_____|_____|_____|_____
_____|_____|_____|_____
_____|_____|_____|_____
_____|_____|_____|_____
_____|_____|_____|_____
_____|_____|_____|_____
_____|_____|_____|_____
_____|_____|_____|_____
_____|_____|_____|_____
_____|_____|_____|_____
_____|_____|_____|_____
_____|_____|_____|_____
_____|_____|_____|_____
_____|_____|_____|_____
_____|_____|_____|_____
_____|_____|_____|_____
_____|_____|_____|_____
_____|_____|_____|_____
_____|_____|_____|_____
_____|_____|_____|_____
_____|_____|_____|_____
_____|_____|_____|_____
_____|_____|_____|_____
_____|_____|_____|_____
_____|_____|_____|_____
_____|_____|_____|_____
_____|_____|_____|_____
_____|_____|_____|_____
_____|_____|_____|_____
_____|_____|_____|_____
_____|_____|_____|_____
_____|_____|_____|_____
_____|_____|_____|_____
_____|_____|_____|_____
_____|_____|_____|_____
_____|_____|_____|_____
_____|_____|_____|_____
_____|_____|_____|_____
_____|_____|_____|_____
Process Normal Yes/ No:_____ Total Shot |
------------------------------------------------------------------------------
Notes:


_____ Cam. Assistant: _____
```

FIGURE 28-2

Camera log for film production.

SOUND RECORDER LOG Production Title_____ Page_____
Mike Op. _____ Recorder_#_____ Tape Type_____Roll #_____
Location_____ Date ___/___/_____
Setup Take Comments   Mike(s) Sync?

Notes:

Recordist:

FIGURE 28-3

Sound recorder log for film or video double system production.

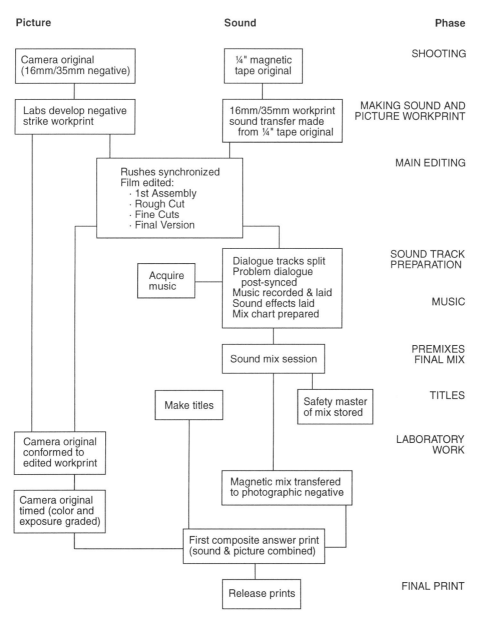

FIGURE 28-4

Flowchart for a production shot on film (double system).

```
V I D E O    L O G  Production Title_____ Page_____

Cam. Operator_____ Camera_____ Date__/__/____
Location_____ Roll # _____

Counter│Scene│                                               │
reading│# and│         Description                           │ Remarks
_____│take │_____│_____
_____│_____│_____│_____
_____│_____│_____│_____
_____│_____│_____│_____
_____│_____│_____│_____
_____│_____│_____│_____
_____│_____│_____│_____
_____│_____│_____│_____
_____│_____│_____│_____
_____│_____│_____│_____
_____│_____│_____│_____
_____│_____│_____│_____
_____│_____│_____│_____
_____│_____│_____│_____
_____│_____│_____│_____
_____│_____│_____│_____
_____│_____│_____│_____
_____│_____│_____│_____
_____│_____│_____│_____
_____│_____│_____│_____
_____│_____│_____│_____
_____│_____│_____│_____
_____│_____│_____│_____
_____│_____│_____│_____
_____│_____│_____│_____
_____│_____│_____│_____
_____│_____│_____│_____
_____│_____│_____│_____
_____│_____│_____│_____
_____│_____│_____│_____
_____│_____│_____│_____
_____│_____│_____│_____
_____│_____│_____│_____
_____│_____│_____│_____
_____│_____│_____│_____
_____│_____│_____│_____
Notes:

                            Signed:
```

FIGURE 28-5 ──

Log for video production.

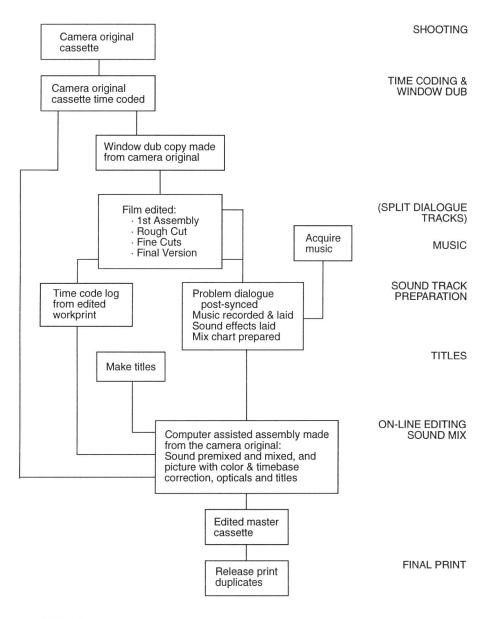

SHOOTING

TIME CODING &
WINDOW DUB

(SPLIT DIALOGUE
TRACKS)

MUSIC

SOUND TRACK
PREPARATION

TITLES

ON-LINE EDITING
SOUND MIX

FINAL PRINT

FIGURE 28-6

Flow chart for a production shot on video (single system).

DIGITAL POSTPRODUCTION AND TIME CODE

No matter whether a production is shot on film or video, editing and even the whole postproduction process are rapidly moving to digital (computerized) methods. The key to this lies in timecoding the film or tape camera original so that subsequent editing can produce an Edit Decision List by which the final will be retrieved and assembled. The order of operations for the different processes (see the flow chart in Figure 28-7) is as follows:

a) Camera original is on tape which is either time coded automatically by the camera, or time coded afterwards. The camera original is fed into a digitizer which compresses the vast amounts of luminance, chrominance, sound, and

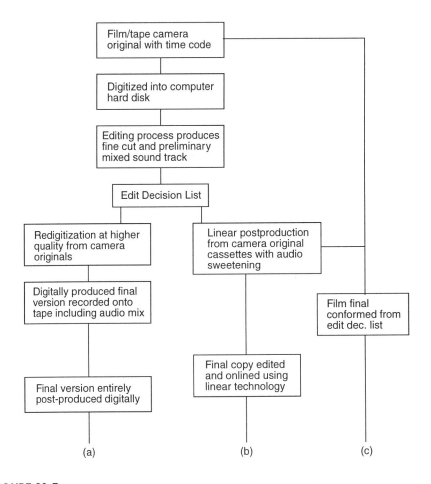

FIGURE 28-7

Flow chart for film and/or tape production. Final copies may be: a) tape from digital post-production, b) tape from digital offline and linear online, c) film after digital offline and camera original retrieved via EDL.

other video information into a minimal record on a hard disk. Now on a computer equipped with a digital editing program, the film is assembled on a time line rather like a word document can be edited using cut and paste methods. The computer lists all your decisions as timecode in and out points in the Edit Decision List (EDL). By redigitizing only the chosen segments at a higher quality (which takes up more memory, which is why the lower quality was used the first time around), the computer can now reassemble, using the EDL, the entire film at or near broadcast standards. The final print is on linear tape.

b) Same as above, but the EDL is instead used to control conventional linear on-line production in which linear machines re-record, a section at a time, from the camera original to a linear recorder. Then comes an audio mix and the final print is issued on tape.

c) Film is digitized complete with its Keycode™ numbers (a Kodak bar code which functions as a new timecode for each film frame, unlike film edge numbers which appear only every half-foot). From the digital version stored in the computer hard disk, an edited final version is produced. This is immensely quicker than labor intensive traditional methods using a flatbed editor working from film trims. The resulting EDL is used to conform the camera original and to prepare sound tracks. Note that only Keycoded film can be used.

With digital editing methods and hardware developing at brushfire speed, we can soon expect to see picture editing, sound editing and sound mixing entirely handled at computer workstations. Digital programs are already capable of color correction and a range of sophisticated optical transitions and filtering (color to black-and-white, for instance). At the time of writing, editing programs are held back by computers that aren't fast enough, and memory and hard disks which are expensive. This will change since the potential markets in the professional and consumer areas are enormous. What is exciting about digital production generally is that digital rerecording does not degrade the image as linear re-recording does. A fiftieth generation copy looks the same as a second generation. The other huge benefit is that it massively decreases the time and labor required to assemble, reassemble, view, and complete productions.

The prophets of doom talk darkly of plummeting artistic standards when editing becomes so easy, but to me this is like equating Shakespeare's genius with his quill pen and alleging he would have been ruined had he used a word processor.

LOG MUST RECORD EQUIPMENT USED

In all cases, logs must identify the serial numbers of equipment used. Should a strange electronic sound be later discovered in the sound, or scratching turn up on a film negative, you must be able to withdraw the offending machine for examination.

SCRIPT SUPERVISOR AND CONTINUITY REPORTS

Directing means being wholly occupied within each moment during the shoot. You have planned your coverage in advance with your script supervisor and now it would be counterproductive to waste your precious energy ensuring that the coverage is being fulfilled. That is your script supervisor's job. He or she must see that the editor is supplied with adequate coverage and ensure that matching shots really match. Which hand a character used to open the suitcase, how long his cigarette was when he stood by the window, and which direction he turned as he left for the door must be consistent between adjacent shots.

In the event of changes or economies, the script supervisor needs to know how the revised footage could be edited together and must at all times guard against omissions.

For a feature shoot, the script supervisor produces reports that are often masterpieces of observation. Each setup has its own sheet to record the following:

- production, personnel, and date
- slate and take number
- script scene number
- camera lens in use
- action and dialogue variations, successes and flaws for each take, and which are to be printed up by the lab (big-budget films are able to print selectively)
- any special instructions from the director to the editor

Not surprisingly, a script supervisor needs fierce powers of concentration and the ability to do huge amounts of typing in spare moments. When everyone else has gone to sleep on location, you will hear the script supervisor still at work. Because one cannot replay an exposed film as one can a recorded video tape, the script supervisor's work is supremely important to feature filmmaking. Its quality later determines how readily the cutting rooms can locate a given shot in their filing system and how well it fits together with its complementaries.

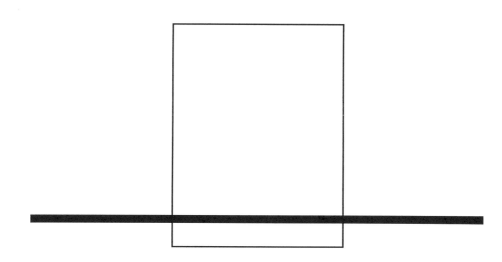

C·H·A·P·T·E·R 29

DIRECTING THE ACTORS

Shooting is a time of euphoria and despair for the director, who, unlike anyone else, must scan many people's work. A supportive, enthusiastic cast and crew will endure and triumph together, but under the best of conditions this will be a time of great stress. Hardest is fulfilling the actors' needs for feedback while also trying to direct the crew. A DP with leadership qualities is a godsend.

SENSORY OVERLOAD

The director's occupational hazard is sensory overload. In a typical take when you must watch the actors keenly you will also hear a lamp filament humming and a plane flying nearby. Can the sound recordist hear them? Insulated inside her head-phones, she only looks back at you questioningly. Next you see a doubtful camera movement, and wonder if the operator will call, "Cut!" Your heroine turned the wrong way when leaving the table and your mind races as you figure out whether it can possibly cut with the longer shot. Now to further boggle your mind the camera assistant holds up two fingers. Only two minutes of film left. At the end of the take your cast looks at you expectantly. How was it? Of course you hardly know. If you are working on tape or have a video assist, you can replay their work, but if you do that too often it will double the shooting schedule. More prac-tical is to ruthlessly prioritize how you use your energy. Ideally, a competent crew will catch all the sound, camera, and action problems and report what you need to rectify. The union crew coming from a system with an emphasis on keeping a small number of specialists working constantly produces highly reliable workers.

But a casual labor system produces a larger number of freelances who generally lack experience. A film school produces some quite brilliant people but their lack of practice will still lead them into mistakes and omissions. No way around it: you get what you pay for, and if you can't pay, you have to work twice as hard.

ACTORS NEED FEEDBACK

Actors learn from acting school and theater experience to depend upon audience signals. There are few in filming, for the director is the sole audience and must somehow try to give each actor the sense of closure normally acquired from an audience. Actors are not fooled by empty gestures. Your brain has been running out of control trying to factor all the editing possibilities that make the last performance even usable, and now you must say something intelligent to your trusting players, each of whom is (and must be) self-absorbed and self-aware. You manage something and the cast nods intently.

Now your crew needs you and the actors are already asking, "What are we doing next?" The production manager is at your elbow demanding confirmation for the shooting at the warehouse next week. The warehouse people are on the phone and they sound testy.

So there you have it: the true glamour of directing is walking around faint from lack of sleep feeling that your head is about to explode.

PRIORITIZE

The solution lies in setting priorities and delegating as much as possible of the actual shooting to the DP, who directs the crew. Your AD should also take as much of the logistical work off your shoulders as possible.

ACTORS' ANXIETIES AT THE BEGINNING

PREPRODUCTION PARTY

Try to bring cast and crew together for a picnic or pot luck party before production begins, to break the ice.

WARN ACTORS THAT SHOOTING IS SLOW

Thoroughly warn actors *that all filming is slow,* that even a professional feature unit may only shoot between one to four minutes of screen time per eight-hour day. Tell them to bring good books to fill the inevitable periods of waiting.

BEFORE SHOOTING

The time of maximum jitters and minimum confidence for the actors is just before first shooting. Take each aside and tell him or her something special and private. What matters is to be sincere and personally supportive. Thereafter that actor has a special understanding to maintain with you. Its substance and development will reach out by way of the film to the audience, for whom you are presently the surrogate.

TENSION AND ITS CONSEQUENCES

Whatever level of performance was reached in rehearsal now comes to the test when shooting begins. Actors will feel as if they are going over Niagara Falls in a barrel. Wise scheduling puts the least demanding material early as a warm-up. In the first day or two there will be a lot of tension, either frankly admitted or displaced into one of the many behaviors that mask it (See Chapter 20, Actors' Problems). Try not to be wounded or angered; if someone is deeply afraid of failing a task, it is forgivably human to demote the work's importance. It does not mean actors are deficient as a breed (the belief of many film technicians), but rather that actors are normal people temporarily succumbing to vulnerability and self-doubt. Having nowhere to hide, actors can easily feel exposed and humiliated. Filming is incomprehensibly slow, and the crew, enviably busy with their gadgets, seem removed and uncaring. Your appreciation and public recognition given for even small achievements, and your astute catering work wonders for morale in both cast and crew.

GETTING INTO STRIDE

As the process settles into a familiar routine, anxieties subside and actors fall in with the pace and demand of the shooting, arriving eventually at a craftsmanlike pride in being a member of the team. Performances improve so much that you wonder about the usability of the earlier material.

THE DIRECTOR'S AUTHORITY

While actors are visibly working their way through a labyrinth of strong feelings, the director must suffer any similar crises in silent isolation. Because cast members invest such trust in their director, he or she must play the role of the all-caring, comprehending, and supportive parental figure.

The poor novice is racked with uncertainty about whether he or she even has the authority to do the job. How do you wield authority when you feel like a fraud? The secret is that you play the part that the whole film unit wants to believe in. To do this well, limit the area you oversee, be better prepared than anyone else, and keep everyone busy. Your authority with the cast rests mainly on being able to recall and communicate what actors have just given, and to point the way forward. This is your central function, so divest yourself of anything impeding it.

Both cast and crew are apt to try your patience and judgment. This all too human testing procedure goes with all leadership. Behind what seems a sparring and antagonistic attitude may lurk a growing respect and affection, but because of the parental role—supporting, questioning, challenging—you may feel thoroughly alone and unappreciated. You are in authority, and many experience their most ambivalent relationships with such figures. For your cast, "my director" and the other actors may be the most important people in their lives, allies with whom to play out complex and personal issues that involve love and hate, and everything else between. This is just as legitimate a path of exploration for an actor as it is for any other artist.

Finding a productive working relationship with the subtle personalities of your actors is really discovering how best to use your own temperament. There are no rules because the chemistry is always different and changing. If it comes to a choice, you should always aim to be respected rather than liked. Liking comes later if things go well.

The director stands at the crossroads to all important relationships in the making of the film, and must do whatever it takes to keep everyone focused on the good of the common enterprise. There is no set way to handle the many situations that come up, except to demand that everyone remain loyal to the project rather than to any individual.

DIVIDING YOUR ATTENTION BETWEEN CREW AND CAST

Often the director of a student production is using an untried crew and justifiably feels that every phase of the production must be personally monitored. But if you are to direct the human presence on the screen, directing the crew should be entrusted to the DP and the AD.

Your authority with both crew and cast lies in keeping abreast of how the material will work on the screen. One learns to do this well by taping the later rehearsals. By the time you shoot you have learned to recognize instinctively when things are working and when they are not.

Directing is easier (though hardly less stressful) for those who have arrived via professional work in one of the crafts because long years of industry apprenticeship teach people how to work in a highly disciplined team. Without this conditioning, the student director and crew are in a precarious position, but if Truffaut's *Day for Night* (1973) is as representative as I think, a lowering of ideals during shooting is a common experience.

DAILY ORGANIZATION

Be sure everyone is well prepared. This means typed call sheets for cast and crew in advance, a map of how to get to the location, floor plans for camera crew, and preestablished lighting design. Tricky camera setups should be rehearsed in advance and correct props and costumes should be ready to go. Have your scene coverage thoroughly worked out with your DP and script supervisor. Your AD should make lists so you carry nothing in your head and nothing gets forgotten. A smoothly running organization signals professionalism to cast and crew. This is vital if lowly-paid or unpaid people are to have confidence in your leadership.

FOR EACH SHOT

While the crew sets up the next shot, take your cast aside and rehearse intensively. The DP can borrow crew members as stand-ins for lighting and movement checks.

Run through the action and *remind each actor of his character's recent past and emotional state on entering the scene.* This is very important both as information and as implied support. It often needs to be repeated in a few words before every take. Your AD should tell you when the first shot is set up so actors can start with the minimum of waiting.

The AD should call for silence as everyone takes their working positions; important because the players are finding their focus. The director asks, "Ready to roll?" and if everyone is indeed ready, he or she next says, "Roll camera." When equipment is up to speed and stabilized, the camera operator calls back, "Speed!"

Then you say that magic word: "Action!" The word itself is actually your last direction because it can communicate something of what you expect to the actors. It can be said loudly, softly, intimately, aggressively—a hundred ways.

It is normally the director who calls, "Cut!" but the sound recordist or camera operator may do so should a technical flaw known only to them render the take unusable. Actors on the other hand should always complete a scene they think is flawed unless the director decides to abort it.

When another take is necessary, quickly tell each actor what to aim for (whether the same or something different) and run up the camera before the collective intensity dissipates. Sometimes a further take is necessary because of a technical flaw in sound or in camera coverage, but usually you want better or different performances. This may affect each actor in a group scene differently. From one you want the same good level of performance, from another a different emotional shading or energy level. *Each actor needs to know what you expect.*

Actors themselves will sometimes feel they can do better. The best acknowledgment is to call, "We're going for another take. Roll camera as soon as possible." While cast should always be allowed to improve, asking for just one more take can become a fetish or a manipulation of directorial decisions. Sometimes you must insist that the last take was fine and that you want to move on. Actors' insecurity has a thousand faces.

FOR THE NEW SHOT

As soon as you have an acceptable take, brief the DP what the next shot is to be, and turn to the cast to give them what they need, both positive feedback about the last shot and preparation for the next.

DEMAND MORE

In directing, the enemy is one's own passive and gullible tendency to accept what actors give as the "best they can do." Try to instill in yourself the artist's creative dissatisfaction with every first appearance. Treat it as the brilliant surface of a deep pool, a reflective facade covering a teeming, complex life underneath, that will be found by diving deeper. Treat each scene as a "seeming" beneath which hide layers of significance that only skill and aspiration can lay bare.

Always pushing for depth means expecting to be moved by the players, and sometimes it will happen strongly. One is tempted to *make* oneself be moved because one feels guilty that the cast are trying so hard and one's own role is that of pasha. This is not the point; you must resist onlooker's guilt and simply allow yourself to be acted upon. If it works, it works, if it doesn't, why? Feed back to your cast what you felt and to what degree. When your players deliver a real intensity, you are creating as you go, not simply placing a rehearsal on record.

Because you are working in a highly allusive medium, your audience expects metaphorical and metaphysical overtones. To draw us beneath the surface of normality, to get beyond externals and surface banality, and to make us see poetry and conflict beneath the surface, you will have to challenge your actors in a hundred interesting ways. These demands keep the cast and the crew on their toes and make their work challenging and fascinating. *You represent the audience and they work to please you.* They want your approval because your demands personify their own gnawing sense of always somehow being capable of better. This dissatisfaction is as it should be. It will probably be accompanied by an undertow of complaining. Emphasize the positive and think of the grumbling as the noise of the rigging in a ship pushed to capacity. Or think of dancers; they are usually in bodily pain, and the pain comes from pushing themselves to the limit in order to make dance look effortless and wonderful.

FEEDING THE UNKNOWN INTO THE PROCESS

To put tension in a scene that threatens to subside into comfortable middle age, take one or more actors aside and privately suggest to each some small but significant changes that will impact on other cast members. By building in little stresses and incompatibilities, by making sure that cast members are working off each other, you can reestablish the tautness and insecurity that is missing.

SIDE COACHING WHEN A SCENE IS BECALMED

When a scene goes static and sinks to a premeditated appearance, try side coaching to inject tension. This means you interpolate at a quiet moment in the scene a verbal suggestion or instruction, such as, "Terry, she's beginning to make you angry—she's asking the impossible." Your voice injects a new interior process in the character addressed, but it will not work if your actors are caught by surprise. If they are unfamiliar with side coaching, warn them not to break character should you use it.

REACTION SHOTS

Side coaching is most useful when directing simple reaction shots. The director provides a verbal image for the character to spontaneously see or react to, or an idea to consider, and gets an immediacy of reaction by challenging the actor to face something unexpected.

Usually the best reactions are to the actual. If a character must go through a complex series of emotions while overhearing a whispered conversation, make it a rule that the other characters do a full version of their scene even though it is off camera. If, however, your character must only look through a window and react to an approaching visitor, her imagination will probably provide all that is necessary.

One way during casting to test an actor's imaginative resources is to give them a phone and to improvise a conversation around a topic and with another (imagined) person which you specify. You should be unable to tell if there is a real person on the other end or not.

Reaction shots are enormously important, as they lead the audience to infer (that is, create) a character's private, inner life. They also provide vital, legitimate cutaways and allow you in editing to combine the best of available takes. Never dismiss cast and crew from a set without being utterly certain that you have thoroughly covered the reactions, cutaways, and inserts for each scene. And always make certain the sound recordist has shot some presence track, about which more later.

BACKLASH AND CRITICISM

Be prepared for personality problems and other friction during shooting. Actors' preferences and criticisms that were expressed during rehearsal often surface more vehemently under duress. There will be favorite scenes and scenes the actors hate, scenes that involve portraying negative characteristics and even certain lines upon which an actor becomes irrationally fixated. One palliative in serious cases is to allow a take using the actor's alternative wording. Don't offer this until all other remedies have been exhausted, and do it as a one-time-only concession, or your cast will each want to see if they too can command alternatives.

As knowledge of each other's limitations grows, actors can become critical or even hostile to each other. Occasionally two actors who are supposed to be lovers take a visceral aversion to each other. Here, loyalty to the project and commitment to their profession can save the project from utter disaster. Filming makes intense demands on people and a director must be ready to cope with everything human. You can learn hugely about the human psyche under duress and this will make you a better director (also a better human being!). If this sounds scary, take heart. The chances are good that you and your cast will like each other and that none of these horror stories will happen to you—yet.

FROM THE CAST

If the cast is to become a company, creativity cannot flow only from the director. The cast may continue quite justifiably to level criticism at the script, the crew, or the director. It should be acknowledged and, if constructive, acted upon diplomatically and without guilt. A wise director stimulates and utilizes the creativity of all the major figures in the team, aware that organic development and change will always be something of a threat to everyone's security, including her own.

If critical suggestions are incompatible with the body of work already accumulated, you must say so. Remain open-minded but do not swing like a weather vane. The best way to avoid unwelcome criticism is to be so prepared and so full of interesting demands that everyone is too busy to reflect. This won't deter genuinely useful and creative ideas.

FROM THE CREW

Actors find the spectacle of dissent among the crew deeply disturbing, so criticism by them should be discreet and kept from public view. Student crew members are sometimes unwise enough to imply how much better they could direct than the director, and to publicly voice their improvements. This is an intolerable situation that must be immediately corrected. Nothing diminishes your authority faster than for actors to feel they are being directed by a committee at war.

You can guard against this situation ever starting by making sure that territories have been clearly demarcated before the shooting starts. Anyone who now strays should be told privately and very firmly to tend his own area and no one else's. When a crew thinks it has a legitimate beef, it should be routed through the DP.

There will be occasions when you have to take a necessary but unpopular decision. Take it, bite your tongue, and do not apologize. Like a lot of other things, it is a test of your resolve, and the unpopular decision will also paradoxically be the one everyone knows to be right.

MORALE, FATIGUE, AND INTENSITY

Morale in both crew and cast tends to be interlocked. Giving verbal credit and appropriate attention to all members of the team is the best way to create loyalty to the project and to each other. Good leadership trickles down. Even so, immature personalities will fracture as fatigue sets in, or when territory is threatened. Severe fatigue is dangerous not only because people lose their cool but because the work becomes sloppy and essentials get overlooked. Careful and conservative scheduling guards against this.

One simple insurance is to take special care of creature comforts. Your production department should make sure that people are warm, dry, have bathrooms to go to, somewhere to sit down between takes, and food and drink. Avoid working longer than four hours without a break, if only for a ten-minute coffee break. From these primal attentions cast and crew infer that "the production" cares about them. Most will go to the ends of the earth for you when they feel valued.

YOU AS ROLE MODEL

You are the director. Your seriousness and intensity set the tone for the whole shoot. If you are sloppy and laid back, others will outdo you and no film may get made. If you demand a lot of yourself and others but are appreciative and encourage appropriate humor, you will probably run a tight ship. Your vision and how you share it will evoke respect in the entire team. People will follow an organized visionary anywhere.

Present any negative criticism as a request for a positive alternative. Thank people formally and individually at the end of each day's work. Respectful appreciation affirms that you take nobody for granted. By implication you are demanding that respect in return. Under these conditions, people should willingly cede you the authority to do your job.

USING SOCIAL TIMES AND BREAKS

During the shooting period, spend time outside the actual shooting with your cast. It is a mistake to retreat from the intensity of your actors to the understanding comradeship of the crew, however exhausted you may be. Try to keep cast and crew together during meals or rest periods. Frequently, while lunching or downing a beer after work, you will learn something that significantly complements or changes your ideas. The process of filmmaking shakes out many new ideas and perceptions, and it generates a shared intensity and sense of discovery that can bind crew and participants in a sense of intoxicating adventure. Conserved and encouraged, this sense of excitement can so awaken everyone's awareness that a profound fellowship and communication develop. Work becomes a joy.

WHEN AND WHEN NOT TO LET THE CAST SEE RUSHES

Under the usual pressured shooting schedule, show footage only to make a point that cannot be made any other way. I once convinced a player that he was acting instead of being by showing him some surreptitiously shot footage of himself in spontaneous conversation. The contrast between this and him performing a scripted conversation was so striking that he abandoned his resistance to my judgment. This kind of revelation is risky because it is a negative approach. Use it cautiously and supportively only if you cannot get through any other way. The same procedure can be used with the actor of fragile ego who insists on projecting a rich and unnatural acting voice instead of his or her natural range.

The worst hazard of indiscriminately showing footage is that you may end up with five cast members and six directors. With familiarity, actors come to more or less accept how they appear onscreen, but the journey to equanimity can be rough, and should be accomplished in rehearsal as part of learning to trust you, their director. At any time, actors tend to blame their feelings of humiliation on other cast members or you, the director, and their anguish becomes the reason to seek control.

None of this need happen if your cast learns to work from what you communicate rather than what their overcritical eyes read from the screen. It is quite normal to show rushes only to the crew and you should make no bones about doing this if you suspect that anyone in the cast will be undermined by it. Promise the cast a viewing of the first cut, if you like, to assuage their natural curiosity.

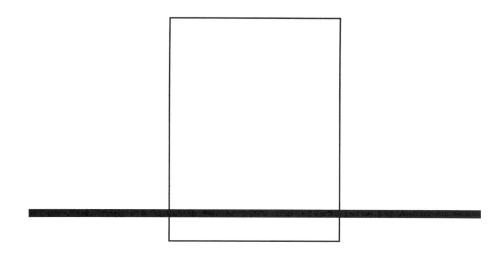

C·H·A·P·T·E·R 30

DIRECTING THE CREW

COMPARTMENTING RESPONSIBILITIES

Beginning directors in film school usually try to monitor the whole crew's work. In search of perfection you will have the urge to set the lights and operate the camera, as well as control a hundred other small details. Too often the human presence on the screen, the one aspect the audience really notices, goes neglected. A check of composition, as we shall see, is absolutely necessary but much else must be off-loaded. The director must be willing to give technicians and production personnel control of their areas, but delegation is a two-way street. For their part, those people must be fully responsible and aware at all times, and take the appropriate initiative without waiting for explicit instructions.

INITIATIVE

Finding crew members who take initiative yet work as a team is not easy. Many people are too passive to act without instructions. Many film students get no further than fulfilling class projects because, already regimented by family and schooling, they can only produce from within a punitive monitoring structure. They are mostly sensitive and intelligent, but their passivity makes them unsuitable to be film crew members. Others take initiative in order to exert control for its own sake. Status and control issues absorb too much of the average person's attention to make him suited for the give and take of teamwork.

Look in a film school's credits for a particular period, and you will find the same few names over and over again in different capacities for different films. These people love the process of filmmaking and will direct one month and be a friend's gaffer or production manager the next. This is the kind of person you should aim to become and these are the people you hope to secure for your crew.

COMMUNICATING

Before shooting begins, each crew member should read and question the script and contribute ideas that belong in his or her own area of specialty. A director should in turn understand the rudiments of each technician's craft, and be able to communicate in the craft's special terms. This is why this book contains so much about the whole production process.

From you or your delegates, *the crew needs positive, concise directions* with as much advance warning as possible. The crew will not rise to genuine crises if things that could have been foreseen go unattended. Avoid thinking out loud, especially when the pace heats up. Try instead to arrive at your conclusions and produce brief, practical instructions worded so they cannot be misinterpreted. Without being condescending, get people to repeat back instructions of any complexity so you know they understand. Everything that can be put in writing in advance should be.

Remember, wherever possible during shooting, the AD and DP should deal with all production and technical questions. This releases you to do your job properly, which is to answer the needs of the actors and to concentrate on building the film's dramatic content.

Relations with Cast and the Public

Every crew member must understand some of the givens of film crew life. When actors privately seek out opinions on the quality of the work, they must react with extreme diplomacy. However flattering this may be, it is probably neurosis and can if wrongly handled become dangerously divisive. To avoid such pitfalls, crew members should only be supportive, which is mainly what actors seek. When actors solicit support for negative attitudes, or communicate something the director should know about, the crew member should remain neutral and afterwards discreetly report the situation up the chain of command. Warn crew never to voice criticism that can weaken anyone else's authority, either on the set or off it. This preserves the all-important working morale.

The same caution should be by everyone in conversation with bystanders on location, who may take it upon themselves to cause trouble or attract unwelcome publicity. Any purposeful questions should be referred to the AD or other crew member delegated to deal with public relations.

LOOK THROUGH THE CAMERA

When a new shot has been set up and before the first take, it is imperative that you look through the viewfinder so you can confer with the camera operator and make sure the starting and other key compositions are as you expect. You may need to do the same at the take's end to check the camera's finishing composition. When there is a lot of moving camera coverage, you will need to agree with your operator on compositions, angle, size of the image, and so on. You should also walk the actors (or stand-ins) through the take, freezing them at salient points to agree with the operator on what should appear in the frame. To stabilize these decisions, your crew will need to make chalk marks on the floor for both actors and camera dolly. Everyone may have to hit particular marks at particular moments in the scene.

Precision of this kind separates the experienced from the inexperienced. Trying to impose this degree of control on an inexperienced ensemble may be an exercise in futility that wastes time and wrecks cast morale. Because framing, composition, lighting, and sound coverage are the formal structuring that translate a live world into cinema, the director needs to keep the strongest possible contact with the outcome on the screen. When shooting video, you can watch the whole take on the monitor during recording and know immediately what you have got. With film however, the results remain in agonizing doubt until the rushes return from the laboratory.

On a film shoot, all you can do to ensure that your vision is being recorded is to clearly brief the technical crew through the DP and to monitor what the camera is doing. One can in fact see from the operator's movements if he/she is in sync with the action. Not to do these things invariably leads to rude shock at the rushes viewing, when it is too late to make changes.

MAKING PROGRESS

Shooting is stop-start work, with many holdups for lighting or camera setups. A crew can easily slow down while everyone waits for A. N. Other. Nobody quite knows what they are waiting for, but everyone knows that *someone* is not ready. Eventually it becomes apparent that everyone is waiting for the notorious and elusive A. N. Other. This character hounds the disorganized and the tired. The good AD is, among other things, a sheepdog who constantly monitors bottlenecks and who barks everyone into action the moment that shooting can continue.

WHEN YOU AND YOUR CREW ARE ALONE

When you are alone with crew members during the shoot, encourage them to discuss the dramatic elements of the shooting. Some members such as grips, electricians, and ADs do their work before shooting and stand observing during the actual take. What they notice may usefully complement your sense of what is really happening. You, after all, have goals from rehearsal to fulfill while they are seeing the action for the first time, and have an audience-like reaction.

The work of the camera operator, DP, and sound recordist demands such localized attention to quality that they cannot be open to dramatic content in the same way. You will therefore get a very mixed bag of observations, some of them way off track. Hear and encourage all views, but do not feel you must act upon or rebuff ideas that imply criticism of your work. If, however, most of the crew, including the women members, find the main female character detached, you should take serious notice.

WRAPPING FOR THE DAY

At the end of a working day, thank actors and crew members personally, and make sure that everything in a borrowed location has been replaced exactly as found. This attention to someone else's property signifies your concern and appreciation. It also helps ensure a welcome should you want to return. Initial reluctance to accept a film crew's presence often arises because people have heard horror stories about boorish treatment of property. On a small crew, those with little equipment should help those with much (lighting for instance) to put their stuff away for the night. Like most human organizations, a film crew personifies class divisions. As their general, you must be concerned for the whole army's welfare especially if you want your footsoldiers' affection and loyalty.

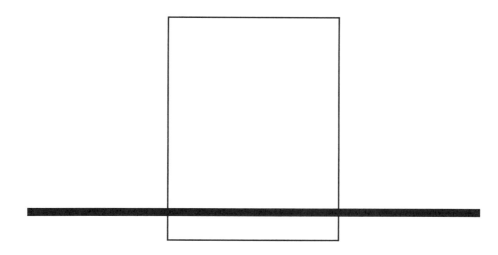

C·H·A·P·T·E·R 31

MONITORING PROGRESS

During the intensity of a shoot, it is easy to lose sight of priorities or to forget important coverage. Where a film's story proceeds by a series of images, or where the narrative is carried by nonverbal actions, directing and keeping track are relatively straightforward. It is when you shoot complex dialogue scenes, especially with several characters, and especially when the scene includes a lot of movement, that errors of screen direction and coverage creep in.

If director, script supervisor, or cinematographer have considerable experience at editing, each forms a film in their heads as shooting progresses. This is good but not infallible. Without methodically tracking coverage it is fatally easy to forget something important. One can just as easily be inattentive to the nuances of the performances. Here are some ideas for staying on top.

KEEPING TRACK OF COVERAGE

A director's nightmare during shooting is that an important angle or shot will be overlooked and then discovered later when it is impossible to reconvene crew and cast. In low-budget filmmaking where a few people must work fast, catastrophes like this are constantly imminent. Working hand-to-mouth, intentions get modified; simply marking off a list of intended shots may not truly reflect what was done, or it may be so covered with changes that the list itself becomes a source of confusion.

Better would be a graphic representation (as always) to show the state of play at a glance. In fact one can use the bracketed script principle to provide a thorough and up to date version.

During the shoot, the script supervisor carries a copy of the bracketed shooting script (see Figure 27-1, page 339). As each setup is completed, the script supervisor inks in what was shot. Where your shoot went as planned, the script supervisor simply overlays the original pencilled planning lines. Where there are changes, new markings demonstrate the difference between intentions and actuality. In association with a ground plan showing camera positions, a color system can be used for different shot sizes or angles (such as blue for wide shots, yellow for medium shots, and red for closeups). The start and finishing point of each setup's span and the angles and groupings it covers all become clearly and immediately visible.

From this anyone can see how the sequence was covered and how it might be edited. Unlike a list of scene numbers, interpreting the graphic requires no cross-referencing or special knowledge. At any point, director or script supervisor can glance at the marked up script to see what alternative permutations will be available should the preferred editing strategy not work out.

MONITORING YOUR RESOURCES

No matter in what order you shoot, your PM should be able to compute how much money has gone out and what should be the current camera roll number (or cassette) if the project is on track.

A production that does not keep some track of resources is like an expedition that eats steak near home and then has to boil its shoes in the wilderness to stay alive. Many beginners' shoots are liberally covered in the first stages but stretched so thin towards the end that the material can hardly be edited. If a scene by scene cost projection was carried out, it is an uncomplicated matter for the PM to track where money and stock are going, and how fast. Knowing early that a complicated sequence has consumed more resources than intended will signal that you must either raise more money, economize to get back on track, or be ready to drop a "luxury" scene.

DRAMATIC QUALITY

There are various levels of thoroughness in monitoring dramatic quality. To see no rushes until the shoot is completed is to not monitor quality at all, except subjectively as the action is shot. For a low-budget film unit away on location, this may seem the only practical solution, although its risks are manifold. Running film rushes on a silent projector is better than nothing, but you should see them synced up. Alternatively, get a cassette copy of the rushes made in home base and see them on a videocassette player at the location. The rushes copy can be shot from the editing machine's screen, or from a projected image. Neither camera nor sound crews will think much of this representation of their work, but it will provide you with feedback on such essentials as acting, coverage, camera handling, composition, and so forth.

For a video production a daily rushes viewing should be obligatory. A unit, however tired, is usually intensely interested in its own work. Do not include the actors who are likely to be thrown by seeing their own work. A feature unit will see its rushes every day (hence the term *dailies* for rushes) so that any reshooting can be done before the set is struck or lighting becomes difficult to reconstruct.

An additional level of quality monitoring is available if the editor starts work from the first day of shooting. As the materials for a sequence come in, he or she makes a rough cut and shows it as soon as possible to the director. Here not only raw materials come under surveillance, but every aspect of the film can be assessed in its edited form—where inconsistencies really show up. Any serious lack of coherency in acting, lighting, framing, sound, or continuity can now be corrected in subsequent shooting, and the director can see if stylistic intentions are working out. A rough assembly of the whole film can be seen a few days after the end of the shoot, avoiding what would otherwise be a delay of weeks or months. Because this assembly method places a premium on speed and requires the director to trust the editor's judgment, it is seldom used by beginners. Digital editing, however, makes it much more possible.

FULFILLING ONE'S AUTHORSHIP INTENTIONS

The big questions during shooting are, am I fulfilling my authorial intentions, and do I have a film? Success is very difficult to measure except in unreassuringly subjective terms. One way to make this easier is break your intentions down into specific goals.

DRAMATIC CLARITY

Earlier in the book I recommended graphing out expectations for a scene in order to clarify the changes that must take place and specify where each new stage is initiated ("Graphics to Help Reveal Dramatic Dynamics" in Chapter 17). Moment to moment, each scene by its action should impart what each character is trying to get or do. The audience needs a sense of each character's will, as he or she strives under ever-changing conditions to realize one desire after another. Keeping these currents alive and flowing should be your major goal. Doing so allows the audience to experience the screen's most tangibly dramatic element. Effective performances make you feel, while you are directing, what the audience should feel. It is something you recognize, not something you have to struggle to see.

It is extremely important to preestablish with your actors the detail in each moment of their performances; otherwise your direction may become rudderless during the shoot. Professional directors acquire so much preparatory experience along the way that their approach is internalized, like the reflexes used by an Olympic slalom skier. For beginners, success lies in developing clear detail and, during the shoot, making sure the detail and clarity of performance is sustained and a series of different emotions emerge. You should be able to feel them; if you have to search for them, or find yourself arguing with yourself that the emotion is there, it isn't.

SUBTEXT

Even when you do all this, there remains something fundamental but less definable to assess. After every scene has been played, there is an elusive imprint left on the observer, one concerning subtext and that is tremendously interesting to your cast, who need to know if their instincts about what took place will reach an audience. To extract impressions as peripheral as this, you'll probably have to ask yourself some special questions. To show how this works, I have applied some typical ones to two takes of a hypothetical scene set in a bus station where, late at night, two stranded passengers start a desultory conversation. Action and dialogue of each take is identical, yet see how each elicits different answers from the director:

Q: What life-roles did the characters adopt?

Take 1: "Two of life's losers unenthusiastically size each other up."

Take 2: "Two depressed, disgruntled people each decide whether they can be bothered with company at this time."

Q: What truth was played out here?

Take 1: "One instinctively despises someone else with the same shortcomings."

Take 2: "Alienated people tend to isolate themselves further."

Q: What metaphor sums up how the scene emerged?

Take 1: "Two neutered cats circle round each other."

Take 2: "Two exhausted convicts decide it is not worth cooperating to break rocks."

Metaphysical questioning forces one to transcend the tunnel vision that prevents one seeing beyond the obvious or the expected. These answers are quite typical and reveal subtle differences between the two takes. They signal that a different subtext is spontaneously emerging from variables in the consciousness of the players at the time.

The difference between the two takes shows how utterly wrong is the idea of a "finished performance." Relationship on or off the camera is (or should be) alive and therefore in flux. All takes on all angles of all learned scenes are still unpredictable of outcome and require this special sensitivity of interpretation. If as a director one brings narrowly focused expectations, such impressions, though immediately available to an audience, remain hidden to the director unless that director deliberately digs them out.

Scene Dialectics

Be aware of the dialectics in each scene and make sure they are well evidenced. By this I mean the paradoxes and opposing polarities of opinion and will that set person against person, movement against movement, idea against idea, and the parts of a person against himself or herself. These are the spars, pressures, and tensions, often insoluble and irresolvable, that stand out like majestic bridge construction from the fog of aimlessness.

My questions, centering as they do on roles, truth, and metaphors are inconveniently metaphysical for the hurly-burly of the set. They are never easy to answer, especially for the uninitiated. But answering such larger questions is the only way to break into that sealed compartment of your consciousness that already knows and recognizes the scene's underlying qualities. Having succeeded, you can be practical in remedying the shortfall between intention and execution.

Keep your intentions clear and keep them handy in list form (see "Crib Sheets" in Chapter 27). Then you'll have access to your objectives and can check before finishing each scene that you have covered all your bases. If my example of intentions for the scene look rather rigid, remember that the list is only a safety net, not a sacred text. It reminds you of what to look for, what to expect, and how to get a decent range of material from the scene. It is a resource that you should appropriate and develop, not a straitjacket.

Keep nothing in your head that can be organized as a checklist on paper. Lists are a godsend when one is too tired to think—a condition that descends rapidly during sustained shooting. At each juncture you may now assess whether you have won or lost each of the individual battles. This is hard and lonely work because one is usually underwhelmed by what takes place before the camera.

MEASURING PROGRESS

Seeing the rushes generally reveals there is a lot more on film than one realized at the time. But during the shoot one often suffers a gnawing doubt just when one is supposed to be feeling creative. This, of course, is not an emotion one dares to share with anybody.

MOVING BEYOND REALISM

The point at which a film moves beyond the literalness of recorded realism, is the point at which cinema links up with its sister arts like music, dance, theater, and literature. There is no set formula for achieving this and you cannot know if your design, worked out in writing and preproduction, is succeeding until the film is fully edited. Your film's inner life comes from the juxtaposition of materials, from assembling them into a provocative antiphony, from the life of the players, from the mood of the company's life together. It is also expressed through sound composition, expressionistic lighting or settings, or by other approaches germane to your piece. It's something you hope for, but is never something over which you can have total and conscious control. If that's what you want, become an animator. If you like accommodating the unexpected into your plans, you'll like making fiction films. If you really love the idea of serendipity and improvisation as ingredients in storymaking, do some *cinéma vérité* documentary in preparation for the more controlled form of fiction (see my book, *Directing the Documentary*, Focal Press, Boston).

CEDING CONTROL

Artistic control is paradoxical because it requires that at a certain moment—usually as the film is coming together in the cutting room—you actually yield control to some intuitively felt sense of truth. Do not worry if nothing like this shows up during the shoot. Usually if you are open-minded your assembled piece will begin to make its own insistent demands, dictating to you and your editor what it wants its final form to be. Like one's children, each of one's films turns out to have its own nature, its own imperfections and integrity, and each will start making its own autonomous decisions. What a shock and delight it is to begin assisting one's film make itself.

Similar capitulation may be required during shooting. A typical situation is an actor producing an unexpected and interesting quality that affects the character's potential or skews a certain situation you are shooting. You must decide whether to rein it in or whether to acknowledge the new direction and live with the consequences. Whatever you decide has an impact on the other players and puts your authority on the line. You will feel your artistic control and the security of your career threatened. Yet to deny these emerging, elusive truths is to choose security over experiment. Directing is never free of moral and ethical dilemmas, nor of compromise.

KEEP THE STORYTELLER ALIVE

The elements of authorship are analyzed in greater depth in Part IV: Aesthetics and Authorship. When you author a movie I contend that you are really using it to recreate some aspect of your own inmost experience, and to vicariously further it. My friend Lois once said, "Nothing is real until I have written about it." Had she been a filmmaker rather than a writer, she would have said, "Nothing is real until I have made a film about it." For we use our medium to extend the boundaries of our own real experience—first for ourselves and also for others. When others are moved, we find something new of ourselves through their recognition.

Thus, when you direct a story with special meaning, you carry responsibility for the voice of the film, that is, the observing witness and Storyteller, this intelligence that is the vital intermediary between the "reality" of the fiction and consciousness of your audience, with whose hearts and minds you are playing in the most purposeful way.

While you direct, you must fight to retain the Concerned Observer's identity that you developed during rehearsals and which the rough edit of taped rehearsals confirmed. As director, you covertly play the most important role, that of the unseen but ever present Storyteller. If you lose your vision of the film, you lose your storytelling identity, and the film loses its voice. This is why it matters intensely to have a clear idea of whom we should see into, and see through, at every stage of the movie. Dialogue sequences are the quicksands where this identity can most easily get lost, which is why so much of this book concentrates on handling the interaction between characters. If you fear this is happening, make sure you shoot enough options to allow shaping options in the cutting room. Single setup coverage for any part of a scene means that no changes in point of view, pacing, or reaction are possible. Always provide yourself with alternatives in case your plans don't work out.

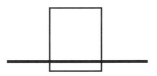

CHECKLIST, PART VI
PRODUCTION

The recommendations and points summarized here are only those most salient or the most commonly overlooked. To find more about them or anything else, go to the table of contents at the beginning of this part, or try the index at the back of the book.

PLANNING ON PAPER

- with the script supervisor, turn the screenplay into a final shooting script
- with your DP, draw a floor plan for each sequence showing characters' movements
- mark in the scene's axis (or axes) and camera positions
- mark up the script to show coverage from each camera position
- plan an establishing shot to clarify scene geography and character placement
- use movement to link angles at action-match cutting points
- make sure there will be plenty of overlap between angles so you will have adequate choice of cutting points
- use characters' eyeline shifts. Follow them with a camera movement or with a point of view shot
- decide where the scene will profit from changes between subjective (near axis) and objective (far from axis) camera angles
- cover any regrouping of characters in a comprehensive shot so that spatial changes can be made evident
- show relatedness through composition wherever possible so you do not have to manufacture juxtaposition through editing
- sketch a storyboard frame for each camera setup to make sure screen direction is maintained
- make up crib sheets for each scene with "must not forget" points listed
- cover important moments of the scene from more than one angle

PLANNING CAMERA MOVEMENTS

For camera movements in general,

- does the camera follow the movement of a character?

- does a moving object in frame permit the camera to pan with it so that camera movement is initiated by action in the frame?
- if a movement lays out a landscape or a scene geography for the audience, what should be most important in the composition?
- is the camera move one that gets closer, and intensifies our relationship with someone or something?
- does the camera move away from someone or something so we see more objectively?
- does the camera by moving reveal significant information?
- is the move really a reframing to accommodate a rearrangement of characters?
- is the move a reaction, panning to a new speaker, for instance?
- what else might motivate this particular camera move?

Using the floor plan to predetermine your camera positions:

- draw in character movements and positions, and draw in scene axis (or "180 degree line")
- draw in other axes if character movements create multiple subject-to-subject lines
- label camera positions A, B, C, etc.
- draw in camera panning and dollying movements using dotted lines leading to new positions
- figure out how best to keep camera positions to one side of each subject-to-subject axis
- when shooting always shoot to show characters' movements
- when shooting, always shoot to show when camera crosses the axis

Whose point of view do you want to engage the audience in? (Remember your Observer's experiences while following the action.)

- when should camera be close to the axis between characters?
- when should the camera come subjectively close to a character's eyeline?
- when should it take an objective stance to the situation (that is, either a distanced viewpoint, or one independent of eyelines)?
- whose story is this sequence if you go by gut reaction?
- with whose point of view will your coverage allow us to sympathize?
- how many psychological viewpoints do you as the Observer share? (Some may be momentary or fragmentary, and perhaps in contradiction to what you are generally seeing.)
- should you be covering the sequence to make alternative povs available to the editor?
- are the audience's sympathies to be structured by camera and editing? Or should they be molded by acting and the situation itself?

When should the camera be used subjectively?

- when do we directly experience a character's point of view?
- are there special reasons for the camera to be seeing subjectively?
- what is the dramatic justification?
- whose point of view is this subjective shot?

What determines camera height?

- a character's general eyeline height?
- intimations of domination or subjugation?
- a foreground through which we see the action?

Are there changes of camera height?

- to accommodate subject matter? (someone going up or down stairs, for instance)
- to make the audience see differently?
- for other reasons?

Review lighting possibilities:

- **mood** conveyed by lighting is _____
- **time of day** requires: day for day/night for night/dusk for night/day for night? _____
- **apparent source** in scene is _____ (natural or artificial source lighting?)
- **style** is high key/low key/graduated tonality?
- **contrast** will be high or low contrast?
- **setup** will be frontal/broad/narrow/back lighting setup?
- **angle** of key light will be high/low?
- **light quality** will give hard/soft edges to shadows?
- **practicals** in the scene are _____
- **lighting continuity** requires that you shoot wide shots first because they may take all available luminaires (lighting instruments). Closer shots can be matched, or "cheated" to match the master shot.

PLANNING THE USE OF SOUND

What sound perspectives might be used?

- complementing camera position (near mike for close shots, far from mike for longer shots, thus replicating camera perspective)?

- counterpointing camera perspective? (an intimate conversation of two characters on the skyline, for instance)
- uniformly intimate? (as with a narration, or with voice-over and "thoughts voices" that function as a character's interior monologue)
- other situations?

What particular sound effects should be shot on location and how will they be used?

- to build atmosphere and mood?
- as punctuation?
- to motivate a cut? (next sequence's sound rises until we cut to it)
- as a narrative device? (in an interior scene, the sound of a child crying off-screen makes a mother hurry to the window)
- to build, sustain, or defuse tension?
- to provide rhythm? (newspaper articles prepared in a montage of brief shots to the rhythmic sound of the printing press)
- to create uncertainty?
- other situations?

To whom will dialogue or narration be addressed? (this could affect how it's acted or recorded)

- by one character to another?
- to himself (thinking aloud, reading diary or letter)?
- to audience (narration, interview, prepared statement)?
- other situations?

EDITING

What will motivate each cut?

- is there an action match to carry the cut?
- is there a compositional relationship between the two shots that makes the cut interesting and worthwhile?
- is there a movement relationship that carries the cut (for example, cut from car moving left-to-right to boat moving left-to-right)?
- does someone or something leave the frame (making us expect a new frame)?
- does someone or something fill the frame, blanking it out and permitting a cut to another frame that starts blanked and then clears?
- does someone or something enter the frame and demand that we cut to a closer shot?
- are we cutting to follow someone's eyeline, to see what they see?

- is there a sound, or a line, that makes us want to see the source?
- are we cutting to show the effect upon a listener
- what defines the right moment to cut?
- are we cutting to a speaker at a particular moment that is visually revealing? What defines that moment?
- if the cut intensifies our attention, what justifies that?
- if the cut relaxes and objectifies our attention, what justifies that?
- is the cut to a parallel activity (that is, something going on simultaneously)?
- is there some sort of comparison or irony being set up through juxtaposition?
- are we cutting to a rhythm (perhaps of an effect, music, or the cadences of speech)?
- other reasons?

SCHEDULING AND RECONNAISSANCE

- be pessimistic when scheduling; you will never have too much time to shoot
- schedule the early shooting for a slower pace
- arrange contingency alternatives (bad weather, etc.)
- crews need a typewritten schedule with map details and phone contact numbers
- PM should double-check lodging and dining arrangements for locations
- to conserve time, bring food to the unit, not the unit to the food
- check location with a compass to assess available light's direction
- when everyone is in transit, make sure there is a central phone contact
- map out electrical supplies, permissible loadings, circuits, and their fuses

GETTING READY TO SHOOT

- remember to include tools and spares
- for location bring first aid and basic medicine kit
- locate nearest toilets and emergency medical facilities if on location
- research nearest point for repairs, spares, and dealers
- PM should prepare daily cost projection
- make sure everyone knows his or her responsibilities. Every area of the undertaking should fall within someone's responsibility
- establish crew protocols for dealing with actors or the public
- hold a potluck party before shooting so you start out with good morale
- warn actors that shooting is slow, and to bring books, chess, yoga mat, whatever

SHOOTING

- check scene's important points on crib card
- have your act together. Your leadership and leadership style set the tone for the shoot
- delegate directing the crew to your DP
- make the decision for a further take quickly, so everyone stays focused
- make allowances for extreme tension in everyone at the beginning
- cater to creature comforts to keep up morale
- give credit publicly to anyone who deserves it
- use breaks for mending fences and picking up loose ends of information
- have personal exchange with all crew members so you are seen as a personal friend
- script supervisor keeps strict watch over coverage and matching
- sound recordist listens for any inadequate lines, and shoots a wild track
- sound recordist can ask for silence to pick up any atmospheres or sound effects on location
- keep dissent away from ears of actors
- ask your crew when you need advice or help
- do not wrap without shooting reactions, cutaways, and location presence track
- replace locations exactly as you found them
- thank everyone personally at the end of each day
- director and key personnel should confer at day's end to plan next day

MISE-EN-SCÈNE

- remember whose point of view audience should sympathize with, moment to moment
- use camera for active storytelling, not just as a passive observer
- check with DP and camera operator the size and framing for each new shot
- look through camera often to check framing, composition, and image size
- during shot stand close to camera so you see more or less what it is seeing
- make the location a character, not a mere container for action
- try wherever possible to create a sense of depth in the frame
- use characters' eyelines as guides for shooting safety cutaways
- use a particular lens for its dramatic revelation potential as well as to cope with limitations imposed by the shooting environment
- decide whether there is a simpler technical means to achieve the same effect
- consider varying camera height from shot to shot

- decide what the camera can legitimately look through
- slow down or simplify character movements if the camera is to follow them

DIRECTING ACTORS

- give actors private, personal feedback and encouragement from time to time
- be careful to be egalitarian toward actors and not to let your preferences or antipathies show
- make each character active in his or her own surroundings
- each situation must reveal something about the characters through behavior
- make sure each character has plenty to do, externally or internally, to avoid self-consciousness
- remind actors often where, emotionally and physically, their character is coming from
- be natural so you do not signal to actors that it is a scare situation
- support, question, and challenge. Make lots of interesting demands
- feed in the unexpected and side coach when a scene needs refreshing

AUTHORSHIP AND MONITORING PROGRESS

- hear and see the scene's actual subtext, not what you want it to say
- make sure each beat is clear so the dialectics of the scene become evident
- cover exposition and other vital points more than one way
- examine the imprint a take has left on you: what life roles were played out? What came from the characters this particular time? What truths emerged?
- check your crib card to see what is being gained and what needs bolstering
- be sensitive to the scene's hidden meaning and energy, and allow it to exert the appropriate control
- expect always to have missed something good. What have you missed this time?
- make sure you have on film the necessary confrontations inherent in your movie's system of issues
- see rushes as soon as possible and more than once. Let them act on you. Don't try to see what should be there. Do let yourself see what is there that you didn't expect (sometimes there are nice surprises!)

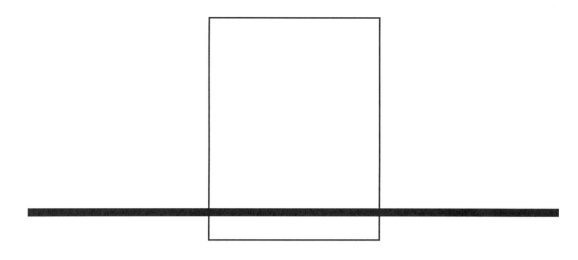

P·A·R·T   VII

POSTPRODUCTION

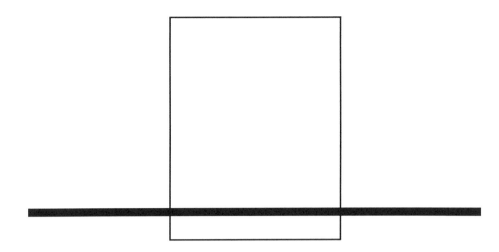

PREPARING TO EDIT

Most of the operations described in this chapter are the editor's responsibility, but a director must know post-production procedures in order to get the best film from the editing stage. Editing is not just assembly, it is like getting a successful performance from an imperfect and incomplete composer's score. This requires one to see, listen, adapt, imagine as one tries to fulfill something to the best of its potential.

EDITING: FILM OR VIDEO?

For speed, good coverage, and inexpensive results onscreen, the beginning director should attempt the first sophisticated work in videotape rather than film. Video equipment of all kinds is being rapidly developed so it would be imprudent to make specific recommendations in this book. However, some generalized information about editing in either medium will be useful.

Few independent filmmakers edit on their own equipment because it is too costly to purchase. Instead, one either rents editing time or talks one's way into being allowed access to free facilities. Quite sophisticated and underutilized equipment may be found at small TV stations and in audiovisual departments in hospitals, police departments, universities, and high schools. You can also rent time from a production house (more expensive) or from a film or video cooperative. Cooperatives are good because they hold prices down and provide a center of activities for like-minded people.

If you can find none of the above, do not despair. It is not unusual for the owner of a commercial operation to allow someone dedicated and impoverished to use the equipment during downtime, either at no cost or for a very modest sum. A surprising number of hard-bitten media types have a soft spot for the committed novice, and many an unlikely partnership has developed from such an initial relationship.

Film has one devastatingly simple advantage over linear tape editing; any part of an edited workprint can be substituted, transposed, or adjusted for length, so long as you remember to make appropriate adjustments to its corresponding sound track. The situation is radically different for linear videotape because it is built up as a series of additions. To shorten the length of an early shot, for instance, means either lengthening the following shot by the deleted amount, or retransferring absolutely everything subsequent to the change.

However, with nonlinear editing the video situation improves radically. After film or tape material is digitized and recorded on a computer hard disk, it can then be called up, assembled, transposed, slowed, speeded up, dissolved, or frozen at will. Everything imaginable can be done with the speed and facility of words in a word processor. While the Avid system is already highly practical and is rendering film editing obsolete, it is expensive and beyond the reach of the independent. Other more modestly priced systems are in development but have yet to prove themselves fully practical. Adobe Premiere for instance works well and has an incredible array of capabilities, but needs a huge hard drive, and a very fast and capacious computer to function without delays for material longer than a few minutes. Part of the problem is that too many systems try to be all things to all users, and end up so internally complex that the system gobbles up memory or must build interminable preview files. They are also maddeningly idiosyncratic to learn and to use, since one must know a lot about the program's housekeeping in order to ration its memory efficiently.

Plainly most of these problems will be solved within two to five years, and low budget filmmakers may soon be using a digital camcorder and a desktop computer for the complete production cycle. We are not there yet, so here's a roundup of the more traditional modes of postproduction.

A POSTPRODUCTION OVERVIEW

Postproduction is that phase of filmmaking in which the raw materials of sound and picture rushes are transformed into the film seen by the audience. Supervised by the editor, both film and video postproduction include the following:

1. For film or double system video recording, synchronizing sound with action.
2. Screening rushes for the director's choices and comments.
3. Marking up the editing script.
4. Logging material in preparation for editing.
5. Making a first assembly.
6. Making the rough cut.
7. Evolving the rough cut into a fine cut.
8. Supervising narration or looping (postsynchronized voice recording).

9. Preparing for and supervising original music recording.

10. Finding, recording, and laying component parts of multitrack sound.

11. Supervising mix-down of these tracks into one smooth final track.

12. Supervising shooting of titles and necessary graphics.

13. Supervising the film lab or video postproduction finalization processes.

In **film** this involves laboratory work to produce a fine-quality release print for projection, including

- conforming (or negative cutting; the original negative is cut and reassembled to match the workprint so that fresh prints may be struck for release)
- having a sound optical negative made by the laboratory from the sound magnetic master. This combined with the picture produces a composite or married print
- timing (or color grading) the picture negative in association with the DP in order to produce the first answer (or trial) print, and
- producing multiple release prints

In **linear video** there are processes analogous to films for producing a broadcast quality tape. After the off-line editing has produced an edit decision list (EDL) the production is ready for on-line editing. A computer controlled rig is used to assemble a high-quality version of the film from camera original cassettes. This matches the much degraded and almost unviewable workprint. This process is the video equivalent of the film process's conforming or negative cutting. It includes:

- timebase correction (electronic processing to ensure the resulting tape conforms to broadcasting standards)
- color correction
- copy duplication for release prints

When **nonlinear video** post-production is used, the camera original material has to be digitized, stored in a computer hard drive, and assembled as segments laid along a time line. Some of the features of nonlinear (digital) editing are:

- a small, poor grade image permits faster handling and a greater amount of material kept in storage
- a full screen image at 30fps (25 in Europe) consumes more memory and pushes the computer to the maximum
- some systems are capable of near-broadcast quality output—plainly the direction of the future since this abolishes the need for on-line editing and all its time and expense
- multiple sound tracks can be laid and levels predetermined so one can listen to a layered and sophisticated track even while editing

- the more sophisticated systems output an EDL which can then be fed into a linear system's computer to make a conventional on-line master
- editing is vastly quicker
- all versions can be stored on disk (as files of access numbers) so earlier or alternative versions can be reviewed at any time
- film editors love these systems for their speed and flexibility

THE EDITOR'S ROLE AND RESPONSIBILITIES

From the number and complexity of the postproduction processes you can see how important the editor is both technically and creatively. For this reason the most common path to directing is by way of being an editor first.

DIPLOMACY

The editor receives the director when the latter is in a state of considerable anxiety and uncertainty, for the film though shot has yet to prove itself. At this time most directors, however confident they appear, are morbidly aware of their material's failures. Many suffer a sort of postnatal depression in the trough following the sustained impetus of shooting. If the editor and director do not know each other well, both will usually be formal and cautious. The editor is taking over the director's baby, and the director often carries mixed and potentially explosive emotions.

PERSONALITY

The good editor is patient, highly organized, ready to experiment endlessly, and diplomatic about trying to get his or her own way.

CREATIVE CONTRIBUTION

The editor's job goes far beyond the physical task of assembly, and the good editor—really a person of author caliber working from given materials—is highly aware of the material's possibilities. Directors are handicapped in this area through over-familiarity with their own intentions. Not being present at shooting, the editor comes on the scene with an unobligated and unprejudiced eye, and is ideally placed to reveal to the director what possibilities or problems lie dormant within the material.

On a documentary production, or an improvised fiction film, the editor is really the second director, since the materials supplied are usually capable of broad interpretation. Putting it more crudely, they are inherently entertaining but lack design. Unlike a scripted production, editing requires that the editor often make responsible subjective judgments. But even in a tightly scripted fiction film the editor needs the insight and confidence to know when to bend the original intentions to better serve the film's underlying goals. Editing is always far more than following a script, just as music is much more than playing the right notes. Composing is in fact the closest analogy to the editor's work.

RUSHES

Feature films usually employ the editor from the start of shooting, so the unit's output can be assembled as fast as it is shot. With low-budget films, however, economics may prevent cutting until everything is shot. This is risky because errors and omissions surface when it is too late to rectify them. One should therefore try to arrange to see dailies. Shooting on video allows rushes to be viewed immediately, so that any reshooting can be scheduled before quitting the location. Many 35mm feature film cameras now make a simultaneous video recording, which allows instant replay and mitigates the unit's absolute dependency upon the script supervisor's powers of observation. The low-budget filmmaker will have no such luxury, but if rushes can be synchronized at home base they can be transferred from the editing machine screen to VHS tape at minimal cost, and seen at the location on a VCR.

PARTNERSHIP

Relationships between directors and editors vary greatly according to the chemistry of status and temperaments, but it is usual for the director to discuss the intentions behind each scene, and to give any necessary special directions.

The editor then sets to work on making the assembly, which is a first raw version of the film. Wise directors leave the cutting room during this period in order to return with a fresh eye for what the editor produces. The obsessive director on the other hand will sit in the cutting room night and day watching the editor's every action. Whether this is at all an amenable arrangement depends on the editor. Some like to be able to debate their way through the cutting procedure. Most prefer being left alone to work out the film's initial problems in bouts of intense concentration over their logs and equipment.

In the end, very little escapes discussion; every scene and every cut is scrutinized, questioned, weighed, and balanced. The creative relationship is intense, often drawing in all the cutting room staff and the producer. The editor must often use delicate but sustained leverage against what he or she senses are those prejudices and fixations that grip every director. Ralph Rosenblum's book *When the Shooting Stops* demonstrates just how varied and even crazy editor/director relationships can be.

DIRECTOR/EDITORS

In a low-budget movie the editor and director are for economic reasons sometimes the same person. This is particularly hazardous for the inexperienced. Another mind in creative tension with the director is an inestimable asset, insuring against an early tumble into the abyss of subjectivity. Because every film is created as an experience for an audience, the director needs the steadying and detached influence of an editor, or that director never gets any distance on the material, and falls prey to subjective familiarity with it. Cuts will get shorter and shorter, and scenes will be interwoven to the point where only the film's progenitors can still understand it. Sometimes this is an indulgent love relationship, but more often it is a self-flagellating dislike in which the director/editor puts the film through contortions in the attempt to mask its imagined deformities.

Sometimes a director will personally edit because he or she was formerly an editor and cannot trust anyone else to "do it properly"; sometimes the director is imbued with the *auteur* theory, and edits believing this will preserve a unified artistic identity for the film. Such impulses signal insecurities about maintaining control. This personality sometimes has great difficulty absorbing criticism, seeing it as an attack on his or her artistic autonomy.

In truth, the scrutiny of the emerging work by an equal, the editor's advocacy of alternative views, and collaboration itself all tend to help produce a tougher and better balanced film than any one person can generate alone. Reflect on this: you may not be the exception.

PREPARING TO EDIT

Working with a professional editor can be intimidating if you do not know what the many procedures are for. All are either necessary or save time and effort, thus allowing the editor to edit instead of search for lost footage.

SYNCING RUSHES

It is beyond the scope of this book to describe the technical process of film rushes syncing, other than to say that the two strips of film—the picture marked at the point where the clapper board bar has just closed, and the sound track marked at the clapper bar's impact—are aligned in a synchronizer or table editor so that discrete takes can be cumulatively assembled for a sync viewing. Every respectable filmmaking manual covers this process (see Bibliography).

KEEPING A RUSHES BOOK

When assembling rushes for either a film or video viewing, make a rushes book, that is, a preparatory log of slate and take numbers. It should be a sturdy notebook in which you divide the pages by sequences and use one line per take. Take scene, slate, and take numbers from the camera log and leave columns for film edge numbers (or video time code numbers) and blank space for cryptic notes during the rushes viewing. Figure 32-1 shows a completed section of the rushes book.

```
                    LAUNDRY SEQUENCE
 1-1  NVG
  -2  End good for David
  -3  Best, but focus change NG (slow)
 2-1  Safety cutaway only
 3-1  NG
  -2  Fair (Liz has interesting dreamy reaction to bad news)
   3  Liz angriest - try to use
   4  Best for consistency - David's reaction best in T2
```

FIGURE 32-1 ——

Typical rushes book notes.

CREW RUSHES VIEWING SESSION

At the completion of shooting, though rushes have been viewed piecemeal, try to let the crew see their work in its entirety. This is how everyone can learn the most for the future, which is important particularly if you expect to work with the same crew again. Screening may have to be broken up into more than one session, since four hours or so of unedited footage is about the longest even the dedicated can maintain concentration. The editor may be present at this viewing, but discussion is likely to be a crew-centered postmortem rather than one useful to the editor.

EDITOR AND DIRECTOR'S VIEWING SESSION

If at the end of shooting nothing has been edited, there should be a rushes showing with the director. It is probably best to assemble the rushes in scene order. Run one sequence at a time, and stop to discuss its problems and possibilities. The editor will need the rushes book (see above) to record the director's choices and to note any special cutting information.

A marathon rushes viewing highlights the relativity of the material and the problems you face for the piece as a whole. You might discover that certain mannerisms are used repeatedly by one actor, and must be cut around during editing if he or she is not to appear phony. Or you might discover that one of your two principals is often more interesting to watch and threatens to unbalance the film.

GUT FEELINGS MATTER

Note down any unexpected mood or feeling. If, during the rushes viewing, you find yourself reacting to a particular character with, "She seems unusually sincere here," then note it down. These are seldom isolated personal reactions. Many gut feelings seem so logically unfounded that it is tempting to ignore or forget them.

Yet what triggered them remains embedded in the material for any first-time audience.

The spontaneous perceptions you note down will be a useful resource when inspiration lags later from over-familiarity with the material. If you fail to commit them in some form to paper, they are likely to share the fate of important dreams, which evaporate if you do not preserve them.

TAKING NOTES

It is useful to have someone present who can take these dictated notes. Try never to let your attention leave the screen, as you can easily miss important moments and nuances.

REACTIONS

There will probably be debates over the effectiveness, meaning, or importance of different parts of the filming, and different crew members may have opposing feelings about the credibility and motivation of some of the characters. Listen rather than argue, for these may be the reactions of your future audience. Remember that crew members are far from objective viewers. They are disproportionately critical of their own discipline and may overvalue its positive or negative effect.

THE ONLY FILM IS IN THE RUSHES

The sum of the rushes viewing is a notebook full of choices and observations (both the director's and those of the editor), and a fragmentary impression of the movie's potential and deficiencies. Absolutely *nothing beyond what can be seen and felt from the rushes is any longer relevant* to the film you are making. The script is a historic relic, like an old map to a rebuilt city. Put it away in the attic for your biographer. You and your editor must find a film in the rushes.

Now that you confront the rushes, you have changed hats. You are no longer the instigator of the material but a surrogate for the audience. Empty yourself of prior knowledge and intentions; your understanding and emotions must come wholly from the screen. Nobody in the cutting room wants to hear about what you intended or what you meant to produce. Keep that for your grandchildren.

SYNC CODING (FILM)

This film process is also known as edge numbering or Dupont numbering. After the rushes have been viewed (to ensure that they are indeed in sync), a film laboratory prints yellow ink numbers every foot or half-foot. Sync code numbers, printed in parallel on both sound and picture, function as unique, unambiguous sync marks, allowing original sync to be restored at any time. Recorded in a log, they also allow almost any length of anonymous-looking film to be reunited with its parent trims or off-cuts.

POOR MAN'S SYNC CODING (FILM)

Because edge coding is expensive and not strictly necessary, subsistence-level film-makers handwrite numbers on the workprint rushes, sound and picture, every three feet or so. Use a three-foot loop in the synchronizer as an interval guide.

TIME CODING AND WINDOW DUB (VIDEO)

When shooting on video, a time coded camera original and a window dub are necessary if you are to later use on-line (computerized) postproduction editing. Time code is either generated at the time of recording and electronically interwoven with the video signal, or (more usual in small-format recorders) the camera original is time coded after shooting. In this process, a digital time code is written in a special vacant area called an address track, or in whichever sound track was unused. If you can choose the time code, start each new cassette from a unique hour number rather than always from zero, that way no two time codes in your rushes are the same.

CAUTION: Be sure you have clearly marked on each cassette which sound track is free or you may lose original sound.

Next make a window dub or window burn-in. This is copy cassette made from each original tape with the time code displayed visually at the bottom of the frame in a window as cassette number, hours, minutes, seconds, and frames (see Figure 32-2). Every frame in your production now has an individual identifying set of numbers, necessary for on-line editing.

FIGURE 32-2 ――――――――――

Time-coded video frame.

DIGITAL EDITING FROM FILM RUSHES

The trend now is to digitize film rushes and to edit on an Avid or D/Vision type of non-linear computer rig. This requires that the picture has its own time code (called KeyCode™) since the resulting EDL will be used to conform, or match-edit, the camera original. There is no margin for error here; once the original is physically cut there is no going back. Film editors, once they have mastered the intricacies of the software program, love the new speed and flexibility. No more filing trims, no more splicing and handling lengths of recalcitrant footage. Alternate versions can be recalled, and a complete sound track can be roughed out before making final judgments.

There is one tricky aspect. With a system that transfers 24 fps of film to 30fps or 60 fields per second of video, you end up with four film frames being represented by five video frames. The process may be complicated by PAL and NTSC equipment that runs at different frame rates, and film cameras that run at either 24fps or 25fps according to whether the material is destined for either American or other TV systems. If you edit on a phantom frame, it can only be approximated at the conforming stage. This means that if your sound track has been completely prepared in the digital mode, over a succession of cuts involving a succession of phantom frames you may accumulatively gain or lose time. Put bluntly, your track may drift out of sync with the conformed film.

Make sure the person handling the equipment is thoroughly aware of the need for clarity about pulldown mode in digitization, and how to avoid unwanted consequences. There is a good description of all this in Thomas Ohanian's *Digital Nonlinear Editing* (Boston: Focal Press, 1993 pp. 279–281). If you think it looks like video's resurrection of the "how many angels can dance on the point of a pin" debate, remember that the consequences of ignoring the problem are dire.

LOGGING THE RUSHES

In any log, since scenes will be shot (and therefore logged) out of order, it is a good idea to start each new sequence on a fresh page so it can eventually be filed in script order. If you type your log into a database, the computer can do the shuffle for you and print in scene order.

In film, every new camera start receives a new clapper board number (see Chapter 28, "Shot and Scene Identification" for a fuller explanation of different marking systems). The clapper exists so the editor can easily synchronize the separately recorded picture and sound. The board usually includes a script scene number, camera setup and take numbers.

In video, since picture and sound are usually recorded alongside each other on the same tape, no syncing up is necessary and a simpler marking system can be employed. Scene numbers (and clapper boards) are not even strictly necessary because videotape editing methods do not permit working materials to be physically uncoupled. While film beginnings and ends are defined by edge or KeyCode™ numbers, video is defined by time code. Logging permits you to trace any piece of action or sound back to its parent take.

THE FILM EDITING LOG

The film editing log may have to facilitate easy access to thousands of small rolls of film. The filing system and the log format will depend upon the editing equipment in use. If an upright Moviola—still the fearsome workhorse of some cutting rooms—is to be used, the workprint will be broken down into individual takes, and filed numerically in cans or drawers. If a table editor such as Steenbeck, Kem, or flatbed Moviola is used, the editor is more likely to withdraw selected sections from large rolls, each containing materials for a single scene. Even then, practice will depend on the work preferences of the editor. If large rolls are used, film logs may be organized like videocassette logs to reflect what is to be found cumulatively in that particular rushes roll.

Film, using separate sound and picture in the cutting room, requires that you log photographic edge numbers and the inked-on sync code numbers (or hand-applied sync code numbers) for the beginning and end of each take. Figure 32-3 is a typical film log entry for script scene 29. A log like this is a mine of useful information. We can see how many takes were attempted, how long (and therefore complete) each scene and each take were, where to find particular takes in camera original rolls if you need to make reprints, even at what points the camera magazine was changed and which magazines started a new day.

The Video Editing Log

The video editing log is a set of cumulative timecode numbers that allows the editor to quickly locate the right piece of action in a cassette that may hold from 20 to 120 minutes of action. It gives the starting point for each new scene and take. Descriptions should be brief and serve only to remind someone knowing the material what to expect. Note that the log (see Figure 32-4) records function, not quality; there is no attempt to add the qualitative notes from the rushes book. To do so would overload the page and make it hard to use.

The figures at the left are minutes and seconds, but might be cumulative numbers from the digital counter on your player deck. When materials are time-coded log by the code displayed in the electronic window.

Scene	Edge #	Sync Code #	Cam Roll	Sound Roll	Date
29-1-1	29J6 434114- 158	000 - 018	14	6	13 Aug 87
2	434159- 207	019 - 038	"	"	"
3	434208- 222	039 - 050	"	"	"
29-2-1	34Z7 945781- 879	051 - 099	15	"	"
2	945880- 904	100 - 151	"	"	"
29-3-1	945905- 965	153 - 186	"	7	"
2	945966- 971	187 - 193	"	"	"
3	945972-6034	194 - 224	"	"	"
29-4-1	21X3 100676- 771	225 - 277	9	MOS	14 Aug 87

FIGURE 32-3 —————————————————————————————

Typical film log book entries.

```
              Cassette 12 SCENE 15: HOTEL LOBBY (NIGHT)

00:00    43-1   WS Henry entering hotel lobby.
00:31     2
00:59     3
01:41    44-1   MS Henry seen through palm tree.
01:51     2
02:24     3
03:02     4
03:35     5        (uses whip pan)
03:54    45-1   CS clerk's hands writing.
04:17    46-1   MCS clerk's face as he works. Stops, smelling smoke.
04:46     2
05:11    47-1   Phone grabbed (4 rounds)
```

FIGURE 32-4 ——

Typical videocassette log entries.

In the log examples there are a number of standard abbreviations for shot terminology which are listed in the glossary. Rule a dividing line between sequences and give the sequence a heading in bold writing. Since the log exists to help quickly locate material, any divisions, indexes, or color codes you can devise will assist the eye in making selections and ultimately save time. This is especially true for a production with many hours of rushes.

MARKING UP THE SCRIPT

When logging is complete, the editor is ready to prepare the script. Each page of the script should end up looking like Figure 32-5. Although the editor's markings appear to duplicate the shooting script (see Figure 27-1) they are made in the peace of the cutting room and reflect only the chosen takes—footage that finally and definitively exists in the cutting room. At a glance the editor can see from the bracketing and notations what angles exist for every moment of the scene, and which takes were considered best. This greatly speeds up assessing alternative cover during the lengthy period of refining the cut. When problem-solving, graphic representation rather than thickets of verbiage save untold time and energy.

To mark up the script, view the rushes for each scene looking at one camera setup at a time. Note that a change of lens is treated as a new setup, for although the camera may not be physically moved, the framing and composition will have changed. Each setup is represented as a line bracketing what the angle covers. Shots that continue over the page end in an arrow. Leave a space in the line and neatly write in the scene number, all its takes (circling those chosen), and the briefest possible shot description. More detailed information can now be quickly found in the continuity reports or rushes book.

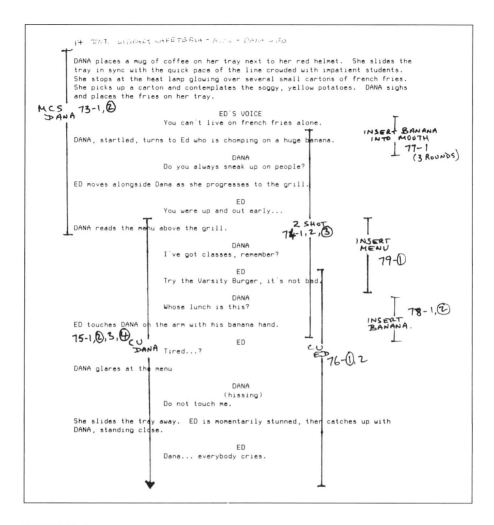

FIGURE 32-5

Editor's script marked up with rushes coverage.

C·H·A·P·T·E·R 33

EDITING THE FIRST ASSEMBLY

THE PHYSICAL PROCESS FOR FILM

MACHINERY

For those unused to handling film, the best editing machine is undoubtedly one of the excellent flatbed table editors such as the Steenbeck (Figure 33-1). It keeps sound and picture in constant sync but allows either to be moved in relation to the other. Sound and picture are simply spliced into the left hand side of the film's passage through the machine.

SOUND TRACK EVOLUTION

Until the fine-cut stage, the sound track is dialogue only, assembled into a single track. This is a temporary compromise, for within a single sequence several mike positions may be cut together and the sound may vary in level and quality. Since the priority at this stage is to achieve a correct dramatic balance, the simplest assembly method is used to allow rapid changes during the lengthy and experimental business of achieving a fine cut. Many table editors permit two or more sound tracks, but editorial changes are proportionately slower when you have more than one sound track to adjust.

Once a fine cut is achieved, dialogue tracks are split apart into separate tracks to allow the appropriate control over each mike position. Sound effects (FX), music, and atmosphere tracks will be laid as appropriate. Some sequences may need

FIGURE 33-1

Steenbeck flatbed table editing machine.

postsynchronizing (also known as looping, automatic dialogue replacement, or ADR) because the original dialogue tracks, perhaps recorded by an expressway, are insufficiently intelligible.

A mix chart is made of all tracks laid, since the sound editor will probably have laid extra tracks to allow for experimental alternatives. Editor, chart, and tracks then go to a sound studio where specialists make the final mix under the director's and editor's guidance. The final mix determines much of the film's artistic effectiveness with an audience.

PICTURE EVOLUTION

The final-cut workprint picture will eventually go to a conformer, who very carefully cuts the camera original (nowadays a negative, but formerly quite often a reversal original) to exactly match what is by now a very tired and beaten up workprint. The conforming process uses cement splices, which require an overlap. While the workprint was butt-spliced with a tape splicer, cement splicers need an overlap and therefore lose frames of camera original whenever a splice is made. While editing film workprint, therefore, *never use adjacent shots without dropping out three frames between them.* These unused workprint frames will ensure that extra frames exist in the camera original to allow cement splice overlaps. Keep the three frames from the workprint (in a "Cutlet" can) in case during editing you later decide to reconstitute the two shots back into one.

CAUTION: Be very clear about this; never using adjacent footage without a minimum of three frames separation allows a conformer to edit the camera original to the butt-spliced workprint. Nothing else will work.

In the lab a photographic sound track is made from the magnetic master, ready to combine with the picture. The A and B rolls of negative are first timed or graded (color- and exposure-graded) then contact-printed. The print stock passes three times through the contact printer to print (1) picture A roll, (2) picture B roll (alternate scenes printed in A roll spaces), and (3) sound negative (sound photographically printed on the edge of the film).

Occasionally there will be additional picture rolls, should titling or subtitling require it. The A/B roll printing process allows a print with no splicing marks showing, with low-cost dissolves and fades.

COMPOSITE PRINTS

The resulting composite print (sound and action) has had adjustments made for inequities of color or exposure in the original and the first print is called the answer print because it demonstrates the viability of these changes. If perfectly acceptable, it becomes the first release print. If further changes are required, they are incorporated into the next answer print. The first acceptable print always becomes the first release print.

FIGURE 33-2

Video editing console.

THE PHYSICAL PROCESS FOR VIDEO

MACHINERY

Linear Editing

The most common format for off-line video editing machines was 3/4″ U-Matic, but 1/2″ VHS editing and more lately Hi8 have become standards. If you shoot in one format and want to edit in another, you simply dub (electronically transfer) from one to the other before editing. Though there is some quality loss especially in picture from one generation to the next, this is a minor consideration since off-line editing leads to final "conforming" by way of an on-line postproduction edit. When you become competent to shoot material for broadcasting, you will need to research the current minimum requirements for each link of the chain; that is, for camera, recorder, editing, time base correction, online, and so on.

Nonlinear Editing

The professional standard is presently the Avid configuration, which uses a Macintosh computer, digitizing card, and a mammoth hard drive as the center of its operations. Many competitors such as D/Vision and Lightworks are in the wings. Since everything in picture and sound is retrieved by numbers, you will need a good logging system to keep track of your materials. The system should put out an EDL for eventual on-lining, but the most advanced systems are rapidly

FIGURE 33-3

Avid Media Composer editing setup. Copyright 1995, Avid Technology, Inc.

approaching broadcast quality. When and if High Definition Television (HDTV) comes along, all video equipment will become obsolete at a stroke. Picture is likely to be originated in film, at least for a while, but some form of nonlinear editing will continue to be used and will be refined to make it as user-friendly as possible.

EDITING MECHANICS

Linear

Linear or cassette-to-cassette editing is quite simple in principle and the mechanics do not take long to master. Essentially it is the progressive transfer of sections from one machine to another. You pick an out-point to material already cut, and then determine in and out-points for the new section to be added on. On pressing the review button, your rig will line up the already recorded and the new material at their cutting points, and in a review pass will let you see how your choice of cut looks and sounds. If you are satisfied and want to record it, you hit the record button and magically, the machine will once again back up, stop, roll forward for five to ten seconds of preroll, and go into record mode at the prearranged cutting point. You see it all on the monitor: the last seconds of previously compiled material, and then the new segment cut onto the old.

With time-code driven machines, you get frame accurate editing and each preview is the same. With control-track editing (where the machine syncs to a count of the sine wave control track) editing decisions are plus or minus a few frames. Worse, as you preview, the decision point may drift even further.

Nonlinear or Digital

Nonlinear or digital editing requires that you learn a whole software program having a long, slow learning curve if you are to know all the program's capabilities. The advantage is in speed of execution and in sound quality. Virtually any imaginable experiment with your footage can be tried in minutes or seconds if you know how to use the program. The best editors are said to be those who learned their aesthetics from film, but film editors seem to be unanimously approving of non-linear's advantages.

SOUND CONSIDERATIONS

Figure 33-4 shows in diagrammatic form how sound in a linear setup is transferred from the feed deck to the recorder. The same process takes place inside a non-linear program, but you use a keyboard and mouse to position an edit point. For sound there is even a graphic representation of the sound track's modulations to show you precisely where sounds and even syllables begin and end, just as one could once see when photographic sound was used before the days of magnetic recording. Non-linear picture and sound tracks are arranged on a time line much as though you were looking down on a set of film tracks laid out in a gang-synchronizer. The system is graphic and allows for level setting and in some systems, equalization settings as well. It is the sound designer's dream.

In my illustration of a generic linear editing setup (Figure 33-4) I have assumed that the original tape was a two-microphone setup, with each mike's output appearing on a separate track. The two tracks are adjusted for level (or volume) at the mixing board, and the mixed result is routed to the recorder. At the

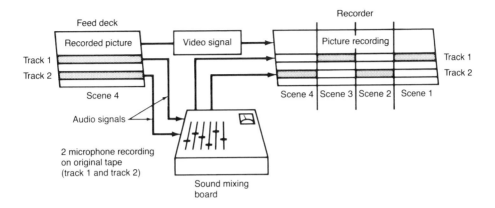

FIGURE 33-4 ───

Two-track dialogue recording mixed and transferred in checkerboard fashion to allow sound mix-down later.

mixing board, you send the mixed track alternately to track 1 and track 2, scene by scene, in checkerboard fashion. At a later stage (Figure 33-5) these individual scenes' tracks can be further mixed down and equalized (made consistent through adjustment of individual tone controls). When also adjusted by level you should get a smooth, seamless sound mix. Figure 33-5 includes a cassette player supplying a nonsync atmosphere (might be wind, traffic, or TV sound coming from an adjacent motel room).

Figure 33-5 shows how at each recording stage two tracks are combined into one. This always leaves an unused track on the newly recorded tape, on which you can in a subsequent pass record additional materials for a further mix. Each stage prior to the final mix is called a premix.

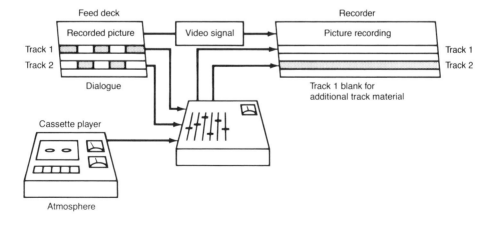

FIGURE 33-5 ───

Checkerboarded tracks mixed with atmosphere track and recorded as a premix.

In non-linear programs one is not limited to two tracks. Adobe Premiere generously provides up to 99 sound tracks. However I suspect that the computer has yet to be produced that could process more than 20 without skipping.

MINIMIZING GENERATIONAL LOSSES

Sound

In analogue recording (that is, nondigital audio) repeated audio premixes as in Figure 33-6 lead to a generational deterioration audible as an increased hiss level and diminished fidelity. It is possible to download tracks into a multitrack recorder using time code. A sync chasing mechanism keeps the multitrack machine, probably a DAT (digital audio tape) recorder/player, in sync with the videotape. Generational loss is kept to a minimum and 24 tracks or more can be mixed at one time.

Picture

Generational losses through retransferring analogue video are disturbingly evident, and show up as increasing picture noise (picture break-up) particularly in shadow areas, color shift (particularly red) and a deterioration in color fidelity and overall sharpness. You can, however, shunt a sixth (or any other) generation sound track back onto an earlier generation picture. The last stage is risky because it involves wiping a track from the second generation combined picture and sound cassette, and replacing it with the sixth generation mix, starting from a common sync start mark.

CAUTION: Practice with unimportant copy tapes before you take risks with vital materials.

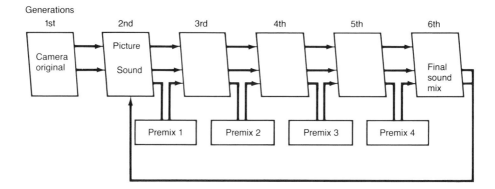

FIGURE 33-6

A succession of video premixes leading to a final sound mix. This is dubbed back onto second-generation picture (caution—see text).

OPTICALS

Rather sophisticated equipment is needed to do picture dissolves and wipes, and fairly advanced electronics are needed to do title and other superimpositions. However, it is perfectly possible to make a professional film without these optical effects. Having access only to a basic editing machine need not hold you back in any significant way.

TIME CODE: ON-LINE AND OFF-LINE EDITING

As described in the previous chapter, time-coding provides every frame of picture and sound with its own unique time code number. The time-code display is likely to show cassette number, hours, minutes, seconds, and frames. The window dub, a copy of the camera original where the time code is displayed in a window (see Figure 32-2), is used as the editing master copy to preserve the camera original from any undue use. The window, with its time-code, copies through to subsequent editing generations. Most importantly, it lets you dub from one generation to another, knowing that when cutting is complete you can make an EDL (edit decision log) from the screen and then use a computerized (on-line) editing setup to recover the sound or action from in the camera original tapes, and to reconstruct a pristine copy. On-line editing is expensive compared with off-line, and the whole process is only economically viable if you have good reason to aim for broadcast quality.

EDITING CONCEPTS

Basic editing can be self-taught using common sense, but both basics and the further reaches of sophistication can be better learned from a detailed analysis of finished films (see Chapter 5, Project 2: "Editing Analysis"). You should also carry out the hands-on shooting and editing projects designed to develop particular skills (Chapter 6, Shooting Fundamentals). What follows here is an overview of the conceptual process.

THE FIRST ASSEMBLY

Putting the material together for the first time is the most exciting part of editing. Don't worry at this stage about length or balance. Experimental adaptation to what you discover is everything. To make a first assembly, work on one scene at a time and put the film together in whatever order is convenient, as follows:

1. Run all the material for the scene to refresh your memory.
2. Referring to the editor's marked-up script, figure out how the coverage might best be assembled. At this stage, use a lot of the master shot, and do not bother yet with closeups or with double-cutting (repeatedly cutting between, say, two speakers when single cuts would adequately relay the action). Nor

should you use any overlap cutting (where a speaker's dialogue, for instance, overlaps the listener before the listener replies).

3.   Assemble the simplest version that is faithful to the script, avoiding any questionable changes in the actors' pacing.

SEE A ROUGH DRAFT FIRST

I believe one should see the whole film as soon as possible in a long, loose form before doing detailed work on any sections. Of course, you will be longing to go to work on a favorite sequence, but fixing details would be avoiding the need to assess the film's overall identity and purpose. Once you have seen the whole ungainly epic, you can make far-reaching resolutions about its future development. These may have to do with performances, pacing, parallel storytelling, structure, or overall meaning. Remember, whatever you originally intended is now irrelevant. This viewing is where you come to terms with what is, and consign to history what was meant to be.

FIRST ASSEMBLY VIEWING

NO INTERRUPTIONS

Run the first assembly without stopping and without interruption of any kind. Make no notes because this will take your attention from the screen. You want to look at the film as an audience would. Someone should "ride gain," that is, adjust sound levels for the smoothest effect.

WHAT DO YOU HAVE?

The assembly viewing will yield some important realizations about the character, dramatic shape and best length of the film. Fundamental issues are now out of the closet. You will sense an overall slowness, that scenes include unnecessary exposition, or hang on beyond a good ending point. You may find you have a film with two endings, one false and one intended, or that one character is unexpectedly stronger than another. A sequence you shot in miserably cold conditions by a river at night turns out to stall the story's advance, and ought to be dropped.

The first assembly is the departure point for the denser and more complex film to come. As a show it is long and crude, yet despite its artlessness it can be affecting and exciting.

RUN THE FILM A SECOND TIME

Now run the film again to confirm original impressions. After further discussion with your editor, collaborate in making a list of aims for each sequence, arranging them by priority.

DIAGNOSTIC QUESTIONING

To question the imprint the film has made and to predict a likely audience response, one must view the film as if seeing it for the first time. At this point one is dealing with the film in its crudest form, so the aim is to methodically elicit one's own dominant reactions.

A useful strategy after seeing an assembly is to rapidly list the memorable material. Now refer to the script and make a second list of whatever you omitted. The human memory discards quite purposefully what it does not find meaningful. All that good stuff you could not recall was forgotten because it simply did not work. This does not mean it can never work, only that it is not doing so at present.

Why does material not deliver? Here are some possible reasons, each suggesting a different solution.

- writing is poor in comparison with other sequences. (Cut the whole scene? Shorten? Rewrite and reshoot?)

- acting is at fault. (Dramatic rhythms are too predictable, actors are not in character or in focus. Help but not cure is available in further editing.)

- scene outcome is predictable. (Scene structure at fault? Too long or too slow? Scene in the wrong place?)

- two or more sequences make a similar point. (Repetition does not advance a film's argument unless there is escalation, so make choices and ditch the redundant.)

- dramatic intensity plummets. (A useful analogy is the idea of a rising or falling emotional temperature. To see material in its context is to see correct relative temperatures more clearly. If your film is raising the temperature then inadvertently lowering it before the intended peak, the viewer's response is seriously impaired. The transposition of one or two sequences will sometimes work wonders. Naturally, this can only be done if the scenes are not locked into a fixed time development.)

- the viewer is somehow set up by the preceding material to expect something different. (We read film by its context, and if the context gives misleading signals or fails to focus awareness in the right area, the material itself will seem flat.)

These areas of examination are all the kind of dramatic analysis used by a playwright or theater producer during rehearsals of a new work. You use the same considerations when analyzing the first audience reactions. Just as a playwright routinely rewrites and adjusts a work based on audience feedback, the filmmaker makes a vast number of adjustments, large and small, before admitting that a work is finished.

Because a filmmaker has no true audience until the work is finished, assessments are hard to make, and they certainly are not objective. First you dig for your own instincts through feeling the dramatic outcome of your material. Later when you have a fine cut and the material becomes showable, you will call in a few people whose reactions and tastes you respect. You will probably find quite a bit of unanimity in what they tell you.

While still in this assembly stage you and your editor begin by examining your own audience reactions and asking basic questions.

- does the film feel dramatically balanced? (If you have a very moving and exciting sequence in the middle of the film, the rest of the film may seem anticlimactic. Or, you may have a film that seems to circle around for a long while until, suddenly, it starts really moving.)
- when is there a definite feeling of a story unfolding, and when not? (This will help locate impediments in the film's development, so you can analyze why the film stumbles.)
- which parts of the film seem to work?
- which parts drag, and why? (Some of the acting may be better than others. Sometimes the problem is that a scene is wrongly placed or repeats the dramatic contours of a previous one.)
- which of the characters held your attention most, and which the least?
- was there a satisfying alternation of types of material, or was similar material indigestibly clumped together?
- which were the effective contrasts and juxtapositions? Are there more to be found? (Sometimes a sequence does not work because the ground has not been properly prepared, or because there is insufficient contrast in mood with the previous sequence. Variety is as important in storytelling as it is in dining.)
- what metaphorical allusions did you notice your material making? Could it make them more strongly? (That your tale carries a metaphorical charge is as important to your audience as a water table is to pasture.)

PRIORITIZE

When you tackle problems showing up in any cut, arrange them by hierarchy and, just like building a scene in rehearsal, deal only with those of the largest dimension. If the film's structure is at fault, reorder the scenes and run it again without making any refinement to individual scenes. If there is a serious problem of imbalance between two characters who are both major parts, go to work on bringing forward the character presently deficient.

LENGTH

Look to the content of your film itself for guidance over length and pacing. Films have a natural span according to the richness and significance of their content, but the hardest achievement in any art form is the confidence and ability to say a lot through a little. Most beginners' films are agonizingly long and slow, and the advice of professionals on a film's proper length is usually painful but valuable. If you can recognize early that your film should be, say, twenty minutes long at the very most, you can get tough with that forty-minute assembly and make some basic decisions.

STRUCTURE

Most of all you need a good dramatic structure to make the movie into a well-told tale. Bear in mind that a good screenplay does not guarantee a satisfying experience for an audience. Other criteria will come into play as a result of the emotional changes and development brought by the cast and the filming itself. These, not your intentions, are what an audience will actually experience, and these become apparent for the first time—to those who can see. The director is often the one whose vision is most impeded by the film's history.

LEAVE THE EDITOR TO EDIT

Having decided what the next round of changes should be, leave the cutting room until summoned back. Not all editors or directors can work this way but it is important to try. The reason is simple: the editor loses objectivity while correcting the many problems and so will any director who remains present. But a director returning with a fresh eye to see a new cut can tell which changes are a positive development. The director acts throughout as a surrogate audience whose keenest tastes must be satisfied.

C·H·A·P·T·E·R 34

EDITING: FROM ROUGH CUT TO FINE

THE ROUGH CUT VIEWING

The cut following the first assembly is called the rough cut. Here the full range of material is deployed toward goals decided from seeing the assembly. No sequence is yet fine-tuned, but the editor tries to make each sequence occupy its right place and be dramatically successful.

The scrutiny you give this new cut is similar to those previous, and it remains important to deal with the large-scale dimensions first.

- Is there adequate, too little, or too much expository detail?
- is exposition integrated with the action or does the film pause to inform the audience?
- what exposition, if excised, could still be inferred by the audience?
- what exposition could be delayed? (always better to make the audience wonder and wait if you can)
- does the film keep up a sense of momentum throughout?
- where does the momentum falter and why?
- does the film breathe so that, like music, each movement feels balanced and inevitable, or is there a misshapen, unbalanced feel to some parts?
- what material feels redundant?

- how logical and satisfying is the development of each major character?
- is anything misleading or alienating about the characters, and needs fixing?
- is there a satisfying balance between interiors and exteriors? (This often means dealing with a claustrophobia the film generates. Well constructed films alternate between intensity and release much as a person must alternate intimacy with solitude, indoors with outdoors, family with work, day with night, and so on.)
- what is the film's present thematic impact?

After seeing the rough cut a second or third time you might ask more localized questions,

- which sequences could have later in-points and/or earlier out-points? (many scenes are better entered or left in action rather than "opened" and "closed")
- what needs to be done for each character to exert maximum impact, and in which sequences?
- which sequences cry out for special attention to rhythm and pacing?
- how effective is the ending?
- are there false endings before (or worse, after) the true one?

Again, ask the editor to fix only the glaring faults before having another showing.

SEE THE WHOLE FILM

Even if work has been done to two sequences alone, make a practice of running the whole film. A film is like a tent: change one pole height or guy-rope length and stresses change throughout the tent's structure. So examine changes to your film in the context of the whole work, and examine it as a whole when you are ready to make further changes.

THE PROBLEM OF ACHIEVING A FLOW

After you have run your evolving cut a few times, it will begin to strike you more and more as a series of clunky blocks of material, with a distressing lack of flow. Dialogue scenes in particular seem to bog down, being centered as they probably are upon showing each speaker. First there is a block of this speaker, then a block of that speaker, then a block of both, and so on. Even sequences themselves go past in a blocky way, like watching boxcars go past in a goods train, each discrete and joined to its fellows with a plain link device. I think of this kind of editing as "boxcar cutting."

How does one achieve the effortless flow seen in the cinema? To move in this direction we must recall our Concerned Observer principle, and reflect on how human perception functions.

EDITING MIMICS AN OBSERVING CONSCIOUSNESS

How and why we cut between speakers in a dialogue scene is based on what in ordinary life makes our attention shift. This is best seen by examining eye contact and eyeline shifts, which are the outward sign of shifting attention. The practiced editor uses these extensively as an editing foundation but it is important to work from human behavior rather than theory alone.

THE MYTH AND THE REALITY OF EYE CONTACT

Take the commonly dramatized situation of two diners having an intimate conversation. Inexperienced actors play this kind of scene by gazing into each other's eyes as they speak. This is an idea of how people converse, but it is not true to life and gives phony results, either for acting or as a guiding principle for editing. Go to a restaurant and do some sleuthing. What really happens is, as always, far more subtle and interesting. It may be unusual for either person to make eye contact more than fleetingly. The situation varies with the individual and with the situation, but generally we reserve the intensity of eye contact for special moments. Eye contact is usually to

- search out information from the other person's expression before we act on them
- check what effect we are having when we are acting on them
- put additional pressure on the other person as we act on them
- see from their body language or expression what they mean when they are acting on us

In each case we glance only momentarily into the other person's face to rapidly gather information. In subtle ways, each speaker is either pressing, or being pressed. Only at crucial moments does one search the other for facial or behavioral enlightenment. Much of the time the listener's gaze rests upon isolated or neutral objects while mentally focusing on what the other person means. Hearing may be totally focused on the other person for the duration of the conversation. Or, it too may wander. Eyes and ears, as we have said, move their attention independently but are always working together feeding information into the overworked brain.

APPLYING THE ANALOGY TO FILM

Film as we have said is unlike literature because it has difficulty in portraying interior life. But where a person looks and what he sees indicates what he feels, so we can and do show these shifts through editing. This way we can imply a special significance to each moment of change. Through editing choices we do in fact have a powerful tool to *imply* inner lives and *suggest* character contours.

Now play the Concerned Observer role again, but this time being very aware of how your own eyeline shifts between the speakers. Notice how

- you often followed the shifts in their eyelines to see what they were seeing, involuntarily switching your gaze from subject to object
- your mind supplied a possible motivation for each eyeline change
- there is a rhythm to your eyeline changes (controlled by the shifting contours of the conversation itself)
- your eyes also made their own judgment about who and what to look at, often on the basis of something on the periphery that demanded a closer look

Independently, your center of attention switches back and forth, often following the pair's action and reaction, their changes of eyeline, and their physical action, but also making choices based on your own evolving thoughts and judgment, not just on outside stimulation alone.

Notice that *your eyes often leave someone speaking to examine his effect on the listener while he still speaks.* Unconsciously, the Observer edits according to his own developing insight, looking for the most telling information.

To film what you have been observing, you would need to cover each speaker's viewpoint of the other, and a third viewpoint, that encompassing both and representing the perspective of you, the Observer. This last is outside the enclosed consciousness of the two speakers and tends to show them in a more detached, storytelling way. Add two complementary over-shoulder shots and you have complete basic movie coverage.

According to choices made in editing, the audience can either identify with one or other of the characters inside the story, or with the more detached perspective of the invisible Storyteller/Observer. While character A talks, the film might allow the audience to look detachedly at either A or B, to share the perspective of either one upon the other, or to look at both of them in long shot. We have said that the Observer turns into the Storyteller after the Observer's faithful, thoughtful watching (such as you might see in a documentary) becomes a more active, manipulative storytelling that has its own distinct attitudes and expectations of the characters.

Flexibility of viewpoint allows the director to structure not only what the spectator sees, but whose point of view and whose state of mind that spectator shares at any particular moment. *This probing, cinematic way of seeing is modelled upon the way we unconsciously delve, visually and imaginatively, into any event that interests us.* The film narrative process is thus never objective but mimics the selective consciousness of a particular observer. This observer may be an involved character in the film, or may be the Storyteller through whose consciousness the film reaches us.

ALTERING PERFORMANCE RHYTHMS

A very significant dramatic control now rests in the cutting room for any scene that has been adequately covered. This concerns not only who or what is shown at any particular moment, but *how much time each character takes to process what he sees or hears.* This timing originates in the actors but is controlled in the cutting room. It contributes hugely to the power and consistency of a scene's subtext.

THE POWER OF SUBTEXT

Let us take the example of a two-person, interior scene where a man asks a simple question of a woman visiting his apartment for dinner: "Do you think it's cold outside?" Depending on the context this could mean several things. He could be saying,

- "As we're leaving, tell me I don't have to change into heavier clothes."
- "Tell me if you think I will be uncomfortable."
- "What clothes do you think I should wear?"
- "Let's not go to the party after all."
- "Do you want to stay the night with me?"

Depending on context and what has previously happened, any of these implications may be present. How do we the audience judge, or even conceive of these possibilities? How the speaker says the line may tell you a lot, but just as much may be inferred from the listener's reactions. An easy and unreflecting "No" is very different from one that is delivered with more difficulty, or one that is long delayed, indicating an internal struggle or perhaps concern over what may come next.

CONTROL IN EDITING

Subtext is always at risk during shooting. From learning lines and from repetition actors tend to drop into a group rhythm of delivery and reaction time. This levels the characters' inner lives to a shared average. Of course this is deadly, and often needs to be varied to recover the changeableness and unpredictability of spontaneous action. Even when performances are uniformly excellent, there is another reason to want to exert fine control over playing rhythms. Editing the scene makes it acquire its own intensity and point of view. It becomes an entity that nobody could quite foresee. So this too requires fine control over the original rhythms of reply, eyeline changes, action, and reaction.

No editor can change a character's rate of speech or, in an unbroken take, the timing of the character's reactions. But the situation changes radically when the scene is covered from more than one angle or image size. Look at Figure 34-1. Diagram A is a representation of the master take, a timing that the actors reproduced in all subsequent takes. The diagram shows picture and sound as separate strands, much as one sees them while cutting film.

In Example B the cut to close-up simply preserves the actors' original timing, though by using it we expect a greater significance in her reply. Example C uses overlap cutting (see below for extended explanation) to make her reply come as quickly as possible. Example D, however, doubles her reaction time by adding together the pauses from both takes. Example E goes still further by double-cutting her thinking and his waiting reaction before cutting back to her thinking and replying. To create this length of delay you will need a complementary closeup reaction shot on him, and a second take on her from which to steal the extra close shot reaction. By using coverage resourcefully we have considerable choice over reac-

```
!2S: Him                              Her
_____
/  "Do you think it's cold out?"        "No"
_____
                     <----t------>
```

Example A: Master Two-Shot (actors' timing "t" as played)

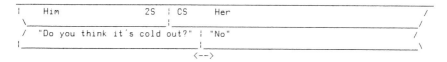

```
\    Him                        2S  ! CS: Her                      !
_____!_____/
/  "Do you think it's cold out?" !     "No"                        !
!_____!_____\
                     <------t---->
```

Example B: Cut from Two-Shot to CS (still actor's timing as played)

```
!    Him              2S  ! CS   Her                              /
_____!_____/
/  "Do you think it's cold out?" ! "No"                          /
!_____!_____\
                     <-->
```

Example C: Reply Now Comes Quickly Using Picture Overlap Reaction

```
\    Him                        2S  ! CS     Her                  /
_____!_____\
\  "Do you think it's cold out?"  !        "No"                  /
/_____!_____/
                     <-------- t x 2 ---->
```

Example D: Reply Delayed by Summing Reaction Time from Both Shots

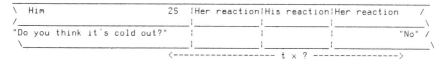

```
\  Him                          2S  !Her reaction!His reaction!Her reaction  /
/_____!_____!_____!_____\
"Do you think it's cold out?"      !          !          !        "No" /
_____!_____!_____!_____\
                     <------------------- t x ? --------------->
```

Example E: Double Cutting Reaction Shots Creates Maximum Delay

FIGURE 34-1

How the original timing of a pause (t) between lines can be removed or augmented to alter the rhythm of dialogue responses.

tion time, though not over the timing of speech itself until digital techniques makes all kinds of manipulation possible.

Intelligent rebalancing of performance reaction times can add massively to the credibility of the characters' inner lives and thus to the believability of the choice and reaction that compels each character into action or speech. In fact, the credibility of all subtexts is very much in the editor's hands. Intelligent editing coaxes our imaginations and lends enormously to the overall impact of the film by aiding and abetting performances and creating the grounds for us to infer thought, feeling, and reaction.

VISUAL AND AURAL EDITING RHYTHMS:
AN ANALOGY IN MUSIC

The interplay of rhythmic elements through editing needs further explanation if the possibilities are to be fully appreciated. Though editing is carried out by the mechanical means of viewing, splicing, or transfer, decisions can no more be made by measuring the script or by calculations with a stopwatch than music can be composed with a metronome.

RHYTHMIC INTERPLAY

Music offers a useful analogy here if we examine an edited version of a conversation between two people. We have two different but interlocked rhythms going. First there is the rhythmic pattern of their voices in a series of sentences that ebb and flow, speed up, slow down, halt, restart, and continue. Set against this, and often taking a rhythmic cue from the sound rhythms, is the visual tempo set up by the complex shifts of visual choice, outlined above and evoked in the interplay of cutting, camera composition, and movement. The visual and aural streams proceed independently yet are rhythmically related, like the relation between music and the physical movements of a dancer.

HARMONY

When you hear a speaker and you see his face as he talks, sound and vision are allied. We could, however, break the literalness of always hearing and seeing the same thing (harmony) by making the transition from scene to scene into a temporary puzzle.

COUNTERPOINT

We are going to cut from a woman talking about her vanished husband to a shot panning across a view of tawdry seashore hotels. We start with the speaker in picture and sound, and then cut to the panning shot while she is still speaking, letting her remaining words play out over the hotels. The effect is this: while our subject is talking about her now fatherless children and the bitterness she feels toward him, we glance away and in our mind's eye imagine where he might now be. The film version of this scene can suggest the mental (or even physical) imagery of someone present and listening. The speaker's words are powerfully counterpointed by the image, and the image lets loose our imagination so we ponder what he is doing, what is going on behind the crumbling concrete facades of the hotels.

Counterpointing one kind of sound against another kind of image has its variations. One usage is simply to illustrate. We see taking place what the woman's words begin to describe: ". . . and the last I heard, he was in Florida. . . ."

Many an elegant contrapuntal sequence in a feature film is the work of an editor trained in documentary trying to raise the movie above a pedestrian script, as Ralph Rosenblum relates in *When the Shooting Stops . . . the Cutting Begins*. Directing and editing documentaries has contributed importantly to the screen fluency of Robert Altman, Lindsay Anderson, Carroll Ballard, Werner Herzog, Louis Malle, Alain Resnais, Alain Tanner, and Haskell Wexler, to name but a few.

DISSONANCE

Another editing technique exploits discrepancies. For instance, while we hear a salesman telling his new assistant his theory of dynamic customer persuasion, we see the same man listing the virtues of a hideaway bed in a monotone so dreary that his customer is bored into a trance. This discrepancy, if we pursue the musical allusion, is a dissonance, spurring the viewer to crave a resolution. Comparing the man's beliefs (heard) with his practice (seen), the viewer is driven to conclude, "here is a man who does not know himself." It is interesting to note that this technique of ambiguous revelation is equally viable in documentary film, where it seems to have originated. Documentary has more of a problem in getting the audience to look critically at certain kinds of reality. People think documentary is just a record when in fact it too is a construct like fiction, and expects the audience to look for critical subtexts and hidden dimensions.

COUNTERPOINT IN PRACTICE: UNIFYING MATERIAL INTO A FLOW

Once you have improved on the script's order for the material, you will want to combine sound and action in a form that takes advantage of counterpoint techniques.

In practice this means bringing together the sound from one shot with the image from another, as we have said. To return on my example where a salesman with a great self-image proved to have a poor performance, one could show this on the screen by merging two sets of materials, one of him talking to his assistant over a coffee break (sequence A), the other of him in the salesroom making a pitch to clients (sequence B).

In editing we can bring these materials into juxtaposition. The conservative, first-assembly method would alternate segments as in Figure 34-2A, a block of explanation then a block of sales talk, then another block of explanation and another of sales, and so on until the point had been made. This is a common though clumsy way to accomplish the objective, and after a few cuts both the technique and the message become predictable.

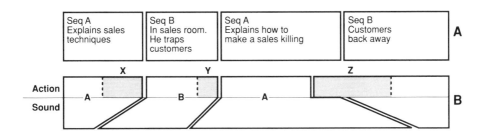

FIGURE 34-2

Counterpointing the content of one sequence against another.

Instead of crudely alternating the sequences, let's integrate the two sets of materials as in Figure 34-2B. Start Harold explaining his sales philosophy (sequence A) during the salesmen's coffee break. While he's showing off to the younger men, we begin fading up the sound from the salesroom (sequence B) in which we hear Harold's aggressive greetings. As he reaches full volume, we cut to the salesroom picture (sequence B) to see he has trapped a reluctant customer and is launching into his sales pitch. After this is established we fade up the coffee break conversation again (sequence A). We hear the salesman say how he first fascinates the customer. We cut to sequence A's picture and see Harold has moved uncomfortably close to his juniors. He tells them one must now make the customers admit they like the merchandise. While the voices continue, we cut back to the salesroom (sequence B) picture only and see the customer backing away angrily. We bring up sequence B's sound as the customer says she only came to buy a pillow.

Notice that in the overlap areas (x, y, and z), picture from one sequence is being countpointed against sound from another. Instead of having description and practice separated as discrete blocks of material, description is now laid against practice, and ideas against reality in a much harder-hitting counterpoint.

The benefits are multiple. The total of the two sequences is shorter and more sprightly. Conversation is kept to an interesting minimum while the behavioral material—the salesroom evidence against which we measure his ideas—is now in the majority. The counterpointing of essentials allows the combination of materials to be pared down to essentials, giving what is presented a muscular, spare quality usually lacking from theatrically conceived film writing. There is a much closer and more telling juxtaposition between vocalized theory and actual performance, and the audience is challenged to reconcile the gap between the man's ideas and what he is actually doing.

Counterpoint editing cannot really be worked out in scripting, because entry and exit points depend on the nuances of playing or even camerawork. But if both scenes are shot in their entirety, one becomes a parallel action to the other. The resulting sequence can be worked out from the materials themselves, and will reliably and effectively compress the two.

There is a shooting/editing project to practice these skills in Chapter 6, Shooting Fundamentals, Project 6-2C, "Vocal Counterpoint and Point of View." This adds a vocal counterpoint to action, but you might want to try improvising the salesman scene used as an example above, using one scene as parallel action to the other and fusing the two in counterpoint.

DRAMA SHOULD TAKE PLACE
IN THE AUDIENCE'S IMAGINATION

By creating a texture of sound and picture that requires an interpretation, a film can juxtapose the antithetical with great economy and kindle the audience's involvement in seeking a resolution to dialectical tensions. The audience is no longer passively identifying and submitting to the controlling will of the movie, but rather stimulated to live an imaginative, critical inner life in parallel with the film.

This critical awareness is what Berthold Brecht, striving to break down the audience's capacity for identification, set out to accomplish in the theater.

THE AUDIENCE AS ACTIVE RATHER THAN
PASSIVE PARTICIPANTS

This more demanding texture of word and image puts the spectator in a new relationship to the evidence presented, encouraging the active rather than passive participation of the dreamer. The contract the storyteller has developed with the audience is no longer just to imbibe diversion but instead a challenge to interpret, to weigh what is seen against what is heard, to balance an idea against its contrary. The film will now sometimes confirm and other times contradict what had seemed true. As in life, the viewer must use critical judgment when, as in our example, a man's ideas turn out to be an unreliable self-image.

But there are yet more interesting ways to use juxtaposition and counterpoint when the basic coupling of sound and picture is altered. For instance, one might show an interior with a bored teenage girl looking out of a store window at people in the street. A radio somewhere offscreen is broadcasting the report of a boxing match as she watches a boy and his mother having a violent argument outside. The girl is too abstracted to notice the counterpoint. Though we see the mother and child, we hear the excited commentator detailing the punishment being inflicted. There is an ironic contrast between two different planes in view; an argument is raised to the level of a public spectacle, yet our main character's consciousness is too naive or too inward-looking to notice. Very succinctly and with not a little humor, both her unconsciousness and a satirical view of mother/child relationships have been compressed into a thirty-second shot. Now *that's* economy!

FILLING IN THE GAPS

Counterpointing visual and aural impressions is only an extension of what was called montage early in film's history. Because film was silent, film grammar developed the juxtaposition of two shots to imply either relatedness or continuity. But the audience's imagination is what supplies the relational links between shots or scenes. It is important to remember that the audience's enjoyment comes not from what it sees and hears, but from what it imagines or projects as it pursues the implied narrative made up of implied subtexts. Few filmmakers seem consciously aware of this. If you grasp this principle and find effective ways to put it into effect, your work will immediately bear the marks of sophistication.

The use of contrapuntal sound came relatively late and was, I believe, developed by documentary editors in search of narrative compression for lengthy actuality materials. In fiction filmmaking, Robert Altman's films from *M*A*S*H* (1970) onwards show great inventiveness in producing a dense, layered counterpoint in their sound tracks. Altman's sound recordist even built a special sixteen track location sound recorder capable of making individual recordings from up to fifteen radio microphones, so the whole problem of miking shots was eliminated. Today you can use two little 8 track DAT machines slaved together if you want to do the same thing.

THE OVERLAP CUT: DIALOGUE SEQUENCES

Another contrapuntal editing device useful to blur the unnatural seams between shots is called the overlap cut. It works like counterpoint between sequences, bringing a speaker's voice in before his picture, or vice versa, and dismantling the procession of level cuts that result when one assembles dialogue material in blocks.

Figure 34-3 is a straight-cut version of a conversation between A and B. Whoever speaks is shown on the screen and before long this becomes predictable and boring. You could alleviate this by slugging in some reaction shots (not shown).

Now look at the same conversation using overlap cutting. Person A starts speaking, but then we hear B's voice (during overlap x). We wait a sentence before cutting to him. B is interrupted by A (during overlap y), and this time we hold on B's frustrated expression before cutting to A driving his point home. Before A has finished, because we are now interested in B's rising anger, we cut back to him shaking his head (during overlap z). When A has finished, B, whom we have seen waiting, caps the discussion and this ends the sequence.

How do you decide when to make overlap cuts (also called lap cuts or L cuts)? Usually it is done at a later stage of cutting, but we shall need a guiding theory. Let's return to our trusty guide for editing, the way human consciousness works. Imagine you are witnessing a conversation between two people; you have to turn your head from one to the other. You will seldom turn at the right moment

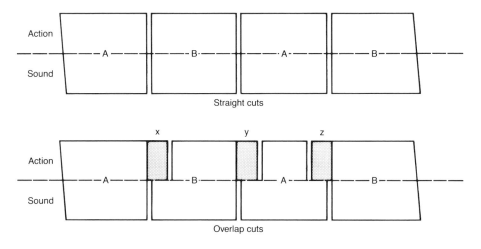

FIGURE 34-3

Straight-cut dialogue sequence and its overlap-cut version.

to catch the next speaker beginning; only a suspiciously omniscient intelligence could be so accurate. Such omniscience in a movie destroys the illusion of watching something spontaneous. Inexperienced or downright bad editors often make neat, level cuts between speakers, and the results give a prepackaged, premeditated effect.

Because in real life one can seldom predict who will speak next, it is hearing a new voice that tells you where to look. If a film or video editor is to convince us that a dialogue sequence comes spontaneously from real life, he or she must replicate the disjunctive shifts we unconsciously make as our eyes follow our hearing, or when our hearing (that is, concentration) catches up late with something we have just seen.

The guideline to effective cutting is always to be found from building the unfolding consciousness of the story's point of view. This is modelled on the motives and intelligence of what I have called the concerned and observant Storyteller. This spectator and guide is engaged not just in hearing and seeing each speaker as he speaks (which would be boring), but also in interpreting what is going on inside each protagonist through clues embedded in moments of action, reaction, or subjective vision. Through what the "concerned observer" notices, through the evidence shown on the screen, the Storyteller's consciousness of the events is subtly established in addition to that of point-of-view characters, and sometimes in contradiction to theirs.

For filmmaking the message is clear. If the editor is to be true to life and to implant in the audience the developing subjectivity of the critical observer, the editor must make sound and picture changeover points as staggered cuts much more often than level ones.

THE OVERLAP CUT: SEQUENCE TRANSITIONS

In the worst and most uncinematic scene transition, a character exits the frame leaving an empty set, and the film cuts to another empty set in anticipation of his arrival. This is really proscenium arch theater, scene shifting that puts a huge hiccup in a film's momentum. Inexperienced directors often engineer scenes to start and stop this way, but a good editor quickly looks for ways to axe the dead footage.

Just as there are dialogue overlap cuts, so are there live transitions from one sequence to another by using the staggered cut. Imagine a scene with a boy and girl talking about going out together. The boy says he thinks her mother will try and stop them. The girl says, "Oh don't worry about her, I can talk her round." Cut to the next scene where the girl asks the question of her mother who closes the refrigerator with a bang and says firmly, "Absolutely not!" to the aggrieved daughter.

First, it is redundant to restate the girl's situation in this way. A level cut would take us instantly from the boy/girl sequence to the mother/girl scene where the mother answers, "Absolutely not!" A more interesting way of leaving the boy/girl scene would be to cut to the mother at the refrigerator while the girl is still saying, ". . . I can talk her round." As she finishes, the mother slams the fridge door and says her line, "Absolutely not!" and the camera pans to show the girl already in the scene.

Another way to create an elision instead of a creaky scene change would be to hold on the boy and girl and have the mother's angry voice say, "Absolutely not!" over the tail end of their shot. You would use the surprise of the new voice to motivate cutting to the mother in picture as the new scene continues.

Either of these devices serves to make less noticeable the coupling between one sequence and the next. Though one sometimes wants to bring a scene to a slow closure, perhaps with a fade-out, more usually one wants to preserve the momentum. Though filmmakers choose dissolves because a level cut jerks the viewer too rudely into a new place and time, the dissolve also inserts a rest period between scenes and dissipates forward momentum.

The answer is the low tech overlap cut; it keeps the track alive, draws the viewer after it, and makes a natural transition while keeping up the pace.

SOUND EFFECTS AS SCENE ELISION

You have seen this overlap technique done with sound effects. It might look like this: The schoolteacher rolls reluctantly out of her bed, then as she ties up her hair we hear the increasingly loud sound of a playground until we cut to her on duty at the school door. Because our curiosity demands an answer to the riddle of children's voices in a woman's bedroom, we do not find the location switch arbitrary or theatrical. Anticipatory sound dragged our attention forward to the next sequence.

Another type of overlap cut makes sound work another way; we cut from the teacher leading kids chanting their multiplication tables to her getting food out of her refrigerator at home. The dreary class sound subsides slowly while she exhaustedly eats some leftovers.

In the first example, anticipatory sound draws her forward out of her bedroom while in the second, holdover sound persists even after she gets home. In both cases, the Storyteller suggests that the din persists in her mind, implying that she finds her workplace unpleasant. This is not just a way of softening transitions between scenes, but a way of suggesting what dominates our schoolteacher's inner consciousness. We could suggest something different by playing it the other way, and let the silence of her home trail out into the workplace, so that she is seen at work with her bedroom radio playing softly before being swamped by the rising uproar of feet echoing in a corridor. At the end of the day, her TV sitcom could displace her voice giving out the dictation, and make us cut to her relaxing at home.

By using sound and picture transitions creatively, we can transport the viewer forward without cumbersome (and in film, expensive) optical effects like dissolves, fades, and wipes. We are also able to scatter important clues about the characters' subjective lives and inner imaginings, something film cannot otherwise easily do.

SUMMARY

In the examples above, we have established that our consciousness can probe our surroundings either

- monodirectionally (eyes and ears on the same information source)
- bidirectionally (eyes and ears on different sources)
- sometimes ears pull eyes forward to seeing a new setting
- sometimes eyes pull ears forward to hearing a new setting.

Film suggests these aspects of consciousness by making the audience share the sensations of a character's shifting planes of consciousness and association. A welcome and money-saving result from creative overlap cutting is that one can completely dispense with the fade or dissolve.

HELP, I CAN'T UNDERSTAND!

These cutting techniques are hard to grasp from a book even though, as I have said, they mimic the way human awareness shifts. If this is getting beyond you, do not worry. The best way to understand editing is to take a complex and interesting sequence in a feature film and, by running a shot or two at a time on a VCR, make a precise log of the relationship between the track elements and the visuals. Chapter 5, Seeing with a Moviemaker's Eye, Project 2: "Editing Analysis" is an editing self-education program with a list of editing techniques for you to find and analyze. Try shooting and editing your own sequences from directions in Chapter 6, Shooting Fundamentals, Projects 6-1 through 6-6. After some hands-on experience, return to this section and it should be much clearer.

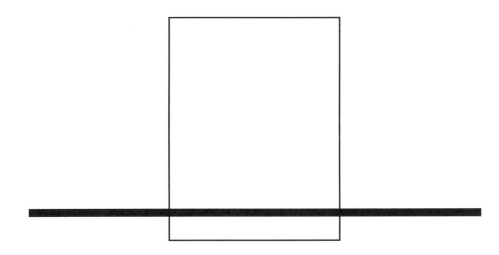

EDITING: FINALIZATION

After perhaps months of sustained editing work on a film, a debilitating familiarity sets in. As you lose objectivity, your ability to make judgments on behalf of an audience departs. Every alternative version begins to look the same. All seem too long, and you may become so obsessed with particular faults in your footage that they seem overwhelming. Not unusually, the director is hanging on to a sequence or a minor character that the editor and others think redundant. These are your darlings, and the director must kill all the darlings if the film is to be consistent and work well.

This disabling condition is particularly likely to overwhelm the hyphenate, the director-editor, who has lived with both the intentions and the resulting footage ever since their inception. But it afflicts the whole editing crew at this stage and is the main reason why one begins to call on other people's reactions to the piece.

DIAGRAMING YOUR FILM

Before you show the cut to outsiders, make an abstract of your film in the form of a block diagram so you can spot anomalies. Some of these you will fix, since diagramming brings not only revelations but ideas for the cure.

DIAGNOSIS: USING A BLOCK DIAGRAM

Whenever one needs to better understand something, it helps to translate it into another form. Statisticians, for instance, know that the full implications of their figures are not evident to the great unwashed public until expressed as a graph, pie chart, or other proportional image.

In our case, we are dealing with the mesmerizing actuality of the film, which, as we view it, concentrates our attention within its unfolding present to the detriment of any sense of overview. It is tempting to regard all of one's earlier production work as something that renders unnecessary any further dramatic analysis, but this is far from being true, especially after you may have altered, abbreviated or transposed much of the original. Through using a block diagram you can in fact regain a fresh and a more objective perspective of your work.

Figure 17-1 (page 231) is a useful dual-purpose form that speeds the job of analysis. To use it, run your film a sequence at a time and make a brief note of each sequence's content in the box (name of characters and what is the main action). Next to the box, write what main point the sequence contributes to the development of the film as a whole. This might be factual information, it might introduce a setting, a character, or a relationship to be developed later in the film, or it might exist to create a special mood or feeling.

Soon you have a flow chart for your film. Like any representation it has limitations, since film sequences are not like a succession of soloists, each singing a self-contained song, but more like the delayed entry of several parts in a choral work. Each entering voice joins and cross-modulates with those preceding. Some foreshadow or make references that will only make sense later. Draw and annotate lines indicating any special relationship existing between each new sequence and those preceding. This may indicate in parallel storytelling, for instance, that one sequence is too far away from its counterpart.

The benefit of analyzing in this way is that one forces oneself to conceptualize what actually comes from the screen, to translate what are conveniently inchoate sensations into hard-edged statements. It is vital, therefore, to do this work from the life on the screen and not from memory or the script. Another useful trick is to give each sequence an impact rating so you can assess the development of the film's dramatic pressures.

Articulating what each sequence contributes will help you to see dispassionately and functionally what is truly there for an audience. What does the progression of contributions add up to? As with the first assembly, you will again find it reveals some of the following:

- the film lacks early impact, or has an unnecessarily pedestrian opening that makes it a late developer (fine for nineteenth-century Russian novels but fatal for a film that may depend on TV showings)
- the main issues are unclear or take too long to emerge (writing problem, but in editing it is sometimes possible to reposition a scene earlier, even ahead of titles, to commit the film to an interesting line of development)
- the type and frequency of impact is poorly distributed over the film's length (feast or famine in dramatic development and progression)
- there is a nonlinear development of basic, necessary information about characters, backstory, and environment, including
- omissions
- duplication
- backdoubles
- redundancy

- information too far ahead of place where audience needs it
- the same kind of dramatic contribution is made in several ways (three consecutive scenes reveal only that the hero has a low flashpoint; choose the best and reposition or dump the others)
- a favorite sequence or character does not contribute to the thrust of the film (this is one of your darlings. Close your eyes and swing the ax)
- the film's resolution emerges early, leaving the remainder of the film tediously inevitable (rebalance or withdraw indicators in the film to keep resolution in doubt, so audience stays interested and working)
- the film appears to end before it actually does (false or multiple endings are a common problem)

Naming each ailment leads to finding the cure. When you have put these remedies into effect, you will sense the improvement rather than see it. It is like resetting a sail; the boat looks the same, but the vessel surges under new power.

DIAGNOSIS: USING THE BLOCK DIAGRAM AGAIN

After several rounds of alterations, make a new block diagram to ensure that housecleaning has not introduced new problems. I cannot overstress the deceit film practices upon its makers. Rest assured that you'll find more anomalies by repeating the process, even when it seems utterly unnecessary.

With some years of practice, most of this formal process becomes second nature and will occur in the earlier stages of the cut. Even so, filmmakers of long standing invariably profit from subjecting their work to such formal scrutiny and much of the discussion during the cutting of a feature film centers on the film's dramatic shape and effectiveness.

A TRIAL SHOWING

Preparing a block diagram brings one more benefit. Having defined what every brick in your movie's edifice is supposed to accomplish, you are excellently prepared to test the film's intentions during a trial show for a small audience.

AUDIENCE

Your audience should be half a dozen or so people whose tastes and interests you respect. The less they know of your aims the better.

PREPARATION

You should warn your audience that it is a work in progress, still technically raw. Tell them that music, sound effects, and titles have yet to be added. Incidentally, it helps to cut in a working title or, in its absence, to tell the audience what it is, since a title legitimately signals a film's purpose and identity to its audience. While the film is running, you may also want to call out a brief description of any vital sound component that is missing.

SOUND CONTROL IS CRITICAL

When you show the film, carefully control the sound levels or you will get misleadingly negative responses. Even film professionals can drastically misjudge a film whose sound elements are inaudible or overbearing.

SURVIVING YOUR CRITICS AND MAKING USE OF WHAT THEY SAY

LISTEN, DO NOT EXPLAIN

Asking for critical feedback must be handled carefully or it can be a pointless exercise. You need to say little and listen much, while retaining your fundamental bearings towards the piece. After the viewing, ask for impressions of the film as a whole. You will probably need to focus and direct your viewers' attention or you may find the discussion quite peripheral to your needs. Avoid the temptation to explain the film in any way. Explanations at this stage are not only irrelevant, they confuse and compromise the audience's own perceptions. Your film must soon stand or fall on its merits, so concentrate on hearing what your audience may be telling you.

Taking in reactions and criticism is an emotionally draining experience. It is quite usual to feel threatened, slighted, misunderstood, and unappreciated, and to come away with a raging headache. You need all the self-discipline you can muster to sit immobile, say little, and listen. Take notes, or make an audio recording of the proceedings so you can listen again in peace.

LINES OF INQUIRY

Because one usually needs to guide the inquiry into useful channels, here are some questions that move from the large issues toward the component parts.

- what is the film really about?
- what are the major issues in the film?
- did the film feel the right length or was it too long?
- were there any parts that were unclear or puzzling? (You can itemize those you suspect fit the description, since audiences often forget anything that passed over their heads.)
- which parts felt slow?
- which parts were moving or otherwise successful?
- what did you feel about _____ (name of character)?
- what did you end up knowing about _____ (situation or issue)?

You are beginning to test the effectiveness of the function you assigned each sequence. Depending on your trial audience's patience, you may be able to survey only dubious areas, or you may get feedback on most of your film's parts and intentions.

BALANCING CRITICS' VIEWPOINTS

Dealing with criticism really means absorbing multiple views and then, after the dust settles, reviewing the film to see how audience members could get such varying impressions. In the cutting room, you and your editor now see the film with the eyes of those who never understood that the messenger was the workmate seen in an earlier scene. You find a way to put in an extra line where the woman asks if Don is still at work, and without compromising the film in any way the problem is solved. Before rushing to fix anything you must, of course, take into account the number of people reporting any particular difficulty. Where comments from different audience members cancel each other out, there may be no action called for. Make some allowance for the subjectivity and acuity of your individual critics.

THE EGOCENTRIC CRITIC

An irritation one must often suffer, especially among those with a little knowledge to flourish, is the person who insists on talking about the film he would have made rather than the film you have just shown. Diplomatically redirect the discussion.

MAKE CHANGES CAUTIOUSLY

Make no changes without careful reflection. Remember that when people are asked to give criticism, they want to leave a contributory mark on your work. You will never be able to please everyone, nor should you try.

HOLD ON TO YOUR CENTRAL INTENTIONS

Never let your central intentions get lost and never revise them unless there are overwhelmingly positive reasons to do so. Act only upon suggestions that support and further your central intentions. This is a dangerous phase for the filmmaker, indeed for any artist. If you let go of your work's underlying identity you will lose your direction. If in doubt, keep listening and think deeply about what you hear. Do not be tempted by strong emotions to carve into your film precipitously. You may need to wait a week for your contradictory passions to settle.

MEA CULPA

It is quite normal by now to feel that you have failed, that you have a piece of junk on your hands, that all is vanity. If this happens, take heart. You might have felt this during shooting, which would have been a lot worse. Actually, things are never so awful as they seem after showing a workprint. Keep in mind that the conditions of viewing invite mainly negative feedback and audiences are disproportionately alienated by a wrong sound balance here, a missed sound dissolve there, a shot or two that needs clipping, and a sequence that belongs earlier. These imbalances and rhythmic ineptitudes massively downgrade a film's impact. The glossy finish you have yet to apply will greatly improve the film's reception.

THE USES OF PROCRASTINATION

Whether you are pleased or depressed by your film, it is always good to stop working on it for a few weeks and do something else. If this degree of anxiety and depression is new to you, take comfort; you are deep in the throes of the artistic experience. It is the long and painful labor before birth. When you pick up the film again after a lapse, its problems and their solutions will no longer seem overwhelming.

TRY, TRY AGAIN

A film of any substance frequently needs a long evolution in the editing room, so you should expect to make alterations and try it out on several new audiences. You may want to show the last cut to the original trial audience to see what changes they report. Sometimes you can get a real sense of progress made during editing.

As a director with a lot of editing in my background, I know that a film truly emerges in the editing process. Magic and miracles appear from the footage, yet even film crews seldom have much idea about what really happens. It is a process unknown and unguessed at by those who have not lived through it, and for the beginner it will be extremely slow. A year of part-time work for a new director to make a thirty-minute film really live up to its potential is not unusual. To abridge this work is like pulling a car chassis off the assembly line and driving away because the engine is connected to the wheels.

KNOWING WHEN TO STOP

Never set a deadline for the end of editing. Instead, be aware of when the learning curve begins to flatten. Some directors will go on fidgeting and fiddling with the cut ad infinitum. This is the fear of letting go. Ending work on your film is like giving up being a shepherd to your children. There's a point where you have to admit that they are as grown up as they are going to be, and you must let them go forward alone, to win friends as they may.

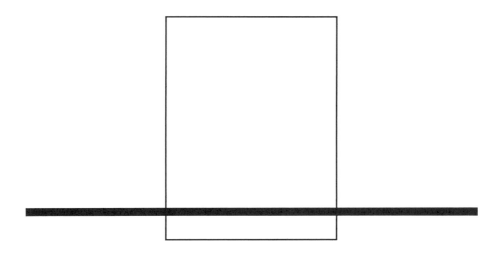

C·H·A·P·T·E·R 36

EDITING FROM FINE CUT TO SOUND MIX

THE FINE CUT

With typical caution, filmmakers call the result of the evolutionary editing process the fine not final cut, for there may still be minor changes and accommodations. Some of these arise out of laying sound tracks in preparation to produce a master mixed track.

SOUND AND MUSIC TREATMENT DISCUSSIONS

Sound is an incomparable stimulant to the audience's imagination, and I give it a full treatment because you should be alert to sound composition possibilities all through postproduction. Depending on the experience and imagination of your editor and sound mixer, you may get only what you insist you want. Poor control of sound can disrupt the dreamlike quality that good film attains so it is vital to develop your own ideas and not to think that sound people are magicians who will pull a rabbit out of the hat. If you haven't monitored and directed the sound treatment throughout, it may be too late to do anything at the sound mix.

Before the editor goes to work splitting dialogue tracks and laying sound effects, there should be a detailed discussion with the director to determine how each sequence should be handled from the sound point of view. How and why music gets used also needs careful thought, and the composer should participate in this. Music is most commonly used as a transitional filler device, or as a mood enhancer, so you will need to agree on the start and finish points. Getting a music segment started is easy, but ending one so the audience does not feel deprived takes careful planning. A good rule of thumb is to conclude or fade out music when something more commanding begins. You might take music out during the first seconds of a noisy street scene, or under the beginning of dialogue. The best guide is to study films that successfully integrate music with the kind of action you have in your film. Never assume that music you like will be available for you to use when you get around to inquiring. Commissioning original music obviates the difficulty of getting (or paying for) copyright clearance on music already recorded.

POSTSYNCHRONIZING DIALOGUE

Postsynchronizing dialogue means creating new speech tracks in lip sync with existing picture, and is variously called dubbing, looping, or automatic dialogue replacement (ADR). It is a procedure to be avoided because newly recorded tracks invariably sound flat and dead in contrast with live location recordings. This is not only a question of lacking background sounds (they can be added) but more a question of sound perspective and location acoustics (impossible to recreate in a studio), and of the artificial situation in which the actor finds himself working to reconstitute a few seconds of dialogue.

SYNC SOUND EFFECTS

Most sound effects can be created wild and fitted afterwards. Repetitive sounds that must fit an action (knocking on door, shoveling snow, or footsteps) can often be recreated by recording the actions a little slower and then cutting out the requisite frames before each impact's "attack." More complex sync effects (two people walking through a quadrangle) will have to be postsynced just like dialogue, paying attention to the different surfaces that the feet pass over (grass, gravel, concrete, etc.). Doing a series of postsync sessions makes one truly understand how critical it is that the location recordist procure good original recordings in the first place.

Sound effects are professionally created, or recreated, in a special effects theater called a Foley stage. On a complex production with a big budget, the cost is economically justified. For the low-budget filmmaker, some improvisation can cut costs enormously. What matters is that sound effects are appropriate (always difficult to arrange) and that they are in sync with the action onscreen. Where and how you record them is not important provided they work well. Sometimes you can find appropriate sound effects in sound libraries but *never* assume that a sound effect listed in a library will work with your particular sequence until you have tried it against picture. Most sound libraries are filled with garbage shot years ago. Many effects tracks are not clean, that is, they come with a heavy ambient background or ineradicable system hiss.

MUSIC

Music sections are logged in minutes, and to the nearest half second. Figure 36-1 shows what a composer's cue sheet looks like.

```
                    "THE WATER-PEOPLE" MUSIC SECTION 4

00:00.0   Music segment begins as Robert jumps in car
00:03.5   Engine starts
00:05.0   Car lurches forward
00:10.5   Cut to Robert checking fuel gauge
00:14.5   Looks in rearview mirror
00:19.0   Frowns, realizing that a motorcycle is behind
00:27.5   Cut to Carl gunning his Harley-Davidson
00:38.0   Cut to Robert staring in mirror, car going off track
00:46.0   Shriek of tyres for 3 seconds as Robert drags car back on to road
00:58.5   Cut to Carl lying forward on motorcycle tank
01:06.5   Cut to BCU Robert's face realizing it's Carl behind
01:08.5   Begin Robert's line: "So you want trouble.  I can give you trouble"
01:12.0   End of line.
01:14.5   Cut to BCU hand opens glove pocket, takes out revolver
01:16.0   Revolver visible
01:17.5   Cut to flashing ambulance light, zoom back and siren drowns out
          music fades to silence and...
01:29.0   music ends here.
```

FIGURE 36-1

Typical scene measurements for a music segment.

COMPOSING AND RECORDING TO SYNC POINTS

An experienced musician will compose to these very precise lengths, paying attention to track features such as the tire screech and the dialogue line so there will be nothing too "busy" at these points in the music that would compete with them. The score will be marked at strategic points with the cumulative timing so that as the music is recorded (normally to picture as a safeguard) there is a running check that the sync points line up. The composer might put a melodramatic "sting" on the first appearance of the pursuing motorcycle at 27.5 seconds and on the appearance of the revolver at 01:16, for instance.

THE SESSION

The editor makes the preparations to record music and attends the recording session because only the editor can say whether a particular shot can be lengthened or shortened to accommodate the slight mistimings that always appear during recording. Adjusting the film is easier and more economical than paying musicians to pursue perfect musical synchronicity.

FITTING MUSIC

After the recording session, the editor fits each music section and makes necessary shot adjustments. If the music is appropriate, the film takes a quantum leap forward in effectiveness.

WHAT THE SOUND MIX CAN DO

After the film has reached a fine cut, the culmination of the editing process is to prepare and mix the component sound tracks. A whole book could be written on this preeminent subject alone. What follows is a list of essentials along with some tips.

You are ready to mix down tracks into one master track when you have:

- finalized your film's content
- fitted music
- split dialogue tracks (a separate track for each mike position in dialogue tracks and sometimes a different track for each speaker, depending on how much EQ will be necessary
- filled in missing sections of background ambience for particular sequences so there are no dead spaces or abrupt background changes
- recorded and laid narration (if there is any)
- recorded and laid sound effects and mood setting atmospheres
- made a mix chart

The mix procedure determines the following:

1. Comparative sound levels (say, between a dialogue foreground track of a voice played against a background of a noisy factory scene).
2. Consistent quality (for example, two tracks from two angles on the same speaker need equalization [tone control adjustments] and level [volume] adjustments to make them sound similar).
3. Level changes (fade up, fade down, sound dissolves, and level adjustments to accommodate new track elements such as narration, music, or dialogue).
4. Equalization (the filtering and profiling of individual tracks either to match others, or to create maximum intelligibility, listener appeal, or ear comfort; a voice track with a rumbly traffic background can, for instance, be much improved by "rolling off" the lower frequencies, leaving the voice range intact).
5. Sound processing (adding echo, reverberation, telephone effect, etc.).
6. Dynamic range (a compressor squeezes the broad dynamic range of a movie into the narrow range favored in TV transmission; a limiter leaves the main range alone but limits peaks to a preset level).
7. Perspective (to some degree, equalization and level manipulation can mimic perspective changes, thus helping create a sense of space and dimensionality through sound).
8. Stereo channel distribution (if a stereo track is being compiled, different elements go to left and right channels to create a sense of horizontal spread).
9. Noise reduction (Dolby and other noise-reduction systems help minimize the system hiss that would intrude on quiet passages).

Be aware that when a manually operated mixing board is used, changes cannot be done instantaneously at a cut from one sequence to the next. Tracks are checkerboarded (meaning, they alternate from track to track) so that a channel's equalization and level adjustments can be set up in the section of silent sound spacing prior to the track's arrival. This is most critical when balancing dialogue tracks, as explained below.

SOUND MIX PREPARATION

Track elements are presented here in the conventional hierarchy of importance, although the order may vary; music, for instance, might be faded up to the foreground and dialogue played almost inaudibly low. When cutting and laying sound tracks, be careful not to cut off the barely audible tail of a decaying sound, or to clip the attack. Sound editing should be done at high volume, so you hear everything that is there.

Laying film and nonlinear digital tracks is easier than in linear video because it follows a logic visible to the eye. Each track section in film is of brown magnetic stock interspersed with different-colored spacing. Fine control is quick and easy since one can cut to the frame (one twenty-fourth of a second). Conceptualizing what one is doing is aided by physically handling the individual tracks. The equivalent operation in a nonlinear program is as easy and logical as film because it is graphic and shows blocks of track laid along a time line.

Because linear videotape editing is accomplished by a transfer process it is more abstract and remote-control, but the working principles remain identical.

NARRATION OR VOICE OVER

If narration is laid to a quiet sequence, you will need to build up the gaps between narration sections with "presence" so the track remains live. Getting actors to make a written narration sound spontaneous is often very difficult, so you should consider using the improv method. Here actors, given a list of particular points to be made, improvise dialogue in character. By judicious side-coaching, or even interviewing, the actor produces a quantity of entirely spontaneous material in a number of passes that can be edited down. Though labor intensive, the result will be more spontaneous and natural than anything read from a script.

DIALOGUE TRACKS AND THE PROBLEM
OF INCONSISTENCIES

Dialogue tracks for video can be checkerboarded during the editing stage (see "Sound Considerations" in Chapter 33), but if this was not the case then you must split dialogue tracks in preparation for the mix. Because different camera positions occasion different mike positioning, a dialogue sequence's tracks played "as is" will change level and acoustic from shot to shot. The result is ragged and distracting when one needs the impression of seamless continuity familiar from feature films. This result is achieved by painstaking and labor intensive sound editing work in the following order:

1. Dialogue tracks should be split (that is, laid on separate tracks) according to the needs imposed by the coverage's mike positioning.

2. In a scene shot from two angles and having two mike positions, all the close shot sound goes on one track, and all the medium shot sound goes on the other. With four or five mike positions, you would need to lay at least four or five tracks.

3. Sometimes tracks must additionally be split by character if one is under- or over-recorded.

4. Equalization (EQ) settings can later be determined in the mix to bring the two into acceptable compatibility, given that the viewer can expect a different sound perspective to match the different camera distances. These settings will now apply to multiple sound sections as they have been grouped according to EQ needs.

5. Special attention must be given to cleaning up background tracks of extraneous noises, creaks, mike handling sounds—anything that doesn't overlap dialogue and can therefore be removed. Gaps must be filled with the correct room tone.

6. If you have to join dissimilar room tones, do it as a quick dissolve behind dialogue, so the audience doesn't notice the change. The worst place to make an illogical sound change is in the clear.

Film and non-linear sound mixing can handle many tracks, but linear video can usually only handle two at a time. Each succeeding section is alternated between the recorder's two available tracks (see Chapter 33, Figure 33-3) to allow prior mixing board adjustments during the sections of silent or blank track. Through rehearsal, the mix engineer can set up the controls for each track section to balance the following,

INCONSISTENT BACKGROUNDS

The ragged, truncated background is the badge of the poorly edited film, its inadequacies of technique stealing attention from the film's content. Frequently when you cut between two speakers in the same location, the background to each is different either in level or quality because the mike was angled differently. Since one angle was recorded after the other, each may have different background activity. Be sure to shoot presence tracks on location so you can add to and augment the lighter track to match its heavier counterpart.

INCONSISTENT VOICE QUALITIES

A variety of location acoustical environments, different mikes, and different mike working distances all play havoc with the consistency of location voice recordings. Intelligent adjusting with sound filtering (EQ) at the mix stage can massively decrease the sense of strain and irritation arising from one's ear having to make constant adjustment to unmotivated and therefore irrational changes.

LAYING MUSIC TRACKS

It is relatively easy to lay music, but remember to cut in just before the sound attack so its arrival isn't heralded by studio atmosphere or record surface hiss prior to the first chords. Arrow A in Figure 36-2 represents the ideal cut-in point; to its left is unwanted presence or hiss. To the right of A are three attacks in succession leading to a decay to silence at arrow B. A similar attack/sustain decay profile is found for many sound effects (footsteps, for instance) so you can often use the same editing strategy. By removing sound between x and y we could reduce three footfalls here to two.

SPOT SOUND EFFECTS

These sync to something onscreen, like a door closing, a coin placed on a table, or a phone being picked up. They need to be appropriate and carefully synchronized. Sound effects, especially tape library or disk effects, often bring problematical backgrounds of their own. You can reduce this by cutting into the effect immediately before a sound's 'attack' (Figure 36-2, arrow A) and immediately after its decay (arrow B), thus minimizing the unwanted background's intrusiveness. Mask unwanted sound changes by placing them behind another sound: an unavoidable atmosphere change could be masked by a doorbell ringing, for example. Sometimes you can bring an alien background unobtrusively in and out by fading it up and down rather than letting it thump in and out as cuts.

Bear in mind that *the ear registers a sound cut-in or a cut-out much more acutely than a graduated change.*

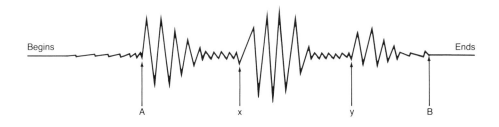

FIGURE 36-2

Sound modulations: attack, three bursts, and decay. Arrows indicate best cutting points.

ATMOSPHERES AND BACKGROUND SOUND

One lays in an atmosphere either to create a mood (birdsong over a morning shot of a wood or woodsaw effects over the exterior of a carpenter's shop) or to mask inconsistencies by using something relevant but distracting. Always obey screen logic by laying atmospheres to cover the entire sequence, not just a part of it. Remember that if a door opens, the exterior atmosphere (children's playground, for instance) will rise for the duration that the door is open. If you want to create a sound dissolve, remember to lay the requisite amounts to allow for the necessary overlap, and listen for any inequities in each overlap.

MIX CHART

Once tracks have been laid to picture, you will need to fill in a mix chart blank (Figure 36-3). In the completed sample (Figure 36-4) each column represents an individual track. By reading down the chart one sees that:

- individual tracks play against each other, like instruments in a vertically organized music score
- the sync pip or "BEEP" at 00:30 is a single frame of tone on all tracks to serve as an aural sync check when the tracks begin running
- segment starts and finishes are marked with timings (or footages for a film mix)
- a straight line at the start or finish represents a sound cut (as at 04:09 and 04:27)
- an opening chevron represents a fade-in (track 4 at 04:10)
- a closing chevron represents a fade-out (tracks 2 at 02:09)
- timings at fades refer to the beginning of a fade-in, or the end of a fade-out
- a dissolve is two overlapping chevrons as at 02:04 to 02:09. There is a fade-out on track 4 overlapping a fade-in for the cassette machine. This is called a cross-fade or sound dissolve
- timings indicate length of cross-fade (sound dissolve), ours being a five-second cross-fade
- it is prudent to lay both tracks longer in case you later decide you would like a longer dissolve
- you may lay up alternative sound treatments, the alternative to be auditioned and chosen during the mix

Vertical space on the chart is seldom a linear representation of time. You might have seven minutes of talk with a very simple chart, then half a minute of railroad station montage with a profusion of individual tracks for each shot. To avoid either unwieldy or crowded mix charts, use no more vertical space than is necessary for clarity to the eye. To help the sound mix engineer, who works under great pressure in the half-dark, shade in the track boxes with a highlight marker.

```
S O U N D   M I X   L O G  Production_____

Date__/__/____  Reel #____  Page # ____  Premix #____  Editor_____
_____
Action    |         |         |         |         |
cues      | Track 1 | Track 2 | Track 3 | Track 4 |Cassette/Disc
_____|_____|_____|_____|_____|_____
          |         |         |         |         |
          |         |         |         |         |
          |         |         |         |         |
          |         |         |         |         |
          |         |         |         |         |
          |         |         |         |         |
          |         |         |         |         |
          |         |         |         |         |
          |         |         |         |         |
          |         |         |         |         |
          |         |         |         |         |
          |         |         |         |         |
          |         |         |         |         |
          |         |         |         |         |
          |         |         |         |         |
          |         |         |         |         |
          |         |         |         |         |
          |         |         |         |         |
          |         |         |         |         |
          |         |         |         |         |
          |         |         |         |         |
          |         |         |         |         |
          |         |         |         |         |
          |         |         |         |         |
          |         |         |         |         |
          |         |         |         |         |
          |         |         |         |         |
          |         |         |         |         |
          |         |         |         |         |
          |         |         |         |         |
          |         |         |         |         |
          |         |         |         |         |
          |         |         |         |         |
          |         |         |         |         |
          |         |         |         |         |
          |         |         |         |         |
          |         |         |         |         |
          |         |         |         |         |
          |         |         |         |         |
          |         |         |         |         |
          |         |         |         |         |
          |         |         |         |         |
          |         |         |         |         |
          |         |         |         |         |
          |         |         |         |         |
          |         |         |         |         |
          |         |         |         |         |
```

FIGURE 36-3 ——

Sound mix blank form.

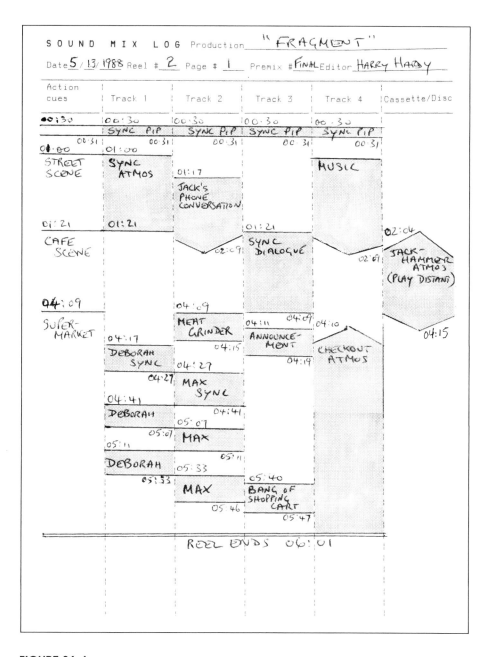

FIGURE 36-4 ────────────────────────────────────

Specimen sound mix log.

SOUND MIX STRATEGY

PREMIXING

One reel of a feature film may comprise forty or more sound tracks. Since only one to four sound engineers operate a mix board, it requires a sequence of premixes. The same principle holds true for a much humbler production, with only a four to eight-track mix, especially if the medium is videotape, where only two tracks at a time can be played off tape. *It is vital to premix in an order that reserves control over the most important elements to the last.* If you were to premix dialogue and effects right away, then a subsequent addition of more effects or music would uncontrollably augment and compete with the dialogue. Since the intelligibility of most films depends on audible dialogue, you must retain control over dialogue-to-background level until the very last stage of mixing. This is particularly true for location sound, which is often near the margin of intelligibility.

Note that each generation of analogue (as opposed to digital) sound transfer introduces additional noise (system hiss). This is most audible in quiet tracks such as a slow speaking voice in a silent room, or a very spare music track. This is particularly true for analogue video sound, which records sound on tracks that are narrow and run at a low tape speed, giving them quality little better than a cheap cassette recorder's. The order of premixes may thus be influenced by which tracks should most be protected from repeated retransfer.

USING A WILD (NON SYNC) SOURCE

To decrease premixing, one can feed in nonsync atmospheres from a CD or cassette player (see sixth column in Figure 36-4). Sound must usually be faded in and out since frame-accurate cut-ins or cut-outs may be impossible.

TAILORING

Many tracks if played as laid will enter and exit abruptly, giving an unpleasantly jagged impression to the listener's ear. This negatively affects how people respond to your subject matter, so it is important to achieve a seamless effect whenever you are not deliberately disrupting attention. The trouble comes when you cut from a quiet to a noisy track, or vice versa, and this can be greatly minimized by tailoring; that is, making a very quick fade-up or fade-down of the noisy track to meet the quiet track on its own terms. The effect onscreen is still that of a cut, but one that no longer assaults the ear (see Figure 36-5).

COMPARATIVE LEVELS: ERR ON THE SIDE OF CAUTION

Mix studios usually use expensive speakers. Especially for video work the results are dangerously misleading, since low-budget filmmakers must expect their work to be seen mostly on domestic TV sets, which have miserably small, cheap speakers. Not only does the unsuspecting consumer lose frequency and dynamic ranges, he loses the dynamic separation between loud and soft, so that foregrounds heard separated in the mix studio become swamped by backgrounds. If you are mixing a dialogue scene with a traffic background atmosphere, err on the conservative

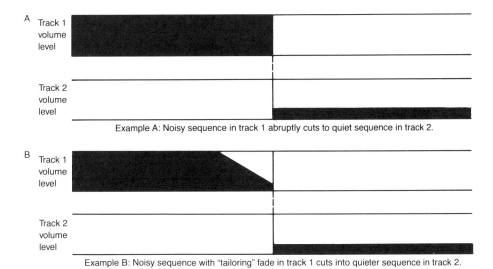

Example A: Noisy sequence in track 1 abruptly cuts to quiet sequence in track 2.

Example B: Noisy sequence with "tailoring" fade in track 1 cuts into quieter sequence in track 2.

FIGURE 36-5

Abrupt sound cut tailored by quick fade of outgoing track so it matches level of the incoming track.

side and make a deliberately high separation, keeping traffic low and voices high. Many mix suites keep a TV on hand and will obligingly play your track through its speaker to give the customer a salutory reminder of what the home viewer will actually hear.

REHEARSE, THEN RECORD

As the director you supervise the mix if you are mixing in a studio rather than doing it on equipment you control yourself. This does not mean you have to know how to do things, only that you and your editor have ideas about how each sequence should sound. To your requests, and according to what the editor has laid in the sound tracks, the mix engineer will probably offer alternatives from which you choose. Mixing is best accomplished by familiarizing oneself with the problems of one short section at a time, and building sequence by sequence from convenient stopping points. It is advisable to check the work as you go, and at the end, it is very important to check the whole mix without stopping.

FILM MIXES

The film medium is sprocketed so tracks or a premix are easily synced up to a start mark in the picture reel leader. The final mix will be transferred by a film laboratory to an optical (that is, photographic) track and photographically combined with the picture to produce a composite projection print. Sometimes television will transmit from double system; that is, picture and the magnetic mix will be loaded on a telecine machine with separate but interlocked sound. The track is taken from the high-quality magnetic original instead of from the much lower quality photographic track. As hi-fi TV catches on, this will happen more often.

VIDEO MIXES

Providing there are unbroken video control tracks, it is possible to transfer in sync using a sync start mark from one tape to another (see Chapter 33, Figure 33-5 and accompanying text). In practice this means that video mixing evolves through a number of generations down from the master edit, with resulting picture degradation. Subsequently, the master mix is dubbed back onto the master cut, which is only a second generation picture. A word of caution: Since eventually this means erasing original tracks to make way for the mix, always first experiment with copies to verify the procedure.

MAKE SAFETY COPIES AND STORE THEM IN DIFFERENT LOCATIONS

Because a sound mix, whether film or video, requires a long and painstaking process, it is professional practice to immediately make safety or backup copies. These are stored safely in multiple buildings. Copies are made from the master mix in the knowledge that should damage or loss occur to it, there are backups.

The same principle should be followed for film picture; keep masters, safety copies, negatives, and internegatives in different places so you don't lose everything should fire, flood, revolution, or act of God destroy what you keep under your bed.

C·H·A·P·T·E·R 3 7

TITLES AND
ACKNOWLEDGMENTS

Although every film has a working title, the final title is often decided late because it must epitomize the final version's concerns and intentions. Remember that your film's title may be the only advertising copy your audience ever sees. TV listings and festival programs rarely have space to describe their offerings, so the title you choose may be your sole means of drawing attention to your film.

A sure sign of amateurism is a film accompanied by an egocentric welter of credit titles. The same name should not crop up in four key capacities, and acknowledgments should be brief. An actor should not be described as "Starring Sherry Mudge" unless Sherry's fame makes the claim realistic. With union actors there will often be contractual specifications for the size and wording of title credits, and these must be scrupulously observed. Many favors are granted filmmakers merely for an acknowledgment in the titles, so be sure you are honoring your debts. Then again, funding often comes with a contractual obligation to acknowledge the fund in a prescribed wording, so this and all such obligations should be carefully checked before titles are specified. Spelling should be carefully gone over by at least two highly literate checkers. The spelling of people's names should receive special care.

Titles should be few in words and short in duration. There are plenty of examples available on TV. Locate models of a length and budget commensurate with your own. Many of the most artistically ambitious European films have brief and classically simple white on black titles. You could do worse.

Appropriate onscreen timings can be assessed by reading the contents of each card (which represents one screen of titling) one and a half times out loud. When you shoot the titles, be sure to shoot at least three times as much as you need. This allows for a title to be extended if needed and for the all-important video editing preroll.

White titles on a moving background are nice, but unless you have access to video superimposition technology they are out of your reach, as will be dissolves and wipes. Plain titles on a colored artwork, or a still photo background can be tasteful and effective.

Titling work has to be done carefully and meticulously, since even small inequities of proportion and straightness show up badly and make titles look amateurish. In general, for video it is best to pay for first rate titles done on an expensive CG (character generator). With film, white titles are easy to overexpose, leading to loss of definition.

Never assume that film titles will be "all right on the night." They are tricky to get right, especially if you are at all ambitious and want fancy effects. Titles, like troubles, are sent to try us, so give yourself plenty of time in case you must reshoot.

Do not forget to include the © symbol before your name and the year as a claim to the copyright of the material. To file for copyright in the United States, write to the Registrar of Copyrights, Library of Congress, Washington, DC 20450, and ask for current information on copyrighting. If you live in another country, be sure to check out the correct copyright procedure. If and when you come to sell your film, legal omissions can be costly or even paralyzing.

LOW-COST FILM AND VIDEO TITLING

If you are meticulous, quite professional-looking film titles can be made using press stick lettering available from art shops and stationers. There is a bewildering choice of typeface, and you should choose one that reflects the nature of your film. Keep in mind that spindly or ornate lettering may be illegible on the TV screen. Lettering size can be adjusted by using either loose or tight framing, always assuming your layout permits the latter within the camera's frame, and assuming that your lens will focus close enough.

White lettering on a graphic background (a still photo or dark-toned painting, for example) can be achieved by using white lettering mounted on an acetate sheet, which is then laid over a choice of still background. The whole sandwich can be lit and shot from the front. You can change white titles on a black ground to any color you want, simply by putting the appropriate filter gel in front of the camera lens, or altering the video camera's color balance. If your camera has inverse video, you can change black letters on white to white letters on black at the flick of a switch.

In video a character generator is a computerized device that electronically produces lettering and symbols on the screen. It is useful for producing rapid, nicely spaced, centered, and legible titling, but the low-priced ones are likely to have an electronic typeface inappropriate for most productions. Computer word-processing programs used in alliance with a good laser printer can produce a variety of typefaces, and give great control over layout.

GETTING TITLES MADE COMMERCIALLY

For more elaborate film titling, talk with the opticals representative at your film lab. Similarly for video, talk with a post-production house. Larger cities have companies that specialize in making up and shooting titles, and it is a wise investment to give a good film professional-looking titles. Since the bulk of optical house work is for wealthy commercials producers, you should check prices carefully in advance, as titling can be vastly expensive. Meet and discuss with the person who will be making them up. Be sure to clarify what further charges you face for reshooting should you be dissatisfied.

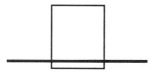

CHECKLIST, PART VII
POSTPRODUCTION

The recommendations and points summarized here are only those most salient or the most commonly overlooked. To find more about them or anything else, go to the table of contents at the beginning of this part, or try the index at the back of the book.

EDITING IN GENERAL

- interesting discrepancies of information drive the audience into an active, problem-solving relationship with the film, instead of the usual passive one
- every call you make to their imagination or judgment is an acknowledgment of the audience as equals, and an invitation to participate in discovery
- are there dramatic advantages to be gained from disrupting the subject's natural advance in time?
- cross-cutting between two stories allows time to be telescoped or stretched, and heightens comparison and irony
- the operative word falling on each new shot helps us interpret the image's meaning
- changing the juxtaposition of words and shots can imply different meanings

- it is easier to shorten a film than to pump substance back into one prematurely tightened
- if an edited version is different from what you expected, see it again before commenting
- stay away from the cutting room and preserve your objectivity

VIEWING RUSHES

- avoid taking your attention away from the screen
- in the rushes book note down chosen takes, special comments, and any ideas and transient impressions; they will be an important resource later
- note down moods and feelings evoked by scenes or individuals
- nothing outside the rushes is relevant to the film you can make
- the director discusses intentions for each sequence with the editor and encourages an early, loose assembly of whole film

PREPARING TO START EDITING

- time spent making a consistent, intelligent log is time liberated for creativity later
- from rushes mark up script to show actual coverage and number of takes for each angle

EDITING PROCEDURE

- when cutting film *never* forget to put aside three frames minimum between adjacent lengths of film to allow for cement splices in conforming
- assemble film workprint sound as one track containing main dramatic elements (dialogue, atmosphere, or music). Later you will split these tracks apart
- assemble video tracks, especially dialogue, in checkerboard fashion to allow early premix with equalization
- leave spaces in dialogue for featured sound effects

FIRST ASSEMBLY

- make first assembly long, loose, and simple using master shots and a minimum of intercutting so you get an early view of the whole film
- see first assembly without interruption and make quick list of what was memorable
- see first assembly a second time and see if your impressions are confirmed

ROUGH CUT

- work on each sequence to make use of all material, but still keep pace slow and cutting simple
- view whole film, and pay attention to material that is not working
- tackle only top level of problems in each pass and see new version before addressing a further level of problems

DIAGNOSTIC METHODS

- make flow chart of whole movie to spot invisible anomalies
- after recutting and viewing, check results by making revised block diagram

FINE CUT

- where necessary, alter performance rhythms in action and reaction to allow the appropriate time that characters need to process particular information
- use eyeline changes and reactions to alert us to those moments of special awareness that yield access to a character's inner life
- where you have multiple angle coverage, experimentally rebalance subjective and objective angles so the sequence feels right
- try counterpointing visuals against speech to suggest a person's subjective vision
- in dialogue sequences, examine coverage for its balance—showing either the actor or the acted upon. Frequently the character acted upon adds more dimension to the exchange
- introduce overlap cutting to set up a visual cutting rhythm that is separate and meaningful in contrast with speech and sound effect rhythms
- tighten transition cuts where action flows from one composition to another
- examine sequence transitions for sound overlap or sound dissolve possibilities
- put the film aside for a week or two, and see it again before deciding the fine cut is final

EVOKING A TRIAL AUDIENCE RESPONSE

- you can't please everyone
- tell your audience the film's title and warn them of what is missing (music, sound effects, atmospheres, etc.)
- in a trial showing, exert maximum control over sound
- direct audience attention to issues over which you need information, but ask nondirective questions and listen carefully for what is really being said

- do not abandon any central intention without long, hard thought
- do not rush into changes of any kind
- expect to feel depressed about the film, that it's failing, etc.

SFX AND MUSIC

- choice of music should give access to interior of character or subject
- music can signal emotional level at which audience should approach the scene
- you cannot know that music works until you try it against the picture
- decide what, if anything, needs postsynchronizing
- start looking for sound effects early; they are part of your orchestra
- plan featured sound effects to go in dialogue gaps (or vice versa)

SOUND MIX

- premix, retaining control over balance of important elements until last
- soften ragged sound cuts by tailoring the louder to the quieter
- when mixing foreground speech with background (music, FX, atmosphere, etc.) err on the side of caution and separate foreground well from background
- check completed mix against picture without stopping
- make at least one sound mix safety copy

TITLES

- keep credits short and few
- each title card should be on the screen long enough to be read aloud one and a half times
- choose a legible, clean typeface that goes with the period and style of your film
- double-check all spelling, especially of people's names
- include acknowledgments, funding sources, dedications, etc. exactly according to contractual obligations
- copyright your film with the Library of Congress or appropriate national authority and put © sign and year at end

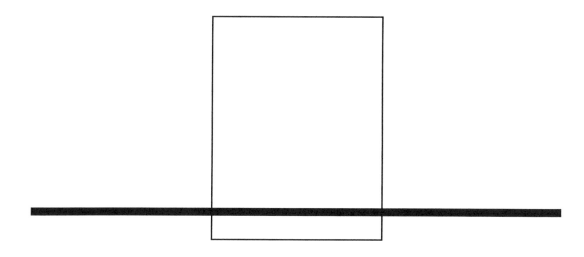

P·A·R·T VIII

CAREER TRACK

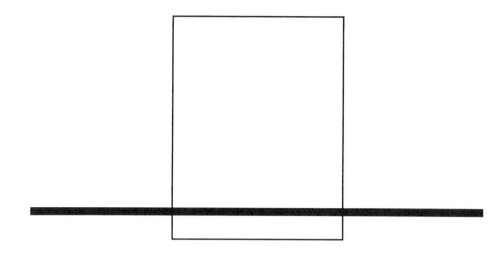

PLANNING A CAREER

Filmmaking, unlike engineering or real estate management, lacks a career ladder with predictable steps for promotion. It is a branch of show business, so how far you get and how long you take to get there depends on your ability, tenacity, and to a smaller degree, your luck. If your primary loyalties are to family, a community, and material well-being, then sustaining a commitment to filmmaking may be impractical because the industry is informally structured, unpredictable, and assumes initiative and complete commitment in the individual.

There are places in the industry for three kinds of person: the craftsman; the craftsman with a visionary inside struggling to get out; and the craftsman who is a fully realized visionary. Only the last is ready to direct, and this is discussed in the next chapter. After years of teaching in a film school, I still can't predict who "has it." Students prove themselves only in the long haul. Unsuited however is anyone lacking the craftsman's attitude—I mean the undisciplined, the unreliable, the nonperfectionist, or those whose egos and insecurities prevent them from working with other people as equals. Filmmaking is long and slow; it is no discipline for those who need immediate gratification. Getting established in the industry is equally slow, but once established, few drop out. After all, where else can the ordinary person so profoundly affect so many lives? Though the profession is insecure, you never have to ask yourself why you go to work every day. If you love the cinema and if you are willing to invest a long and penurious struggle to gain recognition, then you might like working in film very much.

How do you get started? Old-timers used to scorn any form of schooling, but that is changing as film school alumni like George Lucas, Frances Ford Coppola,

Terence Malick, John Milius, Susan Seidelman, Martin Scorsese, Oliver Stone, and Roman Polansky show how a career can follow schooling.

If film school is out of the question, this book shows the way to prepare yourself outside the available educational structures. In any case, the best education will always be that which you give yourself. I think a good school can cut years out of the learning curve, but even here there are drawbacks. Formal schooling is (and must be) geared to the common denominator; it can be frustrating for those who learn more rapidly or who are more than averagely motivated. In short, there are no sure routes, only intelligent traveling.

APPRENTICESHIP AS A BEGINNING

Older people in the film and TV industries may tell you that only on-the-job experience counts. Many of these received no college-level education and believe that it fills young people's heads with idealistic dreams unrelated to the business. Because they tend to value procedural knowledge and professionalism (often deficiencies in recent graduates), they assume schooling fails. Certainly school cannot teach the consistency, tact, and reliability that make up the hallmark of professional responsibility, nor should it drill students in the niceties of industrial procedures at the expense of a conceptual education. Some students eagerly drop their schooling when an industry opening comes their way. It seems like a dream come true, but is almost always a terrible mistake. They should be warned that progress will be slow and their self-esteem will be eroded by the self-serving mystiques propagated by their seniors.

I am myself a scarred survivor of industry apprenticeship. I want to stress the benefits of a purposeful education because I see students in a fifteen-week editing class mastering techniques and using insights that took me ten years on the job to invent for myself. That I learned slowly and in isolation isn't unusual: in the freelance world, know-how and experience are earning power, so workers systemically avoid enlightening their juniors. Most are not secure enough to share their knowledge, or they live highly pressured lives and consider it no part of their job to prepare "the kid" for more responsibility. You have to steal knowledge while serving as the company peon. How much easier if prior schooling has made you ready at any time to assume more complex duties.

WHAT FILM SCHOOL CAN DO

A first rate film/video education imparts:

- a broad cultural and intellectual perspective on your chosen medium
- a knowledge of the history your role grows out of
- the opportunity to relive that history by starting with simple and primal techniques
- some marketable skills
- a lot of hands-on experience

- a can-do attitude that isn't fazed by equipment and technical obstacles
- aspirations to use your professional life for the widest good
- a community of peers with whom you will probably work for much of your life

By encouraging collaboration and unbridled individual vision, the educational process helps you determine early where your talents, skills, and energies truly lie. Most importantly, *by exposing you to a holistic experience of filmmaking, it allows you to form long-range ambitions and to recognize appropriate opportunities when they arise,* something the underprepared worker is mortally afraid to do.

Almost every entering film student wants to be a director. The true visionaries (they are very rare) direct all through film school and go straight into directing when they leave. Others of promise graduate with a useful technical skill and with the beginnings of an artistic identity established. Most on leaving school will be neither ready nor wanting to direct for a number of years.

How does one find out which kind of person one is? Only by going through all the stages of making a film—no matter how badly. Here you will truly see the strengths and weaknesses of your own (and other people's) work. Film being such a dense and allusive language, a director must develop two separate kinds of skill, only one of which can be taught. The first is the slew of human and technical skills to put a well conceived, well composed series of shots on the screen and make them tell a story. The other must be developed by the individual; the skill of knowing oneself, of knowing what one has of value to offer the world, and the capacity to remain true to oneself even when one's work comes under attack.

The beginning filmmaker not only relives and reinvents the history of film, but is shocked to discover how much about personal identity and perception he or she has taken for granted, and how meager and precarious this identity feels when one places it before an audience.

A good film school is the place to have all this experience, for learning is structured and executed in the company of contemporaries. There should be technical facilities and enthusiastic expertise available. Here one can experiment and afford failures. In the industry unwise experiment spells professional suicide. The industry worker must always play it safe, and this is why his development is slow and haphazard.

So film/video school is also the place to:

- learn crafts in a structured way that includes both theory and practice
- get an overview of the whole production process
- use technical facilities
- get mentoring
- experiment
- put work before a (relatively!) sympathetic audience
- become familiar with every aspect of one's medium
- fly high on exhilarating philosophies of filmmaking and of living life
- develop a network of contacts, each tending to aid the others after graduation

FINDING THE RIGHT SCHOOL

Many schools, colleges, and universities now have film courses. Although no serious study of film is ever wasted, be careful and critical before committing yourself to an extended course of study. Many film departments are underequipped and underbudgeted. Often film studies is an offshoot of the English department, perhaps originally created to bolster sagging enrollments. Avoid departments whose course structure shows a lack of interest in field production. Film studies are good in a liberal education for sharpening the perceptions, but divorced from film production they become criticism, not creation. The measure of a film school is what the students and faculty produce. Quite simply, you must study with active filmmakers.

However, there are a number of film teachers whose own films are so far from the mainstream that they lack appeal for almost any audience. During the 1970s some of the more colorful experimentalists got tenured positions in universities and art schools. School administrations welcomed them because they symbolized buccaneering independence to students of the day, and because they were used to working with little equipment and small budgets. Some experimental cinema is undoubtedly significant but much of what passes under the experimental label normally departs from or even despises mainstream forms. Experimentalists are thus equipped neither technically nor philosophically to teach what goes into creating the modern, mass-audience film.

One must also be cautious about film departments in fine arts schools. Usually they undervalue content and craftsmanlike control of the medium and overvalue exotic form presented as personal vision. Instead of working collaboratively, students tend to be reclusive soloists like the painters and sculptors around them. This encourages gimmicky, egocentric production with poor basic control over the medium. Leaving school with no work that film or TV companies can take seriously, the graduate finds developing a career next to impossible.

At another extreme is the trade school, which is more technically disciplined and infinitely less therapeutic. The atmosphere is commercial and industry oriented, concerned with drilling students to carry out narrowly defined technical duties for a standardized industrial product. Union and Academy apprenticeship schemes tend to follow these lines; technically superb but often intellectually arid. They do lead to jobs, unlike the hastily assembled school of communications, which offers the illusion of a quick route to a TV station job. For every occupation there is somewhere a diploma mill. In the TV version expect to find a private, unaffiliated facility with a primitive studio where students are run through the rudiments of equipment operation. Needless to say, it is doubtful whether more than a token few ever find the career they hope for.

A good school balances sound technical education with a strong counterpart of conceptual, aesthetic, and historical coursework. Foundation courses should lead to specialization tracks, such as screenwriting, camera, sound, editing, directing, and production management. Animation is an advantage, but utterly separate from live action filming and closer to the graphic arts in its training. There should be a respectable contingent of professional-level equipment as well as enough basic cameras and editing equipment to support the beginning levels.

Most important of all, a good school should be the center of an enthusiastic film-producing community, where students routinely support and crew for each other. The school's working attitude towards students and how they fit into the film industry is the key. A school that rewards individualist stars or one divorced from working professionals cannot prepare its student body for reality. And a school too much in awe of Hollywood is likely to promote ideas about success that destroy real talent. Oliver Stone's *Wall Street* (1988) stands as a warning not only to young stockbrokers but also to young filmmakers who fly too near the big money. Be warned that some of the big film schools use a competitive system to decide whose work is produced. You may enter wanting to study directing, but find that your work doesn't get the votes, and you end up recording sound for a winner's project.

If the film school of your choice has been in existence for a while, successful former students not only give visiting lectures, but come back as teachers. In turn they either employ or give vital references to the most promising students. In this networking process, the lines separating many schools from real life are being crossed in both directions. The school filmmaking community tapers off into the young (and not so young) professional community to mutual advantage. In the reverse flow, mentors not only give advice and steer projects but exemplify the way of life the student is trying to make his own. Even in the largest cities the film and video community operates like a village where personal recommendation is everything.

Much practical information can be gleaned from the *American Film Institute Guide to College Courses in Film and Television* (Princeton, NJ: Peterson's Guides [Peterson's Guides, Dept 7591, PO Box 978, Edison, NJ 08817]). Being so comprehensive, it allows one to make comparisons and to guess at a department's emphasis. A rousing statement of philosophy may be undercut when you scan equipment holdings and the program structure. Sometimes a department has evolved under the chairmanship of a journalist or radio specialist, so film and television production may be public relations orphans within an all-purpose communications department.

The first attribute of a director is the ability to research a situation and to put together a picture from multiple sources of information. Here are some considerations as you decide whether a particular film school fulfills your expectations:

- how extensive is the department and what does its structure reveal? (Number of courses, number of students, subjects taught by the senior and most influential faculty.)
- how long is the program? (See model syllabus. Below two years is suspiciously short.)
- how much specialization is possible? How far do upper level courses really go?
- how much equipment is there, what kind, and who gets to use it? (This is a real giveaway.)
- how is the school adapting to the massive switch to digital video? (Faculties are sometimes dominated by film diehards.)

- what kind of backgrounds do the faculty members have, and what have they produced?
- are senior faculty still producing, or do they rest on past laurels?
- how experienced are those teaching beginning classes? (Many schools recycle their graduates into teaching before they have had time to develop their own experience.)
- how much equipment and materials are supplied out of tuition and class fees, and how much is the student expected to supply along the way?
- what proportion of those wanting to direct actually do so? (Some schools for budgetary reasons make students compete for top artistic roles and sideline the losers.)
- what does the department say about its attitudes and philosophy?
- what does the place feel like? (Try to visit the facilities.)
- what do the students think of the place? (Speak to senior students.)
- how much are your particular interests treated as a specialty?
- what kind of graduate program do they offer? (An MFA is a good qualification for production and teaching, while a Ph.D. signifies a scholarly emphasis that generally precludes production.)
- if the degree conferred is a BA, how many hours of general studies are you expected to complete, and how germane are they to your focus in film or video?

One way to locate good teaching is to attend student film festivals and note where the films you like are being made. A sure sign of energetic and productive teaching, even in a small facility, is when student work is receiving recognition in competitions.

Some of the larger and well recognized film/video schools in the USA are listed in the next chapter. Also listed are the major film schools around the world since many of this book's users will be from other parts of the globe. Most of these schools only take advanced or specially qualified students. Americans sometimes assume that work and study abroad is easily arranged and will be an extension of conditions in the United States. Be warned that most film schools have very competitive entry requirements, and that self-support through part-time work in foreign countries is usually impossible to arrange. As in the United States, immigration policies exclude foreign workers when natives are underemployed. That situation changes only when you have special, unusual, and proven skills to offer. Check local conditions with the school's admissions officer and with the country's consulate before committing yourself. Also check the length of the visa granted and the average time it takes students to graduate—sometimes these durations are incompatible.

SELF-HELP AS A REALISTIC ALTERNATIVE

Since many can afford neither time nor money to go to school, they must find other means to acquire the necessary knowledge and experience. Werner Herzog has said that anyone wanting to make films should waste no more than a week learning film techniques. Even with his flair for overstatement, this period would appear a little short, but fundamentally I share his attitude. Film and video is a practical subject, and can be tackled by a group of motivated do-it-yourselfers. This book is intended to encourage the reader to learn filmmaking by making films, to learn through doing, and, if absolutely necessary, through doing so in relative isolation.

Self-education in the arts, however, is different from self-education in a technology, because the arts are not finite and calculable. They are based upon shared tastes and perceptions that at an early stage call for the criticism and participation of others. Even the painter, novelist, poet, photographer, or animator—artists who normally create alone—is incomplete until he engages with society and experiences its reaction. Nowhere is public acceptance more important than with film, the preeminent audience medium.

PROS AND CONS OF COLLABORATION

If you use this book to begin active film/video-making, you will recognize that filmmaking is a social art, one stillborn if there is no spirit of collaboration. You will need other people as technicians and artistic collaborators if you are to do any sophisticated shooting, and you will need to earn the interest of other people in your end product. If you are unused to working collaboratively—and sadly education teaches students to compete for honors instead of gaining them cooperatively—then you have an inspirational experience ahead. Filmmaking is an intense, shared experience and no relationship is left untouched. Lifelong friendships and partnerships develop out of it, but on the negative side, flaws emerge in one's own and other people's characters when the pressure mounts.

Somewhere along the way you will need a mentor, someone to give knowledgeable and objective criticism of your work and to help solve the problems that arise. Do not worry if none is in the offing right now, for the beginner has far to go. It is a law of nature in any case that you find the right people when you truly need them.

PLANNING A CAREER TRACK DURING YOUR EDUCATION

Whether you are self-educated or whether you pursue a formal education at school, the way people receive your finished work will indicate whether you are a visionary and it is realistic to try entering the industry as a director, or whether you belong with the vast majority for whom directing is a distant dream. In the latter case *you must develop a craft specialty in order to make yourself marketable and gain a foothold in the industry.* These aspects are the subject of Chapter 40, Breaking into the Industry.

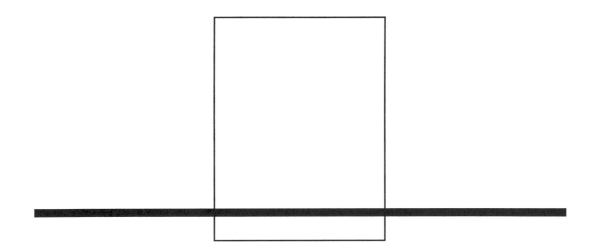

MAJOR INTERNATIONAL FILM/VIDEO SCHOOLS

These are the major film/video schools in their respective countries listed in country then city order. There is no guarantee that they run fiction filmmaking courses, nor that foreign students are accepted. Make appropriate inquiries. The + sign before a phone or fax number indicates the overseas telephone code—011 in the USA—that you dial to make an international call.

ARGENTINA

Centro de Experimentación y de Realización
  Cinematográfica (CERC)
Salita 327
1074 Buenos Aires
Tel: +54 1 38 11785
Fax: +54 1 8143 062

Universidad del Cine
Pasaje Giuffra 330
1063 Buenos Aires
Tel: +54 1 300 1413
Fax: +54 1 782 0473

AUSTRALIA

Victorian College of the Arts
School of Film & Television
234 St. Kilda Road
Melbourne, Victoria 3004
Tel: +61 3 685 9000
Fax: +61 3 685 9001

Australian Film and Television School (AFTRS)
Corner Balaclava Road & Epping Highway
Box 126, North Ryde
N.S.W. 2113
Tel: +61 2 805 6611
Fax: +61 2 887 1030

AUSTRIA

Hochschule für Musik und Darstellende Kunst
  in Wien (HFMDK)
Abteilung "Film und Fernsehen"
Metternichgasse 12
1030 Wien
Tel: +43 1 713 52120
Fax: +43 1 713 52 1423

BELGIUM

Hogeschool voor Audiovisuele Communicatie
Naamsestraat 54
1000 Brussel
Tel: +32 2 511 93 82
Fax: +32 2 502 55 06

Institut National Supérieur des Arts du Spectacle
  (INSAS)
Rue Thérésienne 8
1000 Bruxelles
Tel: +32 2 511 9286
Fax: +32 2 511 0279

St. Lukas Hoger Instituut voor Beeldende
  Kunsten
Paleizenstraat 70
1210 Brussel
Tel: +32 2 217 05 89

Institut des Arts de Diffusion (IAD)
Rue des Wallons, 77
1348 Louvain-la-Neuve
Tel: +32 10 47 80 18
Fax: +32 10 45 11 74

BRAZIL

Escola de Comunicações e Artes
Universidad de São Paulo
Av. Prof. Lucio Martins Rodrigues, 443
Cidade Universitaria CEP 05508-900
São Paulo
Tel: +55 11 818 4020
Fax: +55 11 211 2752

BULGARIA

Nacionalna Academia za Teatraino i Folmovo
  Izkoustvo (NATFIZ)
"Krustyo Sarafov"—Sofia
Rakovski Street 108a
Sofia 1000
Tel: +359 2 87 98 62
Fax: +359 2 89 73 89

New Bulgarian University
Dept of Mass Communications
47 Gurko Street
Sofia 1000
Tel: +359 2 891 203
Fax: +359 2 880 902

CANADA

Université du Québec à Montréal (UQAM)
Module de communications
Case Postale 8888, succursale A
Montréal (Québec) H3C 3P8
Tel: +1 514 987 3759
Fax: +1 514 987 4650

Canadian Film Centre
Windfields
2849 Bayview Avenue
North York, Ontario, Canada M4W 3E2
Tel: +1 416 445 1446
Fax: +1 416 445 9481

York University
Faculty of Fine Arts
Dept of Film & Video
4700 Keele Street
North York, Ontario M3J 1P3
Tel: +1 416 736 5149
Fax: +1 416 736 5710

Ryerson Polytechnic University
Film & Photography Dept
Faculty of Applied Arts
350 Victoria Street
Toronto, Ontario M5B 2K3
Tel: +1 416 979 5167
Fax: +1 416 979 5341

CHINA

Beijing Film Academy (BFA)
Xi Tu Cheng Lu 4
Haidian District
Beijing
Tel: +861 201 2132
Fax: +861 201 2132

CROATIA

Akedemija Dramske Umjetnosti (ADU)
Trg Maršala Tita 5
41000 Zagreb
Tel: +385 1 446 633
Fax: +385 1 446 032

CUBA

Escuela Internacional de Cine y TV (EICTV)
Ap. Aéreo 40/41
San Antonio de los Baños
Tel: +53 7 335196
Fax: +53 7 335341

CZECH REPUBLIC

Akedemie Múzickych Umeni (FAMU)
Filmová a televisni fakulta
Smetanovo Nábr. 2
116 65 Prague 1
Tel: +42 2 24 22 94 68
Fax: +42 2 24 22 23 02 85

DENMARK

Den Danske Filmskole
St. Sondervoldstræde 4
1419 Copenhagen K
Tel: +45 31 57 65 00
Fax: +45 31 57 65 10

EGYPT

Academy of Arts
High Cinema Institute
Pyramids Road
Gamal El Din El Afghany Str.
Giza
Tel: +20 2 537 703
Fax: +20 2 560 1034

FINLAND

Taideteollinen Korkeakoulu
Elokuvataiteen Laitos
Pursimiehenkatu 29-31B
00150 Helskinki
Tel: +358 0 636982
Fax: +358 0 634303

FRANCE

Ecole Nationale Supérieure Louis Lumière
"Ecole de Vaugirard"
Allée de Promontoire
B.P. 22
Marne-la-Vallée
93161 Noisy-le-Grand Cédex
Tel: +33 1 45 92 23 33
Fax: +33 1 43 05 63 44

Institut de Formation et d'Enseignement pour les
    Metiers de l'Image et du Son (FEMIS)
6 rue Francoeur
75018 Paris
Tel: +33 1 42 62 20 00
Fax: +33 1 42 62 21 00

Atelier de Réalisation Cinématographique
    (VARAN)
6 Impasse Mont-Louis
75011 Paris
Tel: +33 1 43 56 64 04
Fax: +33 1 43 56 2902

Ecole Supérieure d'Audiovisuel (ESAV)
Université Toulouse Le Mirail
5 Allées Antonio Machado
31058 Toulouse Cédex
Tel: +33 61 50 44 46
Fax: +33 61 50 49 34

GEORGIA

The Russian State Institute of Theatre and Film
Rustaveli Avenue 19
380004 Tbilisi
Tel: +7 8832 990438
Fax: +7 8832 931824

GERMANY

Deutsche Film-und Fernsehakademie Berlin
  (DFFB)
Pommernallee 1
14052 Berlin
Tel: +49 30 30 30 71
Fax: +49 30 301 9875

Hamburger Filmwerkstatt e.V.
Friedensallee 7-9
22765 Hamburg
Tel: +49 40 3982 6136
Fax: +49 40 3982 6149

Kunsthochschule für Medien
Television and Film Dept
Peter-Weller Platz 2
D-50676 Köln
Tel: +49 221 201 890
Fax: +49 221 201 89124

Filmakademie Baden-Württemberg
Mathildenstr. 20
71638 Ludwigsberg
Tel: +49 7141 969 102
Fax: +49 7141 969 298

Hochschule für Fernsehen und Film
Frankenthalerstr. 23
D-81539 München
Tel: +49 89 68 000 40
Fax: +49 89 68 000 436

Hochschule für Fernsehen und Film "Konrad
  Wolf"
Karl-Marx-Str. 33/34
14482 Potsdam
Tel: +49 331 789 81
Fax: +49 331 75073

GHANA

National Film & Television Institute (NAFTI)
Private Mail Bag—GPO
Accra
Tel: +233 21 71 76 10
Fax: +233 21 77 45 22

GREECE

Hellenic Cinema and Television School Stavrakos
26 Ioulianou Str.
104 34 Athens
Tel: +30 1 8230 124
Fax: +30 1 8237 648

School of Cinema & Television (ETCEH)
Eugégie Hadjikou
Asimaki Fotila Str. 7
114 73 Athens
Tel: +30 1 82 34 236
Fax: +30 1 88 30 871

HONG KONG

Hong Kong Baptist College
School of Communication
Dept of Cinema & Television
224 Waterloo Road
Kowloon
Tel: +852 339 7395
Fax: +852 336 1371

The Hong Kong School for Performing Arts
1 Gloucester Road
GPO Box 12288
Wanchai
Tel: +852 584 1593
Fax: +852 802 4372

HUNGARY

Szinház—es Filmmüvészeti Föiskola
Szentkirályi U. 32/a
1088 Budapest
Tel: +36 1 118 5533
Fax: +36 1 138 4560

INDIA

Development and Educational Communication
  Unit (DECU)
Indian Space Research Organization
ISRO
SAC P.O.
Jodhpur Tekera
Ahmedabad 380 053
Gujarat
Tel: +91 079 42 39 54
Fax: +91 079 42 85 56

Film and Television Institute of India (FTII)
Law College Road
Pune 411 004
Tel: +91 212 33 10 10
Fax: +91 212 33 0416

INDONESIA

Institut Kesenian Jakarta (IKJ)
Fakultas Film dan Televisi
Jl. Cikini Raya No. 73
Jakarta 10330
PO Box 4014
Jakarta 10001
Tel: +62 21 324 807
Fax: +62 21 323 603

Yayasan Citra
Film Centre "Usmar Ismail"
Jl HR Rasua Said
Jakarta 12950
Tel: +62 21 52 07390
Fax: +62 21 51 5027

IRELAND

National Association for Audio-Visual Training
  in Ireland
c/o Irish Film Institute
6 Eustace Street
Dublin 2
Tel: +353 1 679 5744
Fax: +353 1 679 9657

ISRAEL

The Jerusalem Film & Television School
4 Yad Harutzim St.
P.O.B. 10636
Jerusalem 91103
Tel: +972 2 731950
Fax: +972 2 731949

Tel Aviv University
Department of Film and Television
Ramat-Aviv
P.O.B. 39040
Tel: +972 3 640 9483
Fax: +972 3 640 9935

Camera Obscura
School of Art
4 Rival Street
Tel Aviv 67778
Tel: +972 3 537 1871
Fax: +972 3 381 025

ITALY

Ippotesi Cinema
Instituto Paolo Valmarana
Via S. Giorgio, 24
36061 Bassano del Grappa (VI)
Tel: +39 424 500 007
Fax: +39 424 502 139

Zelig
Scuola di televisione e cinema
Via Carducci, 15a
Bolzano
Tel: +39 471 977930
Fax: +39 471 977931

Centro Formazione Professionale per le Techiche
  Cinetelevisive
Viale Legioni Romane, 43
20147 Milano
Tel: +39 2 4048455
Fax: +39 2 48700392

Centro Sperimentale di Cinematografia (CSC)
Via Tuscolana 1524
00173 Rome
Tel: +39 6 72 29 41
Fax: +39 6 72 11 619

JAMAICA

University of the West Indies (CARIMAC)
The Caribbean Institute of Mass Communication
Mona
Kingston 7
Tel: +1 809 927 1481
Fax: +1 809 927 5353

JAPAN

Japan Institute of Visual Arts
1-16-30 Manpukuji
Kawasaki-shi
Kanagawa 245
Tel: +81 44 951 2511
Fax: +81 44 951 2681

Nihon University
College of Art
Department of Cinema
2-42-1 Asahigaoka
Nerima-Ku
Tokyo 176
Tel: +81 3 5995 8220
Fax: +81 3 5995 8229

KENYA

Kenya Institute of Mass Communication (KIMC)
Film Production Training Department
PO Box 42422
Nairobi
Tel: +254 2540 820
Fax: +254 2556 798

LEBANON

Institut d'Etudes Scéniques et Audiovisuelles
   (IESAV)
Université St. Joseph
Faculté des Lettres et Sciences Humaine
Rue Huvelin
Beyrouth
Tel: +961 1 200629
Fax:+961 1 423369

MEXICO

Centro de Capacitación Cinematográfica (CCC)
Czda. de Tlalpan 1670 Esq Rio Churubusco
México 21, D.F. 04220
Tel: +52 5 544 8007
Fax: +52 5 688 7812

Centro Universitario de Estudios
   Cinematográficos (CUEC)
Universidad Nacional Autónoma de México
Adolfo Prieto 721 (Colonia del Valle)
México D. F. 03100
Tel: +52 5 536 02 30
Fax: +52 5 536 17 99

NETHERLANDS

Nederlandse Film en Televisie Academie
Ite Boeremastraat 1
1054 PP Amsterdam
Tel: +31 20 683 02 06
Fax: +31 20 612 62 66

NORWAY

Statens Studiesenter for Film
Storengveien 8b
1342 Jar
Tel: +47 67 53 00 33
Fax: +47 67 12 48 65

PHILIPPINES

Mowelfund Film Institute
No. 66 Rosario Drive
Cubao, 111 Quezon City
Metro Manila
Tel: +63 2 721 7702
Fax: +63 2 722 8628

University of the Philippines
Film Center
UP Film Center
Magsaysay Avenue
PO Box 214
Diliman
Quezon City 1101
Tel: +63 2 96 27 22
Fax: +63 2 99 26 25

POLAND

Panstwowa Wyzsza Szkola Filmova i Teatralna
   (PWSFTV i T)
Targowa 61/63
90-323 Lódz
Tel: +48 42 74 35 38
Fax: +48 42 74 81 39

PORTUGAL

Escola Superior de Teatro e Cinema
Rua dos Caetanos, 29
1200 Lisboa
Tel: +351 1 342 36 85
Fax: +351 1 347 02 73

ROMANIA

Academia de Teatru si Film
Facultatea de Film si TV
Str. Matei Voievod 75-77
Sector 2
73224 Bucuresti
Tel: +40 1 642 47 26
Fax: +40 1 250 98 80

RUSSIA

Russian State Institute of Cinematography
  (VGIK)
Wilhelm Pieck Str. 3
Moscow 129226
Tel: +7 095 181 3868
Fax: +7 095 187 7174

St. Petersburg Institute of Cinema and Television
  (SPIC&T)
Pravda Str. 13
191126 St. Petersburg
Tel: +7 812 315 72 85
Fax: +7 812 315 01 72

SERBIA (AND MONTENEGRO)

Fakultet Dramskih Umetnosti (FDU)
Ho Ši Mina 20
11070 Beograd
Tel: +38 11 140 419
Fax: +38 11 130 862

SINGAPORE

Ngee Ann Polytechnic
Film, Sound, & Video Dept
535 Clementi Road
Singapore 2159
Tel: +65 460 6992
Fax: +65 468 6218

SLOVAKIA

Vysoka Škola Muzickych Umeni (VŠMU)
Filmová a televisna fakulta
Ventúrska 3
813 01 Bratislava
Tel: +42 7 332 306
Fax: +42 7 330 125

SLOVENIA

Akademija za Glendalisce Radio Rilm in
  Televizijo (AGRFT)
Nazorjeva 3
Ljublijana
Tel: +38 61 210 412
Fax: +38 61 210 450

SOUTH AFRICA

Newtown Film & Television School
1 President Street
Newtown, 2113
Johannesburg
Tel: +27 11 838 7462
Fax: +27 11 838 1043

SPAIN

Escuala de Cine y Video (ESKIVI)
Vada. Ama Kandida s/n.
20140 Andoain (Guipúzcoa)
Tel: +34 43 59 41 90
Fax: +34 43 59 40 52

Escola Superior de Cinema i Audiovisuals de
  Catalunya (ESCAC)
Immaculada 25-35
08017 Barcelona
Tel: +34 3 212 40 76
Fax: +34 3 417 86 99

Escuela des Artes Visuales
Fuencarral 45
28004 Madrid
Tel: +34 1 523 17 01
Fax: +34 1 523 17 63

Centro Imagen y Nuevas Tecnologias (CINT)
Adriano VI-9
01008 Vitoria—Gasteiz
Tel: +34 45 13 44 64
Fax: +34 45 14 61 48

SRI LANKA

Sri Lanka Television Training Institute (SLTTI)
100 A Independence Square
Colombo 7
Tel: +94 1 699 720
Fax: +94 1 699 791

SWEDEN

Dramatiska Intitutet (DI)
University College of Film, Radio, Television,
  and Theatre
Borgvägen 5
Box 27090,
102-51 Stockholm
Tel: +46 8 665 13 00
Fax: +46 8 662 14 84

SWITZERLAND

Ecole cantonale d'art de Lausanne (DAVI)
46 rue de l'Industrie
1030 Bussigny
Tel: +41 21 702 92 22
Fax: +41 21 702 92 09

Ecole Supérieure d'Art Visuel
2 Rue Général Dufour
Genève 1204
Tel: +41 22 311 05 10
Fax: +41 22 310 46 36

Focal
Fondation de Formation Continue pour le
   Cinéma e l'Audiovisuel
Stiftung Weiterbildung Film und Audiovision
33 rue St. Lauent
1003 Lausanne
Tel: +41 21 312 68 17
Fax: +41 21 323 59 45

TAIWAN

National Taiwan Academy of Arts
No. 59 Section 1 Da-Kuan Rd.
Pan-Chao Park
Taipei
Tel: +886 2 966 3154
Fax: +886 2 968 7563

UKRAINE

Fakultet Kinomystetstva
Kyïvskoho Instytutu Teatrainoho Mystetstva
   Imeni I.K. Karpenha-Karoho
Yaroslaviv Val St. 40
252034 Kiev
Tel: +7 044212 10 32
Fax: +7 044 210 10 03

UNITED KINGDOM

National Film and Television School (NFTS)
Beaconsfield Film Studios
Station Road,
Beaconsfield, Bucks HP9 1LG
Tel: +044 4946 71234
Fax: +044 4946 74042

London International Film School (LIFS)
24 Shelton Street
London WC2H 9HP
Tel: 01-240-0168
Tel: +44 171 240 0168
Fax: +44 171 497 3718

National Association for Higher Education in
   Film & Video (NAHEFV)
City of London Polytechnic
Dept of Communication Studies
31 Jewry Street
London EC3N 2EY
Tel: +44 181 840 2815
Fax: +44 171 320 3040

Royal College of Art
Dept of Film & Television
Kensington Gore
London SW7 2EU
Tel: +44 171 584 5020
Fax: +44 171 589 0178

University of Westminster
School of Communication
18-22 Riding House Street
London W1 P7PD
Tel: +44 171 911 5000
Fax: +44 171 911 5127

USA

University of Texas at Austin
Department of Radio, Television and Film
School of Communications CMA6.118
Austin, TX 78712-1091
Tel: +1 512 471 4071
Fax: +1 512 471 4077

Emerson College
Division of Communication
100 Beacon Street
Boston, MA 02116
Tel: +1 617 578 8800
Fax: +1 617 578 8804

Columbia College Chicago
Film/Video Department, Columbia College
600 S. Michigan Avenue,
Chicago, Illinois 60605-1996
Tel: +1 312 663 1600 Ext 300
Fax: +1 312 986 8208

American Film Institute (AFI)
PO Box 27999
2021 North Western Avenue
Los Angeles, CA 90027
Tel: +1 213 856 7664
Fax: +1 213 464 5217

Loyola Marymount Unversity
Communications Arts Dept
Los Angeles, CA 90045
Tel: +1 310 338 3033
Fax: +1 310 338 3030

University of California, Los Angeles
School of Theater, Film and Television
East Melnitz
405 Hilgard Avenue
Los Angeles, CA 90024
Tel: +1 310 825 7741
Fax: +1 310206 1686

University of Southern California (USC)
School of Cinema and Television
University Park
Los Angeles CA 90089-2211
Tel: +1 213 743 2235
Fax: +1 213 740 7682

Columbia University
Film Division
513 Dodge Hall, School of the Arts
116th Street and Broadway
New York, NY 10027
Tel: +1 212 854 1681
Fax: +1 212 854 1309

New York University (NYU)
Institute of Film and Television
721 Broadway, Room 1042
New York, NY 10003
Tel: +1 212 998 1700
Fax: +1 212 995 4040

California Institute of the Arts (CALARTS)
24700 McBean Parkway
Valencia CA 91355
Tel: +1 805 253 7825
Fax: +1 805 253 7824

VIETNAM

Truong Dai Hoc San Khau Va Dien Anh
Mai Dich
Tu Liem
Ha Noi
Tel: 43397 (operator service)

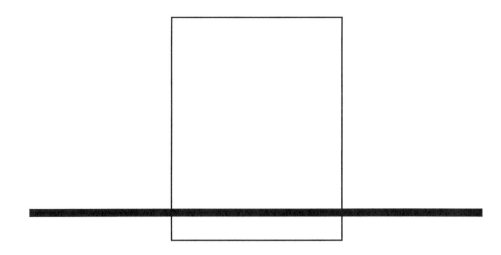

C·H·A·P·T·E·R 40

BREAKING INTO THE INDUSTRY

THE PATH TO THE DIRECTOR'S CHAIR

In Chapter 38 I spoke of there being three good kinds of candidates for working in film/video: the craftsman, the craftsman with visionary potential, and the visionary who is a disciplined craftsman. Everyone entering film school wants to direct, but it soon becomes evident who is equipped with ideas and leadership and who is happier in an interpretive or technical role. Only the craftsman visionary with a fully formed artistic identity is at all likely to go straight from film school into commercial directing. Others face a more gradual ascent through one of the crafts. Most craft practitioners in fact never go on to direct, either because they lack self-confidence, or because they like what they do.

To make best use of your potential, be realistic about which kind of person you are. Look at what you have accomplished by the end of film school, and solicit the opinions of the faculty you respect. Ultimately a degree impresses nobody in the film industry: you are what you have done and what you can show.

THE VISIONARY: DIRECTING STRAIGHT OUT OF SCHOOL

It is very rare to move into directing work straight from school and it happens to people whose early work gains them immediate recognition. If you look at Roman

Polansky's earliest films, *Two Men and a Wardrobe* (1958) and *The Fat and the Lean* (1960), it is apparent that an unusual talent is at work expressing a view of the human condition in surreal allegories.

To be a director is really to be an author, to have something to say. For most people this comes later in life—if at all. For those already deeply marked and deeply ambitious, the time is now. For these few, clarity and urgency will divide the Red Sea. For the rest it will be a slow maturing process while working in less exposed positions.

Developing an artistic identity is not easy and rests on your ability to live life courageously and fully. The resistance to your advancement may seem to lie with those higher up in your film school or higher up the film/television industry, but really it lies within yourself. Most people's lives are centered on mundane matters and they have nothing original to say. When this changes, you will know it and you will be driven to express it. Your identity will be sensed and implicitly recognized by others seeing your work.

Film school is the place to find out whether you have the vision, leadership, and sheer drive to put together outstanding films. Such films win festival prizes and these in turn give you professional momentum. To succeed in the capitalist system you must also be an entrepreneur who can assemble "packages," about which there is much written to help the novice (see Bibliography). You will also, if you expect to be paid for your work, have to have tastes that are shared by a sizeable chunk of the paying public.

You can no more decide to become a popular director than you can decide to become Shakespeare or Elvis Presley. The best you can do is to know yourself (since that is all you have as a creative artist to work with) and to work long and hard.

CRAFTSMAN WORKER

This is the craft worker (camera, sound, editing, production) who does not have a clear and novel vision of life, and knows he or she won't be ready to direct features until more life experience has brought the maturity to figure out what (if anything) they have to say.

Let us suppose that through schooling you acquire a reasonable knowledge and initial experience in the field of film- or videomaking. You want to make the transition from student to paid worker in the medium. If you have an excellent body of work and it has won awards, you might conceivably direct either commercials, educational, or industrial work straight away on commission, and get experience with actors. But it is more likely you will enter the field in a humbler position, so in school you need to develop a craft specialty and make the appropriate industry contacts. Plenty of people get work as grip, assistant editor, camera assistant, or assistant director straight out of school, but it happens *only if you have proven skills, professional discipline, and great references* to prove it. An important facet of any film school is whether they have an industry internship program to help you prove yourself.

PERSONAL QUALITIES REQUIRED

How fast you advance, what responsibilities people care to give you depends on your maturity. If you want to build a positive reputation, everything said in this book about reliability and realism must become your undeviating norm. The committed professional is the person who puts the good of the project before everything.

These stern necessities run contrary to undisciplined and immature personalities who expect others to adapt around their needs. The true creativity behind any film is organized and tenacious, and you will need the same combativeness to get established. If you consistently do good work, on time, and within the agreed parameters, then your reputation will slowly spread through the grapevine, and you will naturally rise. Make a costly mistake, and you will fall back. There are no reliable shortcuts to recognition and reward, for filmmaking is a long, slow, pragmatic business. Like any artform it will only gratify those who value the process as much as the product.

CRAFTSMAN WORKER WITH A DIRECTOR STRUGGLING TO GET OUT

If you are already in the industry as a craft worker and have a frustrated director inside, organize your peers to help you produce independent work. Do *not* listen to the greybeards who say, "Never make films with your own money." They are saying, don't invest in yourself, get someone else to do it. The world doesn't work that way; demonstrate that you believe in your talent, and others are much more likely to agree.

If you are a craft worker recently emerged from film school, contrive to keep producing your own work after you graduate. Keep contact with those whose values you share. Film and video production has always been an area for the self-starter, so unless you are accepted by a going concern as a full time employee, you and your friends must make cooperative efforts to get established. You can form an entrepreneurial film unit around a likely script and shoot some scenes on speculation, knowing that everyone's skills will be furthered even if the piece never finds a backer. If you shoot a complete feature film, make absolutely sure you have a commercially viable script in the first place. With decent acting and professionalism from everyone concerned, there is a fair chance of getting costs back, even of making a modest profit over the long haul. But remember that the labs are full of abandoned feature film negatives.

To acquire a cautionary sense of the market forces at work, grit your teeth and regularly read *Variety* (5700 Wilshire, Ste.120, Los Angeles CA 90036). Study recent low-budget production and its tortuous relationship to distribution by following *The Independent* (AIVF Publications, 625 Broadway 9th Floor, New York, NY 10012). Work your way through recent copies of *International Film Guide* for a sense of international trends. Go to genre festivals and see examples of your kind of work so you know in what area and at what level you are competing.

FREE-LANCING TO GAIN EXPERIENCE

The aspiring director will for a long time have to use his or her craft skills (camera, editing, sound, production management, or writing) to fulfill quite ordinary commercial needs. You may find yourself expending lots of imagination and effort crewing for educational, industrial, training, or medical films, and occasionally even shooting conferences and weddings. Doing this reliably and to high standards will teach you a great deal. A training in industrials and documentaries served Robert Altman and many another director well. Commercials, too, are a good training ground since incredible expense and effort are focused on very limited ends. The superb technical and production knowledge you gain can be transferred to the features setting—if you can let go of the good living that commercials can provide.

In general, American TV produces very little drama itself, unlike its European counterparts (British, German, Scandinavian, and Italian especially) which have nurtured many fine directors and actors. There is a crying need for first rate regional production in the USA to break down the stale formulaic vision of the present production centers. The problem is to convince money sources that "regional" can mean something other than second rate.

Most crew work is free-lance, which means feast or famine (mostly famine) living conditions until demand for your services exceeds supply. As an aspiring director, you must aim to be in the right place at the right time, taking other craft work until something turns up. While making a modest or even good living as a free-lance technician, you try to continue making your own films with contemporaries also struggling to gain experience and recognition. By investing in your own talent and developing it to the point where you have concrete, visible results, you then have something to offer an employer or a sponsor. Once you get a little paid directing work, you start building up a track record and a reputation. It is this and festival prizes alone that recommend you for more interesting and demanding work.

WHICH CRAFTS LEAD TO DIRECTING

Some craft areas lead to directing much more readily than others. Editing is a common route since the editor orchestrates acting, directing, camerawork, sound, and everything else. Writers and directors of photography make the transition, and occasionally actor/writers. However ADs, producers and production managers, handling logistics and organizational details, rarely ever become directors.

If you really want to become a feature film director you should perhaps make a choice between editing or camera, with a strong emphasis on screen writing since you'll never get anywhere as a director without constantly propagating film ideas. If you can contrive to have both spare time and spare cash (usually mutually exclusive for free-lancers) you should try to work with a theater group to gain experience with actors, and with them make several short dramatic films.

DIRECTING DOCUMENTARY FILMS STRAIGHT
OUT OF SCHOOL

If you have studied documentary form and production, you may prefer to enter the film industry through nonfiction filmmaking (documentary, educational, travelogue, industrials, corporate, or promotional films). It will get you out in the world, and working with a small crew you will immediately have the high degree of control and responsibility by which people grow.

If you like this book and want to try documentary work, its sister volume *Directing the Documentary* will tell you how. Look first at the career section. As I have implied all along, documentary and fiction are allied genres, and experience in documentary has been wonderful preparation for many a feature film director. Don't take any notice of the patronizing attitude many in features take towards "docs." They don't know any better.

Being a big fish in a small pool is good for many who are highly motivated but lack the connections or confidence to break into big league. There is plenty of peripheral film and video work to be picked if you are resourceful. These pay a slender living, you will be working for yourself, and you'll get a great further education. Many people with long-term fiction goals start in nonfiction work, or in commercials (if their technical control is good enough), and then try later for fiction work. Many more get stuck for life in one of the good livings encountered along the way, and elect to have children and a mortgage instead of living on the edge while trying to produce art. And who can say this is wrong?

IMPORTANCE OF THE PORTFOLIO

You are what you can show. A film degree is nice (indicating you are educable and committed) but more than anything *you need a portfolio of your work that demonstrates your capabilities* to prospective employers or money backers. If you have some original directing work, this will help you get interviews for feature crew work and perhaps even some modest commissioned work, especially if you have festival awards.

COMPROMISING YOURSELF

Becoming known and fitting into a commercial system may seem like the slipway to compromise. It does not have to be. After all, the films on which we were raised were produced for profit, and some were good art by any standards. Almost the entire history of the cinema has its roots in commerce, with each new work predicated upon ticket sales of the last. If cinema and capitalism go hand in hand, this marriage has a certain cantankerous democracy. Tickets are votes from the wallet that prevent the cinema from being irrelevant or from straying too far from the sensibilities of the common man. Shakespeare and his Globe Theatre company flourished under the same system. Purists got themselves to a monastery.

FINDING FICTION SUBJECTS

Read Chapters 2 and 3 for a full treatment of sources for stories. What follows now places this work in a more commercial perspective.

It is sad but true that people who invest in films mostly do so to make money, not films. Any feature film you want to make must have audience appeal, and you must be able to argue this very persuasively. There are a few cheerfully amoral personalities who will steer instinctively towards pornography and exploitation, but they still need stories, characters, situations, dramatic development, and thematic resolution in order to shore up the sagging fantasies of their clients. Here we are not concerned with exploitation, but with those who are serious and socially responsible and for whom planning their working lives poses difficult questions.

The search for subjects is really a search for counterparts to oneself, the issues that stir one at a deep level. Most of the population will never unlock the shadowy rooms in which those parts are stored, having opted instead to live in pursuit of comfort and happiness. Maybe because this brings deprivation ("The unexamined life isn't worth living") they need you, and live vicariously—by watching lives unfold on a screen.

When you search for subjects that will move a wide audience you are in reality searching for the ways in which you connect with, and represent, a sector of contemporary humanity. You will only do this by plunging into the mainstream of modern awareness. You will need a keen curiosity about the ebb and flow of currents in contemporary society, not just those egocentric concerns circulating within.

This requires you to read omnivorously, to feel that political and international affairs are your responsibility, and to assume that poets, novelists, and songwriters are your equals and share a common endeavor. It means that you must strive to discover the humanity you share with painters and philosophers of the present and past, and that you look for your own history in tales, myths and legends. It means that you have a deep curiosity about the suffering and dreams of other people, and other peoples.

During this quest you will find fellow spirits. Some will be on the other side of the grave, their voices still urgent and speaking to you personally through their works. Some will be very much alive, struggling to make sense and give utterance. Some will become your friends and collaborators, allies with whom you face the world and tell what it's like to be alive—at this moment and in this particular century.

You have probably noticed a strange omission from my list of recommended sources—other films. Of course you will be seeing films and will be influenced by them. Good art always extends a tradition, but its source and its destination is in life, not just in talking to other practitioners. Film subjects and approaches should be developed from life, not from other films; that road leads to derivative and imitative work that lacks identity.

If there is a writer whose tastes and interests you share and with whom you can collaborate, you should jointly explore subjects and make a commitment to meet regularly even if he or she is not currently writing. Truly creative partnerships are tougher, more resilient, and more likely to lead to a strong, marketable story idea than writing solo. The director also retains some objectivity over the evolving script when a writer does the writing.

FORM AND MARKETABILITY

A film is not content alone but also, as I have said all along, a way of seeing. The implication is important: how a film sees is more important than what it sees. There are only a limited number of plots, but infinite ways of seeing—as many as there are original characters. The special subjectivity of characters and of the teller of the tale means that *creativity in form is just as important as ingenuity at finding content.*

To build an artistic identity for yourself, you not only need a subject of interest to an audience, but also a stimulating way of seeing it. Part IV, Aesthetics and Authorship deals with the many issues that affect form.

CONTINUING TO LEARN FROM OTHER PEOPLE'S WORK

It is possible to see other people's films and learn very little. The problem is that good films fascinate us to the exclusion of our critical and analytical abilities. You can overcome this by making films yourself, and by actively analyzing with a VCR whatever films speak to you strongly. A basic study method is suggested in Chapter 5, Project 5-3: "A Scripted Scene Compared with the Filmed Outcome," which you might modify as follows:

- see the whole film through as an audience does, without allowing your expertise to make you reflect upon technique.
- write down dominant impressions, especially what the film conveys thematically. Most importantly, what does it leave you feeling?
- run the film one sequence at a time. Make a block diagram of the movie as a whole.
- analyze each sequence for its contribution to the whole.
- analyze any special technique each sequence uses to achieve its ends, and assess the language or form chosen. Was it appropriate? Could you see a better way of reaching the same communicative ends?
- keep a journal of thoughts, ideas, techniques, and approaches and add to it regularly.

Do this and you will learn an immense amount about the way movies affect you, and how film art is used to create certain kinds of impression. Another priceless outcome is that you can now intelligently question the makers of the film if they happen to appear in your area. Nobody, no matter how famous, who labors to create something so complex as a film, is so secure and aloof that he is indifferent to truly informed questions and comments. Out of such conversations links are formed. Informal though they are, contacts of this nature frequently lead to work of some sort.

If you knowledgeably admire someone's work, he or she will take very seriously your desire to work and learn. Film work is irregular and unpredictable; film crews may suddenly need a gopher or find room for an observer. If your dedication shows you value that position, you become someone special, someone everyone will remember. Film people seldom forget how hard it was to get started; work most often goes to those who earn a warm spot in everyone's heart.

FUNDS, JOBS, AND TRAINING SCHEMES

GETTING A FICTION FILM FUNDED

For anyone who has made a short fiction piece that attracted acclaim there is the possibility of packaging a feature film proposal and setting out to raise money. No set way to do this exists since the laws and regulations that affect investment and fund disbursement are subject to change, but those who follow this route often publish or give interviews about their process. To locate recently successful methods, do a thorough bibliographical search giving particular attention to film periodicals.

In the United States there is a complex and shifting system of federal, state, and private funding agencies, each of which has guidelines and a track record in funding some special area. Usually only local organizations will fund first films. Fund money is good money because you usually are not required to pay it back.

As a general rule, private grant funds prefer to give completion money to films that treat hot social issues and that are shot and viewable. Arts funding, under Presidents Reagan and Bush, has shrunk over many years. This seems to be a trend worldwide.

If you live in the USA, your track record is slender (perhaps a short film that has won a festival award), and you are seeking either preproduction, production, or completion money, you should investigate your state or city arts council, which is probably affiliated with the National Endowment for the Arts. If it does not fund film or video making, its officers usually know what other local sources of funding exist. As with all research, use one expert's knowledge to get to others. The national organization's guidelines can be obtained by writing to Grants Office, National Endowment for the Arts, 2401 E Street N.W., Washington, DC 20506.

Each state has a state humanities committee that works in association with the National Endowment for the Humanities. This agency works to fund groups of accredited individuals (usually academics) producing work in the humanities. Conceivably your film furthers the humanities (literature, for example). National guidelines can be obtained from The National Endowment for the Humanities, 806 15th Street N.W., MS 256, Washington, DC 20506.

Many states and big cities have a film commission or bureau that exists to encourage and facilitate professional filmmaking, which benefits a state's coffers. A full list can be obtained through the American Film Institute (AFI) or through the International Documentary Association's *Membership Directory and Survival*

Guide (IDA, 1551 S. Robertson Blvd, Los Angeles, CA 90035, 310-284-8422). This publication is a mine of information on shooting abroad, insurance, festivals, distributors, archives, TV standards, stocks, state film commissions, and trade and professional organizations. It costs $30 to non-members and $17 to IDA members.

AFI either administers funds or serves as an intermediary, and for anyone looking for internships, funding, or special information, membership of the AFI is imperative. AFI also issues publications and fact files. AFI also administers the Academy of Motion Picture Arts and Sciences annual Internship Program, in which successful applicants spend time observing on shoots by well known directors (AFI, 2021 North Western Avenue, Los Angeles, CA 90027). It has held drama directing workshops specifically for women and, like the Sundance Institute and the Canadian Film Center, functions mainly to educate advanced students. Entry is very competitive.

A good move is to take out a subscription to the monthly *American Cinematographer,* a west coast publication that will keep you abreast of the latest technical innovations, and that also includes news, interviews, and a great deal of useful "who is doing what" information (*American Cinematographer,* American Society of Cinematographers, Inc., PO Box 2230, Hollywood, CA 90078).

The Association of Independent Video and Filmmakers offers books and tapes covering much information on fundraising, copyright, legal issues, budgets, distribution and production. Write for a catalogue to AIVF Publications, 625 Broadway 9th Floor, New York, NY 10012. For a larger view of independent moviemaking, you need to religiously read *The Independent* (AIVF Publications, 625 Broadway 9th Floor, New York, NY 10012).

In the bibliography at the back of this book you will find several books containing a vast amount of interlocking information on the structure of the film/video industry, job descriptions, pay scales, funding agencies, proposals, grants, budgeting, contracts and distribution. Some give case histories and examples; collectively they represent a mine of information.

There are survey organizations to help you find the appropriate private fund or charity to approach. Chicago, for instance, has the Donors Forum (53 W. Jackson Boulevard, Chicago, IL 60604) as a clearinghouse that publishes local information periodically, and in New York there is the Foundation Center (79 Fifth Avenue, New York, NY 10003-3076), a nationwide reference collection for study by those wishing to approach donors and donor organizations.

PRESENTING YOURSELF

Here are some pointers to help you find employment.

1. A good resumé is vital when you seek work. It should be professionally laid out (get a book on resumé writing or take a workshop) and it should show what you have done in the best light. A range of different employment is good and you should have letters of recommendation available from past employers ready for inspection.

2. The most persuasive recommendation will be letters from established film-makers and awards won at festivals. The *AIVF Guide to International Film and Video Festivals* (FIVF Book Sales, 625 Broadway, New York, NY 10012) lists upcoming festivals all over the world, and you should enter your work in as many as you can afford. Most film and video competition entries are abysmal, so with good work you can hope to win. Prizes are inordinately persuasive in swinging votes during a funding application, or in securing an interview. Nothing, they say, succeeds like success, and people with judgmental responsibilities often seem most impressed by prizes and honors. Make sure you get yours.

3. With your resumé, enclose a five minute sample VHS cassette which shows *brief* highlights of your work. The items should be numbered and titled. Collectively they should show the range of work you have done and your professionalism. The aim is to make yourself look as capable, flexible and interesting as possible. Your work should be keyed to your resumé. Some people put together a sample tape targeted for a particular type of job or company.

4. Whenever you approach anyone for help, take pains to learn everything you can about their business or organization. Write to the appropriate individual by name in the company or group. Send with your resume a brief, carefully composed, *individual* cover letter that shows your goals and how you might best contribute to what the company does.

5. After a few days, follow up with a phone call. You will probably be told they have no positions open. Ask if you might stop by for a brief chat in case a position opens up in future.

6. If you are granted an interview, dress conservatively, be punctual, and have all relevant information at hand.

7. Bring copy cassettes of your work with you in case the interviewer is interested in something you have done.

8. At first let the interviewer ask the questions and be brief and to the point when you reply. Don't take up more time than you sense is appropriate, but be ready to open up if you are invited to do so.

9. Don't be afraid to say what you most want to do, and show you are willing to do any kind of work to get there. If absolutely necessary, volunteer to work gratis for a period. It will give you experience, a reference, and possibly a paying job after you've proved yourself. Say concisely what skills and qualities you think you have to offer. Use the interview to demonstrate your knowledge of (and therefore commitment to) the interviewer's business. Be neither grandiose nor humble; try to be realistic but enthusiastic. Energy, realism, and a great desire to learn are attractive qualities.

10. Interviewers often finish by asking if you have any questions. Have two or three good questions ready. This part of the interview can be an opportunity to engage your interviewer in discussion of what their company produces. Most people like their work and are proud of it.

People accustomed to dealing with a volume of job seekers learn to distinguish rapidly between the realists and those naively hopeful souls adrift in alien seas. The *judgment is made not on who you are, but on how you present your-self*—on paper, on the screen, and in person. You'll do this well only if you first do your homework, through resourceful reading and networking on the phone. You don't know the right people? Write this on your cuff: *anyone can get to anyone else in the world in five or less phone calls.* This means that anyone can find out a lot before an important meeting.

If you know that shyness is holding you back, don't wait around for a bene-factor to recognize you. That's hoping for magic. Be proactive and do something about it. Do it now. If you need assertiveness training, get it. If none is available, join a theater group and force yourself to act, preferably in improvisational mate-rial. This will be an impressive addition to your resumé and will do wonders for what you project about yourself.

You alone can make the moves to start believing in yourself. You alone can make yourself different from the herd. Your fingerprints prove you're different, but they won't get you employed. You've got to *actively demonstrate* your worth to the world.

Thank you for using this book. If our paths cross, don't hesitate to tell me if it helped and how I can improve it.

My very best wishes go with you.

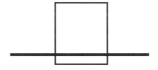

CHECKLIST, PART VIII
CAREER TRACK

The recommendations and points summarized here are only those most salient or the most commonly overlooked. To find more about them or anything else, go to the table of contents at the beginning of this part, or try the index at the back of the book.

To get on target for becoming a director:

- get hands-on knowledge of all the production processes you are most likely to oversee
- accept that you'll need to know writing, acting, camerawork, sound, and editing
- confront your temperament and creative track record for clues about which specialty to take as your craft stepping-stone toward eventual directing
- resolve to make lots and lots of short films

As a director you'll need to,

- become a tough-minded leader
- be able to function even when feeling isolated

- be passionately interested in other artforms
- have original and avidly critical ideas about your times

To make educational progress,

- use short works to argue for your competency at directing longer ones
- be ready to adapt and improvise when working low-budget (people and imagination make films rather than equipment)
- use trial and error in a long developmental process prior to production to arrive at professional-level results

To entertain your audience means,

- giving the audience mental, emotional, and imaginative work, not just moving pictures of externals
- using myth and archetype to underpin anything you want to be powerful
- using screen language that suggests a lot more than it shows, so your audience can imagine

Authorship essentials require:

- using your work to search for your identity, not illustrating what you know
- picking a form after you've found a story—remembering that form follows function
- knowing what marks your life left on you and being ready to make art from them
- knowing the unfinished business in your life and using your art to go into dangerous waters. Only what's scary is really worth doing

Film school:

- a good one will massively accelerate your career, *if* you get established after school
- no school can give you the energy, persistence, intelligence, and drive to succeed
- you can't avoid technical stuff, writing, or bouts of drudgery in filmmaking
- a filmmaking community, finding one's equals, and the immersion of film school are invaluable
- check a school's production facilities, support for production, morale, and attitude to non-star students (the majority)
- check production activity of senior faculty, and experience of those teaching beginner classes (often they are graduate students recycling knowledge only recently acquired)

- only self-starters succeed in freelance arts, so use the school and don't hang about waiting to be recognized. You have to create an identity for yourself and create a visibility through energy and excellence
- plan your life, break tasks down into stages, and set goals and deadlines for yourself. Many will come from the school, but confusion and inertia defeat most people during the time they control themselves. Don't be one of them, and don't depend on anyone showing these signs
- make friends by seeking and using good advice, especially from active faculty
- take little notice of conventional wisdom among students, it's always full of negativity and doom
- don't kid yourself you're keeping your options open by avoiding craft specialization. Decide what you're suited to do and pursue it—it will be your bread and butter
- learn to be creative from those with a positive attitude towards work, authority, and other students
- do not under any circumstances leave film school without saleable skills in something other than directing—that is, production, camera, sound, editing, production design, special effects, etc.
- make sure you have a reel of good and varied work as evidence of your competency. Your parents, not the film industry, care that you got a degree
- get all the internship experience you can, and all the references from film/ video employers possible so you can pump up your resumé
- excellent directing work, prizes to prove it, and a great script may get you into directing straight away, but it's unwise to expect it, and foolish not to prepare for a less dazzling destiny

After film school and when you're looking for work:

- reaching the top rung of film school only qualifies you to apply for the bottom rung of work in the film industry
- send out a professional looking resumé and a 5 minute VHS reel of quotes from your best and most varied work. Follow up with a politely insistent call asking for a chat
- know where you want to work, know who's there, what they do, and keep trying
- don't embarrass employers by overestimating your abilities, importance, or potential
- you are what you have done
- one or two whiz kids make it big, the rest move s-l-o-w-l-y up through the freelance ranks and usually take several years to build up regular employment
- film/video is always a small professional community, even in Hollywood. Everyone watches everyone else. Good people get known the way they do in a village. If you work well and are always a good trooper, you'll come to be valued

- think of starting in non-fiction to gain experience and worldly immersion
- your capital is your reliability, resourcefulness, and capacity for originality. Work night and day at expanding your mind in all the arts, not just cinema
- don't believe in talent, believe in persistent self-development
- learn from others, especially their mistakes (we all make them)
- learn how the funding circus works
- plug into all the information sources and trade information
- don't listen to cynics. They'll tell you the world is going to the dogs and that you will never succeed
- know what you want. People accomplish what matters to them and not much else
- things happen because of personal connections and friendships, not merit alone
- get proficient at networking. Anyone can get to anyone else by personal connection in the world in five or less phone calls
- there are a lot of highly intelligent, kind, and responsible people in the film/video industry. They all work on junk a lot of the time, and you will too until someone genetically re-engineers mass taste. You can win the pros' respect, affection, and help if you earn it
- keep on writing, keep on making short projects, keep on entering them in competitions and festivals
- expect the freelance life in a collaborative medium to take a toll on your personal life
- believe in yourself and work with others who do so too
- keep the faith

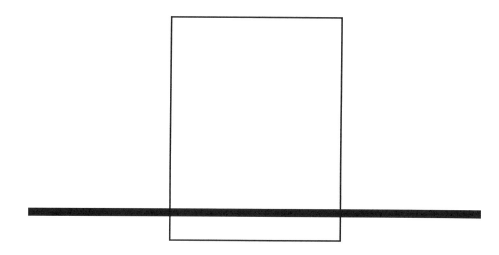

G·L·O·S·S·A·R·Y

More information can often be found by using the Index.

A & B rolls   Two or more rolls of film camera-original from which release prints are struck.

Acetate sheet   Clear plastic sheet used in making titles or animation cels.

Action match cut   Cut made between two different angles of the same action using the subject's movement as the transition.

AD   Assistant director.

Adaptation   The unique way each character adapts to the changing obstacles that prevent him or her from gaining his ends and a prime component in externalizing his or her conflicts.

ADR   Automatic dialogue replacement. *See* Postsynchronization.

Aerial shot   Shot taken from the air.

AFI   American Film Institute.

Ambient sound   Sound naturally occurring in any location. Even an empty, quiet room has its own special atmosphere, since no space is truly silent.

Analogue recording   Any sound or picture recording that records its waveforms as an analogue representation, rather than digitally, when the waveform is registered by digital numbers as in the coordinates for a graph.

Angle of acceptance   The height and width of the subject filmed by a particular lens at a given distance expressed in a lens table either in degrees or as measurements. Photographed image also depends on aspect ratio of the format in use. Wide-screen format will have longer horizontal measurement.

Anticipating   Term used to describe when an actor speaks or acts in advance of the appropriate moment.

Anticipatory sound   Sound brought in ahead of its accompanying picture.

Aspect ratio   The size of a screen format expressed as the ratio of the width in relation to the height. Films made for television are photographed at a ratio of 1.33:1. *See also* Angle of acceptance.

Atmosphere track   Sound track providing a particular atmosphere (cafe, railroad, beach, rain, for example).

Attack (sound)   The beginning portion of any sound.

Audio sweetening   The level and equalization adjustment process that accompanies sound mixing.

Auteur theory   The concept that one mind controls the creative identity of a film.

Axis   *See* Scene axis.

Baby legs   A miniature tripod for low angle shots.

Back lighting   Lighting from behind the subject.

Back story   The events stated or implied to have happened prior to the period covered in the screenplay.

Bars   Standard color bars generated in video systems, usually by the camera.

BCU   Big close up.

Beat   Point in a scene where a buildup of dramatic pressure effects a noticeable change in one or more characters' consciousness.

BFI   British Film Institute.

BG   Background.

Blocking   Choreographic arrangement of movements by actors and camera in relation to the set.

Body copy   Nondialogue descriptive portion of screenplay, usually consisting of stage directions and physical description.

Book, the   Actors' name for the script.

Boom   Support pole suspending the microphone close to the speakers but just out of shot.

Boxcar cutting   Crude method of assembling sound and action segments as level-cut segments for speed and convenience.

Broad lighting   Lighting that produces a broad band of highlight on a face or other three-dimensional object.

Business   The in-character activity generated by actors to fill out their characters' behavior.

Butt splice   Taped film splice made without the overlap necessary to cement splicing.

Buzz track   *See* presence.

Call back   Calling back actors who have successfully passed the first round of auditioning for a second round.

Camera left/right   Method of specifying movement or the placement of objects in relation to the camera: "Davy turns away from camera and walks off camera left." Also expressed as screen right or left.

Camera motivation   A shot or a camera movement must be motivated within the terms of the scene or story if it is not to look alien and imposed. Camera motivation is often answered by asking, "What is the point of view here?"

Camera-to-subject axis   The invisible line drawn between the camera and the subject in the composition. *See also* Scene axis.

Cattle call   The call for a number of actors to try out, often simultaneously, for parts.

Cement splice   A film splice made by cementing two overlapping portions of film together.

Chalk marks   Temporary marks made on the floor to ensure that actor or camera stops at a precise place.

Character biography   The biographical portrait an actor invents as background to the character he or she is to play.

Character generator   An electronic device for producing video titles.

Checkerboarding   The practice during conforming of alternating film scenes with black leader in each A & B roll of camera original. Sound tracks prior to mixing are likewise alternated between channels, with silence separating sound segments. Both black frame and silence allow the operator a grace period in which to adjust printer or sound channel settings before the arrival of the next segment.

Cinema verité   Documentary shooting method in which the camera is subservient to an actuality that is sometimes catalyzed by the director.

Clapper board   Marker board used at the beginning of takes whose bar closing permits separate sound to be synchronized. Also called the slate.

Climax   The dramatic apex of a scene.

Coincidence   Dramatists in a tight spot make things happen or people meet "by coincidence," a crutch overused at the dramatist's peril.

Color bars   Standard electronic video color test, usually generated by the camera.

Color chart   Chart attached to film slate board as color reference for laboratory processing technicians.

Color temperature   Light color quality is measured in degrees Kelvin. Common light sources in moviemaking contain a different mix of colors. The eye compensates effortlessly, but film and video cameras (or lighting itself) must be adjusted to prevailing color temperature if white objects are to be rendered as white on-screen. Mixing daylight (around 5,400°K) and studio lights (3,200°K) in the same scene leads to an unnatural lighting effect. One source must be filtered to make its output match the other, and the camera must likewise be filtered or electronically color balanced for all scene colors to be rendered faithfully.

Comm   Commentary.

Communion   The principle by which actors react to the unforeseeable nuances in each other's performances in order to regain the spontaneity of real life during a rehearsed performance.

Complementary shot   A shot compositionally designed to intercut with another.

Composite print   A film print combining sound and picture.

Compression   Sound with a wide dynamic range can be proportionately compressed so that loudest and softest sounds are closer in volume. All TV transmissions and most radio transmissions, with the exception of high-fidelity music stations, are compressed. Cinemas usually give you the authentic range between whispers and the roar of battle.

Concept   The dramatic *raison d'être* underlying the whole screenplay.

Conforming   The process in which the film camera original is edited in conformity with the fine-cut workprint prior to making release prints.

Confrontation   Bringing into final collision those people or forces representing the dramatic piece's main conflict.

Contingency percentage   A percentage usually between ten and fifteen percent superadded to a budget to provide for the unforeseeable.

Contingency planning   Scheduling alternative shooting for any scenes threatened by weather or other imponderables.

Continuity   Consistency of physical detail between shots intended to match.

Continuity script   Script made after postproduction as record of film contents. Useful in proving piracy or censorship.

Continuity supervisor   See script supervisor.

Contrast   Difference in brightness between highlight and deep shadow areas in an image.

Contrast ratio   Ratio of lightest to darkest areas in an image.

Controlling point of view   The psychological perspective (a character's or the storyteller's) from which a particular scene is shown.

Counterpoint   The juxtaposing of antithetical elements, perhaps between sound and picture, to create a conflict of impressions for the audience to resolve.

Coverage   The different angles from which a given scene is covered in order to allow variations of viewpoint in editing.

Crab dolly   Wheeled camera support platform that can roll in any direction.

Craning   A boom supporting the camera which can be raised or lowered during the shot.

Crash zoom   Very fast zoom in or zoom out.

Crib notes   Director's notes listing intentions and "don't forgets" for a scene.

Crossing the line   Moving the camera across the scene axis. Can be problematical.

Crossplot or Scene breakdown   A chart displaying the locations, characters, and script pages necessary to each scene.

CS   Close shot.

CU   Closeup.

Cutaway   A shot, often a character's physical point of view, that allows us to cut away momentarily from the main action.

Cut-in   Magnified detail within an existing shot.

Dailies   The film unit's daily output, processed and ready to be viewed. Also called rushes because of the rush involved in readying them.

DAT recorder   Digital audio tape recorder

Day for night   Special photography that allows a sunlit day shot to pass as moonlit night.

Decay   The tapering away of a concluding sound.

Deep focus   Photography that holds objects both near and far in sharp focus.

Degradation   A picture, either video or photo, becomes degraded when it passes through several generations of copying. Affects analog sound as well.

Depth of field   The depth of the picture that is in acceptably sharp focus. Varies widely according to lens and f-stop in use.

Deus ex machina   The improbable event imported into a story to make it turn out right.

Diagetic sound   Sound that belongs naturally with what we see in picture.

Diffused light   Light composed of disorganized rays that casts an indistinct shadow.

Digitizing band (also known as capturing)   The process of turning an analogue signal, whether audio or video, into a digital record. This usually involves using an algorhythmic formulation to compress the information so as to avoid wasteful recording of similarities from one frame to the next.

Direct cinema   A low-profile documentary style of shooting that disallows any directorial intrusion to shape or instigate incidents.

Dissolve   Transitional device in which one image cross-fades into another. Also called a lap dissolve. One sound can dissolve into another.

DOF   Depth of field.

Dolby   A proprietary electronic recording system that produces low-noise sound recording, that is, having a lowered systemic hiss.

Dolly shot   Any shot on a wheeled camera support.

Double-system recording   Camera and sound recorder are separate instruments.

DP   Director of photography.

Dramatic dynamics   The ebb and flow of dramatic pressure through the length of a scene or of a whole piece.

Dramatic interpretation   The selection of a dominant meaning for a particular text.

Dub   To copy from one electronic medium to another. Can be sound or video picture.

Dutch angle   Shot made with camera deliberately tilted out of horizontal.

Dynamic character definition   Defining a dramatic character by what he or she wants and is trying to accomplish.

Dynamic composition   Pictorial composition as it changes within a moving shot.

Echo   Sound reflections that return after a constant delay time.

Edge numbers   Code numbers imprinted on the edge of camera original film and printing through to the work print.

Edit decision list   Sound and picture edit decisions in a movie defined as a list of timecode or Keycode numbers. Taking camera originals and a standard EDL to a postproduction facility allows them to make a perfect facsimile of the workprint.

EDL   *See* Edit decision list.

Effects   Sounds specially laid to augment the sound track of a film.

Emotional memory   An actor who carefully devises specific actions to fit a particular mood of his character finds, when he performs, that he spontaneously experiences the character's emotions.

Emotional transition   Emotional change during a scene. Scripts often challenge actors by calling for leaps from one mood to another in a shorter time than is normal in life.

Energy level   Both scenes and performances have their own energy levels. A director will often call for a change in energy level when a scene is not working out, or when actors are getting tired.

EQ   *See* Equalizing.

Equalizing   Using sound filters to reduce the discrepancy between sound tracks that are supposed to match and sound seamless.

Establishing shot   A shot that establishes a scene's geographical and human contents.

Exposition   The part of a scene or a story in which basic information is relayed to the audience. Good exposition is buried within action and goes unnoticed.

Expressionism   A mode in art in which verisimilitude is laid aside in favor of techniques that evoke the subjective vision either of a character or of the storyteller.

Ext   Exterior.

External composition   The compositional relationship between two images at the point of cutting between them.

Eye light   Small wattage light mounted on camera to put a liquid sparkle in actors' eyes.

Eyeline   The visual trajectory of a character in a scene.

Fade down   Lower sound level.

Fade to white   Fade an image to white instead of to black.

Fade up   Raise sound level.

Falling action   *See* Resolution.

FG   Foreground.

FI   Fade in.

Fill light   Diffused light used to raise light level in shadows cast by key light.

Flash forward   Moving temporarily forward in time, the cinematic equivalent of the future tense. This quickly becomes a new form of present.

Flashback   Moving temporarily backwards in time; a cinematic past tense that soon becomes an ongoing present.

Floor plan   *See* Ground plan.

FO   Fade out.

Focal distance   Distance between camera and subject.

Focus (acting)   Seeing, hearing, thinking in character. When an actor loses focus he or she becomes self-conscious and aware of participating in a make-believe world.

Foley   Generic name for a process in which sound is recreated to picture.

Foreshadowing   A somewhat fatalistic narrative technique by which an outcome is hinted at in advance. Helps to raise expectant tension in the audience.

Form   The means and arrangement chosen to present a story's content.

Freeze frame   A single frame arrested and held as a still picture.

Frontal lighting   Key light coming from the direction of the camera and showing the subject virtually without shadows.

FTs   Footsteps. Often must be recreated.

FX   Sound effects

Generation   Camera original (in film or video) is the first generation, and copies become subsequent numbered generations, each likely to show increased degradation of the original's fidelity.

Genre   A kind or type of film (horror, sitcom, cowboy, domestic drama, et cetera).

Givens   Whatever is nonnegotiably specified in a text.

Grading   *See* Timing.

Graduated tonality An image composed of mid tones and having neither very bright nor very dark areas.

Gray scale Test chart useful to camera and lab technicians that shows the range of gray tones and includes absolute black and white.

Grip Location technician expert in handling lighting and set construction equipment.

Ground plan Diagram showing placement of objects and movements of actors on a floor plan. Also called floor plan.

Gun/rifle mike Ultradirectional microphone useful for minimizing the intrusiveness of ambient noise.

Hard light *See* Specular light.

Headroom Compositional space left above heads.

High angle Camera mounted high, looking down.

High contrast Image with large range of brightnesses.

High down Camera mounted high, looking down.

High-key picture Image that is overall bright with few areas of shadow.

Highlight Brightest areas in picture.

Hi-hat Ultralow camera support resembling a metal top hat.

Improv Improvisation. A dramatic interaction that deliberately permits an outcome to emerge spontaneously. Improvs can involve different degrees of structure, or may set a goal to be reached by an undetermined path.

Insert A close shot of detail to be inserted in a shot containing more comprehensive action.

Int Interior.

Interior monologue The interior thoughts voice an actor will sustain to help himself or herself stay in character and in focus.

Internal composition Composition internal to the frame as opposed to the compositional relationship existing between adjacent shots, called external composition.

Irony The revelation of a reality different from that initially apparent.

Jump cut Transitional device in which two similar images taken at different times are cut together so that the elision of intervening time is apparent. From this the audience infers that time has passed.

Juxtaposition The placing together of different pictorial or sound elements to invite comparison, inference, and heightened thematic awareness on the part of the audience.

Keycode™ Kodak's proprietary system for bar coding each camera original film frame. This facilitates digitizing by assigning each frame its own timecode. Later after digital editing, the coding permits negative cutting (conforming) from a digitally produced EDL.

Key light A scene's apparent source of illumination, and the one creating the intended shadow pattern.

Key numbers *See* Edge numbers.

Keystone distortion   The distortion of parallel lines that results from photographing an object from an off-axis position.

LA   Low angle
Lap dissolve   *See* Dissolve.
Lavalier mike   Any neck or chest microphone.
Lead space   The additional compositional space allowed in front of a figure or moving object photographed in profile.
Legal release   A legally binding release form signed by a participant in a film that gives permission to use footage taken.
Leitmotiv   Intentionally repeated element (sound, shot, dialogue, music, et cetera) that helps unify a film by reminding the viewer of its earlier appearance.
Lens speed   How fast a lens is depends on its maximum aperture.
Level   Sound volume.
Lighting ratio   The ratio of highlight brightness to shadow illumination.
Limiter   Electronically applied upper sound limit, useful for preventing momentary transient sounds like a door slamming from distortion through overrecording.
Line of tension   Invisible dramatic axis, or line of awareness, that can be drawn between protagonists and important elements in a scene.
Lip sync   Recreated speech that is in complete sync with the speaker. Singers often lip sync to their recordings and fake a singing performance on television.
Looping   *See* ADR.
Lose focus   *See* Focus.
Low angle   Camera looking up at subject.
Low-contrast image   Small differences of brightness between highlight areas and shadow.
Low-key picture   A scene that may have high or low contrast but which is predominantly dark overall.
LS   Long shot.

Magazine   Removable light-proof film container for a film camera.
Mannerisms   An actor's idiosyncratic and repeated details of behavior. Very hard to change or suppress.
Master mix   Final mixed sound, first generation.
Master shot   Shot that shows most or all of the scene and most or all of the characters.
Match cut   *See* Action match cut.
MCS   Medium close shot.
Metaphor   A verbal or visually implied analogy that ascribes to one thing the qualities associated with another.
Midtones   The intermediate shades of gray lying between the extremes of black and white.
Mimesis   Action that imitates the actuality of life.
Mise-en-scène   The totality of lighting, blocking, camera use, and composition that produces the dramatic image on film.
Mix   The mixing together of sound tracks.

Mix chart   Cue chart that functions like a musician's score to assist in the sound mix.

MLS   Medium long shot.

Montage   Originally meant editing in general, but now refers to the kind of sequence that shows a process or the passage of time.

Montage sequence   *See* Montage.

MOS   Short for "Mit out sound," which is what the German directors in Hollywood called for when they intended to shoot silent. In Britain this shot is called mute.

Motif   Any formal element repeated from film history or from the film itself whose repetition draws attention to an unfolding thematic statement. *See also* Leitmotiv.

Motivation   Whatever plot logic impels a character to act or react in a particular way, usually a combination of psychological makeup and external events.

MS   Medium shot.

Murphy's Law   "Whatever can go wrong will go wrong." Applies also to people.

Mus   Music.

Music sync points   Places in a film's action where music must exactly fit. Also called picture pointing and can be overdone.

Mute shot   *See* MOS.

Narr   Narration.

Narrow lighting   Lighting which in portraiture produces a narrow band of highlight on a face.

Negative cutting   *See* Conforming.

Noise   Noise inherent in a sound recording system itself.

Noise reduction   Recording and playback technique that minimizes system noise. *See also* Dolby.

Normal lens   A lens of a focal length that, in the format being used, renders distances between foreground and background as recognizably normal.

Obligatory moment   The moment of maximum dramatic intensity in a scene and for which the whole scene exists.

Off-line edit   Manual, noncomputerized video editing. *See also* On-line edit.

Omniscient point of view   A storytelling mode in which the audience is exposed to the author's capacity to see or know anything going on in the story, to move at will in time and space, and to freely comment upon meanings or themes.

On-line edit   Video editing assisted by a computer that can locate and line up specific time-coded frames in the process of assembling a final cut.

Optical   Any visual device like a fade, dissolve, wipe, iris wipe, ripple dissolve, matte, superimposition, et cetera.

Optical house   A company specializing in visual special effects.

Optical track   A sound track photographically recorded.

OS   Offscreen.

Over the top   Expression signifying a performance carried out with a surfeit of emotion.

Overlap cut   Any cut in which picture and sound transitions are staggered instead of level-cut.

Parallel storytelling   The intercutting of two separate stories proceeding through time in parallel. Useful for abridging each and for making ironical contrasts.

Pan   Short for panorama. Horizontal camera movement.

Perspective   The size differential between foreground and background objects that causes us to infer receding space. Obviously distorted perspective makes us attribute subjective distortion in the point of view being expressed.

Picture pointing   Making music fit picture events. Walt Disney films used the device so much that its overuse is called "Mickey Mousing."

Picture texture   This can be hard or soft. A hard image has large areas in sharp focus and tends toward contrastiness, while a soft image has areas out of focus and lacks contrast.

Playwriting   One actor's tendency to take control of a scene, particularly in improv work, and to manipulate other actors into a passive relationship.

Plot   The arrangement of incidents and the logic of causality in a story. Plot should create a sense of momentum and credibility, and act as a vehicle for the thematic intention of the piece.

PM   Production manager.

Point of view   Sometimes literally what a character sees (a clock approaching midnight, for instance) but more usually signifies the outlook and sensations of a character within a particular environment. This can be the momentary consciousness of an unimportant character, or that of a main character (*See* Controlling point of view). It can also be the storyteller's point of view (*See* Omniscient point of view).

Postsynchronization   Dialogue or effects shot in sync with existing action.

POV   Point of view. When abbreviated thus it nearly always means a shot reproducing a character's eyeline view.

Practical   Any light source visible in the frame as part of the set.

Premise   *See* Concept.

Premix   A preliminary pass in which subsidiary sound elements are mixed together in preparation for the final mix.

Preroll   The amount of time a video editing rig needs to get up to speed prior to making a cut.

Presence   Specially recorded location atmosphere to authentically augment "silent" portions of track. Every space has its own unique presence. Also known as buzz-track, ambience, or room-tone.

Prop   Property.

Property   Physical object handled by actors or present for authenticity in a set. A term also used of a script to which someone has secured the rights.

Rack focus   Altering focus between foreground and background during a shot. Prompts or accommodates an attention shift (a figure enters a door at the back of the room, for instance).

Radio microphone   A microphone system that transmits its signal by radio to the recorder and is therefore wireless. Famous for picking up taxis and CB enthusiasts at inopportune moments.

Reader's script   Transcript of a finished film presented in a publisher's format that makes maximum use of the page.

Reconnaissance   Careful examination of locations prior to shooting.

Release print   Final print destined for audience consumption.

Research   Library work and observation of real life in search of authentic detail to fill out fictional characters and situations.

Resistance   Human evasion mechanisms that show up in actors under different kinds of stress.

Resolution   The wind-down events following the plot's climax that form the final phase of the plot's development. Also called falling action.

Reverberation   Sound reflections returning in a disorganized pattern of delay.

Rising action   The plot developments, including complication and conflict, that lead to a plot's climax.

Room tone   *See* Presence.

Rushes   Unedited raw footage as it appears after shooting. Also called "dailies."

Rushes book   Log of important first reactions to performances in rushes footage.

Scene axis   The invisible line in a scene representing the scene's dramatic polarization. In a labor dispute scene this might be drawn between the main protagonists, the plant manager and the union negotiator. Coverage is shot from one side of this line to preserve consistent screen directions for all participants. Complex scenes involving multiple characters and physical regrouping may have more than one axis. *See also* Crossing the line.

Scene breakdown or crossplot   A chart displaying the locations, characters, and script pages necessary to each scene.

Scene dialectics   The forces in opposition in a scene which usually require externalizing through acting, blocking, composition, visual and aural metaphors, et cetera.

Scene geography   The physical layout of the location and the placing of the characters when they are first encountered. *See also* Master shot.

Screen direction   The orientation or movement of characters and objects relative to the screen (screen left, screen right, upscreen, downscreen).

Screen left/right   Movement or direction specifications. *See* Screen direction.

Screenplay   Standard script format showing dialogue and stage direction but no camera or editing instructions.

Script Supervisor   Also called continuity supervisor, this person notes the physical details of each scene and the actual dialogue used so that complementary shots, designed to cut together, will match.

Segue   (pronounced "seg-way") Sound transition, often a dissolve.

Set light   A light whose function is to illuminate the set.

Setup   The combination of particular lens, camera placement, and composition to produce a particular shot.

SFX   Sound effects.

Shooting ratio   The ratio of material shot for a scene in relation to its eventual edited length. 8:1 is a not unusual ratio for dramatic film.

Shooting script   Screenplay with scenes numbered and amended to show intended camera coverage and editing.

Sidecoaching   During breaks in a scene's dialogue the director can quietly feed directions to the actors, who incorporate these instructions without breaking character. Most often used when shooting reaction shots.

Sightlines   Lines that can be drawn along each character's main lines of vision that influence the pattern of coverage so it reproduces the feeling of each main character's consciousness.

Silhouette lighting   Lighting in which the subject is a dark outline against a light background.

Single shot   A shot containing only one character.

Single-system recording   Sound recording made on film or video that also carries the picture. *See* Double-system recording.

Slate   *See* Clapper board.

Slate number   Setup and take number shown on the slate, or clapper, which identifies a particular take.

Soft light   Light that does not produce hard-edged shadows.

Sound dissolve   One sound track dissolving into another.

Sound effects   Nondialogue recordings of sounds intended either to intensify a scene's realism or to give it a subjective heightening.

Sound mix   The mixing together of sound elements into a sound composition that becomes the film's sound track.

Sound perspective   Apparent distance of sound source from the microphone. Lavalier mikes, for instance, give no change of perspective when characters move or turn because they remain in a fixed relationship to the wearer.

Specular light   Light composed of parallel rays that casts a comparatively hard edged shadow. Also called hard light.

Split page format   A script format that places action on the left hand side of the page and its accompanying sound on the right.

Stage directions   Nondialogue screenplay instructions, also known as body copy.

Stand in   Someone who takes the place of an actor during setup time or for shots that involve special skills, such as horse-riding, fights, et cetera.

Static character definition   Giving a character static attributes instead of defining him in terms of dynamic volition.

Static composition   The composition elements in a static image.

Steadicam   Proprietary body brace camera support that uses counterbalance and gimbal technology so the camera can float while the operator walks.

Step outline   Synopsis of a screenplay expressed as a series of numbered steps, and preferably including a definition of each step's function in the whole.

Sting   Musical accent to heighten a dramatic moment.

Storyboard   Series of key images sketched to suggest what a series of shots will look like.

Strobing   The unnatural result onscreen resulting from the interaction of camera shutter speed with a patterned subject such as the rotating spokes of a wheel or panning across a picket fence.

Structure   The formal organization of the elements of a story, principally the handling of time, and their arrangement into a dramatically satisfying development that includes a climax and resolution.

Style   An individual stamp on a film, the elements in a film that issue from its makers' own artistic identity.

Subjective camera   An angle or camera handling that implies the physical or psychological point of view of one of the characters.

Subtext   The hidden, underlying meaning to the text. It is supremely important and actors and director must often search for it.

Superobjective   The overarching thematic purpose of the director's dramatic interpretation.

Surrealism   Also a movement in art and literature. Concerned with the free movement of the imagination particularly as expressed in dreams, where the dreamer has no conscious control over events. Often associated with helplessness.

Sync coding   Code marks to help an editor keep sound and action in sync.

Tag   An irreducibly brief description useful for its focus upon essentials.

Take   One filmed attempt from one setup. Each setup may have several takes.

Telephoto lens   Long or telescopic lens that foreshortens the apparent distance between foreground and background objects.

Tense, change of   Temporary change from present to either past, future, or conditional tenses in a film's narrative flow. Whatever tense a film invokes speedily becomes a new, ongoing present. For this reason screenwriting is always in the present tense.

Thematic purpose   The overall interpretation of a complete work that is ultimately decided by the director. *See* Superobjective.

Theme   A dominant idea made concrete through its representation by the characters, action, and imagery of the film.

Three-shot/3S   Shot containing three people.

Thumbnail character sketch   Brief character description useful either in screenwriting or in recruiting actors.

Tilt   Camera swiveling on a vertical axis, tilting up and down to show the height of a flagpole, for instance.

Time code   Electronic code number unique to each video frame.

Timebase correction   Electronic stabilization of the video image, particularly necessary to make it compatible with the sensitive circuitry used in transmission over the air.

Timing   The process of examining and grading a negative for color quality and exposure prior to printing. Also called grading.

Tracking shot   Moving camera shot in which the camera dolly often runs on tracks like a miniature railroad.

Transitional device   Any visual, sound, or dramatic screen device that signals a jump to another time or place.

Treatment   Usually a synopsis in present tense, short story form of a screenplay summarizing dialogue and describing only what an audience would see and hear. Can also be a puff piece designed to sell the script rather than give comprehensive information about content.

Trucking shot   Moving camera shot once shot from a truck. The term is used interchangeably with tracking.

Two-shot/2S   Shot containing two people.

Unit   The whole group of people shooting a film.

VCR   Videocassette recorder.

Verbal action   Words conceived and delivered so as to act upon the listener and instigate a result.

Video assist   A video feed taken from the film camera's viewfinder and displayed on a monitor usually for the director to watch during shooting.

Visual rhythm   Each image according to its action and compositional complexity requires a different duration onscreen to look right and to occupy the same audience concentration as its predecessor. A succession of images when sensitively edited exhibits a rhythmic constancy that can be slowed or accelerated like any other kind of rhythm.

VO   Voice over.

Volition   The will of a character to accomplish something. This leads to constant struggle of one form or another, a concept vital in making dramatic characters come to life.

VT   Videotape.

WA   Wide angle.

Whip pan   Very fast panning movement.

White balance   Video camera setup procedure in which circuitry is adjusted to the color temperature of the lighting source so that a white object is rendered as white onscreen.

Wide-angle lens   A lens with a wide angle of acceptance. Its effect is to increase the apparent distance between foreground and background objects.

Wild   Non sync.

Wild track   A sound track shot alone and with no synchronous picture.

Window dub   A transfer made from a time-coded video camera original that displays each frame's time code number in a window near the bottom of the frame.

Wipe   Optical transition between two scenes that appears on screen as a line moving across the screen. An iris wipe makes the new scene appear as a dot that enlarges to fill the screen. These effects are overused on the TV screen.

Wireless mike   See radio microphone.

WS   Wide shot.

WT   Wild track.

XLS   Extra long shot.

Zoom lens   A lens whose focal length is infinitely variable between two extremes.

Zoom ratio   The ratio of the longest to the widest focal lengths. A 10 to 100mm zoom would be a 10:1 zoom.

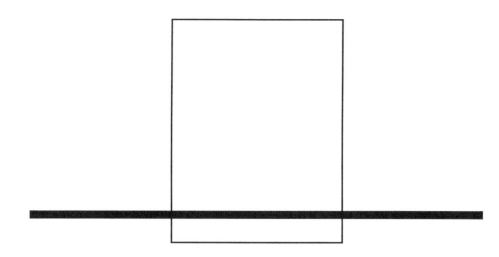

B·I·B·L·I·O·G·R·A·P·H·Y

ACTING

Barr, Tony. *Acting for the Camera.* New York: Harper and Row, 1982. "Learn the role—not the lines."

Bernard, Ian. *Film and Television Acting.* Boston: Focal Press, 1993.

Blum, Richard. *Working Actors: The Craft of Television, Film, and Stage Performance.* Boston: Focal Press, 1989.

Caine, Michael. *Acting in Film: An Actor's Take on Moviemaking* (Videocassette). NY: Applause Theatre Book Publishers, 1990.

Callow, Simon. *Simon Callow on Acting in Restoration Comedy* (Videocassette) NY: Applause Theatre Book Publishers, 1987.

Earley, Michael & Philippa Keil. *The Classical Monologue: Men.* NY: Routledge Theatre Arts Books, 1992.

Harmon, Renee. *Teaching a Young Actor: How to Train Children of All Ages.* NY: Walker, 1994.

Harrop, John. *Acting.* London, NY: Routledge, 1992.

Hodgson, John and Ernest Richards. *Improvisation.* New York: Grove Press, 1974. Emphasizes the connection between acting and living.

Katz, Steven D. *Film Directing Shot by Shot.* Boston: Focal Press in association with Michael Wiese Productions, 1991. Invaluable for blocking and framing.

Malkin, Michael. *Training the Young Actor.* South Brunswick: A. S. Barnes, 1979.

Marowitz, Charles. *The Art of Being: Towards a Theory of Acting.* New York: Taplinger, 1978.

Moore, Sonia. *The Stanislavski System.* New York: Viking Press, 1965. Later revisions available, but I like this version best.

Moore, Sonia. *Stanislavski Revealed.* NY: Applause Theatre Books, 1991

Morris, Eric and Joan Hotchkis. *No Acting Please.* Los Angeles: Spelling Publications, 1979. Concentrates on the emotional honesty that is so important to the film performance.

Naremore, James. *Acting in the Cinema*. Berkeley: U. of Calif. Press, 1988.

Smith, Marisa & Jocelyn Beard, Eds. *Contemporary Movie Monologues*. NY: Fawcett Columbine, 1991.

Spolin, Viola. *Improvisation for the Theatre*. Evanston: Northwestern University Press, 1985. Seminal work.

Zucker, Carole, Ed. *Figures of Light: Actors and Directors Illuminate the Art of Film Acting*. NY: Plenum Press, 1995.

Zucker, Carole, Ed. *Making Visible the Invisible* (Anthology) Metuchen, NJ: Scarecrow Press, 1990

SCREENWRITING

Bergman, Ingmar. *Four Stories by Ingmar Bergman*. Garden City: Anchor Press, 1977. Four documents that were the starting point for films in Bergman's nontraditional screenwriting process.

Blacker, Irwin R. *The Elements of Screenwriting*. New York: Macmillan, 1986. Brief and to the point.

Blum, Richard A. *Television and Screen Writing: From Concept to Contract 3rd Ed*. Boston: Focal Press, 1995.

Cooper, Pat & Ken Dancyger. *Writing the Short Film*. Boston: Focal Press, 1994. Writing for the short form has been neglected till recently.

Dancyger, Ken and Jeff Rush. *Alternative Scriptwriting: Writing Beyond the Rules 2nd Ed*. Boston: Focal Press, 1995.

Dmytryk, Edward. *On Screen Writing*. Boston: Focal Press, 1985. Conversational, good examples but conceptual and not procedural.

Edmonds, Robert. *Scriptwriting for the Audio-Visual Media*. New York: Teachers College Press, 1978. Survey of screenwriting forms and their applications.

Field, Syd. *Screenplay: The Foundations of Screenwriting*. New York: Dell, 1982. A favorite.

Field, Syd. *The Screenwriter's Workbook*. NY: Dell, 1984.

Horton, Andrew. *Writing the Character-Centered Screenplay*. Berkeley: U. of Calif. Press, 1994.

Howard, David. *The Tools of Screenwriting*. NY: St. Martin's Press, 1993.

Hunter, Lew. *Lew Hunter's Screenwriting 434*. NY: Perigee Books, 1993.

Johnson, Mary C. *The Scriptwriter's Journal*. Boston: Focal Press, 1994.

Mehring, Margaret. *The Screenplay: A Blend of Form and Content*. Boston: Focal Press, 1990.

Phillips, William H. *Writing Short Scripts*. Syracuse, NY: Syracuse Univ. Press, 1991. Writing the short form has hitherto been a neglected area.

Rosenthal, Alan. *Writing Docudrama*. Boston: Focal Press, 1994.

Swain, Dwight and Joye Swain. *Film Scriptwriting: A Practical Manual*. 2nd ed. Boston: Focal Press, 1988.

Vale, Eugene. *The Technique of Screen and TV Writing*. New York: Simon and Schuster, 1982. Considered the classic text: compares film, theater, and novel forms.

Vogler, Christopher. *The Screenwriter's Journey: Mythic Structures*. Studio City, Calif: Michael Wiese Productions, 1992.

ADAPTATION

Bluestone, George. *Novels into Film*. Berkeley, CA: University of California Press, 1957. Discusses formal limits and specific films.

Boyum, Joy Gould. *Double Exposure: Fiction into Film*. NY: New American Library, 1985.

Brady, Ben. *Principles of Adaptation for Film and Television*. Austin: U. of Texas Press, 1994.

McDougal, Stuart Y. *Made into Movies: From Literature to Film*. New York: Holt Rinehart and Winston, 1985. Theory, texts, and case studies.

Orr, John & Colin Nicholson, Eds. *Cinema and Fiction: New Modes of Adapting 1950–1990*. Edinburgh: Edinburgh Univ. Press, 1992.

Portnoy, Kenneth. *Screen Adaptation*. Boston: Focal Press, 1991.

Richardson, Robert. *Literature and Film*. Bloomington, IN: Indiana University Press, 1969. Intelligent discussion of the relationship between the two forms.

DIRECTING

Bresson, Robert. *Notes on Cinematography*. New York: Urizen, 1977. Tantalizingly brief entries from the notebook of the French veteran director tackling many fascinating issues.

Crisp, Mike. *The Practical Director*. Boston: Focal Press, 1993.

Lumet, Sidney. *Making Movies*. NY: Knopf/Random House, 1995. The whole process clearly explained by a master who never talks down.

Mamet, David. *On Directing Film*. NY: Viking, 1991. Some important articles of faith well explored here.

Rabiger, Michael. *Directing The Documentary, 3rd Ed*. Boston: Focal Press, 1997. The documentary equivalent to this book.

Rea, Peter and David Irving. *Producing and Directing the Short Film and Video*. Boston: Focal Press, 1995. Attention for the short form at last.

Richards, Ron. *A Director's Method for Film and TV*. NY: Grove Weidenfeld, 1990.

Sherman, Eric. *Directing the Film: Film Directors on their Art*. Los Angeles: Acrobat Books, 1988. Stellar directors talking their craft, but sight of the job remains fragmented and remote.

CONTINUITY

Miller, Pat P. *Script Supervision and Film Continuity, 2nd Ed*. Boston: Focal Press, 1990.

Rowlands, Avril. *The Continuity Handbook: For Single Camera Shooting, 3rd Ed*. Boston: Focal Press, 1995.

LIGHTING

Box, Harry. *The Set Technician's Handbook: Film Lighting Equipment, Practice, and Electrical Distribution*. Boston: Focal Press, 1993.

Brown, Blain. *Motion Picture and Video Lighting, Revised Ed*. Boston: Focal Press, 1995.

Carlson, Verne and Sylvia Carlson. *Professional Lighting Handbook, 2nd Ed.* Boston: Focal Press, 1991.

Ferncase, Richard K. *Film and Video Lighting Concepts.* Boston: Focal Press, 1994.

Ferncase, Richard K. *Basic Lighting Worktext for Film and Video.* Boston: Focal Press, 1992.

Fitt, Brian and Joe Thornley. *The Control of Light.* Boston: Focal Press, 1993.

Fitt, Brian and Joe Thornley. *Lighting by Design: A Technical Guide.* Boston: Focal Press, 1993.

Lyver, Des and Graham Swainson. *Basics of Video Lighting.* Boston: Focal Press, 1995.

Malkiewicz, Kris. *Film Lighting.* NY: Prentice Hall, 1986.

Millerson, Gerald. *The Technique of Lighting for Television and Film, 3rd Ed.* Boston: Focal Press, 1991.

Ritsko, Alan J. *Lighting for Location Motion Pictures.* New York: Van Nostrand Reinhold, 1979. Covers every aspect of the lighting and rigging problems that beset films made on location. Presumes no prior knowledge.

Samuelson, David W. *Motion Picture Camera and Lighting Equipment: Choice and Technique.* Boston: Focal Press, 1986. Specifics and use of a wide range of equipment; discusses special situations.

Viera, David & Maria Viera. *Lighting for Film and Electronic Cinematography.* Belmont, Calif: Wadsworth, 1993.

VIDEO CAMERAS AND RECORDING

Hodges, Peter. *The Video Camera Operator's Handbook.* Boston: Focal Press, 1995.

Lyver, Des and Graham Swainson. *Basics of Video Production.* Boston: Focal Press, 1995.

Millerson, Gerald. *Video Production Handbook, 2nd Ed.* Boston: Focal Press, 1992.

Millerson, Gerald. *Video Camera Techniques.* Boston: Focal Press, 1994. Handling, operation, and use of video cameras.

Ward, Peter. *Basic Betacam Camerawork.* Boston: Focal Press, 1994.

Watkinson, John. *The Digital Videotape Recorder.* Boston: Focal Press, 1994.

Watkinson, John. *Digital Compression in Video and Audio.* Boston: Focal Press, 1995.

Watkinson, John. *The Art of Digital Video, 2nd Ed.* Boston: Focal Press, 1994.

CINEMATOGRAPHY AND MOTION PICTURE TECHNIQUES

Arijon, Daniel. *Grammar of the Film Language.* Los Angeles: Silman-Janus, 1991. Good for understanding camera placement and framing to ensure smooth editing.

Beacham, Frank, ed. *American Cinematographer's Video Manual.* Hollywood: American Society of Cinematographers. Videographer's bible.

Bernstein, Steven. *Film Production 2nd Ed.* Boston: Focal Press, 1994. Conceptual and practical overview.

Carlson, Sylvia and Verne Carlson. *Professional Cameraman's Handbook 4th Ed.* Boston: Focal Press, 1993.

Detmers, Fred, ed. *American Cinematographer's Handbook.* Hollywood: American Society of Cinematographers. Issued regularly, the cinematographer's bible contains an incredible breadth of professional-level information. Accessible even to the beginner.

Happe, L. Bernard. *Basic Motion Picture Technology.* Boston: Focal Press, 1978. Good at explaining working principles.

Maier, Robert G. *Location Scouting and Management Handbook.* Boston: Focal Press, 1994.

Malkiewicz, J. Kris. *Cinematography: A Guide for Film Makers and Film Teachers 2nd Ed.* New York: Prentice Hall, 1989. Superlative text for intermediate filmmaking that extends from cameras, filters, lighting, and sound recording through editing and production.

Olson, Robert. *Art Direction for Film and Video.* Boston: Focal Press, 1993.

Pincus, Edward and Steven Ascher. *The Filmmakers Handbook.* New York: Plume, 1984. Classic for the beginner, lots of information both technical and conceptual. Good for the experimental filmmaker.

Samuelson, David W. *The Panaflex User's Guide.* Boston: Focal Press, 1990.

Samuelson, David W. *"Hands-On" Manual for Cinematographers.* Boston: Focal Press, 1994.

Samuelson, David W. *Motion Picture Camera Techniques.* Boston: Focal Press, 1979. Information on a wide range of camera-related topics clearly presented.

Ward, Peter. *Picture Composition for Film and Television.* Boston: Focal Press, 1995.

MICROPHONES, RECORDING, AND SOUND

Baert, Luc, Luc Theunissen, Guido Vergult. *Digital Audio and Compact Disk Technology 3rd Ed.* Boston: Focal Press, 1995.

Bartlett, Bruce. *Stereo Microphone Techniques.* Boston: Focal Press, 1991.

Borwick, John. *Sound Recording Practice 4th Ed.* Oxford & NY: Oxford University Press, 1994.

Borwick, John. *Microphones: Technology and Technique.* Boston: Focal Press, 1990.

Borwick, John. *Loudspeaker and Headphone Handbook 2nd Ed.* Boston: Focal Press, 1995.

Clifford, Martin. *Microphones: How They Work and How to Use Them.* Blue Ridge Summit, PA: Tab Books, 1977. Thorough and user-friendly for a relatively technical work.

Ford, Ty. *Advanced Audio Production Techniques.* Boston: Focal Press, 1993.

Forlenza, Jeff & Terri Stone, eds. *Sound for Picture: An Inside Look at Audio Production for Film and Television.* Milwaukee, WI: Hal Leonard Publishers, 1993.

Hubatka, Milton C., Frederick Hull, and Richard W. Sanders. *Audio Sweetening for Film and TV.* Blue Ridge Summit, PA: Tab Books, 1985. Techniques and equipment rather than applied artistry.

Huber, David Miles. *Microphone Manual: Design and Application.* Boston: Focal Press, 1988.

Lyver, Des. *Basics of Video Sound.* Boston: Focal Press, 1995.

Nisbett, Alec. *The Use of Microphones, 4th Ed.* Boston: Focal Press, 1994.

Nisbett, Alec. *The Sound Studio, 6th Ed.* Boston: Focal Press, 1995.

Nisbett, Alec. *The Technique of the Sound Studio, 3rd Ed.* Boston: Focal Press, 1989.

Pendergast, Roy M. *Film Music: A Neglected Art, 2nd Ed.* NY: W. W. Norton, 1992.

Pohlmann, Ken C. *Principles of Digital Audio.* Carmel, Ind: Sams, 1991.

Rumsey, Francis. *Digital Audio Operations.* Boston: Focal Press, 1991.

Rumsey, Francis. *Sound and Sound Recording: An Introduction 2nd Ed.* Boston: Focal Press, 1994.

Watkinson, John. *The Art of Digital Recording, 2nd Ed.* Oxford & Boston: Focal Press, 1994.

Watkinson, John. *An Introduction to Digital Audio.* Boston: Focal Press, 1994.

White, Glenn D. *The Audio Dictionary.* Seattle: University of Washington Press, 1987.

EDITING

Anderson, Gary H. *Video Editing and Post Production: A Professional Guide.* White Plains, NY: Knowledge Industry Publications, 1993.

Browne, Steven E. *Videotape Editing: A Postproduction Primer 2nd Ed.* Boston: Focal Press, 1993.

Burder, John. *The Technique of Editing 16mm Films.* Boston: Focal Press, 1988. Practical introduction to tools and concepts.

Dancyger, Ken. *The Technique of Film and Video Editing.* Boston: Focal Press, 1993. Concepts as well as procedures. Highly recommended.

Hollyn, Norman. *The Film Editing Handbook.* Beverly Hills, Calif: Lone Eagle, 1990. Deals with feature film editing. Very good on organization and method in the cutting room.

Kerner, Marvin. *Art of the Sound Effects Editor.* Boston: Focal Press, 1989.

Ohanian, Thomas A. *Digital Nonlinear Editing.* Boston: Focal Press, 1993. Avid intensive.

Reisz, Karel and Gavin Millar. *The Technique of Film Editing.* Boston: Focal Press, 1968. Still the standard work for the concepts of editing, full of good information, but cramped in layout and with oppressively dated examples.

Rosenblum, Ralph. *When the Shooting Stops . . . the Cutting Begins.* New York. Penguin, 1980. Personal and funny account of the professional editor's way of life.

Walter, Ernest. *The Technique of the Film Cutting Room.* Boston: Focal Press, 1982. An A to Z of the physical process of the cutting room.

FINANCE, PRODUCTION, AND DISTRIBUTION

Gates, Richard. *Production Management for Film and Video, 2nd Ed.* Boston: Focal Press, 1995.

Goodell, Gregory. *Independent Feature Film Production: A Complete Guide from Concept Through Distribution.* New York: St. Martin's Press, 1982. Legal, business, facilities, services, distribution, and a lot of production aspects, too.

Levison, Louise. *Filmmakers and Financing: Business Plans for Independents.* Boston: Focal Press, 1994.

Matza, Aleks. *The Video Production Organizer.* Boston: Focal Press, 1995. Disk included; save your fingers.

Randall, John. *Feature Films on a Low Budget.* Boston: Focal Press, 1991.

Rosen, David. *Off-Hollywood: The Making and Marketing of Independent Films.* NY: Grove Weidenfeld, 1990.

Russo, John. *How to Make and Market Your Own Feature Movie for $10,000 or Less.* NYC: Barclay House, 1994.

Singleton, Ralph. *Film Scheduling.* Los Angeles: Lone Eagle, 1991. A must for your production manager.

Wiese, Michael. *Film and Video Marketing.* Boston: Focal Press, 1989.

Wiese, Michael and Deke Simon. *Film and Video Budgets.* Boston: Focal Press, 1995 (various format computer disks available, saving hours of keyboard bashing).

Wiese, Michael. *The Independent Film and Videomaker's Guide, Revised and Enlarged Edition.* Boston: Focal Press, 1990. Finding investors, preparing the prospectus, researching the market, producing, and distributing.

Wiese, Michael. *Film and Video Financing.* Boston: Focal Press, 1991.

EDUCATION AND CAREER POSSIBILITIES

Angell, Robert. *Film and Television: The Way In.* London: British Film Institute, 1988

Bayer, William. *Breaking Through, Selling Out, Dropping Dead.* NY: Limelight Editions, 1989.

Bone, Jan. *Opportunities in Film Careers.* Lincolnwood, IL: VGM Career Horizons, 1990.

Horwin, Michael. *Careers in Film and Video Production.* Boston: Focal Press, 1990.

Laskin, Emily, ed. *Getting Started in Film.* NY: Prentice-Hall. 1992.

Lazarus, Paul. *Working in Film.* NY: St. Martin's Press, 1993.

O'Donnell, Gail & Michele Travolta, eds. *Making It In Hollywood.* Napierville, IL: Sourcebooks, 1994.

Peterson's Guides to Graduate Programs in the Humanities, Arts, and Social Sciences. Princeton, NJ: Petersons (periodically published). Comprehensive listing of institutions, their faculty, philosophy, equipment, and core courses.

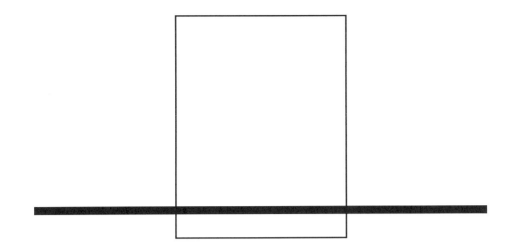

I·N·D·E·X